In Quest of Justice

The publisher and the University of California Press Foundation gratefully acknowledge the generous support of the Ahmanson Foundation Endowment Fund in Humanities.

In Quest of Justice

ISLAMIC LAW AND FORENSIC MEDICINE
IN MODERN EGYPT

Khaled Fahmy

UNIVERSITY OF CALIFORNIA PRESS

University of California Press, one of the most distinguished university presses in the United States, enriches lives around the world by advancing scholarship in the humanities, social sciences, and natural sciences. Its activities are supported by the UC Press Foundation and by philanthropic contributions from individuals and institutions. For more information, visit www.ucpress.edu.

University of California Press
Oakland, California

Library of Congress Cataloging-in-Publication Data

Names: Fahmy, Khaled Mahmoud, author.
Title: In quest of justice : Islamic law and forensic medicine in modern Egypt / Khaled Fahmy.
Description: Oakland, California : University of California Press, [2018] | Includes bibliographical references and index. |
Identifiers: LCCN 2018010666 (print) | LCCN 2018017543 (ebook) | ISBN 9780520971721 (Ebook) | ISBN 9780520279032 (cloth : alk. paper)
Subjects: LCSH: Medical jurisprudence—Egypt. | Evidence, Expert—Egypt. | Chemistry, Forensic—Egypt. | Criminal justice, Administration of—Egypt. | Medical jurisprudence (Islamic law) | Evidence, Expert (Islamic law) | Criminal justice, Administration of (Islamic law) | Islam and justice.
Classification: LCC KRM4700 (ebook) | LCC KRM4700 .F34 2018 (print) | DDC 347.62/067--dc23
LC record available at https://lccn.loc.gov/2018010666

Manufactured in the United States of America

27 26 25 24 23 22 21 20 19 18
10 9 8 7 6 5 4 3 2 1

Dedicated to the memory of ʿIṣām ʿAṭā and the countless other victims of police brutality in Egypt, and to the brave men and women of Egypt's human rights movement

CONTENTS

ILLUSTRATIONS

ACKNOWLEDGMENTS

I started research on this book many years ago, and it has taken many twists and turns since. But in the fall of 2011, an incident happened that drew the book's main argument into sharper focus. Over the previous nine months, I had gone to Tahrir Square in Cairo countless times to participate in the mass uprising that had erupted on January 25, the day that the Egyptian state had designated National Police Day, when people in the capital and elsewhere in Egypt had taken to the streets to protest against police brutality. While at Tahrir Square, I had learned about many cases of torture in police stations, but there was one particular case of state violence that drew my attention. It was the case of 'Iṣām 'Aṭā, a young man who had been illegally arrested, tried with no legal counsel, and sentenced by a military tribunal to three years in prison. On October 25, 2011, after eight months of incarceration, he died under suspicious circumstances, and there were rumors the prison wardens had tortured him to death. Two days after 'Iṣām's death, his body was sent to Qaṣr al-'Ainī, Cairo's main hospital, where the family was gathered and deliberating whether to press for an autopsy, a step that would inevitably invite the wrath of the authorities.

It was to show solidarity with 'Iṣām 'Aṭā's family that my friends and I decided to go to the Zeinhum Morgue in Cairo. On entering that awful place, I saw a young man in the courtyard talking on his mobile phone, insisting on an autopsy. "We will open him, come what may," he declared. I later discovered that this was 'Iṣām's brother, Muḥammad, who was arguing with his uncle on the phone. Watching this scene, I was immediately hit with a poignant sense of déjà-vu. Given that this was my first visit to the morgue, I wondered where the feeling had come from. On reflection, I realized that what I was witnessing was not something I had seen before but rather something I had read about. Over the previous few years, I had been conducting research in the Egyptian National Archives, where I was consulting police and hospital records that told the stories of people in nineteenth-century Egypt—humble, brave, and upright individuals like Muḥammad ʿAṭā—who were willing to violate many taboos related to death and insist on autopsies in one last attempt to bring to justice those they suspected had been responsible for the death of their loved ones. It is this quest for justice that suddenly became crystal clear to me on that fateful day and animated and inspired me to write this book.

I would first and foremost like to acknowledge the bravery and integrity of the activists who stood by ʿIṣām ʿAṭā's bereaved family that day in October 2011: Aida Seif al-Dawla, Gamila Ismail, Nadia Kamel, Nawwara Negm, and Ahdaf Soueif. Ever since the beginning of the Egyptian Revolution on January 25, 2011, these brave women, and many other men and women activists in Egypt's vibrant human rights movement, have taken courageous stances defending the victims of state violence and standing by their quest for justice, often at huge cost to themselves and their loved ones. In this regard, the work of the staff at Al Nadeem Center for Rehabilitation of Victims of Violence and at the Egyptian Initiative for Personal Rights (EIPR) has been exemplary. Of particular note is Hossam Bahgat, the founding director of EIPR, whose integrity and honesty have been most inspirational.

It also gives me deep pleasure to acknowledge the love and friendship of many of my Tahrir companions, who, more than they realize, helped me hone my ideas about the history of the modern Egyptian state and its wanton use of violence: Nassef Azmi, Ziad Bahaa Eldin, Madiha Doss, Dina El-Khawaga, Hala Galal, Ahmed Gharbeia, Amr Gharbeia, Naira Ijjeh, Nadia Kamel, Azza Khalil, Wael Khalil, Sohail Luka, Malak Rushdi, Reem Saad, Akmal Safwat, Randa Shaath, and Hania Sholkamy. I have also found the writings of Alaa Abd El-Fattah, Amr Adly, Ismail al-Bahar, Basma El Husseiny, Alia Mosallam, Mohamed Naeem, Aly El Raggal, Sarah El Serry, and Ashraf El Sherif to be very enlightening.

The research for this book and several colloquia related to it have benefited from support I received from the Egyptian National Archives, the Egyptian Historical Association, New York University, the American University in Cairo, Columbia University, Harvard University, and l'Institut d'études de l'Islam et des sociétés du monde musulman at l'École des hautes études en sciences sociales. I owe a considerable debt to my colleagues, students, and friends who read parts of this book or discussed ideas with me that found their way in it, particularly Lila Abu-Lughod, Hussam Ahmed, James Baldwin, On Barak, Nadia Benabid, Chloe Bordewich, Guy Burak, Omar Cheta, Mary Elston, Kouross Esmaeli, Belal Fadl, Bruce Ferguson, Michael Gilsenan, Greg Halaby, Will Hanley, John Halliwell, Shireen Hamza, Emad Helal, Ibrahim El-Houdaiby, Choon Hwee, Alice Hu, Shehab Ismail, Aaron Jakes, İbrahim Kalkan, Mina Khalil, Tamer el-Leithy, Mahmood Mamdani, Brinkley Messick, Adam Mestyan, Shana Minkin, Salmaan Mirza, Timothy Mitchell, Anne-Marie Moulin, Jakub Novak, Hussein Omar, Roger Owen, Leslie Peirce, Jamil Sbitan, Paul Sedra, Amr Shalakany, Kathryn Schwartz, Laura Thompson, Başak Tuğ, and Leonard Wood. Ruud Peters kept me company during many years of research in the Egyptian National Archives, and his work on Egyptian legal history was foundational for this book. Zach Lockman and Judith Tucker read the entire manuscript closely and provided invaluable critical suggestions to sharpen its argument and improve its style. Over a decade ago, Niels Hooper became interested in this book's project, and I thank him for his patience and for introducing me to the world of the University of California Press. I also thank Genevieve Thurston for her diligent copyediting work.

I have the deepest gratitude for my family's support: my parents, Soheir and Mahmoud, who have always encouraged my academic endeavors; my brother, Tamer, for his unmatched kindness and integrity; my twin sister, Rania, who is a source of constant inspiration; and, finally, my nephews, Karim, Mazen, Seifalla, and Ziad, who are a source of endless joy and for whom I wish happiness in a kinder and gentler Egypt.

Cambridge, England
April 29, 2018

Introduction

IN A MUSEUM OF MEDICAL HISTORY in Cairo hangs a curious unsigned painting (see figure 1). A faded old card explains that it depicts the first anatomy lesson performed in Egypt. The momentous event took place in 1829 at a medical school that had recently been founded in Abū Za'bal, to the northeast of Cairo. The painting shows a black male cadaver laid out on a dissection table in the middle of a large amphitheater, the walls of which are adorned with the Arabic names of Greek and Muslim physicians: Galen, Jābir Ibn Hayyān, Hippocrates, and Ibn al-Bayṭār, among others. Next to the dissection table stands a turbaned physician clad in oriental costume, pointing with one hand to the cadaver and with the other to a skeleton hanging next to him, as if illustrating the inner structure of the human body. In the background sit some hundred students, also turbaned, listening attentively to the anatomy lesson. Surrounding the dissection table is a group of animated religious scholars, one of them leaning over the cadaver. A military officer is standing at the foot of the body, and an armed sentry guards the entrance to the room.[1]

Like the event it commemorates, this painting is one of a kind, and it is difficult to situate it in an art historical context that can help explain the artist's meaning. Even though classical Arabic medical literature is replete with manuscripts containing anatomical illustrations, these illustrations do not depict anatomy lessons; rather, they represent a "highly schematic approach to human anatomy, [and] . . . could serve as a reasonable *aide memoire* for the user, even though they might give an inadequate representation of the structures themselves."[2] However, by comparing our painting to early European Renaissance woodcuts that illustrate anatomy lessons, especially those lessons that were performed in Italian medical colleges, a central

FIGURE 1: Strekalovsky, *The First Dissection Lesson in Egypt, 1829*. Museum of the History of Medicine, Qaṣr al-ʿAinī Medical School, Cairo. Photo by Mazen Attalla.

feature presents itself as a possible clue. Down the centuries, these European images point to an ongoing dialogue, if not a tension, between the dissected body and the medical text being recited aloud by a lector sitting behind an elevated lectern, the text authored by medical authorities that can be traced all the way back to Galen, the second-century-CE Greek physician.[3] Some of the earliest European anatomical illustrations expressed this tension quite vividly, for they "do not show so much what . . . had [been] seen as what [was known] to exist."[4] Simply put, this tension was about what has precedence over the other: the text or the cadaver? Are the senses (especially those of touch and sight) to be trusted enough to replace the word? Is the corpus of classical medical literature to be discarded in favor of direct observation of a dissected cadaver, or does a corpse only corroborate the teachings of the ancients?

By contrast, our Egyptian painting lacks explicit references to any text except the names of classical medical authors running along the amphitheater walls. However, there is another poignant, if subtle, reference to the tension between cadaver and text at the very center of the painting. Surrounding the cadaver is a group of *ʿulamāʾ*, or custodians of the Text (i.e., the Quran), one of them gesticulating excitingly at what is taking place in front of him. Compared to the figures in the much more famous dissection scene depicted on the frontispiece of Vesalius's *De humani corporis fabrica* (1543), neither the anatomist nor the dissected cadaver in the Egyptian painting demand our attention.[5] Rather, the group of religious scholars occupies center stage, and the painter arranges them in such a way as to obstruct both our view and that of the students, preventing direct access to the cadaver, ostensibly the source of knowledge about the internal structure of the human body. Autopsy, which literally means "to see with one's own eyes," is thus thwarted by religion.

This reading of the painting, wherein religion stands in the way of science, gains further credence when we identify the artist and date of the painting. Anne Marie Moulin, who studied the history of nineteenth-century Egyptian medicine, has identified the artist as a certain Strekalovsky, a Russian painter who worked in Egypt in the 1930s and 1940s.[6] With more than a century separating him from the event he was commemorating, there is little doubt that Strekalovsky derived his understanding of the circumstances surrounding the opening of the medical school, where instruction was based on dissection, from the copious writings of Dr. Antoine-Barthélémy Clot, the French founding director of the school. The turbaned teacher depicted in the painting is almost certainly Dr. Clot himself, or Clot Bey, as he famously came to be known.[7]

In his memoirs, Clot Bey wrote that soon after he had been entrusted by Egypt's ruler, Mehmed Ali Pasha (r. 1805–48), to found a medical school, he explained to the Pasha that the medical education he had in mind had to be firmly based on human dissection. To his dismay, he received a firm directive that cadavers were not to be touched. Undeterred, the French doctor used all of his rhetorical and political skills to overcome this formidable barrier. He recounted this campaign in his memoirs:

> I harbored the hope that one day I would vanquish this prejudice, even though I clearly noted the profound disgust of the students and the fanatical opposition of the *ulémas,* with whom I had had communication on the subject. I applied myself to winning the confidence of Cheikh El Islam al-Arusi, an important person who enjoyed a high reputation for holiness in the country. . . . When I approached the question of anatomy, he would not give a single concession. His principal argument was that, according to religion, cadavers could feel pain, to which I concurred, but added that bodies would decompose and become the prey of worms soon after death. . . . [The Shaykh then argued that medical treatises] published on such subjects should suffice for the instruction of the students. . . . [I responded] that the theory provides no more than incomplete notions: a watchmaker, I told him, who has to repair watches, does he not need to understand their whole mechanism?

Moreover, does he not have to put together and take apart the various pieces before he can understand how they operate? This image struck him, . . . [and] I managed to obtain a tacit agreement to study anatomy but to act with the greatest discretion and to do so in secret.[8]

After he had managed to placate the *'ulamā',* Clot Bey had to face the hostility of his own students. One day, he wrote, a student approached him with a letter. No sooner had he started reading the letter than the student attacked him with a knife. Instinctively, Clot Bey raised his right arm, which received a deep wound. The attacker was immediately grabbed and disarmed, and Clot Bey ordered him to be detained. During the ensuing interrogation, the same students who had earlier disarmed the attacker backed their colleague's version of events "after being made to understand that a believer should not be given up for a Christian dog." After only eight hours in detention, the attacker was released and allowed to walk scot-free. This left Clot Bey completely demoralized: "I admit that from the time I was hit by the fanatic young man a deep despondency seized me. . . . Sacrificing one's life, giving up one's peace in order to conquer the prejudices of a people, to develop their intelligence, to extend to them the benefits of civilization only to be rewarded by indifference, if not hatred, this thought overwhelmed my soul."[9]

Nevertheless, and after being consoled by Jean-François Mimaut, the French consul in Egypt, Clot Bey decided not to resign. Instead, he became even more committed to continuing the mission that he had come to Egypt to complete. Through perseverance and hard work, he finally succeeded in overcoming not only the students' "huge veneration of Aristotle" but also their "fanaticism" and dogmatic resistance to dissection; eventually, they "no longer considered anatomical dissection to be a profanation."[10]

A century later, Dr. Naguib Bey Mahfouz, the assistant dean of the school's Faculty of Medicine, gave a slightly different version of this dramatic event, and his text did much to bolster Clot Bey's image as a beacon of enlightened thought in a sea of darkness. In his English-language *History of Medical Education in Egypt,* he wrote that

the practice of dissection provoked much antagonism, not only from the Ulemas [*sic*] but also from the students themselves. By steady perseverance the Ulemas were induced to give their consent. . . . The dissecting rooms were surrounded by guards, who were kept ignorant of what was going inside. On one occasion one of the medical students, infuriated at seeing the bodies dissected, attempted to kill Clot Bey, stabbing him on the forehead and chest.

> By a fortunate movement of the arm Clot Bey evaded the attack. The other students soon intervened and the student was taken into custody. Clot Bey calmly completed his lecture, to the great admiration of the class.[11]

Gripping as it may be, this account of a European man of science determined to win over Muslim *'ulamā'* and overcome their opposition to dissection raises many questions. Who was this Dr. Clot, and why did he end up in Egypt? Why did Mehmed Ali entrust him with founding a medical school? If the purpose was to found a medical corps for the Pasha's new army, would it not have been cheaper and more expedient for Clot Bey to invite more of his countrymen to join him in Egypt? Was Clot Bey correct in sensing that his Muslim interlocutors' opposition to dissection was doctrinally based? Did the *'ulamā'* he reached out to really believe that cadavers could feel pain, or were there other reasons for their opposition to dissection? And given that this was not a freak show but a lesson in a medical school that surely had professors teaching other branches of medicine, who were the other professors? Did they share Clot Bey's belief in his *mission civilisatrice?* And returning to our painting, who were the animated students following this historic lesson, and how did they end up in the school? What careers did they pursue after graduation, and what social status did they enjoy as bearers of medical diplomas? More importantly, did they share their professor's belief that science and religion represented two distinct fields of thought, or did they agree with classical Muslim physicians—whose names adorned the walls of their classrooms—in rejecting such a binary distinction?

In light of the ostensible opposition of the *'ulamā'* to dissection as well as Mehmed Ali's directive to Clot Bey not to use dissection, the presence of the guards points to the purported hostility of the wider society to what was going on inside the hallowed halls. Did dissection elicit negative reactions from non-elite Egyptians? And if so, what was their understanding of modern medicine and of the Abū Za'bal Medical School, which was rebranded as the Qaṣr al-'Ainī Medical School and Hospital after 1838, when it was relocated to a district by that name closer to Cairo? Furthermore, since cadavers were routinely dissected not only for the purposes of medical pedagogy but also for legal purposes, to ascertain cause of death, how did non-elite Egyptians react to this encroachment on what was, literally, a matter of life and death? Moreover, dissections and postmortem examinations were part of a much larger set of practices that were being used by the newly evolving modern state in the 1830s to control Egypt's population. These practices included registration at birth; vaccination against smallpox; branding of criminals; routine medical examination of students, workers, sailors, and soldiers; conscription; and carrying stamped passports (*tadhākir*) when moving from village to village. How did non-elite Egyptians understand and react to these diverse examples of corporeal surveillance?

The newly constituted police, moreover, routinely practiced autopsies to aid in criminal investigations. The detailed forensic medical reports that police doctors prepared were then presented to courts of law, which based their final rulings squarely on them. But these courts were not the familiar shari'a courts that had existed for centuries in Egypt, just as they had in many other parts of the Ottoman Empire. These were new "legal councils" that were central components of a rapidly evolving legal field. What were these councils, and what was the legal logic that allowed them to accept forensic medicine as prime means of establishing probative proof? How did the public approach these councils and react to the entire legal system, of which they were part? Finally, what was this state that was implementing all these innovations in the medical and legal fields? Who was behind it, and how was it formed? What animated it, and how did it evolve? Did its unprecedented techniques of corporeal surveillance constitute it, or did these techniques simply aid it in placing Egyptian society firmly under its surveillance?

This book attempts to answer these questions by putting the human body at its focal point, and it asks how one can study the twin practices of dissection and autopsy as a way of rethinking the universalistic category of modernity in a non-Western context. As seen from the short excerpt of Clot Bey's writings quoted above, by the beginning of the nineteenth century opening up human cadavers was universally deemed an essential aspect of medical pedagogy. A few years later, prying open the human body to determine cause of death became a standard procedure in criminal investigations within the rapidly evolving legal field. Dissections and autopsies thus came to play pivotal roles in an Egyptian modernity that can be seen to have two central pillars, namely medical and legal reform. This book therefore adopts a corporeal history of the nineteenth-century project of modernization known as *al-Nahḍa* and follows dissections and autopsies—as well as postmortems, burials, quarantines, and legal torture—as a way of understanding how non-elite Egyptians thought of and reacted to modernity.

To explicate further the questions that this book raises and spell out its methodology and approach, it may be useful to refer to four bodies of scholarly literature with which it engages.

EGYPTIAN HISTORIOGRAPHY OF MODERN EGYPTIAN MEDICINE

In his study of the conditions surrounding the establishment in Egypt of history as an academic field, Yoav Di-Capua follows the endeavors of Shafīq Ghurbāl, the founder of twentieth-century Egyptian historiography, as he struggled to distinguish his profession from both the historical school coalescing around the ʿĀbidīn royal palace and the nationalist, nonprofessional historians who were animating the field in the 1920s and 1930s.[12] Di-Capua explains that Ghurbāl went against the latter group by insisting that his students accept objectivity as a cardinal principle and underscoring for them the importance of using archival sources. At the same time, he and his students distanced themselves from the "royal historians," those European historians that King Fu'ād (r. 1923–36) had commissioned to "lend support to the saga of state formation under [Mehmed Ali] and his successors."[13] Accordingly, in contradistinction to royal historians, who concentrated on power politics and stressed the royal dynasty's accomplishments in warfare and diplomacy, Ghurbāl directed his students to study the social and institutional reforms that were believed to have helped Egypt on its path toward modernity. Thus, ʿAlī al-Giritlī studied industrialization; Aḥmad al-Ḥittā learned about agricultural reforms; Ahmad ʿIzzat ʿAbd al-Karīm wrote about education; Jamāl al-Dīn al-Shayyāl examined translation; Abul-Futūḥ Raḍwān worked on the advent of the printing press; and Ibrāhīm ʿAbduh researched the advent of the journalistic press.[14] Notably, medical reforms were not the subject of any of the independent studies conducted by the first generation of Egyptian academic historians. It is as if Qaṣr al-ʿAinī and the many modern medical practices associated with it were of only secondary importance compared to industrial, economic, or educational reforms.

Nevertheless, both ʿAbd al-Karīm's study of education and al-Shayyāl's treatise on translation have lengthy sections on the Qaṣr al-ʿAinī Medical School and Hospital.[15] These sections exhibit certain assumptions about modernity and Egypt's relations with Europe that, as Di-Capua deftly shows, were characteristic features of the first generation of Egyptian academic historians and that could also be traced back to the intellectual production of subsequent generations of academic historians. Ghurbāl's students accepted the chronology of the royal historians, in which Mehmed Ali appeared as a great founder of modernity, with the result that a before-and-after approach was strictly followed. Before Mehmed Ali, Egypt had gone through a long period of Ottoman rule that, according to this view, was best left unstudied and ignored. After Mehmed Ali, Egypt evolved along a modern European nation-state model.[16] The only slight variation that the academic historians made to the "founder paradigm" when they addressed medical reforms was to add Clot Bey alongside Mehmed Ali, describing the former as a great reformer who used enlightened, modern medicine to put an end to the quackery and superstition of Ottoman times.

For example, in his 1938 study of education during Mehmed Ali's reign, 'Abd al-Karīm describes Clot Bey's efforts as being instrumental in "spreading modern medicine in the deep Egyptian countryside ... and lifting the clouds of ignorance that had been hovering over the country for long centuries."[17] For his part, al-Shayyāl was deeply impressed by the manner in which Clot Bey dealt with the formidable challenges he encountered in his "enlightening mission." Al-Shayyāl goes to enormous lengths to explain how Clot Bey made "every effort to overcome [these challenges] until he finally succeeded."[18] Behind the French doctor's ceaseless efforts, al-Shayyāl argues, was the unflinching support of Mehmed Ali, who realized "from the instant he ascended to the Egyptian throne[19] that he had to implement a new plan of reform to lift Egypt from the destruction and corruption of the Ottoman era and ... do so by borrowing from the West and its sciences."[20] Of equal significance is al-Shayyāl's description of the overall context in which this process of medical reform was taking place:

> For nearly three centuries, that is, during the Ottoman period, Egypt had been looking inward, sitting behind closed doors and windows, after its contact with the outside world, especially Europe, had been severed.... Toward the end of the eighteenth century, however, the West had become impatient with this isolation ..., and rather than invite Egypt to open its windows and doors to allow in European light and civilization, this European West took it upon itself to do so with brute force.... And hence Egypt awoke from its long, deep slumber. But its awakening was not a spontaneous or gentle one; rather, it was an abrupt, forceful awakening. As for the lights that the French brought with them, the lights of arms, civilization, and science, these were so bright that they blinded the eyes of the Egyptians and baffled their most learned man, the famous chronicler 'Abd al-Raḥmān al-Jabartī, when he visited the French library and institute and said, "And they have strange and marvelous matters and equipment, which our limited minds cannot comprehend."[21]

The first generation of Egyptian academic historians, therefore, typically stressed the staunch determination of Clot Bey, his patron Mehmed Ali, and a few of their "enlightened" assistants to overcome superstitious belief and popular, "unscientific" remedies. As I illustrate in chapter 1, these accounts followed Western Whiggish narratives about the progress of medical science through the ages and its triumph over popular superstition and religious dogma by resorting to metaphors of light and darkness when describing the efforts to institute dissection as standard practice in medical pedagogy. However, within Egyptian historiography, this Manichean struggle between light and darkness was not limited to the field of medical history; rather, it suffused the much larger historiographical field of Egypt's relationship with Europe. As Di-Capua has illustrated, the first generation of Egyptian academic and nonacademic historians saw Bonaparte's invasion of Egypt in 1798 as a momentous event that ushered in European modernity to an Egypt that had been shrouded in centuries of Ottoman darkness.[22] Before we follow the story through the second half of the twentieth century to see how Egypt's encounter with European science and modernity was approached, it is important to stop at an influential study published in the late 1960s that dealt with the French Expedition. Although not written by a professional historian, this study had a profound influence on subsequent generations of Egyptian academic historians.

Two years after the June War (1967), Luwīs 'Awaḍ (1915–90), an essayist, literary critic, cultural historian, and professor of English literature at Cairo University, published a two-volume study titled the *Tārīkh al-Fikr al-Miṣrī al-Ḥadīth* (History of modern Egyptian thought), in which he sought to understand the reasons for Egypt's crushing defeat:

> The reason for our weakness was that we had not completed our tools of modern life. As is well known, Egypt did not exit the darkness of medieval times that had been spread by the Ottoman Empire to all its dominions until 170 years ago [i.e., in 1789], when Egypt had its first direct encounter with Europe. This is a very short period in the life of peoples and civilizations. Why, Europe herself began her renaissance around 1500 [CE], that is, five centuries ago; and if she has surpassed us in maturity, this is only because she started the process of modern state-building five hundred years before us.[23]

In the second volume of his study, 'Awaḍ closely examines the works of various nineteenth-century literati and follows the way they understood and reacted to notions such as the rule of law, women's liberation, self-rule, liberalism, and democracy, among others. But the contours of 'Awaḍ's argument become manifest in the first volume, where, rather than following the trajectory of certain ideas, he investigates the conditions that allowed Egyptians to think of themselves as Egyptians—that is, as a group that is distinct from the wider Ottoman, Muslim, and/or Arab world. For him, "Bonaparte's expedition to Egypt was a watershed separating two diametrically distinct worlds. [On one side of the divide,] there was a medieval world that extended throughout the Turkish-Mamluk period and ended in 1798. During this period, [Egypt] witnessed a number of purely economic uprisings which, however, did not produce any political, social or cultural thought. [On the other side,] there was a world in which no social or political action occurred except if it was associated with a clear political persuasion, distinct social ideology, and/or definite cultural trend."[24]

To illustrate the gulf that separated the "medieval" world of Turkish-Mamluk Egypt from the modernity that the French Expedition ushered in, 'Awaḍ zooms in on the Institut d'Egypte, the scientific institute that Bonaparte founded in Cairo in the house of Ḥasan Kāshif, one of the vanquished Mamluk emirs. 'Awaḍ's aim is not simply to document the French efforts to display their *mission civilisatrice* but also to trace the contrasting reactions of conservative and "enlightened" Egyptian intellectuals to modern science. He quotes an account from a French source of an experiment performed at the institute by the chemist Claude Louis Berthollet, of modern chemical nomenclature fame, and notes that this experiment was witnessed by some *'ulamā'*. This account describes Berthollet showing how acids interact with each other and how electricity is generated, only to be asked by an incredulous shaykh: "Can you be present in Marrakesh and Cairo simultaneously?" 'Awaḍ comments that Berthollet must have been stunned by this nonsensical question and unaware that the shaykh meant to ridicule the science displayed by the French savants. It is, 'Awaḍ argues, as if the shaykh was saying, "Do not be haughty with your intelligence. You might have arrived with your wondrous material sciences, but you forget that they are but childish tricks compared to our spiritual exercises that enable . . . our holy men to exist in more than one place at the same time." 'Awaḍ concludes by commenting, "In this episode, we see an entire civilization confronting another."[25]

To provide a contrast "to this conservative faction," 'Awaḍ devotes an entire chapter to the famous chronicler 'Abd al-Raḥmān al-Jabartī (1753–1825), depicting him as

> one of the pioneer Egyptian intellectuals of this strange and wondrous time in which the culture of the Middle Ages was crumbling the way an egg

hatches and out of which emerges a phoenix's cocoon. Not only did Jabartī see contemporary sciences, whether they were theoretical, experimental, or exact, as essential for nation-building; he also exceeded that position to stand in awe in front of the arts that had been rejected by his conservative milieu . . . such as painting and sculpture. . . . . As to embracing the foundations of modern material life, including exact, experimental, or technological sciences—this is an easy matter even for reactionaries, *salafī*s, and conservatives. For the history of civilizations has taught us that people espouse their material, this-worldly interests faster and more easily than they appropriate what can lead to their intellectual, moral, or spiritual wellbeing. This cultural schism that manifests itself in accepting material rejuvenation but rejecting its spiritual counterpart is a sign of civilizational rupture that often afflicts societies and individuals in moments of transition. So when we see someone like ʿAbd al-Raḥmān al-Jabartī who accepted the possibility of social reform, both materially and intellectually, then it is incumbent upon us to stand in front of him with great respect.[26]

ʿAwaḍ's *Tārīkh al-Fikr al-Miṣrī al-Ḥadīth* was a bombshell, and for decades it shaped the contours of Egyptian discussion not only about the French Expedition but also about modern Egyptian cultural and intellectual history. As we will see shortly, the book's polemical style, its preference for discursive analysis over institutional or sociohistorical investigation, and its insistence on viewing three centuries of Ottoman rule as Egypt's "dark ages" were all features that greatly influenced the field of academic inquiry into Egypt's supposed "first modern encounter with Europe."[27]

Chief among the Egyptian historians who were influenced by ʿAwaḍ was Ra'ūf ʿAbbās (1939–2008), a prolific historian of modern Egypt who started his academic career pioneering a new mode of nineteenth-century agrarian social history based on meticulous archival research,[28] and who, years later, was drawn to writing an intellectual history comparing Mehmed Ali's Egypt to Japan during the Meiji period. In the latter, ʿAbbās compares the career of one of Egypt's leading intellectuals, Rifāʿa al-Ṭahṭāwī (1801–73), with Japan's Fukuzawa Yukichi (1835–1901).[29] As interesting as that study is, it is an earlier study Abbās published in 1987 that has a direct bearing on our analysis.

Titled "Qudūm al-Gharb: Bidāya lil-Nahḍa am Ijhāḍ Lahā?" (The advent of the West: A beginning or an abortion of renaissance?), this article is a synthesis of many of ʿAbbās's ideas to date that dealt not only with Egypt's encounter with Europe during the French Expedition but also with the entire trajectory of nineteenth-century Egyptian history.[30] ʿAbbās repeats the now familiar trope of the Ottoman dark ages by arguing that when the

Ottomans occupied the Arab provinces in the sixteenth century, "they caused a cultural decline by imposing a complete isolation . . . that prevented Arabs from resuming their dialectical relationship with the West. . . . In addition, the Ottomans were originally Bedouins with no tradition of founding a civilization."[31] This isolation was finally broken by Bonaparte's expedition, and 'Abbās argues that one needs to distinguish between two waves of Western encroachment on Arab lands: the first toward the end of the eighteenth and the beginning of the nineteenth century, and the second starting in the second half of the nineteenth century.

It is in his analysis of the first wave that 'Abbās's debt to 'Awaḍ is most apparent, for he says that the French Expedition had a positive impact on "awakening Arabs to the reality of their decline, . . . [for] by participating in the councils that Bonaparte had established, . . . the perception of the elite to [political] power changed, so did their understanding of the rights of the subjects vis-à-vis their rulers, and the responsibilities of the rulers towards their subjects."[32] Building on 'Awaḍ's argument that participating in Bonaparte's councils had far-reaching consequences,[33] 'Abbās contends that it was the resulting heightened self-confidence that allowed the "popular leadership" in 1805 to defy the Ottoman sultan and insist on instating a man of its choice, Mehmed Ali Pasha, as governor of Egypt. Mehmed Ali, 'Abbās argues, adopted "a political project of founding a strong Arab Islamic state that would encompass the Arab east under his command and would be a bastion frustrating the West's designs."[34] This project entailed a well-thought-out process of completely overhauling the economy, one that led to the formation of state capitalism wherein the state controlled the agricultural sector, introduced modern industry, and sent student missions to Paris and other European capitals, thus resuming cultural links between Egypt and the West. However, 'Abbās maintains, due to the fact that this political project was elitist and state-led, its "social aspect was absent and people's daily lives were not altered."[35] Accordingly, in 1841, when the European powers put pressure on Mehmed Ali to abolish the monopolies that underpinned his control of the economy, the first attempts "at renaissance crumbled at the blows it received from Western imperialism. Thus, the second advent of the West was an abortion of the renaissance project, as it entailed a ferocious imperialist attack aimed at maintaining the status of cultural decline and allowing but minor adjustments to the infrastructure of Arab society, adjustments that were designed to deepen the economic, political, and cultural dependency ties [that linked Egypt to the Western metropole]."[36]

Despite the fact that 'Abbās later revised his negative assessment of the Ottoman period and even became the convener of a weekly seminar held at the Egyptian Historical Society that was devoted to social history during that period, the Whiggish approach to Egyptian history that informed his work had a deep impact on the field of Egyptian history.[37] Furthermore, the lack of scholarly attention to medical reforms continued to be a noticeable feature of the Egyptian historiographical scene. A significant exception is Amira El Azhary Sonbol's study *The Creation of a Medical Profession in Egypt, 1800–1922*, which, as its title indicates, deals specifically with medical reform. Sonbol believes that there was once "a golden age of Arab medicine" in Egypt. However, sharing with 'Abbās a negative assessment of the Ottomans, she argues that this age was followed by an Ottoman dark age, a period of "stagnation and deterioration" that, by the end of the seventeenth century, left no "medical training worth the name."[38] Like 'Abbās, she argues that this moribund state of affairs was shattered by the enlightened policies of the Pasha and the energetic efforts of his chief medical adviser, Clot Bey. Relying primarily on the latter's writings, she traces the early efforts taken to found the Abū Za'bal Medical School and argues that the school quickly became "a center of civilization that was to have an enlightening effect on the country as a whole."[39] But, again like 'Abbās, she says that due to the elitist, state-led nature of these medical reforms, "the country was still steeped in ignorance in the mid-nineteenth century."[40] So when the British took control of the school and the adjoining hospital in the 1890s, restricting the number of students, changing the language of instruction from Arabic to English, and establishing a yearly fee after decades of free education, the fortunes of the school declined rapidly as there was no one to defend it. The regulations the British set up, she argues, "could only have one result, that is, the reduction of the number of Egyptian doctors and confinement of membership in the profession to one elite group, which would moreover be English speaking. It was upon just such groups that the British colonial system depended to maintain British control over occupied nations, Europeanized colonial elite groups of this sort were expected to identify more with Europeans than with their countrymen."[41]

As important as this last insight is, Sonbol does not treat us to any detailed analysis of how the Egyptian graduates of the medical school might have identified with their patients *before* the British takeover. Her study, moreover, lacks a comprehensive account of the social reaction to the introduction of modern medicine to Egypt. Despite her argument that "medicine is perhaps the most appropriate [profession to study the understanding of the dynamic of modernization] because of the importance of health and medicine in the religious, social and economic affairs of Islamic society,"[42] there is no exploration of how this "Islamic" society was affected by modern medicine.

The Egyptian school of historiography therefore exhibits a number of Whiggish features when dealing with the story of how modern medicine was introduced in the first half of the nineteenth century, features that, as the above analysis demonstrates, also apply to the way that this school tackled the much larger issue of Egypt's relationship with Europe during and immediately following Bonaparte's expedition. This school believes that before this proverbial confrontation with the West, and due to the "uncivilized" policies of the Ottomans, Egypt was cut off from any direct contact with Europe, which, significantly, it considers to be the true provenance of science and knowledge. But Europe became impatient with this isolation, and Bonaparte's invasion is seen as an expression of this frustration and its determination to put an end to it. Bonaparte's civilizing mission, however, was short-lived, and what he left unfinished was eventually restarted by Mehmed Ali, who restored Egypt's contacts with Europe and implemented an ambitious, well-thought-out plan for national rejuvenation. This plan, however, was thwarted not only by Western imperial designs but also by one fatal flaw: its top-down approach effectively excluded the natives from government and restricted educational and other reforms to the production of only those bureaucrats and technocrats that the government needed. Unlike Bonaparte's expedition at the end of the eighteenth century, therefore, this second instance of the West knocking on Egypt's doors did not trigger a national awakening, for there was no social base that had an interest in defending the reforms that had been initiated by Mehmed Ali. Despite highlighting the radical nature of the many reforms brought about by the Pasha and his successors, Egyptian studies on the history of modern medicine do not offer a detailed understanding of the impact the introduction of modern medicine had on non-elite Egyptians.

In contrast to this historiography, this book, although it is interested in discovering the Pasha's intentions behind founding a medical school in Egypt and looks closely at the medical publications of Clot Bey and his many Egyptian students, is primarily concerned with charting the reactions Egyptians from all walks of life had to the many innovations their society witnessed during the middle decades of the nineteenth century. By zooming in on medical, legal, and public hygienic reforms, this book asks how our understanding of Egyptian modernity would differ if we examined it not by studying schools, newspapers, and printing presses, but by taking a close look at cemeteries, slaughterhouses, and cesspools. Methodologically, it follows intellectual and conceptual transformations by placing them within their institutional settings. *In Quest of Justice* also takes as axiomatic the assumption that one cannot understand nineteenth-century Egyptian developments except by viewing them within their wider Ottoman context. Building on the work of Jane Hathaway, Ehud Toledano, Alan Mikhail, Adam Mestyan, and James Baldwin, this book sees Egypt in the khedival period (1805–79) as still very much part of the Ottoman Empire—its politics, economy, and culture being shaped by developments within that empire—and argues that Cairo's growing connections with Paris and London should be seen in light of its historic relationship with Istanbul.[43]

COLONIAL MEDICINE AND COLONIAL SUBJECTIVITY

The triumphalist visions and hagiographic narratives that depict Clot Bey and his patron, Mehmed Ali Pasha, as motivated by a high-minded humanitarian zeal to put an end to the ignorance, superstition, and inertia of Egyptians raise the question of whether it is accurate to characterize Qaṣr al-ʿAinī as a "colonial medical institution," to think of Clot Bey as a "colonial official," or to label the medicine that he introduced as "colonial medicine." What makes medicine colonial, and what is colonial about colonial medicine? This is a question that many scholars working on British India and colonial Africa, among other places, have struggled with.[44] On the most basic level, and especially in the tropics, medicine was instrumental in enabling the European conquest of many parts of Africa, Asia, and the New World. The use of quinine prophylaxis as a malaria preventative, for example, is often cited as one of the prime "tools of empire." Without quinine, "European colonialism would have been almost impossible in Africa, and much costlier elsewhere in the tropics."[45]

But what makes medicine colonial is also the different ways in which Western medicine was closely tied to a wide range of military, administrative, and economic activities of the colonial state. The management of colonial labor, especially in mines and armies, and the struggle to protect the lives of native workers, sailors, and soldiers meant that medicine was very often associated with the work of the policeman, the recruiting sergeant, the tax collector, and the many other officials of the colonial state. Moreover, the diffusion of Western medical theories and practices were intricately bound up with the increasingly interventionist colonial state, and as David Arnold has argued, colonial India demonstrated "in a manner unparalleled in Western societies, the exceptional importance of medicine in the cultural and political constitution of its subjects."[46] This close association between medical knowledge and colonial power is what prompted Indians to resist British approaches to healing, disease prevention, and public health, and it was what led Frantz Fanon to comment that "Western medical science, being part of the oppressive [colonial] system, has always provoked in the native an ambivalent attitude. . . . With medicine we come to one of the most tragic features of the colonial situation."[47]

The racial exclusiveness of medical service in European colonies is yet another feature of colonial medicine. In British India, for example, Europeans, Eurasians, and native Christians were overrepresented in the medical colleges. By offering instruction only in English and requiring students to take their exams in London, medical colleges in British India admitted very few Indians, and it took a century after the founding of Calcutta's medical college in 1835 to overturn the racial exclusiveness of the Indian Medical Service.[48]

Furthermore, medicine, along with education, was often used by colonial officials to justify colonialism. Western medicine in particular was depicted as the quintessential evidence of the West's superiority as it was made to stand for rationality and progress "while indigenous society foolishly cherished superstition and witchcraft, was ruled by ignorance and cruelty, and held beliefs and practices Europe had left behind with the Dark Ages."[49] In Tunisia, for example, Western medicine became an integral part of the French *mission civilisatrice,* and a 1905 article in the *Revue Tunisienne* observed that "the doctor is the true conqueror, the peaceful conqueror. . . . It follows that if we wish to penetrate their hearts, to win the confidence of the Muslims, it is in multiplying the services of medical assistance that we will arrive at it most surely."[50]

Finally, some scholars have contended that the single most important aim of colonial medical policy was protecting the white colonial enclave. Most notably, Radhika Ramasubban has argued that in British India, the protection of the army and the European civilian population was "at all times the highest priority" of colonial health policy.[51] With the shift from miasmatic theories about disease etiology to germ theory, "disease came to be identified, not as in the past, with pathogenic landscapes, but with living 'native reservoirs' of diseases."[52] This eventually gave rise to a policy of segregation and isolation using criteria of soil, water, air, and elevation. To protect the white, colonial community, residential areas were established away from the "native" quarters, and, occasionally, sanitary cordons were set up to enforce segregation of the colonial enclave from the natives. In 1859, a Royal Sanitary Commission was set up to "lay down elaborate norms for the creation of distinct areas of European residence, and the 'cantonment', . . . regulated by legislation, developed into a colonial mode of health and sanitation based on the principle of social and physical segregation."[53]

With these characteristics of colonial medicine in mind, we can now revisit the questions of whether Qaṣr al-ʿAinī can be seen as a colonial medical institution and whether Clot Bey can be viewed as a colonial medical official. At first glance, it would appear that Clot Bey could certainly be considered such given the clear manner with which he viewed his effort in Egypt as a belonging to civilizing mission and the frequency with which he congratulated himself for conquering the religious superstitions of a backward people and for enlightening them about the glorious benefits of Western science.[54] However, there is more to that characterization than meets the eye. For one thing, although he was French, Clot Bey had not been dispatched to Egypt by the French government and was not an official of the French state. Despite the fact that he had been introduced to Mehmed Ali by the French consul, he was eventually employed by the Pasha, and throughout his long career in Egypt, which spanned some two decades, he remained an official of the Egyptian state, received his salary from Cairo, and never answered to the Quai d'Orsay or to any other agency of the French state.

For another, unlike Fort William, in the shadow of which the Calcutta Medical College was built in 1835, the Jihād-Abād military camp, which was close to the initial site of the medical school (before it was moved to Qaṣr al-ʿAinī in 1838), was not a military outpost of a European colonial power occupying Egypt. Rather, it was a large camp that Mehmed Ali had built to prepare his army for his own dynastic military adventures. Despite the fact that the Pasha later sought the assistance of the French state in building this army and ended up employing many French officers, his army was not deployed in a European colonial enterprise. After turning down a request to help the French navy occupy the Barbary States of Tripoli, Tunis, and Algiers, Mehmed Ali directed the full wrath of his military machine to the north.[55] In 1831, he launched a spectacularly successful attack on the Ottoman Empire's troops in Syria, thus inaugurating an occupation of the Syrian provinces that would last for some ten years and that would pose a serious threat to the very existence of the Ottoman Empire.[56] And as is discussed in more detail in chapter 1, the Qaṣr al-ʿAinī Medical School was primarily founded to serve the Pasha's army. In fact, one of the main arguments that this book makes is that Qaṣr al-ʿAinī should be viewed within an Ottoman context rather than a European one.

Moreover, the medicine that Clot Bey introduced did not have as its main aim the protection of a European army of occupation. As such, what can be called "khedival medicine," that is, the medicine that was introduced and supported by Egypt's khedives, was not enclavist but universal. Indeed, and as illustrated in chapter 4, Clot Bey struggled hard against calls from members of the European diplomatic corps residing in Egypt to restrict health reform policies to the European community. Instead, he pushed for the establishment of a public health policy that had as its main target all the inhabitants of Egypt, not only those living in the European enclaves in Cairo, Alexandria, and other main cities, the populations of which were expanding thanks to rising trade with Europe.

Furthermore, on accepting Mehmed Ali's commission to found a medical military corps (discussed in more detail in chapter 1), Clot Bey told the Pasha that securing the medical services of Frenchmen would cost him dearly; it would be wiser and cheaper, he advised, to establish a medical college to train hundreds of native doctors and pharmacists. Crucially, he argued, these native doctors should receive their education in Arabic so that they would be able to communicate with their patients. It is important to ponder the significance of this momentous decision: Clot Bey, a Marseilles-trained, French-speaking doctor, advising Mehmed Ali, a Kavalla-born, Turkish-speaking Ottoman governor, to establish a medical school in Egypt where the Arabic-speaking natives would receive state-of-the-art medical education in their mother tongue. This does not square easily with a typical colonial venture.

In thinking about the supposed colonial nature of Qaṣr al-ʿAinī, one also needs to distinguish between, on the one hand, Clot Bey and his European colleagues, who, for the first few years of the institution's history, constituted the institution's teaching staff, and, on the other hand, the Egyptian students, some of whom would go on to assume teaching positions at their alma mater and even become directors of the school. It is clear from even the short excerpts of Clot Bey's writings quoted above that he shared with many of his nineteenth-century European contemporaries the belief that science had had a teleological progression since its inception in antiquity. According to this traditional view, science was believed to have had its origins in ancient Greece, when philosophers broke away from the myths of their forebears. A long period of stagnation ensued with the rise of Christianity, when science suffered a setback as a result of the church having a strong hold on intellectual and cultural life, reaching a nadir in the Middle Ages. But then science witnessed a triumphant comeback with the scientific revolution of the seventeenth century.[57] Throughout the centuries, a deep anticlerical hostility pervaded this viewpoint, and Clot Bey's occasional resentment of the *'ulamā'* might be seen as part of this overarching animosity to religion in general, which he saw as distinct from, and antithetical to, science.[58] But the question remains as to whether Clot Bey's Egyptian students shared with him the belief that science and religion represented two distinct fields of thought or whether they agreed with classical Muslim physicians in rejecting such binary distinction.[59] Furthermore, while Clot Bey depicted himself in many of his publications aimed at a Western audience as transferring Western knowledge to Egypt, it is not clear if his Egyptian students and colleagues believed that they were "diffusing" European science into their country,[60] or if they thought that Qaṣr al-'Ainī was a "contact zone" where European scientific ideas were exchanged and got circulated.[61] As suggested in chapter 1, Clot Bey's Egyptian students repeatedly argued in their Arabic translations of European textbooks that by opening a modern medical school, Mehmed Ali was neither bridging the gap with the West nor trying to catch up with Europe but rather reviving an art that had once flourished in Egypt and renewing a form of science that had once thrived there.[62]

But even if we set aside for the moment the question of the purported colonial subjectivity of Clot Bey's Egyptian students and how they thought of their racial, religious, and gendered positioning within Qaṣr al-'Ainī, Clot Bey's own views and those of his European colleagues about the supposed colonial project in which they were involved merit some closer investigation. Again, the comparison with India may be instructive. In his study of how both the British and Indian nationalist discourses viewed the Indian body, Gyan Prakash asks a crucial question: "What was colonial about the colonization of the body?"[63] By this he means to investigate not only the nature of colonial medicine but also the nature of the colonial state. Building on Foucault's elegant triad of sovereignty, discipline, and governmentality, Prakash argues that what made nineteenth-century Indian medicine colonial was the British denial of the possibility of governmentality in the colony. If sovereignty is concerned with territory, legitimacy, and the law, and if discipline is associated with such institutions as the factory, the prison, the school, and the hospital, then governmentality is defined as "pastoral power" that functions by setting up "economy at the level of the entire state, which means exercising towards its inhabitants, and the wealth and behavior of each and all, a form of surveillance and control as attentive as that of a head of a family over his household and his goods."[64] Prakash then says that what was specific about colonialism was the denial of sovereignty: "British India was marked by the absence of the elegant sovereignty-discipline-government triangle that Foucault identifies in Europe. Fundamentally irreconcilable with the development of a civil society, the colonial state was structurally denied the opportunity to mobilize the capillary forms of power. Thus, colonial governmentality developed in violation of the liberal conception that the government was part of a complex domain of dense, opaque, and autonomous interests that it only harmonized and secured with law and liberty."[65]

In other words, since the presence of these autonomous interests was denied in the colony, and since colonialism, to start with, was predicated on, and justified by, denying the colonized the possibility of self-rule and self-knowledge, it follows that the medical policies adopted by the colonial state reflected this denial of the possibility of governmentality. Accordingly, what distinguished colonial medicine from medicine applied in Europe was not merely the colonial state's deployment of medicine in such a way as to make the Indian body a site of power that witnessed a range of Indian responses (resistance, accommodation, participation, and appropriation), for these responses were not restricted to the colony.[66] Rather, what made medicine colonial, Prakash argues, was the colonial governmentality that was informed by stereotypical images of "Indians as diseased, unhealthy, unhygienic, superstitious, and unscientific."[67]

This view of the colonized as essentially lacking in the liberal faculties of self-knowledge and self-rule is what Partha Chatterjee famously labeled "the rule of colonial difference."[68] Although I find this idea about the very nature of the colonial project illuminating, and while I judge Prakash's critique of the nature of colonial governmentality to be equally insightful, I mention them here not to indicate their applicability to the Egyptian case but, on the contrary, to point to their possible limitations. For ever since the rise of the cultural turn within the field of modern Middle Eastern history, there have been a plethora of studies that approach nationalism in terms of cultural construction, and the work of the Indian Subaltern Studies Collective has been rightly very influential in raising new questions with which to approach the rise of nationalism as a new form of collective subjectivity. The expanding cottage industry of subjectivity studies, however, has all too often made implicit (sometimes explicit) equations between Egypt and India, paying little attention to the differences that set the Egyptian colonial experience apart from the Indian one.

By contrast, this book starts from what should be a commonsensical assumption, namely that Egypt was never an Indian province, let alone a Bengali one. Despite the fact that many post-1882 British officials saw Egypt through an Indian lens, the nature of khedival Egypt should have made these officials realize the fallacy of their comparisons.[69] Furthermore, pace Timothy Mitchell's *Colonising Egypt,* a book that rightly continues to illuminate and rejuvenate the field of modern Middle Eastern studies, I question if it is reasonable to refer to pre-1882 Egyptian society as colonial.[70] Given this chapter's discussion of the nature of Mehmed Ali's dynastic project, Clot Bey's medical venture, and the evolution of Qaṣr al-ʿAinī as the center of a wide-ranging public hygiene establishment, I question the degree to which "colonial medicine," a phrase that describes the experience of India in the nineteenth century, captures the reality of khedival medicine. For as shown in this book, neither Clot Bey nor his students argued that the Egyptian body was *essentially* diseased, unhealthy, or unhygienic; indeed, a deep belief in the pedagogical impact of Qaṣr al-ʿAinī informed the efforts of hundreds of Egyptian doctors and hygienists during the middle decades of the nineteenth century.

LEGAL MEDICINE, POSTSECULAR CRITIQUE, AND IMPOSSIBLE STATES

As stated at the beginning of this chapter, dissections were performed at Qaṣr al-ʿAinī not only for the purposes of medical instruction but also for legal investigations of criminal cases. Specifically, the police routinely requested autopsy reports in their investigations of suspicious cases of homicide and other cases of violent crime. These autopsy reports, together with the results of police investigations, were then included in the dossiers that were forwarded to the legal councils that adjudicated criminal cases. Accordingly, in addition to tackling the issue of the supposedly fraught relationship between Islam and modern medicine and of the colonial nature of khedival medicine, *In Quest of Justice* also raises the question of medicine's intimate connection to law. Indeed, this book primarily offers an account of the history of legal medicine in nineteenth-century Egypt, and it relies heavily on forensic medical reports that were prepared by the police and forwarded to legal bodies responsible for adjudicating cases of violent crime.

Notably, these legal bodies were not shari'a courts, even though shari'a courts were as fully operational in the nineteenth century as they had been for centuries.[71] Given that the shari'a courts were competent to deal with cases of violent crime, such as homicide, battery, and sexual assault,[72] and despite the fact that, as shown in chapter 5, both *fiqh* (Islamic jurisprudence) and legal practice in shari'a courts readily admitted medical expertise in adjudicating certain kinds of cases, the forensic medical reports that the Qaṣr al-'Ainī doctors prepared were not forwarded to these courts. Rather, they were forwarded to legal bodies called *majālis al-siyāsa*. In modern-day Arabic, this phrase would translate as "councils of politics." But these councils were legal, not political, bodies; they were created in the late 1840s and early 1850s with a mandate to adjudicate cases of serious crime, among other offenses. What, then, were these councils, and how did they relate to the shari'a courts? What is the connection between *fiqh,* shari'a courts, *siyāsa* councils, and medicine? How can the study of the introduction of forensic medicine shed light on the transmutations that shari'a witnessed in nineteenth-century Egypt and help us understand the history of modern Egyptian law?

Chapter 2 offers a full account of nineteenth-century legal change in Egypt, but it may be helpful to summarize the standard narrative here and follow a particular critique it generated. According to the standard narrative, legal change is subsumed under the general rubric of secularization. Starting with the assumption that what existed in Egypt before the onset of this secularization was something called shari'a, both Egyptian secularists and Islamists see the jurisdiction of this type of shari'a as having been steadily truncated due to the gradual encroachment of Western, mostly French, legal principles and practices.[73] The decisive turning point is believed to have come in 1876, with the establishment of the Mixed Courts (al-Maḥākim al-Mukhtalaṭa) (so called because they adjudicated disputes between natives and foreigners and also because their judges were from various European nations). The last chapter in this process of legal change came in 1883, when new courts known as the National Courts (al-Maḥākim al-Ahliyya) were inaugurated. These applied legal codes that had been translated from French into Arabic. These codes covered a wide range of fields, such as criminal, commercial, civil, administrative, and constitutional law. So deep was the European influence on Egyptian law that by the end of the century, shari'a's jurisdiction had been restricted to the field of personal status.[74]

In his *Formations of the Secular,* Talal Asad offers an incisive critique of this narrative, which I will follow here. Instead of seeing secularism as a result of the gradual restriction of shari'a jurisdiction and the growing adoption of Western civil codes, Asad argues that secularism needs to be seen as having initiated a radical and formal separation of ethics from the authority of the law. Accordingly, the task should be not to study the gradual curtailment of shari'a but rather to trace the "changes in the *concept* of the law in colonial Egypt that helped to make secularism thinkable as a practical proposition."[75] Although it deals with the transformations that shari'a underwent in nineteenth-century Egypt, Asad's analysis in *Formations of the Secular* is part of a much larger critique of the very idea of an anthropology of Islam that he launched more than three decades ago. Ever since Asad put forward the notion of "discursive tradition," a generation of anthropologists have creatively interacted with his critical inquiries about the nature of the secular project, of the role of ethics in shaping Muslims' lives, and of the cultivation of affect, piety, subjectivity, self-formation, and governmental rationality.[76] At the core of the research project launched by Asad and his interlocutors is an incisive critique of liberalism and secularism aimed at highlighting the coercion, silencing, and exclusion that inhere in the alleged universality of Western traditions.[77] As productive and necessary as this postsecular research project is, it has not been without its detractors. One of the most notable reservations is that articulated by anthropologist Samuli Schielke, who points to the fact that one needs to "look beyond the elegant but narrow confines of piety and tradition and to include the messier but richer fields of everyday experiences, personal biographies and complex genealogies."[78]

To elaborate on this reservation, it may be helpful to take a closer look at Asad's critique of how the process of legal reform in nineteenth-century Egypt is commonly approached. This process of legal reform, Asad argues, "has been represented by historians as the triumph of the rule of law, or as the facilitation of capitalist exploitation, or as the complex struggle for power between different kinds of agents—especially colonizing Europeans and resisting Egyptians." Asad is not interested in checking which one of these perspectives is correct; rather, he is concerned with exploring "what is involved when *conceptual* changes . . . make 'secularism' possible."[79] As stated above, Asad is also skeptical of the standard narrative, which equates the process of legal reform with the abridgment of shari'a and the limiting of its jurisdiction to "personal status." Unlike the advocates of an Islamic state, Asad is not concerned with showing how this abridgment has deprived shari'a of political authority. Rather, he is interested in studying the conceptual and paradigmatic shifts within shari'a when it has been truncated in this manner. To document this transmutation of shari'a and the various rearticulations of basic concepts such as law, morality, ethics, religion, and human agency, Asad subjects a few legal texts from the very last years of the late nineteenth and early twentieth century to a close reading. This allows him to detect how an intellectual space was opened up that made secularization thinkable. Specifically, he traces transmutations of the concepts of the individual and the family and studies how these transmutations brought about a distinction between morality and law. It is this separation between morality and law and the concomitant ascendance of the principle of self-governance, he argues, that are the bulwark of the secular state, a state that has at its disposal the authority of the law to "civilize" entire populations.[80]

As a critique of the liberal project predicated on self-government and human agency, Asad's intervention is effective. However, methodologically, the import of the critique is circumscribed by the fact that it is restricted to tracing conceptual transmutations of such terms as law, morality, and ethics. Asad, in fact, acknowledges that his book is "not a total history of legal reform"[81] but rather a study that takes as its subject matter leading intellectuals and would-be reformers who penned reports, articles, and books at the end of the nineteenth century. In his reading, these intellectual works are indicative of the paradigmatic shift that is characteristic of secularism, namely the wrenching apart the twin concepts of morality and law that are believed to be central to shari'a. In response to historical studies that suggest that some of the characteristics of secularism might be traced to the premodern Muslim society, Asad insists, "The issue here is not an empirical one. It will not be resolved simply by more intensive archival research, just as understanding the place of the secular today requires more than mere ethnographic fieldwork.... A careful analysis is needed of culturally distinctive *concepts* and their articulation with one another."[82]

By contrast, *In Quest of Justice* is based on a methodological assumption that zooming in on conceptual changes to try to understand the process of legal change is of limited value, as this approach tells us that the law has changed but not specifically how these changes occurred. Rather than dismissing "intensive archival research," this book argues that it is precisely such a methodological approach that can help us understand how and when the law changed. Intensive archival research, furthermore, can tell us how people in the past, who might or might not have been pious and who might or might not have written probing tracts, reacted to legal change in their daily lives.

This book, therefore, follows a particular society (Egyptian) in a particular period (the middle decades of the nineteenth century) to trace particular transformations undergone in particular institutions (the legal and medical institutions). It closely studies a number of practices in which the two fields of law and medicine intersected—primarily legal medicine but also torture, urban planning, and food control. *In Quest of Justice* presents a detailed study of the evolution of these messy practices, but it does not intend to trace how conceptual transformations wrenched apart the concepts of morality and law (for, as this book argues, these concepts have always been separate within *an* Islamic discursive tradition). Rather, the book intends, firstly, to trace these conceptual transformations, not genealogically but by locating them in the institutional, social, political, and intellectual contexts that gave rise to them, and secondly, to grasp the messiness of daily lives (and deaths), and chart the myriad ways in which average Egyptians understood, reacted to, and shaped the many forces that were rapidly altering their society in the mid-nineteenth century.

I also take issue with Asad's *Formations of the Secular* on empirical and theoretical grounds. Asad's critique of secularism's separation of morality from law derives its poignancy from the assumption that "secularism did not exist in Egypt prior to modernity" and that prior to modernity, "the moral subject [was] not concerned with state law as an external authority."[83] Within Muslim tradition, Asad argues, "the capability for virtuous conduct, and the sensibilities on which that capability draws, are acquired by the individual through tradition-guided practices. . . . *Fiqh* is critical to this process not as a set of rules to be obeyed but as the condition that enables the development of the virtues."[84] But was *fiqh* the only constituent component of the law, or did the law also embody the political calculations and interests of the state? In other words, were law and morality wrenched apart from one another only by modernity, or is it conceivable to think of law and morality as uncoupled within a premodern shari'a legality? As important as empirical details are in understanding how the law was practiced and applied, not only imagined and thought, this is not merely an empirical question. Rather, it is a theoretical and conceptual question, one that goes to the very definition of shari'a. For Asad is positing a notion of shari'a legality that is a *fiqhī* (Islamic jurisprudential) one in the double sense that it is a product of the discursive tradition of the *fuqahā'* (jurists) and is based solely on ethics and aimed at the cultivation of the virtues, with no role in state politics, or *siyāsa*. This *fiqhī* understanding of shari'a legality does indeed belong to *an* Islamic discursive tradition; it is doubtful, however, that it belonged to *the* Islamic discursive tradition, and *In Quest of Justice* raises the possibility that there might have existed other conceptions of shari'a legalities that belong to other Islamic discursive traditions, traditions that allowed for *fiqh* to be conjoined with *siyāsa*. Put differently, this book questions whether *fiqhī* morality was the only morality in Egyptian society, and it asks if a *siyāsī* morality can be imagined, one that derives from the rich *siyāsa* literature and the reciprocal rights and duties that this literature stipulates for rulers and ruled alike.

The idea that shari'a is synonymous with *fiqh* is also what informs Wael Hallaq's oeuvre on Islamic law. In his most recent book, *The Impossible State: Islam, Politics and Modernity's Moral Predicament,* Hallaq critiques the notion, held by secularists and Islamists alike, that a modern state can be regarded as "Islamic" if it applies Islamic legal norms.[85] As the title of his book implies, Hallaq argues that an "Islamic state" is a logical, conceptual, and even metaphysical impossibility. Hallaq sees shari'a as a worldview that is essentially incompatible with the modern nation-state and its version of rule of law. Whereas "in its day [shari'a] was at once moral, legal, cultural, and deeply psychological," and whereas "Islamic governance rests on a moral, legal, political, social and metaphysical foundations that are dramatically different from those sustaining the modern state," the modern state with its European provenance is predicated on a "distinction, indeed separation, between Is and Ought."[86] The modern state, Hallaq argues, is based on the Enlightenment philosophical paradigm that separates fact from value and destroys any possible harmony between law, morality, governance, and human consciousness. In contrast to the disenchanted world in which Enlightenment thinkers lived, "the pre-modern Muslim intellectuals inhabited a world that was, more or less, 'enchanted.'"[87]

Like Asad, Hallaq points to the tension, indeed the violence, that inheres in the modern state paradigm, with its separation of ethics from law, and to how this new paradigm brought about the "structural death" of the shari'a "epistme."[88] Also, like Asad, Hallaq's premodern Muslim society is a *fiqhī* society in the sense that it is difficult to locate it except in the minds of the *fuqahā'*, the jurists who produced the copious *fiqh* manuals that he studies. It is not that this society is a mythical one or that Hallaq's account of it is "nostalgic," as he himself preemptively says, anticipating skeptical highbrows.[89] Rather, it is a *conceptual* society, one that is constructed in the minds of jurists and may or may not bear a resemblance to the messy realities that Muslims lived outside the neat pages of the elegant tomes of the *fuqahā'*. As pointed out by an observant critic, Hallaq's Muslim past "has no real space for conflict, contestation or suppressed alternatives . . . for the study of *power* in pre-modern Islam."[90]

But as with Asad, I take issue with Hallaq, not only with his preference of the paradigmatic over the historical[91] but also with his *fiqhī* understanding of shariʿa. In *The Impossible State,* and even more so in his earlier work *Sharīʿa: Theory, Practice, Transformations,* Hallaq presents a complex picture of the relationship of Islamic law and legal practice. He makes use of the copious scholarship produced by Ottomanists that relies heavily on the *sijills*, or registers, of shariʿa courts that the Ottoman Empire kept throughout its long history. Above all, however, he draws valuable insights from his commanding reading of the voluminous *fiqh* literature produced by jurists, who, he insists, worked independently of rulers. As such, Hallaq sees Islamic law as a "non-state, community-based, bottom-up, jural order."[92] And while he acknowledges the importance of *siyāsa sharʿiyya,* that is, the discretionary power of the ruler in upholding and implementing the judgments of the *qāḍī* in shariʿa court, he insists that this was a limited concept and that it was restricted to the fields of "tax collection, public order, land use, and at times criminal law and some aspects of public morality that could affect social harmony."[93] Similarly, he recognizes the historical fact that rulers of Islamic polities had to regularly enact legislation that was meant to act as a "supplement . . . to the Sharīʿa in what was known as the *qānūn.* . . . [The latter added] to the religious law, especially in areas having to do with public order, the bedrock of any successful regime. Public order was enforced by extra-*sharʿī* legislation pertaining to highway robbery, theft, bodily injury, homicide, adultery and fornication (and accusations thereof), usury, taxation, [and] land tenure."[94] However, even though he acknowledges the centrality of *qānūn* in maintaining public order, calling it "the bedrock of any successful regime," he insists that "the *qāḍī* stood as the exclusive agent of the *qānūn*'s enforcement. On the ground, he was the ultimate administrator and final interpreter of the *qānūn.*"[95]

By contrast, this book views *siyāsa* and *qānūn,* not only *qaḍāʾ* and *fiqh,* as central to our understanding of Islamic law. It builds on the copious literature that considers *siyāsa* as a legal-political concept as well as a lived practice. According to this literature, Muslim polities, from the very beginning of Islamic history, have always sought to supplement the *fiqh* that the jurists defined with extra measures intended to maintain peace within the realm and uphold the interests of the state. Therefore, in addition to privileging legal practice over legal thought, this book follows this legal practice in *siyāsa* councils rather than in *qāḍī* court. By examining the copious correspondence of a particular *siyāsa* system, that of nineteenth-century Egypt, *In Quest of Justice* builds on a growing body of original and insightful scholarship that has challenged the heavy reliance on *sijills* within Ottoman legal historiography and insisted on seeing the qadi court as but one of many legal bodies with overlapping jurisdictions.[96] Furthermore, by relying primarily on reports of forensic medicine, which not coincidentally was called "*siyāsa* medicine" (as it was used in *siyāsa* councils, not in qadi courts), this book asks if it is possible to view *siyāsa* and *qānūn* not as extra-*sharʿī* but as extra-*fiqhī* concepts and questions how our understanding of shariʿa differs if we include *siyāsa* as a constituent component of it.

ISLAMIST HISTORIOGRAPHY OF MODERN EGYPTIAN LAW

One particular aspect of the standard narrative of nineteenth-century legal reform, namely the supposed curtailment of shariʿa, has been the source of deep consternation for generations of Egyptian Islamists. Interestingly, and as Leonard Wood has shown in his study of the formation of modern Egyptian law, it took a while for an "Islamic legal revivalism" to gain traction among Egyptian legal practitioners and scholars, and it was only in the 1920s and 1930s, that is, a full half-century after the establishment of the National Courts, that we see a concerted effort to challenge this Westernization and attempt to bring about a revival of Islamic law in the face of European incursion.[97]

By offering a detailed reading of forensic medicine in nineteenth-century Egypt, *In Quest of Justice* engages with Egyptian Islamist historiography of modern Egyptian law. While this historiography is understandably voluminous, I will give a close reading of two studies by Egyptian Islamists that deal with the history of modern Egyptian law and that had a profound impact on shaping the weltanschauung of generations of Egyptian Islamists and their understanding of the place of shariʿa in a modern state context. As this reading shows, although Egyptian Islamists are concerned with what they believe was a Western onslaught aimed at replacing shariʿa governance with Western positive law, they are unconcerned with following the precise mechanisms through which this ostensible onslaught was carried out. Instead, their scholarship is informed by a deep anxiety about identity and the dangers to cultural authenticity that the adoption of positive law threatened. By contrast, this book questions if this Islamist obsession with identity forwards our understanding of the precise ways Egyptian law evolved in the khedival period.

The first study was penned by ʿAbd al-Qādir ʿAwda. After graduating in 1930 from the law school of King Fu'ād University (later renamed Cairo University), ʿAwda joined the Muslim Brotherhood. Meanwhile, he occupied key positions in the judiciary and eventually became a judge. In 1949, he resigned his government posts and devoted his full energy to working for the Brotherhood. During the struggle for power between Gamal Abdel Nasser and Muḥammad Nagīb in February and March 1954,[98] ʿAwda was arrested and sent to prison. A few months later, following the failed attempt to assassinate Nasser in October 1954, he was charged with attempting to overthrow the new revolutionary regime. After a swift trial, he was given a death sentence and hanged on December 7, 1954, guaranteeing him a prominent place in the pantheon of Muslim Brotherhood martyrs.[99]

Five years before his death, ʿAwda published a two-volume study of more than eight hundred pages on Islamic criminal law. Titled *Al-Tashrīʿ al-Jināʾī al-Islāmī Muqāranan biʾl-Qānūn al-Waḍʿī* (Islamic criminal legislation compared to positive law), the book is structured not like classical *fiqh* tomes but according to the logic of modern, positive law.[100] Despite its format, which resembles the layout of the textbooks he studied in university, the work's content was a distillation of the criminal elements of the four *sunni madhhabs* (schools of thought). In the preface, ʿAwda explicitly states his reason for choosing this particular layout for his book:

> I have to confess that I began studying Islamic shariʿa only in 1944. . . . Studying the criminal side [of the four *sunnī maddhabs*] was an arduous task as I had no prior experience with *uṣūl* [*al-fiqh,* i.e., principles of Islamic jurisprudence], and also lacked knowledge of *fiqhī* terminology. . . . [Studying the four *sunnī madhhabs* in a comparative manner] did me a lot of good as it made it easier to understand the bases on which each jurist had built his theory. . . . After I had realized the amount of effort that a man with a background in [positive] law has to undertake to comprehend the principles of shariʿa, after I had seen the glaring results that I had obtained [from my own study of shariʿa], and after I had seen the tragicomic conclusions that we had reached [by arguing that Islamic shariʿa is incompatible with modern times], I felt that I had an urgent obligation to shariʿa, to my legal colleagues, and to anyone who had received a nonreligious education, namely to inform [them]

> of the principles of Islamic criminal law in a language that would be accessible and understandable, to correct the information that legal specialists [*rijāl al-qānūn*] have about shari'a, and to make public the facts that ignorance had hidden from us for a long time.[101]

'Awda's purpose was to show that "by conducting a comparison between the most modern legal theories and the ancient principles of shari'a, . . . [it is clear that] the static ancient is better than the variable modern, and that despite its age, shari'a is more sublime than to be [even] compared to modern positive laws. . . . The modern can never reach the perfection of the classic [since this is akin to] comparing what people create to what the Master of all people has created."[102] Nearly three-quarters of a century after the inauguration of the National Courts, 'Awda's book articulated what many legal practitioners of his generation had started to believe, namely that there was much to learn from shari'a and that it was wrong to assume that it was incompatible with modern times. The political import of 'Awda's tome could not be mistaken, for in addition to providing the Brotherhood with proof that what they were striving for—that "implementing God's law" (*taṭbīq shar' Illāh*) was scientifically sound—it also brought home the folly of replacing a "perfect, superior, and permanent" legal system with what has been shown to be a deeply defective one.[103]

Equally significant is 'Awda's denial of history. Starting from the assumption that shari'a was of divine origin, he argues that it "did not start as simple laws that were gradually augmented. It did not start as some scattered principles that then got collected either. Nor as rudimentary principles that got complicated. Shari'a was not born [like an infant] that gradually grew and developed; rather, it was born agile, complete, [as it was] revealed by God as a whole, perfect, all-inclusive, self-referential shari'a that has no wrongs or imperfections."[104] It is this denial of the historicity of shari'a that *In Quest of Justice* engages with. By examining forensic medicine during the khedival period, this book investigates shari'a as it was practiced in a particular historical period, that of khedival Egypt, and challenges the identitarian lens through which Islamists view legal reform in that period. Specifically, by taking *siyāsa* practices seriously and by viewing *siyāsa* as a constituent component of shari'a, this book asks if, instead of viewing the reforms to the Egyptian legal system in the nineteenth century as an example of a Western attack on Muslim identity, it may be more useful to see these reforms as constituting a stage in shari'a's historical evolution.

Some forty years after ʿAwda's death, another Egyptian Islamist jurist and judge, Ṭāriq al-Bishrī, offered a scathing critique of how Western law achieved its hegemony in Egypt by marshaling historical evidence and engaging closely with the historical record. In addition to being one of Egypt's top jurists, al-Bishrī is also a prominent historian.[105] Like ʿAwda, al-Bishrī did not study shariʿa at an academic institution; rather, he acquired his knowledge of *fiqh* and shariʿa after graduating from Cairo University's School of Law. His early historical writings do not evince any particular interest in Islam or shariʿa. Following Egypt's defeat in the June War, however, a fundamental shift occurred in his outlook on Egyptian politics and history, and he subjected his own writing to severe self-criticism. In 1981, when he was preparing the second edition of his classic book *Al-Ḥaraka al-Siyāsiyya fī Miṣr, 1945–1953* (The political movement in Egypt, 1945–1953), which had originally appeared in 1972, he decided not to change a single word of the original text. However, he famously wrote a new preface in which he subjected his own earlier work to scathing criticism. This seventy-two-page preface was one of the most daring examples of autocriticism penned in Egypt after the 1967 defeat. It focused on his earlier downplaying of the role played by the Muslim Brotherhood and the "Islamic movement" at large in Egyptian politics in the first half of the twentieth century. And at the core of the older al-Bishrī's critique was the young al-Bishrī's inability to understand the significance of the Muslim Brotherhood's call to implement Islamic shariʿa:

> We used to engage in arguments [with the Muslim Brotherhood, telling them,] "Why shariʿa? Should [implementing it] be the goal we should strive toward? We consider the legislative system [only] as a way of upholding justice and freedom, . . . regardless of whether it had its origins in Islamic shariʿa or Roman law." . . . My two chapters on the Muslim Brotherhood in this book reflected this logic, a logic that is prevalent among secularists, who assume an agnostic stance regarding the ideological and cultural struggle between what we inherited and what reached us from the West, and who do not differentiate between the historical and cultural roots of their countries, on the one hand, and the values and ideas that had been introduced by the invaders, on the other. Despite the fact that we received adequate education about Islamic shariʿa in our law schools, the reference point, as far as the curricula were concerned, was always those principles that had been imported from the West, especially from France. . . . The typical student thus learns that the history of his law can be traced back to the Romans, then to European ecclesiastical law, then to the Napoleonic Codes. . . . Shariʿa, however, is relegated to the field of personal status. We have called the process of excising shariʿa and

> introducing French legislation "legal and legislative reform." It is true that we were in need of reform; however, in this, as in other fields, we neither reformed nor modernized. Instead, we managed to destroy the structures and edifices [of our own system of law]. We then upheld aspects of the foreign imported [system] that was chosen for us and imposed them upon ourselves.[106]

This scathing double critique—of the delusional attitude of the opponents of the Muslim Brotherhood and their inability to understand the significance of the Brotherhood's call to implement shari'a, and of his own earlier inability to question this delusional attitude—has been the subject of many subsequent works that al-Bishrī published in the 1980s and 1990s. In these later publications, he strives to show that modern Egyptian law is not the result of a natural, endogenous evolution but was coercively implanted by European powers and Europeanized elites and that shari'a, despite its flexibility and malleability, was not allowed to grow and develop within the Egyptian legal environment but was deliberately and cynically uprooted and displaced. According to al-Bishrī's analysis, four factors are primarily responsible for this misguided effort to replace shari'a with Western law. The first (and here we see traces of the familiar depiction of the Ottoman period as an era of intellectual sterility) was the hardening (*jumūd*) of shari'a-derived jurisprudence and the lack of intellectual originality among the *'ulamā'* that lasted until the end of the eighteenth century.[107] The second was that European powers ruthlessly pressed the Ottoman Empire to launch the Tanzimat "reforms" and manipulated Egypt into establishing the Mixed Courts with the aim of furthering their influence in the heart of Islamic lands. These legal innovations were ostensibly needed, European powers argued, to introduce the principle of equality into the legal system so that non-Muslims would be granted the same rights and duties as Muslims. In practice, however, these reforms were the thin end of the wedge that allowed European powers to interfere in the domestic affairs of the Ottoman Empire and Egypt and to act as patrons of non-Muslim subjects.[108] This "ferocious European assault" also necessitated changing legal and judicial structures to accommodate the changing power relations with Europe.[109] The third factor was that the Ottoman and Egyptian elites uncritically accepted Western ways and began a wholesale process of mimicry:

> [It was so thorough] that we became like Europeans, despite the differences that separate us from them in reality. With regards temporality, by believing that we share with them the same time, . . . a split was affected in the way we

think of our present whereby we appeared to have two presents: their present, which has become our future, a future we strive to achieve in our own countries, and our present, which has become in our consciousness one that we strive to get rid of. Many of us fell between these two presents in an abyss of agnosticism and the absurd.[110]

The fourth factor behind the extensive adoption of European legal codes and institutions that started in the last third of the nineteenth century, al-Bishrī argues, was not solely the work of Egyptian secularists infatuated with the West; the *'ulamā'* themselves were also to blame. As evidence of this, al-Bishrī quotes a story narrated by Rashīd Riḍā in his biography of Muḥammad 'Abdu that shows Khedive Ismā'īl turning to the shaykhs of al-Azhar and asking them if they would write a book of civil and criminal law based on the shari'a in the form of a positive law code that would be suitable to the times. The shaykhs turned down his offer, fearing that they would draw public scorn and be accused of impiety. As a result, the new National Courts were founded on the basis of French codes and not on the basis of shari'a, and there was a sharp reorientation of Egyptian law toward European legislation.[111]

Al-Bishrī's critique revolves around the binary of *al-mawrūth,* that which had been inherited and passed on from generation to generation,[112] and *al-wāfid,* that which had been imported (from the West). Al-Bishrī is careful to clarify that he does not mean by *al-mawrūth* a pristine, uncontaminated essence, and he insists that Islamic civilization thrived by constantly borrowing from other cultures throughout its long history. However, faced with the challenge of Western hegemony in the nineteenth century, Ottoman and Egyptian elites lost all sense of direction and reversed their priorities of what to preserve and what to borrow:

The question that is posed nowadays revolves around what to take and what to leave from *al-mawrūth* and *al-wāfid.* This question has been constantly raised over the past hundred years. However, I argue that the choice offered by this question is now based on different criteria. In the past, our default position has been that of *al-mawrūth,* and we used to argue about what aspects of Western civilization are compatible with that default position. Later, our default position became that of *al-wāfid,* and we started talking about *al-turāth* in the third person. . . . Now our internal debate revolves around what to retrieve from *al-turāth,* whereas our fathers used to argue about what to accept from *al-wāfid.* . . . By arguing about what to take and what to leave from *al-mawrūth* and *al-wāfid,* we are effectively establishing

> an equivalency between these two terms as if they both occupied the same distance from us. We are thus treating them as if they were merchandise in a storefront.[113]

It is in this language of cultural authenticity and civilizational encounters that al-Bishrī couches his critique of how Western law has established its hegemony in Egypt. It is a critique that centers around a double indictment of Egyptian elites: first, for putting *al-mawrūth* and *al-wāfid* on the same footing, "as if they were merchandise in a storefront," and then for equating *al-wāfid* with modernity and *al-mawrūth* with being backward-looking (*raʾʾī*).[114] Al-Bishrī, therefore, gives a highly original and perceptive critique of the typical story of how Egyptian law was supposedly modernized. It is a critique that has provided the Islamist movement in Egypt with a sharp, articulate indictment of a central pillar of the modern state, namely its legal system. Al-Bishrī's scathing critique is centered not on the efficiency, integrity, or popularity of that legal system but on its purported inauthenticity. His analysis repeatedly comes back to this central point: the current legal system did not develop from within the Egyptian cultural, political, and social environment but rather was imposed by European powers and by their Egyptian acolytes, who had been dazzled by the West and ensnared by its might.

Despite the originality and importance of al-Bishrī's analysis,[115] however, there are two curious omissions in the way he narrates the story of modern Egyptian law. The first is that, while he occasionally refers to courts, whether shariʿa courts or the newly established National Courts, he makes no attempt to describe in any degree of detail how these courts functioned, how the process of legislative changes might have affected the way they handled cases, or how their procedures have changed over time as a result of imported ideas or imposed institutional changes. Instead, throughout his analysis there is a preference to document changes in legal thought and a near total disregard for documenting judicial practice. This privileging of legal thought over judicial practice is a clear reflection of al-Bishrī's deep belief that "more than anything else, the great jurists of Islam [*jumhūr fuqahāʾ al-Islām al-ʿiẓām*] represent the genius of Arab-Islamic intellectual production."[116] As a result, despite his attempt to historicize his critique of the standard narrative of legal reform, his own analysis pays little attention to institutional developments and concentrates on how key intellectual figures (jurists, Azharī shaykhs, lawyers, politicians, journalists, etc.) responded to the increased hegemony of Western law. The second, which is also another example of privileging intellectual over institutional analysis, is that al-Bishrī hardly ever refers to the *siyāsa* system, even though it was the dominant legal system in Egypt during the four decades immediately preceding the introduction of Western law. Despite his insistence that Western law replaced shariʿa in the last third of the nineteenth century, al-Bishrī does not give a detailed account of how shariʿa, as the quintessential *mawrūth,* functioned in courts or of how it interacted with Western laws, the paradigmatic *wāfid.* Also conspicuously absent is any analysis of whatever role the *siyāsa* councils might have played in negotiating the relationship between shariʿa and Western legal thought and practice. In fact, the only time al-Bishrī referred to the *siyāsa* councils was to argue that these new legal bodies grew next to the *qāḍī* courts but in a completely unrelated fashion: "These *majālis* [councils] implemented whatever laws had been issued by the governor [of Egypt] and disregarded shariʿa."[117]

In Quest of Justice, relying as it does on the copious documentation of the *siyāsa* system, questions al-Bishrī's dismissive assessment of what should be seen as a central component of shariʿa as it was practiced in khedival Egypt. By closely reading the records of this branch of the legal system, this book also asks if the emphasis Islamists place on identity and cultural authenticity as the prime causalities of what they perceive as a Western legislative onslaught is the best way to evaluate the nature and effect of legal change in khedival Egypt.

THE BODY OF THE MODERN EGYPTIAN STATE

To tell the story of legal and medical reform in khedival Egypt, *In Quest of Justice* relies primarily on documents culled from the Egyptian National Archives (ENA). This archival material offers a detailed picture of how shariʿa was actually implemented, how the criminal system functioned, and how *siyāsa* councils interacted with *qāḍī* courts in daily practice. The records of the *siyāsa* councils housed in the ENA comprise more than four thousand ledgers, and this archive of a complex and highly efficient legal system has seldom been studied before. As I will discuss further in chapter 2, earlier *siyāsa* systems throughout Islamic history have been described in detail by contemporary observers, subsequent historians, and political and legal detractors and supporters of this intriguing component of shariʿa. *In Quest of Justice,* however, offers the first full account of the *siyāsa* system based on the system's own records, revealing its internal logic and relying on its discourse.

This book also uses the records of the Qaṣr al-ʿAinī Medical School and Hospital and those of a number of related medical and public hygienic institutions to explain how new scientific-medical knowledges and practices were introduced in Egypt. Since these records contain bureaucratic correspondence about the daily workings of a multitude of medical institutions (hospitals, public clinics, dispensaries, chemical labs, etc.), the picture that emerges complements the neat one that is usually encountered in the writings of medical practitioners and public health officials. Very often, this bureaucratic correspondence reveals fascinating accounts of the tactical maneuvers that non-elite Egyptians pursued in actively and creatively engaging with modern medical and public hygienic practices and discourses.

By offering a detailed account of how the disciplines of both medicine and law developed in the nineteenth century, *In Quest of Justice* examines what the founding of a modern state specifically entailed and how Egyptians came to experience it in a corporeal way. The modern Egyptian state, this book argues, was constituted by devising techniques that enabled it to touch and control the bodies of its subjects, such as vaccinations, the collection of vital statistics, quarantines, torture, and dissection. Egyptians therefore found their bodies being monitored and controlled in unprecedented ways, literally from birth to death and beyond. This book charts how these novel practices were introduced and then refined and calibrated through time and also examines how non-elite Egyptians understood, reacted to, and/or resisted this unprecedented control of their bodies.

Again, my purpose is not to trace the trajectory of such concepts as "the state," "the constitution," or "justice" from their origins in Europe to their diffusion in Egypt; nor is it my intention to show how such concepts might have been transmogrified in the course of their translation. In charting out the evolving concepts of law, the state, public health, personal hygiene, and justice and tracing the discursive shifts that these concepts underwent, this book embeds these shifts within administrative and institutional contexts. At the same time, I pay close attention to the ethnic, linguistic, financial, political, and cultural tensions that infused these administrative and institutional bodies in the nineteenth century. As the following chapters show, these tensions informed the manner in which the two fields that this book concentrates on—law and medicine—evolved during the khedival period.

This book takes the human body as its unit of analysis and looks at how it can be studied as a site on which both state power and non-elite resistance were performed. Throughout this book, the corporeality of the body is stressed to show how the newly reconstituted fields of law and medicine attempted to subject the body to the authority of the state, and to follow non-elite Egyptians in their reactions to these incessant attempts at subjectification. Accordingly, and to emphasize the centrality of the body both as a product of hegemonic discourses of medicine and law and as a site of resistance, the chapters of this book are structured around the five senses and are arranged in the traditional hierarchy in which they typically appear in both Islamic and Western medical systems: sight, sound, smell, taste, and touch.

It is important to stress, however, that the five chapters do not offer a social or cultural history of the senses. Rather, the senses are used merely as heuristic devices to introduce the two main tropes of this book—law and medicine—and to structure five different arguments, one in each chapter, that deal with the relationship between science and religion. Chapter 1, therefore, uses the sense of sight to introduce the practice of autopsy (literally, "to see with one's own eyes") and describe the intricate means by which anatomoclinical medicine was introduced in Egypt. The chapter charts the reaction of non-elite Egyptians to dissection and quarantines, two practices associated with the newly constituted medical field. More specifically, it raises the question of how different segments of Egyptian society understood and accommodated to these practices. The chapter revolves around the question of whether non-elite Egyptians saw the dissection lessons conducted in the Qaṣr al-'Ainī Medical School and Hospital as a profanation to the sanctity of the body or if they were more concerned with the fact that this medical institution was a military hospital. In other words, was it the religious or the military context that shaped how Egyptians reacted to modern medicine?

Chapter 2 introduces the second main trope of this book, law, through the theme of sound. Tracing a hypothetical legal case through all stages of litigation, concentrating on penal law, it describes the *siyāsa* legal system and discusses how it interacted with the traditional shari'a courts. The chapter challenges the traditional way that nineteenth-century Egyptian legal history is described as undergoing an indelible process of secularization. It asks if the development of Egyptian law in the nineteenth century can be viewed as a shift not from religious to positive law but from the audible, spoken word to the silent, written one. Accordingly, the chapter asks if secularization is the right lens through which to view the significant transformations Egyptian law has witnessed, or if bureaucratization might be more apt. Furthermore, having described the *siyāsa* system in action, so to speak, and having presented the *siyāsa* councils as belonging to an old shari'a tradition, it asks what was modern about the specific instance of coupling *siyāsa* with *fiqh* in khedival Egypt.

Chapter 3 follows with an analysis of public hygiene and of how the complex public health program that was launched in Cairo and throughout Egypt was informed by notions of miasma and bad air. As in Europe, the medical profession in Egypt was split between those who believed in contagion and those who thought that diseases spread through effluvia and vapors that arose from decomposing bodies, which they believed altered the nature of air and rendered it foul. The chapter imagines how differently the history of nineteenth-century Cairo could be told if vision were dethroned as a guiding sense and smell were privileged instead. It also investigates whether the medicine that was practiced at Qaṣr al-ʿAinī could be described as colonial medicine.

Chapter 4 deals with the sense of taste, tracing the ways that Cairo's food markets were monitored and policed in the nineteenth century. Monitoring comestibles was only part of the job of the *muḥtasib,* the market inspector, and so this chapter takes a close look at *ḥisba,* an elaborate concept in Islamic law that refers both to market inspection and to moral censorship. The chapter traces the history of the *muḥtasib* and examines the way the intricate process of inspecting food in Cairo's markets was gradually transferred from the *muḥtasib* to the newly founded professions of the sanitary police and forensic chemistry. In addition to explaining how these two professions came to be, the chapter checks the validity of the claim that the abandonment of *ḥisba* was one of the results of secularization.

Chapter 5 features the sense of touch. Specifically, it deals with flogging as torture and closely studies a decree passed in 1861 that banned the use of the whip both as a means of extracting confessions and as legal punishment. The chapter argues that torture was banned because its two main functions were rendered obsolete by the appearance of alternatives, namely forensic medicine (which was a more reliable means of establishing legal proof) and prisons (which ceased to be places of exile and/or death). By looking closely at the central role forensic medicine came to play in the evolving penal system, the chapter also follows the complex legal and institutional structures within which forensic medicine was deployed and argues that understanding these structures is indispensable for any accurate understanding of the profound conceptual changes that eventually made secularism thinkable.

ONE

Medicine, Enlightenment, and Islam

IN 1827, A HUGE STRUCTURE SPRANG out of the desert of Abū Zaʿbal, to the northeast of Cairo (see figure 2). It was a square, one-story building with sidewalls measuring two hundred meters and a large botanical garden in the central courtyard. The structure housed a medical complex comprising a school and a hospital serving the nearby large military camp of Jihād-Abād. The Abū Zaʿbal Medical School was the first medical establishment to be built in Egypt in over five centuries,[1] and it is one of only two institutions dating from Mehmed Ali Pasha's time to have survived till the present day, the other being the Būlāq Press.

The director of this impressive new institution was a French doctor from Marseilles, Antoine-Barthélémy Clot, known as Clot Bey (see figure 3), whom Mehmed Ali had hired two years earlier to be the chief medical officer of his newly founded army.[2] During a number of meetings with the Pasha, Clot Bey had explained that experience had shown that the ravages of disease were more ruinous to soldiers than wounds suffered in combat and argued that the best way to protect the new army would be to train local doctors rather than solicit the services of European ones. To this end, Clot Bey suggested that the Pasha found a medical school that, in time, would supply the army with doctors, surgeons, and pharmacists.[3]

In 1833, *The Lancet* published a glowing article praising Clot Bey for his efforts in Egypt and describing his "yet brief career" as having "no parallel in medical history." The editor, Thomas Wakley, even went as far as to say that Egypt "now boasts of a well-organized medical government, essentially superior in many respects to that of a nation which vaunts of its multitude of chartered corporations, professedly devoted to the cultivation of medical science."[4]

FIGURE 2: Strekalovsky, *Abū-Za'bal School and Hospital.* Museum of the History of Medicine, Qaṣr al-'Ainī Medical School, Cairo. Photo by Mazen Attalla.

The following year, a British traveler visited the Abū Za'bal Medical School and wrote a very favorable account of the establishment. "The school of medicine," he averred, "is without doubt one of the most extraordinary of all the Pasha's establishments. . . . [The school contains] a museum, dissecting-rooms, a theatre for lectures, a laboratory, a dispensary and dependencies, with store-rooms and baths. . . . [There is also] a lithographic printing-office where the young Arabs are constantly employed in printing Arabic translations of the best European works on medicine." In clean and well-lit lecture halls whose walls had been decorated with "designs illustrative of science," students were instructed in history, geography, arithmetic, botany, chemistry, and "the theory and practice of medicine and surgery." Lectures were delivered in French and subsequently translated into Arabic "by able interpreters who, from their long employment in the hospital, are themselves tolerably well aquatinted with the science. . . . Practical knowledge is acquired by attending the sick."[5]

In 1837, that is, ten years after the school was founded, Clot Bey told the Pasha that the teaching hospital was too far away from Cairo, which meant that patients incurred considerable cost to reach it, and he therefore suggested moving the medical complex closer to the city.[6] After some hesitation, Mehmed Ali gave orders for the school to be relocated to Qaṣr al-'Ainī, in Cairo's western environs, and the new medical complex was named the Qaṣr al-'Ainī Medical School and Hospital.

FIGURE 3: Antoine Barthélémy Clot Bey. Image courtesy of the Wellcome Collection.

During the first ten years of its existence, the Qaṣr al-ʿAinī Medical School trained around 420 doctors for the Pasha's army and navy.[7] After the size of the army was radically reduced in the early 1840s, Qaṣr al-ʿAinī became the center of an extensive medical establishment that reached well beyond the confines of the military (see chapter 4). The hundreds of doctors who had been trained at the school were appointed to positions throughout the country. Some worked at clinics in Cairo, where they offered free medical services to the poor and needy; others were sent to the city's police stations or to the administrative headquarters of Egypt's various provinces, where they took on forensic duties. An ambitious and highly successful nationwide campaign against smallpox was conducted under the supervision of alumni of the school, which required the implementation of an elaborate system for collecting and updating vital statistics.[8] In 1848, a comprehensive census that counted individuals and not just households was successfully carried out.[9] During the second half of the nineteenth century, a highly efficient public hygiene apparatus was gradually shaped that used quarantines, among many other measures, to attempt to control the deadly epidemics of cholera and plague that ravaged Egypt throughout much of the nineteenth century (see chapter 3).

This chapter tells the story of how different segments of Egyptian society understood and reacted to the founding of a modern medical and public hygiene regime, which was represented by the Qaṣr al-ʿAinī Medical School and Hospital. After describing how the introduction of modern medicine in khedival Egypt is typically analyzed in terms of enlightenment versus superstition or vision versus blindness, the chapter argues that these significant medical reforms should instead be viewed as part of the larger military reforms that were part of Egypt's dynastic struggle with the Ottoman Empire.

The chapter then challenges the argument that the introduction of "modern" medicine in Egypt was opposed by Islam by analyzing the practices of dissection and postmortem examinations, two central components of the new medical and public-hygiene regime, and looking at how non-elite Egyptians reacted to them.

DAZZLING LIGHTS

Many earlier works on the history of Qaṣr al-ʿAinī describe the novel practices that attended the founding of the hospital, such as quarantines and dissections. For the most part, these works adopt an elitist approach that concentrates on the logic, motivation, and policies of "great men." Clot Bey invariably occupies an important place in these narratives, and his publications—both his technical writings, which were intended for medical professionals, and his polemical writings, which were aimed at a larger audience—have formed the basis for many studies of the history of medicine in nineteenth-century Egypt.[10] Mehmed Ali Pasha appears in these accounts as the great reformer credited with introducing many beneficial medical reforms.[11]

This historiography is infused with metaphors of light and enlightenment when it depicts how modern medicine was introduced to Egypt. As we saw in the introduction, Clot Bey viewed himself as someone who strove hard "to conquer the prejudices of [the Egyptian] people, to develop their intelligence, to extend to them the benefits of civilization."[12] Even though he insisted that the "sudden, abrupt and spontaneous" appearance of "civilization in the East" had "not proceeded from the mass of the people" but rather was the result of a "grand accidental cause . . . [that] appears to us [as] . . . the expedition of the French in Egypt,"[13] he felt obliged to pay homage to his patron, Mehmed Ali, who, he declared, resurrected "this science [of medicine] that had died in Egypt"[14] by opening the Qaṣr al-ʿAinī School of Medicine, thereby helping Clot Bey in the fight against a whole gamut of "quacks" (*dajjālūn*) that had sprung up to treat the sick with their unscientific remedies and thereby cause them harm, just like a "blind man who brandishes a saber in the midst of a crowd so that few escape uninjured."[15]

The importance of using metaphors of light, vision, and knowledge was not lost on Mehmed Ali in his ceaseless efforts to dazzle his European visitors and thereby influence Western public opinion. In an oft-quoted statement made to a British official who had been sent by Lord Palmerston to report on the Pasha's finances and system of government, Mehmed Ali said:

> Do not judge me by the standard of your knowledge. Compare me with the ignorance that is around me. We cannot apply the same rules to Egypt as to England: centuries have been required to bring you to your present state; I have only had a few years. . . . I have much to learn, and so have my people; and I am now sending . . . fifteen young men to learn what your country can teach. *They must see with their own eyes;* they must learn with their own hands; . . . they must discover how and why you are superior to us; and when they have been among your people a sufficient time, they must come home and instruct my people.[16]

Aḥmad al-Rashīdī was one of those young men sent to Europe on an educational mission. He studied at al-Azhar, then at the newly founded Qaṣr al-ʿAinī Medical School, and later in Paris, where he was sent to further his medical education. He acknowledged that if it were not for Mehmed Ali's determined efforts, modern medicine would not have stood a chance of being resurrected in Egypt. In his introduction to the Arabic translation of Sir William Lawrence's *A Treatise on the Diseases of the Eye* (1833), he argued that "medical science had all but disappeared from Egypt . . . and was practiced by all kinds of quacks who . . . did not understand anything about medicine, its rules, or its foundations. . . . [This continued] until God sent us the greatest reformer on earth, . . . Mehmed Ali, . . . who was determined to resurrect this science by opening medical schools."[17]

Muḥammad al-Shāfiʿī, who was also an Azharī and had also been sent to France to further his medical education, and who, in 1847, became the first Egyptian director of Qaṣr al-ʿAinī, agreed that "after Mehmed Ali had founded the medical school, great benefits accrued to rich and poor, and this dissipated much superstition that had gripped the minds of Egyptians for ages." Like al-Rashīdī, and indeed like most other Egyptian doctors who translated French medical texts, al-Shāfiʿī did not use metaphors of "borrowing from the West" to describe what was taking place in his medical school, as others would a generation later. Rather, he stressed the fact that in opening a hospital and a medical school based on anatomical medicine, Mehmed Ali was resurrecting, phoenix-like, an art that had once thrived in Egypt but that by that point "had completely disappeared and that exists only in name."[18] He then gave a long list of folk remedies, stressing the widespread reliance on self-medication, a point that the doctors accompanying Bonaparte's army had remarked on earlier.[19] He commented that oculists (*kaḥḥalūn*) "are ignorant about ophthalmia and cannot differentiate between different types of it, and know nothing about the anatomy of the eye."[20]

Western medicine's purported capacity to rescue Egypt from superstition and quackery is a theme that many observers continued to dwell on following the start of the British occupation in 1882. British observers who studied the history of the Qaṣr al-ʿAinī Medical School, for example, stressed that a sharp break differentiated the medical "science" taught and practiced in the school from the "quackery" that had been widespread before the foundation of the school in 1827, a quackery that, they lamented, was still prevalent. They did acknowledge that the art of medicine had its origins in Egypt, but unlike the Egyptian doctors who had studied at Qaṣr al-ʿAinī and who saw it as their role to revive the medical art that had once thrived in their country, the British observers rejected the notion that this art had ever held the potential of a sui generis development in Egypt. Dr. F. M. Sandwith, for example, who in 1884 became codirector of the newly formed Sanitary Department under the British occupation, admitted that the "earliest triumphs of the art of healing were celebrated in Egypt." Yet, he hastened to add, "the most remarkable thing about Egyptian medicine of that day was its non-progressive character. . . . The learned Egyptian was above all things a scribe, . . . but the Greek physician, on the contrary, was a man of speech and argument."[21] Sandwith was repeating the idea, which had been widespread since the time of the philosophes of the Enlightenment, that, unlike the Greeks, the ancient Egyptians (and the peoples of other Near Eastern civilizations) were incapable of critical thought. According to Diderot, "[Ancient] Egypt, for all the shrewdness of its priests and its instinct for preserving knowledge, remained a breeding ground for superstitions, an ideal country for magicians and fortune tellers and for the worship of cats and onions."[22] Sandwith shared this view of Ancient Egyptian medicine as stagnant and uncritical, and after providing a brief survey of the development of Arabic medical knowledge, he applauded the efforts of Clot Bey in "restoring to Egypt the modern fruits of that knowledge which was, for so many years, almost a monopoly in the famous cities of Memphis, Heliopolis and Alexandria."[23]

While Sandwith credited Clot Bey with founding modern medical services in Egypt, his compatriot, the Earl of Cromer, the British consul-general for the first quarter-century of the British occupation of Egypt, stressed that his own efforts were the real impetus behind the medical reforms: "On the whole, although of course much remains to be done, it may be said that, insofar as medical instruction and organization, veterinary administration and the proper maintenance of hospitals, dispensaries and lunatic asylums are concerned, an amount of progress has been realized which is as great as could be reasonably expected. The very capable Englishmen who have devoted their energies to the making of this department . . . have at all events succeeded in introducing the first commonplace elements of Western order and civilization into the country."[24] Like Clot Bey before him, Cromer believed that his civilizing mission was met with nothing but strong resistance from the natives. However, he noted that this resistance "was powerless to arrest the progress of medical instruction." Paraphrasing Molière, he insisted that "with characteristic Anglo-Saxon energy, the Englishman set to work to make the Egyptian 'un médecin malgré lui.'"[25]

THE ARMY AND THE ORIGINS OF THE EGYPTIAN MEDICAL ESTABLISHMENT

Rather than beginning the story of the founding of the Egyptian medical establishment with Clot Bey enlightening Mehmed Ali as to the benefits of modern medicine, it may be more appropriate to start by discussing the Pasha's lingering dark anxieties about his position in Egypt. Having arrived in Egypt at the age of thirty-one as a member of a large contingent of troops that the Ottoman sultan had gathered from the Balkans to evict the French army from his most prized province, Mehmed Ali knew very well that he was neither a *sharīf,* who could claim descent from the Prophet, nor a *ghāzī,* who could base his legitimacy on having won Egypt by the sword.[26] He was aware that his humble origins and the fact that he was a complete stranger to the country—and an illiterate one at that—meant that his sole source of legitimacy as governor of Egypt was the *firman* that the sultan sent in July 1805, which bestowed on him the coveted governorship following the departure of the French army and the ensuing power vacuum. He also knew that the sultan had issued this *firman* with reluctance after earlier attempts to assign other governors had failed. Moreover, unlike previous governors of Egypt, who had typically come from within ruling circles in Istanbul and had thus been known within the leading households in the imperial capital, and for whom the governorship of Egypt would have been but a step in their advancement within the empire's bureaucracy, Mehmed Ali was a completely unknown quantity to the ruling factions in Istanbul. Furthermore, Egypt was too important a province to be entrusted to an outsider, and he knew that it was only a matter of time before Istanbul would try to remove him from this prized province. The way he was regarded in Istanbul was a source of deep anxiety for Mehmed Ali.

It was this anxiety that prompted him to build a military force to defend his coveted position. His initial efforts in 1815 to train the unruly Albanian troops that had arrived with him in Egypt back in 1801 failed when they mutinied and went on a rampage. Five years later, he turned to Sudan to gather men for his intended army. In 1820, he dispatched two expeditions to the region, totaling some ten thousand Moroccans, Bedouins, Albanians, and Turks. The campaigns proved disastrous, though, mainly because of the lack of medical services. The troops succumbed to all kinds of diseases; in September 1821, the number of the dead reached 600, and it rose to 1,500 the following month.[27] Moreover, the nonexistent medical services and the lack of any effective means of transportation resulted in thousands of African slaves perishing before they ever reached Egypt. Even more shocking is the fact that out of the twenty thousand slaves who did make it to Aswan in 1824, only three thousand survived the following months. The others perished in Egypt, "like sheep with the rot."[28]

The lack of medical services became a problem once again after the Pasha took the fateful decision in February 1822 to conscript Egyptians into his new army. With no census available and no reliable medical services to screen the peasants, conscription officers sent from Cairo ended up gathering many men who were later found to be too old or infirm for military service. This caused serious disruption not only to the training of new battalions but also to the agricultural sector, as many farmers were snatched from their fields and dispatched to distant training camps only to be deemed unfit and rejected by the army.[29]

Mehmed Ali's fabled encounter with Clot Bey in December 1824, therefore, in which the Frenchman purportedly convinced him of the importance of opening a medical school, was not a road to Damascus conversion, as the French doctor would have us believe. Mehmed Ali had already learned that he needed a military medical corps the hard way, after incurring huge losses.

In the years that followed, the Pasha became convinced that he needed to train doctors locally and assign them to military units, and thus the connection between the army and the budding medical establishment proved to be a lasting one. As illustrated in this chapter, the military beginnings of the khedival medical establishment shaped the very nature of the establishment and dictated the way it developed. Students in the medical schools were given military ranks. The first doctors trained at the schools became army doctors; when they graduated, they were given a military rank and sent to serve in army units. Female doctors and nurses also carried military ranks. Hospitals were run in a military style, and doctors conducted their daily rounds as army drills. Even after the Pasha's army was reduced in size in the wake of the 1841 settlement with the Ottoman sultan and army medical officers were appointed to civilian clinics (see chapter 4), Shūrā al-Aṭibbā, or the Doctors' Council, which was the central administrative body that oversaw medical matters, and which was headed by Clot Bey, continued to function as a division of the War Department. The Qaṣr al-ʿAinī Medical School, despite acquiring new objectives during a quarter-century of evolution, "never lost its character as a service agency for the military establishment."[30] From its inception, therefore, the nineteenth-century Egyptian medical establishment was intricately connected to military power and shaped by military logic, organization, and discipline.

RECEPTION OF MODERN MEDICINE

Instead of using the copious archival material generated by the military-medical complex to corroborate (or challenge) the traditional ocular-centric narrative of the introduction of modern medicine in Egypt, this section takes a close look at how the unprecedented medical policies that Egypt witnessed in the nineteenth century were experienced by lower-class Egyptians. Specifically, the following pages single out two practices that constituted the backbone of the nationwide medical establishment, namely quarantines and postmortem examinations.

Quarantines

Like the story of opening hospitals and medical schools, the story of enforcing quarantines and the reaction non-elite Egyptians had to them is commonly told as a variation of the larger enlightenment theme.[31] In this case, it is usually Muslim fatalism that is stressed to illustrate how religious dogma put up a fierce fight against modern science.[32] Alexander Kinglake, an English traveler who visited Cairo at the peak of the 1835 plague epidemic and gave a vivid account of how it ravaged the city, described his skepticism of the European residents' self-imposed quarantines as resembling "the Mahometan's feelings [toward] these little contrivances for eluding fate."[33] Francesco Grassi, the medical director of the Consular Board of Health in Alexandria (which is discussed in more detail in chapter 4), argued that the isolation measures put in place to combat the cholera epidemic of 1848 failed partly due to the "Mussulmen's . . . want of faith in medicine and to their fanaticism."[34]

Rather than viewing quarantines as part of the enlightenment narrative that considered religious fatalism and fanaticism to be obstacles to modern scientific measures, it may be useful to view quarantines within the larger military perspective of Egyptian history during the first half of the nineteenth century and to identify questions informing the wider medical context in which these scientific measures were introduced. These include questions about the nature of communicable diseases, most significantly cholera and the plague, and whether these diseases were endemic to Egypt.

Quarantines and the "Problem of Population" in Ottoman Egypt. Bonaparte's military expedition to Egypt is usually cited as the context in which quarantines were first introduced. On March 24, 1799, placards were put up throughout Cairo with regulations issued by the French military authorities announcing the imposition of quarantines in Cairo. The placards read as follows:

> An address to the people of Cairo, Būlāq, Old Cairo and vicinity. You shall obey, uphold and observe, without opposition, the orders. Anybody oppos-

ing them will encounter abundant vengeance, painful punishment and severe retribution. They are precautions against the disease of the plague. In the case of anybody whom you know certainly, or believe, imagine, or suspect to be suffering from this illness in any place, house, caravansary or building, it is your duty and obligation to establish a quarantine, and the place must be closed off. The elder of the quarter or street in which this occurs must immediately inform the French officer who is the district supervisor. . . . Any of the chiefs of sections, elders of quarters, and police of districts who has information concerning this disease and does not record it will be punished as the commandant sees fit. Neighborhood elders will be punished with 100 lashes for failure to report. It is also decreed that anyone who is infected, or in whose house a case occurred among his family or relatives, and who moves from his house to another place to somewhere else, shall suffer capital punishment.[35]

Before elaborating on the military nature of these regulations, it is important to interrogate their novelty and investigate the reasons why the Ottoman authorities in Egypt, before Bonaparte's expedition, never imposed similar regulations, even though quarantines had been known throughout the Mediterranean world, and even though Egypt had suffered periodical devastating epidemics since the fourteenth century.

Ottoman policies in Egypt were informed by what can be called an "exaction logic," and Istanbul's attitude toward the population of Egypt never developed to take the population as the "end and instrument of government."[36] As this section demonstrates, there was indeed a concern about the "populousness" of Egypt—that is, the overall well-being and tranquility of the residents of this wealthy province of the empire. However, the Ottoman sultan was interested in the residents of Egypt primarily insofar as they represented an index of the wealth of his empire. The sultan, his viziers, and his governors were also concerned about Egypt's ability to feed the empire and provide enough food for poor and needy pilgrims during the annual Hajj. Remarkably absent from the Ottoman administrative mind, however, was an effective means of dealing with the repeated plague epidemics that had been striking the country every nine years since the middle of the fourteenth century.[37] Indeed, Nāṣir Ibrāhīm, who studied the social and economic crises that Egypt suffered during the seventeenth century, remarked that it was very rare for Ottoman governors to pay any attention to matters of public hygiene and that it was "absolutely impossible to notice any significant presence of an overall administrative policy in light of the near total absence of specialized bodies [that provided] . . . health services."[38]

It is not that the Ottoman authorities were not concerned about health matters in Egypt or that they did not worry about the devastating impacts of plagues on such an important province. Egypt was considered the breadbasket of the Ottoman Empire, and the Ottomans had set up a complex administrative and economic system that guaranteed that grain from Egypt was regularly sent to Istanbul and to Hijaz to support the annual Hajj. Any disruption of this vital food supply was taken very seriously. Furthermore, both contemporary chroniclers and records of the orders sent from Istanbul to the governors in Cairo show that Ottoman authorities were principally concerned about the breakdowns of law and order that generally followed low Niles, famines, and plague epidemics.[39] Following the 1695 drought, for example, an angry mob stormed the Citadel of Cairo demanding that the authorities provide food rations. When the governor failed to contain these disturbances, Istanbul summarily dismissed him and appointed a new governor in his place.[40]

Related to this security concern was the fear that lack of order in Egypt following plagues and famines would make it easier for fugitives from the central authorities to seek refuge in the remote province. In 1791, using very strong language, Ottoman authorities ordered those Ottoman leaders still present in Egypt to prevent any fugitives from entering Egypt to hide there.[41]

But the Ottoman administration was primarily worried about revenue from one of its wealthiest provinces, and this concern shaped the immediate reaction of the administration to news of plague outbreaks in Egypt. For example, the chronicler Aḥmad al-Damurdāshī (d. 1755) says that in the wake of the 1695–96 plague, the Ottoman governor was quick to collect the administrative tax paid on *ḥulwān* (title deeds), from peasants who were keen to get hold of lands left vacant after the owners had died.[42] After the devastating plague epidemic of 1791, an imperial *firman* was sent to the governor in Cairo ordering him to provide information about which Ottoman officials had fled the country so that the state could seize their property and money.[43] Al-Jabartī writes that after the 1801 epidemic, the Ottoman governor ordered the Mamluk emir Muḥammad Bey al-Alfī to "seize the inheritance of those who had died of the plague."[44]

However, various Ottoman governors were aware that a balance needed to be struck between this "exaction logic" and the need to preserve the peace after a plague epidemic. Thus, we see Maksūd Pasha, the Ottoman governor of Egypt in 1643, ordering the officials of Bayt al-Māl—a government body responsible for, among other things, registering the legacies of the deceased—

to suspend their normal business activities during the plague. Al-Bakrī (d. 1650) noted that by issuing this order, the governor was hoping to lift the financial burden from the families of plague victims. He added that to avoid any delays in burials, the registration of the legacies of the deceased (*al-kashf ʿalā al-amwāt*) was canceled, and survivors were told to bury their dead without registration.[45]

Thus, although the Ottomans were very aware of the significance of Egypt and its productive capacities for the wealth and well-being of their empire, they never developed a policy that could be interpreted as signaling an understanding of what Foucault called "the problem of population." They were indeed concerned about maintaining the productivity of Egypt, but they did not put any specific measures in place to account for or increase the productivity of the province's population. The Ottoman sultans and their governors in Egypt ruled according to what Foucault would call "the reason of state," which, although it involved a concern with "numbering the people" (i.e., taking stock of the population as an index of the wealth of the realm), did not express an interest in the "population" as an abstraction.[46]

Accordingly, the quarantine measures mentioned above, which the French imposed shortly after their arrival, constituted a radical shift in how the population of Egypt came to be viewed. Cut off from home after Nelson destroyed their fleet in the Battle of the Nile (August 1798), the French saw the 1799 outbreak of plague in Egypt as a grave threat that could very well decimate their army. Therefore, the imposition of quarantines in March 1799 and the draconian measures taken to implement them spelled out in the decree quoted earlier in the chapter were not the result of scientific advances that revealed the pathogenic agent that caused plague or of data that showed statistically that quarantines were effective in controlling the epidemic. Rather, they were the result of the firm belief of the occupying army that its survival, and indeed the success of Bonaparte's imperial enterprise in the Orient, depended on protecting the population of Egypt from the ravages of the plague. It became painfully clear that this was indeed the case when the plague contributed to the defeat of the army in Palestine in 1800.

The connection between the enforcement of quarantines and the needs of the military was clear to contemporary observers, most prominently al-Jabartī. As Kuhnke noted, al-Jabartī's reaction to the health measures imposed by the French was complex and nuanced. Given that he saw plague as a periodically recurring disease caused by miasmas (fetid vapors arising from the ground, discussed in more detail in chapter 3), he raised no objections in his chronicle to the preventive measures the French had imposed, which were based on their belief in miasmatic principles. Specifically, he approved of regulations prohibiting intramural burial and those ordering that all clothing, furniture, and other effects pertaining to deceased persons be aired on rooftops. These measures, he argued, "dissipate the bad odors which could have engendered plague." He even admonished the masses, who, "in their ignorance, saw here only a means of finding out what others possessed. However, they [the authorities] had no other objective but to destroy miasmas and to prevent an epidemic." Nevertheless, al-Jabartī was opposed to the government decree because it stipulated severe punishments for noncompliance with quarantine regulations.[47] He was also opposed to the French order to bury those who had died of the plague with their clothes on by simply throwing them into a pit and shoveling dirt over them.[48]

Mehmed Ali's Quarantine Policy: The Early Years. The 1799 quarantine measures imposed by the French were part of a larger effort to introduce hygienic reforms that aimed at "improv[ing] the condition of the population, [and] increas[ing] its wealth, its longevity."[49] These policies included the implementation of many public hygiene measures based on miasmatic principles and a ban on intramural burials.[50] After the departure of the French and the rise of Mehmed Ali, the brief moment in which the population was seen as the "end and instrument of government" came to an end, and for some time there was no attempt to impose quarantines to combat epidemics. While it is true that the Pasha accepted the advice of his European doctors and imposed quarantines in 1813 for the first time during his reign, it would be a mistake to see this as a continuation of the same policies adopted by the French during their short-lived occupation.[51] For in contrast to the nationwide quarantine policy that the French implemented, the 1813 quarantines were imposed only on the Pasha's palace, which prompted al-Jabartī to remark sardonically that by doing so, the Pasha was showing his "desire for the life of this world and the fear of the plague."[52]

For the first fifteen years of his long reign, Mehmed Ali did not evince any real concern with improving the conditions of Egypt's population, increasing their productivity, or improving their well-being. In fact, during these early years, he behaved as the quintessential Foucauldian sovereign whose main task was to strengthen the link between himself and his principality.[53] His first act as Pasha was to summon to Egypt his sons and other members of his immediate family from Kavala and its environs. He put these sons, nephews, uncles, and other relatives in charge of important provinces throughout Egypt. He then unleashed a ruthless campaign to stamp out any opposition to his power and wipe out all competing centers of power within Egypt. Most infamously, in March 1811, he invited to his *dīwān* all heads of rival households and their retainers and ordered his men to slaughter them. Over four hundred Mamluks perished on that single day, and the Mamluk presence in Egypt was wiped out forever.

With Egypt now his and his alone, the Pasha ordered his men to squeeze every *para* out of the inhabitants of Egypt. Al-Jabartī commented: "The Pasha increased [his] zeal for accumulating property by all possible means, after expropriating the whole country, nullifying cession, sale, and purchase except for unclaimed land, along with the confiscation of fodder and stored grain. Anyone who died in possession of an *iltizām* share, endowment income, or a stipend lost all right to such, and it was recorded and transferred to the Pasha's bureau."[54]

As mentioned above, the decision in 1822 to conscript the fellahin of Egypt into an army that was hoped would fulfill Mehmed Ali's dynastic aspirations radically altered the meaning and significance of the population of Egypt. Following the fateful decision to create a regular, standing army based on conscription, the Pasha's *dīwān* employed a new logic that was not limited to differentiating between "the scarce and the numerous, the submissive and the restive, rich and poor, healthy and sick, strong and weak"; rather, this new logic now necessitated distinguishing between "the more or less utilizable, more or less amenable to profitable investment, those with greater or lesser prospects of survival, death and illness, and with more or less capacity for being usefully trained."[55] In other words, it was the army that effected the shift from, to use Foucault's terms, sovereignty to governmentality, and it was in this military context that the "problem of population" appeared in Egypt.

The Army and the Development of the Quarantine Policy. After incurring huge expenses and taking great risks to raise a conscript army, Mehmed Ali had to make sure that his investment was properly taken care of. As mentioned above, his interest in opening a medical school derived first and foremost from his need to protect the lives of his soldiers. Likewise, his interest in quarantines derived from his need to protect his actual fighting units and his potential fighting units (i.e., the population at large), especially given the scale of the epidemics that hit Egypt in the 1830s. The first of these devastating epidemics was the cholera epidemic, which hit in August 1831 and lasted for only a few weeks but claimed between 150,000 and 190,000 lives. A British traveler, James A. St. John, described the frustration of a village shaykh and a Turkish official who, together, could not raise enough taxes from a particular village, as its population had been reduced from 6,000 to 2,500 by the epidemic.[56] Cairo was hit particularly hard: in less than a month, thirty-six thousand of its estimated quarter of a million inhabitants, 14.4 percent of the population, were dead, with mortality figures fluctuating between five hundred and six hundred deaths per day. These numbers far exceeded losses in Paris, where the epidemic struck one in every nineteen residents and killed over eighteen thousand.[57] Barely four years later, Egypt was visited by another devastating epidemic, the plague, which struck with a vengeance in November 1834. It lasted until October 1837, claiming some two hundred lives, among them a third of Cairo's population and over half the Muslim population of Alexandria.[58] After a minor epidemic in 1840, the plague mysteriously disappeared, but Egypt was hit by cholera again four other times: in 1848, when thirty-thousand succumbed to the disease; 1865, when twice that number died; 1883, when between eighty and a hundred thousand died of the disease; and finally the epidemic of 1895–96, which claimed sixteen thousand victims.[59]

With the public hygiene system still in its embryonic stage, the pathogenic agents that caused these epidemics still unknown, and so much at stake, the authorities relied heavily on quarantines as a bulwark against these devastating epidemics. In 1831, for example, when cholera was detected in Mecca and the Egyptian 19th Regiment stationed there reported heavy causalities in the wake of the pilgrimage season,[60] quick measures were taken to intercept the pilgrims on their way back from Quṣayr and Suez, and lazarettos were established in these two port cities. However, pilgrims managed to breach the perimeter, and Cairo soon became infected. It was at this point that Mehmed Ali proposed that the European consuls in Alexandria form a quarantine board to protect the city from the sweeping disease.[61] Even though the Pasha placed twenty thousand troops at the consuls' disposal to help implement a *cordon sanitaire* around the city, the epidemic soon spread to Alexandria, and in a few days' time the board disbanded itself after recognizing that its quarantine policies came too late and were ineffective.

However, Mehmed Ali never abandoned his belief in the efficacy of quarantines. Indeed, concerned mostly about his army, which was poised to invade Syria, he issued strict orders for the different military units in Cairo and in the Delta to be isolated from the urban population. When this policy proved effective, sparing the army the worst effects of the epidemic, the Pasha became even more adamant in insisting on the strict implementation of quarantines. In the following years, he issued orders for quarantines to be built for Muslim pilgrims returning from Mecca and for Russian Orthodox pilgrims heading to Jerusalem.[62] A lazaretto was founded in Alexandria in January 1833, and the Pasha seems to have given it much attention.[63] When he was approached by merchants complaining about the delays that the quarantines were causing and how ruinous the policy was to their business,[64] he consistently turned a deaf ear and argued that the salvation of the country and the population depended on quarantines.[65] During the 1834–37 plague epidemic, he ordered the members of his *dīwān* to be quarantined.[66] He advised his son, Ibrāhīm Pasha, who was in Syria at the time, to quarantine his harem in Egypt.[67] Strict quarantines were imposed on all factories and schools throughout Egypt.[68] When the head of the Alexandria hospital and his deputy argued that plague was not contagious and that the quarantine measures were useless, Mehmed Ali wasted no time in firing them.[69] All caravans entering Egypt from the east had to pass through quarantines in either al-ʿArīsh or Suez; quarantine officials who were negligent were punished by three-month prison terms, and those who were corrupt and accepted bribes to allow the caravans to circumvent the quarantines were sentenced to prison for three months to one year.[70]

Mehmed Ali's firm adherence to the quarantine system was not based on any scientific understanding of the contagiousness of cholera or the plague; rather, it stemmed from his empirical observations of the efficacy of quarantines and from the realization that these measures proved to be successful in limiting the spread of epidemics and lessening their devastating impact.[71] He was also keenly aware that although quarantines suspended trade and therefore hurt his finances, which were dependent on strong commercial ties with Europe, they actually improved his business prospects in the long run. As a matter of course, ships originating from Egypt were routinely subjected to long detention periods in European ports. Therefore, Mehmed Ali's decision to impose quarantines on ships in Alexandria rather than in European ports did not prolonging the overall time ships had to remain in port. Rather, by being so diligent in imposing quarantines throughout Egypt and concurring with the Quarantine Board of Alexandria, he was not only defending the Egyptian hinterland with its many villages, which "were the bases of our prosperity and security," but also protecting the commercial foundations of his state.[72]

Ironically, the Pasha's chief medical advisor, Clot Bey, had little faith in quarantines. Being a noncontagionist and a believer in miasmas, he was deeply suspicious of quarantines and thought they were useless in combating epidemics. Nevertheless, given his patron's unflinching adherence to the practice and realizing the risks involved in disobeying orders, Clot Bey had to instruct his subordinates, "Whatever your opinion, you are to consider plague a contagious disease and to act accordingly."[73] In a medical treatise that was distributed in 1832 to army doctors, he wrote, "Most people believe that plague is contagious. However, this opinion, despite its prevalence, is not conclusive, for many clever doctors looked closely into this disease and denied that it is contagious. . . . Be that as it may, it is recommended that military doctors use caution and isolate those afflicted with plague until one of these two opinions [on the contagiousness of the plague] wins out. By failing to do so [i.e., failing to isolate plague-stricken soldiers], the doctor may inadvertently help in spreading this scourge even further."[74] Three years later, when plague had broken out in Egypt, Clot Bey wrote another special treatise devoted solely to the plague and the stringent quarantine measures that had to be strictly enforced. Published in Arabic by Būlāq Press, this treatise stated: "Given that plague is widely believed to be contagious, i.e., that it spreads by touch, all people and objects suspected to be afflicted with the plague should be treated as if they are in fact afflicted. Accordingly, people suspected of carrying the disease should be isolated."[75] Clot Bey then gave detailed instructions about how strict quarantine measures were to be implemented.

In his French and English publications and lectures, however, Clot Bey expressed his deep skepticism about, if not utter disbelief in, quarantines. For example, in a lecture he gave at l'Hôpital de la Pitié in Paris in 1840, he argued that theories of etiology point to decomposing animal and vegetable matter as sources of disease; accordingly, miasmas must carry the infection, and any preventative measure that failed to take the exciting cause, or miasma, into account would be unsuccessful. He ended by making it clear that he regarded quarantines as altogether useless.[76] In a letter published in *The Lancet* in 1839, he reported that the British consul in Egypt had publicly expressed his increasing skepticism about the quarantine policy that was being rigorously enforced in Egypt. He concluded by saying, "We have the pleasure of seeing the number of contagionists daily decrease, and I trust that the day is not far off when quarantine regulations will be completely reformed, if not altogether abolished."[77]

Clot Bey's contradictory position regarding quarantines (he forcefully executed them as per his patron's orders even though he believed them to be ineffective) reflected a division within the scientific community about the communicability of plague and the best means of confronting the disease. Just as cholera was believed to be endemic to India, Egypt was thought by many Europeans to be the cradle of plague, and it was feared that the country's environment was responsible for the repeated outbreaks of deadly epidemics. Some attributed the high prevalence of illness to noxious miasmas emanating from soil in which human corpses were decomposing, a theory that came to be known as the "cadaveric virus theory." Clot Bey refuted this theory and argued that meteorological circumstances peculiar to Egypt had endowed plague with a "pestilential constitution."[78] He remained convinced, however, that plague was not communicable and that it instead spread through miasmas; hence, he believed that quarantines were ineffective to combat it. By contrast, Francesco Grassi, the medical director for the Consular Board of Health in Alexandria, was a committed contagionist who firmly believed that "Egypt never was and never will be the cradle of plague, and that every time that it was subjected to it, it was always imported from elsewhere."[79]

Attitudes toward quarantines and plague in nineteenth-century Egypt, therefore, should not be summarily seen as reflecting Muslim fatalism and fanaticism, for as we have seen, the scientific community itself was divided about the pathology of the plague and how best to combat the disease. Nevertheless, the argument that quarantine efforts were thwarted by Muslim fatalism should not be dismissed outright. European travelers and physicians working in Egypt were not the only ones making this argument. Indeed, the fiercest debates on this topic were those Mehmed Ali engaged in with his administrators and the *'ulamā'* of Alexandria, who were alarmed by the health measures taken to combat the 1834–37 plague epidemic. A close look at official correspondence may shed light on the reasons behind this opposition to quarantines and specifically on the "Muslim fatalism" that supposedly frustrated public hygiene efforts.

In December 1834, in a rare act of defiance, the *'ulamā'* of Alexandria presented a petition to the Pasha complaining about the health measures enforced to combat the epidemic. They were purportedly opposed to the removal of the family members of those who were suspected of having caught the disease to special areas outside the city, where they were placed under strict quarantine. The petition concluded that "quarantines will never succeed among Muslims as they are not afraid of plague."[80] In response, Mehmed

Ali wrote to Zakī Efendi, the governor of Alexandria, telling him that he could not accept such a petition and that he had to inform the Quarantine Board via the city's police commissioner, who was the Egyptian liaison officer on the board, not to take it into account.[81] Eventually, he gave a stern response to the people of Alexandria and their *'ulamā'*. In a letter to Zakī Efendi, he wrote: "People's avoidance of health measures and of quarantines is the result of their ignorance. I have previously said that prevention [of the epidemic] within the precepts of the shari'a requires us to undertake certain measures. This epidemic is a sign of God's wrath, and fleeing from His wrath to His mercy is not contrary to the shari'a. Didn't God say in His Book, 'Do not throw yourselves with your own hands into destruction'? [2:195] and didn't the Prophet say 'Flee the leper as you flee a lion'?" He added that there were many Quranic verses and Prophetic hadiths that substantiated his position, and if the residents of Alexandria needed a fatwa concerning quarantines, he could secure one for them. He ended by insisting that the quarantine and other hygienic measures would be unrelentingly applied.[82]

A few months later, he ordered the governor to summon the *'ulamā'* and the city notables and to make clear to them that he was determined to move plague-stricken residents outside the city. The rich would be allowed to take whatever they needed while in quarantine, while the government would take care of the needs of the poor during their period of isolation. Those who hid plague-stricken patients at home and did not inform the authorities of their presence would be executed.[83] When he doubted the accuracy of the mortality figures reported daily, he asked Ḥabīb Efendi, his chef du cabinet, if death reports were compiled after a doctor had actually conducted a postmortem examination or if the statistics were based on hearsay.[84] To make sure that no fraud took place, he ordered the governor of Alexandria to be personally present while postmortem examinations were conducted.[85] However, since there was at that time a shortage of female doctors who could conduct these exams, he made a concession that spared the bodies of dead women.[86] He insisted, though, that all male corpses be examined.[87] When informed during the peak of the epidemic that the *'ulamā'* of Cairo had the intention of gathering city residents in group prayers to supplicate for divine mercy, he rebuked the religious leaders, saying that such large gatherings in crowded places would only spread the epidemic further; if people wanted to pray, he added, they could do so privately and individually.[88] Finally, he ordered the governor of Alexandria to ask the *'ulamā'* for a fatwa to build a new Muslim cemetery outside the city and to prevent intramural burial, as this practice was ruinous to public hygiene.[89] He said that there would be no need to move the corpses of those Muslims already buried within the city because, first, this would be contrary to shari'a and, second, the bodies would have already decayed.[90]

The Pasha stuck to his near dogmatic belief in the efficacy of quarantines and his determination to reject the protests of the *'ulamā'* when a minor plague epidemic broke out in Damascus in 1840, during the very last months of the Egyptian occupation there. In March 1840, the governor of Syria, Mehmed Şerif Pasha, wrote to Ibrāhīm Pasha, Mehmed Ali's son and commander in chief of his army, saying that when a quarantine was imposed on five or six houses in the city where plague cases had been detected, the *'ulamā'* complained that such measures were against shari'a. He added that the *'ulamā'* went about spreading rumors that the dead had been denied ritual washing and had been buried unwashed, that no funerary prayers had been recited, and that quicklime had been poured on their remains. One particular shaykh, Shaykh Ḥāmid al-'Aṭṭār, spoke on behalf of his fellow *'ulamā'* when he challenged the health measures by quoting the Quran: "So when their time has come, they will not remain behind an hour, nor will they precede [it]" (7:34); "Wherever you may be, death will overtake you, even if you should be within towers of lofty construction" (4:78); "Say, 'Never will we be struck except by what Allah has decreed for us; He is our protector'" (9:51). Şerif Pasha denied that the health regulations entailed the use of quicklime or burial without ritually washing the corpse. He also rebutted the cited Quranic verses with a favorite verse of his own: "And do not throw [yourselves] with your [own] hands into destruction" (2:195). But given the fierce resistance from the locals, he was at a loss as to what to do and indicated that he was leaning toward lifting the quarantine but feared Mehmed Ali's wrath.[91] In response, Ibrāhīm Pasha told him to stand fast and under no circumstances lift the quarantine.[92] Two months later, the *'ulamā'* gave their consent to quarantines after receiving assurances that no quicklime had been used on the bodies of dead Muslims and that proper burial rituals had been observed. In fact, they agreed that the new health measures, including quarantining the poor (*aṭrāf al-nās*) outside the city and the rich (*wujūh al-nās*) in their homes, were within the confines of shari'a, and they wrote to Şerif Pasha asking him to convey their best wishes to "the Benefactor" (*Walii al-Ni'am*), for "his everlasting and victorious state."[93]

At around the same time, Mehmed Ali received a fatwa from the mufti of Alexandria stating that quarantines were in conformity with shari'a. To support their ruling, the mufti cited a *sunna* from Caliph ʿUmar that showed him refraining from entering a town called Sargh in Syria when he heard that it had been struck by plague and subsequently urging his followers to leave the area.[94] When one of the Companions of the Prophet questioned his decision, arguing that by leaving he was, in fact, trying to evade God's destiny, ʿUmar rebuked him, saying, "We evade God's destiny [only] to God's destiny [*innamā nafirru min qadari illāh ilā qadari illāh*]." The mufti added that there was also a hadith in which the Prophet says, "If you hear of a plague-stricken place, then do not enter it; and if the place you are in is struck by plague, then do not flee it." Based on these *sunan*, the mufti opined that the shariʿa position regarding quarantines falls somewhere between "being mandated and being desired [*bayn al-wujūb wa'l-istiḥbāb*]"—with the proviso, however, that the necessary measures be implemented in a way that would not violate any religious precepts. He explained: "The European practices of imprisoning those who may be present in the house of the plague-stricken patient, appointing guards to watch over them in a way that is difficult for the weak among those people to bear, evicting them [to areas outside the city] in a frightening manner, burning their belongings, burying the dead in their clothes [without ritual washing and without wrapping them in a shroud], pouring quicklime on their bodies and unveiling the private parts of the bodies of dead Muslim—none of this is approved of by shariʿa." The mufti ended by adding a medical reason for opposing these measures. These frightening measures, he opined, were contrary to the principles of quarantines as "they evoke fear and anxiety, and these feelings are the strongest causes of diseases and the plague."[95]

Far from being an example of Muslim fatalism, this fatwa represents a measured response by the *ʿulamāʾ* of Alexandria to the unprecedented quarantine measures that had been enacted to deal with the plague, and this viewpoint was probably shared by a large segment of the city's population. As is clear, the fatwa was not against imposing quarantines in principle if it meant abstaining from entering or fleeing an infected locality. Rather, it was adamantly opposed to using force to evict people from the city or sequester them in their houses. It also declared that suspending proper death rituals (washing, shrouding, and burying the bodies) was against shariʿa. It was also clearly opposed to allowing the bodies of dead women to be exposed to the gazes of even "Christian women [doctors], as this is tantamount to being seen by an unknown man [*ajnabī*]."

It is not clear what Mehmed Ali's direct response to this fatwa was, but a month later, in a letter to the governor of Cairo, ʿAbbās Pasha, who was his grandson, he indicated that it was class and not religious matters that he was mostly concerned about when thinking about how to amend his quarantine policy. In this letter, he also wrote that while the rich could afford to be quarantined in their own homes, the poor should be sent to the Civilian Hospital, al-Isbītāliya al-Mulkiyya, for treatment, but only after their houses were put under quarantine.[96] The following year he issued a decree titled General Regulations Concerning the Public Health at Alexandria, the second chapter of which dealt exclusively with quarantines. The principles applied in Alexandria were also applied in Cairo: well-to-do people who were afflicted with plague had to have their houses quarantined until "1. the patient shall have recovered and have quitted the house and gone to another to perform a *spoglio* of thirty-one days; 2. when the patient shall be conveyed to the Lazaretto; [or] 3. after the death of the patient." The regulations went on to declare: "Indigents without means to support themselves in their own houses during the quarantine will be sent to the Lazaretto where they will be granted the same ration of daily bread the government grants to indigent passengers."[97] During the same period, strict orders were repeatedly issued forbidding intramural burial,[98] and in a couple of orders that show the authorities shared the mufti of Alexandria's belief that fear was a health hazard as it predisposed bodies to the epidemic, the professional wailers who brought up the rear of funeral processions were banned because "other denizens get terrified"[99] by their wailing and shrieking, which resembles the "ugly sound of donkeys."[100] Regarding burials, although the authorities repeatedly denied the use of quicklime and insisted that proper rituals were being carried out, all bodies had to be inspected before they were buried to ascertain the cause of death. In an attempt to placate those opposed to the bodies of dead women being examined by non-Muslim doctors, the female graduates of the School of Midwives, Madrasat al-Qābilāt, which was located within the Azbakiyya Civilian Hospital, were entrusted with this important task.[101]

Despite the fact that reactions to quarantines were verbally expressed in religious terms, there are many indications that opposition to the practice was triggered by the way the quarantine regulations were perceived to have affected the lives of the living and not only by how the *'ulamā'* viewed them as violating the rights of the dead. European diplomats, and Clot Bey, remarked that indigent citizens were so fearful of being transported to the lazarettos that they hid disease-stricken family members at home and rarely reported illness to the Quarantine Board until it ended in death. They also feared that removing the sick to the lazarettos, where they were entrusted to the state, effectively meant denying family members the right to take care of each other in sickness. In their December 1834 petition against the quarantine regulations, the *'ulamā'* said that quarantining the family members of plague victims outside the city meant removing them from work and depriving them of their daily bread, which clearly indicates that the *'ulamā'* were concerned about the economic livelihood of the denizens of the city and not only about their spiritual wellbeing. Furthermore, the manner in which families were carted off by torchlight under cover of darkness was particularly alarming, and the *'ulamā'* objected to these sinister convoys, which shattered the peace and stirred up terror. These fears compelled people to bury their dead in courtyards or under the floors of their houses, practices that carried the punishment of execution.[102] Another common practice that clearly shows that the inhabitants of Alexandria were more concerned about their livelihoods than upholding religiously sanctioned burial rites was the depositing of dead bodies in the streets after nightfall to avoid identification and spare the families of the dead from being transported to lazarettos outside the city. Finally, forbidding professional wailers from practicing their trade and preventing both Muslims and Christians from visiting cemeteries during feast days, as was their custom,[103] further denied the poor the right to mourn their dead and violated their traditional funerary rituals (which were not necessarily religiously sanctioned).[104] It appears, therefore, that given the specific manner in which quarantine regulations were carried out, it was concern about the well-being of the living rather than sensitivity about the treatment of the bodies of the dead or a fatalistic stance that triggered and shaped people's reaction to the quarantines.

Dissection and Postmortem Examinations

The argument that the *'ulamā'* were at the root of the opposition to the "enlightened" efforts to improve health conditions in Egypt is most forcefully made in the case of dissection, autopsies, and postmortem examinations in general. As shown in the introduction, Clot Bey spared no effort in arguing how opposition to dissection was the most important obstacle he had to overcome if his new medical institution was to have any chance of success, and he insisted that this opposition could have halted the entire project were it not for his perseverance, determination, and political acumen.[105]

Before we proceed to look closely at how religious scholars, medical students (who had been educated in Azharī schools), and lower-class Egyptians reacted to dissection, it is important to point out that in Clot Bey's post-Enlightenment view, religion in general, not just Islam, was an impediment to rational, scientific thinking. As is well known, Enlightenment thinkers consistently stressed that the church was the most serious obstacle to the opening up of cadavers for scientific ends and that there always existed a deep-seated taboo against prying open the human body. Opening up the body was considered sacrilegious mainly because it was seen as challenging God's will to maintain the inscrutability of all that was hidden from human eyes. Dissection, therefore, was seen as violating a divine prohibition on forbidden knowledge, and as such, "the prohibition of dissection was not [only] the first prohibition on knowledge itself, [it was] the model of all such prohibitions."[106]

Recent scholarship, however, has convincingly shown that blaming the church for being behind the opposition to dissection is based on a myth. However, although ample evidence has been marshaled that shows that the opposition to dissection was rooted in nonreligious factors, this myth, "like the flat-earth myth, with which it is often associated, has proved protean and apparently impossible to kill."[107]

According to this critical scholarship, the suspicion of, and resistance to, dissection did not stem from a religious taboo as such: "It lay rather in the dramatic violation of personal and family honor involved in dissection."[108] It is no accident, for example, that all statutes regulating dissection in early modern European medical schools stipulated that only the bodies of condemned criminals and foreigners could be dissected. Katharine Park argues that "these people were dissected in the first place qua foreigners rather than qua criminals, . . . [i.e., as people who] had no relatives nearby with an investment in a conventional and honorable funeral and usually no money to guarantee for themselves."[109] In his study of Italian dissection manuals published in the fifteenth and sixteenth centuries, Andrea Carlino shows that the prohibition against dissection was not the result of a religious doctrine. Rather, he contends, it was linked to "the transgression of certain anthropological codes such as the inviolability of the deceased, the integrity of the body, and the avoidance of contamination arising from contact with blood and death."[110] Furthermore, he argues that scholastic rigidity revered the canonical authorities on medicine, namely Galen and Aristotle, and that this is what was behind the strong academic hostility to dissection in medical schools. Professors who conducted dissections did so not to learn directly from the open cadaver but to illustrate the validity of the ancient authors, and when they occasionally found a discrepancy between classical authors and the dissected body, they "often did not believe what was actually before them," with the result that it took two centuries (from Mondino to Vesalius) for sensory perception to establish itself decisively over the textual authority of the ancients.[111] The disturbances that occasionally accompanied the dissection lessons, therefore, were not rooted in a perceived violation of church dogma about the inviolability of the human body; rather, they "might have been provoked by relatives and friends who protested the profanation of the remains of their loved ones; by spectators at dissections, by barbers and surgeons over the exorbitant entrance fees, or by the controversies that could arise from the assignment of places normally distributed on the basis of the positions, seniority and 'dignity' of those present."[112]

It is also germane to refer to Foucault's explanation of why medical history insisted that there was a strong resistance to dissection when none existed: "In the history of medicine, this illusion has a precise meaning; it functions as a retrospective justification: if the old beliefs had for so long such prohibitive power, it was because doctors had to feel in the depths of their scientific appetite, the repressed need to open up corpses."[113] In other words, the constant insistence by scholars and historians that dissections in early modern Europe were carried out under cover of darkness and against strong prohibitions was itself a cover-up that helped conceal the internal inability of the medical establishment to see what Xavier Bichat (1771–1802), the famous pathologist and histologist,[114] eventually proved, namely that pathological anatomy could unravel the mysteries of the human body.

Finally, in her study titled "Attitudes towards Dissection in Medieval Islam," Emilie Savage-Smith surmises that "just as great as a religious deterrent was perhaps the general human dread of cadavers and the revulsion of the sight of human dissection, combined with a climate most unfavorable for such an undertaking before the days of refrigeration.... Cutting into a corpse, especially a human one, is a messy and painstaking endeavor which, under the best of conditions, requires a strong motivation to carry out."[115]

After this short detour through the critical studies of the myth of doctrinal opposition to dissection, we can now revisit Clot Bey's account of the opposition he ostensibly faced from senior *'ulamā'* and students alike. That there was a stigma associated with dissecting bodies at Qaṣr al-'Ainī is not in doubt; nor is it contested that Clot Bey was attacked by one of his students. The question, rather, is how correct Clot Bey was in arguing that this opposition to dissection stemmed from an Islamic doctrinal prohibition to opening up cadavers. For one thing, Clot Bey's allusion to the natural theology argument of the divine watchmaker betrays a presupposition that the violation of the divine prohibition on opening the inscrutable body was behind the opposition to dissection, a presupposition that, as we have seen, has been seriously challenged in European societies such as Renaissance Italy and Enlightenment France.[116] For another, his paraphrasing of Shaykh al-ʿArūsī's argument that "cadavers could feel pain" seems to be based on a misreading of the Prophetic hadith "Breaking the bones of a person when dead is like breaking them while living," which can be understood as censuring grave robbers rather than prohibiting opening cadavers per se.[117]

What follows, therefore, is an analysis of the relationship between Islam and dissection that looks closely at four specific areas: what classical Islamic *fiqh* had to say about the permissibility of opening cadavers; the opinions nineteenth-century Egyptian *ʿulamāʾ* had about the topic; how dissection was understood by the first generation of Qaṣr al-ʿAinī graduates, who had been students in Azharī schools; and finally, the reaction of non-elite Egyptians to autopsies.

Dissection in Postclassical Fiqh. Savage-Smith has investigated the position of Islamic *fiqh* regarding dissection.[118] In an attempt to find out whether there was a prohibition against dissection in Islamic thought, she analyzes three bodies of literature. First, after studying the vast hadith literature, she argues, "In none of the early writings on jurisprudence or in the collections of *hadith*s does there seem to be any mention of anatomy/dissection (*tashrih*), either approvingly or disapprovingly."[119] She then moves on to the manuals for market inspectors, *adāb al-muḥtasib,* which give advice on procedures to be followed by these inspectors when monitoring physicians, barbers, pharmacists, phlebotomists, cuppers, surgeons, and oculists.[120] She reaches a similar conclusion: "From a legalistic viewpoint, human post-mortem dissection was not an impossibility within the medieval Islamic world. It seems that there was no actual prohibition in Islam against dissection or post-mortem examination."[121] Finally, she analyzes early (i.e., ninth century) Islamic medical literature to ascertain if it is averse to dissection. After a lengthy discussion of how Galen's writings on anatomy were translated and received by Arab authors, she concludes: "It is evident that there was no revulsion to the basic idea of human dissection on the part of the translator [referring to Ḥunayn Ibn Isḥāq, who translated Galen's *On Anatomical Procedures* into Arabic in the ninth century]. Such an unambiguous and uncritical rendering of references to human dissection implies that, in ninth-century Baghdad, at least among the community of Christian physicians, the idea may not have been repugnant or unthinkable."[122] Dealing with a later period of translation, she argues, "No criticism of these Galenic statements [on dissection] has been found in the extant Arabic medical literature that has been surveyed, and in fact, many of the ideas and themes are repeated by later Islamic writers."[123] Elsewhere, Savage-Smith reiterates the position that there was no "explicit legal or religious strictures banning it [dissection]. Indeed, many Muslim scholars lauded the study of anatomy, primarily as a way of demonstrating the design and wisdom of God."[124]

The argument that there does not seem to have been a consensus on the prohibition against dissection among premodern *fuqahā'* is reiterated in a study by the influential Shaykh 'Abd al-'Azīz Ibn 'Abdallāh Ibn Bāz (1910–99), the former mufti of Saudi Arabia. In a 1982 book devoted solely to the subject of dissection, Ibn Bāz noted that the majority of postclassical Muslim jurists gave a positive answer to the question of whether opening cadavers was permissible.[125] Naturally, postclassical jurists were never making rulings for medical or forensic purposes. Rather, the issue was typically brought up to illustrate some *fiqhī* principle and clarify the hierarchy of various *fiqhī* rules. For example, to stress the importance of the principle of the right of the property owner to his or her property, postclassical jurists raised the hypothetical question of whether it was permissible to open the belly of a dead man who had swallowed some coins or jewelry to return them to their rightful owner. The jurist Abū Muḥammad ʿAlī Ibn Aḥmad Ibn Saʿīd Ibn Ḥazm (994–1064) gave an affirmative answer to this question, arguing that the actual property, rather than compensation, should be given back to the property owner whenever possible.[126] Many jurists also responded in the affirmative to the question of whether it is permissible to eat human flesh when no alternative is available and not doing so would result in starvation. In justifying this position, they argued that maintaining life is paramount and should take precedence over dignifying the dead.

Needless to say, in asking these questions, the jurists were not responding to actual cases; rather, they were asking hypothetical questions to illustrate the proper course of action in undoubtedly confusing circumstances. In general, there was little unanimity in such ambivalent matters. The question of what should be done if faced with the case of a dead pregnant woman whose unborn baby could be ascertained to be still alive offers a good example of the scholastic controversies that were often triggered by these questions. The Shāfiʿite al-Nawawī (1233–77) and Ibn Ḥazm, for example, approved of opening up her cadaver to save her fetus, arguing that protecting human life is sacrosanct according to the Quran ("If any one saved a life, it would be as if he saved the life of the whole people," 5:32) and should take precedence over the principle of dignifying the dead. The Ḥanbalī Ibn Qudāma (1147–1233), by contrast, refused to allow for this possibility, and he strictly upheld the principle of the sanctity of the dead body and its inviolability in all circumstances. Even if there were available midwives, he argued, and even if it were determined that the baby was still alive, under no condition should the body of its dead mother be opened. But due to the impermissibility of burying people alive, he reasoned, enough time would have to elapse before burial to ensure that the unborn baby had died and would not be buried alive.[127]

Much later, in the early twentieth century, Rashīd Riḍā (1865–1935), gave an affirmative answer to the question of whether Islam allows postmortem examinations. In 1908, and again in 1910, Riḍā issued two fatwas in response to queries put to him by readers of his influential *Al-Manār* magazine to the effect that it was permissible, even mandatory, to conduct postmortem examinations on Muslim cadavers. In both fatwas, Riḍā opined that postmortem examination was allowed since it was a "worldly matter [*min al-masā'il al-dunyawiyya*] . . . and not a religious one [*laysat 'ibāda*]." The *fiqhī* principle alluded to was that of "casting off harm and attracting the beneficial [*dar' al-mafāsid wa jalb al-maṣāliḥ*]." The 1908 fatwa referred explicitly to the health regulations that that were in place in Egypt at the time and said that postmortem examinations, which were aimed at determining a person's cause of death, were considered a public good (*maṣlaḥa 'āmma*) and that this reasoning should thus take precedence over the principle of dignifying the dead (*takrīm al-mayyit*). The 1910 fatwa reiterated that line of thinking and said that the *sunna* of prompt burial could be disregarded if there existed the slightest doubt in determining cause of death. Referring to the remote possibility of a person being buried alive because fainting was mistaken for dying, "and thus suffering from the most horrible kind of death," the fatwa said that conducting a postmortem examination is permissible even if it meant that a male doctor needed to examine the body of a dead woman.[128]

The question of the permissibility of postmortem investigations was raised again in the 1940s, when Shaykh Ḥasanayn Muḥammad Makhlūf, the chief mufti of Egypt, was asked to give his fatwa on the following question: "According to the *sharī'a*, is it permitted to perform postmortem examination for scientific purposes or in criminal cases?" After careful consideration, Shaykh Makhlūf gave an affirmative answer:

> Our opinion must be in accordance with the public good which agrees with the spirit of Islamic Law in each place and generation and which guarantees happiness in this world as well as in the world to come. Therefore, we say: Whoever views postmortems as necessary, it is because in certain circumstances, such as when a person is accused of a crime against another and he is acquitted when the examination shows that the "victim" was not criminally attacked; or when a person is criminally attacked, and then, in order to conceal the crime, he is thrown into a well, etc., postmortems are mandatory. Add to that the progress to science that accrues from postmortems, progress which humanity as a whole may enjoy and which may bring relief to many who almost died or suffered terrible pains so that they are like living dead. We say: the general picture as well as the details must lead to the conclusion that postmortems are permitted, since the benefits outweigh the disadvantages.[129]

Dissection and Nineteenth-Century Egyptian 'Ulamā'. The preceding short detour into the writings of postclassical Muslim *fuqahā'* does not necessarily imply that Islamic *fiqh* informed the reactions of nineteenth-century Egyptian *'ulamā'* to dissection. For one thing, it is not known to what degree students at al-Azhar were familiar with the writings of, for example, Ibn Ḥazm and al-Nawawī; for another, there is no explicit doctrinal formulation by a nineteenth-century Egyptian *'ālim* on the question of the permissibility of dissection. Earlier, in the eighteenth century, Shaykh Aḥmad al-Damanhūrī, the rector of al-Azhar from 1768 to 1776, penned a treatise urging doctors (*al-mutaṭubibīn*) to study dissection and anatomy, collectively referred to as *tashrīḥ*. Titled "Muntahā al-Taṣrīḥ bi-Khulāṣat al-Qawl al-Ṣarīḥ fī 'Ilm al-Tashrīḥ," the treatise starts by giving a definition of the word *tashrīḥ:* "Linguistically, it means explication and description [*al-kashf wa'l-bayān*]. Idiomatically, it means describing the [different] parts of the human body and knowing their locations and their uses to attain knowledge of the Supreme Creator, His power, and His delicate wisdom."[130] However, a close reading of the treatise reveals that it does not refer to dissection as opening up a cadaver or cutting flesh but rather as the knowledge of the technical anatomical literature, beginning with Aristotle and Galen and ending with the numerous Arabic commentaries on Ibn Sīnā.

Later, in 1813, Ḥasan al-'Aṭṭār, who in 1830 would become rector of al-Azhar, wrote a treatise that came very close to extolling dissection, although it did not do so explicitly and did not take the form of a manual guiding students to the actual practice of dissection. The treatise, titled "Sharḥ al-'Aṭṭār al-Musammā bi Rāḥat al-Abdān 'Alā Nuzhat al-Adhhān fi 'Ilm al-Ṭibb," was written as a commentary on a minor work by Dāwūd al-Antākī

(d. 1599). According to Peter Gran, in this manuscript al-ʿAṭṭār was rallying the authority of both Ibn al-Nafīs (d. 1288) and al-Rāzī (d. 925) to launch "a critique of the Ibn Sīnian tradition of medicine." In a later work dating from 1830, al-ʿAṭṭār wrote, "While Ibn Sīnā was the great doctor of the theory of medicine, al-Rāzī was the great practitioner. The distinction was itself significant, especially because of his [i.e., al-ʿAṭṭār's] linking practice to dissection, and his obvious preference for practice as opposed to theory."[131]

The only explicit doctrinally based position of nineteenth-century Egyptian *ʿulamāʾ* regarding dissection and postmortem examinations in general that we have evidence of in the archival record relates not to the issue of the inscrutability of dead bodies but to the issue of delayed burial, which was the inevitable result of these examinations. Facing repeated complaints by members of the *ʿulamāʾ* about delayed burials,[132] ʿAbbās Pasha (r. 1849–54) issued strict orders that forensic doctors had to conduct their postmortem examinations promptly, and he set down clear punishments for any doctors who caused an unnecessary delay in burial.[133] The General Health Council, which was in charge of all public hygiene matters, issued stern warnings to the resident doctors in all quarters of Cairo and in other cities not to delay in checking any reported death and instructed them to give the matter their utmost priority. The directive specified that postmortems should be conducted during daytime, from one hour after sunrise to one hour before sunset.[134] Those who violated these regulations were severely punished: records indicate that punishments ranged from a ten-day detention to being discharged from service altogether.[135] At the same time, however, strict orders were issued to local authorities not to be too hasty in burying the dead. A waiting period of eight hours in summer and ten hours in winter was mandated. However, deaths had to be certified by the neighborhood or village physician to avoid the grave error of mistaking fainting for death and thus burying someone alive.[136]

It does not appear, therefore, that the few cases in which members of the *ʿulamāʾ* voiced their opposition to dissection were based on Islamic doctrine. There is no evidence in the records that the *ʿulamāʾ* believed that Muslim corpses could feel pain, as Clot Bey claimed. As mentioned above, the only point of doctrine that was occasionally mentioned in the opposition of the *ʿulamāʾ* to dissection concerned delays in burial, which was not connected to any theological principle related to the sanctity of the human body, such as fear of opening up corpses or suspicion that dissection jeopardized one's chances of resurrection. This is not to say that this opposition was negligible or unimportant; as we have seen, it was occasionally effective in forcing the government to alter its position on some issues related to public hygiene. However, this opposition can better be seen as stemming from the increasingly marginalized position that the religious establishment found itself in during the nineteenth century. With the new regulations stipulating that doctors were responsible for defining death, some *'ulamā'* must have felt that their monopoly on matters of death and burial was being challenged by Qaṣr al-'Ainī graduates.[137]

Dissection and the Azharī Students of Qaṣr al-'Ainī. Besides studying the position of the *'ulamā'* on dissection, one can gauge the reaction of Egyptian society to this delicate issue by following the writings of the first generation of Qaṣr al-'Ainī graduates, who, it has to be remembered, had been students at Azharī schools before attending the new medical school. A number of these students were later sent to France to continue their medical education, so their writings offer an important insight into the relationship between Islam and science in nineteenth-century Egypt and allow us to examine what these former Azharī students might have thought of dissection and how they reconciled their beliefs with their new medical profession.

One of these students was 'Issawī al-Naḥrāwī, who entered Qaṣr al-'Ainī when it opened in 1827. After graduating in 1832, al-Naḥrāwī was immediately sent to France in the first student mission of that year. When he returned to Egypt in the mid-1830s, he took a teaching position at his alma mater. He eventually became the head of the Azbakiyya Civilian Hospital. Later, he was appointed director of the School of Midwives, which, despite its misleading name, trained women not only to become midwives but also to assume important roles in the forensic medical establishment and effectively become forensic doctors in their own right. While still in France, al-Naḥrāwī translated Pierre Augustin Béclard's *Elémens d'anatomie générale, ou Description de tous les genres d'organes qui composent le corps humain,* which had originally been published in Paris in 1827. On al-Naḥrāwī's return to Egypt, Būlāq Press published his translation under the title *Al-Tashrīḥ al-'Āmm* (General anatomy), and it quickly became a staple textbook for Qaṣr al-'Ainī students, with a second edition appearing in 1845.

A brief look at this anatomy textbook reveals something about how al-Naḥrāwī thought of the connection between dissection and Islam. After a short rhyming introduction in which he praises God, al-Naḥrāwī states his purpose in translating his tome: "This is a book on general anatomy, which is the basis of both medicine and forensic science. It is a book unique in Egypt and aids its reader to understand the composition of the human body, which is the most noble of all animal bodies. It is an indispensable book for any physician for it helps him to diagnose illnesses, and whoever reads it will strengthen his faith [in God] as he will marvel at the precision of the Maker's creatures."[138] In a later section that introduces the general differences between human and other mammal anatomies, he says, "The main difference between humans and other mammals is the mental faculties that constitute humanity. What most distinguishes man is the determination for an act, rationality, will, and feeling and confessing to the presence of God Almighty."[139]

This attitude of not seeing a contradiction between personal belief and Islamic doctrine, on the one hand, and modern medicine and the practice of dissection, on the other, is also found in the works of a colleague of al-Naharāwī's, Muḥammad al-Shabāsī (see figure 4).[140] On returning from his student mission in France, al-Shabāsī worked on two anatomical texts. The first was an Arabic translation of Jean Cruveilhier's two-volume work *Anatomie pathologique du corps humain* (originally printed 1829–42), which he published under the title *Al-Tanqīḥ al-Waḥīd fī al-Tashrīḥ al-Khāṣṣ al-Jadīd.* Al-Shabāsī also wrote a one-volume textbook, *Al-Tanwīr fī Qawā'id al-Taḥḍīr,* as an aid for his students on how to prepare corpses for autopsy and how to conduct the autopsy itself.[141] It was this latter work that was the basis of his fame. *Al-Tanwīr* was presented to the General Health Council, which ordered a thousand copies to be printed.[142] If we are to believe what the author says of the book's effects on his students, it appears to have been a smashing success: Al-Shabāsī wrote that students were in the habit of taking corpses to their lodgings to learn more about human anatomy and noted that they did not find it problematic to sleep in the same rooms where dead bodies were kept, regardless of the criticism that this behavior triggered.[143] As odd as this may seem, the anecdote has two illustrious antecedents: Galen, in the first book of his *De anatomicus administrationibus,* mentions how he secured, for his own personal edification, the body of an outlaw that had been stripped of its flesh by ravenous birds, and Vesalius mentions in his *De humani corporis fabrica* how his thirst for knowledge impelled him to acquire a cadaver illicitly.[144] In her study *Death, Dissection and the Destitute,* Ruth Richardson has documented numerous cases of bodysnatching by surgeons and anatomists in England, the earliest dating from the late seventeenth century.[145]

In the preface to his second book, al-Shabāsī states explicitly: "It is common knowledge among civilized nations that medicine cannot advance

FIGURE 4: Muḥammad al-Shabāsī. Image from Amīn Sāmī, *Taqwīm al-Nīl* (Cairo: Dār al-Kutub, 1936), vol. 2, opposite p. 596.

except by practicing dissection."[146] "Opening cadavers," he adds, "has many benefits. Among them are acquiring the knowledge of how healthy organs might have looked like immediately prior to death. It also enables us to identify pathological transformations that affect each organ and to compare them to symptoms detected just before death, and thus helps us diagnose illness. It can also be useful in problems related to forensic medicine, such as burns, poisoning, homicide, drowning, falling [from a high place], and dangerous wounds. Moreover, it can be of use in pointing out dangers that should be avoided while conducting small or major surgical operations." Al-Shabāsī has no problem adding a religious benefit to this list: "Marveling at the precise functioning of the organs and meditating on God's creatures, which deepens and strengthens one's faith."[147] He then paraphrases Galen: "Reading anatomy books is the greatest of all acts of worship, and it forces one to acknowledge God's oneness."[148]

Throughout his book, al-Shabāsī follows the tradition of medieval Muslim physicians, who saw no contradiction between their personal faith and their medical profession. This harmonious view of his religion and his practice of dissection is seen most clearly in the conclusion of the book, where he dwells on the importance of dissection for forensic medicine:

> What we have just explained should enable the forensic doctor to be sufficiently alert so that he can distinguish between apparent death and real death [*mawt ḥaqīqī*]. [Another value of dissection can be illustrated by] the example of three people who all drowned at the same time. Consequently, a problem of [Islamic] inheritance arises, a problem that can only be resolved if we determine who died first. Specifically, one person may have died after suffering from blood coagulation in the brain and then died of a stroke, the second by fainting [*ighmā'*], and the third struggled with drowning for some time and eventually died of asphyxiation. In this case, the forensic doctor can deduce from the condition of the arteries, the veins, the heart, the lungs, and the brain certain rational conclusions based on visual signs [*mushāhdāt*], not on guessing and surmising [*ẓann wa takhmīn*]. The same can be said in other similar cases, such as when many people die at the same time in an earthquake, the collapse of a building, or a fire. [In all these cases, the forensic doctor] must be careful to make clear that his results are not absolute truths [*barāhīn qaṭi'yya akīda*] but only plausible, relative matters.[149]

In his very last remark, al-Shabāsī reminds his students of the importance of diligence in their work and cautions them not to jump to easy conclusions:

> When the forensic doctor comes across a dead body in the street, he should be very careful in determining the cause of death. For if he says that the victim died as a result of a brain stroke [i.e., a natural death], but death was [actually] caused by something else [i.e., unnaturally], then two errors will have been committed: first, the shari'a-stipulated capital punishment, retaliation [*qiṣāṣ*], of his murderer is prevented, and second, this case would be recorded wrongly in the death registers [*'adam ẓabṭ qawā'im al-mawtā*].[150]

The ease by which this former Azharī student, who held the chair of professor of the Department of Physiology and Pathological Anatomy at Qaṣr al-'Ainī, could combine his understanding of *fiqh* with his belief in the value of human dissection is a far cry from Clot Bey's assertion that "religious superstitions" hampered his medical work in Egypt. In this remarkable book, which is written in a nonpolemical, matter-of-fact style and was intended not for the general public but for medical students, al-Shabāsī clearly explains how dissection could be of aid not only to medical education but also to the proper collection of vital statistics and, most remarkably, to upholding the Islamic principle of retaliation for a *medically* proven case of homicide.

Al-Shabāsī was not alone among his colleagues at Qaṣr al-ʿAinī in having this harmonious attitude toward his faith and his profession. Indeed, they did not see these two fields of thought as distinct from one another. The eloquent introductions they wrote for the books they translated from French into Arabic show not only how much they viewed their scientific endeavors as deepening their belief in God but also how these endeavors themselves were part of their faith. They paid homage to Bichat and Lavoisier; they extolled Ibn Sīnā, Galen, and Hippocrates; and they profusely thanked the khedives for reviving an old science that, they believed, had been born in Egypt. Above all, however, they thanked God. Every single medical and chemical book that Būlāq Press published in the first fifty years of its history started with a rhymed, spirited introduction praising God for His bounty and marveling at His creation. These introductions are craftily written, playing on some of God's attributes that are relevant to the topic of the book. For example, the translators and editors of Bayle's anatomy book, *Traité élémentaire d'anatomie,* which was published under the title *Al-Qawl al-Ṣarīḥ fī ʿIlm al-Tashrīḥ,* wrote in their introduction: "Praise be to Him Who has created man in such good form; Who composed his body of bones, nerves, veins, and cartridges; Who expanded the chest of[151] [*sharaḥta,* i.e., inspired] whoever wants to marvel at its form and constituent parts."[152] A book on apothecary published in 1840 opened with the following words: "You Whose mere mention is the best remedy for man, and Whose praise is the best antidote for hearts and bodies, . . . glory be to Your Majesty in which the bodies of those who love You dissolve. . . . The mere mention of You is a balsam that can cure all their ills, and praying to You is an elixir that can remedy all sickness."[153] Finally, Muhammad al-Tūnisī, Muḥammad al-Harrāwī, Darwīsh Zaydān, and Ḥusayn Ghānim, who translated and edited Nicolas Perron's *Al-Djawāhir al-Saniyya fī'l-Aʿmāl al-Kīmāwiyya,* wrote in their introduction, "You to Whom pure souls rise, and of Whose Majesty bodies dissolve, and on the thresholds of Whose mercy bodies prostrate, Your Exalted Being knows neither composition nor decomposition, and Your Sublime Attributes do not change or morph. There is no god but You, who has created for us Earth with its metals, plants, and animals, and has brought into being food that is sweet, sour, tasty, and salty."[154]

Moreover, the position of these doctors on dissection and on the medical profession they were establishing in Egypt was shaped more by an acute awareness of their social position in Egypt than by any religious anxiety about the profanity of dissection. The 1827 decision to use Arabic as the language of instruction in the newly established Qaṣr al-'Ainī Medical School had far-reaching political, social, and cultural repercussions, for this decision meant that only Arabic-speaking natives were recruited to the school and members of the Turkish-speaking military-bureaucratic elite and members of the country's different ethnic minorities (e.g., Armenians, Circassians, Greeks) were excluded. At the same time, the medical school, and indeed the entire medical and public hygiene establishment, lacked financial and administrative independence. Starting in 1837, when different government departments were set up, Qaṣr al-'Ainī fell under the jurisdiction of the Department of Public Instruction (Dīwān al-Madāris), while the Shūrā al-Aṭibbā, through which Clot Bey managed the far-flung medical establishment, was a branch of the War Department. Both of these departments were controlled by members of the Turkish-speaking military-bureaucratic aristocracy. Moreover, within the medical establishment, European physicians and pharmacists occupied the most senior positions. It was only in the early 1840s that the Arabic-speaking Egyptian graduates of the school started to be able to compete with their European superiors for these coveted positions because in that decade the first Egyptian graduates of Qaṣr al-'Ainī started returning from their student missions in France, and those graduates who had served in the army were released from military service, having acquired considerable experience working in field hospitals (see chapter 4).

These Egyptian doctors found that they had to compete with their European and Turkish superiors while simultaneously struggling to distinguish themselves from their compatriots, and they realized that it was necessary to distance themselves as much as possible from their humble rural origins. In their fierce determination to elbow themselves up the social ladder, they saw science as a tool that enabled their upward mobility. For them, science was a universal language that established equivalence between themselves and their European colleagues. But science, and specifically the medicine, pharmacology, and chemistry that they were practicing, was a skill that was effectively denied to their Turkish-speaking superiors, even though these superiors, because they had the power of the purse, controlled the medical profession.

Dissection and Non-elite Egyptians. Neither the *'ulamā'* in nineteenth-century Egypt nor the doctors of Qaṣr al-'Ainī seem to have posed serious objections to dissection, and non-elite Egyptians appear not to have resisted or dismissed it outright either. To be sure, the sight of or contact with dead bodies must have evoked feelings of horror, disgust, and shock, and the decision of the authorities to rely on dissection to ascertain cause of death must have been viewed as a deeply disturbing practice by the general public. However, police and court records show that as disturbing as they might have considered autopsies, non-elite Egyptians were often willing to resort to the practice when they suspected that a loved one had been murdered and that the only way to achieve justice was by asking for an external postmortem examination, even if this entailed exhuming the body. Indeed, in some cases, Egyptians were willing to go so far as to ask that the body of a loved one, be it a daughter, husband, or father, be sent to Qaṣr al-ʿAinī for an autopsy.

Naturally, in most cases, the first things that people did when faced with a death were performing funerary rituals and having the body properly buried. This was what happened in the case of a fifteen-year old boy named Muḥammad Ibn Muḥammad ʿAbdallāh. In February 1860, the boy was sent by his father to learn the Quran with two shaykhs, Shaykh Maḥmūd and Shaykh Ibrāhīm, who had a Quran school (*kuttāb*) in al-Imāmayn, the southern cemetery of Cairo. When young Muḥammad did not return home to his parents at the expected time, his father went to the school in person, where he was told that his son had died three days previously in the mill (*tāḥūna*) that was attached to the *kuttāb*. At the mill, he found his son's bloodstained clothing and was told that his son's body had already been buried. He then went to the Cairo police headquarters and demanded that the two shaykhs be summoned. When they appeared, he and his wife accused them of murdering their son. In the subsequent trial in the shariʿa court, the *qāḍī* dismissed the case because the plaintiffs could not present a shariʿa proof—that is, a confession by the defendants or an eyewitness account. As in most similar cases, the parents dropped the charges and did not insist on an autopsy. Police investigations later revealed that there was no suspected foul play, as the boy had been in the habit of sleeping in the mill and, on that fatal night, had fallen and been caught between the wheels. When the two shaykhs were questioned about why they had not informed the authorities after discovering the body the following morning, they said that they thought that "delaying this matter [i.e., burial] would have been improper [*al-taʾkhīr ʿan dhālik laysa min al-ṣawāb*]."[155]

In numerous other cases, however, where foul play was suspected, plaintiffs, in their quest for justice, were willing to ask for an autopsy to prove their case against whomever they suspected of killing their loves ones. Consider, for example, the case of ʿAlī al-Shīmī, from Shubrā al-Nakhla, who was buried after the resident doctor of Bilbays had examined him and found no suspicious signs on the body. Al-Shīmī's relatives, however, insisted that death was unnatural and that ʿAlī had been murdered by a certain Jāhīn al-Shāʿir. Confronted with the family's persistence, the authorities ordered the body exhumed and reexamined.[156]

By the 1850s, only one generation after the foundation of Qaṣr al-ʿAinī, the centrality of forensic medicine in investigating crimes was readily understood and appropriated by non-elite Egyptians. In fact, an order by the health authorities from 1859 explicitly refers to this common understanding when it states that autopsies should be conducted not only when the authorities were suspicious but also when "the relatives of the deceased remain adamant that their relative had died an unnatural death. . . . In such cases, the doctors should go ahead and perform autopsies [*al-ʿamaliyya al-tashrīḥiyya*] to uncover the truth [*li-ẓuhūr al-ḥaqīqa*] so that both parties [involved in the case] are satisfied [with the verdict]."[157]

In fact, Egyptians believed so firmly in the practice that they were occasionally willing to request autopsies even if the result was that legal charges might be brought against members of their own family. For example, in the summer of 1858, a thirty-five-year-old woman named Ḥanīfa bint Muwāfī, from Bāb al-Lūq in Cairo, died. On conducting the postmortem, the forensic doctor—in this case the *ḥakīma* (female doctor) responsible for the quarter—learned that Ḥanīfa's husband had beaten her and that this might have been the cause of her death. She decided to send for a more senior *ḥakīma* from the Cairo police headquarters. The second *ḥakīma,* however, reported that the woman had died of natural causes. A death certificate was issued to that effect and the body was buried. Shortly thereafter, however, Ḥanīfa's mother grew suspicious and filed a report with the police requesting that her daughter's body be exhumed, claiming that she had evidence that her daughter had not died of natural causes.[158]

The strong faith that non-elite Egyptians had in dissection and postmortem examinations is further illustrated by a dramatic case from 1875. It involves the residents of the newly founded city of Port Said, who presented a petition requesting the replacement of the European doctor in charge of examining the dead, as they believed he had been in the habit of issuing burial certificates without conducting postmortem examinations in person (see figure 5). What triggered the petition was the suspicion that the doctor

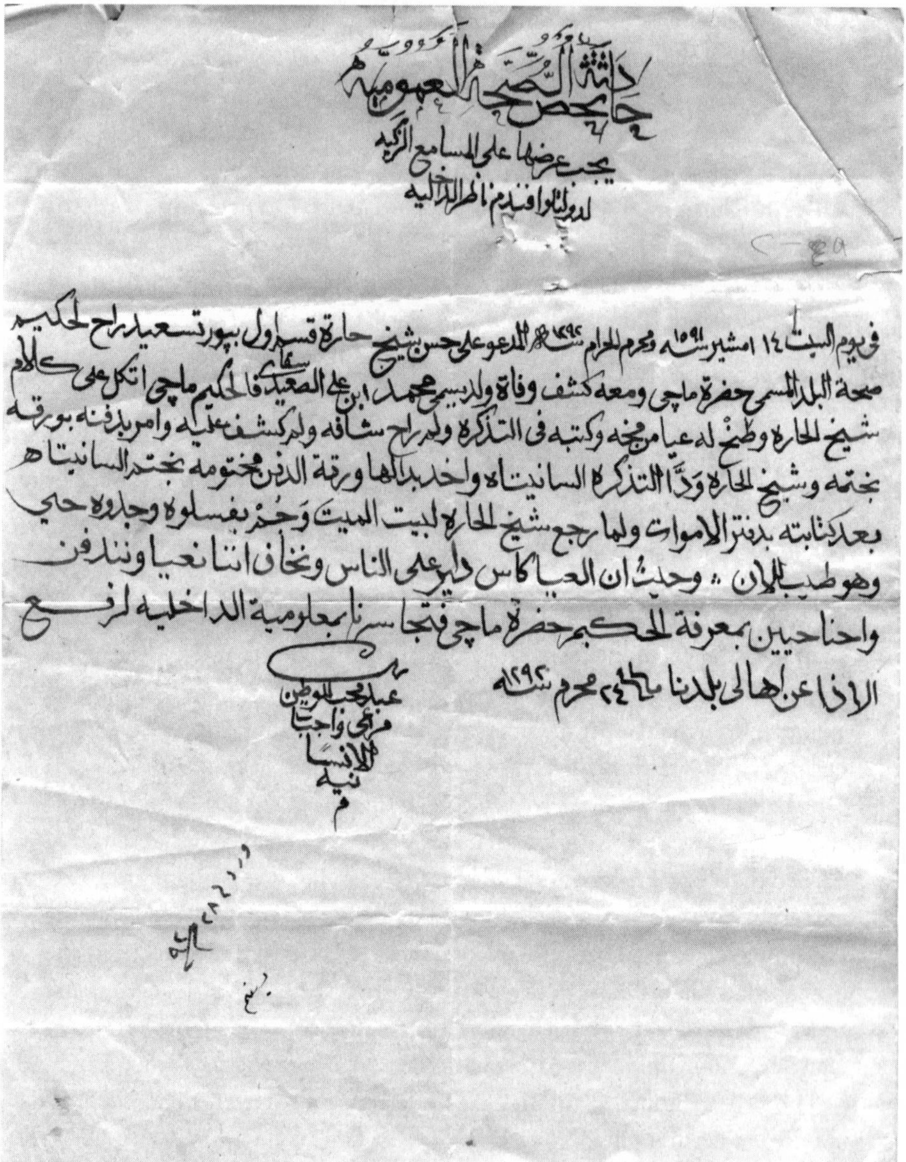

جانب مجلس الصحة العمومية دامت

يجب عرضها على المسامع الزكية

لدولتلو افندم ناظر الداخلية

في يوم السبت ١٤ امشير سنة ١٥٩١ ه محرم الحرام سنة ١٢٩٤ المدعو علي حسن شيخ حارة قسم اول ببورت سعيد راح الحكيم
صحة البلد المسمى حضرة ماچي ومعه كشف وفاة ولد يسمى محمد ابن علي الصعيدي سقاي فالحكيم ماچي اتكل على كلام
شيخ الحارة وطبع له عيا من نخه وكتبه في التذكرة ولم راح شافه ولم كشف عليه وامر بدفنه بورقه
بختمه وشيخ الحارة ودا التذكرة السانيتاه واخد بدالها ورقة الدفن مختومه بختم السانيتاه
بعد كتابته بدفتر الاموات ولما رجع شيخ الحارة لبيت الميت وجد بغسلوه وجدوه حي
وهو طيب الان . وحيث ان العيا كاس دليل على الناس ونخاف اننا نعيا وننذفن
واحنا حيين بمعرفة الحكيم حضرة ماچي فتجاسرنا بعلومية الداخليه لرفع
الاذا عن اهالي بلدنا ما ٢٤ محرم سنة ١٢٩٤

عبيد محب الوطن
من محبي واحبا
الانسا
نية
م

FIGURE 5: Petition from the residents of Port Said, 1877. Reproduced courtesy of Dār al-Wathā'iq al-Qawmiyya (Egyptian National Archives), Cairo.

had wrongly issued a death certificate to a six-day-old baby boy who "came back to life" when his relatives were about to bury him. In their petition, the residents of Port Said said that "illness is like a goblet that goes around for all to drink from" (*naẓaran li-ʾanna al-ʿayā kās dāyir ʿalā al-nās*), and since the doctor was supposed to be diligently preserving the community's health but had not been performing his job properly, resulting in one of their own children almost having been buried alive, they requested that he be replaced by a physician they could trust.[159]

Studying the intricate practice of dissection in nineteenth-century Egypt shows that there is no evidence that the introduction of anatomoclinical medicine was resisted by Islam. After studying the opinions of religious men, the writings of medical students who had received deep religious training, and the actions of a variety of non-elite Egyptians from Cairo and the provinces, it appears that postmortem examinations and dissection were met with little resistance in Egypt. Contrary to what Clot Bey wrote in his oft-quoted polemical works, the archival record shows that opening cadavers was not a controversial issue that had to be delicately handled to placate local religious sensibilities. Egyptians certainly believed in the sanctity of death. They may have been deterred from autopsies by fear of death and revulsion to corpses, but on numerous occasions, their determination to conduct autopsies in their quest for justice overrode any anxieties they might have had regarding religious or traditional beliefs about death and its sanctity.

CONCLUSION

Having studied how anatomoclinical medicine was introduced in Egypt, we are now in a position to critically assess the common view that sees these fraught processes as a struggle between European enlightenment and Islamic beliefs. For one thing, such a simplistic depiction of an alleged Manichean struggle between the modern and the traditional, the scientific and the emotional, the rational and the spiritual does not even begin to capture the complex reactions that many segments of Egyptian society had to such practices as imposing quarantines and performing dissections. By concentrating on the translatability of the epistemes of European modernity, these theories fail to take into account the complex local, institutional, ethnic, and class contexts in which these translations took place. They also fail to acknowledge that nineteenth-century Egypt was not only dealing with rising European imperialism and the expansion of capitalism but also launching its own dynastic struggle for autonomy within the Ottoman Empire. And as we will see in subsequent chapters, this larger struggle was an important factor that shaped the Egyptian *nahḍa* of the nineteenth century.

By ignoring the larger Ottoman context and overlooking Mehmed Ali's desire to establish hereditary rule in Egypt and found a conscription-based army for that purpose, previous scholars have chosen to tell the story of Qaṣr al-ʿAinī and medical reform in nineteenth-century Egypt as one of a few determined, enlightened men determined to open the eyes of Egyptian society to the endless benefits of modern medicine. Repeatedly, these histories contrast the enlightened, altruistic efforts of these men to introduce modern medicine with society's superstition, fatalism, and fanaticism. As shown above, the metaphors of light, vision, and enlightenment suffuse these accounts of borrowing and resistance.

Rather than engage with these polemics by investigating whether Qaṣr al-ʿAinī and its affiliate institutions were practicing "Egyptian" or "European" medicine, the preceding account stressed the larger Ottoman context and followed the specific manner in which practices such as quarantines and dissection were performed. The purpose was to highlight that the discourse of European enlightenment vis-à-vis Islamic fanaticism has blinded us to what has always been lurking behind glittering surfaces. A more sinister, military aspect had always been part of Egyptian medicine in the nineteenth-century. This connection to naked power informed people's understanding of Qaṣr al-ʿAinī and its affiliate institutions and is best expressed by a commemorative plaque that dates back to 1813, when the building that would later be occupied by the Qaṣr al-ʿAinī Medical School functioned as a military barracks. Tellingly, the inscription, which remained above the main entrance after the building had been converted to a medical school and hospital, referred not to vision but to its exact opposite. It reads as follows:

> Muḥammad Ali Pasha, prince of Egypt, victory's son
> Ordered this noble barrack to be built, and lo! it is done
> So may the foes' eyes blinded be, whene'er this pile they scan.[160]

TWO

Siyāsa, *the Forgotten Code*

THE STILLNESS OF THE NIGHT was pierced by a loud gunshot. Ibrāhīm ʿAbd al- Raḥmān rushed to the barn, where the sound had come from, only to find his brother, Muḥammad, bleeding to death on the ground. He picked up the body and, together with a few companions, marched toward his brother's house. When they saw Muḥammad's blood-soaked clothes, all members of his household—his wife, his mother, his father, his children—burst out wailing and crying. After the clamor had subsided, rumors started circulating in the village (Mīt Yazīd, in Gharbiyya Governorate in the Nile delta) that the person who had shot dead Muḥammad ʿAbd al-Raḥmān was Ḥammād Zalaṭ, a local strongman. By the morning, a heavy blanket of silence fell on the village. When Ibrāhīm went to the house of the village head (*ʿumda*) to report his brother's murder, he found the village shaykhs and local sentries all gathered together. They told him to hold his tongue, saying that no good would come out of reporting the incident to the governorate headquarters (*mudīriyya*). The local barber surgeon was summoned and coerced into issuing a forged burial certificate (*tadhkarat dafn*) recording diarrhea as the cause of death. The resident scribe in the local health office took out his monthly register and duly recorded the death as natural. Muḥammad was then hastily buried after a small, hushed funeral. "Intimidated by the village *shaykh*s, the victim's relatives could not go to the government to report the incident" (*min khawfihim min al-mashāyikh lam amkanahum al-tawajjuh lil-ḥukūma wa'l-tashakkī*).

However, people started whispering that a body had secretly been buried with no proper medical investigation. Three days after the incident, the governor got wind of what had happened. When he arrived on the scene on July 25, 1876, his investigation was frustrated by the silence that enveloped the village, as no one was willing to step forward to say what exactly had taken place. Eventually, Ibrāhīm approached the governor and "told him secretly" (*akhbarahu sirran*) that he was the brother of the deceased and that he knew where the body was buried. The head doctor of Gharbiyya Governorate and one of his assistants were quickly fetched and, after the body had been exhumed, they conducted a postmortem examination. Their detailed report left no doubt that Muḥammad had not died a natural death. With the matter no longer a secret, the family decided to press murder charges in the local shari'a court, Maḥkamat Ṭanṭā. The qadi ascertained the heirs' identities according to shari'a rules (*ba'd tahaquq ma'rifatihim shar'an*) and proved that they were the sole heirs of the deceased and that no *ḥājib* existed that would prevent them from receiving the inheritance. The heirs then accused Ḥammād Zalaṭ of murdering Muḥammad 'Abd al-Raḥmān with intent (*'amdan*).[1] They asked for their shari'a-stipulated rights, including the right to question Ḥammād about the incident. When Ḥammād was questioned, he denied the accusations. As the heirs were not able to provide an eyewitness, the qadi asked them if they had a *bayyina* (*shar'ī* evidence) to prove their case. They replied that they lacked a *bayyina*. Consequently, the qadi ordered them to drop the charges and "stop obstructing the defendant" (*muni'ū al-mudda'īn . . . min mu'āradatihim lil-mudda'ā 'aliyhi*). Having failed to prove their case in the shari'a court, the heirs "relegated the matter to the government" (*fawwaḍū al-amr lil-ḥukūma*).

While the qadi was conducting the case in his court, the *mudīriyya* had been conducting its own detailed investigations: witnesses were summoned, suspects arraigned, reports written, and testimonies recorded. The resulting voluminous documentation was forwarded to a judicial administrative body called the *majlis* (council), in this case Majlis al-Gharbiyya (the Council of Gharbiyya Governorate), which found Ḥammād Zalaṭ to be the prime suspect, despite the fact that he had denied the accusations. Based on the forensic medical report, the testimony of various witnesses, and the claims of the plaintiffs, the majlis sentenced Ḥammād to seven years in prison per Article 11 of Chapter 1 of the Humāyūnī Criminal Law of 1852. All the other suspects in the case—the sentries who had not rushed to the scene when they heard the gunshot; the barber surgeon who had forged the burial certificate; the scribe who had recorded the wrong cause of death in his monthly register; the corpse-washer who had seen the bullet wound on the dead body while preparing it for burial but had not reported it—were handed various prison sentences that ranged from thirty days to six months.

The case was then forwarded to a higher appeals council, Majlis Isti'nāf Baḥarī (the Appeals Council of Lower Egypt), which reduced the prison sentence passed against Ḥammād Zalaṭ from seven to five years. Finally, the case was forwarded to Majlis al-Aḥkām (the Council of Judicial Ordinances), the highest council in the land, which ratified the revised verdict of Majlis Isti'nāf Baḥarī.[2]

As detailed as this account of the 1876 murder case may appear, it is but a brief summary of a copious narrative that unfolds over several large folios of one ledger of Majlis al-Aḥkām, which was the most supreme legal body in Egypt for most of the nineteenth century. As will become clear as we review other cases in this and subsequent chapters, criminal cases similar to Muḥammad 'Abd al-Raḥmān's were adjudicated by a penal system that was complex and highly organized. Specifically, this penal system relied on an increasingly efficient police force that arraigned and interrogated suspects; prepared detailed and lengthy reports of these interrogations; used circumstantial evidence—most notably forensic medicine—in conducting their investigation; and adjudicated cases in judicial administrative councils that were arranged in a multitiered fashion, with councils of "first instance," appeals councils, and at the top of the judicial apparatus, Majlis al-Aḥkām. Most significantly, this intriguing penal system coupled *fiqh* with its detailed rules in penal matters, with *siyāsa,* a legal system with a long lineage in Ottoman and Islamic history and that, in nineteenth-century Egypt, referred to the discretionary powers exercised by Mehmed Ali and his descendants to adjudicate cases in special bodies called *majālis siyāsiyya* (*siyāsa* councils).

The records of this complex legal system—which functioned for some forty years, from the early 1840s to the early 1880s—are now housed in the Egyptian National Archives. Together, these ledgers—there are over four thousand of them—contain copious correspondence of the different institutions of the *siyāsa* system, written in clear, legible script. The thousands of cases these ledgers contain shed light on the intricate inner workings of this complex legal system: how petitions were accepted, how the police went about investigating cases, how central forensic medicine was in police investigations, and how sentences were passed and punishments carried out. This voluminous documentation makes it possible to follow a given case from the initiation of legal action, through various levels of adjudication, to sentencing. Most interestingly, these ledgers clearly show how the *siyāsa* legal system, with its governorate councils, worked in tandem with the shari'a courts and how *siyāsa* verdicts were passed only after a shari'a verdict (*i'lām shar'ī*) had been issued.

Despite the very detailed and voluminous documentation produced by it, the *siyāsa* system has evaded the attention of most scholars, and with very few exceptions, the historiography of nineteenth-century Egyptian law has not accorded it the attention it deserves.[3] As this chapter will show, this intriguing, complex, and original legal system does not feature prominently (if at all) in historical accounts of how Egyptian law is believed to have developed in the nineteenth century. For the most part, these accounts prefer to see Egyptian law progressing teleologically along secular lines, starting with Bonaparte's invasion in 1798 and ending with the inauguration of the Mixed Courts in 1876 or the National Courts in 1883 and their adoption of French law lock, stock and barrel. There is no place in this story of triumphant secularization for the *siyāsa* and its *majālis*.

This chapter tells the story of an intriguing missing chapter of Egyptian legal history. It does so by relying on the copious documentation of this legal system, specifically on records of actual criminal cases, mostly homicides. Before doing so, though, the following section offers a detailed overview of the historiography of nineteenth-century Egyptian law with the aim of highlighting how and why there has been a deafening silence in the literature on *siyāsa*. To understand the underlying logic of the *siyāsa* system, this chapter offers various examples of how *siyāsa* was coupled with *fiqh* in the daily functioning of the *siyāsa* councils and takes a closer look at the copious records of the *siyāsa* councils to see how the two branches of the criminal law system, *siyāsa* and *fiqh* handled the various stages of adjudicating typical criminal cases. The chapter concludes by presenting some thoughts on the significance of nineteenth-century Egyptian legal reforms, revisiting the question of how the *siyāsa* system was excised from the historical record, and explaining how this system came to be seen as playing no part in the formation of modern Egyptian law.

THE HISTORIOGRAPHY OF NINETEENTH-CENTURY EGYPTIAN LAW

The specter of Europe haunts the historiography of nineteenth-century Egyptian legal reform. When discerning what might have prompted the khedives to pass new legislation,[4] analyzing the logic that might have informed judicial practice,[5] or describing the changes that legal education and training have undergone,[6] most scholars have been primarily concerned with detecting European influences that have ostensibly affected the changes in the Egyptian legal environment. Compared to what are assumed to be quintessentially European principles of secularism, juridical equality, and rule of law, Egyptian legal practice is found lacking and inadequate. This local practice, together with the long Ottoman legal tradition from which it emanated and on which it is based, is easily dismissed in such accounts as unjust, arbitrary, and/or despotic. In true Whiggish fashion, the long process of legal reform in the nineteenth century is seen as motivated by a desperate attempt to catch up with the West and effect a transition to European-inspired legal principles. The final outcome of the reforms is depicted as the steady and gradual adoption of Western- (mostly French-) inspired legal codes that covered civil, commercial, administrative, penal, and procedural law. The result, it is unanimously agreed, was the gradual curtailment of the jurisdiction of shari'a, so that by the end of the century it was left covering little more than personal status.

This Eurocentric narrative stresses the rugged path that the process of legal reform followed, and accounts of the reforms invariably include a section that deals with popular opposition to what are always depicted as beneficial changes. In describing how secularism was gradually introduced throughout the Ottoman Empire, J. Anderson, for example, argued that the systematic replacement of shari'a by "codes derived largely from the West . . . was far less the result of any popular demand for reform . . . than imposed upon the people from above. . . . The conservative opposition to these reforms was challenged by a variety of arguments put forward by the more progressive elements in the countries concerned."[7] In other words, according to this view, these ideas eventually triumphed because members of "progressive" circles finally realized the moral weakness of their own society. By launching persuasive arguments and by persevering in the face of bigoted and reactionary public opinion, these few enlightened men ultimately managed to institute legal reforms that had a far-reaching impact on nearly all aspects of Ottoman society.[8]

In its Egyptian context, the story typically starts with Bonaparte's invasion of 1798. Aḥmad Fatḥī Zaghlūl, who in 1900 published a book that went on to play a canonical role in shaping historical consciousness about nineteenth-century Egyptian law, flatly asserted that before the arrival of the French, "Egypt lacked a judicial system."[9] Farhat Ziadeh, for his part, took

Bonaparte's establishment of a commercial court, Maḥkamat al-Qaḍāyā, as "a complete innovation . . . [that] set the pattern for later reforms by Muhammad Ali and his successors in the field of judicial organization."[10] According to Ziadeh, the French innovations were particularly significant because there was "very little in the Islamic background of Egypt that was conducive to the rise of constitutionality or the rule of law."[11] Concluding his short excursus on Egyptian law before the arrival of the British, Lord Cromer argued that "any system of justice, properly so called, was unknown in the country. The divorce between law, such as it was, and justice was absolute."[12]

European influence is seen as having continued unabated during the long reign of Mehmed Ali. The Pasha sent students on missions to Europe to acquire various skills, and although law is not usually mentioned as one of these skills, accounts usually highlight the role subsequently played by Rifāʿa al-Ṭahṭāwī, the imam of one of the early student missions, in founding the School of Translation and in translating, together with many of the graduates of the school, numerous legal codes from French into Arabic.[13] More significantly, Mehmed Ali is often described as having been deeply inspired by European legal systems. Laṭīfa Sālim, for example, in her detailed history of the modern Egyptian legal system, argues that when the Pasha established the Judicial Committee (Jamʿiyyat al-Ḥaqqāniyya) in 1842 as the capstone of his legal institutions, he "had finally achieved his goal of following in Europe's footsteps in the legal field."[14] Furthermore, in their influential works on nineteenth-century Egyptian law, both ʿAzīz Khānkī and Aḥmad Fatḥī Zaghlūl quote the Pasha as saying, "We are bound to take Europe as a model in legal matters."[15]

Europe's imprint on Egyptian law is seen to have become both deeper and irreversible under Mehmed Ali's successors. During this era, it was not only the khedive and a few men around him who fell under the spell of Western law; wider segments of the Egyptian elite are described as looking to Europe for inspiration. In the words of Muḥammad Nūr Faraḥāt, a prominent legal scholar, "Given the fundamental social changes that [Mehmed Ali] had implemented, [European legal principles] were adopted by middle-class intellectuals who had recently returned from their educational missions to Europe, thus providing budding Egyptian capitalism with intellectual support and enlightened culture."[16] In this narrative, the decisive turning point that sealed the future of Egyptian law was the founding of the Mixed Courts in 1876. Anxious to find a way to limit the jurisdiction of consular courts, which adjudicated disputes between Europeans living in Egypt and between

Europeans and Egyptian subjects, creating an environment of legal chaos and seriously curtailing the sovereignty of the Egyptian state, Nūbār Pasha, Khedive Ismāʿīl's chief minister, worked doggedly for ten years to convince European consuls to renounce their various consular courts and replace them with a single court. The resulting compromise was the foundation of the Mixed Courts, which appointed European judges, applied French codes, and firmly upheld the principle of the separation of the judiciary and the executive.[17] Seven years later, in 1883, the final step toward the complete triumph of European law in Egypt was taken when the principles of the Mixed Courts were extended to the newly founded National Courts, which adjudicated disputes between Egyptians. These new courts are seen to have seriously encroached on the jurisdiction of the traditional shariʿa courts, which were left to hear little more than personal status disputes.

Curiously absent in this standard narrative is any serious analysis of *siyāsa*. On the few occasions when it is mentioned, it is either described as a muddled attempt to Westernize Egyptian law or dismissed outright as a corrupt, inefficient, slow, and inherently unjust legal system. As noted in the introduction, ʿAbd al-Qādir ʿAwda and Ṭāriq al-Bishrī, two prominent Egyptian Islamists, had next to nothing to say about nineteenth-century *siyāsa* councils. What are worth noting, though, are two historical studies written by lawyers during the first half of the twentieth century that decisively shaped the general understanding of the pre-1883 *siyāsa* system. The first is *Al-Muḥāmāh* (Lawyering), by Aḥmad Fatḥī Zaghlūl (see figure 6), which was published in 1900 and shortly thereafter assumed canonical importance in the historiography of modern Egyptian law. When he published this volume, his most significant work, Zaghlūl was president of the Cairo National Court, one of the new National Courts, which had been founded in 1883. He had earlier translated a number of classical European legal and psycho-ethnic works that demonstrated his infatuation with Enlightenment thinking, including Jeremy Bentham's *An Introduction to the Principles of Morals and Legislation*[18] and Edmond Demolins's *A quoi tient la supériorité des Anglo-Saxons.*[19] He was extremely ambitious but generally overshadowed by his more famous brother, the nationalist leader Saʿd Zaghlūl. He was obsessively jealous of Saʿd, who had been selected to receive the portfolio of the Ministry of Justice instead of Aḥmad. This was in spite of the fact that Aḥmad had done the British a great favor by serving on the infamous Dinshiwāï tribunal in 1907. The excessively brutal sentences that this tribunal summarily passed on a number of peasants who had been accused of shooting a British soldier

FIGURE 6: Aḥmad Fatḥī Zaghlūl. Image courtesy of Hussein Omar.

triggered a fierce anticolonial movement that engulfed the whole country and tainted Aḥmad Fatḥī Zaghlūl's name forever.[20]

Al-Muḥāmāh, however, earned him an influential role in the historiography of modern Egyptian law. It is a study of advocacy in European nations, but contains a long section on the history of the Egyptian legal system in the nineteenth century, with an extensive appendix that includes reproductions of more than twenty original khedival orders pertaining to various legal aspects. The book, therefore, has been taken as a primary source, and there are hardly any studies on the history of modern Egyptian law that do not consider it an indispensable guide. Given his training and sentiments,

Zaghlūl does not spare any effort in depicting the legal system before the founding of the National Courts as corrupt and inefficient. He cites some examples of legal cases reviewed by the *siyāsa* councils to argue that the detailed records they kept were clear signs of inefficiency and cluttered bureaucracy. This inefficiency, he goes on to assert, was what caused the councils to frequently take inordinately long periods to look into some cases, sometimes even more than a decade, leading the public to lose confidence in the whole legal system.[21] All in all, the book is a damning indictment of the entire legal system, which is consistently described as despotic and inherently unjust. Although he recounts the story of the establishment of the councils by reproducing the original khedival orders that founded them, Zaghlūl fails to uncover the logic that informed their activity, and he cannot help but reiterate his modernist view that they failed to live up to Western legal principles. Specifically, he blamed the *siyāsa* system for not upholding the principle of separation of powers, criticizing the fact that many councils that were founded in the 1850s, 1860s, and 1870s were presided over by local governors, which blurred the distinction between the executive and the judiciary.[22] He also wondered how a legal system could ever claim to be just if it did not uphold the principle of equality before the law; lacked any clear notion of procedural law and the difference between it and substantive law; and denied litigants the right not only to legal counsel but also to appear in front of the legal tribunal reviewing their case. Given the positive law perspective of these arguments, it is no wonder his book still appeals to many scholars of Egyptian legal history.

The second study that is of comparable significance is the elegant two-volume *Al-Kitāb al-Dhahabī lil-Maḥākim al-Ahliyya* (The golden book of the National Courts), which was published on the occasion of the semicentennial of the National Courts, and which emulated the *Livre d'or: Les jurisdictions d'Egypte, 1876–1926*, which had been published on the occasion of the semicentennial of the Mixed Courts a few years earlier. *Al-Kitāb al-Dhahabī* contained a number of original essays by various authors pertaining to different aspects of Egyptian legal history, such as the history of the office of the public prosecutor (*al-niyāba al-ʿumūmiyya*), the prisons department (*maslaḥat al-sujūn*), the law school (*kuliyyat al-ḥuqūq*), and advocacy (*al-muḥāmāh*). Regardless of the topic, all the essays shared the assumption that the beginning of Egyptian legal history, strictly defined, could be traced back to the founding of the National Courts and argued that whatever existed before then could be described as legal chaos at best and as outright despotism at worst. This unambiguous conflation of Westernization and civilization can best be detected in 'Azīz Khānkī's essay "Al-Tashrī' wa'l-Qaḍā' Qabl Inshā' al-Maḥākim al-Ahliyya" (Legislation and adjudication before the opening of the National Courts).[23] Providing a scathing assessment of the pre-1883 legal system, this essay proved nearly as influential as Zaghlūl's tome. Khānkī enumerates five features that rendered the entire legal system inherently unjust: the Pasha's influence over judicial and legal matters; the control of the judiciary by the executive branch; the military's domination of civilian aspects of administration; the conflicting sovereignties of both the Ottoman sultan and the pasha of Egypt over who had the right to pass death sentences in Egypt; and the fact that judges and administrators lacked competence in classical Arabic. He concludes by stating, "Legislative powers during Mehmed Ali's time, and then during the rules of 'Abbās, Sa'īd and Ismā'īl emanated from the governor and from him alone; executive powers were also monopolized by him. Justice in these times was not consistent, for maintaining the courts or removing them depended on the whims of the ruler. Laws were passed to protect the rights of the state not the individual. Laws back then were a mixture of backwardness and barbarism, on the one hand, and refinement and civilization, on the other."[24]

That these two studies were written not by historians but by legal practitioners (Zaghlūl was a judge and Khānkī was a lawyer) is not coincidental. As Yoav Di-Capua has shown, the history of legal reforms, like the that of medical reforms, was not one of the subjects that historians working in the royal palace or King Fu'ād University (later renamed Cairo University) were interested in.[25] The absence of historical studies on nineteenth-century legal reform written by historians is partly the result of the way legal sources were classified in the Royal Archives (Qism al-Maḥfūẓāt al-Malakiyya bi-Qaṣr 'Ābidīn), the prototype of the present National Archives.[26] When the Royal Archives were first constructed in the late 1920s, a select collection of documents from the older archival depository in the Citadel (Daftarkhānah) was transferred to 'Ābidīn Palace, but neither the voluminous registers of the shari'a courts nor the copious records of the *siyāsa* councils were included. It is relatively easy to understand the logic of leaving behind the shari'a court registers given that these documents were created before the ostensible date of the foundation of modern Egypt and were therefore, by definition, premodern and consequently did not fit within the royal mandate of collecting only documents relevant to the royal family's efforts to found a modern state. By contrast, however, the reason the registers of the *siyāsa* councils were left behind is intriguing. It seems that reserving the word *maḥkama* for the qadi court and calling these new administrative bodies *majālis* gave the impression that the *siyāsa* councils were municipal councils rather than courts of law.[27] And neither royal nor academic historians were interested in collecting documents pertaining to municipal councils that they erroneously believed dealt with such mundane matters as garbage collection, neighborhood security, and local administration.

But this diagnosis of archival omission, if it is true, reflects a more substantive blind spot in the way the story of legal reform in nineteenth-century Egypt is told. Simply put, this narrative is informed by an explicit Eurocentric assumption that the adoption of Western (and specifically French) laws and Western-style courts are the teleological end to which any process of legal reform should aspire. Accordingly, any legal system in which shari'a played even a small role and that did not respect the principle of the separation of powers would, by definition, be considered unfit for a modern state. As we will see shortly, these were precisely the reasons the legal system applied in Egypt for most of the nineteenth century was ignored by historians in their incessant quest for modernity. And these were also the reasons judges and lawyers trained in a positive law tradition could easily characterize this legal system by a series of lacks: lack of the principle of separation of powers, lack of distinction between substantive and procedural law, lack of justice, and so on.

In contrast to this deafening silence about the role played by *siyāsa,* the following analysis paints a vivid picture of Egyptian law during a period that witnessed significant and long-lasting reforms. This chapter does not present an archaeology of conceptual shifts or a close reading of a few legal texts penned by key intellectual figures. Rather, it examines the copious archive of the *siyāsa* legal system to trace the history of a number of the bureaucratic and scribal rearticulations that gave rise to new legal practices that, in turn, allowed for a new notion of the individual as someone who has been detached from a shari'a context and inserted into a newly imagined *siyāsa* world. It is by describing this *siyāsa* world that one can best understand what secularism meant in nineteenth-century Egypt.

The *siyāsa* archive that I rely on in this chapter has rarely been used before. Historians of the Middle East are now thoroughly familiar with the shari'a court archives, which have been tapped as a rich source for writing social,[28] economic[29] and legal histories.[30] The *siyāsa* archive, by contrast, has scarcely been noticed. This is partly because, as pointed out above, it was not chosen to be part of the Royal Archives and partly because of the ambiguous and confusing term by which it was known: *siyāsa*. Referring to the councils of the *siyāsa* system as *majālis siyāsiyya* or *majālis al-aqālīm* has led archivists and scholars to mistake these judicial councils for either political or provincial ones.

The main aim of this chapter is to analyze how the two branches of the pre-1883 Egyptian legal system went about adjudicating homicide cases. By insisting on studying *siyāsa* in conjunction with *fiqh,* the following analysis raises questions about the narrative of triumphant secularism that is usually used to describe the history of modern Egyptian law. To anticipate the conclusion, I argue that rather than describing the Egyptian legal system as having undergone a steady process of secularization, it would be more fruitful to look at the system as having undergone a process of bureaucratization whereby the written word played an increasingly crucial role in adjudicating criminal (and other) cases and whereby the spoken word slowly but surely lost its supremacy. As this chapter will demonstrate, the main difference between the qadi court and the *siyāsa* council was not that the first was religious and the second secular but that the first was a very vocal arena where disputes were articulated verbally, whereas the second was a closed, silent office where cases were adjudicated mostly on the basis of written evidence. This difference between the orality of the qadi court and the textuality of the *siyāsa* council is reflective of deeper epistemological differences between *fiqh* and *siyāsa*.

Framing the argument about how Egyptian law was modernized in the nineteenth century around the tension between orality and text rather than secularization highlights the salient tensions between the written and the spoken word that were present in different measures in both the *fiqh*-based qadi court and the *siyāsa*-based council. Furthermore, the struggle between the written and the spoken word echoes the tension between legal thought and judicial practice, a tension that has, for the most part, also been sidelined in the existing scholarship. This framing will also allow us to assess the relative importance of the Ottoman and European influences on Egyptian law.

NECROPOLITICS: MURDER, *SIYĀSA,* AND SHARIʿA

As stated above, *fiqh* and *siyāsa* each approached homicide differently, and studying how homicide cases were adjudicated will afford us an opportunity to see how these two branches of the legal system worked in tandem. In order to highlight the differences between them, we will follow the different stages of a typical homicide case: initiating legal action, establishing juridical identity, conducting criminal investigation, and passing a verdict.

Initiating Legal Action

The main criminal code operative in Egypt during the period under investigation was the Humāyūnī Law (also known as the Sultanic Law), which was promulgated in 1852. As its names suggests, this law was copied from the Ottoman Criminal Law of 1850. After intense negotiations with the Sublime Porte that resulted in the original laws being altered to fit the Egyptian context, the new law was applied in Egypt.[31] This law clearly stated that murder cases had to be investigated thoroughly in shariʿa court and that no death sentence could be passed except after a qadi had issued a *qiṣāṣ* (lex talionis) sentence following strict *fiqh* procedural rules.[32] Crucially, the *fiqh* considers adjudicating homicide to be "claims of men" (*ḥuqūq al-ʿibād*) and not "claims of God" (*ḥuqūq Allah*). As Rudolph Peters points out, "This means that the plaintiff is the *dominus litis* and that the prosecution, the continuation of the trial and the execution of the sentence are conditional upon his will."[33] In other words, it is the victim's heirs who have the exclusive right to initiate legal action and to press charges. Bernard Weiss explains the significance of the premodern sociological context of the patriarchal family and kinship ties that informed the Islamic approach to homicide:

> Homicide does not belong within the domain of criminal law, strictly speaking; it is not an offense against society as such calling for public prosecution. Rather, it belongs under the rubric of a *lex talionis* in which the family unit—or, more precisely, the *ʿāqila,* which comprises certain male agnates—is the primary actor; it is an offense against the family, and the family must decide how to deal with it. . . . Within the setting of patriarchal family life as envisioned by the Muslim jurists, the talio operates as a highly effective deterrent to homicide and as a means of preserving life. Every individual, including the one inclined to take the life of another, is part of a tightly knit extended family unit. The murderer therefore does not act alone but rather represents his family in an act inimical to another family, for the victim too represents a family. All human life is embedded in the web of kinship. . . . When one kills without cause, one therefore is as much accountable to one's own family, which incurs responsibility for appropriate action, as to the family of the victim. Therein lies the deterrent force of the talio within a society founded on ties of kinship.[34]

The archival record corroborates this insight, showing that as far as *fiqh* is concerned, it was indeed the victim's heirs who consistently initiated legal action in the qadi court. The only exceptions were the rare cases when the victim had no heirs. When this happened, according to the Humāyūnī Law, the qadis upheld the *fiqhī* principle of *al-sulṭān walii man lā walii lahu*—that is, the governor or ruler is the guardian of he who has no guardian.[35] In other words, the sultan, or other leader, acts as proxy for the victim's heirs and could thus initiate legal proceedings. The following case provides a good example of this process. In 1862, a young soldier named Ḥasan, who was originally from Alexandria but had been stationed in the Qaṣr al-Nīl barracks in Cairo, was caught stealing sixteen bars of soap. On discovering the theft, his commanding officer, who was a Turk by the name of Khālid Efendi, decided to make an example of him: he tied Ḥasan to a tent pole and lashed him on the buttocks so severely that the solider died three days later from his wounds. Given that the victim's family could not be located in Alexandria, the case could not be heard in the shari'a court until the governor of Cairo stepped in and acted as proxy to initiate legal proceedings and press charges against Khālid Efendi.[36]

A more serious implication of this principle is that heirs sometimes decided not to step forward to press charges because they were afraid of potential repercussions. The records of Majlis al-Aḥkām contain many cases in which the key suspect was a local strongman, most often the *'umda* (village chief) or one of his relatives. In these cases, the victim's relatives were often intimidated into silence for fear of retaliation by the *'umda*'s henchmen. The case with which this chapter opened is a good example of this. Another example is a case that came to light on April 4, 1864, when, during a regular inspection tour of his governorate, the governor of the Fashn Governorate in Upper Egypt heard peasants whispering about a grave matter that had occurred in one of the villages. Two weeks earlier, birds of prey had been noticed hovering strangely above a plot of land. The local village *shaykhs* were promptly informed, but they failed to notify the governorate authorities. The rumor was that the local *'umda* had murdered two men from outside the village who had been on their way north to sell cattle. When the *'umda* realized that the makeshift graves in which he had buried his victims had been discovered, he had ordered the bodies to be swiftly exhumed and reburied in the village cemetery. On hearing these rumors, the governor promptly went to the village cemetery and ordered the graves to be opened. What he saw immediately gave credence to the rumors: the two bodies had been buried without shrouds, the jaws were open, and the legs and arms were stretched out, all in violation of Islamic burial rituals and a clear sign that the bodies had been buried in haste. A forensic doctor was fetched and his detailed report conclusively stated that the two men had not died a natural death.[37]

Since the case had already come to light and *siyāsa* investigations had already been initiated, the relatives of the victims were urged to press homicide charges. They therefore approached the local shari'a court and accused the *'umda* of killing the two men. Once they did this, the qadi asked them to provide their evidence. However, they failed to produce any witnesses willing to testify against the all-powerful *'umda,* a man named Muḥammad 'Umar. Furthermore, neither the *'umda* nor any of the other suspects (mainly his two brothers, Qāsim and Jād al-Mawlā, who were *'umad* of neighboring villages) would give a confession. Lacking a confession or an eyewitness account, the qadi could not find for the plaintiffs and thus ordered them to drop their charges against the *'umda.*[38]

Once it was suspected that a murder had occurred, the case would be forwarded to the shari'a court (the term often used was *tuḥāl al-da'wa 'alā al-shari'a*), and the victim's heirs would be encouraged to press for charges there. Crucially, however, as noted above, the local authorities would also start their own proceedings, which were consistently referred to as *siyāsa* (e.g., *al-taḥqīqāt al-siyāsiyya*, "the *siyāsa* investigations"). A decree passed in November 1865 giving detailed guidelines on how the main criminal laws were to be implemented stated that the purpose of its promulgation was to save people the trouble of chasing after the governors asking them to look into their cases, effectively encouraging litigants to initiate legal action in the *siyāsa* councils. The decree stipulated that police stations in the cities (*ḍabṭ iyyāt*) and in the countryside (*mudīriyyāt*) had to accept petitions presented by the public in criminal matters and start their own investigations immediately.[39]

The records of the Cairo and Alexandria police provide countless examples of people approaching the police to present petitions (*'arḍḥālāt*), thus initiating *siyāsa* legal action. However, the police often did not wait to be approached by the public to spring into action, and the records show that in many cases, in sharp contrast to the shari'a courts, it was the police who initiated proceedings, conducted investigations, and pressed charges. The police had a wide range of agents working for them, which allowed them to monitor suspected activities and initiate legal action if they hit on something suspicious. The investigation into the case of Khālid Efendi mentioned above, for example, started when a Turkish-speaking *qavvās* (sentry) discovered the dead body of a thirty-year-old man lying in front of the Sayyida Zaynab Mosque in Cairo. It must have been a strange sight, for a crowd of onlookers immediately gathered and the body was quickly sent to the Cairo Police Department (Ḍabṭiyyat Miṣr) in Azbakiyya, where a preliminary postmortem investigation was conducted. The investigation, however, could not conclusively identify the cause of death, so the body had to be sent to Qaṣr al-ʿAinī Hospital for an autopsy. The result of the second autopsy was conclusive: this was an unnatural death that had been caused by severe beating on the buttocks. The next steps were identifying the dead man, figuring out how his body had been dumped near the mosque, and finding the culprit. It is at this point that the police's network of spies and local government agents became useful, for when the shaykh of the nearby quarter, Darb al-Gamāmīz, was asked what he knew about the case, he immediately called on the help of the shaykhs of the local neighborhoods, Shaykh Salīm of Ḥārat al-Ḥilmiyya and Shaykh Sulaymān of al-Sayyida Zaynab, and Aḥmad al-Qāḍī, head of the local guild of donkey drivers, in an attempt to locate a young boy who was rumored to have been leading a donkey with the body of a dead man on it. After long, detailed interrogations of numerous witnesses, the police managed to identify a young donkey boy, who, in turn, identified numerous witnesses, some from the remote quarter of Būlāq, at the other end of the city. These detailed and lengthy *siyāsa* investigations led the police to identify the dead man as Ḥasan and the culprit as Khālid Efendi.

We thus see a system of double jurisdiction: in any murder case, both shariʿa courts and *siyāsa* councils would get into gear and follow their separate rules and proceedings. From this brief review of the procedures of initiating legal action, the first major difference between the two branches of the legal system can already be identified. Because *fiqh* considers punishing murder crimes to be "claims of men" and not of God, it grants the right to press charges only to the victim's heirs. The *siyāsa* system, by contrast, which was created to keep public order, included a mechanism whereby agents of the state, mainly the police, could initiate legal action and press charges. In this respect, the *siyāsa* system differs from the *fiqh* system in one very important respect: *fiqh* effectively deals with murder as a matter of private law, whereas *siyāsa* insists that society and the state also have claims and that murder cases should not be left to the interests of the immediate parties concerned. Therefore, the prime agent of the *siyāsa* councils, the police, was given the right not only to investigate cases but also to prepare them for trial.[40] As such, the police acted in a way akin to the present-day Egyptian *niyāba,* the French *parquet,* or the US public prosecutor, institutions that have no parallel in *fiqh.*

Nevertheless, and despite their contrasting approaches to murder, and crime in general, both *siyāsa* councils and shariʿa courts collaborated very closely in handling murder cases. This close collaboration was reflected in an 1865 decree issued by the vice-regal cabinet, al-Maʿiyya al-Saniyya, which stated: "Since the shariʿa court personnel [*muwaẓẓafī al-maḥākim al-sharʿiyya*] and the *siyāsa* council employees [*al-maʾmūrīn al-siyāsiyyīn*] interact with each other closely, such as in the case of taking down a deposition or recording a testimony, it is necessary that their offices be located in close proximity to one another."[41]

Juridical Identification

The contrast between the *fiqh* and *siyāsa* systems can also be seen in the next stage that a typical murder case would go through: the process of establishing the identity of litigants.

The Court Witnesses. *Fiqh* has elaborate rules governing how personal identity is established. Like other premodern legal systems, *fiqh* identifies individuals by locating them carefully in their social settings and taking note of their embodied relations.[42] In his court, the qadi would do this by relying on upright individuals who had good reputations in their community and who would be able to vouch for those people living in a given area who used the court to settle their disputes. Indeed, the jurists (*ʿulamāʾ* or *fuqahāʾ*) agreed that a qadi could not accept the testimony of witnesses unknown to him unless their probity had been established by reputable individuals.[43] Those reputable individuals, known as *shuhūd ʿudūl,* were an essential part of the court, and "the entire weight in the identification of witnesses rested on the human links of interpersonal knowledge" that they provided.[44] Accordingly, they were often considered part of the regular personnel of the court, and shariʿa court records often mention qadis' orders appointing them to their courts.[45] Their functions included establishing the probity (*ʿadāla*) of the witnesses;[46] recording oral testimonies, affidavits, and contracts;[47] witnessing and furnishing proof of the proceedings of the court and of the qadi's judgment;[48] and being delegated by the qadi to accompany his deputy (*nāʾib*) to gather probative evidence from a crime scene.[49]

Alongside these *'udūl* witnesses, the court also had another set of witnesses called *shuhūd al-ḥāl*. These were respected members of the community who often added their signatures to judgments, thereby attesting to the fairness of the court procedures.[50] Most crucially, they helped the judge identify litigants. The following 1865 entry from the shari'a court of Manṣūra, in the Delta, is a good example of how the *shuhūd al-ḥāl* helped the judge establish the identity of the individuals who appeared in his court: "Al-'Adawī Ṭāhā al-Maghallāwī of Manṣūra, the son of the late Hajj Ṭāhā al-Saqqa [the water carrier], arrived in the shari'a court of Manuṣūra, and after he had been identified by the testimony [*ba'da thubūt ma'rifatihi bi-shahādat*] of both the honorable [*al-mukarram*] 'Abd al-Mit'āl Shāhīn al-Ḥāyik, the son of the late al-Mitwallī Shahīn, and Sayyid Aḥmad al-Maghallāwī, the son of the late 'Alī Sayyid Aḥmad, both from Manṣūra, he confessed and testified [*aqarra wa i'tarafa*]."[51]

As can be seen in this typical entry, a litigant's name is not sufficient to serve as identification. Nor is it enough for a litigant to mention his or her town of residence or father's profession. This information has to be corroborated by two *'udūl* witnesses whose patronymic names are also recorded. The two witnesses named in the entry, 'Abd al-Mit'āl Shāhīn al-Ḥāyik and Sayyid Aḥmad al-Maghallāwī, are residents of the same city, Manṣūra, and it can be assumed that they knew the litigant in person. This allowed them to help the qadi with the crucial task of establishing the identity of the litigants. In other words, this initial stage of a legal case, that of establishing the identity of litigants, was based on reputation, social standing, and communal recognition.

Patronymic Names By contrast, the *siyāsa* system did not employ any of these complex mechanisms for identifying litigants and witnesses. Instead, it appears that the *siyāsa* authorities used an individual's name, father's name, and domicile to establish juridical identity. Occasionally a profession was also stated. It was therefore typical for a *siyāsa* record of a criminal case to start by simply stating: "An individual [*shakhṣ*] named Khalīl Sāba, the Greek grocer who lives in Ṭanṭa [a large city in the Delta], filed a complaint with the governor of the city [*mu'āwin al-bandar*] that two people had come to his drinking hole [*khammāra*], one named As'ad Dāghir and the second named 'Abdallah Ṭanūs al-Dayrūṭī, and they were soon joined by Ibrāhīm 'Abdallāh al-Bayrūtī, ... Khalīl al-Dīb, and Milḥim al-Sammāsh, all from Syria [*min al-diyār al-shāmiyya*]."[52]

Sometimes the father's name was not even mentioned, as in the case of "the woman [*al-ḥurma*] named Alfiyya who lives on Ḥārat Bahlawān in the

Sayyida Zaynab district [*khuṭṭ*]," who presented a petition to Dīwān Kethuda (Arabic: Katkhuda) accusing a certain Hajj Khidr of killing her son, Ḥasan.[53]

Naturally, because *ʿudūl* witnesses were not used in *siyāsa* courts, there was room within the system for people to lie about their true identity or assume different names. This was sometimes done for innocent reasons, as was the case with a woman caught stealing in Cairo who claimed her name was Khadra and said she was originally from al-Munṣūriyya, Gīza, and was the daughter of the late Muḥammad al-Kharrāt.[54] When she was sent back to her village, the Gīza Governorate wrote back to Cairo to say that her true name was Sayyida and that she was the daughter of Khadra. Asked why she had lied, she answered that she went by that name but that it was in fact her mother's name, not hers.[55] However, in some cases, individuals used false names to evade punishment. For example, in one case, a man who said his name was Maḥmūd Muṣṭafā from the town of Damanhūr in the Delta was caught red-handed stealing cloth in Cairo. At the police station, he confessed that his real name was Khalīl Abū Ṭūr and that he had previously been convicted of theft, imprisoned, escaped from prison, and was currently on the run. Knowing that prior records were crucial in determining punishment (as shown below), Khalīl was probably hoping to hide his earlier conviction and thus receive a lighter punishment.[56]

To get around the problem of people hiding their true identity by changing their name, it was common to add domiciles and professions as further markers to help with identification. For example, when the Cairo Governorate (Muḥāfaẓat Miṣr) wrote to the Cairo Police Department to fetch a certain Muḥammad Badawī for some legal dispute,[57] the latter wrote back saying that "without specifying this person's profession and his domicile, it is impossible to locate him, as there are many people who carry this name."[58] It was only after receiving information that the man in question was a carriage driver (*sāyis*) who had worked on the estate of the late Ibrāhīm Pasha Yeğen that the police could identify and arraign him.[59]

It was also common for people to assume different names not as a means of evading prior convictions but in an attempt to better their social standing. And in a society that was highly hierarchical, with a legal system that was not based on the principle of equality before the law, this was a very serious offense. A decree passed in 1845 stipulated that "anyone who uses a false name or a false title in order to appear dignified and respected [*fī maẓhar al-iʿtibār waʾl-waqār*] or who puts on airs of being a feared person . . . will be sent to prison for a period not less than a year and not exceeding five years in addition to paying a fine ranging from 200 piastres to 12,000 piastres."[60]

Domicile Without an identity-establishing institution like the shari'a *shuhūd 'udūl,* and lacking modern technologies such as picture IDs, fingerprinting, DNA tests, and so on, the *siyāsa* authorities were extremely anxious about drifting identities.[61] This anxiety was most acute when it came to people who roamed the city with no fixed residence or profession. As far as the authorities were concerned, these people could only mean trouble, and as Daniel Lord Smail has noted, "The very idea that identity can be attributed to geographical location is an essential intellectual component of administrative concerns about bandits, Bedouins, vagabonds, beggars, and other mobile populations, concerns that typically develop in centralizing political jurisdictions."[62] *Siyāsa* records contain many expressions of this concern about people with no known domicile.[63] A man called Ibrāhīm Muḥammad, for example, was accused of petty theft, and the records state, "He is [originally] from Cairo but has no known domicile, no relatives, works as a laborer in the morning and sleeps in the streets and in empty places [at night]," which was enough to convict him.[64] In another case, a man named Muḥammad Darwīsh persuaded a military cadet to drop out of school and go with him to Alexandria to spend a good time together. The cadet's military school sent out a circular with his physical description, and both young men were caught. When Darwīsh was interrogated, it was found out that he was unemployed (*min dūn sinā'a*) and had no home (*lā maḥall yatawaṭṭan fīhi*), and he was sentenced to one year in prison.[65] Prison records would specify if a certain prisoner was "with no domicile" (*lam yakun lahu ma'wā*).[66] This anxiety about drifters and people with no known domicile is also easily detectable in laws of the era. Mehmed Ali's first criminal legislation (issued in 1829) had a section about "gypsies who are wandering around unemployed in Cairo, . . . [others] who are harmful to the people and inhabitants of Cairo and the villages, . . . people from Hejaz and Sudan, and . . . slaves, fortune-tellers, magicians, and treasure-hunters" It went on to say that of these people, those "who are healthy are to be removed and sent to the ironworks, those of them who are young to the troops, and those of them who are very unfit to remote regions, i.e., places like Esna [in Upper Egypt]."[67] In 1863, shortly after he became governor of Egypt, Ismā'īl Pasha wrote to Majlis al-Aḥkām ordering it to send "those unemployed who roamed around as they pleased" to the War Department (Dīwān al-Jihādiyya) to be put to work by officers in a special platoon of convicts (*firqat al-mudhnibīn*).[68] In 1880, a general circular was issued stating that "given that it has been known that there are [people] in the cities and ports who are homeless and unemployed and who roam around as they please, and since these drifters have no purpose except to harm people, it was decided that such people should be arrested, pressed into the army, or sent to serve in eastern Sudan to get rid of their evil deeds [*wiqāyatan min shurūrihim*]."[69] Finally, in 1891, a special order was issued giving a precise legal definition to vagabondage and imprisoning people who were defined as vagabonds (*al-mutasharridīn*) for a period ranging from fifteen to forty-five days with the possibility of exile.[70]

Tadhkara. While the requirement to have a legal domicile made sense in an urban setting, the authorities had another technique to keep track of people living in the countryside. To identify itinerant peasants, the authorities mandated that they carry with them stamped a certificate, or "passport," called a *tadhkara.* These *tadhākir* were first mentioned in the 1820s, when they were used to catch army deserters. The certificates stated the first name, the patronymic name, the village, and a physical description of its bearer. If caught without a *tadhkara,* a peasant would be immediately arrested and repatriated to his or her village.[71] When it was found out that a black market for these documents had developed and that civilians were selling their passports to soldiers and sailors, Mehmed Ali issued an order to use different stamps for different types of certificates.[72] Precise orders were issued in 1833 to the Cairo Police Commissioner to arrest any peasant, even village shaykhs, who arrived in Cairo without a *tadhkara.*[73] By the early 1850s, concern about the growing number of Europeans arriving in Egypt led to the establishment of a Passport Department (Qalam al-Basabūrtū) in Alexandria. Whenever a new ship from abroad arrived at the port, this new department would compile a register with the names, physical descriptions, and characteristics (*asmā wa awsāf wa shamāyil*) of those on board who were disembarking and proceeding to Cairo. This register was then sent to the Cairo police.[74] A similar department was established in Suez.[75]

Ḍamān. In addition to demanding that town dwellers have a legal domicile and that peasants carry their *tadhkara* with them when moving from one location to another, the authorities established another practice that proved effective in giving rise to new concepts of individual identity. Starting in the 1840s, people were required to present a piece of paper called a *ḍamān,* or voucher, which was issued by someone who had good standing in his or her community, most typically the neighborhood head (*shaykh al-ḥāra*) or the master of a guild (*shaykh al-ṭā'ifa*), and vouched for its bearer. There were two types of *ḍamān*. The first was called a *ḍamān ḥuḍūr,* or "presence voucher," which obligated the person bearing it to fetch a given person who had been summoned by a public authority (e.g., the police, a government office, a public school, etc.). The second was a *ḍamān ghurūm,* or "fines voucher," which guaranteed that the person issuing the voucher would be responsible for paying any fines or debts incurred by the bearer.

A quick look at some laws and police cases may illustrate how the *ḍamān* worked and what place it had in the legal system. The Humāyūnī Law, for instance, stipulated that "evildoers who . . . cause disturbance to the populace should be sent to prison in iron chains for a period of a year. . . . After the end of this period, they could be released if it becomes evident that they had been disciplined [*ḥaṣal iltimās ta'dībihi wa tarbiyatihi*] and if they manage to secure someone who can vouch for them [*ḍāmin min al-ahālī*]."[76] The police records show that when prisoners failed to secure such a guarantor (known as a *ḍāmin*), which occurred most often when prisoners were newcomers to a neighborhood, they would remain in jail until they could find a guarantor who would vouch for them; if none could be found, they would be sent back to their original village or neighborhood.[77] In 1853, Majlis al-Aḥkām issued a circular stipulating that individuals were forbidden to sell things in the market unless they could produce a *ḍamān* that stated that the merchandise had not been stolen.[78] When renting out a flat, the landlord or the *shaykh al-ḥāra* was obligated to ask for a *ḍamān* from the new tenant; failure to do so would make him or her legally liable.

Even leaving for the annual pilgrimage to Mecca required a *ḍamān*. To receive the *tadhkara* necessary for disembarking from Suez or Quṣayr on the way to Hijaz, pilgrims had to procure a *ḍamān* from their local police station.[79] The police issued strict orders to the heads of the neighborhoods and to the shaykhs of the guilds to issue *ḍamānāt* to the prospective pilgrims only after verifying that they had no outstanding taxes or other unfulfilled obligations (*khuluww ṭaraf*). These *ḍamānāt* were needed to make sure that pilgrims would return home after the pilgrimage season was over. Only thus, an 1853 order added, could the requirements of progress and growth (*asbāb al-'amār*) be achieved.[80]

It is true that these bureaucratic innovations—obliging citizens to use patronymic names, requiring all persons to have a legal domicile, issuing *tadhākir* and *ḍamānāt*—were not specific to the legal system. Nevertheless, they had very significant legal implications, for the *siyāsa* councils repeatedly relied on these bureaucratic devices to establish legal identity. In interactions with police stations, people would produce a *ḍamān,* a *tadhkara,* or a vaccination or conscription certificate to establish their identity. In contrast to the qadi courts, which used *'udūl* witnesses, effectively embedding individual identity in a communal and local setting, the *siyāsa* councils relied on complex and efficient bureaucratic methods to embed individual identity in a new textual order, that of *siyāsa.* These new devices gave rise to a new notion of the individual that was independent of social and communal setting. These scraps of paper with government stamps and seals on them allowed the state to deal with individual using its own textual devices. As we will see below, this bureaucratization of the individual had far-reaching implications on how the legal system came to be conceived of and how such basic notions as law, justice, and the individual came to be thought of.

Investigation

The contrast between *siyāsa* and *fiqh* becomes most apparent in the third stage that a typical criminal case went through: investigation. The Humāyūnī Law of 1852 stipulated that capital punishment (*qiṣāṣ*) was not to be carried out unless a shari'a verdict (*i'lām shar'ī*) had been issued. However, it also states that the "conclusive inquiries and thorough examinations should be done according to both shari'a and *qānūn.*"[81] Moreover, a supplement to that law made clear that *siyāsa* would play a large role in investigating homicide cases:

> Preliminary investigation and examination in cases of homicide must be carried out by the administrative headquarters [*mudūriyya*] of the governorate in which the case has taken place. The case should then be forwarded with most scrutiny to [one of] the regional councils [*majālis al-aqālīm*] in the presence of the [*majlis*'s] mufti and the members of the council. As soon as the case is clear [i.e., as soon as a verdict is reached], the shari'a sentence, together with the transcript of the case, should be sent to Majlis al-Aḥkām for ratification [*taṣdīq*]. From there, the transcript [together with the ruling of Majlis al-Aḥkām] should be sent to Majlis al-Khuṣūṣī and from there to the Viceroy [*al-wālī*].[82]

As this article indicates, homicide cases were reviewed simultaneously by both shari'a courts and *siyāsa* councils, resulting in two distinct tracks of investigation. As we have seen with the process of establishing juridical identity, both branches used separate but related techniques and procedures, and as we will see below, each was based on different doctrines of truth and distinct conceptions of legal proof.

One of the striking differences between *fiqh* and *siyāsa* is the role of interrogation. In the *fiqh* system, interrogation is essentially absent, whereas in the *siyāsa* system, the interrogation of witnesses, the plaintiff, and the defendant constituted one of the most crucial tasks the police performed in preparing a case for a ruling. This difference is very revealing of the logic that informed these two branches of the legal system. Within the *fiqh* system, it is the duty of the plaintiff to provide witnesses for his claim, to bring them to court, and to obtain confessions from them.[83] Baber Johansen has convincingly shown that the *fiqh* principle of limiting the judge's role to ascertaining the identity of witnesses and to making sure that the strict rules of procedure are applied is intended to protect both the qadi and the rights of the defendant: "[By] delegating responsibility for establishing the facts to the parties . . ., [the formalistic character of the judicial process] relieves the judiciary of [that responsibility], and shield[s] the judge from pressure exerted by the litigants who want to see the truth recognized."[84] In listening to the utterances of the plaintiff, the defendant, and the witnesses, the qadi is presented with contradictory claims, and if he "wants to determine whether the speakers are sincere or mendacious, [he] has to look for an external factor that tips the balance in favor of one or the other interpretation."[85] The process of establishing the probity of witnesses, *jarḥ wa taʿdīl,* is important precisely because it provides the qadi with a procedural means of tipping this balance, which helps him decide which evidence to accept.[86] The qadi, in turn, establishes the probity of witnesses by checking "their social and religious reputation carefully before he admits their testimony in his court session." In short, in passing his judgment, the qadi "depends not on his grasping the truth of the facts but on his abiding by formal rules of procedure. . . . According to classical Sunni doctrine, the qadi should establish the facts on the basis of the testimony of witnesses and the acknowledgement [i.e., confession] of the defendant. He is not entitled to initiate an investigation: he has no power of inquisition."[87] In fact, as Leslie Peirce has argued in her study of the Aintab shariʿa court in the early sixteenth century, "the work of the [court,] while dependent upon the presence of the judge, could not be accomplished without the testimony of local people, which the shariʿa regarded as the core input into a judge's ruling. The testimony of individuals, in other words, can be said to be the flesh on the skeletal structure of procedural rules."[88]

At the core of these procedural rules, moreover, is the principle that the witness's testimony must be given complete, whole, and uninterrupted. The witness is not to be interrogated or cross-examined. The necessity of allowing for the unimpeded flow of the witness's narrative is, in turn, based on the assumption that a direct link has to be established between the speech act of delivering a witness account and the act or event that had been witnessed. As Brinkley Messick has remarked, in Arabic, both these events—that is, the initial sensory perception of the event in question and the subsequent testimony of an eyewitness in front of a qadi—have the same word, *shahāda,* which stresses how in *fiqhī* legal thinking, the qadi should establish as direct a link as possible between the original sensual perception and the subsequent verbal production—that is, the testimony in court.[89]

Given that the witness's testimony must be heard uninterrupted, it follows that it must also be delivered in camera—that is, in the qadi's court.[90] The plaintiff's testimony, which typically initiates legal action, must be presented in the presence of the defendant (*fī wajhihi,* literally "in his face").[91] The primacy of the court is a fundamental feature of the system, and "testimony is not legally given except if it occurs before a judge or before an individual ordered by the judge to hear it."[92] The care taken to remove any obstacles to the transmission of full witness accounts is also what lies behind the suspicion of written documents, which is "a well-known characteristic of Islamic law."[93] Until recently, it was believed that "doctrine discourages their use [i.e., the use of written documents] by refusing to allow documents as legal proof, and accepting only the oral testimonies of witnesses."[94] This privileging of witness testimony is based on the fundamental belief that nothing supersedes the physical presence of the witness, a presence that guarantees that the qadi will receive the unmediated speech act of the witness. This view, which privileges the medium of speech and casts suspicion on the written word, is further expressed by the fact that a written document could be accepted as proof in shari'a court only if two witnesses attest to having seen the actual process of it being written and deliver spoken testimony to that effect in court.[95] In other words, "writings must be converted to spoken testimony to have evidential value."[96] This privileging of the spoken over the written word was eventually legally codified in the late nineteenth-century Ottoman civil code, the *Mecelle.*[97]

The *siyāsa* procedures stand in sharp contrast to all of this. As Rudolph Peters has remarked, a *fiqh* "trial was in principle a public trial of an accusatory nature: Plaintiff and defendant would fight a legal battle with the qadi as a referee. [By contrast, the] procedure before the [*siyāsa*] councils was essentially inquisitory. There was no office of public prosecutor and the council would function both as prosecutor and judge, whereas the defendant was not a party in the trial, but rather the object of an investigation."[98] Crucially, this investigation relied squarely on the written word, and the *siyāsa* system demonstrates a clear privileging of the written over the spoken word. In fact, one fundamental feature of the whole *siyāsa* system is the effective silencing of the person, whether claimant, defendant, or witness. In contrast to the central place occupied by the spoken word in the *fiqh* system, the written word reigns supreme within the *siyāsa* system. In other words, there is a fundamental difference between the two systems as far as legal proof is concerned: whereas the *fiqh* system insists on the necessity of the physical presence of a witness and on his or her sensory perception of the act in question to be translated in the qadi court in an unmediated manner in the form of uninterrupted oral testimony, the *siyāsa* system clearly privileged written documents, especially those that relied mostly on circumstantial evidence.

This does not mean, however, that the *siyāsa* councils did not hear witnesses. As mentioned above, the police were tasked with receiving petitions from the public and acting on them immediately. A typical criminal case involved a thorough investigation by the police, a process that invariably included detailed interrogations of suspects. As opposed to the uninterrupted flow of a witness's testimony in a qadi court, however, police interrogations took the form of meticulous back-and-forth interview sessions, during which the plaintiff, defendant, suspect, or witness was subjected to close scrutiny, and in which her or his deposition was constantly interrupted. The following is an example of one such interrogation session, where the suspect, Ḥajj Khidr, was being questioned about the death of a man called Ḥasan:

> Police: You have to give a detailed account of how you hit Ḥasan.
>
> Ḥajj Khidr: Ḥasan, the son of the woman [called] Alfiyya, was talking to Muṣṭafā, the carriage driver of Ḥasan Efendi, our supervisor, concerning *usṭā* Sa'īd. I told Ḥasan, "You have no business [talking to the supervisor directly.]" At that, he suddenly took out a wooden plank and tried to hit me with it. I managed to free it from his hand. We then grabbed each other. I don't know who hit him. This is my answer.
>
> Police. How can you say that? . . . Ḥasan brought the wooden plank to hit you with, and you managed to get it from his hand, and then you found him beaten and then claim that you don't know who hit him. This is inconceivable, since it is not likely that one would hit oneself. Moreover, his mother stated [in her deposition] that your colleagues witnessed you beating him. You have to give up pretending and give an honest answer.

Khidr: What happened is as I have stated. And if my colleagues come to testify against me that I beat Ḥasan, then I would be guilty of beating him, and their words [i.e., testimony] would be applied to me.[99]

It is therefore clear that the status of witness testimony is fundamentally different in shariʿa court and *siyāsa* councils. Within the adversarial procedure of the *fiqh* system, the witnesses are called by the parties, not the court, and the judge does not carry out any questioning of the witnesses, let alone a cross-examination. The judge's role is limited to ascertaining the probity of the witnesses and making sure that proper procedure is being followed.

By contrast, within the *siyāsa* councils, the witnesses are sought out and questioned by the police during their interlocutory proceedings preparing the case. While the shariʿa court relies on the immediacy of oral testimony, the *siyāsa* councils based their work on procès-verbaux. The law establishing one of the earlier councils, Majlis Aḥkām Mulkiyya (1833), stated: "The scribes of the council and their assistants should go out at two o'clock in summer (three o'clock in winter) and receive orders from the Viceroy as well as all [other] correspondence and documents arriving from the different government departments. [They should then] hand in [these documents] for translation. The scribes should [then] prepare all the documents that the council will read when it convenes."[100] One of the first orders of Majlis al-ʿUmūmī, which was established in 1847, was to issue an order stating: "During deliberations in the council it was suggested that since the cases that will be forwarded to the council will necessitate interrogating [*istinṭāq*] both plaintiff and defendant as a preliminary step [*min al-ibtidā*] to clarify the cases, and since summoning them to the council will delay other affairs, it was decided to understand [i.e., listen to] the aforementioned and write down their cases one by one in a separate room. Thereafter, the documents will be forwarded [to the council], together with both plaintiff and defendant."[101]

Subsequently, litigants were prohibited from appearing in front of the councils that were trying their cases: the ordinance establishing Majlis al-Aḥkām in 1849 stipulated that the council was to read transcripts of only those cases that had been submitted to it.[102] Most clearly, the ordinance establishing the regional councils (*majālis al-aqālīm*) in 1852 stipulated: "A box will be placed outside the door of [each governorate] council for petitions to be deposited therein. This box will be opened in the presence of the president of the council and its members, and [the petitions inside it] will be read."[103]

In contrast to the primacy of voice in shari'a and the very public nature of qadi court sessions, the 1849 ordinance establishing Majlis al-Aḥkām stressed the importance of secrecy and silence: "Since it is necessary to prevent the deliberations of the council from leaking out, mute servants will be appointed to the deliberating rooms when the council is in session."[104]

From the above, it becomes clear that shari'a courts and *siyāsa* councils had very distinct manners of investigating criminal cases. There were clear differences between the courts and councils when it came to how the identity of litigants and witnesses was established, and how litigants appeared (or did not appear) in front of the two legal bodies. Whereas shari'a can identify individuals only if they are embedded in their communal context and if their gender, religion, age, reputation and social standing in the community and whether they were free persons or slaves is known, the *siyāsa* system embedded the individual in a textual context of its own making. And whereas *fiqh* was clearly biased toward the spoken word, the *siyāsa* system gave the written word pride of place.

Sentencing

The contrast between *fiqh* and *siyāsa* can further be seen by examining the fourth and final stage of a typical criminal case: sentencing. As has been pointed out in this chapter, and as will be discussed further in chapter 5, a qadi's verdict is only valid if it is based on information revealed in his court, and it cannot be based on a confession extracted under duress.[105] And while the qadi's private knowledge of the circumstances of any given case (*'ilm al-qadi*) can be sufficient proof for a sentence for a non-*ḥadd* offense (offenses for which there is no clear-cut punishment stipulated in the Quran), it is not enough in homicide and *ḥadd* cases.[106] Similarly, circumstantial evidence is not admitted in homicide and *ḥadd* cases.[107] Moreover, according to the hadith "Waive the fixed penalties because of doubt,"[108] any element of doubt (*shubha*), such as a discrepancy in a witness's testimony or an individual's failure to use certain words in giving a confession, can prevent a qadi from issuing a guilty verdict.[109] Finally, in the *fiqh* system, although litigants have the right to approach more than one qadi to maximize their chances of getting a verdict to their liking, the qadi's ruling within any one court is final and cannot be appealed.

The *siyāsa* system stands in sharp contrast to all of this. The following section illustrates four main features of *siyāsa* verdicts that distinguish them from *fiqh* ones.

Admitting Circumstantial Evidence. The *siyāsa* councils often based their verdicts on circumstantial evidence, which was in contrast to the shari'a courts, which require a confession or two upright (*'adl*) male witnesses to bring charges in homicide and *ḥadd* cases.[110] The Five-Article Circular, which was passed in 1858 and considered a supplement to the Humāyūnī Law of 1852, stated that homicide cases in which *qiṣāṣ* (retaliation) verdicts could not be passed due to lack of *fiqh* evidence should be adjudicated in the *siyāsa* councils, where circumstantial evidence could be considered. It added that prison sentences passed in such cases should be commensurate with the strength of the circumstantial evidence presented—the stronger the circumstantial evidence, the longer the prison sentence. Chief among the types of permissible circumstantial evidence (which, significantly, is called *adilla siyāsiyya,* or "*siyāsa* evidence"[111]) were the reports written by forensic doctors, who were called *ḥukamā' al-siyāsa,* or "*siyāsa* physicians."[112] We have already seen many cases that relied on forensic medicine throughout this chapter, and more of them will be discussed in chapter 5. What needs to be discussed here, though, is how the *siyāsa* councils based their verdicts on these forensic medical reports.

The following case of miscarriage serves as a good example. The case involved two women, Hānim bint Muḥammad and Zannūba al-Baṣīra, who were married to the same man. One night, the two women had a fight, during which Hānim pushed Zannūba, who was pregnant, so that she fell onto a metal bed and began to bleed. She was rushed to the hospital, where the *ḥakīma* certified that she had suffered a miscarriage.

Zannūba filed a case against her co-wife in the shari'a court, accusing her of causing the miscarriage. In court, the plaintiff provided only one witness, a man who testified that he had seen Hānim holding Zannūba from behind. He was not sure, however, if Hānim had in fact pushed Zannūba. Hānim herself did not deny that the fight had occurred, but she claimed that she had given her co-wife only a small push, which, since Zannūba was blind, had caused her to trip over and fall on the metal bed.[113] Eventually, the husband and Zannūba decided to drop the charges, and so the case was closed according to the shari'a court.

When the *siyāsa* council viewed the case, however, it issued a different verdict. The police asked the Azbakiyya Civilian Hospital to clarify whether falling on a metal bed could cause a miscarriage. The answer was clear: "Causes of miscarriages are numerous. They include falling on a solid object, the body [of the pregnant woman] being beaten by a solid instrument, falling from a great height, blows to any part of the body, [and] strong psychological tribulations [*al-infiʿālāt al-nafsāniyya al-shadīda*]." Based on this medical report, the *siyāsa* council issued the following ruling:

> Since it was established that Zannūba al-Baṣīra suffered a miscarriage as a result of the fight she had [with her co-wife], . . . and since witnesses have testified that the fight did in fact take place, and given that the medical report counted falling on a solid object among the reasons that can cause a miscarriage, . . . it was decided that even though no one was convicted when the case was heard according to shariʿa because the plaintiff had pardoned [*musāmaḥat*] [the defendant], matters regarding miscarriage are important, and since it is clear (*muttaḍiḥ*) that the miscarriage was caused by the fight with her co-wife and her falling down as a result, and since the defendant acknowledged that she had had a fight, . . . she is hereby sentenced to two months' imprisonment in the Iplikhane Workshop[114] after deducting the cost of treating the woman in the hospital (i.e., 22.75 piasters).[115]

Another case in which forensic medicine proved crucial in a conviction involved a group of men who had been playing cards in a Greek grocer's shop in Ṭanṭā. According to the testimonies the men gave during the police investigation, one of them, Asʿad Dāghir, who was originally from Kisriwān in Mount Lebanon, asked for a glass of water, and after drinking it, he fell to the ground unconscious. A physician was fetched, and he pronounced Asʿad dead. Finding this story incredible, the police ordered an autopsy. The autopsy report stated that there were signs of external pressure on the neck, as well as evidence of a brain concussion, which, it concluded, was the cause of death. The men were then questioned again, and when confronted with the forensic report, they confessed that a brawl had erupted after Asʿad had won in a card game. One of the men, Ibrāhīm ʿAbdallāh al-Bayrūtī, grabbed Asʿad by the neck with one hand and beat him hard with the other. Asʿad then left the grocery shop but soon came back woozy, asked for a glass of water, and collapsed after drinking it.

The authorities then contacted the *mutaṣarrif* of Mount Lebanon to fetch the victim's heirs in Beirut so that they could press for charges in the shariʿa court. The victim's heirs could not be located, so the case had to be heard by *siyāsa* council in their absence. Majlis Ṭanṭa adjudicated the case and, based on the new testimonies that had been prompted by the forensic report, found Ibrāhīm guilty and sentenced him to five years in the *līmān* (hard labor prison) of Alexandria. The Appeals Council of Lower Egypt (Majlis Istiʾnāf Baḥarī) upheld the verdict. However, on reviewing the case, Majlis al-Aḥkām found the verdict to be faulty, as it deemed the action to have been manslaughter and not intentional homicide (*qatl khaṭa' lā 'amd*); accordingly, the sentence was reduced to only one year of prison.[116]

Admitting Doubt (Shubha) The *siyāsa* councils saw no problem in basing their verdicts on doubt (*shubha*); indeed, they sometimes explicitly stated this in the wording of the verdicts themselves.[117] By contrast, the qadi courts would consistently uphold the Prophetic hadith "Waive the fixed penalties because of doubt." The following two cases are good examples of this difference between shari'a and *siyāsa*.

On August 24, 1863, a woman called Sitt Ikhwatha went to the provincial police station in Aṭfīḥ, near Fayyūm, to report the murder of her brother-in-law, Sayyid Aḥmad Badr, who was blind and who had arrived in her village with his son a few days earlier to sell a cow that he owned. The buyer, she claimed in her deposition, was a man called 'Awaḍ, who had agreed to pay the price of the cow in cash. On their way back from the village market after finalizing the sale, both 'Awaḍ and Sayyid wanted to perform their ablutions by washing in a nearby canal, and they told Sitt Ikhwatha not to wait for them. No sooner had she left them than her nephew came running to inform her that 'Awaḍ had stabbed his father to death and then threw the body in the canal. 'Awaḍ himself then approached Sitt Ikhwatha and threatened her with the same knife he had used to killed her brother-in-law and warned her that he would kill her if she told anyone. Frightened and intimidated, she remained silent for four days, but then she went to the local village shaykhs and told them what had happened.

The case was viewed by the Banī Sweif shari'a court, where Sitt Ikhwatha's sister, the deceased man's wife, brought charges against 'Awaḍ, claiming that he had stabbed her husband in the neck with intent (*'amdan*) and that her husband had died instantaneously as a result. She then asked for the shari'a-stipulated punishment. But since the defendant denied the charges, and since the claimant could not present any witnesses, the qadi offered her the chance of asking the defendant to give an oath.[118] When the defendant gave an oath denying the charges, the qadi issued a verdict "preventing her from her claim."

However, the *siyāsa* council, Majlis Banī Sweif, convicted 'Awaḍ without absolute certainty that he had intentionally murdered Sayyid Aḥmad Badr. "From the *siyāsa* investigations," the council reasoned, "it is *apparent* [*mutarā'ā*] that the accusations against the defendant are true. [This is based on] the depositions of the victim's sister-in-law, of his son, and of the shaykhs of the neighboring villages. . . . It is *likely* that he undertook this act to satisfy his desire to take the 370 piasters that the victim carried and which was the price of the cow." Despite the lack of absolute certainty, the councils sentenced ʿAwaḍ to deportation to the White Nile in the Sudan. Majlis al-Aḥkām increased the sentence to ten years.[119]

The following case is even more revealing of how the *siyāsa* councils often based their verdicts on reasonable doubt. The case started when a Coptic woman went to her village *ʿumda* to inform him that her daughter, Ghazziyya, had left home ten days earlier with her brother, Barsūm, and never returned. When she questioned Barsūm about his sister's whereabouts, he initially denied knowing anything, but he later said that Ghazziyya's husband, Mīkhā'īl Rūfā'īl, had shot her with a gun while the siblings had been gathering firewood. In the subsequent *siyāsa* investigations, Barsūm could not provide any evidence that his brother-in-law had shot his sister dead. It also transpired that Mikhā'īl had been estranged from his wife for the previous six years after having accused her of dancing at weddings, adultery, and prostitution. He had even sought an annulment of his marriage by petitioning the Coptic Patriarch (*al-baṭrak*) in Cairo. When the qadi of Asyūṭ adjudicated the case in his court, he asked the plaintiffs for evidence, and when they failed to produce any, he gave them the right to ask for an oath from the defendant. Under oath, the defendant denied the charges, and the qadi consequently ordered the case closed. The *siyāsa* council, however, issued the following verdict:

> Since it is *apparent* [*muttaḍiḥ*] that the victim had been practicing prostitution [*muttabiʿa fiʿl al-fāḥisha*] and had deserted her husband for years; that her husband had complained about her to the heads of their religion; that [in the ecclesiastical investigations] witnesses corroborated his claims against her; . . . that in the meantime she had disappeared while going with her brother, Barsūm, to gather firewood, and when she did not return and when her mother inquired from the brother about her whereabouts, the brother first denied any knowledge [but] then confessed [*iʿtaraf*] that her husband had killed her, [from all the above] it can be *deduced* [*fa-yu'khadh*] from [the brother's initial] silence and from the animosity of the husband . . . that [both men] conspired to kill her. This is what happened. Her brother's claim that it was Mikhā'īl alone who killed her is baseless, for if this were true, he would not have been silent about the incident and not told his mother [about his sister's murder] for days.[120]

Remarkably, without an eyewitness testimony, a confession, or even a corpus delicti, Majlis Asyūṭ sentenced both men to prison for five years each. The Majlis al-Aḥkām upheld this verdict.[121]

Considering Administrative and Bureaucratic Details. A third difference between *fiqh* and *siyāsa* verdicts was how the latter occasionally looked beyond the purely criminal facts at hand to address administrative details that were only tangentially related to the case. This was typical procedure, and it reflected the fact that these councils were not purely legal bodies: they were manned by administrators who had been empowered to adjudicate legal disputes. As a result, their verdicts often contained administrative measures that dealt with tangential aspects of a case that had been revealed during the investigation. The councils took both bureaucratic and criminal points into account in their attempt to maintain order in their governorates. The comprehensive purview of the councils is illustrated in a case of abduction and religious conversion that was closely studied by Rudolph Peters. The case involved a couple with different religions who lived together but were not married. The man, Filippo, was an Ottoman subject of Greek ethnicity, while the woman, Siteta, was a Muslim girl. The couple met in Alexandria, where Siteta's father was the doorman (*bawwāb*) of the tenement house in which Filippo lived. The couple fell in love and decided to move to Cairo. Filippo went first and rented an apartment in the Muskī area, a neighborhood with a high concentration of foreigners. Shortly thereafter, Siteta fled her parents' house in Alexandria and boarded a train to Cairo to move in with her lover. The couple lived together for some time until they were discovered by the police, who had received a petition from Siteta's brother to locate her.

The *siyāsa* council found Filippo and Siteta guilty of violating Articles 2 and 6 of Chapter 2 of the Humāyūnī Law, sections that deal with the injuring of a person's honor and abducting a girl, respectively. They were both sentenced to prison: Filippo to one year of hard labor in the *līmān* of Alexandria, and Siteta to one year in the Iplikhane Workshop. Significantly, the district head of the neighborhood that Filippo had moved to in Cairo, a man named ʿIsā al-Ḥabbāk, was also interrogated by the police. The interrogation revolved around why he had not demanded a *ḍamān* from Filippo when he moved to the neighborhood. Based on these interrogations, the *siyāsa* council found ʿIsā guilty of violating Article 7 of Chapter 5 of the Humāyūnī Law,[122] and they ordered him to be dismissed from his post and sentenced him to two months in prison.[123]

The case of Sayyid Aḥmad Badr, mentioned earlier, is a further example of how the *siyāsa* councils often took administrative, as opposed to strictly legal, matters into account when dealing with criminal cases. In this case, in addition to sentencing the murderer to ten years in the Sudan, the council ordered that all peasants from the village be disarmed and also passed various light prison sentences on different guards and sentries for their laxity in apprehending the culprit. In the case of the death, ruled a manslaughter, of Zahra from the Kūm al-Shaykh Salāma neighborhood of Cairo (reviewed in chapter 5), it is interesting to note that the deliberations of the different councils and the final verdict were not limited to the details of the defendant's act, which allegedly led to Zahra's death, but also included another significant aspect of the case, namely the supposed negligence of the *ḥakīma*. The *siyāsa* council also found Amna Efendi, the *ḥakīma* who had conducted the postmortem exam on Zahra's body, guilty of negligence. Specifically, the council was surprised by the discrepancy between her postmortem report, in which she said that there was nothing suspicious about Zahra's death, and the subsequent autopsy report, which reached the opposite conclusion. The council reasoned that the *ḥakīma* should have sought a second medical opinion instead of issuing a definitive report that, as it turned out, was faulty. Amna was therefore sentenced to ten days' imprisonment according to Article 7 of Chapter 5 of the Humāyūnī Law.[124]

Means of Establishing Reputation. Another difference between how the two branches of the legal system passed their verdicts was the process each used to establish the legal reputation of the defendant. As pointed out earlier in this chapter in the section dealing with how juridical identity was established, a qadi had to rely on the local community, as represented by *'udūl* witnesses, to identify the litigants appearing in his court. But as Leslie Peirce noted in her study of the Aintab shari'a court in the sixteenth century, those representatives of the community not only verified the identity of witnesses but also attested to their reputation:

> How was a community to judge the morality of its members? If spiritual commitment was ultimately knowable by the individual alone, observable conduct was the basis for the only concrete measure of morality: one's reputation. Aintabans were regularly consulted concerning their neighbors' reputations: when Hamza sexually assaulted a woman in his village (he climbed into her bed), his fellow peasants were questioned about his character; they told the judge that "once before he was involved with a woman in this village; he has a record of immoral behavior." . . . This role of the collective—the neighborhood, the village, the tribe—as moral arbiter was also reflected in its legal accountability for the moral climate in its domain.[125]

It was the living memory of the community and its oral record that established an individual's reputation, and it was this communally based reputation that often made a decisive difference in how the qadi reached his verdict. In English, the word "fame is essentially an oral concept: [the Latin root] *fama* means talk."[126] Arabic retains the same connection between orality and reputation: both *sum'a* (reputation) and *sama'* (hearing) derive from the same root. And as Peters has argued, these verbal acts had profound implications on establishing reputation and, by implication, guilt and innocence: "By giving evidence about the character and reputation of a person, these communities had far-reaching powers over their members: their testimonies to the effect that the accused was a habitual offender could be the deciding factor for passing a death sentence or for a sentence banishing him from the neighborhood or village where he lived."[127] It is true that people occasionally approached the qadi to tell their own version of events, thereby effectively erasing from the written record of the court a known offense or a communal suspicion that had tarnished their reputation.[128] The vocal nature of establishing reputation remained fundamental.

By contrast, the *siyāsa* councils relied firmly on textual, bureaucratic devices in the form of criminal records (*sijillāt al-sawābiq*), not to establish reputation but to identify recidivists, the idea being that these individuals had not been deterred by previous punishments and therefore deserved harsher sentences.[129] In certain cases, the police had to consult these records and report the information to the *siyāsa* councils so that the councils could pass stricter sentences on previously convicted felons. This was necessary for a number of offenses (mostly theft), as the laws made a distinction between first-time offenders and recidivist offenders. Article 5 of Chapter 2 of the Humāyūnī Law, for example, stipulated that if drunkards and gamblers "perform their offense once and twice, and if they are not deterred [by previous punishment] from following their whims and insist on [recommitting] their offense, then they should be exiled or sent to prison chained [in shackles] until they repent."[130] Article 11 of Chapter 3, furthermore, stipulated that "he who has stolen three times, been punished and has not been deterred, then it should be understood ... that he is incorrigible [*ghayr qābil li'l-istiqāma*] and is incapable of proper behavior. Accordingly, he should be exiled and banished to the Sudan."[131] For another example, Article 19 of Chapter 3, which deals with market offenses, stipulated that those who cheated with prices or weights should be given between three and seventy-nine lashes with a stick on the first offense. On the second offense, the punishment was to be increased to imprisonment, which would involve them "closing down their shops and losing their means of subsistence." If they persisted and repeated the offense a third time, "they should pay any debts that they might have incurred and then be sent back to their villages in order not to be counted as merchants."[132]

The registers of the *siyāsa* councils provide countless examples of how these articles were interpreted. In March 1864, for instance, a lad named ʿAbd al-Majīd stole a golden watch and pawned it to pay a debt he owed to a jail guard. When he was caught, it was discovered that he had two priors: he had received the first in June 1861, when his father, irked by "his recalcitrant behavior" (*naẓaran li-shaqāwatihi*), had brought him to the police station, where he was given a number of strikes by the cane as legal punishment, and had gotten the second the following month, when he admitted to stealing a large amount of money from his father. During the investigation into the stolen money, however, he escaped, but he was later found in a brothel. His father resolved to send him to Medina, in the Hijaz, where the father had family, "so that he rectifies his behavior." When the Police Council (Majlis al-Ḍabṭiyya) reviewed the case of the stolen watch, ʿAbd al-Majīd was sentenced to eighteen months of hard labor in the Department of Industry (Dīwān al-Wābūrāt wa-l-ʿAmaliyyāt), which was used as a labor pool for work in factories and quarries,[133] according to Article 11 of Chapter 3 of the penal code. Majlis al-Aḥkām approved the verdict.[134]

In this case, it was the father who testified that his son was a recidivist offender; more typically, this was determined by checking the criminal record of the defendant at the police station. For example, in March 1878, a man named Maḥmūd Aḥmad was caught stealing from a warehouse in Alexandria. In the police station, it was discovered that he had two prior incidents listed in his criminal record (*sijil al-sawābiq*). The police thus wrote to the Alexandria Council, stating that "since Maḥmūd Ahmad had been caught red-handed while stealing, and since he had two priors in his records, the Majlis can now decide on his case."[135] In a similar case, a man was caught red-handed stealing the sum of seventeen pounds from another man who was praying in the Sayyida Zaynab Mosque in Cairo. At the police station, his records were checked and it was discovered that he had seven previous convictions. He was therefore permanently exiled to the Sudan according to Article 11 of Chapter 3 of the Humāyūnī Law.[136]

FIQH AND *SIYĀSA*

Having seen the sharp differences between *fiqh* and *siyāsa*—in how legal action is initiated, how identity is established, how criminal cases are to be investigated, and how verdicts are reached—it is important to stress that we are not dealing with two competing and internally contradictory systems with different jurisdictions, with the masses subject to *fiqh* while the elite and the rulers were subject to *siyāsa,* as has been recently argued.[137] Rather, these were two components of one legal system, a system, moreover, that was predicated on making sure that its two components worked seamlessly together. It's also incorrect to argue that *siyāsa* represented a step in the long march of the modernization of Egyptian law, which started clumsily and hesitantly under Bonaparte and ended with the adoption of European codes and legal systems in the 1880s. In fact, the recently rediscovered archive of the *siyāsa* councils suggests that Egypt witnessed one of the most imaginative and persistent efforts in Islamic history to implement shariʿa and bring it in conformity with *siyāsa.* Later in this chapter, we will investigate the historical origins of the *siyāsa,* but first, the following section highlights three instances that demonstrate that *siyāsa* and *fiqh* were part of the same legal system. Far from being a way to sidestep or circumvent *fiqh, siyāsa* was an important, indeed crucial, tool to bolster and implement it.

Defining the Murder Weapon

As Rudolph Peters, the pioneering scholar of this exciting chapter of Egyptian law, has argued, the different legal innovations witnessed before 1883 indicate that "there was no trend towards restricting the application of Islamic law. On the contrary, the government seems to have been keen on ensuring the correct application of Hanafite law."[138] While it is true that Peters argued that Egyptian legislators and administrators in the middle decades of the nineteenth century were aware of contemporary European legal trends and even occasionally attempted to copy some European codes, he nevertheless concluded that whatever European influence that can be detected "remained a matter of form and not of content."[139]

Examples of how closely the government adhered to the principles of shariʿa are numerous. As we have seen, the main penal code, the Humāyūnī Law of 1852, referred explicitly to shariʿa when dealing with homicides and other serious crimes. Most crucially—unlike the 1850 Ottoman Penal Code from which it was copied, with some modifications—this legal code did not allow the death penalty to be applied except in murder cases that had been adjudicated by a qadi court and in which a *qiṣāṣ* sentence had already been passed according to strict *fiqhī* rules.[140] It is significant to note, for example, that when, soon after promulgating this penal code, Majlis al-Aḥkām was confronted with new evidence that there was a significant rise in murder cases in the Egyptian countryside, they did not attempt to replace the relevant articles in the code that referred to shari'a and its strict rules about how a *qiṣāṣ* sentence should be issued with a more lax set of rules. Specifically, there was an alarming rise in the number of murder cases that involved the *nabbūt,* a thick wooden stick that men in the Egyptian countryside, and in Upper Egypt in particular, carried. Majlis al-Aḥkām feared that people were using the *nabbūt* to kill their opponents (especially in land disputes) because they knew that the shari'a qadis would consider such cases *qatl khaṭa'* (unintentional killings), and accordingly get away with a *diyya* (blood money) sentence instead of a *qiṣāṣ* (lex talionis) sentence. The problem for the members of the Majlis al-Aḥkām was that Abū Ḥanīfa, the founder of the Ḥanafī doctrine, which was predominant in Egypt and in the Ottoman Empire at that time, did not agree that wooden sticks embodied the intention to kill.[141] A general meeting of all the muftis working in Majlis al-Aḥkām was convened to discuss the matter. After lengthy deliberations, the muftis decided that even though Abū Ḥanīfa had rejected the *nabbūt* as a homicidal weapon, his two disciples, Abū Yūsuf and Muḥammad b. al-Ḥasan, as well as the three other imams Mālik, al-Shāfi'ī, and Ibn Ḥanbal, all considered the *nabbūt* to embody homicidal intention in the same way that a knife does. Henceforth, Majlis al-Aḥkām ruled that any murder case involving a *nabbūt* would be treated as a case of homicide and not of manslaughter and that the individual who had wielded the *nabbūt* could be sentenced to death (*qiṣāṣ*) if it was demonstrated, according to shari'a methods of establishing proof, that he had used it.[142]

Establishing Judicial Oversight of Qadi Courts

Another element of the legal system that shows that the authorities were keen to uphold the principles of *fiqh* by supplementing them with *siyāsa* principles rather than circumventing the former, is that the *siyāsa* councils were authorized to check the validity of qadi rulings in criminal cases. In what can be described as a system of judicial oversight, the *siyāsa* councils repeatedly overturned sentences issued by shari'a courts on the grounds that the sentences had not properly followed the principles of Ḥanafī doctrine. The fact that the councils had muftis among their permanent members enabled them to spot mistakes and discrepancies in shari'a court rulings and to return them to the qadis for revision and correction.[143] The following homicide case, which was reviewed by the Ma'iyya Saniyya (Vice-Regal Cabinet), is a good example of this process of judicial oversight.[144]

The case started on May 28, 1860, when the heirs of a man named al-Sayyid Muḥammad in Idfū, Upper Egypt, went to the shari'a court of al-Fashn to press charges against a *dhimmī* (non-Muslim) man, accusing him of killing al-Sayyid Muḥammad. In court, they employed all the right formulae for a valid homicide charge: they testified that the defendant had used a wooden stick to intentionally hit the victim on the left side of the head; that the blow had cut the skin, broken the bones, drew blood, and spilled out the brain; and that the victim had walked home after the beating, stayed alive for one day, and then died as a result of the beating.

After hearing the heirs, the qadi asked if they could provide proof of their accusation. They produced one Muslim man and two *dhimmī* men as witnesses. The qadi then attempted to establish the probity (*'adāla*) of the witnesses, but the way he did so was most unusual. He asked the Muslim man about prayer and whether he prayed regularly. The witness answered that he did pray, but only occasionally, as his business got in the way. The qadi then turned to the two *dhimmī* witnesses and asked them "about their faith and their rituals." They answered that they knew nothing about their faith; they explained that they were "farmers who work in the fields and who know nothing [about their religion]." They insisted, however, that they were Christian. Based on these answers, the qadi decided that the testimonies of the *dhimmī* witnesses could not be accepted and asked the heirs for new evidence. When they said that they had none, the qadi offered them the chance to ask the defendant to take an oath. They refused to do so, and the case was dropped as a result.

When the Ma'iyya reviewed the case, however, it decided that the qadi's actions were inadmissible:

> By asking questions that [can only] lead to the heirs' and the witnesses' inability to establish proof [*ta'jīz*], and by doing so himself [rather than] asking the defendant to challenge [the probity of the witnesses and the accusations of the plaintiffs, this qadi has allowed] this murderer to go unpunished [*tarattab minhu ihdār damm al-maqtūl*]. This cannot be accepted, according to shari'a. In order to safeguard against the qadis' committing such acts, and

in order to guarantee that the [qadis] adjudicate the subjects' cases [*daʿāwā al-raʿiyya*] according to the Luminous Shariʿa and prevent forfeiting the rights of the subjects, the Maʿiyya saw fit to write to all local governors so that they [in turn] can write to the qadis in their governorates to make sure that the qadis avoid such pitfalls, to urge them to be diligent in adjudicating cases according to the shariʿa, and to warn them that they will be punished if they violate these instructions.[145]

In fact, so important was *fiqh* in the daily functioning of the *siyāsa* councils and so integral was the councils' practice of judicial oversight of shariʿa courts that Majlis al-Aḥkām's records contain an entire subsection exclusively dedicated to records of shariʿa court sentences (*iʿlāmāt sharʿiyya*) that were reviewed by the Majlis. The following entry is a good example of Majlis al Aḥkām's judicial oversight of shariʿa courts. The first section is a summary of the shariʿa verdict in an 1852 homicide case. The second section is Majlis al-Aḥkām's 1854 review and comments on the shariʿa verdict.

> I. The case of the murder of Aḥmad Sulaymān al-Sahrqāwī, from the village of Shnieṭ in Sharqiyya, and his killer is Dāwūd Ḥanna, from Ṣa'l-Ḥajar, based on [Dāwūd's] confession [that he had] stabbed [Aḥmad] with a knife and [that Aḥmad had] died as a result of that. A shariʿa verdict was issued by the qadi of al-Maḥalla al-Kubrā dated 6 Ṣafar 1269 [November 18, 1852] stipulating that *qiṣāṣ* be applied on Dāwūd Ḥanna, the abovementioned defendant. The verdict was based on the opinion of . . . Abū Ḥanīfa. This shariʿa verdict was ratified by the *ʿulamāʾ* of the Second *Siyāsa* Council of Lower Egypt [Majlis Thānī Baḥarī]. . . .
>
> II. We have reviewed the case of the murder of Ahmad Sulaymān al-Sharqāwī, . . . and we have understood its contents. . . . [We noticed that] the qadi had not explicitly stated in his verdict whether he had established the probity of the witnesses, privately and publicly [*sirran wa ʿalanan*], before issuing the *qiṣāṣ* ruling. It is necessary to establish the probity of witnesses, privately and publicly, before issuing a *qiṣāṣ* ruling, as we had previously made clear in a [similar] case. . . . This is because *qiṣāṣ* is similar to *ḥadd* punishments, and both [types of punishment] are to be avoided by doubt as much as possible, as stated in *kitāb al-shahādāt* [i.e., the chapter on witness testimonies in Ḥanafī *fiqh* books]. God is All Knowing.[146]

Supplementing Fiqh with Siyāsa *Punishments*

It should be clear by now how serious the authorities were in their desire to uphold rather than to circumvent shariʿa. Engaging with Ḥanafī doctrine to come up with a more inclusive definition of what constitutes a murder weapon; appointing muftis to the *siyāsa* councils who were competent enough to oversee the proper implementation of *fiqh* in shari'a courts; streamlining and improving the shari'a judiciary[147]—all these measures were aimed at bolstering shari'a and not intended to sideline or marginalize it. It was this creative combination of *fiqh* and *siyāsa* that allowed Mehmed Ali and his successors to establish a state of law and order in Egypt and to use law to strengthen and exhibit the sovereignty of the centralized state that they were creating.

As early as September 1829, when he passed his first penal legislation,[148] and years before he first expressed his desire for official independence from the Ottoman Empire in the late 1830s, Mehmed Ali was using law, and penal law in particular, to carve out an independent realm for himself where his laws and his bureaucracy would reign supreme. Hasanaine al-Besumee, one of the Egyptian students Mehmed Ali had sent to Britain in the early 1830s, for example, felt comfortable arguing that "a Christian's head is as safe on his shoulders at Cairo as it is in London, and his purse safer in his pocket."[149] Similarly, an anonymous British author writing in 1852 made a credible case for how tranquil and secure Egypt had become over the previous two or three decades:

> The state of Egypt presents a striking contrast to that of Turkey. Everyone knows the good order and security which there prevail; it would be idle to speak on this point.... In Egypt [Mehmed Ali] had compiled a code, had adapted it to the manners of the people whom he governed, had established tribunals, and no person could be executed in Egypt without a previous trial and sentence passed according to certain prescribed rules, and confirmed by the Viceroy himself. The principles of the Hatti Sheriff (of Gulhané of 1839), which forbids any functionary to put a person to death arbitrarily, existed in Egypt even before the young sultan, who established it in Turkey, was born: in that... Egypt preceded Constantinople.[150]

It was this legacy of establishing a state of law and order in Egypt that 'Abbās Pasha successfully defended when he entered into negotiations with the Sublime Porte on how to implement the Ottoman Penal Code of 1850 in Egypt. After revising two chapters of the original law to fit the Egyptian context, the issue was raised as to who had the right to issue execution orders on murderers who had committed crimes in Egypt and against whom a *qiṣāṣ* verdict had already been issued. The sultan insisted that this should be his own right and that his Sublime Porte should have the right to ratify these death sentences. ʿAbbās, however, argued that sending *qiṣāṣ* verdicts to Istanbul for ratification would take so much time that the deterrent effect of the punishment would be significantly weakened. He therefore insisted that Egypt retain the right to pass death sentences on convicted murderers without approval from Istanbul. In the end, a compromise was reached whereby ʿAbbās was given a grace period of seven years, during which time he could pass death sentences himself, provided that the murder victim had heirs who demanded execution; if the victim had no heirs, then the sultan had the right to ratify the *qiṣāṣ* sentence and issue the execution order. This provision, however, remained a dead letter, for neither during nor after the grace period did Cairo ever send *qiṣāṣ* sentences to Istanbul for ratification.[151]

Like the examples mentioned above (e.g., engaging with classical Ḥanafī *fiqh* to expand the definition of a murder weapon, and empowering the *siyāsa* councils to have judicial oversight of shariʿa courts), this particular episode of ʿAbbās's negotiation with Istanbul serves as further proof that the Egyptian authorities embraced shariʿa and were not attempting to circumvent it. However, in their efforts to make sure that the principles of *fiqh* were properly understood and that the qadi courts were efficiently run, the Egyptian state came to realize, like countless other Islamic states before it, how upholding *fiqh* in criminal matters, especially in adjudicating homicide cases, had serious drawbacks for a state keen on spreading its hegemony and intent on maintaining order in its realm.

I have already discussed instances in which principles of *fiqh* were strictly upheld but simultaneously deemed to be insufficient, specifically with regard to homicide cases. To recapitulate, there were three instances in which *fiqh* was found to be insufficient and measures were taken to complement it. Firstly, given that the state was increasingly looking at homicide as an attack on its sovereignty, the fact that *fiqh* effectively treated homicide as private law was seen as particularly problematic, specifically with regard to who had the right to initiate legal action. As noted above, the newly created police force was given the right to press charges and launch investigations into suspected homicides and other criminal cases, both in the urban centers and in the countryside.

Secondly, the very high bar established by *fiqh* for what constitutes admissible evidence in court and how *fiqh* defines valid legal proof was problematic. By necessitating the testimony of two Muslim, upright, male witnesses or the confession of the defendant, *fiqh* established too high a barrier for conviction.

For instance, in a study of the records of one shari'a court in Upper Egypt, Rudolph Peters found that only 2 percent of homicide cases ended in a successful conviction with a *qiṣāṣ* sentence and that only 5 percent ended in a *diyya* sentence. He found only one sentence of amputation of a defendant's hand for theft, which was rejected after an appeal.[152] It was the keen desire of the state to supplement *fiqhī* methods of establishing legal proof that led circumstantial evidence, primarily forensic medicine, to be admitted as a valid means of establishing proof, and this became heavily relied on in the *siyāsa* councils.

Thirdly, in the rare cases where a successful conviction was passed in a homicide case, the principle of private justice that shari'a effectively uses to deal with homicide gave the victim's next of kin the option to pardon the defendant by not asking for the *qiṣāṣ* sentence to be carried out or by accepting blood money instead. These possibilities were deeply inimical to the interests of a state fiercely trying to assert its right to prosecute murderers and to establish its sovereignty in the name of the law and by means of the law. Therefore, to make sure that homicide crimes did not go unpunished and that society at large, not only victims' next of kin, had a say in how convicted murderers were punished, the state ordered that shari'a sentences were required to be coupled with *siyāsa* sentences. Article 11 of Chapter 1 of the Humāyūnī Law stipulated that "murder acts that should have received capital punishment [*qiṣāṣ*] but in which a blood money [*diyya*] verdict was issued instead because of [the next of kin agreeing to] a pardon or settlement [*'afw al-waratha aw al-muṣālaḥa*] . . . will be punished by imprisonment for a period of five to fifteen years."[153]

THE SIGNIFICANCE OF EGYPTIAN *SIYĀSA*

It should be clear by now how central shari'a was in the Egyptian legal system before the advent of the Mixed Courts and National Courts. Nothing could be further from the truth than arguing that Mehmed Ali and his successors were trying to "catch up with Europe" in legal matters and were keen on adopting European legal systems. Throughout much of the nineteenth century, the Egyptian legal system had shari'a as its main reference point, both in terms of legislation and court practice. The legal system gave *fiqh* a very prominent place in the field of criminal law: the texts of the main penal code repeatedly referred to it; the qadi courts played a central role in adjudicating crime; there was a consistent insistence that no death sentence could be passed until a *qiṣāṣ* verdict had been issued by a qadi; and meticulous mechanisms were put in place to make sure that qadis abided by the strict rules of *fiqh,* especially in homicide cases. All of this casts doubt on the commonly held narrative that nineteenth-century Egyptian law steadily and indelibly marginalized shariʿa.

However, the shariʿa that the Egyptian legal system so consistently applied throughout much of the nineteenth century was not the shariʿa that had been defined by the *fuqahāʾ*. Despite ʿAwda's insistence that shariʿa was born complete, comprehensive, and perfect (*kāmila, shāmila,* and *sāmiya*)—an insistence dogmatically reiterated by many Islamists—the shariʿa that was implemented in nineteenth-century Egypt was flexible and evolving, and it was found lacking in many respects. With regard penal matters, *fiqh* was found particularly problematic because it effectively dealt with murder as a matter of private law. Also deeply troublesome was the very high bar set by classical *fiqh* to establish legal proof.

Furthermore, and again contrary to ʿAwda's popular ahistorical view about the immutability of shariʿa, the Egyptian nineteenth-century historical record shows that shariʿa was highly flexible and adaptable to changing times. However, this was not the result of the intellectual originality of nineteenth-century Egyptian *fiqh,* nor was it derived from an authentic mindset that was true to the nation's heritage (*mawrūth*) or critical of imported thought (*al-wāfid*), to use al-Bishrī's language. Rather, the shariʿa that was implemented in the nineteenth-century Egyptian legal system derived its flexibility and adaptability from coupling *fiqh* with *siyāsa.* This was mainly done by founding *siyāsa* councils alongside qadi courts and by empowering these councils to adjudicate criminal cases, as well as other types of cases.[154] New laws were promulgated to help these councils in their job, and as explained above, clear guidelines were issued to guarantee that the councils would coordinate their work properly with the qadi courts. Most significantly, these councils were established not to sideline *fiqh* but to complement it. Thus, whereas *fiqh* only gave a victim's next of kin the right to initiate legal action, *siyāsa* laws gave police departments and governors the power to do so. In contrast to *fiqh*'s insistence on establishing legal proof through *bayyina,* which is effectively a verbal act (in the form of an eyewitness account or a defendant's confession), the *siyāsa* councils accepted all kinds of circumstantial evidence, most importantly written forensic medical reports. Whereas qadis courts were constantly reminded not to impose any penalty if there was any doubt (*shubha*) that all the conditions for demanding a penalty had been met, the *siyāsa* councils explicitly, and as a matter of policy, based their verdicts on reasonable doubt. Finally, and in contrast to retaliation and blood money, the main *fiqhī* punishments for homicide, prison sentences were the main punishment meted out by the *siyāsa* councils, since the councils were motivated by the need to establish deterrence, as opposed to restitution, as the main purpose of punishment.

Therefore, far from being an arbitrary, inherently unjust legal system, as claimed by Zaghlūl and his countless followers, the pre-1876 Egyptian legal system was a self-confident, authentic one that, at least in criminal matters, was based on a very consistent and highly imaginative attempt at coupling *fiqh* with *siyāsa*. Furthermore, this *siyāsa* was not some alien *wāfid* imposed on society by a disenchanted and misguided elite who had lost confidence in their *mawrūth,* as al-Bishrī has polemically argued. Rather, as the fourteenth-century Mālikī jurist Ibn Farḥūn argued, *siyāsa* "is a sure way to implement the objectives of shari'a" (*yutawwaṣal bihā ilā maqāṣid al-sharī'a*).[155] Moreover, as Colin Imber has shown in his study of Ebu's-Su'ud, who was the chief jurist of Sultan Süleyman (known as the Lawgiver) in the sixteenth century, there was a long and venerable tradition in the Ottoman Empire of complementing *fiqh* with *siyāsa*.[156] Furthermore, it had always been known that *fiqh* rules were, in many respects, impractical, and the need to supplement the system with parallel legal mechanisms had always been felt. Baber Johansen has shown, for example, that a serious deviation from *fiqh* doctrine on proof and procedure was effected during Mamluk times. Judging classical *fiqh* to have been encumbered by rigid formalism, the two towering late-classical jurists of the Mamluk era, Ibn Taymiyya and Ibn Qayyim al-Jawziyya, argued for an epistemology of truth that would make it possible to institute new kinds of trials, trials of suspicion (*da'āwā al-tuham*). Johansen notes, "Under the *siyāsa* doctrines of . . . the Mamluk period, these trials are considered legitimate whenever a suspect, be he a plaintiff, a witness or a defendant, cannot be convicted according to the procedural law of classical *fiqh* doctrine."[157] It was this *fiqh*-based argument that allowed circumstantial evidence to be admitted in *siyāsa* councils. Most crucially, what Ibn Taymiyya, Ibn al-Qayyim, and the many other *fuqahā'* following them had accomplished was nothing less than bestowing legitimacy on *siyāsa,* a practice that had hitherto been widely implemented but lacked a crucial *shar'ī* cover. By coining the phrase *siyāsa shar'iyya* (shari'a-sanctioned *siyāsa*), both Ibn Taymiyya and Ibn al-Qayyim introduced into the Sunni Muslim mainstream the argument that *siyāsa* was necessary not only to defend and protect the interests of the state but also to uphold and complement shari'a.

In addition to analyzing *fiqhī* prescriptive treatises that shed light on the logic of *siyāsa* in Mamluk times, Jørgen Nielsen has studied historians' chronicles to produce a detailed account of how *siyāsa* was actually applied during the Mamluk period and examined how the *siyāsa* councils, which were also known as *maẓālim* courts, were an integral part of the Mamluk system of justice.[158] Recently, Yossef Rapoport has shown how central *siyāsa* was in the Mamluk legal system. Similarly to Johansen, Rapoport argues that the shari'a courts were encumbered by the rigid formalism of the *fuqahā'*. It was this rigid formalism, he argued, that gave rise to the need to complement the shari'a courts with institutions that could also uphold equity and to "offer justice, not just law."[159] Rapoport also convincingly argues that the Mamluk *siyāsa* system was a popular one and was seen by the public as legitimate since "the authority of *siyāsah* magistrates was founded on popular notions of equity."[160] Most importantly, Rapoport cites many examples that show that while it is true that some *fuqahā'* objected to the *siyāsa* courts,[161]

> not all members of the judiciary objected to the expanded jurisdiction of the *siyāsah* courts, even if it came at the expense of the courts of the *qadis*. Admittedly, other jurists and religious scholars condemned *siyāsah* justice as a symptom of decay and corruption, sometimes in very harsh words. But other, more nuanced, approaches are evident in writings of the ulama. The problem with *siyāsah* justice was usually not that *siyāsah* is illegitimate per se, but that it was left in the hands of incompetent and corrupt officials. The principle of *siyāsah* was acceptable or even necessary, but without the guidance of the *shari'ah*, it allowed significant room for abuse.[162]

Furthermore, recent scholarship has persuasively shown that coupling *fiqh* with *siyāsa/maẓālim* was a practice that far predated the Mamluks and that it can in fact be traced all the way back to the 'Abbāsids.[163] Finally, and as al-Māwardī (d. 1058) argued in his famous *Al-Aḥkām al-Sulṭāniyya,* the practice of relying on *siyāsa* to administer justice can even be traced further back in time, to the Umayyads.[164] So it can safely be said that even though it was not legitimized as part of shari'a until the end of the twelfth century, *siyāsa* was practiced from the very early stages of Islamic history and has always existed in conjunction with *qaḍā'* (the administration of justice in the shari'a courts).[165]

The *siyāsa* system that was implemented in nineteenth-century Egypt, therefore, was no *bid'a* (innovation); rather, it had a long and venerable pedigree in Islamic tradition. It was not imposed on society by colonial powers or a misguided, disillusioned elite either. The fact that it does not feature in al-Bishrī's *mawrūth* (which privileges *fiqh* and to a far lesser extent, *qadā'*) is a reminder of how arbitrary in al-Bishrī's mind the boundaries are that define this *mawrūth* and demarcate it from *al-wāfid*.

It is along these lines that the significance of the Egyptian nineteenth-century *siyāsa* can be appreciated. As this chapter has attempted to illustrate by relying on the records of this system, *siyāsa*'s voluminous documentation gives us a unique perspective on how *siyāsa* functioned in practice. Previous scholars of *siyāsa* have relied on either prescriptive treatises that provided an idealized, normative description of the system (e.g., Māwardī and Ibn al-Farra'[166]) or on chroniclers who described, sometimes secondhand, what took place in *siyāsa* or *maẓālim* courts.[167] The archive of the Egyptian *siyāsa* system from the nineteenth century, by contrast, is unique, not only because we know of no other *siyāsa* system with records that have been so comprehensively preserved but also because the sheer size of the archive—which contains over four thousand ledgers—and the exceptionally careful way in which it is organized have allowed us to understand the highly sophisticated manner in which the system functioned and the very systematic way that it complemented and engaged with *fiqh*. As such, this impressive archive provides ample documentation of how shari'a evolved and adapted to changing times in a specific historical context.

The significance of nineteenth-century Egyptian *siyāsa*, furthermore, derives from what it can tell us about the proverbial closure of the gates of *ijtihād*, which is famous in Orientalist scholarship on Islamic law. As is well known, students of this subject generally assume that the process of laying the foundations of Islamic law was completed in the tenth century and that this law became static soon after its earliest formative centuries. They have been able to make this claim by relying mainly on the *mutūn*, the textbooks that explicate the dominant doctrine of the schools of Islamic law. This claim has been seriously challenged by many scholars using different methods.[168] Some attempted to find signs of doctrinal innovation beyond the date of the supposed closure of the gates and the ossification of *fiqh*.[169] More recently, Johansen has shown that the traditional position that *fiqh* ossified after the tenth century ignores the important signs of flexibility and originality shown in literary genres other than the *mutūn*. He specifically stresses the importance of commentaries (*shurūḥ*), responses (*fatāwā*), and treatises on particular questions (*rasā'il*).[170] Moreover, historians of the Middle East, especially those working on the Ottoman period, have also highlighted the importance of the voluminous records of the qadi courts in understanding not only social, economic, and cultural realities[171] but also points of law and doctrine.[172] As this chapter has shown, the records of the *siyāsa* system can be added to this list of sources—which includes *fiqh* books, *shurūḥ, fatāwā, rasā'il,* and qadi court records—that can be used to define the form and content of Islamic law.

Finally, the voluminous records of the nineteenth-century Egyptian *siyāsa* councils shed light on how Islamic law could be implemented and made compatible with modern times. Recent scholarship in this field has pointed to two prominent Egyptian jurists, ʻAbd al-Razzāq al-Sanhūrī (1895–1971) and Chafik Chehata, who had a firm grounding in both European and Islamic law. Given their training, these two jurists applied comparative private law to *fiqh* texts "to disengage from their casuistry the principles that govern the *fiqh*'s legal reasoning and which can be translated into a sufficiently abstract and general form to be applied in the codification of modern national law."[173] As pointed out above, the Egyptian *siyāsa* councils, while following a well-trodden path within Islamic history, have embraced quintessentially modern practices. Examples include the use of forensic medicine as circumstantial evidence and the employment of bureaucratic devices such as the *ḍamān* and the criminal record as tools to establish personal identity. While council members produced no treatises that could provide ontological reflections on the strategic acceptance of such modern medical and bureaucratic practices and on the implications of this acceptance on notions of proof, evidence, justice, and law, the huge archive that the *siyāsa* system produced is nevertheless invaluable for the information it provides on how *siyāsa* very imaginatively combined with *fiqh* in the context of a modern state structure.

SIYĀSA AND THE CRITIQUE OF SECULARISM

In critiquing the Orientalist thesis of the "closure of the gates of *ijtihād*," Asad insists that "argued change was important to the shariʻa, and its flexibility was retained through such technical devices as *ʻurf* (custom), *maslaha* (public interest) and *darūra* (necessity)."[174] This chapter suggests that *siyāsa* can be added to Asad's list of devices that guaranteed shariʻa's flexibility over the centuries, for the *siyāsa* archive discussed here shows that nineteenth-century Egypt witnessed what is arguably one of the most creative experiments in implementing shariʿa in Islamic history. By establishing *siyāsa* councils and setting precise guidelines on how they collaborated with qadi courts in adjudicating crime, what we see is a consistent, flexible legal system that was as confident in embracing modern bureaucratic and medical measures as it was proud of standing in the shadow of an old, indigenous legal tradition. But *siyāsa*'s confident and steady acceptance of modern medical and bureaucratic techniques had a profound impact on the entire legal system, which might have unwittingly led to the triumph of secularism. To elucidate this point, it might be useful to revisit Asad's critique of the secularization thesis one last time.

Asad is deeply critical of the popular narrative that shariʿa was abandoned by the process of legal reform in nineteenth-century Egypt. His critique centers on showing that the traditional narrative, by limiting its analysis to examining how shariʿa was gradually marginalized until only matters of personal status were under its jurisdiction, misses out on the transformations that shariʿa underwent during that process: "When the shariʿa is structured essentially as a set of legal rules defining personal status, it is radically transformed. . . . What happens to the shariʿa is best described not as curtailment but as transmutation. It is rendered into a subdivision of legal norms (*fiqh*) that are authorized and maintained by the centralizing state."[175] Through a critical reading of a few very late nineteenth-century normative texts calling for legal reform in family law, Asad is able to show how this process of legal reform was aimed, in fact, at instituting a process of governance that would have as its purpose the normalization of social conduct in a modern, secular state. Central to this process was the legal reconstitution of the family as the basic unit of society, where the individual was to be physically and morally reproduced as a "private" being. For this to happen, Asad argues, following Foucault, the family had to be subjected to the state's concern in the form of new knowledge (political economy) and toward a new object (population). At the same time, the individual had to be pedagogically encouraged to govern him- or herself as befits the citizen of a secular, liberal society. Asad argues that contrary to the commonly held position that colonial governments were reluctant to interfere with family law because it was the heart of religious doctrine and practice, "the shariʿa thus defined is precisely a secular formula for privatizing 'religion' and preparing the ground for the self-governing subject."[176]

CONCLUSION

The material presented in this chapter suggests not only that the constitution of the family was transformed but also that the very notion of the individual witnessed a radical alteration as a result of combining *siyāsa* with *fiqh*. For as explained above, lacking the meticulous means of establishing identity that were deployed in the qadi courts, which had been theorized by the *fuqahā'* and perfected in practice over the centuries, the *siyāsa* councils had to resort to alternative mechanisms to make sure that the litigants whom they dealt with were who they claimed to be. Instead of *'udūl* witnesses, who were effectively the linchpin between the qadi and the community, and who could establish not only the identity of litigants and witnesses but also their reputation, the *siyāsa* councils relied on the textual devices mentioned above: the census record, the *ḍamān,* the *tadhkara,* legal domicile, and simple patronymic names.

But these new textual devices also led to the appearance of a new concept of identity altogether. In contrast to the qadi courts, which embedded individual identity in a communal setting, relying on the community (the tribe, the extended family, the neighborhood, the village, etc.) to establish the probity and reputation of individuals, the *siyāsa* councils, by relying on the textual devices of the modern state, could dispense with the communal context altogether and find alternative means of establishing identity, ascertaining probity, and checking reputation.

It was this newly forged individuality, embedded firmly not in the communal context but in the textual setting of the modern bureaucratic state, that made it possible for the idea of equality to be thinkable. As Lawrence Rosen has remarked, the concept of *'adāla* in *fiqh,* which forms the basis of the process of *'udūl* witnessing, means both "to be straight" and "to be balanced." This concept is based on a notion of individual reputation, which is embedded in a host of socioeconomic ties that the individual has constantly to maintain. At the same time, the community to which the individual belongs "derives its legitimacy from those very networks of embedded dependencies through which individual effort is given social utility."[177] In this *fiqhī* world, the relationship that binds different entities together is not equality but equivalence. There is a "larger, almost Aristotelian, notion . . . at work here, namely, that entities which are different should be treated differently, that justice lies precisely in recognizing and validating these differences, and that injustice would flow from a contrary position."[178]

Accordingly, and as is well known, the qadi does not see individuated, isolated entities when passing his judgments but is entreated to consider the social and communal relationships, the relationships of reciprocity, that bind individuals to each other, and before passing a ruling, he has to consider such factors as the gender, the religion, the sanity, and the age of the litigants and witnesses appearing in his court, as well as whether they are free or slaves. The sum of blood money, the number of witnesses to be heard, the amount of inheritance an heir is to receive—all these and other questions cannot be addressed until the qadi has paid close attention to whether his litigant is a man or a woman, a Muslim or a non-Muslim, a slave or a free person. By contrast, because it had at its disposal the bureaucratic devices mentioned above, the *siyāsa* council could deal with individuals irrespective of their freedom, gender, or religion. It is not that the *siyāsa* archive has no mention of religion, gender, or other personal qualifications, but these factors did not have a bearing on how a case was viewed, and they were not central in how people presented themselves to the police or in the manner in which they articulated their cases.

Therefore, the idea of equality before the law in Egyptian legal thinking, which is so central in most accounts of secularization, was not born out of any deep belief in the Enlightenment ideals of the value of each and every individual. Nor was it the result of pressure applied by European diplomats on leading intellectuals in Istanbul or Cairo to treat their Muslim and non-Muslim subjects equally. Furthermore, the concept of equality (as opposed to equivalence) that was established between members of the same polity in Egypt was made thinkable not because, as Asad has argued, morality was divorced from the law, for this had happened when *fiqh* was combined with *siyāsa*—that is, in the very early days of shari'a. Rather, legal equality was born as a result of *siyāsa*'s successful attempt to uphold and maintain *fiqhī* principles and to do so by embracing modern medical and bureaucratic devices. In other words, shari'a became secularized in khedival Egypt not because it was limited to the realm of personal status but because its partner in crime, the *siyāsa* councils, were successful in embracing the bureaucratic and medical techniques of the modernizing, centralizing state. The following chapters elucidate what other implications these medical and bureaucratic techniques had on the legal, ethical, and social world of khedival Egypt.

THREE

An Olfactory Tale of One City

CAIRO IN KHEDIVAL TIMES

ON THE MORNING OF A SPRING DAY IN 1878, a child playing with his friends close to the Qaṣr al-Nīl barracks overlooking the Nile to the west of Cairo noticed a stray dog sniffing a buried old rag. When the children realized that the dog had unearthed a suspicious body, they rushed to the head of the neighborhood, who was as puzzled as they were at what they saw. He summoned the resident doctor from the nearby police station, who was equally perplexed. The contents of the rag were then sent to the Qaṣr al-ʿAinī Hospital for forensic examination, and the hospital's report came back saying that the rag contained the female remains of either a stillborn baby or a fetus; the uncertainty stemmed from the fact that the body was in an advanced stage of putrefaction, making it impossible to ascertain whether death had occurred before or after birth.

The head of the neighborhood and the local authorities immediately set out to investigate how the body had been buried in such a manner, who the mother was, and what the conditions of this death had been. After some brief interrogations in the neighborhood, an eighteen-year-old woman named Faḍl Wāsiʿ was questioned, and she eventually confessed that she was the one who had buried the body in this hasty, crude manner. She explained that she was from the town of Jirjā in Upper Egypt and that she had gotten pregnant there by a soldier who later deserted her to join his battalion in Cairo. She traveled to Cairo alone after her pregnancy started to show to search for her child's father, and she gave birth there two months prematurely. After talking to the local midwife and questioning two men who had taken pity on Faḍl Wāsiʿ and given her refuge, the police decided not to press charges for murder or manslaughter against Faḍl Wāsiʿ and her accomplices. It turned out that

Faḍl Wāsiʿ had endured a long and dangerous labor. After her ordeal, she and her "husband" (one of the men who had offered her shelter pretended to be the father of the baby) decided not to register the newborn because they could not afford to pay the registration fees and because Faḍl Wāsiʿ could not report the name of the real father. It was also revealed in the course of the police investigation that soon after the baby's death, Faḍl and her "husband" found themselves in a difficult situation since they could not report the death of a person who, as far as the authorities were concerned, was nonexistent. Accordingly, they decided to bury the body without performing any rituals and without informing the authorities.

In spite of the fact that the police did not press murder or manslaughter charges, Faḍl Wāsiʿ and her "husband" were still accused of violating three ordinances regarding public health. Specifically, they had violated the requirement that all newborns be promptly registered, the requirement that all deaths be reported, and the ban on intramural burial. Faḍl Wāsiʿ was found guilty of the offenses, and her case was forwarded to Majlis Ibtidāʾī Miṣr, the Cairo Council of First Instance, for a ruling.[1]

This chapter does not deal with teenage pregnancies, forensics, or policing. It deals, rather, with urban planning and public hygiene in nineteenth-century Cairo. So why open a chapter on the modernization of Cairo with a sad story of an unfortunate girl who lost her baby in what must have appeared to her to be an intimidating, large city? There are two reasons for this. The first is that Faḍl Wāsiʿ's story took place in what proved to be a highly strategic location that was full of symbolic significance for the history of modern Cairo and of modern Egypt at large. Close to the barracks where Faḍl Wāsiʾ buried her stillborn child, a new bridge across the Nile, the Qaṣr al-Nīl Bridge, had been built just seven years earlier. This bridge, the first steel bridge ever to be built across the Nile, features prominently in the historiography of modern Cairo. The bridge was erected, along with many hastily constructed buildings, to celebrate the inauguration of the Suez Canal in 1869. It was intended to be used exclusively by the illustrious guests attending the extravagant celebrations, who would be staying at the newly constructed palace across the river on the island of Jazīra (al-Jazīra Palace, now the Marriott Hotel), which the Egyptian ruler, Khedive Ismāʿīl (r. 1963–1879), had reserved for them.[2] Traditional historiography on this exciting period of Egypt's modern history stresses how Ismāʿīl's financial policies were ruinous to Egypt and highlights the disastrous economic impact of the celebrations accompanying the inauguration of the Suez Canal as an example of these imprudent policies. John Marlow, for example, argues that even though it was Ismāʿīl's insolvency and not his extravagance that turned Europe against him and helped depose him in 1879, his indebtedness could not have been helped much by such ostentatious display of wealth.[3] The story of the construction of Qaṣr al-Nīl Bridge, therefore, although a mere anecdote in the larger story of Ismāʿīl's extravagance and of the modernization of Cairo, fits perfectly into the grand narrative of elites, power politics, colonialism, and nationalist struggle. Faḍl Wāsiʿ's story, on the other hand, provides an antidote to this elitist historiography, reminding us that equally, if not more, profound stories were taking place *under* the bridge and suggesting that no narrative of Cairo's modernization in the nineteenth century is complete if it does not take Faḍl Wāsiʿ and others like her into account.

The second reason for starting with this rather sad story is that it is a story about odors and the olfactory sense. If it were not for the dog sniffing around, the children playing nearby would not have discovered the body, and the whole case would have literally remained buried, sharing the same fate as countless other similar incidents that went unnoticed by the authorities. Faḍl Wāsiʿ's story, therefore, points out the importance of smell in our telling of Cairo's grand narrative of modernization. Like the people under the bridge, the olfactory sense has been treated unjustly by historians of modernity. Consistently privileging sight over smell, historians of modern Cairo have all too often purged their accounts of the lingering stink of the city they write about, preferring to dwell on expansive views from imposing monuments; point out the insightful visions of city planners, cartographers, and landscape engineers; and describe the sublime sights of breezy, open-air promenades. Faḍl Wāsiʿ's story reminds us that an alternative story of the city can be told: a collective story of its inhabitants, who appear as lively, vibrant denizens and subjects of their own lives, not simply objects of some city planner's schemes or mere spectators to what was going on in their city. The olfactory sense can be our guide to writing the story of nineteenth-century Cairo by inviting us to revel in the fetid ooze lurking underneath the official history. This chapter attempts to detect in the records of the city's official history the accounts of mundane, quotidian life, full as it was with eating, defecation, urination, fornication, death, rot, and regeneration, and therefore to reintroduce Cairenes and their stench into the sanitized narratives of how their city was modernized.

VISION TRIUMPHANT: THE TRADITIONAL NARRATIVE

As we saw in chapter 1, the story of the modernization of medicine is infused with clear ocular-centric and Eurocentric features. As with the larger story of Egypt's modernization, this narrative typically begins in 1798, when the French under Bonaparte came to Egypt, bringing with them not only a mighty army but also the printing press and ideas of liberty, equality, and fraternity. The Egyptians, who had ostensibly been slumbering during the long, dark, Ottoman centuries, were shaken out of their complacency and idleness and urged to catch up with modernity. With regard to the modernization of Cairo, the French reorganized the city's administrative districts and consolidated the city's thirty-five *ḥarāt* (neighborhoods) into eight *atmān* (or *arrondissements*), and made changes to the city's street pattern. These so-called improvements, while motivated purely by military considerations, left their mark on the city for a long time to come.[4]

The next part of the traditional narrative of how Cairo was modernized is typically the long reign of Mehmed Ali Pasha. Mehmed Ali is usually described as having spared no effort in pulling Egypt into the modern age, and many of his policies appear to be modeled after those of the French and even of Napoleon himself. Yet this man, who is often dubbed the "founder of modern Egypt"[5] and is famed for his imaginative and dynamic reforms, was no Napoleon when it came to city planning and urban design. Except for making minor alterations to some open squares and constructing a couple of straight boulevards that the French had initially planned but could not execute due to standing buildings, Mehmed Ali goes down "in the history of Cairo in the rather prosaic role of housekeeper. Cairo and its problems never seemed to have captured his imagination."[6]

His successor, ʿAbbās I, earned an even more ignominious role in the annals of Cairo. Suspicious that the French and British had designs on his wealthy province, reputed to be a homosexual, and rumored to have a strange proclivity for Arabian horses and desert palaces, ʿAbbās attracted the wrath of historians and went down in history as a mad pervert.[7] Under his reign, ʿAbbās neglected Cairo, preferring to spend his resources on strange, eerie palaces.[8] ʿAbbās's successor, Saʿīd (r. 1854–63), fared only slightly better, appearing in nationalist historiography as a lethargic and opulent despot fond of eating pasta and addicted to everything French. Cairo didn't seem to interest him either, and with the exception of constructing a few buildings (most notably the Nuzhah Palace in Shubrā, to the north-west of Cairo, and the Qaṣr al-Nīl Barracks, which is where this chapter started and where the Ritz-Carlton Hotel is now located), Sa'īd does not seem to have been that concerned with his capital city.

1867: THE BIRTH OF "PARIS ALONG THE NILE"

It is only when Ismā'īl came to power that Cairo seemed to finally receive the full attention of Egypt's ruler. Ismā'īl radically transformed the city during the fifteen-odd years of his reign, not only by carving straight boulevards into its old core but also by building a completely new neighborhood, appropriately called Ismā'īliyya, to the west of the existing city. Most of the new construction radiated out of Azbakiyya (the area where the French occupation authorities had established their military headquarters), which thus became a nodal point connecting the old city with the new, French-inspired neighborhood of Ismā'īliyya. The story of the construction of Ismā'īliyya and the redesigning of Azbakiyya is interesting enough to warrant going through in some detail.[9]

It is very common to date the rapid transformation that Cairo witnessed in the late nineteenth century to an event that took place four years into Ismā'īl's reign, namely his visit to Paris to attend the International Exposition of 1867 and inaugurate the Egyptian pavilion there.[10] Ismā'īl had studied in Paris, so he was familiar with the Paris of the 1840s, but he was impressed by what Baron Haussmann, Napoleon III's enterprising prefect of the Seine, had accomplished in the French capital. Haussmann's successful street planning efforts had transformed the city's twisted, dank streets into wide and clean boulevards that crisscrossed at fixed intervals, giving rise to the famous places and roundabouts.[11] Soon after his return from this trip, Ismā'īl embarked on a feverish wave of construction activity with the aim of turning Cairo into a "Paris along the Nile" and giving it a facelift in preparation for the huge celebrations that he was planning for the inauguration of the Suez Canal the following year.[12]

To help him transform Cairo, Ismā'īl relied on 'Alī Mubārak (see figure 7), an old school friend who had studied with him in Paris, whom he appointed to head the Department of Public Works (Dīwān al-Ashghāl). In much of the scholarly literature that deals with the history of Cairo during this period,

FIGURE 7: ʿAlī Mubārak. Image from Amīn Sāmī, *Taqwīm al-Nīl* (Cairo: Dār al-Kutub, 1936), vol. 3, opposite p. 920.

Mubārak is portrayed as an impressively energetic official, one of nineteenth-century Egypt's most remarkable public servants. As the narrative goes, modern Cairo owes its very shape to his diligent, imaginative efforts. Born in a village in the Delta in 1823, he enrolled in one of the newly established government schools, a move that proved decisive in propelling him to become one of the most significant *fallāḥ*-born Egyptians to assume a senior public post. ʿMubārak was chosen to join a government-funded student mission to Paris in 1844, and he spent his five-year sojourn there studying French, engineering, and the principles of administration. He quickly distinguished himself. After returning to Egypt, he first assumed some menial posts, but after Ismāʿīl became ruler, he was given a prime appointment and rose to meteoric heights, eventually heading the prestigious Department of Railways (Dīwān al-Murūr wa'l-Sikka), Department of Public Instruction (Dīwān al-Madāris), Department of Religious Endowments (Dīwān al-Awqāf), and Department of Public Works, at times in charge of two or even three of the agencies simultaneously.[13]

The traditional accounts of Cairo's modernization also stress the fact that although Mubārak was not part of the large entourage that accompanied Ismā'īl to Paris in 1867, he did travel to Paris that year. Relying mostly on Mubārak's autobiographical sketch in his magisterial *Al-Khiṭaṭ al-Tawfīqīyya al-Jadīda,*[14] these accounts point out that in October 1867, a month after being appointed director of the Department of Pubic Instruction, Mubārak joined Ismā'īl at the International Exposition, where the Egyptian pavilion was reputed to have been among the most popular pavilions.[15] Officially, Ismā'īl sent Mubārak to Paris on a mission concerning finances, but it is plausible that Mubārak's actual assignment was to check out the Augean stables that Haussmann had cleansed with the aim of emulating Haussmann's urban planning efforts.

The trip that Ismā'īl and Mubārak made to Paris in 1867, therefore, occupies a central position in the story of modern Cairo, and it is usually seen as a decisive step in prompting the khedive to redesign Cairo along Parisian lines. Indeed, 1867 is considered a central date in the modernization of Cairo, just as 1798 is considered a crucial year in the modernization of Egypt at large. Immediately after returning to Cairo in late 1867, Mubārak was appointed head of Department of Public Works and entrusted with the daunting task of giving Cairo a facelift in preparation for the celebrations of the inauguration of the Suez Canal that would take place in two years' time. Realizing that the entire city of Cairo could not be "Parisianized" in such a short period, both the khedive and his energetic public works minister decided to limit their efforts and revamp Azbakiyya, the neighborhood in the west of the city where many elite Egyptians had their homes.[16] Specifically, Ismā'īl entrusted Mubārak with three main tasks: developing Azbakiyya; designing and executing a plan for the huge area that lay between the Nile and the western edges of the old city, which would be called Ismā'īliyya; and drawing up a master plan for Cairo. During 1868, just over five months later, Mubārak was busy working on the first of these three tasks: an opera house was constructed; the squares of al-'Ataba al-Khadra, Opera, and al-Khazindār were planned; and the park at the center of the quarter was completely redesigned by Jean-Pierre Barillet-Deschamps, the landscape engineer who had planned the Bois de Boulogne and the Bois de Vincennes in Paris.

Mubārak set about accomplishing the second task with equal diligence. A grid pattern for the new neighborhood of Ismā'īliyya was chosen, and, as in

Paris, statues of public figures would be erected, starting in the 1880s, in the roundabouts that were created at the intersections of vertical, horizontal, and diagonal streets.[17] Members of the Turkish-speaking ruling elite, as well as Arabic-speaking members of the government bureaucracy, were granted plots of land in the new district at nominal prices, and to prevent speculation, they were prohibited from selling their land for five years. During this period, the government reserved the right to retake the land if the owners showed no signs of initiating construction. Strict building codes were established to ensure that the planned villas and mansions were European, and not oriental, in style.

As impressive as these developments were, Mubārak's third task, drawing up a master plan of the entire city of Cairo, took a very long time, and the attempt to open up the heart of the old city for modern transport took even longer. A master plan for the city that was created in 1874 shows a series of main thoroughfares that were never constructed. Muḥammad 'Alī Street, which linked Azbakiyya to the Citadel, took thirty years to complete (1845–75). Work on Al-Muskī Street, also known as Al-Sikka al-Gadīda, the idea for which originated during Bonaparte's expedition, commenced in 1845, but the construction inched along at such a slow pace that ten years later it extended only to al-Naḥḥāsīn, less than half the way to the desert in the east.

THE TWO CAIROS

This is the condensed version of the standard narrative of Cairo's transformation in the nineteenth century. After many centuries of neglect, Cairo finally received the attention it deserved, and an ambitious urban development scheme was launched, the likes of which the city had not seen since Mamluk times. However, this attention was not distributed evenly throughout the city. In fact, Mubārak's efforts are seen to have led ineluctably to a dichotomous development in the city: on the one hand, a rapid transformation of the new area named Ismā'īliyya, extending from the western walls of the city to the Nile, took place, and on the other hand, a very slow and cumbersome opening up of the old city occurred. By the end of the century, Cairo did indeed look like a colonial dual city: to the east lay the "Oriental" city, with inward-looking, clogged, twisted alleyways and closed cul-de-sacs, and to the west lay the "Western" city, with open squares, straight boulevards, and clean air.

The visual separation of Cairo into two distinct halves was something that prompted contemporary travelers and travel guides, as well as subsequent historians, to refer to Cairo as a dual city, one that was divided and clearly segregated.[18] At the turn of the twentieth century, for example, a European visitor noted that "European Cairo . . . is divided from Egyptian Cairo by the long street that goes from the railway station past the big hotels to Abdin [Palace]. . . . It is full of big shops and great houses and fine carriages and well-dressed people as might be a western city. . . . The real Cairo is to the east of this . . . and . . . is practically what it always was."[19] The divide between the two Cairos appeared to be so absolute that an English visitor in 1889 remarked, with what Janet Abu-Lughod, preeminent English-language historian of Cairo, rightly characterizes as matchless condescension, "With the polo, the balls, the races, and the riding, Cairo begins to impress itself upon you as an English town in which any quantity of novel oriental sights are kept for the aesthetic satisfaction of the inhabitants, much as the proprietor of a country place keeps a game preserve or a deer park for his own amusement."[20] Abu-Lughod comments, "The old native city had been left relatively intact from the premodern age. . . . A new European-style city had developed parallel to it on the west and began to encircle it on the north, but this community remained socially and physically distinct. Each city had a predictable continuity of its own."[21]

1867 OR 1876?

This traditional account of the modernization of Cairo rests squarely on Mubārak's account as recounted in his *Khiṭāṭ,* and it is best expressed in Abu Lughod's magisterial 1970 study of Cairo as well as in numerous Arabic publications.[22] In the 1990s, however, Jean-Luc Arnaud questioned many of the central points of this narrative in his study *Le Caire, mise en place d'une ville moderne, 1867–1907.*[23] Specifically, Arnaud argues that Cairo owes its shape not so much to Ismāʿīl's visit to Paris in 1867 but to Egypt's bankruptcy in 1876 and the establishment, in that year, of the Caisse de la Dette Publique, which assumed control over the finances of the Egyptian government. Arnaud provides convincing evidence that many of Ismāʿīl's grand projects were abandoned at that point and taken over by private companies and speculators, which Arnaud argues precipitated the uneven development of the city and the lack of a coordinated urban policy.

Furthermore, Arnaud argues that very significant urban projects were completed in Cairo before Ismāʿīl's visit to Paris, thus challenging the centrality of that visit, which is usually seen as having affected the subsequent development of the city. Significantly, Arnaud's research was based on the Wathā'iq 'Aṣr Ismā'īl (Documents of Ismā'īl's reign), a large archival collection of mostly French documents housed in the Egyptian National Archives that has only rarely been consulted before. Arnaud uses these documents to vividly illustrate Ismā'īl's relations with foreign companies, private investors, different branches of his administration, and key figures in charge of developing Cairo. Unlike Mubārak's *Khiṭaṭ,* which naturally stresses the role played by the Department of Public Works, which Mubārak headed, Arnaud's study contends that the Wathā'iq 'Aṣr Ismā'īl documents shed light on other departments that contributed significantly to the development of Cairo. Among them were the Water Company, which was initially entrusted with important street-planning duties; the Department of Roads (Maṣlaḥat al-Ṭuruq), which was initially established within the Governorate of Cairo, and which fell under the jurisdiction of the Department of the Interior (Dīwān al-Dākhiliyya) and not of the Department of Public Works; and the Department of Public Parks (Maṣlaḥat al-Mutanazzahāt). The documents also highlight the important roles played by many individuals who had hitherto been viewed as only nominally involved in modernizing Cairo, such as Nūbār Pasha, who was head of the Department of Public Works before Mubārak took over; Jean-Antoine Cordier, the head of the Water Company; and P. Grand Bey, the head of the Department of Roads. Relying on these documents, Arnaud raises serious doubts about Mubārak's narrative, in which he is depicted as the sole mastermind of Cairo's development, and in doing so he presents a different picture of the city's evolution. Arnaud specifically criticizes Mubārak for attributing to himself many of the accomplishments of Grand Bey and argues that as far as modern Cairo is concerned, "Mubārak plays not an insignificant role; his, however, was only a secondary one."[24]

As valid as many of Arnaud's critical points may be, his account leaves many of the implicit assumptions of the old narrative unchallenged. By arguing that Grand Bey and Cordier rather than Mubārak should be credited with the pioneering work done in setting a street plan for the city, Arnaud makes an important correction to the historical record. However, important questions are left unasked: What were the reasons behind this urban reconstruction (regardless of who undertook it), and was it aesthetics or other considerations that informed it? Furthermore, while some of the public works that took place before 1867 are highlighted in Arnaud's study, the centrality of Ismāʿīl's visit to Paris is not effectively questioned, and consequently, the Eurocentric implications of the Paris-as-model argument are left intact. If anything, that argument gains more credibility from Arnaud's near exclusive dependence on the French documents of the Wathā'iq 'Asr Ismāʿīl, which, by their very nature, give rise to a picture wherein European companies dictate the shape of the city at least from 1876 onward.

Finally, the ocular-centric narrative of the modernization of Cairo is also left intact, if not bolstered. While Abu-Lughod attributes the apparent division of Cairo into two cities to the positive impact 1860s Paris had on Ismāʿīl and to the fact that the khedive did not have enough time to transform his entire capital into Paris on the Nile and thus had to satisfy himself with giving a facelift to the elite quarter of Azbakiyya, Arnaud argues that the uneven development of the city was due to the 1876 bankruptcy and the subsequent inability of the central government to implement its master plan for the city, which forced it to allow European companies to take over. Abu-Lughod and Arnaud suggest different reasons for the division of the city into two unevenly developing halves, but both take as their starting point a visual sign, the *apparent* division of the city as evident from the map. In other words, both arguments depict the city as a text that can be read backward, as it were, to reveal the underlying urban policies (or lack thereof) that gave it its modern shape. By privileging sight, therefore, this ocular-centric narrative is blind to the possibility that other hidden concerns and subterranean fears might have informed urban policies, which, in turn, might have shaped the city in unseen ways.

A TRIP TO THE BELLY OF THE CITY

We get a whiff of what these other concerns and fears might have been, interestingly enough, by reading Mubārak's account of his 1867 trip to Paris, which is embedded in the autobiographical section in his magisterial *Khiṭaṭ*. Unlike his compatriot Rifāʿa al-Ṭahṭāwī, who described his own trip to Paris some forty years earlier in a text[25] that dwelled at length on visual themes, with extensive descriptions of spectacles, theatrical performances, and mirror-lined cafes,[26] Mubārak's description of Paris contains hardly any visual descriptions of the City of Light, even though he was seeing Haussmann's radical reconstructions for the first time. Indeed, what is remarkable about Mubārak's narrative is that it says nothing of the wide boulevards, the new department stores that lined them, or the luminous cafés and restaurants that were frequented by middle- and upper-class flâneurs. Nor does Mubārak, who had already been appointed as head of the Department of Public Instruction, describe his visits to the city's schools and libraries in much detail, devoting only two lines to these institutions of learning.

What did pique his interest, however, were Paris's sewers. "These are huge constructions," he explained, "with very high vaulted roofs, built beneath the streets of the city, to which one can have access through stairwells that open to the streets and which also allow in air and light." After describing in detail the subterranean canals through which water flowed and the boats that carried curious passengers on tours of the sewers, and after giving a detailed account of the mechanism that propelled these boats, he marveled at how the water that circulated in the sewers, which was composed of nothing but the "refuse of toilets and kitchens and rain water, had been flushed in a precise manner that rendered it odorless in spite of its volume and sheer quantity." He concluded by remarking how "beneficial this construction is, by which the city managed to get rid of the heavy rainwater, its refuse and its filthy smell."[27]

Mubārak was commenting on what was universally recognized as one of Haussmann's most marvelous achievements. The prefect of the Seine had consciously opened the newly constructed sewers to the public so that they could "experience an otherworldly environment devoted to mastery of a former locus of fear and disgust."[28] Visitors, including important dignitaries and even foreign royalty, marveled at how the old reeking, dirty, and dangerous *égouts* and *cloacas* of Paris were transformed into the tidy and orderly new sewers where only the water was unclean: "Everything else, walls, flooring, roofing, the cars [where the visitors sat], the boats, the clothing of workmen, all are the perfection of neatness."[29]

This lengthy reference to sewage and very brief mention of libraries and schools by one of celebrated men of the Egyptian nineteenth-century Enlightenment is not surprising. For in addition to being one of the most enterprising ministers of the Department of Public Instruction and rightly famous for his efforts in efforts in spreading education, founding schools, and establishing libraries, Mubārak was also a civil engineer, and as director of the Department of Public Works, he was among the many designers of modern Cairo. More importantly, Mubārak was also one of Egypt's main public hygienists, and his contemporaries recognized that his attention to issues of public health emanated from his conviction that these issues constituted some of "the most important national matters."[30] Mubārak's extensive report on the Paris sewers was therefore more than an observation of the fascination these sewers triggered from the wider public. Given Mubārak's intimate familiarity with Cairo's public health problems, which were not dissimilar to those Paris had suffered from during his student years, his detailed description of the Paris sewers is testimony to his recognition that Haussmann's subterranean olfactory achievements were no less significant than his ocular accomplishment of reordering of the streets of Paris, and one can even detect in Mubārak's account a faint trace of envy.

THE PREHISTORY OF MODERN CAIRO

Soon after his return from Paris, Mubārak handed Ismā'īl an ambitious thirty-four-article plan to reorganize the street pattern of Cairo and control the construction companies working in the city.[31] The goal was to thoroughly organize the building activity within Cairo by dividing the city into eight districts, starting with the core of the old city and ending with the most remote suburbs. Even though this plan fell short of the minimum requirements for the city's development, such as having "a sufficient budget and precise, intelligent [urban] legislation,"[32] it was hailed as a pioneering attempt to remedy Cairo's problems, given that it "at least identified the problem and, in so doing, suggested the beginning of a solution."[33]

In spite of the fact that it was turned down by the khedive and thus never implemented,[34] this plan is revealing of the desire to overcome many of the administrative problems facing Cairo, which included inadequate funds, an insufficient number of administrators, delays in adjudicating legal cases as a result of new city planning ordinances, and violations of Tanẓīm codes.[35] Drafted in 1868, the plan can be seen as giving credence to the argument that the International Exposition of 1867 in Paris, attended by Ismā'īl and his minister of public works, "provided a model for the new city and stimulated the motivation for it."[36]

Nevertheless, it would be an exaggeration to argue that this plan ushered in a new phase of state concern about street planning and construction activities in Cairo. In fact, as is argued below, there is ample evidence that Egypt's rulers had been concerned about Cairo's streets, buildings, and even its appearance long before the Ismā'īl's visit to the French capital in 1867. André Raymond, for example, shows how Ottoman governors during the seventeenth century paid considerable attention to cleaning up rubbish mounds and clearing the Ḥākimī and Nāsirī canals.[37] And ʿAbd al-Raḥmān al-Jabartī mentions the case of Mehmed Pasha, the Ottoman governor of Egypt from 1699 to 1705, who ordered the awnings of shops to be removed to widen the roads and the markets. He also ordered the streets to be leveled and excavated "until the foundations were uncovered."[38]

1844: THE FIRST CAIRO PLANNING COUNCIL

During Mehmed Ali's reign, contrary to Abu Lughod's argument that the Pasha paid no attention to Cairo, there is compelling evidence that many ordinances were passed to improve the capital city. In late 1843, a key institution was founded to oversee the organization of the city. This was the famous Majlis Tanẓīm al-Maḥrūsa (Cairo Planning Council), or simply the Tanẓīm, which was to play a very significant role in such activities as street planning, issuing building and renovation permits, dealing with religious endowments (*awqāf;* singular *waqf*), and implementing and revising many ordinances pertaining to public hygiene. Unlike the Majlis al-Urnāṭū, Alexandria's municipal council, which had been established in 1834, the Tanẓīm has never been the subject of an independent study, even though it is often referred to in secondary literature.[39] This may be due to the fact that the Tanẓīm was never an independent council but always a branch of a larger administrative body. For the first twenty years of its existence, it was part of the Department of Public Instruction.[40] In 1863, it was taken under the jurisdiction of the Cairo Governorate, and in 1866, it became part of the Department of Public Works.

This lack of financial and administrative independence notwithstanding, the Tanẓīm indelibly marked Cairo, not only after 1863, the year of Ismāʿīl's ascension, but even during its first twenty years of its existence.[41] As far as can be ascertained, the first decree related to this important municipal body was the founding decree, issued in December 1843 by ʿAbbās Pasha in his capacity as governor of Cairo and addressed to the head of the Department of Public Instruction. In this decree, ʿAbbās stipulated that the new council take Alexandria's Majlis al-Urnāṭū as a model and concern itself with beautifying Cairo and setting its streets straight.[42] A short time later, the Tanẓīm was formed and presided over by Edhem Bey, head of the Department of Public Instruction. Its members included the Cairo Police Commissioner (Ma'mūr

Ḍabṭiyyat al-Maḥrūsa); Clot Bey, head of the Health Council; Hekeyan Bey, former head of the School of Engineering; director of the Department of Public Buildings; Linant Efendi, the chief engineer of the Nile Barrages (al-Qanātir al-Khayriyya); Muṣṭafā Bahjat Efendi, head of the Engineering Unit (Ra'īs Qalam al-Handasa) within the Department of Public Instruction; Dr. Duvigneau, a member of the Health Council; and Charles Lambert, head of the School of Engineering.[43]

This council was to meet every Sunday morning to go through the many requests for building permits presented by the public.[44] One of the council's main criteria was that all new construction and all renovations be build along straight lines. Another issue that the Tanẓīm frequently had to address was how to deal with *waqf* buildings. In the absence of general guidelines, the Tanẓīm dealt with such issues on a case-by-case basis.[45] Another duty of the council was to evaluate property that was designated for demolition to make room for new streets.[46] The Tanẓīm was also entrusted with the mammoth task of naming streets, numbering houses, and installing street signs.[47]

THE 1859 DECREE OF CAIRO STREET PLANNING

Under Sa'īd and Ismā'īl, a number of decrees predating Mubārak's 1868 decree about building codes were passed aimed at organizing Cairo's streets and easing traffic. The first of these decrees was issued by Majlis al-Khuṣūṣī (the Privy Council), in 1859.[48] The preamble to this decree mentions that an earlier draft had been prepared the previous year by Linant Bey, the chief architect and head of the Architecture Unit (Sirr Muhandiss wa Nāzir Qalm al-Handasa). The earlier draft included many stipulations regarding organizing Cairo (*tanẓīm al-Maḥrūsa*), widening its streets and alleyways, and easing its traffic. The earlier draft, the preamble states, also stipulated the payment of taxes on the city's carriages and on protruding balconies. It also set pecuniary punishments in the form of fees for violations of building codes and traffic laws and for obstructing free passage in streets and alleyways. When these stipulations were presented to the Ma'iyya (the Khedive's Cabinet), serious objections were raised to the idea of fines, and an alternative system of punishments was suggested. As to the funds needed to compensate landlords whose property had been expropriated, the Ma'iyya suggested setting aside a fixed sum of five hundred *kīsa*s annually for that purpose. No exact figure was set for funding for other large city planning projects (such as building new streets), but the Department of the Interior was instructed to write to the Maʿiyya directly with an estimate of the amount needed. Once approved by the Maʿiyya, an order would be issued to the Department of Finance (Dīwān al-Māliyya) to release the monies needed.

With these general guidelines established, a committee composed of the directors of the Department of Religious Endowments, the Department of the Interior, the Department of Finance, and the Department of Foreign Affairs was formed within the Privy Council, and it came up with a comprehensive decree with nine sections and a conclusion. Named the Decree of Neighborhood Planning (Qānūn Tanẓīm al-Ḥārāt), it formed a ten-member Tanẓīm Committee (Mashūrat al-Tanẓīm) headed by Linant Bey and including among its members a chief architect (*miʿmār*), the Cairo Police Commissioner, the deputy of the Department of Health Inspection (Wakīl Mufattish al-Ṣiḥḥa), and a building inspector (*mufattish al-tanẓīm*). This committee was entrusted mainly with the important task of widening and straightening the existing streets as well as planning new streets and squares. The committee was authorized to use maps that were to be drawn by a special Cartography Unit (Firqat al-Rusūmāt), which would supervised by the committee, and it was to rely on these maps in its street planning activities. Different types of streets with specific widths were designed, and different regulations were applied to them. For example, all *kharjāt* (protrusions) had to be elevated at least 4.5 meters above street level. On streets that were 8 to 10 meters wide, *kharjāt* could not extend over 1 meter; on streets that were 6 meters wide, *kharjāt* could not extend over 0.75 meters; and on streets that were 3 to 4 meters wide, *kharjāt* could not extend over 0.5 meters. Strict regulations were set to prevent any obstruction of passage in the streets. Special attention was given to the rubble produced by building and construction activities, and certain locations were specified to dump this rubble in. Vegetable and fruit sellers were prohibited from exhibiting their merchandise in thoroughfares. Carpenters, barrel makers (*barmīlgiyya*), coppersmiths, marble cutters, and people engaging in any activity that could block the main street were likewise prevented from obstructing traffic. There was also an attempt to set speed limits on carriages passing through different kinds of streets, although these limits were necessarily imprecise (the decree refers to "medium speed" and "slow speed").

The decree also established an important Inspecting Unit (Taftīsh al-Tanẓīm) that was headed by an inspector (*mufattish*) whose job was to conduct inspections with a team of architects of all buildings to be renovated, refurbished, or demolished. He also regularly toured the city's streets to make sure that the building codes and Tanẓīm lines were strictly followed.

With regard to punishments, the decree stated that persons who carried out unauthorized construction on their property would be required to demolish the new structures at their own expense. Owners had three days to remove the rubble resulting from construction activities on their property, after which they would be sentenced to *ta'zīr,* the shari'a-stipulated physical punishment that varies according to the status of a person and his or her social standing. The same punishment was stipulated for merchants of all trades who did not remove their merchandise from public thoroughfares. Owners of coffeehouses were similarly punished if they put chairs and tables in the main street; however, they were given special dispensation during religious festivals (*mawlids*), when pilgrims from rural areas came to the city and swelled its population. In fact, *ta'zīr* was the preferred punishment for most offenses, and, as has been said above, the decree avoided establishing pecuniary penalties.

Finally, the decree allowed for the expropriation of property only in exchange for monetary compensation. The amount of the compensation was established case by case by experts chosen by both the landlord and the Tanẓīm. A landlord who wanted to build on a piece of land that he owned needed to apply to the Tanẓīm for a building permit. If the council decided to expropriate a portion of the land to comply with Tanẓīm lines, no compensation would be paid if the area was less than one-fifth of the owner's total land area; however, if it exceeded one-fifth, then the Tanẓīm would pay the market price of the area in excess of one-fifth of the area.

THE 1866 *WAQF* DECREE

Seven years after this important decree had been issued, another significant decree was passed concerning *awqāf* that dealt specifically with the question of whether or not shari'a allowed for the possibility of exchanging *waqf* domains.[49] Since it was commonly believed that once a building had been designated as *waqf,* it could never be dealt with as private property again and therefore could never be expropriated for urban planning purposes, the decree referred to *waqf* "as one of the most important obstacles to urban development [*'umāriyya*]." In an attempt to get around this obstacle, Khedive Ismā'īl wrote to the Privy Council to discuss the matter, and the council, in turn, asked 'Alī Efendi al-Baqlī, the mufti of Majlis al-Aḥkām, to give his opinion on this delicate matter. Al-Baqlī issued a detailed fatwa in response in which he opined that if the originator of the *waqf* (*al-wāqif*) had specifically ruled out the possibility of exchange (*istibdāl*), then the *waqf* could never be exchanged. However, if *al-wāqif* had not made such explicit stipulation, and if the *waqf* domain had fallen into ruin over the years so that it no longer yielded any income for its upkeep and for the benefit of its beneficiaries, it would be legal to exchange it for a more profitable domain or even for cash. If the domain in question was not completely ruined, al-Baqlī added, according to the great jurist Abū Ḥanīfa and his first disciple, Muḥammad Ibn al-Ḥasan al-Shaybānī (d. 805), it could not be exchanged. But according to Abū Ḥanīfa's second disciple, Abū Yūsuf (d. 798), an exchange was still possible if a different domain could be found that would yield a higher income (presumably in the case of agricultural land) or that was better located (in the case of urban property). Al-Baqlī went on to cite other leading religious authorities, including the Palestinian jurist al-Ramlī (1585–1671) and the Damascene scholar Ibn 'Abidīn (1783–1836), to give weight to his argument that it was indeed lawful to exchange *waqf* domains, in some cases even for cash.[50]

On receiving this unambiguous opinion, the Privy Council issued a recommendation to Ismā'īl to allow for the exchange of *waqf* properties, "as this will lead to urban development and the public good" (*kamāl al-'umāriyya wa al-manfa'a al-'umūmiyya*).

THE 1866 TANẒĪM ORDINANCE

In 1865, Ismā'īl remarked in an order to his interior minister that he had read a draft decree that had been prepared by the Department of Public Works that standardized the width of streets. However, he did not find that draft to be satisfactory as it could not guarantee "the free circulation of air, which is the main cause for good public hygiene," nor was it clear enough to ease traffic congestion. Ismā'īl also remarked that he had recently viewed a report about slums (*hīshān*) within the city in which packs of riffraff (*ri'ā'*) were piled on top of each other. "Given how crowded these slums are," Ismā'īl wrote, "and given their filthy, squalid condition, they pose a grave danger to the health of their inhabitants and to people residing close by." He concluded by suggesting that the slums be emptied and that their inhabitants be moved to buildings specially constructed for this purpose in each quarter, even if this entailed considerable expense.[51]

On receiving this order, the Privy Council set up a committee composed of the deputy of the Department of Public Works (Wakīl Diwān Ashghāl 'Umūmiyya), the chief architect of the Tanẓīm (Mi'mār wa Nāẓir Qalm al-Tanẓīm), the deputy of the Architecture Unit (Wakīl Qalm Handasa), the chief health inspector of Cairo (Mufattish al-Ṣiḥḥa), the chief investigator of the Tanẓīm (Mufattish al-Tanẓīm), and the building inspector (Ma'mūr Kashf al-Amākin). The committee came up with the Tanẓīm Ordinance (Lā'iḥat al-Tanẓīm), which is composed of six sections. Unlike the 1859 Decree of Cairo Street Planning, which it effectively replaced, this new decree was not concerned only with Cairo; it set out to establish *tanẓīm* councils in Alexandria and other towns and cities (*mudun wa banādir*).[52]

One of the clear features of this decree was the importance it gave to maps. Section 2 of the decree stipulated that general maps be made for each city to the scale of 1:1000. These maps were to be used by the *tanẓīm* councils of each city to demarcate the lines of new streets and *mīdān*s and the lines of the old streets. The decree acknowledged that this process would take a considerable amount of time, stating, "In order for the tasks of the *tanẓīm* councils not to be delayed until the completion of these maps, whenever a landlord requests to demolish or build his property overlooking public streets, the chief architect of the *tanẓīm* council has to draw a detailed map to the scale of 1:500 of the property in question extending to fifty meters from either side of the said building." Like the previous decree, the new one established various widths for different kinds of streets. Furthermore, it stated, "every care should be given to straighten old streets as much as possible; new streets have to be absolutely straight. Old buildings such as mosques, synagogues [*hayākil*], water fountains [*asbila*], and cemeteries [*maqābir*] are not to be demolished."[53] The new decree followed the previous one in stipulating that expropriated property be compensated by the government if its size exceeded one-fifth of the original plot. One major deviation from the previous decree was the punishment system: the new decree contained no mention of *ta'zīr* and instead specified a system of fines and administrative penalties.

'UMĀRIYYA, SHARI'A, AND PUBLIC HYGIENE

While the abovementioned decrees are in no way an exhaustive list of the laws and ordinances that concerned Cairo during the khedival period, they do highlight a number of challenges to the traditional narrative of how Cairo was modernized in the nineteenth century. One of these is that concern about the city and its development predated Ismāʿīl's much celebrated visit to Paris in 1867. As we have seen from this small sample of decrees pertaining to city planning, Egypt's rulers from the time of Mehmed Ali onward and the countless officials and bureaucrats who worked for them were acutely concerned about al-Maḥrūsa, or the "Protected City," the name by which Cairo was known for much of the period under consideration. As shown above, and as is discussed further below, decrees were issued as early as the 1830s to improve the status of the city's public health, security, markets, streets, and buildings. Therefore, to bemoan the fact that Cairo has always lacked an independent municipal body that would allow it to control its own destiny rather than be at the mercy of the whims of Egypt's rulers[54] is to concentrate on what Raymond has called the Orientalist description of a "noncity," a city which is seen only through the prism of what it lacked in comparison to European cities, namely the regularity and institutions of the cities of antiquity and the communes of medieval towns.[55] Such a view (of which Gabriel Baer is the best representative)[56] overlooks the significant efforts of the numerous administrative bodies established to improve Cairo's public hygiene, security, and economic development.

However, the problem with the argument that Paris served as the model for Cairo's development is not solely that it ignores all the city planning efforts that predated Ismāʿīl's visit to the French capital in 1867. The main problem is that the traditional narrative fails to identify what motivated these efforts and explain how these motivations might have evolved over time. In other words, while the above-quoted city planning decrees from the late 1850s and early 1860s show a concern about straight lines and exhibit a clear understanding of the intricate connection between cartography and urban design, concerns that assume paramount importance under ʿAlī Mubārak and Grand Bey in the late 1860s and early 1870s, what informed these earlier concerns is still not explained, and it would be erroneous to assume that they simply prefigured the later ones in a teleological manner.

So what informed these early concerns about city planning that Egypt's rulers and their numerous bureaucrats expressed long before Ismāʿīl and his energetic minister of public works visited Paris in 1867? Without ruling out aesthetic considerations altogether, undoubtedly one major consideration was a concern about urban growth and expansion. We find evidence of this concern in the term *ʿumāriyya,* which can be translated as construction, urban development, urbanity, and even civilization, and which was ubiquitously mentioned in numerous decrees and government correspondence. The preamble of the April 1866 decree mentioned above concerning *waqf*, for example, mentions that "khedival thoughts have always been directed to whatever would bring *ʿumāriyya* and enhance it."[57] The October 1866 decree states that "demolition permits are being given to tear down walls overlooking the public thoroughfares with the pretext of renovating property and therefore [these permits should be stopped as they] make it difficult to set streets straight and therefore prevent the enhancement of *ʿumāriyya*."[58] An 1870 decree issued by the Privy Council approving a recommendation of the Legislative Assembly (Majlis Shūrā al-Nuwwāb) stated that "one of the prime objectives of the khedive is . . . the enhancement of progress [*taqaddum*] and *ʿumāriyya*."[59]

Besides the obvious definitions of growth and expansion, *ʿumāriyya* also denotes productivity. As Timothy Mitchell has explained, productivity and abhorrence of waste were key concepts that were assuming increasing importance in the mindset of Egyptian officials in the khedival period,[60] and we find them shaping much of government policy regarding not only urban planning but also agriculture, education, the military, and numerous aspects of social life.[61] In addition to these modern connotations, *ʿumāriyya* clearly has strong echoes of Ibn Khaldūn's famous key term *ʿumrān*, and it would not be farfetched to argue that the meaning of *ʿumāriyya* has been directly influenced by it.[62]

Moreover, the different city planning decrees and regulations passed in the nineteenth century paid close attention to shariʿa principles as elaborated in classical *fiqh*. There are many examples in the decrees mentioned above that testify to the importance town planners gave to shariʿa. Mention has already been made of the extreme care that was given to finding a shariʿa-based solution to *waqf* domains, which were seen as an obstacle to *ʿumāriyya*. Rather than declaring *waqf* to be an obsolete system not conducive to modern aims of urban planning, the nineteenth-century town planners and administrators solved the problem with the shariʿa notion of *istibdāl*.

The stipulation that violations to building codes and traffic regulations be punished by *taʿzīr* rather than by a system of fines is another example of how administrators did not consider *fiqh*-based principles to be inherently contradictory to the goals of modern city planning. A further example of how shariʿa informed many city planning ordinances under the khedives is the stipulation in the 1859 decree that a religious scholar, and in this case specifically Shaykh Ismāʿīl al-Ḥalabī of Majlis al-Aḥkām, be on the Tanẓīm committee.[63] Lastly, the 1859 decree referred explicitly to shariʿa when it stated that the qadi courts, rather than the *tanẓīm* councils, were competent to consider cases of disputes over breaches of privacy that resulted when a person opened a window on another person's property.[64]

As was discussed in chapter 2, it is commonly argued that shari'a was increasingly marginalized in nineteenth-century Egypt (and in the Ottoman Empire at large) and that it lost ground to secular laws in the fields of state organization and legislation. However, the many ordinances pertaining to city planning and the copious government correspondence related to it dating from the 1830s to the late 1870s clearly illustrate that shari'a was not only upheld but actually informed many measures regarding city planning and urban policy.

PUBLIC HYGIENE AND CITY PLANNING

Apart from being informed by the concept of *'umāriyya* and the principles of *fiqh,* many of the decrees, laws, and ordinances that governed Cairo in the nineteenth century were mostly shaped by an incessant desire (one can even call it an obsession) to improve public health. Indeed, I argue that concern for public hygiene was the most important factor influencing urban planning and that the fear of epidemics and the measures taken to combat disease and improve public hygiene were much more significant than the aesthetic concerns implied in the Paris-as-model argument. Due to the paramount significance of public hygiene, the rest of this chapter reviews a number of the most important public health measures that had a direct bearing on how Cairo was shaped throughout much of the nineteenth century.

The Cairo that 'Alī Mubārak directed his seemingly inexhaustible energies to helping was suffering from serious problems, including an antiquated street system that could not cope with the increased volume of traffic, weak municipal structures that had to confront the mammoth task of redesigning the city, inadequate funds, and an insufficient number of administrators. However, as was the case in pre-Haussmannian Paris, one of Cairo's most acute problems, which was readily recognizable to Mubārak and, as will be shown below, to many urban planners before him, was the deplorable state of public health. More than any aesthetic improvements Ismā'īl made to impress his foreign visitors, it was the concerted efforts to ameliorate the city's health condition and improve public hygiene that shaped Cairo's dramatic transformation in the nineteenth century. Chief among these public hygiene problems was getting rid of the city's waste, a problem that the gradually evolving public health policy aimed to tackle. Other problems that were targeted with equal diligence were the practice of intramural burial; the lack of strict regulations on slaughterhouses, butchers, and fishmongers; and the dilapidated state of water management in a city that had within it many bodies of water that were stagnant for most of the year. Common to all these issues is that they were considered to be sources of bad stench, which was feared literally like the plague as it was thought to carry within it the very essence of death.

BAD AIR

The notion that stench was responsible for spreading disease can be traced all the way back to Greek medical writers and classical and medieval physicians, who considered illness to be the result of some disturbance in the natural balance of the four bodily humors: yellow bile, black bile, phlegm, and blood. The Greeks believed that imbalance of these four humors caused the symptoms of disease, but the question was, what caused the misbalance of the humors in the first place? A concept that seemed to provide the answer to this crucial question was that of miasma, a concept that was of an imprecise nature and that had shifting definitions over time but that was related, in its original Greek meaning, to pollution or a polluting agent. Linked to the belief, prevalent since the days of Hippocrates (c. 450–370 BCE), that the environment affected health and disease, miasma seemed to provide an explanation for how disease occurred: air tainted by miasma caused outbreaks of disease, as those who inhaled or were exposed to this contaminated air experienced an imbalance of their humors and subsequently fell ill.[65]

While the precise nature or character of these miasmas remained undefined, it was generally thought that they could be detected by their foul smell. The "thick airs" or miasmas (referred to as *'ufūna, aryāh, awkhām,* etc.) emanating from stagnant lakes, decomposing animal or human bodies, excreta, decaying vegetables, and sick persons were thought to carry the very essence of disease.[66] This connection between the environment and etiology remained in place well into the nineteenth century, when it was challenged by the so-called contagionist theory, which argued that disease was an exogenous entity that attacked specific organs or structures of the body. For most of the nineteenth century, the battle between these two rival theories could not be decisively won. If anything, the miasmatists seemed to be gaining ground as they could point out that even though miasmas could not be detected by scientific instruments, they revealed their existence through their smell.[67] It is this common understanding of the nature of "thick airs," miasmas, and the olfactory sense on which Mubārak and many public hygienists before him based their campaign against such sources of stench as cesspools, stagnant lakes, tanneries, cemeteries, slaughterhouses, fishmongers, and refuse dumps. The idea was that the fetid smell of these places was not simply offensive to the olfactory sense but was morbidly dangerous, and therefore no effort should be spared in making these places more salubrious.

In Egypt, the story of the preeminence of the miasmatic theory in the nineteenth century is a checkered one. From the time he founded the Qaṣr al-'Ainī Medical School in 1827, Clot Bey was more inclined toward the contagionist model in matters related to training medical students. He modeled instruction at the new institution on the Paris school of medicine, which embraced Giovanni Battista Morgagni's focus on individual organs as the site of pathology. In his writings, Clot Bey seems to have rejected the idea that miasmas caused disease:

> Disease is a condition contrary to health that arises from one or more organs of the human body undergoing a change which in turn results in a deficiency in the function of this or these organs. . . . The causes of some diseases are known, while others are unknown, . . . [but] every disease has its symptoms that signify its presence. . . . Some people delve into the nature of disease [only] by guessing. Some say it is caused by a corruption in the humors or an increase in their quantity. . . . Some say it is due to unknown miasmas. The sane person, however, has to reject these views and to know that the human body is composed of liquids and solid substances, the latter being more numerous. It has been determined by experiment that most diseases originate in the solid parts and only rarely in the liquids. Even when the liquids undergo some change, this change is not independent but is a result of a change already undergone in the tissues. It has to be known, therefore, that it is the solid parts that are affected by disease and not the liquids.[68]

In some respects, the Egyptian medical establishment in the nineteenth century followed these general principles, which were ultimately influenced by techniques closely associated with the Paris school, namely comprehensive medical examinations, scrupulous autopsies, and regular recording of morbidity and mortality statistics.[69]

However, although he followed the contagionist model when teaching, Clot Bey was a staunch miasmatist when it came to matters related to public health. In this realm, he was deeply suspicious of the contagionist viewpoint, to the point of being dogmatic. In 1840, for example, he asserted that "all enlightened men, 'except Italians and Spaniards,' had abandoned the idea of contagion for scrofula, scabies, leprosy, ophthalmia, phthisis, dysentery, typhus, yellow fever, and cholera as well as the plague. He shuddered at the 'ridiculous and barbarous custom' of the Romans who segregated pulmonary consumption patients from other patients in their hospitals."[70] In simultaneously holding on to these contradictory positions (contagion theory in matters of medical instruction and miasmatic theory in matters of medical practice and public hygiene), Clot Bey was sharing in the confusion of many of his contemporaries when it came to understanding what caused disease. During the first half of the nineteenth century, the techniques of medical training associated with the Paris school had become standard in hospital procedure, emphasizing localized, specific pathological phenomena, but "the majority of practitioners [in France] continued to follow the Greco-Roman humoral system, relying on the time-honored purges, emetics, sudorifics, and above all, blood-letting of traditional depletion therapy."[71] Even someone like Xavier Bichat, who more than anyone else contributed to the final triumph of clinical medicine, held similar self-contradictory views. While he insisted on isolating disease and localizing it in tissues, he strongly believed that miasmas also carried disease. He believed, for instance, that the odor of the wind he broke while dissecting corpses was affected by the putrid air emanating from the cadavers, explaining that corrupt air emanating from the corpses must have penetrated his skin while he conducted his autopsies.[72]

MIASMAS AND OTHER DEADLY VAPORS

If one discards vision and instead allows the olfactory sense to be one's guide to the history of Cairo, then one can easily realize that concern over Cairo's poor public health—a concern that was informed by the miasmatic theory and that predated Ismā'īl's fabled visit to Paris—shaped the city in more important ways than the ostensibly aesthetic ones that are stressed in Paris-as-model accounts. Worry about the stench of Cairo's streets can be detected in various sources even before the nineteenth century. Al-Jabartī, for example, quotes his favorite poet and close friend, Ḥasan al-Ḥijāzī, complaining of the filth and stench of the streets of Cairo which, the sardonic poet said, contained "seven evils: urine, feces, mud, dust, rudeness, noise, and the inhabitants of the streets themselves, who resemble ghosts of a cemetery."[73] During much of the Ottoman period, even though Cairo lacked a municipal authority that could coordinate the efforts of street cleaning, cleanliness was not completely ignored, and it was left to local residents to sweep and water the streets, sometimes with the help of professional sweepers (*zabbālīn*).[74] In the nineteenth century, however, stress was put on public hygiene, and the cleanliness of the streets of Cairo assumed unprecedented importance. The campaign to found a municipal authority became closely tied to efforts to improve the city's sanitation. In 1830, for example, the Department of Civil Affairs (Dīwān Khidīwī) ordered the superintendent of Cairo's Department of Public Works (Ma'mūr Ashghāl al-Maḥrūsa) to implement a new ordinance aimed at cleansing the streets of the city. "Due to the state of public safety that Cairo currently enjoys," the ordinance read, "every effort should be directed to cleaning the streets and alleyways of the city as this will undoubtedly have an impact on the city's general appearance and on its public hygiene. Accordingly, the heads of the neighborhoods [*mashāyikh al-atmān*] will henceforth order the residents to sweep and water the area in front of their houses. Sentries will go on regular rounds to check on the cleanliness [of the city] and to punish the recalcitrant with light beating."[75]

Five years later, a more detailed decree was issued to control the stench of Cairo's streets. It said that in spite of the existence of latrines (*murtafaqāt*) in the city's many mosques, rural migrants and the poor and the blind were in the habit of relieving themselves in the streets:

> Since these nasty deeds contribute to increasing stench and the emission of various miasmas [*al-'ufūna wa-l'awkhām al-muta'didda*], causing harm to the dwellers of the city, and since it has also been noticed that the dwellers of houses overlooking the Khalīj [the main waterway that bisected the city] are flushing their dirty waters into it [*biyuṭliqū murtafaqāt al-manāzil*], . . . it was decided to appoint a special police officer who will head a force of six soldiers and who will pass regularly by the streets and alleyways of the city to make sure that they remain clean. On spotting anyone easing nature in the public way, [he will punish this person severely,] and on catching anyone dumping rubbish either in the Khalīj or on the streets, he will have the door of this person's house nailed for three days.

The ordinance added that seven years previously, the fields flanking the main road leading to Būlāq had silted up due to people dumping their garbage there. A special police force composed of soldiers paid a monthly salary of thirty piastres each was created to stop this habit.[76] Health officials on regular inspection tours would write reports to the head of Cairo's police to inform him of the filthy spots where people urinated and defecated so that he could make sure that measures were taken to prevent this practice.[77] Particular attention was given to areas that were partly hidden, which gave some degree of privacy, such as the latrines attached to mosques[78] and the old gates of the city, which "have ceased to function as such and which are now used as spots behind which people urinate, making them a source of miasmas [*awkhām*]."[79] Under 'Abbās, and contrary to traditional accounts, which depict him as having been uninterested in Cairo, the city's health conditions, and especially the quality of the air circulating in its streets, continued to receive official attention. In 1852, for example, 'Abbās's deputy issued a decree revising an earlier one that required all streets to be sprinkled with water to settle the dust: "Since people are in the habit of throwing dirty water from their windows onto the streets and thus rendering them dangerous because of miasmas [*al-'ufūna*], and since the winter sun is not strong enough to dry these streets which are usually already damp, it is heretofore decreed that streets are to be only swept [and not sprinkled with water] during winter months. Wide streets, [on the other hand,] that receive enough sunshine and whose dust can be settled only by watering can be sprinkled with water according to the regulations."[80]

This and other decrees reflected a general distrust of water and humidity, since it was believed that humidity "relaxed the fibers, thinned the humors, and therefore . . . resulted in susceptibility to putrefaction."[81] At the same time, however, there was also what appeared to be a suspicion of dust. Given the general fear of miasmas, subterranean soil constituted a deep source of danger. As in Paris, what lay under the streets of Cairo was thought to contain "the excremental past of the city, ready to burst forth again at any opportunity: a fissure in the ground, the digging of a well, an excavation for a building foundation."[82] Thus, the repeated orders that were issued to make sure people who were carrying out renovations or demolitions removed the resulting rubble were aimed not only at preventing obstructions to traffic[83] but also, as was explicitly mentioned, at avoiding dust, because leaving this rubble in the middle of the streets was "contrary to health principles" (*mukhālif li-uṣūl al-ṣiḥḥa*).[84] Sprinkling streets with water, as harmful as it was thought to be if done in excess, "was necessary to settle the dust and prevent the resulting mephitis" (*li-ajl hubūṭ al-atribah wa man' al-wakhāma al-ḥāṣila*).[85] Extreme vigilance had to be used in making sure that the "carts used to remove the rubble to outside the city limits be tightly covered, for it has been noticed that these carts lose half their freight in the streets and alleyways before reaching their destination. Moreover, to save themselves the trouble of going to the designated dump areas outside the city, the drivers of these carts deliberately open the lids of their carts and dump their cargo on the way."[86]

This suspicion of dust also lay behind the repeated orders to whitewash buildings. Walls were thought to be dangerous surfaces that, through capillary action, sapped the subterranean noxious effluvia and released them into the air. In Paris, the city's stone and brick buildings were a source of alarm due to their porous nature, which drew the "mephitic sap . . . though the foundation . . . and released [it] into the atmosphere."[87] In Egypt, where houses were often built with limestone and sometimes even with unbaked mud bricks, walls were considered to be infinitely more dangerous. Clot Bey, therefore, insisted that all buildings in Cairo be whitewashed to prevent "miasmas and filth" (*al-ʿufūna wa-l-qadhūrāt*).[88] It seems that his repeated ordinances to that effect were taken too seriously, for he received information that people were not only whitewashing the exterior walls of buildings but also painting wood and marble columns in mosques. He responded that people should desist from this practice, as it had no obvious health benefit. "This is like gold-platting diamonds, . . . [and it] will be the butt of jokes by [European] tourists," he added in his typical sarcastic manner.[89]

Decomposing bodies were another source of grave danger to the city. Throughout the nineteenth century, a perceptible move to segregate the living from the dead was taking place. Strict ordinances were issued forbidding burial within cities, and these ordinances were vigorously applied in Cairo.[90] Burials in cemeteries that were within the city limits were stopped, and residents who used to bury their dead there were offered alternative places that were thought to be at a safe distance and where the earth had been leveled properly.[91] Once interned, bodies were not to be exhumed unless very special orders had been issued.

Like human remains, human waste was a source of acute concern for the health authorities, and Cairo's cesspools and latrines were the subject of numerous decrees and ordinances, which attempted to limit the morbific vapors emanating from them. The issue was how frequently these cesspools were cleared, for in spite of orders that the waste be cleared regularly, inspection visits by the health officers occasionally discovered cesspools that had not been cleared for months on end. In one such visit, a health inspector found out that a given cesspool had not been cleaned for 150 years, and "given that this cesspool was not tightly sealed and was on the path of the wind, it is feared that it becomes a source for material that will corrupt the air and cause epidemics."[92] According to miasmatic theory, cesspools should be cleared only at night, "for fear of the health of the inhabitants."[93] The reasoning was that fewer people passed through the streets at night and the danger of them "inhaling the disgusting smells" was therefore at its minimum. The dangerous waste matter should then be transported to designated spots outside the city, where it would be buried and covered carefully with dust, "thus the miasmas and mephitis would be prevented, saving people from danger" (*fa-ʾalā hadhā tamtaniʿ al-ʿufūna wa-lʾrāyḥa al-karīha wa-lʾmuḍirra ʿan ʿibād Illāh*).[94] Other regulations were issued to make sure that cesspools were clearly marked to prevent people from accidentally falling into them and incurring serious injuries.[95]

Food sellers trading in items that emitted pungent smells, especially butchers and fishmongers, had their merchandise subjected to scrutiny. Inspection tours by the Department of Health Inspection of Cairo (Dīwān Taftīsh Ṣiḥḥat al-Maḥrūsa) would typically report any activity in food markets that they considered to emit "miasmas that are harmful to public health" (*ʿufūna . . . muḍirra biʾl-ṣiḥḥa al-ʿumūmiyya*).[96] All such food vendors were required to have a special permit before opening their shops.[97] *Fisīkh,* a particularly pungent type of salted fish, attracted close attention, and its sellers were prohibited from opening their shops on main, crowded thoroughfares. It was suggested that such shops be lumped together in one area, as had been done with butcher shops.[98] Above all, slaughterhouses and tanneries were a nightmare for authorities. Given their particularly dangerous nature, as they dealt with animal parts that were considered prime sources of miasmas, tanneries had been the subject of acute concern even since Ottoman times. According to Raymond, both the governor and the chief judge of Cairo were instructed as early as 1552 by the imperial center in Istanbul to "move the tanneries to a corner of the city . . . where they will not be noxious to the city within walls."[99] Throughout the second half of the nineteenth century, repeated inspections of slaughterhouses and tanneries revealed that these workshops were causing great harm to the city because they did not have proper ventilation inside, were located on the path of the wind, or had poor drainage systems, resulting in stagnant ponds that exacerbated the threat of miasmas.[100]

As dangerous as the dank streets of Cairo were, and as alarming as its cesspools, cemeteries, butcheries, and slaughterhouses were, the most serious threat to the city's health was thought to come from the many bodies of water that dotted it. Even though Cairo did not extend to the shores of the Nile until late in the nineteenth century, the city had numerous lakes, which were fed by an intricate but antiquated canal system that was connected to the great river. When the annual floodwaters receded, the lakes were left stagnant, emitting what were believed to be dangerous fumes and miasmas. These marches and lakes, which had played a central part in the lives of Cairo's denizens for centuries, were now viewed by the health authorities with grave suspicion and deep concern. Even Azbakiyya Lake, the largest lake in the city, around which the country's elite had built their houses at the end of the eighteenth century and throughout the first half of the nineteenth century, was considered a threat. From as early as 1846, Clot Bey's Health Council was concerned about the water in the lake. One of its reports stated that it "had acquired characteristics harmful to public hygiene" (*iktasabat al-awṣāf al-muḍirra lil-ṣiḥḥa*).[101] The following year, Mehmed Ali himself ordered Edhem Bey, the head of the Department of Public Instruction, to look into the source of the miasmas emanating from the lake and take necessary measures to deal with the dangerous effluvia.[102] Plans to reorganize the canal system of Cairo made it feasible to drain the lake,[103] and this was done in 1848.[104] Yet even after the lake had been filled in and turned into a park, the small ponds that the landscape engineers had retained were still considered a threat to public health. During one of their regular tours of the city, the director of the Department of Health Inspection of Cairo and Grand Bey, director of the Cairo City Planning Council, discovered that the water in these ponds was stagnant and could cause serious health hazards. Both men wrote to the Cairo Governorate asking for an engineer to be fetched immediately to devise ways to make the water flow constantly so that it did not stagnate in the ponds.[105]

Furthermore, in the late 1840s and early 1850s, the lakes of al-Raṭlī, Qāsim Bey, and al-Fīl were filled in.[106] Regular inspection tours did not spare so much as a small puddle that was discovered in front of the house of a certain Khurshid Pasha in the elite quarter of Azbakiyya.[107] Even public fountains whose troughs were discovered to be leaking were a cause of alarm as the resulting puddles were thought to emit "filthy miasmas that are harmful to public hygiene" (*rawāyiḥ ʿafina wa muḍirra li-ṣiḥḥat al-sukkān*).[108] All in all, according to one of the staunchest miasmatists, Muḥammad Ali al-Baqlī, who was one of Clot Bey's most illustrious students and eventually became the director of the Qaṣr al-ʿAinī Medical School, a total of 605 lakes were drained in Egypt between 1866 and 1867, and 3304 lakes would later be filled in.[109]

THE PROBLEM WITH THE KHALĪJ

Although the miasmatists triumphed in their all-out campaign against the stench, filth, and morbific effluvia of Cairo's numerous lakes, they were less successful in combating the dangers posed by the Khalīj (see figure 8), the narrow waterway that bisected the city from south to north, drawing its water from the Nile. The Khalīj had been constructed long before the nineteenth century.[110] Dry for most of the year, it was filled only during the flood season, when the ancient ritual of dam-cutting at Fumm al-Khalīj ("the mouth of the canal") was performed with great pomp. After this annual ceremony, the water would flow through the canal, supplying water to the city's numerous water carriers, who supplied water to the different residential quarters and government buildings until 'Alī Mubārak succeeded in creating a relatively reliable municipal water delivery system. (In *Al-Khiṭaṭ,* he boasted that thanks to his efforts, 150,000 meters of pipes had been laid out, supplying 10,764,580 cubic meters of water to the city each year.)[111] But it was during the dry season that the Khalīj was considered a serious health hazard to the city.[112] The inhabitants on both banks of the narrow canal were in the habit of throwing their rubbish into it, and every winter, after the floodwater had receded and the mouth of the Khalīj had been closed, complaints came pouring in of the dangerous fumes rising out of the waterway.[113]

One of the remedies suggested was that the whole Khalīj be lined to create an inclining slope so that the water would constantly run through it and not stagnate or acquire a bad smell.[114] Eventually, however, it was decided that the Khalīj would be cleaned manually each year by night soil men who had experience in cleaning cesspools.[115] However, these measures were not successful, and in 1870, after seventy-one "doctors and Europeans" (*ḥukamā' wa khawāgāt urubāwiyyīn)* presented a petition urging the health authorities to do something about the suffocating stench of the waterway, the original ban on flushing toilets and throwing refuse into the canal was reimposed "to forestall the possibility of an outbreak of an epidemic."[116] The controversy about the Khalīj and how to resolve its health hazards continued for much of the nineteenth century, ceasing only in 1898 when the canal was finally drained and filled in and its route used to construct Cairo's first tram line.[117]

FIGURE 8: Al-Khalīj, c. 1870. Image from Marcel Clerget, *Le Caire: Étude de géographie urbaine et d'histoire économique* (Cairo: Schindler, 1934), unnumbered page at the end of vol. 1.

PROBLEMS WITH THE MEDICAL ESTABLISHMENT

Part of the reason it took such a long time to deal with this grave source of danger was the oscillation between these two alternatives: draining the Khalīj or keeping it permanently flooded. Each option presented its own engineering and financial challenges. On the one hand, flooding the canal all year round posed the danger of turning it into a source of miasmas if the water did not run smoothly, which, as has been shown, the authorities were struggling to do. On the other hand, draining the Khalīj would have meant doing away with the annual dam-cutting ceremony, a ceremony that was presided over by the ruler of Egypt and occupied an important place in the Egyptian political, social, and religious calendar going back to Mamluk times, if not earlier. Mostly, however, the draining option seems to have been opposed by wealthy people with houses overlooking the Khalīj, who drew water from the canal in the flood season to water their gardens and used it as a dumping ground for their refuse during the remainder of the year, thus saving on the cost of paying water carriers and building cesspools. Year after year, the health authorities received complaints that the owners of houses lining the banks of the Khalīj were throwing their refuse into the canal, and Clot Bey realized as early as 1847 that the owners of these houses were the ones opposing his efforts to have the Khalīj filled in.

In one of his typically sardonic letters, Clot Bey gave a concise assessment of the social and even international context of his department's efforts to improve Cairo's olfactory situation. The letter was addressed to the Department of Civil Affairs, which acted as the interior ministry, and which shortly thereafter incorporated his own department, Shūrā al-Aṭibbā, as one of its branches. Clot Bey started by saying that water had stopped flowing in the Khalīj for sixteen days and that in spite of this, the inhabitants of houses overlooking the canal were dumping their refuse in it, causing the emanation of heavy fumes that were adversely affecting the entire city. He added that he entered into similar correspondence with the Department of Civil Affairs each year but that no actions were ever taken. He added: "We have to insist that some miasmas [*aryāḥ*] should not be considered a private matter, for they have an impact on public health. [I concede that] the subject of the water that is used to irrigate private gardens does not fall squarely within the issue of [public health and] the spread of disease. Yet the Shūrā and the Quarantine Board have both come to the conclusion that there is nothing that causes a greater danger to the public health of Cairo than the Khalīj." He threatened that he would have no option but to inform a delegation of French doctors about to visit the country that in Egypt, "the principles of public hygiene are forgotten and none are applied." Quarantine restrictions would result in delays in the free movement of persons and goods from Cairo. He advised that the canal be drained into the Nile and its bed cleaned of filth and rubbish and then planted with barley and that strict orders should be given and enforced that no refuse was to be deposited there.[118]

Clot Bey's frustration at his inability to carry out his public hygiene plans was not restricted to the Khalīj; he encountered less than encouraging understanding from his superiors in many other areas as well. For example, after being entrusted by Mehmed Ali to design a nationwide plan for the reconstruction of Egypt's villages and to rebuild peasant dwellings to be more hygienic, he was baffled by the subsequent series of petty bureaucratic queries from his superiors. Missing out on the fundamental purpose of the plan and dwelling instead on minute, inconsequential details, the Department of Public Instruction (which supervised some aspects of Clot Bey's Shūrā al-Atibbā) wrote to the French doctor inquiring about the recommended length of the reeds needed for the roofs of the proposed new peasant houses. Clot Bey responded with clear frustration:

> I have received the letter concerning the reeds needed for the rooftops of the newly renovated peasant houses. I have to admit that I could not understand the connection between health matters and this question. Nevertheless, I venture with the following answer as far as my mind allows me. First, no roof can be covered except by using wooden beams. Second, as far as health matters are concerned, there is no difference between short and long reeds that would be necessary to cover these wooden beams. Third, if the intention of dwelling on the length of reeds is to argue that they could be used instead of wood and could therefore help in cutting down on cost, then this would mean that these houses would necessarily have to be so small as to render them unhealthy and unfit for human habitation. Since Your Excellency was kind enough to address us concerning this matter, we are more than delighted to remind Your Excellency that the intention of His Highness [Mehmed Ali] was to rebuild and renovate the villages in the entire country of Egypt. For this purpose, he has allocated the sum of 50,000 purses, and this is something that has been published in *Al-Waqā'i' al-Miṣṣriyya* [the official gazette] and was reported by all European newspapers. Ultimately, the aim is to improve the health of the population [*ṣiḥḥat al-'ibād*]. But now we have spent a whole year with only three villages being rebuilt. Accordingly, and God willing, at this pace we will need four thousand years to renovate the villages of Egypt.[119]

While these rancorous letters are partly a reflection of Clot Bey's fiery temperament, they are also revealing of serious structural problems that plagued the Egyptian public health establishment, which Clot Bey complained of in numerous other letters. One such problem that has already been alluded to was the lack of financial and administrative independence of the Shūrā al-Aṭibbā, the main medical body that supervised medical and public hygiene matters from 1825 until it was disbanded in 1856.[120] During its existence, the Shūrā was a division first of the Department of War and then of the Department of the Interior (first called Dīwān Khidīwī and later changed to

Dīwān al-Dākhiliyya). Furthermore, in supervising the Qaṣr al-ʿAinī Medical School, the only teaching hospital in the country, the Shūrā was headed and controlled financially and administratively by a third department, the Department of Public Instruction. It was a lack of coordination between the different government bodies to which it had to report that frustrated the Shūrā and its head, Clot Bey.

Moreover, beneath this tension lurked a more basic social and political struggle between the different ethnic and linguistic groups vying for dominance in khedival Egypt. When, back in 1825, Clot Bey had managed to convince the Pasha to found a medical school to train the doctors needed for the army, he made a strategic decision to use Arabic, rather than Turkish or French, as the language of instruction. As we saw in the introduction, his logic was that this was the only way to ensure that the country's doctors could communicate with their patients. This decision had serious consequences as it meant that Arabic-speaking Egyptians, often with rural origins, had the opportunity to acquire a skill that was proving to be of crucial significance for military, educational, and urban planning purposes. The medical diplomas that the Qaṣr al-ʿAinī graduates received allowed them to elbow their way up the social ladder and challenge the power and status of the Turkish-speaking aristocracy. One cannot help but notice that Clot Bey's frustration might have stemmed from the fact that the Department of War and the Department of the Interior (and to a lesser degree the Department of Public Instruction) were dominated by members of this Turkish-speaking aristocracy. Even though he repeatedly stressed that "members of the Shūrā [and by implication, the entire medical establishment] had no purpose in mind except to serve this [medical] establishment and could not be accused of nepotism or favoritism,"[121] it is possible to detect in his letters an attempt to protect the budding medical establishment, which was composed mainly of Francophile Arabic-speaking doctors, in its competition with the Turkish-speaking aristocracy. Furthermore, the fact that members of the Turkish-speaking aristocracy had the power of the purse did not make this latent socioethnic struggle any easier.

On a different level, Clot Bey's correspondence reveals another tension within the medical and public health establishments, a tension that was directly related to matters of urban planning. This tension sprang from the question of whether it was the physician or the engineer who was best suited to undertake the mammoth task of supervising the process of urban reconstruction, and it was clearly felt within the Tanẓīm, the first municipal body to improve the condition of Cairo. Although the Tanẓīm was entrusted with handling many public hygiene issues, the fact that the body had six engineers and only two physicians on its nine-member board (the ninth member was a police officer) was an indication of the relative importance given to engineers in urban planning. This caused Clot Bey to feel increasingly marginalized, and when he saw that that his recommendations on issues literally concerning life and death were not heeded, he stopped attending the meetings of the Tanẓīm altogether, prompting a rebuke from the head of the Tanẓīm. Clot Bey penned the following response:

> I received your letter in which you requested my presence next Tuesday,[122] . . . and [noted] that I had been missing a number of meetings. . . . It is therefore necessary to remind Your Excellency that the reason that I am counted among the members of the Tanẓīm [in the first place] is because of [my expertise in] health matters. I have attended several meetings in which we discussed matters pertaining to public hygiene, such as removing tanneries, draining lakes, and finding a way to make sure that the water of the Khalīj flows regularly. . . . However, none of these matters has been resolved. So if there is some vital matter that requires my presence, then I will obediently attend. But to the best of my knowledge, there are no public health matters more important than those that I have just mentioned. And since we have already discussed these matters and our decisions have not been implemented, [then there is no need for my presence], and if you request my presence to discuss such matters as straightening streets or organizing some shops, then this could be done by the engineers, as this is their specialty.[123]

This struggle between engineers and physicians does not mean that matters of public hygiene were dismissed. Rather, and as was the case in England and France at the time, it was believed that the role of physicians was to identify the source of dangers threatening the city, whereas the role of engineers was to devise ways to combat those dangers. At the same time that Clot Bey was struggling to empower his physicians in their competition with engineers, Edwin Chadwick in London was convincing the public in England that sanitation problems were best tackled by engineers, not physicians. In 1865, he wrote: "The great preventives—drainage, street and house cleansing by means of supplies of water and improved sewerage, and especially the introduction of cheaper and more efficient modes of removing all noxious refuse from the towns—are operations for which aid must be sought from the science of the civil engineer, not the physician, who has done his work when he has pointed out the disease that results from the neglect of proper administrative measures, and has alleviated the sufferings of the victims."[124]

These struggles between physicians and engineers and between the Arabic-speaking, Francophile graduates of Qaṣr al-ʿAinī Medical School and members of the Turkish-speaking aristocracy helped shape Egypt's emergent public hygiene policy. To add to the complexity of the situation, this policy was also shaped by the lack of administrative and financial independence of the medical establishment.

THE ESSENCE OF CAIRO

Taking the olfactory sense seriously casts serious doubt on the validity of the Paris-as-model ocular paradigm; moreover, it also leads us to question the dual-city paradigm that sees Cairo as having developed in a bifurcated manner that gave rise to two unevenly growing halves. As shown above, the urban planners, influenced as they were by the miasmatic theory of etiology, did not limit their energy or restrict their activity to the new western half of the city. From as early as 1830, the heads of Cairo's ten neighborhoods were required to supervise the sweeping and watering of the streets in their districts. By 1846, a special police force had been established that included public health physicians and made daily rounds of all streets in each neighborhood. On finding anything that could potentially be a health hazard, the inspectors would immediately summon the head of the neighborhood to resolve the matter.[125] By the early 1870s, this system had evolved into a meticulous regime whereby the resident doctor of each neighborhood (*ḥakīmbāshī al-tumn*) conducted a daily round each morning accompanied by "health soldiers" (*ʿasākir khidmat al-ṣiḥḥa*) to inspect the cleanliness of the neighborhood. Residents with rubbish found in front of their houses were fined 20 piastres; shopkeepers with "water or rubble and the like" in front of their shops were fined 5 piastres.[126] The copious records of the Department of Health Inspection of Cairo attest to the thorough manner in which all neighborhoods of the city, not only the newly constructed Ismāʿīliyya, were subjected to close sanitary scrutiny. On the map, the city might have appeared divided into two halves, but despite this visual division, the miasmas that wafted through Cairo were not held by demarcation lines, real or imagined, and the health authorities and urban planners therefore felt obliged to direct their seemingly inexhaustible energies to all districts of the city.[127] The "Oriental" half of the city was not left to rot in filth and squalor.

Nevertheless, the division that appeared on the map was a real and not imagined one. However, it had its logic in class distinctions and not in an essential racial otherness that often informed colonial dual-city policies. As discussed earlier in this chapter, the building codes that were established for Ismāʿīliyya were intended to turn the new quarter into a neighborhood for the rich and famous. Furthermore, considerations of class and not race were what shaped many of the measures that attempted to regulate and control the smells drifting through the city. One thing that immediately comes across from reading the petitions presented to the Department of Health Inspection is that the upper classes, whether the Europeans residing in Egypt, the Ottoman-Egyptian class, or the local indigenous urban elite, shared the new sanitized olfactory sensibilities introduced by the authorities more than members of Cairo's lower classes did. For example, even after special areas of the city had been designated for the sale of *fisīkh,* a number of Europeans complained that they found the odor so offensive that they could not even tolerate the passage of the *fisīkh* merchants down the streets on their way to their new shops.[128] Similarly, a man named Ḥusayn Efendi Hāshim, who, judging by his title, Efendi, was probably an upper-middle-class government employee, complained about the two food shops beneath his upper-story apartment. The Department of Health Inspection investigated and found out that, indeed, a *fisīkh* merchant and a grilled meat vendor (*kabābjī*) had opened their shops on the street level. Neither of them had a license to open such shops in the residential neighborhood, and both were fined, the first twenty piastres and the second, forty.[129] ʿAbdallāh Efendi Muṣṭafā, a senior official in the Department of Finance, presented a petition complaining of the "heavy air" emanating from the vacant land (*kharāba*) adjacent to his house in the elite quarter of Azbakiyya; the Department of Health Inspection wrote to the resident doctor of the neighborhood to investigate the area at once.[130] Ḥasan Pasha Sirrī complained of the vapors emanating from the lake in front of his house in Būlāq.[131] An Englishwoman by the name of Mrs. Elite, who was living in an apartment beneath the Kūm al-Shaykh Salāma Mosque in al-Muskī, the Frankish quarter, went to the police station in person to complain about the stench and dangers vapors emanating from the cesspool of the mosque. When the Department of Health Inspection investigated, her complaint was found to be "in its place," and prompt action was taken to improve the smell of the area.[132]

The class dimension of these complaints and indeed of many of the health measures themselves can also be detected in the numerous reports that the

Department of Health Inspection wrote summarizing the findings of regular inspection tours throughout the city. While the department routinely reported all cases of what they considered to be violations of the stringent health standards that had been established, regardless of location or perpetrator, they often made sure to point out if any given offense was taking place outside the house of a notable individual, along the regular route of the khedive, or to the north (i.e., on the "wind path" [*'alā rīḥ*]) of the palatial dwelling of a pasha or a society lady (*sitt*).[133] These class considerations are explicitly mentioned in reports referring to the health condition of the elite quarter of Azbakiyya. For example, one stated that "this quarter should be cleaner than all other quarters . . . since it is where the European residents live and it is where the European consulates are located."[134]

HOW COLONIAL WAS MEDICINE IN KHEDIVAL EGYPT?

The dual-city model, therefore, appears not to be applicable to khedival Cairo, not only because of its confining ocular illusions and its inability to factor in olfactory considerations but also because the racial matrix that typically informs this model in such places as the colonial cities of French North Africa and the British Raj was missing in Cairo. Although the visual division of the city into two halves was strikingly similar to divisions in colonial North African cities, Cairo's urban planners were neither informed by the same principles that informed the French colonial urban administrators in North Africa nor burdened by the same concerns and political imperatives as those French administrators. The rationale behind urban polices in late nineteenth-century Egypt was strikingly different from those in, say, colonial Morocco, where there was a need to draw a contrast between the "modernist vision of formal order [as represented by] smooth white planes of building facades aligned along broad straight boulevards, and an exotic dream of voluptuousness" as represented by the "Islamic" medina.[135] For even though Cairo appeared to be divided into two halves at the end of the nineteenth century, the urban policies that gave rise to this division did not derive from the incessant desire to create a sharp distinction between a European city that represented rationality and order and a Muslim city that stood for tradition and backwardness. In other words, neither Khedive Ismā'īl nor 'Alī Mubārak nor even Lord Cromer was moved by the same principles that inspired Hubert Lyautey, the French resident-general in Morocco, namely using architecture and urban design to illustrate the innate differences between the Orient and the Occident and "protect certain aspects of cultural traditions while sponsoring other aspects of modernization and development, all in the interest of stabilizing colonial domination."[136]

Cairo's development in the nineteenth century does not seem to have been informed by the same principles that gave rise to British urban policies in India either. In Indian cities, British health officials and urban planners could not visualize a unified Indian social body. Rather, they insisted on seeing the cities of the Raj as bifurcated into two sections: one for the white British colonists and the other for the colonized natives. Given their deeply entrenched belief that India was the breeding ground of disease, the British felt the need to segregate the colonial elite from the colonized masses and create hygienic European havens "that were separated from the swampy, malarial grounds of the native population. . . . Such hygienic enclaves were expected to reduce the threat to European health posed by Indians."[137] Furthermore, this anxiety about the health and security of the empire was based not only on the belief that India was a distinctly diseased *environment* but also that Indians were an inherently diseased *people*. Their customs and habits, beliefs and rationality, and bodies and souls were found lacking.[138] It was on these shortcomings that the British colonial project was predicated. Since they believed that the Indians were unable to inculcate habits of self-discipline and internalize European notions of sanitation and personal hygiene, the British felt obliged to shoulder the burden of governing India and civilizing the natives. In the process, however, they had to protect themselves from succumbing to the very dangers that they had come to alleviate. This led to the development of an urban policy whose main task was "to seal the cordon sanitaire, not to improve the conditions of the populace."[139]

The health policies that were developed in Egypt in the nineteenth century were not predicated on these ideas. Nowhere do we see Clot Bey, his European or Egyptian colleagues, or any of the Egyptian, Arabic-speaking medical students arguing that the Egyptians were *inherently* diseased. Egyptians might have had many unhealthy habits, their environment might have been unhygienic, and their bodies might have succumbed to endemic disease, yet there was nothing elemental or natural about this state of affairs. There was no essential obstacle that prevented Egyptians, in Cairo or elsewhere, from adopting healthier habits or living in more salubrious environments. There was no one in the Egyptian health establishment who argued that the Egyptians were "inoculated by time and habit" against innovation, as the chief commissioner of Benares in India said of Indians in 1888.[140]

The medical self-help literature that seems to have flourished in Egypt from the 1870s onward similarly shows that although the ignorance and poverty of the Egyptians seriously alarmed the establishment, there was nothing in the religious or cultural beliefs of the populace that was thought to constitute an insurmountable obstacle to raising health standards. When the medical community had identified the main pathogens of disease and the different public health authorities had implemented ambitious hygienic measures, the authors of these countless self-help pamphlets, most of them practicing doctors, directed their attention to the daily practices of Egyptians that they thought were amenable to change. Gradually, the abject poverty of the lower classes appeared as the main culprit.[141] "The ignorance of some people" (*jahl baʿḍ al- ʿāmma*) was the reason rubbish, dead animals, and the contents of toilets were dumped in the Nile and its many canals, resulting in "the greatest harm."[142] Peasants were reproached for living in dark, damp rooms and for raising chicken, geese, and rabbits inside their houses.[143] Attention was therefore directed away from slaughterhouses, stagnant lakes, and cemeteries and toward the interior of houses. "To achieve the cleanliness a house," a popular 1893 booklet about how to combat cholera asserted, "it is not enough to whitewash its external surface. . . . Rather, the interior of the house . . . should also be cleaned, especially the kitchens of large households, latrines, and the dwellings of the poor."[144] Special consideration was given to the quality of air inside the house: windows should be opened at certain times of the day to allow for proper ventilation;[145] overcrowding should be avoided at all costs;[146] plants, flowers, and food should not be allowed inside bedrooms;[147] and so forth. Domestic latrines received the closest attention, with specific recommendations made about the amount of water needed to flush toilets,[148] the shape and weight of the ideal toilet cover,[149] the best time of year to clear the cesspools, and so on.[150]

While much of this literature singled out ignorance (especially of peasants and the urban poor) as the main cause of disease, one cannot help but notice a basic, fundamental belief in the possibility that the poor could abandon unhealthy practices and adopt more hygienic ones. Nowhere do we see these doctors bemoaning the fact that the poor were sticking to their unhealthy habits. If anything, doctors often pointed out that with proper guidance, the poor were quick to pick up proven medical remedies. One doctor remarked, for example, that during the 1882 cholera epidemic, the entire population of the Sayyida Zaynab neighborhood, totaling some 150,000 residents, were all spared the ravages of the disease because they frequented his clinic and used a particular remedy he had concocted.[151] Similarly, these doctors never saw Islam as an obstacle to a more hygienic lifestyle; in fact, many of them spared no effort in proving that their modern medical practices were supported by numerous verses from the Quran and hadiths of the Prophet.[152]

Cairo's public health officials, therefore, as well as the administrators of the medical establishment of the country at large, did not base their practice on a belief in the absolute otherness of Egyptians in the way medical authorities during the Indian Raj did. Even when the miasmatic theory of disease etiology was prevalent, neither the French doctors in Egypt nor their Egyptian colleagues ever thought of Egypt as a distinctly diseased environment. More importantly, even if Cairenes, and Egyptians in general, were thought to have been living amid their own filth and to have been mired in their own squalor, they were not trapped by unreformable habits nor shackled by their religious beliefs. In the countless memos, ordinances, and laws that were written and issued by public health officials with the aim of improving the health standards of the country, we do not find any reference to the Egyptian body as a "specter of filth and error,"[153] which is largely how the Indian body was imagined. Rather, the laws, regulations, pamphlets, and books that dealt with public hygiene reveal an impressive belief in the capability of Egyptians to change their filthy habits, give up their unhygienic practices, follow healthy regimens, and function as self-governing, self-knowing citizens. The elegant sovereignty-discipline-governmentality triangle that Foucault identified for Europe seems to be equally applicable in khedival Egypt, where, unlike in India, medicine could not be described as colonial.[154]

CAIRO AS A EUROPEAN CITY

A good example of how racial anxieties did not inform urban planning policies in Egypt can be found in a detailed 1874 report on the public hygiene dangers confronting Cairo and how best to deal with them. Written by Cairo's chief health inspector (most likely Martini Bey) and submitted to Khedive Ismāʿīl, the report is important enough to warrant a close look.[155]

The report listed five major sources of dangerous stench—the Khalīj, cemeteries, slaughterhouses, sewers, cesspools—and proposed practical ways to

TABLE 1 Deaths in Cairo, AH 1284–88

Year	Number of deaths
AH 1284 (1867–68 CE)	14,911
AH 1285 (1868–69 CE)	15,155
AH 1286 (1869–70 CE)	16,161
AH 1287 (1870–71 CE)	16,570
AH 1288 (1871–72 CE)	16,365

SOURCE: DWQ, Majlis al-Khuṣūṣī, S/11/8/22, doc. no. 10, pp. 12–14, AH 17 Shawwāl 1291 / 27 November 1874 CE.

deal with each of them. The report recommended that strict orders be issued forbidding people from throwing their rubbish into the Khalīj to prevent it from silting up. It advised that cemeteries be moved beyond the city limits and that all intramural burials be banned. It suggested that the northern slaughterhouse be closed down as it was close to the daily route of the khedive and on the path of the northern winds, thus causing harm to the city. It recommended that the southern slaughterhouse be renovated and enlarged so that it could accommodate the hygienic slaughtering of all animals needed for the entire city. Finally, with respect to sewers and cesspools, it recommended a drastic rearrangement of collecting the *qalta*—the solid refuse in the city's cesspools. The report calculated that Cairo, with a population of 450,000 inhabitants, produced 225,000 tons of feces annually, and it argued that the city needed at least four hundred carts to remove that amount of human waste. However, the report noted that the number of carts currently available was sufficient for only one of Cairo's ten quarters. Moreover, the sites designated as dumping ground for this refuse were deemed dangerously close to the city, and there were vacant plots within the city that were littered with human excrement. The report therefore recommended fencing off the vacant plots of land within the city in which people defecated, increasing the number of carts to remove *qalta,* hiring more people to do this job, dumping the *qalta* at faraway sites, and turning the *qalta* into manure so that it could be productively reused.

As detailed as these observations of the olfactory condition of Cairo were, what is most significant about the report is how it reached the conclusion that the most serious threat to the city's salubriousness was not the Khalīj, cemeteries, or cesspools but overcrowding. The report reached this conclusion by

TABLE 2 Deaths in Cairo by neighborhood, AH 1289–90

	Deaths in AH 1289 (1872–73 CE)					Deaths in AH 1290 (1873–74 CE)				
	Adults		*Children*		*Total*	*Adults*		*Children*		*Total*
Neighborhood	M	F	M	F		M	F	M	F	
Azbakiyya	465	510	729	627	2,331	461	469	740	671	2,341
Bab Al-Sha'riyya	332	422	589	564	1,907	356	407	618	548	1,929
'Ābidīn	208	344	415	402	1,369	212	293	444	424	1,373
Darb al-Gamāmīz	666	478	397	336	1,877	694	454	400	401	1,949
Al-Darb al-Aḥmar	219	324	363	357	1,263	200	315	434	426	1,375
Jammāliyya	335	444	476	453	1,708	311	423	564	447	1,745
Qaysūn	167	269	211	237	884	129	266	259	197	851
Khalīfa	270	328	439	417	1,454	255	336	562	534	1,687
Būlāq	469	422	745	640	2,276	425	476	844	788	2,533
Old Cairo	147	201	307	268	923	163	154	421	336	1,074
Total	**3,278**	**3,742**	**4,671**	**4,301**	**15,992**	**3,206**	**2,593**	**5,286**	**4,772**	**16,857**

SOURCE: DWQ, Majlis al-Khuṣūṣī, S/11/8/22, doc. no. 10, pp. 12–14, AH 17 Shawwāl 1291 / 27 November 1874 CE.

looking closely at Cairo's overall mortality statistics over a period of five years, from AH 1284 to 1288 (1867/8–1871/2 CE) (see table 1).

It went on to provide a quarter-by-quarter breakdown of these figures for the previous two years, AH 1289–90 (1872–74 CE) (see table 2).

Finally, it showed the death rate in Cairo compared to the death rates of major European and American cities (see table 3).

The report noted that whereas the overall crude death rate of Egypt was lower than that of "most foreign countries," the crude death rate of Cairo did not compare favorably: "Accordingly, we had to investigate the reason behind this discrepancy. We acknowledge that His Highness, the Khedive, has accomplished major beneficial improvements such as opening up new boulevards, planting trees, laying out public parks throughout the city, all to improve the quality of air and elevate public hygiene standards. . . . However, it has been revealed that the main factor affecting mortality rates [*mīzāniyyat al-mawtā*] is overcrowding [*ijtimā' al-nufūs*]." The chief health inspector reached this decisive conclusion after studying the mortality figures of five European cities (see table 4) and comparing their crude death rates to the number of inhabitants per house.

"With regard to large European cities," the report stated, "it has been noticed that the smaller the number of inhabitants per house, the lower the

TABLE 3 Death rates in Cairo and select European cities

City	Death rate[1]	Death rate (per 1,000 individuals)[2]
London	51.9	19.2
Madrid	36	27.7
St. Petersburg	34.9	28.6
Palermo	33	30.3
Boston	31.1	32.1
Amsterdam	31	32.2
Paris	30.6	32.6
Naples	29	34.4
Brussels	25.5	39.2
Berlin	25	40
Rome	24.1	41.4
Vienna	22.5	44.4
Cairo	28	35.7

SOURCE: DWQ, Majlis al-Khuṣūṣī, S/11/8/22, doc. no. 10, pp. 12–14, AH 17 Shawwāl 1291 / 27 November 1874 CE.

[1]Number of living "souls" (*nufūs*) for every death.

[2]The numbers in this column are my own calculations.

TABLE 4 Inhabitants per household and mortality rates in five European cities

City	Inhabitants per house	Deaths per 1,000 inhabitants
Berlin	32	25
London	8	24
Paris	35	28
St. Petersburg	52	40
Vienna	55	47

SOURCE: DWQ, Majlis al-Khuṣūṣī, S/11/8/22, doc. no. 10, pp. 12–14, AH 17 Shawwāl 1291 / 27 November 1874 CE.

overall death rate." The report then compared the mortality rates of each quarter of Cairo separately and reached a similar result: Qaysūn, the least crowded quarter, had the lowest mortality figures. Specifically, the large houses of that particular quarter, the distance separating each house, and the small number of inhabitants within each house made Qaysūn the most salubrious of Cairo's quarters. The report concluded that such new quarters as Ismā'īliyya, 'Abbāsiyya, and Shubrā, which had been recently built around Cairo, would help in lowering the population density of the traditional neighborhoods and "result in great improvements to public hygiene for the entire city."

What is most impressive about this report, which was presented to the Privy Council and then submitted to the khedive, is the confidence it displayed in the public hygiene administration. The report not only offered an estimate of the overall population of Cairo (450,000) but also gave precise mortality figures for each quarter and showed their progression over time. The Egyptian public health officials could use these figures to read the city, so to speak: they could map them out to detect which neighborhoods were more salubrious than others and then deduce conclusions and make specific policy recommendations.

Equally important was how easy the report made it for Cairo's chief health inspector to compare the public hygiene situation of his city to that of major European cities. Although he enumerated many factors that he deemed harmful to Cairo's air (the Khalīj, sewers, cesspools, cemeteries, and slaughterhouses), his final analysis was that there was no fundamental difference between Cairo and other major cities. With reliable figures at his fingertips, he was able to compare Cairo's mortality figures with those of European cities, and he concluded that overcrowding, as measured by the number of inhabitants per dwelling, affected the salubriousness of the city more than any cultural, religious, or climatic factors. Cairo's *essence* might have been foul, but there was nothing *essentially* different about the beliefs or the behavior of Cairenes that fundamentally set them apart from Parisians, Londoners, or Viennese. In other words, if Egypt was ever to be part of Europe (as Ismā'īl is famously quoted to have said), and if Cairo was to be imagined as a European city, it would not be because Cairo looked like "Paris along the Nile" but because the city could be viewed using the twin sciences of statistics and cartography.

CONCLUSION

It was the work of the miasmatists, who were obsessed with foul odors and determined to rid the city of all sources of deadly miasmas, rather than Ismā'īl and 'Alī Mubārak's fabled visit to Paris in 1867, that informed the reorganization of Cairo in the nineteenth century. The relocation of cemeteries to sites outside the city; the close regulation of food vendors, butchers, and fishmongers; the careful monitoring of demolition, construction, and renovation activities that involved moving dust and rubble; the meticulous inspection of the cleanliness of streets, alleyways, and cul-de-sacs; and the filling in of the Khalīj and of the city's numerous ponds, which had played an important part in the lives of its inhabitants for centuries—all of these acts transformed daily life in the city in fundamental ways. Without belittling the impact of the reorganization of Azbakiyya, the laying out of Ismāʿīliyya, or the other acts that traditional accounts attribute to Khedive Ismāʿīl, with his desire to build a Paris on the Nile, the disappearance of the Khalīj and the lakes of Azbakiyya, al-Fīl, and al-Raṭlī had a more profound impact on the city. These public hygiene measures, which were informed by olfactory concerns, may not have been as glamorous as building the Khedival Opera House or as visually stunning as extending straight streets that intersected at roundabouts adorned with statues of national heroes. Nevertheless, their impact on the daily lives of Cairenes was as unprecedented as it was deep, for these measures profoundly affected Cairenes and touched their daily lives in unprecedented ways. They reshaped the way that Egyptians registered their babies, built their houses, ate and drank, urinated and defecated, and buried their dead. None of the acts that are celebrated by the traditional accounts of how Cairo was redesigned—supposedly to acquire a Parisian look—was as significant or long lasting.

While these olfactory obsessions were not new, and while miasmatic concerns could be detected in the urban policies adopted by Egypt's Ottoman governors in the seventeenth and eighteenth centuries, what was novel about khedival public hygiene policies was that officials employed cartography and statistics in devising an overall plan for Cairo's rejuvenation. More remarkably, the urban policy that was implemented in khedival Cairo was never predicated on a Manichean logic that attempted to protect a white, colonial enclave from the unhealthy, unreformable dirty masses. The policies that appeared to divide the city into two halves at the end of the nineteenth century did not originate in a colonial mentality informed by the racist dual-city model. Rather, the obsession with miasmas and the incessant need to eliminate all sources of malevolent vapors meant that the urban and health authorities insisted on treating the city as one organic whole. Moreover, the inhabitants of the city were seen as capable of self-discipline and self-improvement.

FOUR

Law in the Market

ḤISBA AND FORENSIC CHEMISTRY

IN HIS TWELFTH-CENTURY *ḤISBA* MANUAL, *Nihāyat al-Rutba fī Ṭalab al-Ḥisba,* ʿAbd al-Raḥmān Ibn Naṣr al-Shayzarī (d. 1193) gave the *muḥtasib* (market inspector) detailed instructions on how to inspect the quality of food in markets. When visiting bakeries, he stipulated, the *muḥtasib* was required to make sure that the baker had wiped the inside of the oven with a clean cloth. The *muḥtasib* was also instructed to verify that the dough kneader did not knead with his feet and that he was "veiled in case he sneezes or speaks and some drops of spittle or nasal mucus fall into the dough." Shayzarī instructed the *muḥtasib* to make sure that, at the end of each day, butchers sprinkled ground salt "on the chopping board so that dogs do not lick it or any vermin crawl on it." Fryers of fish needed to wash "daily the baskets and trays with which they carry the fish. . . . They must [also] thoroughly wash the fish after slicing it open, cleaning it out, and scraping off its skin and scales." Sausage makers were required to have someone with them with a fly swatter to keep the flies away when mincing meat.[1]

In the nineteenth century, the techniques used to inspect food markets were markedly different. In September 1864, for example, while conducting a regular inspection tour of Cairo's food markets, the police became suspicious of a particular shack selling cooked food (*ṭabīkh*). They took a sample and sent it to the Qaṣr al-ʿAinī Chemical-Pharmaceutical Lab for analysis. After concluding that the sample showed traces of arsenic acid, the lab said that henceforth, the police should not send suspicious food "samples except after putting them in a glazed earthenware, or better still, in a sealed glass vessel. Under no circumstances should they send food in copper pans, even if these pans have been coated with tin, given that [chemical] reactions [*iḍṭirabāt*] with copper may take place, and especially given that copper may react with the acids contained in the suspected material."[2]

On the face of it, these two accounts seem to be dealing with the same thing, namely inspecting food in the marketplace. Although nearly seven centuries separate them, they ostensibly reflect the same concern of monitoring the quality of comestibles prepared and sold in the marketplace. However, was the chief concern of the twelfth-century *muḥtasib* the same as that of the doctors and chemists who manned the 1864 chemical lab? Or did the twelfth-century *muḥtasib* and the nineteenth-century chemist have diametrically different concerns?

By investigating whether Shayzarī's *muḥtasib* had the same concerns as Cairo's nineteenth-century chemists, this chapter uses taste as a heuristic device to raise a number of questions about *ḥisba* and its meaning through the ages. First, by concentrating on mechanisms of food control, we will try to figure out what happened to *ḥisba* and what caused its demise. Modern-day Islamists bemoan the disappearance of *ḥisba* and the *muḥtasib* as another sign of sad times that "have seen men's valor declining, [and] their strength of faith waning, with the result that *ḥisba* ended up being one of the first central duties of Islam to be abandoned."[3] Is *ḥisba*'s disappearance a sign that Muslims have abandoned their venerable Islamic traditions? Was its decline the result of shari'a being steadily marginalized and ultimately withdrawn from daily life in Muslim societies, as Islamists claim?

This chapter also inquires about the chemists who ostensibly replaced the *muḥtasib:* Who were they, and where and how were they trained? What did their expertise consist of, and how did they acquire it? To what purposes did they apply their scientific expertise, and how were they authorized to do so? What effect did these chemists have on the food markets of nineteenth-century Cairo, which were considerably larger and more complex than those examined by traditional writers on *ḥisba?*

Finally, this chapter looks at how markets were affected when their regulation passed from the *muḥtasib* to chemists, policemen, and public hygienists. These public hygienists were chiefly concerned with adulterated food, deadly poisons, dangerous drugs, and "sophisticated" drinks.[4] But although they appear to have shared a common concern with the early *muḥtasib,* did these hygienists see the marketplace the same way the *muḥtasib* did?

To answer these questions, this chapter offers a preliminary reading of the history of *ḥisba* in nineteenth-century Egypt and argues that *ḥisba*'s demise was caused not by the introduction of the civil law tradition but by the ascendency of a complex and far-reaching public health system that deployed forensic Lavoisian chemistry to monitor food markets. After an introductory section that deals with conceptual and methodological questions raised by two recent studies on the crisis of secularism in modern Egypt, the chapter is divided into two halves. The first half deals with *ḥisba* in the Islamic textual tradition and starts with a brief survey of lexicographical definitions of the term *ḥisba*. This is followed by a close reading of four foundational *fiqh* texts that describe in some detail the manner in which *ḥisba* was supposed to be practiced in markets. It ends with a commentary on the role violence occupied in the *fiqhī* understanding of *ḥisba*.

Following this first section, there is a short interlude that looks closely at a pivotal decree issued in 1841 pertaining to public health and market inspection. This decree is significant because it was one of the last times the *muḥtasib* made an appearance in official correspondence.

The second half of the chapter deals with the fate of *ḥisba* in nineteenth-century Egypt and how the role of the *muḥtasib*, as far as regulating inspections of markets for comestibles is concerned, was taken over by chemists and policemen. The material presented in this second half is therefore qualitatively different from that dealt with in the first half. Instead of examining *fiqh* treatises and *ḥisba* manuals, this section relies on chemical textbooks, public hygiene decrees, and police reports. It looks at how the overt violence that accompanied the practice of *ḥisba* in *fiqhī* theory and in actual practice was replaced by a subtler violence practiced by policemen in collaboration with forensic chemists when monitoring the increasingly complex market for food and beverages.

ḤISBA, SHARIʿA, AND THE COERCIVE POWER OF THE STATE

In a recent study of the paradox that inheres within the very nature of secularism, Hussein Agrama offers a convincing critique of the principle that sees it not as the separation of religion from politics but as the fashioning of religion into an arena of state management and intervention.[5] Relying mostly on twentieth-century texts,[6] Agrama argues that *ḥisba* "in its classical *Shariʿa* elaborations, was part of a form of reasoning and practice connected to the cultivation of selves," and that *ḥisba* was "intended to maintain conditions necessary for the success of the Muslim community, [and thus] is one such practice of disciplined moral criticism."[7] He goes on to argue that due to "the influence of civil law tradition," *ḥisba* got incorporated into the judicial system of the state and thus became part of the state's coercive power.[8]

Similarly, in his most recent study on tradition, Talal Asad argues that *ḥisba,* which is based on the Quranic principle of "commanding right and forbidding wrong" (*al-amr bi'l-ma'rūf wa'l-nahy 'an al-munkar*), can be seen as a practice equivalent to "what is known historically in Christian history as 'pastoral care' [but what within Islam] is . . . diffused among all Muslims in relation to one another."[9] To illustrate his point, Asad relates a conversation he had with the *khaṭīb* of Sultan Ḥasan Mosque in Cairo that revealed this shaykh's views on the formation of personal virtue in Islamic tradition. This is what the shaykh told him:

> The process by which human beings were formed (*takwīn al-insān*) was what formed intentions, and therefore the possibility of a just social life: The constitution of intentions by behavioral and verbal action takes place in various contexts of social life. He went on to talk about the education of good character (*tahdhīb al-akhlāq*) through the practices of devotion and discipline, but insisted that the ethical formation of the individual was not a matter for the individual alone, that it took place through interactions among people and things in several social locations: "household, school, mosque, the media, and the street."[10]

Later in the text, Asad explains that what he "found intriguing about [the shaykh's] discourse was the attempt to tie *amr bi-l-ma'rūf* to the virtue of 'friendship' (*suhba, ikhwa*), to present it as a matter of responsibility and concern for a friend rather than simply of policing. The language and attitude in which one carried out that duty was integral to what *amr bi-l-ma'rūf* was, because, 'Every Muslim is a brother to every other Muslim.'"[11] He then adds that "one implication here—although [the] shaykh . . . did not articulate it—is that speaking harshly . . . may sometimes be necessary to make even a friend change his or her behavior."[12]

In critiquing the secularists' dismissal of ritual, bodily comportment, and disciplined behavior as evidence of blind obedience to authority, Asad makes a compelling argument. His insistence on viewing the so-called Islamic Awakening (*al-Ṣaḥwa al-Islāmiyya*) within Islamic tradition is equally powerful. However, when it comes to dealing with that historical tradition by reading its texts and engaging with these texts' authors, Asad's analysis raises an important issue. When referring to Ghazālī's ideas about *al-amr bi'l-ma'rūf* (commanding right), Asad directs his readers not to the foundational chapter on that principle in Ghazālī's influential *Iḥyā' 'Ulūm al-Dīn* (discussed later in the chapter) but to another book of Ghazālī's, one about friendship that has little to do with *ḥisba*.[13] Like Agrama, Asad views *ḥisba* as a mode of moral criticism that had no connection to the coercive power of the state, and he argues further that the relationship between the two was formed only with the creation of the modern state and with the fundamental transformations that shari'a witnessed in modern times.

The idealized view of *ḥisba* that Agrama and Asad present bears some resemblance to the view adopted by many modern-day Islamist proponents. These Islamists maintain that *ḥisba* was "a masterpiece of Islamic legislation" (*rā'i'a min rawā'i' al-tashrī' al-Islāmī*) that was guaranteed to "protect rights, uphold justice, safeguard . . . piety, . . . and protect society from evil."[14] They contend that it is a "binding religious duty" (*ḥukm shar'ī bi'l-wujūb*)[15] and insist that it is a *farḍ 'ayn*, not a *farḍ kifāya*—or in other words, that it is incumbent on all Muslims and not just on some of them.[16] They argue that the *muḥtasib*'s functions were equivalent to those of the present-day "public prosecutor, the traffic police, the vice squad, the ministry of health with its technical labs, the ministry of trade, the ministry of supply, the weights and measurements agency, and the municipal and village administrative agencies," and assert that the *muḥtasib* fulfilled his functions in a highly efficient, just, and equitable manner.[17] They also call for Arab governments to reapply *ḥisba* so that the "[Arab] nation can regain its great position, repossess its power and restore its glory—[acts that can only be accomplished when] society has been restored to righteousness, and when moral and religious principles have been observed in daily behavior and in [social] transactions."[18]

But are all these accounts of *ḥisba* faithful to shari'a as a textual tradition? Or are the accounts themselves the result of discursive transformations brought about by the creation of the modern state? Specifically, is it true that *ḥisba* functioned within the Islamic textual tradition as a form of moral criticism that was diffused within the Muslim community and that was unrelated to the state's coercive power? What exactly is the connection between moral criticism, violence, and the law? And was the connection between *ḥisba* and violence formed with the foundation of the modern state and the introduction of the civil law tradition, or was it an integral part of the functioning of Islamic state even before the onslaught of modernity?

First we must ask, what exactly is *ḥisba,* and how did it evolve over time?[19] To answer these questions, we need to take a detour to discuss *fiqh* treatises and manuals for the *muḥtasib* before turning to archival sources from the nineteenth century, which is when the *muḥtasib* delivered his swan song and when his role as surveyor of markets was taken over by chemists and uniformed policemen.

Lexicographical Glosses on a Curious Root

The first thing to point out about *ḥisba* is that the word has a deeply ambivalent linguistic root. Ibn Manẓūr's thirteenth-century lexicon, *Lisān al-ʿArab,* for example, gives the following possible meanings for and derivatives of *ḥ.s.b.,* which is the root of the word *ḥisba*: counting, generosity, honor, sufficiency, value, reward, and precision.[20] The fourteenth-century lexicon *Al-Qamūs al-Muḥīṭ,* by Fayrūzabādī, adds two more definitions: compensation or wages (*ajr*) and management (*tadbīr*).[21] In his popular eighteenth-century lexicon, *Tādj al-ʿArūs,* Zabīdī ruminates on why the word *ḥisāb* was chosen to refer to market transactions: "The reason for using the word *ḥisāb* in people's [commercial] transactions is that it refers to what is considered sufficient, that is, that which does not go above or below the precise amount [*al-miqdār*]."[22] Ibn Manẓūr adds another interesting gloss when commenting on the connection between the impersonal, objective act of counting and enumeration on the one hand and the socially determined value of honor and prestige on the other: "A man's . . . . pedigree is referred to as *ḥasab* because [when] a man boasted [about his lineage and pedigree in olden times], he would count and enumerate his honorable acts and those of his ancestors. And given that *ḥasb* means counting and enumeration, then *ḥasab* is that which is counted [which, in this case, is honor and pedigree]."[23]

Two main themes become evident from these glosses. The first is the intimate connection between the root *ḥ.s.b.* and numbers, enumeration, arithmetic, and calculation. The second is the equally intimate connection that the term has with concepts like justice, management, and honor. This conflation of two sets of meanings, one precise and abstract and the other subjective and socially constructed, is indicative of an inherent tension within *ḥisba* as a concept and as a practice, a tension that the rest of this chapter attempts to elucidate.

The reason for including this analysis of the linguistic meaning of the term *ḥisba* is to point out a tension between two contrasting ways in which *ḥisba* has been understood through the centuries. On the one hand, *ḥisba* was used to refer to the practice of communal moral regulation, a practice that was based on the Quranic principle of commanding right and forbidding wrong. At the beginning of his study of this principle in Islamic thought, Michael Cook cites eight Quranic verses that mention it.[24] Present-day proponents of *ḥisba* often single out one of them (Quran 3:104) that they interpret as indicating clearly that commanding right is a cardinal duty in Islam.[25] The verse reads: "Let there be a community of you calling to good and commanding right and forbidding wrong" (*wa-l-takun minkum ummatun yadʿūna ilā al-khayri wa-yaʾmurūna biʾl-maʾrūfi wa-yanhawna ʿani ʾl-munkar*). Turning to Prophetic Traditions, there are numerous hadiths on the subject, the most famous being the one related by the companion Abū Saʿīd al-Khudrī (d. 693): "Whoever sees a wrong and is able to put it right with his hand, let him do so, if he can't then with his tongue; if he can't, then with [or in] his heart."[26] According to this view, therefore, *ḥisba* is believed to be a duty sanctioned by both the Quran and Prophetic Tradition, and there is near unanimity among the *ʿulamāʾ* about the fact that it is obligatory; the only slight disagreement was whether the duty was also grounded in reason.[27]

On the other hand, there were those who believed that there was a "need to tame the revolutionary potential of the *ḥisba,* and [to consign it] as a precisely defined job to a government-appointed official."[28] Accordingly, *ḥisba* was given a drastically different meaning, that of market inspection, and hence the market inspector came to be referred to as *muḥtasib.* This official was in charge of monitoring all activities taking place "not so much [in] a particular market as [in] any space in which public life and commercial transactions occurred."[29] Until recently, it was believed that the *muḥtasib* was a continuation of the late Roman *agoranomos,* or market inspector.[30] However, this belief has now been refuted, and it is now commonly thought that a long period of time passed between when the *agoronomos* existed and when the *muḥtasib* was established, and that the latter is based not on Greek or Roman precedents but on the Quranic principle of commanding right and forbidding wrong.[31] Regardless of whether the *muḥtasib* was a revived *agoranomos* or a genuinely new Islamic market inspector, the main point is that according to this second view, he derived his authority from the state and not from the community.

Ḥisba *in the* Shar'ī *Textual Tradition*

So does *ḥisba* denote a moral duty incumbent on all Muslims as per the Quranic principle of commanding right and forbidding wrong? Or is it an official institution tasked with monitoring commercial transactions in the public marketplace? I raise these questions to investigate the assumption, made recently by Asad and Hallaq, among others, that law was coupled with morality in premodern times and that they were divorced only with the onset of modernity. In an attempt to answer these questions, I will provide a brief survey of four *fiqh* texts on *ḥisba* that deal with market regulation and that belong to different shari'a discursive traditions, not only *fiqhī* ones.

Yaḥyā Ibn 'Umar's Aḥkām al-Sūq. The first *ḥisba* text we will look at, which is also the oldest, is *Kitāb Aḥkām al-Sūq,* by Yaḥyā Ibn 'Umar (d. 902).[32] This Andalusian Mālikī text is the earliest known *ḥisba* manual. Two features stand out immediately when reading it. The first is that Yaḥyā Ibn 'Umar uses the term *ṣāḥib al-sūq,* or "governor of the market," instead of *muḥtasib.* The second is the format of the text, which takes the form of answers to anonymous questions posed to Yaḥyā Ibn 'Umar about different market transactions. In responding to these questions, Yaḥyā Ibn 'Umar occasionally refers to founding figures of the Mālikī *madhhab,* including Mālik himself, although these references are to the eponym's oral tradition rather than to his *Muwaṭṭa'.*[33]

Yaḥyā Ibn 'Umar's text contains many details about how *ṣāḥib al-sūq* should monitor public morals in the marketplace. For example, women are not allowed to wear squeaky sandals (*khifāf ṣarrāra*) because they attract attention in the streets. If a woman is caught breaking this rule, her sandals are to be cut at the seams (*tushaqq khirāzat al-khuff*), and she is to be beaten.[34] Women are allowed to march in funerals, but they are forbidden from wailing and crying loudly.[35] Public bath attendants have to wear a towel while working.[36] Christians and Jews are forbidden from wearing clothes similar to those worn by Muslims; if they fail to comply, they are to be given twenty lashes each and then imprisoned.[37] Shopkeepers who sprinkle too much water in front of their shops so that streets become slippery, which can cause carriages passing by to break and spill their cargo, must compensate the damaged goods.[38] Cloth merchants are required to clear their cloth of lice if the buyer complains; if, however, the sold cloth is so infested with lice that the merchant is unable to remove all the insects, then this is considered cheating and the merchant has to exchange the cloth for money.[39]

But the regulations monitoring the sale of comestibles are where Yaḥyā Ibn ʿUmar's text most plainly reveals the logic informing *ḥisba*. These regulations show not only a keen interest in guaranteeing smooth economic transactions but also a desire to uphold morality and ensure fair play in the marketplace. A deep concern with enforcing a moral and just economy is clearly evinced. Thus, and given the stern Quranic prohibition on tampering with scales (Quran 83:1–3), Yaḥyā Ibn ʿUmar's text has repeated injunctions against cheating with weights,[40] and the strongest punishments (beating, imprisonment, and expulsion from the market) are reserved for merchants who tamper with scales.[41] *Ṣāḥib al-sūq* is instructed to warn butchers against mixing lean and fatty meat.[42] Butchers who blow water into the stomachs of slaughtered animals to make them appear fatter and those who mix mutton with goat meat are to be warned. If they don't desist, they are to be expelled from the market, a punishment "more severe than beating [*ashaddu min al-ḍarb*]."[43] Merchants who sell grains and pulses (e.g., wheat, barely, beans, lentils, and chickpeas) are to sift their grains before selling them.[44] Fruit sellers are not to sell unripe fruit as this may impact the volume of the following season's harvest.[45] The practice of waxing figs to add to their weight is banned, and fruit sellers who persist will have their merchandise confiscated and distributed to the poor.[46] Milkmen should not mix the milk of cows with that of sheep, "for this is cheating," and those who continue this practice after being warned, as well as those who add water to their milk, will have their milk confiscated and distributed to the poor.[47]

Bread receives the closet attention, and Yaḥyā Ibn ʿUmar describes how the different stages of its production are to be monitored. Millers who damage wheat by using defective millstones will have to pay a fine (*ḍamān*).[48] Bakers who, despite being warned, do not desist from selling underweight bread will be expelled from the market and their bread will be confiscated and distributed to the poor.[49] The same punishment is applied to bakers who mix low- and high-quality wheat.[50]

In general, *ṣāḥib al-sūq* is to ensure that fairness and equity rule the market. Fixed prices (*tasʿīr*) are to be avoided,[51] but so too are artificially depressed prices and high ones set by merchants seeking excessive profit (*ishtiṭāṭ*).[52] If a merchant with lower quality foodstuffs enters the market and offers his products at a low price, then *ṣāḥib al-sūq* has no right to force this low price on other merchants; but if that merchant intends to harm the market (*arāda bidhālika fasād al-sūq*), then *ṣāḥib al-sūq* has to offer him the choice of either following other merchants' higher prices or being expelled from the market.[53]

Cornering the market (*iḥtikār*) is also prohibited. A food merchant who aims to corner the market will be forced to sell his products; he is allowed to recoup his capital, but the profit will be forfeited and distributed as charity to the poor (*yutaṣaddaq bihi*).[54] Merchants can get together and withdraw from the market in order to help a young colleague who needs to start his business and support his new family; but they should be prevented from doing so if this leads to harming the consumers (presumably through ratcheting up prices).[55]

Māwardī's Al-Aḥkām al-Sulṭāniyya. The same concern with fairness and equity in the marketplace can be detected in the second *fiqh* text to be discussed, *Al-Aḥkām al-Sulṭāniyya,* by Abū'l-Ḥasan al-Māwardī (974–1058 CE), the last chapter of which is devoted entirely to *ḥisba.*[56] Throughout his book, which is arguably one of the most influential political treatises in the *fiqhī* textual tradition, Māwardī focuses on the state-appointed official, for whom he reserved the title *al-muḥtasib.* A state official himself,[57] Māwardī was very concerned about opening the field of *ḥisba* to all Muslims. While he did not make practicing *ḥisba* conditional on the consent of the ruler, he obviously thought that giving Muslims the right to take the law into their own hands opened the door to chaos. He therefore devotes the largest section of the chapter to the officially appointed *muḥtasib,* clearly indicating his preferences as to who should perform this cardinal duty.

In delimiting the range of the *muḥtasib*'s duties, Māwardī makes it clear that these duties include matters of orthodoxy (right belief) as well as orthopraxy (right behavior).[58] Thus, the *muḥtasib* is mandated to make sure that people perform the Friday communal prayer.[59] He must ensure that prayers are conducted in the proper fashion and chastise people who conduct prayers wrongly, such as those who vocalize prayers that are meant to be silent or those who are silent during vocalized prayers.[60] He is also to oblige women, if divorced, to wait the prescribed period before remarrying.[61] With regard the public display of liquor (*al-khamr*), Māwardī reviews different opinions about what should be done: "Jurists have differed with respect to the spilling [of confiscated liquor]. Abū Ḥanīfa argued that it should not be spilled because it is, in his view, part of the [non-Muslims'] stipulated and rightly guaranteed property. Al-Shāfiʿī's view is that it should be spilled" since in his view, neither a Muslim nor a non-Muslim is allowed to sell liquor in public. Regarding musical instruments used in public, the *muḥtasib* should "break them up until they are reduced to harmless timber boards; discipline [those who play them] in public; but not damage [the instruments] if their wood could be used in other things than amusements."[62]

With regard orthopraxy, it is market transactions that Māwardī is interested in, and like Yaḥyā Ibn 'Umar, he is mostly concerned with cheating: how to detect it, how to stop it, and how to punish it. This section is of particular relevance to our purposes here and therefore deserves a careful look. Māwardī starts the section by giving this example of cheating: "The practice of not milking cows for a while until their udders are swollen with milk at the time of sale." He then writes, "One of the main concerns of the office of market supervisor is preventing the practices of tipping scales or tampering with weights on account of the warning by the God Almighty forbidding such practices."[63] In addition to advising the *muḥtasib* to harshly and publicly punish those who engage in such practices, Māwardī suggests that the *muḥtasib* test and calibrate scales used in the market if he doubts them, noting that "it would be more prudent and correct were he to imprint on those [scales] he has calibrated a stamp [*ṭābiʿ*] of his own that is recognized by the public." In what appears to be an interesting afterthought, he writes, "If the country is large enough for its population to require calibrators of weights and measures and controllers [*kayyālīn wa wazzānīn wa nuqqād*], the market supervisor should select [such people], carefully screening out any but the ones he approves for their honesty and trustworthiness."[64]

Most significantly, Māwardī offers an original taxonomy of fraudulent market practices and makes his own suggestions of ways to check and punish them. He says that there are three kinds of workers in the marketplace that the *muḥtasib* has to deal with. First, there are those whose work must be judged in terms of care or negligence, such as physicians and teachers; second, there are those whose work must be judged according to their honesty or dishonesty, such as "jewelers, tailors, bleachers, and dyers"; and third, there are those whose work is judged by whether it is of good or poor quality. Māwardī proposes that the *muḥtasib* make sure that only qualified people practice jobs that fall into the first category. Thus, "only those who are knowledgeable and whose method [of teaching or medicine] should be approved, while those who fall short and perform poorly should be kept from engaging in that which would corrupt souls or be detrimental to morals." With regard the second category of workers, Māwardī suggests that the *muḥtasib* "look for those who are honest and trustworthy among them and approve them." And finally, he says that the *muḥtasib* should pay particular attention to those in the third category of workers, as they "are the special concern of market supervisors." The *muḥtasib* should "take them to task for poor and shoddy workmanship even if no one complains of it. If a contending party complains to him of a commissioned piece of work, . . . [claiming] that it has been done shoddily and [that he has been] cheated, [the *muḥtasib*] should respond to that with censure and reprimand."[65]

Ghazālī's Iḥyā' 'Ulūm al-Dīn. Māwardī's *Al-Aḥkām al-Sulṭāniyya* has proven very influential in shaping the theory of *ḥisba*. However, before checking how Māwardī's text informed many subsequent *ḥisba* manuals, it is important to have a close look at Abū Ḥāmid al-Ghazālī (1058–1111 CE) and his equally influential understanding of *ḥisba*. In a certain way, Ghazālī's chapter on *ḥisba* in his monumental *Iḥyā' 'Ulūm al-Dīn* can be seen as a powerful critique of Māwardī and as an impassioned challenge to the caliphs' attempt to monopolize the duty of *ḥisba*. In contradistinction to Māwardī's clear preference that *ḥisba* be performed by a state-appointed official, Ghazālī's belief is that *ḥisba* is not only an inalienable right but also a duty of the individual believer, even if she or he is a sinner.[66] As such, although both authors use the same word, *muḥtasib,* to refer to the person practicing *ḥisba,* Māwardī makes it clear that he means the state-appointed official, whereas Ghazālī insists that he is referring to *every* Muslim.

Arguably one of the most influential texts in the entire history of the Islamic discursive tradition, *Iḥyā' 'Ulūm al-Dīn* is Ghazālī's magnum opus, and he devotes an entire chapter of it to the duty of commanding right and forbidding wrong. This chapter has proven to be highly influential through the centuries: some of the scholars and students who were followers of Ghazālī's school, the Shāfi'īs, memorized the work by heart, and numerous others wrote summaries of it. At least one of them proceeded to write a manual for the work of the *muḥtasib* in the market in which he quoted extensively from Ghazālī and made extensive use of his treatment of the subject.[67] More remarkable is the fact that *Iḥyā' 'Ulūm al-Dīn* was the subject of many epitomes written by scholars belonging to other schools, including Shī'ites. Among modern-day scholars, Ghazālī's treatment of the duty has proved to be equally influential.[68] Given the profound importance of this chapter, it is worthwhile to have a close look at it, specifically at how it lays down an argument for *ḥisba* acting as a guide for how the Muslim community could be self-governing and self-policing.

In the introduction to his formidable elaboration of how *ḥisba* is to be practiced, Ghazālī makes clear that he considers it the main pivot of the faith (*al-quṭb al-aʿẓam fī 'l-dīn*) and the main reason God sent His prophets.[69] He insists that *ḥisba* is an inalienable right of individual Muslims and that it should be performed by every legally competent Muslim person who is capable of performing it (*mukallaf, muslim, qādir*),[70] even if he or she is a persistent sinner (*fāsiq*),[71] and, significantly, even if it is unauthorized by the political authority (*al-imām* or *al-wālī*).[72] The examples he cites of when and how *ḥisba* is to be performed go a long way in describing how the Muslim community is to govern itself and in explaining the enduring popularity of the text. For example, according to Ghazālī, a *muḥtasib* has the duty to instruct the ignorant about the proper way of performing prayers: "Every person who sits at home [minding his business] is complicit in the wrong [that may be committed in public] . . . as he has thus been negligent of guiding and informing people about what is good. Most people, for example, are ignorant about the proper way to perform prayer. This is so even in cities, let alone in villages and remote areas."[73] The same applies to the many offenses that are committed daily in the marketplace: if the *muḥtasib* is capable of putting a stop to these offenses, then he is not allowed to exempt himself from this duty by staying at home.

The offenses themselves are equally noteworthy because they explain how *ḥisba* continues to inspire people as a practice that upholds the moral, economic, and political integrity of the community of believers. One such transgression is when a merchant lies about defects in commodities he sells in his shops; similarly, any passerby who is aware of such defects has a duty to inform buyers of it, and if he remains silent to curry favor with the merchant, he will be considered an accomplice to cheating. Adding balconies to houses or benches to shops that obstruct free passage in the street is also forbidden, as this encroaches on the right of pedestrians to have unhindered access to the thoroughfare. Piling supplies of wood in front of a house is permitted but only of a reasonable quantity; if there is more wood than necessary, it is considered a nuisance to the public. "Streets are for communal use," Ghazālī states, "and no one has the right to have exclusive use of them." Leading pack animals carrying sharp-edged loads that could tear the clothes of passersby is a wrong that must be stopped. So is it when a butcher slaughters animals on the street instead of in his shop, firstly because splashed blood may defile whomever it touches, and secondly because people, by nature, abhor filth. The muezzins were not spared Ghazālī's criticisms. Their habit of stretching the calls to prayer, especially the one at daybreak, when people are asleep, is considered a nuisance that serves no one, and the habit of one muezzin starting his call to prayer in the middle of another's is deemed a cacophony (*tadākhul al-aṣwāt*) that confuses the congregation. Quacks and sellers of amulets inside and outside mosques are to be banned and their activities stopped, as "every sale transaction that entails lying, cheating or hiding defects from the buyer is illicit [*ḥarām*]."[74]

Shayzarī's Nihāyat al-Rutba fi Ṭalab al-Ḥisba. The last *ḥisba* text to look at is 'Abd al-Raḥmān Ibn Nasr al-Shayzarī's *Nihāyat al-Rutba fi Ṭalab al-Ḥisba,* with which this chapter opened. Written a little less than three centuries after Yaḥyā Ibn 'Umar's *Aḥkām al-Sūq* and less than a century after Ghazālī's *Iḥyā',* Shayzarī's *Nihāyat al-Rutba* is surely the mother of all *ḥisba* manuals, having left its mark on many subsequent *ḥisba* manuals.[75] Some later authors borrowed not only its classification scheme—organizing their manuals according to market practices and professions (e.g., bakers, cooks, sellers of sheep heads)—but also its title.[76]

Shayzarī's detailed listing of the many fraudulent practices that go on in the marketplace and his numerous prescriptions for how the *muḥtasib* is to detect and punish these practices are what assured his manual's long-lasting influence. With regard to bakers, Shayzarī writes, "The *muḥtasib* must take into account the way they adulterate the bread with vetch and beans, for these turn the crust red. Some bakers adulterate the bread with the flour of chickpeas and rice because this makes it heavy, but undercooked."[77] When discussing *zalābiya* (a kind of confection made with honey and almonds), he warns, "When the *zalābiya* turns black, this occurs due to the frying pan being dirty, or perhaps only fine flour being used and no semolina or it being fried in old oil. . . . The *muḥtasib* must keep an eye on [the producers] regarding all these things."[78] Shayzarī lists many fraudulent practices butchers engage in: "Some of them cut the flesh from the stomach [of the slaughtered animal] and blow water in. They know places in the flesh in to which to blow water. Thus the *muḥtasib* must keep an eye on the slaughterers in the *'arīf*'s [i.e., his aide's] absence. There are others who parade fat cows in the markets and then slaughter other ones. This is fraud."[79] In the chapter devoted to sellers of roast meat (*al-shawwā'īn*), he alerts the *muḥtasib* that he "should examine the meat when it is being weighed to make sure that the meat roasters have not hidden iron or lead weights in it. . . . Some of the meat roasters smear the carcasses with honey and then put them in the oven. In this way they very quickly go brown and give off an aroma, so they must be examined to make sure they are properly cooked."[80] A seller of sheep heads (*rawwās*) "must put his fingers in the noses [of the slaughtered sheep] after crushing the bridge, wash inside them, and take out all the impurities, dirt, and maggots if there are any."[81] With regard to fryers of fish, Shayzarī writes that if the "*muḥtasib* is absent, the *ʿarīf* should check the frying pan every hour in case they fry fish with oil mixed with the fat coming from the fish's stomach. The best thing to fry fish with is sesame oil. They must not fry it with used oil whose smell has become rancid or remove the fish from the frying pan until it is properly cooked, but not overcooked or burned."[82] As for the makers of *harīsa* (a thick pottage made of cooked wheat and meat pounded together), Shayzarī writes that the *muḥtasib* "must watch out for the methods of adulterating the oil [used to make the *harīsa*]. Some of them take the bones and skulls of cows and camels and boil them thoroughly in water until a lot of oil comes out of them, then they mix this with the oil used for *harīsa*. The way to identify this is to drop a little of it onto a tile; if it does not congeal or is transparent, then it has been adulterated with the things we have mentioned. . . . But God knows best."[83]

From this brief analysis of Shayzarī's *Nihāyat al-Rutba,* it should be easy to see why this manual of *ḥisba* has proven to be influential over the centuries. More fleshed out than the skeletal frames of Māwardī's and Ghazālī's *fiqh* chapters on *ḥisba,* and more exhaustively and better organized than Yaḥyā Ibn ʿUmar's much earlier *ḥisba* manual, it offered the *muḥtasib* an extensive list of the trades he was likely to encounter and the tricks tradesmen were likely to perform to swindle, cheat, and scam and also offered detailed suggestions for how to detect and punish common, and not so common, fraud. More than any other *ḥisba* manual, Shayzarī's *Nihāyat al-Rutba* has not ceased to fascinate its readers, prompting many modern-day proponents of *ḥisba* to bemoan the loss of the office of the *muḥtasib* and yearn for its revival.

Violence and the Official Muḥtasib. There is no doubt that the theory of *ḥisba* as described in the *fiqh* texts analyzed so far presents a serious attempt to think about the complexity of pre-modern markets and how to monitor them. For example, Māwardī's suggestion that the *muḥtasib* use calibrated scales that have been stamped with his seal was an original and, judging from the historical record, effective means of standardizing weights and measurements and controlling and detecting counterfeit currency in markets that were increasing in size and complexity.[84] By coupling a meticulous mechanism of monitoring market transactions with "a form of care of the self [that is] initiated by someone concerned about another's behavior,"[85] *ḥisba* presents itself as a remarkable moral system that maintained the cohesion of the community, upheld internal peace, preserved the integrity of markets, expanded personal piety, and elevated the ethical standards of society. Not for nothing do Islamists believe that the practice of *ḥisba* resulted in "tranquility [*ṭuma'nīna*] spreading all over the Abode of Islam, where the inhabitants reveled in serenity [*sakīna*]."[86]

With regard to market control, what is most noteworthy about *ḥisba* is its prohibition of grain hoarding, windfall profits, adulterated products, and noncustomary prices. Its continued popularity over time can be explained by the fact that it harks back to a traditional view of social norms and obligations and insists on commonly shared notions of the proper function of several parties within the community. The *ḥisba* discourse about a moral economy that is characterized by just prices, fair markets, and a concern for the poor and needy has a seductive appeal especially in modern times, when markets have been disembedded from society, agrarian relations have been commercialized, and the centralized state has failed to provide adequate protection to the marginalized.

Yet despite its appeal, the *fiqhī* theory of *ḥisba* contains a very unsettling trait: according to this theory, the morality of the market is maintained not with friendly words of advice or by appealing to the shared values of the community but with a remarkable degree of extreme violence.[87] Modern-day proponents of *ḥisba* often ignore the fact that *fiqh* treatises on *ḥisba* explicitly authorized the *muḥtasib* to resort to violence as a necessary means of enforcing market regulations; these treatises considered appealing to morality, communal values, or local tradition insufficient and inadequate. In his influential description of the position's qualifications, for example, Māwardī writes that the *muḥtasib* must be "free [i.e., not a slave], upright [*'adl*], with a say in the matters of the faith, and knowledgeable about the evident breaches of the moral codes (*al-munkarāt al-ẓāhira*)," but he notes that he need not be "a religious scholar well versed in matters of the law" (*'ālim, min ahl al-ijtihād*). But he should have "vigor and firmness" (*ṣarāma wa khushūna*).[88] Māwardī justifies the need for such firmness by saying that the *muḥtasib*'s "office is created to intimidate, so that [demonstrating] overbearingness and harshness in the exercise of it may not be considered to exceed the limits or break the rules." The subject matter of *ḥisba*, he explains, "is the awe associated with sovereign audacity and the sternness of power."[89]

Shayzarī, for his part, stresses how important it is for the *muḥtasib* to use violence, and he lists some of tools that can be used to enforce regulations:

> Among these things are the whip, the *dirra* [a special stick, described below] and the *ṭurṭūr* [headgear]. As for the whip, the *muḥtasib* should choose one of moderate thickness, neither too thick nor too thin and soft but rather something between the two. This is so that it does not harm the body and there is no fear of injury. As for the *dirra,* it should be made of ox or camel hide and filled with stones. As for the *ṭurṭūr,* this should be made of felt, variegated with colored pieces of cloth, adorned with onyx, seashells, bells, and the tails of foxes and cats. All these instruments should be hung on the *muhtasib's* booth for the people to see, so that the hearts of the wicked will tremble and swindlers are restrained.[90]

Indeed, so much was violence associated with *ḥisba* that the poet Nizāmī described the *muḥtasib* as a *dirra*-wielding demon in the late twelfth century.[91] Moreover, the fact that violence was an essential ingredient not only of the theory of *ḥisba* but also of its practice is indicated by the frequent references in historical chronicles to the *muḥtasib* beating commoners and merchants, almost always excessively and brutally. In his *Al-Nujūm al-Zāhira,* Ibn Taghrī Birdī mentions the case of a certain *muḥtasib* of Damascus, Ibrāhīm Ibn ʿAbdallah,

> who, when he beat a man with the *dirra,* the man said "This was on the back of Abū Bakr's head." When he struck him again, he said, "Thus was on the back of ʿUmar's head." Then he struck him again, and he said, "This was on the back of ʿUthmān's head." Then he struck him again, and the man did not know what to say. The *muḥtasib* said to him, "You don't know the order of the Companions. I will teach them to you, and the best of them are the people of [the Battle of] Badr. Let me beat you their number." So he beat him 316 *dirra* strokes. Then the man was carried away and died a few days later.[92]

In his *Badāʾiʿ al-Zuhūr,* Ibn Iyās mentions an order by a certain *muḥtasib* in 1472 that women wear headscarves with particular specifications; those who defied the order were beaten up and paraded down the thoroughfare with the scarves dangling from their necks.[93] In his *Sulūk,* Maqrīzī mentions the case of the *muḥtasib* Ibn al-Aṭrūsh, who in 1348 summoned some bakers who had been selling bread too cheaply and had them pelted with stones by the public.[94] He also mentions a curious case of a married couple that devised a ruse with a poor shaykh, pretending that a wall in their house was speaking and answering questions set to it by individuals high and low. The local *muḥtasib,* Jamāl al-Dīn Maḥmūd al-ʿAjamī, was sent to investigate this curious case, which was attracting the attention of the public and causing confusion and excitement. When he planted a spy in the house and discovered that it had been an elaborate scheme, he reported the culprits to the governor, who ordered that the three be severely beaten. Maqrīzī specifically described the woman's punishment: she was given six hundred lashes of the cane and then had her hands nailed to a cross (*tasmīr*) and was sat on a camel and paraded through the market. When the sultan rewarded the *muḥtasib* for his diligence, people cursed him, showing sympathy for the woman.[95]

Perhaps there is no better commentary on the violence inherent in the practice of *ḥisba* than that of Sibawayhi al-Miṣrī, the wise fool of Cairo and Fusṭāṭ during Ikhshīdī and Fatimid times (i.e., the late tenth century). The contemporary historian Ibn Zawlāq[96] wrote that once while Sibawayhi was riding his donkey in Fusṭāṭ, he ran into the local *muḥtasib,* who was surrounded by his *aḥrās* (aides or guards). This is what he told him: "What are these guards, you impure scoundrels!? By God, you have not upheld what is right, nor adjusted a price, nor punished a criminal, nor honored those who are famous. You are only content on ringing bells[97] when imposing wrongful acts, when slapping people at the back of their necks, and when tearing their pants. May God not protect he who appointed you *muḥtasib.* May He not have mercy on your father or his. May He unleash upon both of you someone who can inflict on you severe pain."[98]

To analyze the repeated references in the Mamluk chronicles and biographical dictionaries to the *muḥtasib*'s frequent use of violence, Jonathan Berkey conducted a thorough prosopographical study of the *muḥtasib* over the entire period of Mamluk rule.[99] Berkey's main explanation for the violence resorted to by the *muḥtasib,* as mentioned in these historical sources, is that a gradual but decisive evolution took place in the character of the office over the two and a half centuries of the Mamluk sultanate. At the beginning of the sultanate, the office of the *muḥtasib* was thought of as a religious office (*waẓīfa diniyya*), with those appointed to the post coming from the ranks of the *ʿulamāʾ*. By the mid- to late fifteenth century, however, the military elite had effectively monopolized the post, so much so that Ibn Taghri Birdi, whose chronicle ends in the year 1467, lists the *muḥtasib* among political and military appointees in a carefully graded list, placing him "just above the *wali* [i.e., governor] of Cairo, and just below the *nazir al-jaysh* [head of the army]."[100] Looking at the professional background of those appointed to the office of *muḥtasib* in the fifteenth century, Berkey remarks that they "were increasingly unsuited, both professionally and temperamentally, for a religious or legal post,"[101] with the result that by the fifteenth century, "evidence of a strictly ethical or religious character [of the post] all but disappears from the chronicles."[102] As the sultanate stumbled toward its fall, the office of the *muḥtasib* could less and less be considered a *waẓīfa dīniyya,* and the *muḥtasib*'s authority "possessed an increasingly arbitrary, coercive, political character."[103] "By the fifteenth century, then," Berkey remarks, "the *muḥtasib* functioned as much as a tax collector as a market inspector, let alone as the guardian of public morals which al-Ghazālī, al-Māwardī and others have envisioned. . . . Under the Mamluk sultanate, driven by a shrinking tax-base with no proportionate decline in expenditures, the collection of revenue became an ever more arbitrary practice. It was a process in which the *muḥtasib* participated; he became . . . 'an arm of the royal extortion network.'"[104]

Concluding his study, Berkey writes that by the end of the Mamluk sultanate, the position of *ḥisba* had degenerated so much that the *muḥtasib* effectively became a "royal 'inquisitor,' not in matters religious, but in financial matters; more specifically, he imprisoned, flogged, tortured, even unto death, those whom the sultan had fined but refused to pay, or those who, simply by means of their wealth, tempted extortion." Commenting on these atrocities, Berkey wonders, "Could al-Māwardī or al-Ghazālī even have recognized the office? Would not even Ibn al-Ukhuwwa have been shocked?"[105]

Kristen Stilt's study of *ḥisba* during the Mamluk sultanate, while primarily concerned with the larger question of studying the application (as opposed to the theory) of *ḥisba,* still has important things to say about the *muḥtasib*'s routine recourse to violence.[106] By relying not only on *fiqh* sources but also on letters of appointment to the position of *muḥtasib*, biographical dictionaries, and Mamluk-era chronicles, Stilt investigates whether the *muḥtasib* derived his authority from legal doctrine (i.e., *fiqh*), which would mean that his position was akin to that of the qadi and the mufti, or from policy-based considerations (i.e., *siyāsa*), which would indicate that his position was associated with the sultan and his viziers. She follows a number of practices, such as price-setting, public consumption of alcohol, monitoring the quality of comestibles, regulation of non-Muslims, and the regulation of currency and taxation, to investigate how the *muḥtasib* went about his business in Mamluk Cairo. Stilt argues that unlike the judge or the mufti, who worked predominantly within the principles of *fiqh,* the *muḥtasib* worked within *siyāsa,* which she views as an essential component of shariʿa, a component that existed alongside *fiqh* with remarkably little tension.

Disregarding the fact that *fiqh* sanctioned and mandated resorting to violence in practicing *ḥisba,* Stilt prefers to view the *muḥtasib* as a *siyāsa* official. Given the fact that *siyāsa*'s rules for accepting evidence were less stringent than those of *fiqh* and that *siyāsa* had a wider latitude than *fiqh* when it came to applying corporal punishment (see chapter 2), it is not surprising that the Mamluk-era *muḥtasib* that Stilt studied often resorted to violence to impose peace and security. Regarding the hoax of the speaking wall mentioned above, for example, even though it was the sultan, not the *muḥtasib,* who carried out the horrific punishment of *tasmīr,* the logic of resorting to this kind of violence is clear: "This seems to have been a case of policy-based punishment, punishment *siyāsatan.* . . . Policy-based punishments typically . . . have the goal of restoring public order and deterring future breaches by displaying publicly the consequences suffered by the violator."[107]

Whether we look at the *muḥtasib* as a *siyāsī* official or as a *fiqhī* one, and whether we prefer to see *ḥisba* as a *waẓīfa diniyya* or a *waẓīfa siyāsiyya,* the fact remains that violence was an integral part of the theory and practice of *ḥisba.* It is true that the *muḥtasib* was entrusted with maintaining the moral good of society, but his way of doing so was not friendly words of brotherly advice, pace Asad, but the whip, the *dirra,* and the cross.

Violence and the Private Muḥtasib

If we turn to the other dimension of the duty—that is, *ḥisba* as moral self- and communal policing—violence appears to play an equally important role. A close look at the chapter on *ḥisba* in Ghazālī's influential text *Iḥyā 'Ulūm al-Dīn,* which still informs the *ḥisba* practiced by many private *muḥtasib*s, reveals how central violence is in this text. To recapitulate, Ghazālī, in contradistinction to Māwardī, insists that *ḥisba* is the duty of each Muslim and that it does not need a license from the ruler to be practiced. When he elaborates on how and when *ḥisba* should be practiced, Ghazālī gives many examples that entail a chilling amount of violence. In one section, he gives an excursus about the confusing issue of whether it is permissible for an inferior to perform *ḥisba* on a superior—for example, a son on his father, a slave on his master, a wife on her husband, a pupil on his teacher, or a subject on his or her ruler—in the same unqualified way it is performed in the other direction. The answer Ghazālī gives is important enough to warrant quoting in full:

What we see is that both cases are similar in principle, but there are differences in detail. To explain, we take the son and the father as an example, and we say: We have explained that there are [various] levels for the performance of *ḥisba*. The son is authorized to use the first [two levels, namely] informing and polite counsel. He has no right to perform *ḥisba* through harsh language or the threat or use of violence. . . . But does he have the right to perform *ḥisba* . . . [by using physical action against offensive objects] in such a way as to lead to the father's aggravation and anger [*ḥaythu tu'addī ilā adhā al-wālid wa sukhṭihi*]? This requires consideration [*hādhā fīhi naẓar*]. He [i.e., the son] can, for example, smash his [i.e., the father's] lute, spill his liquor, loosen the seams of his silk garments, return to its [rightful] owners money he robbed or stole, . . . erase pictures drawn on his walls, or those that are carved into his house's wood, and break the golden and silver vessels [that he keeps in his house]. His performing these acts does not relate to the person of the father, unlike the use of violence or harsh language. The father is aggrieved and angered [by his son carrying out the abovementioned acts], but the son's act is right, and the father's aggravation is due to his love of error and the illicit [*ḥubbuhu lil-bāṭil wa'l-ḥarām*]. By using analogy, it becomes most likely [*al-aẓhar fī'l-qiyās*] that the son is authorized to act in this manner. Indeed, he is obliged to do so.[108]

Ghazālī's frequent references to violence in his account of how to practice *ḥisba* raise a number of issues. The first problematic feature of Ghazālī's text is his instruction that all Muslims should practice *ḥisba* without being authorized to do so by their ruler, a position that he shared with his mentor, Imām al-Ḥaramayn al-Juwaynī.[109] He even goes so far as to allow the private *muḥtasib* to carry weapons and to join others in forming an armed gang to stop manifest wrongdoing, something his mentor disproved of[110] and that some of his commentators, among them Ḥanbalīs, Ḥanafīs, Māliksī, Zaydīs, and even Shāfi'īs, were quite alarmed by, given that it entails the possibility of bloody strife.[111]

The second problematic point raised by Ghazālī's text is that the duty of commanding right and forbidding wrong, even if it requires the use of violence, is entrusted to—nay, incumbent on—the layman (*al-'āmmī*), someone who, by definition, is ignorant of the intricacies of the law. According to Ghazālī, a passerby has the right to storm into a private home if the owner is drinking wine and break his head, but should he do so if he is informed by two upright Muslim men (*yukhbirāhu*) that wine is being drunk therein?[112] Or should he remember the general rule against spying? What if he receives, in an unsolicited manner, information (*khabar*) about an illicit act that is being committed in private? Strictly speaking, this is not considered spying.

Should a guest at a wedding loosen the seams of the silk robe worn by a male youth if that youth is found at the banquet, or should he leave the youth alone on the grounds that he is not yet of age? How can a son measure the anger felt by his father when he spills his father's wine, smashes his musical instruments, or breaks his silver and golden vessels, especially given the high value of such damaged property? "These are delicate points," Ghazālī admits—so delicate that specialized knowledge is required to deal with them. Yet it is precisely these delicate points that the layman is mandated to handle, and he is allowed to use violence in doing so. And even though Ghazālī warns the layman against meddling in ambiguous cases and implores him to stick to clear cases (*al-jāliyyat al-maʿlūma*) like drinking wine, committing adultery, and failing to pray, the problem remains of how the layman distinguishes the ambiguous cases that he should steer clear of from the open-and-shut cases he believes he is obliged to handle.[113]

The third problematic feature of the deployment of violence in practicing *ḥisba* that Ghazālī's formidable text evinces pertains to the very purpose of such violence. Despite the fact that the first four stages—recognition, instruction, counsel, and rebuke—that Ghazālī stipulates for the proper performance of *ḥisba* suggest that the main aim of the duty is to reform the wrongdoer by convincing him of the gravity of his offense, the numerous examples of offenses (*al-munkar*) that Ghazālī cites leave little doubt that he believes the real aim of the duty is to stop the offense rather than to "produce Muslim selves, possessed of the correct desires and passions."[114] Crucially, *ḥisba* is concerned not with inner selves but with the manifest wrong, *al-munkar*. Accordingly, the practice is focused not on producing and caring for inner selves but on policing and monitoring outward behavior, and no attention is paid to the connection between these two forms of self-control. This is most clearly expressed in a short passage in which Ghazālī asks the intriguing question of what the proper course of action should be if one is confronted by a man who intends to sever his own limb and who will not desist except if he is fought, something that carries with it the possibility of his own death: "Should he be fought even if [some people think] that this is wrong, arguing that [fighting him] in an attempt to save a limb will result in the loss of life, and that the loss of life necessarily means the loss of limb?" Ghazālī's answer to this intriguing question is as unambiguous in its wording as it is revealing of the very purpose of *ḥisba:* "He should be prevented from this [i.e., severing his own limb], and he should be fought [to prevent him from doing so], for our purpose is not only to save his life and his limb, but to prevent the wrong and the sin [*ḥasm sabīl al-munkar wa'l-ma'ṣiya*]. For killing him as *ḥisba* is not a sin, [whereas] his severing his own limb is [*qatluhu fi'l-ḥisba laysa bi-ma'ṣiyatin wa qat'u ṭarafi nafsihi ma'ṣiyatun*]."[115]

It is thus clear that *ḥisba* is as infused and informed by violence when practiced by a private *muḥtasib* as it is when practiced by a public, officially appointed *muḥtasib.* In both types of *ḥisba,* there is clear recognition that brotherly words of advice are not enough to deter the wrongdoing (*al-munkar*), and both types of *muḥtasib*s are enjoined to resort to violence in an extreme manner.

Conclusion of Ḥisba *in the Islamic Discursive Tradition*

The above excursus via lexicons, *fiqh* treatises, *ḥisba* manuals, and pre-modern chronicles was not intended to offer an exhaustive survey of the history of *ḥisba* as a concept and as a practice. Nor was it intended to argue that the *muḥtasib's* position as market inspector was a failure—the thriving urban culture of different Islamic polities over the centuries, from Cordova to Samarkand, indicates that the *muḥtasib* did contribute to the safety and prosperity of many Islamic cities. A further indication of the utility of the office of the *muḥtasib* can be found in how it was resurrected, with some important modifications, in southern European cities after the Reconquista.[116] However, a quick look at the theory of *ḥisba* reveals that it contained serious tensions that are a far cry from the idealized image that posits it as a technique of producing Muslim selves, endowed with the correct desires and passions, or as a system of peaceful communal self-policing practiced among friends. At issue are two points, the first being the fact that the *muḥtasib* lacked effective independence from the state, and the second being the central role violence plays in the theory of *ḥisba.* It may be true, as many modern-day proponents of the practice contend, that *ḥisba* is "a masterpiece of Islamic legislation" (*rā'i'a min rawā'i' al-tashrī' al-Islāmī*), the implementation of which is guaranteed to "protect rights, uphold justice, safeguard . . . piety [*ḥimāyat . . . al-faḍīla*], . . . and protect society from evil."[117] But given how central violence is in the theory of *ḥisba,* it is difficult to agree with Asad's claim that *ḥisba* is connected "to the virtue of 'friendship' [*suhba, ikhwa*], . . . [and that] it as a matter of responsibility and concern for a friend rather than simply of policing,"[118] or with Agrama's contention that "*ḥisba* is a disciplined practice of moral criticism intended to produce proper Muslim selves, possessed of the correct desires and passions."[119] Rather, *ḥisba* is firmly tied to the *siyāsa* prerogative of the Muslim state to maintain peace and take any measure to doing so, including restoring to extreme physical violence.

INTERLUDE: THE *MUḤTASIB*'S SWAN SONG:

We've now had a quick look at the violence that lies at the center of the theory of *ḥisba,* but the question remains as to when exactly the *muḥtasib* disappeared from Egyptian public life and who replaced him in the important task of monitoring the market. When and how did *ḥisba* fall into disuse? While a complete history of the practice of *ḥisba* through the ages awaits a thorough study, a number of laws and regulations from the specific context of nineteenth-century Egypt point to the fundamental transformation *ḥisba* underwent in conjunction with the creation of the modern state.

From as early as 1830, Egyptian authorities were determined to deal with the shortcomings of the *muḥtasib*'s position and to devise alternative mechanisms for monitoring the market. That year, a top-level council, al-Majlis al-ʿĀlī, held a meeting to discuss the problem. It summarily dismissed the present *muḥtasib,* Selim Ağa, and decided to replace him with a more assiduous official. The council also noted that Cairo was such a large city that it could not be monitored by one *muḥtasib,* no matter how diligent. No sooner had the city's merchants agreed to the *muḥtasib*'s prices than they violated them. The council recommended appointing undercover agents to roam the markets and report wayward merchants to officers of the newly formed police force. A daily report was to be compiled and forwarded to the Majlis, which would decide what future action was to be taken.[120]

A few years later, the entire office of the *muḥtasib* was abolished. The Siyasetnameh law of 1837 stipulated that the *muḥtasib*s of Cairo and Alexandria would henceforth be dismissed and that their duties would be taken over by the Dīwān Khīdīwī and Dīwān al-Baḥr, respectively.[121] However, we do find the *muḥtasib* mentioned in a subsequent law, one dating from 1841 that indicates that this important office was phased out in stages rather than abolished with one stroke. In August 1841, following a minor outbreak of plague in Alexandria, a decree titled General Regulations Concerning the Public Health in Alexandria and the Interior was issued, and what was significant about it was that it explicitly assigned the public health physician to examine the quality of all kinds of food sold and consumed in the market.[122] Equally significant was the stipulation that the physician be accompanied on his daily rounds not only by a "man of the police" but also by the city's *muḥtasib.* This marked a clear turning point in the power and prestige of the *muḥtasib,* and in just a few years his age-old position as the prime overseer of the markets disappeared without a trace. It is therefore worth our while to take a close look at this decree, for it indicates a pivotal moment in the long history of the *muḥtasib* in Egyptian history and marks the point at which his duties were taken over by a wide range of new officials.

While this decree covered many aspects of public hygiene, including checking the bodies of the dead, sweeping streets, and demolishing huts "that have been built on a plan opposed to the rules calculated for salubrity," it also contained an entire chapter titled "Sanitary Police of the Environs." This chapter included an entire section on food control that warrants quoting in full:

> There being a physician for inspecting the cattle killed for account of government and preventing sick or unhealthy animals from being killed; it shall be his business to inspect also the cattle which are killed at the same place for account of private individuals. The said physician shall be accompanied by a *cavass* [sentry] of the police.
>
> On certain days, in the hot season, fish being sold in a stale and putrefied state, to the detriment of the population and the public health, it shall be the business of the physician inspecting meat to inspect also the sales of fish, and not finding it fresh and fit for sale, to deliver the fish and the seller to the Man of the Police for punishing the latter severely and throwing the fish into the sea.
>
> There are, besides, places in the city where meat, stale fish, fruits, vegetables, grains, etc., are sold, which are kept in such a state as would injure the health of those who purchase them. This shall be prevented and it shall be done in the following manner.
>
> The physician appointed over butchers, etc., not being employed for more than two hours every morning in inspecting the different denominations of meat, when he has thus discharged that duty, shall join the Mohzasse [*sic;* i.e., *muḥtasib*] of the city in his rounds, and happening to meet any stale meat, grain, fruits or anything else, he shall collect all such articles of provision and deliver them up to the police, together with the seller thereof. He shall also inspect the market of the public cooks, and there visit and ascertain the quality and the condition of the victuals and of the utensils in which they are cooked and finding either in a state that could injure the public health, he shall deliver up the utensils containing such meats, as also the seller thereof, the latter for being punished.

> The water which serves for ablutions in the mosques remaining some days without being changed, corrupts and stinks; to prevent which the heads of the mosques shall be invited to change it once in three days.
>
> The stores of salt fish called *Fisich,* and other such articles noxious to public health, shall be removed from the city and placed at the Mahmoudié to the south of the huts of the *barrani* [foreigners].
>
> Cattle which yield milk, such as buffaloes, cows, goats, etc., abound in the interior of the city, and of inhabited houses and of the stores belonging to them. These also shall be removed to the vicinity of Pompey's pillar gate, into stables or enclosures at a distance from inhabited places, in order that exhalations caused by their excrement may create no harm.[123]

What is striking about this decree is the reduced role that the *muḥtasib* played in monitoring comestibles. Gone were the days when his appearance in the market was marked by fear and awe; the decree effectively reduced him to a local informant who merely assisted the police in checking the quality of food sold in the market. In addition to the central role played by the police and the correspondingly diminished role played by the *muḥtasib* in the daily rounds of the food markets, what is significant here is the type of hygienic concerns with which the physician—accompanied by the policeman—is preoccupied.

ḤISBA IN KHEDIVAL EGYPT

Chapter 3 examined how the concern about miasmas informed public hygiene policies throughout the middle decades of the nineteenth century. The remainder of this chapter will study how these ideas and inquiries shaped medical theory, specifically with regard to diet and food control, and how medical theory, in turn, informed public hygiene policy with respect to market inspection. This will bring us into the Qaṣr al-ʿAinī Medical School, where we will take a close look at the curriculum and follow the school's students after graduation. Such a tour of the prime medical institution of nineteenth-century Egypt is necessary if we are to find out who replaced the *muḥtasib* in his central task of monitoring comestibles sold in the markets.

From Morals to Humors

The lengthy quote cited above from the 1841 health ordinance illustrates, among other things, a dramatic shift from concerns about market fraud, pubic morality, and weights and measures to an acute anxiety about public hygiene. This shift is further demonstrated by the following excerpts from two different texts that deal with the same topic: the consumption of alcohol. In his twelfth-century *ḥisba* manual, Shayzarī states that the *muḥtasib* must make sure that non-Muslims do not "display any alcoholic drinks or pigs."[124] He instructs the *muḥtasib* to give Muslims caught drinking wine publicly forty lashes with the whip. He adds, "If he thinks that public interest will be served by giving him eighty lashes, then he may do so. This is because ʿUmar b. al-Khaṭṭāb gave eighty lashes to someone drinking alcohol . . . The *muḥtasib* should strip off the man's clothes, lift the hand holding the whip until the white of his armpit can be seen, and distribute the lashes on the man's shoulders, buttocks, and thighs."[125]

By contrast, the following account from *Al-Minḥah fi Siyāsat Ḥifẓ al-Ṣiḥḥah,* an 1834 Qaṣr al-ʿAinī medical textbook written by a certain Dr. Bernard, illustrates the radically different language used to talk about alcohol in the nineteenth century:

> All simple alcoholic beverages [e.g., wine] . . . are suitable for people with a lymphatic temperament. They are also beneficial for people whose stomachs are irritable, those who do manual labor, and the elderly. They are also useful during times of cold weather or during extreme heat, which is dilapidating. [These drinks are also beneficial when eating] food that is difficult to digest, that is, food that does not stimulate the stomach strongly. At the same time, these drinks should be avoided by people who have bilious or sanguine temperaments; at times when the organs, especially the stomach, are stimulated; when performing gentle physical exercise [*ar-riyāḍa al-laṭīfa*]; during adolescence; when struggling with mental work [*al-kadd fi taḥṣīl al-ʿulūm*]; or during temperate weather. We are not talking here about the [harmful effects of drinking] adulterated wine and other alcoholic beverages.[126]

There is no reference here to holy writ or prophetic utterance; nor is this new approach to alcoholic drinks informed by ethical concerns or historical precedents from Islamic history. Rather, what we see here is a deep concern about public hygiene and the role that consuming food played in a reconstituted world—reconstituted, that is, along medical and hygienic lines. To understand clearly how this new world was shaped and how the *muḥtasib* lost his place in it, we need to look at how books like Dr. Bernard's shaped generations of Egyptian physicians and chemists and at how these young medical men believed that they had at their disposal an objective, reliable tool that enabled them to monitor food markets.[127] The following is therefore an inquiry into the way the medical world of nineteenth-century Egypt viewed and treated comestibles: Who were these physicians and chemists that were charged with investigating food sold in the marketplace? How and where were they trained? What medical theories did they subscribe to and how did these theories enable them to perform their food inspection duties? We need to follow these men from the schools in which they were trained to the labs in which they worked. We also need to follow the policemen they worked in tandem with to the streets that they roamed, to the coffee shops they descended on, and to the brothels they raided in their ceaseless attempts to investigate the quality of food and beverages sold and consumed therein.

From Humors to Tissues

The numerous medical books published by Būlāq Press in the first fifty years of its existence offer an invaluable insight into the medical world of nineteenth-century Egypt.[128] Although most of these books were translated from French and therefore only tangentially reflected medical beliefs in Egypt, the translators, who themselves were professors at Qaṣr al-ʿAinī, often wrote extensive introductions in which they commented on prevalent medical practices in Egypt. Two of these books deserve special attention as they were written specifically for an Egyptian audience and also because they both had extensive sections on food. More significantly, given that they were written ten years apart, they show the transformation that had occurred in medical doctrine at the Qaṣr al-ʿAinī medical establishment. The first, *Al-Minḥah fī Siyāsat Ḥifẓ al-Ṣiḥḥah,* referred to above, was published in 1834, making it the third medical book to be published by Būlāq Press. Its author, Dr. Bernard, had been professor of hygiene and forensic medicine at Qaṣr al-ʿAinī since the foundation of the school in 1827.[129] Although translated from French, *Al-Minḥah* had not been published before because it had been commissioned specifically by Clot Bey to be used as a textbook for his students.[130] The second book, *Kunūz al-Ṣiḥḥa wa Yawāqīt al-Minḥa,* was written by Clot Bey and intended to educate a wider, nonspecialist public about general principles of public hygiene.[131]

Both Bernard's *Al-Minḥa* and Clot Bey's *Kunūz* played crucial roles in shaping public opinion regarding food and diet as well as influencing official government policy on food control and investigations of coffee shops, food vendors, and food markets. Comparing these two books also shows that there was a marked shift from humoralism, represented by Bernard's

Al-Minḥa, to anatomopathological medicine, represented by Clot Bey's *Kunūz al-Ṣiḥḥa.*

The importance of diet in *Al-Minḥah* can be clearly seen by the fact that Bernard starts the first section—on personal hygiene ("Aṣ-Ṣiḥḥa al-Infirādiyya")—of his four-section book with a discussion of the digestive system and the various dietary regimens that he believed should be followed to ensure good health.[132] The theoretical basis on which Bernard constructs his dietary regimen does not derive from a mechanistic model of the body, one that sees the body as nothing "but a statue, an earthen machine," as Descartes put it.[133] Accordingly, he does not believe that there is one dietary regimen that is suitable for all bodies.[134] Rather, he believes that human bodies come in numerous forms and shapes due to the multiplicity of natural factors that affect them; so numerous are these factors, he contends, that if taken seriously, they will result in as many classifications as there are human bodies, and it "would then be necessary to prescribe health regimens for each individual body." However, he states that there are seven natural factors that should inform any system of classification: age (*al-asnān*), gender (*al-dhukūra wa'l-unūtha*), habits and customs (*al-ʿādāt*), humors (*al-amzija*), occupations (*al-ṣanāyiʿ*), hereditary predispositions (*al-istiʿdādāt al-mawrūtha*), and idiosyncrasies (*idiūsinkrāsia*).

Of these natural factors, Bernard considers humors to be the most significant. Showing clear signs of humoralism, he assumes that the body contained humors whose different blends, or temperaments, are responsible for the various functions of the different organs. However, in a sharp contradistinction to the Greek Galenic and the Arab/Persian Avicennian theories that believed in the existence of four humors (i.e., blood, phlegm, yellow bile, and black bile), Bernard writes that scientists "in our age believe in [only] three temperaments: the sanguine, the nervous, and the lymphatic." He then gives a brief description of each:

> The sanguine temperament is that in which the sanguine organs reign supreme. It is likely to lead to inflammatory diseases. People with this temperament should avoid all stimulants that result in exciting the circulation of blood. They should also avoid agents that help transform chyle [*al-kīlūs*] into blood as this may lead to blood clots, which, depending on [an individual's] age, can appear in different parts of the body. They should avoid different kinds of fatigue.... At the same time, they should stay away from idleness, rest, and inactivity.
>
> The nervous temperament results from being prone to the agitation of the entire spinal cord, especially the nerves serving the brain.... People with this

> temperament should avoid undertaking any activity that can increase the vital forces in the nervous system. . . . They should also avoid physical exercise and should spend extensive time in cerebral contemplation [*tafakkurāt ʿaqliyya*]. They should avoid all stimulants, . . . like alcoholic drinks, tea, and coffee. . . .
>
> The lymphatic temperament is known by the excessive appearances of lymphatic nodes and vessels. Scrofula and scoliosis are the two ailments that are mostly the result of the pathological preponderance of this temperament [*al-tasalṭun al-raḍi li-hādhā al-mizāj*]. . . . The best prophylactic measures to follow are to live in hot, dry climates; to preserve the skin energy by covering it with woolen clothes; to consume small quantities of nutritious food; and to continuously perform physical exercise in hot, sunny places.[135]

The epistemology of Bernard's *Al-Minḥa* is clearly that which sees "the theory and principles of humoral pathology . . . as given in natural science . . . and their investigation [as] off-limits to the physician."[136] Like all humoralists, furthermore, Bernard is careful not to argue that these temperaments exist in pristine form: "Rather, they are usually mixed together in the same body, and rarely do we find the preponderance of any one of them over the others."[137] Nevertheless, it is in the right balance of these temperaments that health resides and it is restoring this balance, if it is temporarily lost, that is the prime duty of the physician. As a public hygienist, however, Bernard is not concerned with prescribing "individual health measures" (*waṣāya ṣiḥḥa khuṣūṣiyya*)[138] but with setting down principles of public hygiene and identifying general rules of how to prevent the natural balance of the body from tipping over into imbalance. Like ancient humoralists, he is concerned with the six "non-naturals" of the traditional *regimen sanitatis* literature—that is, the six categories according to which the body could be restored to health. These *sex res non-naturales* were believed to be air; food and drink; exercise and rest; sleeping and waking; repletion and excretion; and emotional well-being.[139] Above all, he is concerned with food and drink, and specifically with the conditions in which they are consumed in such a way as not to cause a "change in temperament" (*taghayyur mizāj*).[140]

Thus, and as we have seen, alcoholic drinks are to be avoided by people with a sanguine or a bilious and nervous temperament. Milk and milk products are to be avoided by people with a lymphatic temperament and by those living in low, humid countries that have bad air circulation.[141] Food rich in albumin, like eggs, oysters, snails, brains, liver, and blood, is good for those with irritable stomachs, the elderly, women, and "those who lead a life of laziness and inactivity, like scholars."[142]

By contrast, Clot Bey's *Kunūz al-Ṣiḥḥa* does not evince such a belief in humors. With the exception of a small section on humors and how they affect individual health,[143] the entire book appears to have been written with a clear aim in sight: the categorical renunciation of humoralism. In introducing the section on pathology, Clot Bey makes his stance clear:

> Most people believe that disease is the result of the corruption of, or the excess of, humors. They believe the humors to be bile, blood, yellow phlegm, and black bile. Others say [disease is the result of] unknown natural vapors. The sane person has to reject this talk and understand that the [human] body consists of fluids and solids, the latter being more numerous. It has been empirically shown that most diseases are formed in the tissues, which are considered among the solid parts [of the body], and rarely are they formed in the abovementioned fluids. Even when a change is detected in these fluids, this change is not a primary one but a consequence of [morphological] changes that occurred in the tissues. Therefore, . . . pathogenesis originates in the organs [and not in the fluids]. . . . Most of the morphological changes take the form of an inflammation. . . . The inflammation of the lungs, for example, results in the secretion of phlegm, and when this [phlegm] is excreted in excess, this means that it [i.e., the phlegm] is but a symptom, whereas the lung is the seat of disease. The same is true about bile, which is a consequence of an inflammation of the liver.[144]

Given his rejection of humoralism, when he turns to a discussion of food and drink, Clot Bey appears not to address their impact on temperaments. For example, in contrast to Bernard's discussion of alcoholic drinks and their suitability, or unsuitability, for people with different temperaments, Clot Bey points out that

> drinking wine is not a human necessity, for there are many regions in which it is unknown, or where those who know it abstain from drinking it; yet they lead a healthy life. It may even be said that [drinking] wine, even in small quantities, is harmful in hot climates. This is in contrast to colder climates, where it is useful, and if drunk in moderate quantities, helps in digestion, affects the skin [positively], and warms the body. Many people have got so accustomed to [drinking] it that it has become a necessity for them. *'Araqī* [an anise-flavored alcoholic drink], on the other hand, is the nastiest of alcoholic drinks [*aqbaḥ al-ashriba al-khamriyya*] for it is harmful to health. And what is really strange is that despite its harmful nature, it is widely used in Egypt. [Moreover,] those who drink it do so not out of necessity but only to get drunk, unlike the Europeans who say that there is no harm in drinking it in small quantities to help with digestion. . . . All nations have out-

> lawed the imprudent drinking of alcoholic beverages [*qad ajmaʿat al-milal wa'l-niḥal ʿalā ḥurmat istiʿmāl al-muskir iʿtibāṭan*], as drunkenness is harmful and degrading to man. Indeed, the drunkard is on the same level as the lowest of animals. How many illnesses are attributable to excessive drinking? Indeed, excessive drinking can lead to a stroke, which is a fatal illness, and how many drunkards have died suddenly [as a result of drinking]!?[145]

In addition to the clear moralistic tone assumed toward the end of his diatribe, what is noteworthy in Clot Bey's analysis of the harmful effects of alcoholic beverages is the absence of any reference to humors and how alcohol may be harmful to people with different temperaments. Having based his understanding of pathology on the study of morphological changes within tissues, there was no place in Clot Bey's thinking for humors and how they might affect the human body. Although at times he leans toward the notion of dietary management, avoidance of gluttony, and regular exercise,[146] he does not seem to be linking his ideas about dietary regimens to humoral temperaments. Instead, the new theories of morbid anatomy that had been expounded in Paris in the 1790s by Xavier Bichat informed Clot Bey's views of pathology and physiology. Like Bichat, Clot Bey specifically rejected older Aristotelian and Avicennian notions of souls or "vital spirits" and accepted that the human body could best be understood by analyzing tissues (*ansijah*), whose comparable structures, even if found in different organs, provided a new map of the human body. In another work, a short treatise on general anatomy in which he explicitly cited Bichat, Clot Bey argued that these tissues "can be further divided into cellular tissues, muscular tissues, and nervous tissues," and even though he disagreed with Bichat's conclusion that the human body is composed of twenty-one types of tissues, he nevertheless based his entire understanding of the human body on Bichat's new approach, which took tissues to be the building blocks of anatomy, physiology, and pathology[147] and saw them as "the real organizing elements of our bodies, whose nature is constantly the same wherever they may be found."[148] Furthermore, in *Kunūz al-Ṣiḥḥa,* Clot Bey argued, "The human body is like a machine composed of tissues that, in turn, form the different organs.... These tissues are distinct from the fluids that may be in these organs. The body is also composed of solid substances, like bones, and of less solid substances, such as cartilages, tendons, sinews, nerves, arteries, veins, lymph nodes, ... and cellular tissues."[149]

Chemical Pathology

Comparing Bernard's *Al-Minḥa* with Clot Bey's *Kunūz al-Ṣiḥḥa* shows that a paradigmatic shift occurred in Qaṣr al-ʿAinī's medical discourse. By discarding Bernard's humoralism, Clot Bey followed Bichat's new theories, which were based on morbid anatomy and held that disease attacks tissues rather than humors. This had significant implications for both personal and public hygiene. According to these beliefs, a healthy diet is not one that restores the balance of the humors but one that "revitalizes the human body by restoring, through digestion, bodily organs."[150] Likewise, food sold in markets should be monitored not to catch fraud, as the *muḥtasib* was instructed to do, or to avoid pungent smells, as humoralists insisted, but to verify its nutritional value and freshness. Clot Bey, accordingly, cautioned against eating old fish as it "may be as harmful as poison."[151]

The Centrality of Chemical Pathology in Medical Training In addition to Bichat's theories of pathology, Lavoisier's chemical revolution also had a profound impact on the medical worldview of Qaṣr al-ʿAinī's students, and it may be instructive to look at how the school's curriculum prepared graduates to handle the chemical investigations that were conducted on adulterated food and to perform postmortem investigations in criminal cases in which poison was suspected.

Chemistry was central in the education of Qaṣr al-ʿAinī's students, and a quick look at medical textbooks printed by Būlāq Press for the school's students immediately shows how foundational Lavoisian chemistry was for the curriculum. In *Kunūz al-Ṣiḥḥa,* for example, Clot Bey argued that chemistry was much more reliable in explaining and treating poison than the prevalent medical beliefs, which he traced back to Ancient Egypt, Galen, and Dāwūd al-Anṭākī.[152] Muhammad al-Shāfiʿī, who translated Clot Bey's *Kunūz al-Ṣiḥḥa,* wrote a book on diagnostics in which he argued that chemistry was one of the necessary sciences that the doctor had to master to be able to give a correct diagnostics.[153] *Ghāyat al-Marām fī Adwiyat al-Asqām,* a veterinary textbook published in 1839 that comprised the lecture notes of a certain Dr. Grégoire, who taught veterinary science at Qaṣr al-ʿAinī, started with a lengthy introduction extolling the new science of chemistry and praising its founder, Lavoisier. In a section titled "The History of Air," he ridicules the ancients (*al-aqdamūn*) for having thought of air as composed of four elements and argues instead that air is a gaseous liquid (*sayyāl ghāzī*).[154] The following section, "On Water," reads: "The ancients used to think that water was one of the four elements, along with air, fire, and earth. A long time later, chemists wondered about the composition of water, and in 1783 Lavoisier figured out its composition. Two years later, four chemists [corroborated] the aforementioned scientist's [i.e., Lavoisier's] method, and succeeded in adding a certain amount of hydrogen to a certain amount of oxygen to produce an ounce of water."[155]

The most important chemistry book printed by Būlāq Press, however, was an Arabic translation of Nicolas Perron's lecture notes titled *Al-Djawāhir al-Saniyya fī'l-A'māl al-Kīmāwiyya* (The sublime jewels in chemical tools), published in 1844.[156] The centrality of chemistry in medical education is spelled out clearly in the book's preface, which states, "Chemistry is fundamental to the science of medicine and healing bodies. It is like a mother to this science, whereas physics is the father."[157] In the introduction, Perron provides a lengthy summary of the history of chemistry that starts with ancient Egypt and goes on to mention the unintended beneficial outcomes of alchemy, give a detailed explanation of the Arab contribution to chemistry, and then highlight the contributions of such scientists as Paracelsus, Albertus Magnus, Bacon, van Helmont, Becher, Stahl, Herman Boerhaave, Marggraf, Reoulle, Cavendish, Priestley, Guyton, and Lavoisier, among others. He ends the introduction by paying homage to his own teacher, Mathieu Orfila, the father of toxicology,[158] and highlighting Orfila's contribution to the advancement of toxicology.[159]

The Qaṣr al-'Ainī Chemical-Pharmaceutical Lab. Having seen that the physicians who attended Qaṣr al-'Ainī were trained in Bichatian pathology and Lavoisian chemistry, we move our attention to the nationwide public health system, where these physicians worked after graduation. At the core of this system, certainly as far as food quality control was concerned, was the Qaṣr al-'Ainī Chemical-Pharmaceutical Lab, located close to the Qaṣr al-'Ainī Medical School and Hospital, which is where the chemical compounds needed for the school were prepared.[160] European travelers who visited this lab noted how organized and well run it was. In 1840, William Wilde (the dramatist Oscar Wilde's father) visited Qaṣr al-'Ainī and wrote that the "pharmacy was on a scale of great magnificence; beautifully clean, in comparison with such establishments in England, and had in it all the most valuable and approved medicines, many of which were prepared in the laboratory by native hands."[161] Thirty years later, the Qaṣr al-ʿAinī Chemical-Pharmaceutical Lab had gained such fame that it warranted a special mention in Baedeker's *Egypt: Handbook for Travellers:* "Cairo also possesses . . . a Chemical-Pharmaceutical Laboratory, presided over by M. Gastinel, a French chemist, and possessing an excellent pharmaceutical collection. The medicines required for all the hospitals in the country are prepared in large quantities at the laboratory, and the yield of the twelve saltpeter manufactories of Egypt (about a thousand tons per annum) is tested here."[162]

Known in Arabic as Maʿmal al-Kīmyā, and also sometimes referred to as al-Kīmyākhāna, this lab analyzed suspicious food samples that the police gathered from the markets, and it is this lab that addressed the police with the cautionary remarks mentioned at the beginning of this chapter about how food samples should be packaged. Before we delve into how this lab went about investigating the quality of food samples, it may be useful to have a quick look at its staff and their qualifications.

A document dating from September 1864 gives a detailed account of the composition of a typical ad hoc chemical committee (*jamʿiyya kīmāwiyya*) established at the Qaṣr al-ʿAinī Chemical-Pharmaceutical Lab to investigate a sample of food sent by the police.[163] Chairing the committee was Antonio Figari Bey, chief pharmacist and head examiner (*kashshāf bāshī*). Figari was an Italian pharmacist and botanist who taught botany and materia medica (pharmacology) at Qaṣr al-ʿAinī. He was born in Genoa in 1804, graduated with a diploma in pharmacy in 1825, and arrived in Egypt in 1829.[164] In 1833, he was put in charge of all Qaṣr al-ʿAinī laboratories. Six years later, he became inspector of pharmacies, and in 1858, he was promoted to the position of head of the Department of Pharmacology at the medical school and given the honorific title Bey. He was an avid collector of plants and managed to amass a large collection of natural history specimens while on official expeditions to Sinai, Upper Egypt, the Western Desert, Sudan, Nubia, and Palestine, expeditions he was dispatched on to search for marble and coal. In 1865, he donated his entire collection of thirty thousand specimens to the city of Florence. In 1863, his annual salary was eight thousand piasters, one of the highest salaries in the entire medical service. In 1867, he went to Paris as part of the official delegation in charge of organizing the Egyptian pavilion at the International Exposition of that year. He published many books related to his work in Egypt, including a plan to establish model farms in Egypt[165] and two textbooks on botany written for the students at Qaṣr al-ʿAinī.[166] His most important work, however, was his 1865 account of Egyptian natural history, *Studi scientifici sull'Egitto e sue adiacenze, compresa la penisola dell'Arabia Petrea*. In 1870, he returned to Genoa, where he died in November of that year.[167]

Also serving on the committee was J. B. Gastinel, who was mentioned above in the Baedeker *Guide to Egypt* quote. Gastinel started out as a professor of chemistry, physics, and natural history at Qaṣr al-ʿAinī and was later promoted to the position of director of the School of Pharmaceutics.[168] He was described in an 1858 official report as "a chemist and a pharmacist who studied in France; served in Egypt for many years; [and] participated in the Syrian campaign [1831–1840]. . . . He then opened a pharmacy in Cairo that was reputable for its good medicines. He is famous for his scientific discoveries and is universally acknowledged to be of good and upright character. He currently teaches natural history at Qaṣr al-ʿAinī."[169] Gastinel was a prolific writer, with studies under his name on hashish, opium, glutens, and the Helwan mineral waters.[170] But his most important book was a three-volume textbook on chemistry, which Būlāq Press published in translation in 1870 under the title *Nukhbat al-Adhkiyāʾ fī ʿIlm al-Kīmiyāʾ*.[171]

Another member of the committee was Aḥmad Efendi Nadā, who had studied at the Qaṣr al-ʿAinī Medical School.[172] After graduating in 1845, he was sent to France to study chemistry. He returned in 1847 and was employed as a professor at many government schools, including his alma mater. He was a prolific translator; his translations include Figari's *Ḥusn al-Barāʿa* and Gastinel's *Nukhbat al-Adhkiyāʾ*. He also authored a book on botany and another on geology.[173]

The committee also included Ṣāliḥ Efendi ʿAlī, assistant professor of chemistry and physics at Qaṣr al-ʿAinī. Ṣāliḥ Efendi had studied at Qaṣr al-ʿAinī, specializing in pharmacology. He graduated in 1845 and was sent to France in 1862, but he returned after only one year. He was then employed as a pharmacist at the Qaṣr al-ʿAinī Hospital and as a professor at the adjoining medical school.[174]

It would thus appear that this lab was a centralized government body that had been tasked with coordinating all matters pertaining to drugs and chemicals needed for Qaṣr al-ʿAinī Medical School and Hospital. The chemists and physicians who managed it had been educated in the newly reconstituted sciences of physiology, chemistry, botany, toxicology, and so on; they also taught at the medical school, often using textbooks that they had written or translated themselves. This coupling of practical expertise and academic knowledge allowed the scientists of the Qaṣr al-ʿAinī Chemical-Pharmaceutical

Lab to play a decisive role in sidelining the *muḥtasib* insofar as the delicate task of monitoring food was concerned.

Medical Policing

From what has been said so far, it should be clear that the *muḥtasib* as an inspector of food markets was gradually losing his position as the new field of Lavoisian chemistry was becoming known in Egypt. This new discipline was the product of a complex set of institutional and pedagogical efforts that allowed it to play an increasingly effective role in monitoring comestibles. To get a fuller picture of how chemistry was deployed in Cairo's food markets, we have to zoom out of Qaṣr al-ʿAinī and its chemical lab and take a look at the Cairo police. Viewing this larger picture of public hygiene will help us understand how *ḥisba* as a form of market inspection was ultimately replaced by Lavoisian chemistry and how the physical violence that was a central component of the *muḥtasib*'s profession was replaced by the latent violence of the law as enforced by the police.

Development of the Public Health System. As stated above, the Qaṣr al-ʿAinī Chemical-Pharmaceutical Lab was the centerpiece (as far as food investigation was concerned) of the Egyptian public health system. The centralized activities of this system, through which the state (rather than neighborhood associations or charitable organizations) assumed responsibility for matters of public hygiene, seem to have much in common with the ideas of Johann Peter Frank (1748–1821), the German pioneer of public health and social medicine, whose *System einer vollständigen medicinischen Polizey* (A complete system of medical police), published in nine volumes between 1779 and 1827, laid the groundwork for the systematic analysis of the health problems of community life.[175] Although Frank's influential book was not translated into Arabic, many of its ideas can be detected in both Bernard's *Al-Minḥa* and Clot Bey's *Kunūz al-Ṣiḥḥa*. Having seen how notions of dietary regimens, were reflected in the Qaṣr al-ʿAinī curriculum and how the concern about nutritious food was one of the factors behind the need to monitor the quality of food sold in the markets, we now need to look at how these concerns were translated into institutional practice. What follows, therefore, is an account of the evolution of how the public health system handled food and drug control.

As noted in chapter one, there is no evidence that any serious steps toward social medicine were taken before the 1830s. It was the cholera epidemic of

1831, which killed between 150,000 and 190,000 people over a few months, that triggered the first institutional response to the country's public hygiene problems. After the devastating effect of the epidemic became clear, Mehmed Ali Pasha suggested to the European consuls in Alexandria that they form a quarantine board to protect the city. The result was a five-man committee called the Quarantine Board of Alexandria. The Pasha put at its disposal twenty thousand troops and gave it carte blanche for expenditures.[176] The board, however, failed to check the spread of the epidemic and had to disband itself only ten days after its formation. Nevertheless, in October 1831, after the epidemic had started to wane, the European consuls reassembled the board and, with the backing of the Pasha, imposed tight restrictions on maritime traffic. This incarnation of the board remained in existence until the early 1880s, although it assumed different titles, the most widely used of which were the General Board of Health (Majlis 'Umūm al-Ṣiḥḥa) and the Quarantine Board (Majlis al-Karantīnā). Regardless of its name, the body's main task was to impose and regulate quarantines, and it had only a tangential concern for the general health conditions of the country at large.[177]

More relevant and influential was the medical council that Clot Bey headed in Cairo, the Shūrā al-Aṭibbā, which also went by the name Mashūrat al-Ṭibb.[178] Clot Bey was never happy about the influence that the Alexandria board had over Mehmed Ali, and he viewed its members as laymen who were ignorant of the sensitive medical matters in which they were dabbling. For their part, the members of the Alexandria board took a dim view of Clot Bey's anticontagionist policies and were alarmed by the public statements he made in lectures and in publications that favored the admission of plague patients to public hospitals. But the conflict between the Alexandria board, on the one hand, and Clot Bey, the European members of his Shūrā, and the Egyptian students who had started to return from their student missions in France, on the other hand, was not limited to doctrinal differences about the nature and communicability of the plague. More fundamentally, the conflict centered around the desirability and possibility of creating a public health system on a national level. Whereas the Alexandria board restricted itself to quarantine services, the Cairo-based Shūrā thought that the precautionary measures taken against plague were too narrow and believed that a genuine public health system, one that stressed preventive medicine, should be founded. This conflict came to a head in 1841 with the resolution of the conflict between Mehmed Ali and the sultan and the subsequent drastic reduction of the size of the army.[179] With the sudden availability of hundreds of army doctors, surgeons, and pharmacists, Clot Bey argued that the time was ripe for the creation of a public health system that could cover the entire country. The Alexandria board, however, saw these qualified and trained doctors as an opportunity to expand the quarantine services.[180]

A minor outbreak of plague in Alexandria gave Clot Bey the pretext that he needed to push for his own proposal. While the members of the Quarantine Board of Alexandria argued that it was the right time to expand quarantine measures, Mehmed Ali was aware of the growing dissatisfaction among European merchants at the inevitable delays in trade that quarantines entailed. He seems also to have been notified by his informants in Istanbul[181] that the British ambassador there was making strong protestations against quarantine measures and asserting that "the plague is much aggravated, if it is not actually generated by the want of cleanliness in the streets, by the want of sufficient ventilation in houses, and by the want of proper drainage in places contiguous to habitations."[182] In August 1841, Mehmed Ali accepted Clot Bey's proposals for the expansion of health measures that went beyond imposing quarantines, passing the comprehensive public health measures reviewed above, which marginalized the *muḥtasib.*

Science in Action. To complete our picture of *ḥisba,* chemistry, and food, we add one last element: the Department of Health Inspection of Cairo (Dīwān Taftīsh Ṣiḥḥat al-Maḥrūsa). Part of the Governorate of Cairo but also supervised by Shūrā al-Aṭibbā, this department had as its centerpiece the health offices (*makātib al-ṣiḥḥa*) that were opened in all of the ten neighborhoods (*atmān*) of Cairo in 1842. Not only did these offices function as public clinics, providing free consultations for the sick and needy, they were also responsible for the following important tasks: collecting vital statistics, administering smallpox immunizations, and imposing quarantines. In addition, as noted in the 1841 public hygiene ordinance quoted earlier in the chapter, issued by Mehmed Ali, these offices were mobile in the sense that their chief resident doctors made daily rounds of the city to supervise such tasks as street cleaning, refuse disposal, and marsh drainage.[183] But these health officials did not roam the market equipped only with science; they were always accompanied by armed policemen. The health officials used the coercive power of the law to seize suspected food samples and send them to the chemical lab at the local health office for preliminary examination. If this examination proved inconclusive, then further testing would be conducted by the chief pharmacist (*ajzajībāshī*) of the Azbakiyya Civilian Hospital (see figure 9).[184] If that

FIGURE 9: Strekalovsky, *Azbakiyya Civilian Hospital.* Museum of the History of Medicine, Qaṣr al-ʿAinī Medical School, Cairo. Photo by Mazen Attalla.

examination was also inconclusive, then the suspected sample would be sent to the Qaṣr al-ʿAinī Chemical-Pharmaceutical Lab.

An 1874 medical circular gives further details about how resident physicians should perform the daily inspections of the food markets: "These inspections should be conducted every few days, randomly, and with no prior warning, so that the merchants could not be forewarned. Any suspicious material should be immediately confiscated, and a sample should be sent, after being sealed [with the seal of the Department of Health Inspection], to the local police station so that they, in turn, can take the necessary measures."[185] This eventually prompted the Department of Health Inspection to ask the police how it should deal with foreign merchants: should they, too, be subjected to these unannounced inspections, or should their merchandise be inspected only after informing their consulates?[186] The police initially replied that the consulates should be forewarned and that inspections should be conducted only in the presence of a delegate from the consulate. However, the Department of Health Inspection complained that this would give foreign merchants a chance to sell or hide their merchandise and insisted that all foreign merchants be subjected to the same regulations imposed on locals "given that no exceptions are ever to be made in matters of public hygiene as these are matters of public utility applied in all provinces and in every city."[187]

The archives of the Department of Health Inspection contain countless reports of chemical examinations of suspected samples gathered from the Cairo food markets performed in neighborhood health offices, the Azbakiyya Civilian Hospital, or the Qaṣr al-ʿAinī Chemical-Pharmaceutical Lab. Cooking oil[188] and spices[189] were among the food products that were inspected for adulteration. As if heeding Clot Bey's warning against eating unripe fruit,[190] officials seized vegetables and fruit that were suspected of not being ripe enough.[191] One can get a glimpse of the way these food inspections were conducted by following one particular item that was of special concern to health officials: coffee. In 1863, a regular examination conducted on coffee collected from fifteen coffee merchants revealed that all were adulterated: some had been mixed with starchy cereals, others contained ground hazelnut shells, and still others were nothing but a mixture of roasted chickpeas and barley. The report by the Department of Health Inspection stated that coffee "is a nutritious substance and very helpful for health when pure but can be very harmful to the human body if adulterated or mixed with impure substances."[192] Another examination conducted a few years later of four samples of coffee revealed that all but one were adulterated, although no poisonous substances were found. The report did declare that those who mixed coffee with other substances were akin to thieves, but given that its chief concern was health and not morals, it hastened to add that since coffee is a "stimulating, healthy substance," adulterating it is harmful to health, especially the health of manual workers who frequent coffee shops after a long day's work.[193] On receiving a sample of what was suspected to be adulterated bread, the doctors at the Qaṣr al-ʿAinī Chemical-Pharmaceutical Lab conducted their investigations, and their report contained the following: "On checking the sample, it was discovered that it was of bread that had been baked using coarse wheat. On examining it, we discovered black spots that on further investigation under the microscope were discovered to be small pieces of insect wings, probably of beetles. . . . The bread had no poisonous substances. However, the disgust [*al-karāha*] that would necessarily result from finding traces of insects [in items of food] requires bread to be diligently investigated."[194]

The way the physicians and chemists (assisted by the Cairo police) conducted their chemical investigations in their scientific laboratories is a far cry from how the *muḥtasib,* as envisaged by either Ghazālī or Māwardī, carried out his job monitoring fraud in the marketplace. Due to the significant expansion of the size of Cairo markets in the second quarter of the nineteenth century and the concomitant increased sophistication of commercial transactions, markets had to be monitored and controlled differently. Simply put, a small market where tradesmen and customers are neighbors and anonymity is rare could indeed be viewed through a moral prism, and it would be easy to imagine the applicability of Ghazālī's dictum that a passerby who is aware of a defect in a particular product on sale in a shop but remains silent and does not inform buyers is complicit in fraud (*khiyāna*), as "he would then be content to see the squandering of his Muslim brother's money. This is illicit."[195] However, the complexity of modern food production, distribution, and sale and the growing separation of producers and consumers invited fraud that could not be monitored simply by moral probity. Without factoring in the increased complexity of the marketplace in the first half of the nineteenth century, it would be difficult to understand how easily the *muḥtasib* lost what little power he still had in monitoring the market.

Forensic Chemistry. The detailed chemical investigations that were carried out by the Qaṣr al-'Ainī Chemical-Pharmaceutical Lab in the middle decades of the nineteenth century were a clear sign of the degree to which chemists and physicians had taken over the *muḥtasib*'s delicate task of monitoring increasingly complex food markets. The years of training that the medical students received at Qaṣr al-'Ainī; the care with which medical and chemical books were translated, edited, and printed by Būlāq Press; the high degree of coordination between the Cairo police and the Department of Health Inspection in monitoring the markets for comestibles—all of this helped create a professional establishment that contrasted sharply with the *ḥisba,* which was centered around the *muḥtasib* and his assistants.

The transition from *ḥisba* to chemistry in khedival Egypt can be further illustrated by looking at how forensic chemistry got involved in the intricate gastronomic world. While chapter 5 will look at the role forensic medicine played in establishing probative evidence in criminal cases, the following case is meant to highlight another function of forensic medicine, namely the role chemistry in particular came to occupy a central place in police investigations of cases that involved alcohol, poison, or drugs.

The case in question took place in 1877, and it involved a man named Ibrāhīm al-Miṣrī, who had arrived in Alexandria earlier in that year with his mother to look for a job in the bustling city. He soon found employment as a tailor in a shop owned by a merchant called Ḥanīn Usṭūfān. A few days later, Ibrāhīm went missing, and his mother started looking for him all over the city. In the meantime, the body of a young man was found in the courtyard of a house inhabited by twenty-two Jews. The face of the man was bruised and his clothes were smeared in mud. When the mother was informed that the physical description of the man matched that of her missing son, she went to the police station and identified the body. She then accused his employer, Ḥanīn Usṭūfān, of murdering him.

The police went about investigating the case in their typical diligent manner. A forensic doctor was fetched who, detecting rigor mortis, concluded that death had occurred twenty-four hours earlier.[196] The body was then sent to the hospital for an autopsy. Significant traces of alcohol were found in the stomach, and the brain showed signs of asphyxiation. The lungs showed signs of an unusual inflammation. The autopsy report therefore concluded that the death must have been caused by excessive drinking. The alcohol had caused severe indigestion, which had led to the blocking of the larynx, resulting in asphyxiation. The police accepted the findings of the autopsy report, which basically concluded that Ibrāhīm had drowned in his own vomit, and in their own report they explained that the contusions on the face and the muddy clothes must have been caused by excessive drunkenness, which had caused Ibrāhīm to trip over repeatedly and end up in a house of complete strangers. In other words, the police dismissed the possibility that the bruises on the body might have been signs of a physical attack. As a result, the Alexandria police concluded that Ibrāhīm al-Miṣrī's death was accidental, and no one was charged.[197]

This case, which involved beverages and a police investigation, serves as a real-life example to end this analysis of *ḥisba* and illustrate the degree to which the marketplace had been removed from the purview of the *muḥtasib* by the late nineteenth century and was monitored instead by chemists, public hygienists, and policemen. There are police reports of innumerable other cases that involved poison or drugs, but the *muḥtasib* was not summoned in connection to any of them; rather, these cases were handled by experts working in such institutions as the Qaṣr al-ʿAinī Medical School and Hospital, the Cairo Police Department, the Qaṣr al-ʿAinī Chemical-Pharmaceutical Lab, and the Department of Health Inspection.

Having seen how these different officials and institutions worked together, it is now possible to understand the degree to which the process of monitoring comestibles had been organized in such a way that by the early 1850s, there was no place left in it for the *muḥtasib*. The Qaṣr al-ʿAinī Medical School had managed to train a critical mass of doctors in Bichatian pathology and Lavoisierian chemistry. Clot Bey won his battle to establish a nationwide public health system and staff it with the doctors that had been released from military service after the reduction of the size of the army in 1841, and many of them were appointed to the new public health offices in Cairo and other cities as well as to provincial health offices in the countryside. At the same time, the Qaṣr al-ʿAinī Chemical-Pharmaceutical Lab supervised the different analyses of food samples sent by the Department of Health Inspection in collaboration with the Cairo police.

Together, these institutions produced new bodies of knowledge and devised a set of intricate policies that made it possible for the state to control food markets in more subtle ways than those envisaged by Yaḥyā Ibn ʿUmar or Shayzarī. Gone were the days in which the market could be controlled by a *muḥtasib* roaming the streets with his assistants, capturing merchants caught adulterating food and punishing them by beating them up, closing down their shops, or seating them backward and bareheaded on a donkey and then parading them disgracefully through the *sūq*. By the end of the nineteenth century, the duty of monitoring food markets had fallen to a number of officials, most notably public hygienists working in tandem with policemen. Together, these "health policemen" would seize suspicious food material and send samples to chemical labs, where chemists analyzed them and wrote up detailed forensic reports of their findings. While the implications of the textual nature of the work of these new forensic specialists are teased out in chapter 5, what is worth noting here is that by the middle decades of the nineteenth century, the supervision of food markets gradually moved away from the personal, direct surveillance of the *muḥtasib* and his assistants to the impersonal and indirect knowledge of market malpractices of chemists and physicians, mediated by such institutions as the Cairo Police Department and the Department of Health Inspection.[198]

CONCLUSION

This chapter examined food sold and consumed in the marketplace as a way of studying the Islamic duty of *ḥisba* and the institution of the *muḥtasib*. The aim was to engage critically with two sets of critics working on *ḥisba:* on the one hand, Islamists who view the regime of *ḥisba* in Islam as a perfect system that catered faultlessly to society's needs and fell into disuse only when secularizing elites in the Muslim world abandoned their traditions and adopted Western lifestyles lock, stock, and barrel; and on the other, Western academics who view *ḥisba* as an example of a functioning system of moral critique and character building in which ethical formation was not a matter of individual concern but one that took place through social interaction in the household as much as on the street. In addition to sharing an idealized view of *ḥisba* in premodern times, these two views pay little attention to the intricate historical process with which *ḥisba* lost its centrality as a regime of both ethical and agoranomic discipline. More importantly, both views skip over the central role played by violence in the theory of *ḥisba;* instead, they offer a seamless picture of a practice that ostensibly aimed at the moral cultivation of Muslim selves.

By contrast, this chapter's analysis of the history of *ḥisba* in Egypt started with a close reading of four influential texts that dealt with that central principle in Islamic thought: Māwardī's *Al-Aḥkām Sulṭāniyya,* Ghazālī's *Iḥyā' 'Ulūm al-Dīn,* Yaḥyā Ibn 'Umar's *Al-Aḥkām al-Sūq,* and Shayzarī's *Nihāyat al-Rutba.* These texts played a foundational role in shaping the Islamic textual tradition on *ḥisba.* This close reading revealed how central violence was in the theory of *ḥisba* and how both the private *muḥtasib* envisaged by Ghazālī and the official *muḥtasib* championed by Māwardī were strongly enjoined to use violence in commanding right and forbidding wrong. Equally important, the analysis revealed that when dealing with what can be described as "the care of the self," the *ḥisba* literature is concerned more with stopping the wrong (*al-munkar*) than caring for the self of the wrongdoer. Moreover, if there was a self that the *ḥisba* literature was keen to care for, it was the self of the *muḥtasib* (i.e., the performer of *ḥisba*) not that of the *muḥtasib 'alayhi* (i.e., the one on whom *ḥisba* is performed).

By concentrating on the other side of *ḥisba,* namely market inspection, the analysis in this chapter concentrated on food markets and gave a close reading of Yaḥyā Ibn 'Umar's and Shayzarī's *ḥisba* manuals in conjunction with Māwardī's seminal treatise on *ḥisba.* This reading of these foundational texts showed another serious problem with the nominal theory of *ḥisba* in the Islamic tradition, namely that very little effort was made to stop *ḥisba* from being used by political leaders and to prevent the *muḥtasib* from effectively being a financial inquisitor. The analysis then moved from the prescriptive treatises laying down how *ḥisba* was supposed to be practiced to a brief overview of how it was practiced under the Mamluks.

Finally, the chapter took a close look at the wide range of medical, police, and public hygiene institutions that gradually took over from the *muḥtasib* the important task of monitoring food markets. The argument was not that these modern institutions worked perfectly or without any problems. Nor was it that these modern institutions deployed no violence in monitoring the markets for comestibles. On the contrary, they were ridden with their own internal problems, such as tensions between competing scientific theories and rivalries among ethnic and professional groups. Moreover, the fact that these institutions worked in tandem with the police highlights that violence was ever-present. But as the following chapter illustrates, the khedival state was struggling to contain this violence, calibrate it, and practice it in ever-subtler forms. Indeed, it is this deep anxiety about the naked use of physical violence, as exemplified by the manner in which the *muḥtasib* performed his job, that lay at the very center of the modern state's efforts to constitute itself and establish its hegemony.

Contrasting the way the *muḥtasib* went about monitoring the marketplace with the way forensic chemists checked comestibles has provided the reader with important correctives to the manner with which *ḥisba* is commonly believed to have changed in modern times. For one thing, *ḥisba* was never that ideal system that dealt decisively with all ills in the marketplace, as many modern-day Islamists believe. Nor was it an ethical practice that helped Muslims care for their selves, as its Western proponents claim. For another, *ḥisba*'s demise was not brought about by the introduction of the civil law tradition in Egypt and the shrinking of the area governed by shariʿa. Nor did it fall into disuse because modern-day political and intellectual elites of the Muslim world became so enamored by the West that they were eager to abandon their Islamic tradition. Rather, *ḥisba* has always entailed an inordinate amount of violence, a feature that was just as troubling to many premodern thinkers as it is to present-day Islamist revisionists.[199] And among those premodern thinkers who were troubled by *ḥisba,* we find not only Muslim statesmen who were keen to deny the *fuqahā'* the right to sanction violence but also such luminary *fuqahā'* as Imām al-Ḥaramayn al-Juwaynī, whose position on this matter contrasted sharply with that of his student Ghazālī, who sanctioned Muslims to form armed gangs and roam marketplaces commanding right and forbidding wrong without their ruler's authorization. This wanton use of violence was the central problem of *ḥisba* that the modern state sought to address. With the introduction of forensic medicine, forensic chemistry, modern police, and a public health system founded on Bichatian pathology and Lavoisian chemistry, the khedival state finally had at its disposal a set of institutions with which it could monitor the marketplace without resorting to naked violence. As the following chapter shows, while the state succeeded in devising new ways to monitor markets by practicing violence in subtler—and more efficient—ways, these markets and the entire world in which they belonged were irrevocably altered.

FIVE

Justice without Pain

ON NOVEMBER 6, 1858, an estate belonging to a member of the ruling family witnessed a dramatic event that could be seen as marking a significant moment in the history not only of Egyptian law but also of the foundation of a modern state in Egypt. On that day, twenty-seven black slaves employed by the estate of Ilhāmī Pasha, the grand-nephew of Egypt's governor, Sa'īd Pasha, marched en masse several kilometers to the Cairo Police Department headquarters, Ḍabṭiyyat Miṣr, to present a deposition against the overseer of the estate's stables, a high-ranking dignitary by the name of 'Umar Bey Waṣfī. In their deposition, they stated that 'Umar Bey had ordered one of their fellow slaves, Sulṭān, to be flogged after he had gone missing for two days. They claimed that the flogging was so excessive that some of the slaves lost count of the number of lashes. They all agreed that flesh was peeling off Sulṭān's buttocks and back and that he was screaming and spitting blood throughout the ordeal. When the flogging was over, 'Umar Bey had Sulṭān's legs chained in iron fetters and molten lead poured on the locks. Sulṭān was then taken to the stables, where he was denied water and food for three days. On the third day, he expired. The slaves said that 'Umar Bey had previously beaten to death two other slaves and that they were fearful that he might turn on any one of them next. They demanded that the "government take necessary action" (*ann al-ḥukūma tujrī majrāhā*).

On hearing this deposition, the Cairo Police Department decided to send one of its senior officers, Ṣāliḥ Efendi, to the estate to investigate the matter. As a further sign of the seriousness with which they viewed the case, the police also sent the chief doctor (*ḥakīmbāshī*) and his assistant to fetch Sulṭān's body. When he reached the estate, the doctor found out that the employees of the estate had tried to wash the corpse and put it in a shroud in preparation for burial to cover up the beating, but the other slaves who had stayed behind had prevented them from doing so. The undertakers of the neighborhood, moreover, had refused to go to the estate when summoned as word had reached them that this had not been a natural death and that there was suspicion of foul play.

When Ṣāliḥ Efendi arrived, he had a significant encounter at the gate of the property. The encounter was revealing of the power dynamics between the central government, represented by Ṣāliḥ Efendi, and the ruling dynasty, represented by Ilhāmī Pasha. After being told by the director of the estate's servants (*nāẓir mamālīk al-sarāya*) that 'Umar Bey had left for his house in the Ḥilmiyya quarter of Cairo,[1] the officer asked for the exact location of the house, but the servants feigned ignorance. As the officer was leaving, he chanced upon 'Umar Bey, who was returning to the estate in his carriage. But 'Umar Bey slipped away from the officer's grip, entered the estate, locked himself up inside, and issued orders to the porters not to allow the officer in. Baffled, Ṣāliḥ Efendi stood at the gate, jotted his questions down on a piece of paper, and requested that the servants deliver it to the bey. However, the servants refused, claiming that 'Umar Bey had left the estate using a back door. Frustrated, Ṣāliḥ Efendi returned to the Cairo Police Department and reported to his superiors that 'Umar Bey had refused to come back with him for interrogation.

The Cairo Police Commissioner (Ma'mūr Ḍabiṭiyyat Miṣr) then dispatched another senior police officer, Muḥammad Efendi, to fetch 'Umar Bey from "wherever he happens to be." This second officer also failed to arraign the bey, so the commissioner went to the estate in person and ordered his men to storm in and arrest him. Realizing that hiding in the estate would not grant him the protection he sought, the bey slipped out the harem gate and fled toward the city in his carriage. The commissioner saw him trying to escape, and a Ben-Hur-esque carriage chase through the desert followed, which ended with the commissioner jumping onto 'Umar Bey's carriage, grabbing him, and escorting him to the police headquarters in Azbakiyya for interrogation.

Once there, 'Umar Bey denied any wrongdoing. He admitted that he had indeed ordered Sulṭān to be beaten to punish him for disappearing without a permit. But he insisted that he had never intended for the slave to die. He claimed that the real reason behind Sulṭān's death was not the beating but the slave's "frail constitution" (*ḍa'f al-binya*), which was the result of excessive drinking. He also argued that the police commissioner should not believe the slaves' exaggerated testimonies about the beating, calling them "a bunch of drunkards who are knee-deep in smoking hashish." The broad allegations they were making against him, he added, were a reaction to his repeated attempts to discipline them. The police then confronted him with the testimony of one slave, Bakhīt al-Sāyis, who averred that Sulṭān had been lashed 1,500 times. To prove his point, Bakhīt said that he had been carrying his string of prayer beads throughout the beating and that he marked every lash with one bead. Every time the string of ninety-nine beads made one full whole loop, he would extend a finger; by the end of Sulṭān's flogging, he had extended his finger fifteen times. In response, ʿUmar Bey said that Bakhīt was lying, for if he was sincere in his prayers he could not have been paying attention to the number of lashes. He then reiterated his argument that the slaves' testimonies should not be admitted, saying that "the justice of the government does not permit untruthful statements [*ʿadālat al-ḥukūma lā tasmaḥ li-qawl al-muftarī*], and [given that] establishing right is a condition of justice [*iqāmat al-ḥaqq fī wujūb al-ʿadl*]."

While ʿUmar Bey was being interrogated, his scribe paid the Cairo Police Commissioner a surprise visit. The scribe produced a purse containing one hundred and fifty Majīdī pounds, a very large amount of money, and placed it on the commissioner's desk. The commissioner immediately summoned the chief accountant of the Cairo Police Department and ordered him to record the flagrant attempt at bribery in his records.

In the meantime, the doctor finished conducting his postmortem examination. He concluded that although there were clear signs of beating on the buttocks and the beating had affected some vital internal organs, he could not reach a conclusive opinion about the cause of death and recommended a full autopsy. However, the autopsy report did not establish the exact cause of death either, even though it stressed that serious external signs of beating could be seen and that an internal hemorrhage had occurred.

After Majlis al-Aḥkām received the case file, which included the police commissioner's report and the reports of the postmortem examination and the autopsy, which had been carried out at the Qaṣr al-ʿAinī Hospital, it conducted a serious deliberation, after which, and probably given the gravity of the case, it decided not to issue its own verdict, as was customary, but to write a strong recommendation to Saʿīd Pasha, the governor of Egypt, in person. The reasoning and the wording of the recommendation are significant enough to warrant quoting at length:

After studying this case in the Majlis, it became evident that Sulṭān had indeed been excessively flogged at the order of ʿUmar Bey, as is clear from the [testimony of the] estate employees who had witnessed and carried out the flogging and from the doctors' reports. Moreover, ʿUmar Bey himself admitted ordering the flogging of the abovementioned slave. He only denied the severity of the flogging, a denial that should not be taken seriously given the fact that the doctors' reports had established that [signs of] excessive beating [*kathrat al-ḍarb*] could be seen on the deceased's body, leading to the abovementioned slave's death.

It is also clear that ʿUmar Bey had earlier caused the death of two slaves, one by beating, . . . and the other by imprisoning him with no food or water. Accordingly, and since homicide cases are adjudicated by both shariʿa [courts] and *siyāsa* [councils], and since according to shariʿa . . . there are three possible outcomes—conviction, acquittal, or pardoning by the plaintiffs—then even if the case ends in acquittal or pardoning according to *siyāsa,* it has already been established that ʿUmar Bey is guilty, as he forcefully ordered [the beating to death of Sulṭān] and thus *has attacked and squandered the sanctity of the government* [*taʿaddā wa ḍayyaʿ ḥurmat al-ḥukūma*] and the government should not forsake its right . . . but should avenge itself for his *violating its sanctity* [*faʾl-ḥukūma . . . lā budd min akhdh ḥaqqihā minhu naẓīr taʿddīhi fī hatk ḥurmatihā*], it has been agreed in the Majlis that ʿUmar Bey is guilty and deserves to be punished, but his punishment should be decided on by the Sublime Thresholds [i.e., by Saʿīd Pasha].

Three months after receiving this strongly worded recommendation from Majlis al-Aḥkām, Saʿīd Pasha ordered ʿUmar Bey Waṣfī to be banished from Egypt, and letters were sent to governors of ports to deny him entry should he try to return.[2]

. . .

The importance of this dramatic case in the history of law and of state-formation in Egypt cannot be exaggerated. Firstly, it vividly illustrates how central the police had become in the lives of Cairenes. By the late 1850s, although it was no more than thirty years old, the Cairo Police Department had become an effective body in charge of controlling crime, monitoring epidemics, and collecting vital statistics.[3] As a result, Ḍabṭiyyat Miṣr, located in Azbakiyya, at the northwestern edge of Cairo, became an important center of power in the nascent state that the khedives were struggling to found in Egypt. However, Ḍabṭiyyat Miṣr also presented itself as a place of universal justice where even black slaves could reasonably expect to have their grievances against high-ranking notables redressed. In this particular case, the slaves were petitioning not just against any notable but against a bey employed in the household of Ilhāmī Pasha, who was the khedive's grandnephew and who also happened to be married to Princess Münire, the daughter of the Ottoman sultan. In other words, this is a case in which black slaves used the recently founded institutions of the police and the *siyāsa* councils to convict a high-ranking notable working for a prince who was part of the very core of the ruling family, and indeed the Ottoman Empire.

Secondly, the case is testimony to the central role played by forensic medicine in the rapidly expanding legal system. Like the police, the medical establishment and forensic medicine were no more than thirty years old. With little tradition or experience to build on, forensic doctors approached their difficult tasks with professionalism and diligence, and, as this case illustrates, and is shown by more cases below, their reports played a decisive role in legally convicting the rich and powerful. Equally remarkable was the public awareness of how important forensic medicine was in establishing probative evidence, as illustrated by the fact that the slaves guarded Sulṭān's body and prevented the employees of the estate from burying it until the police doctors had arrived.

Thirdly, the case points to the centrality of law in the fraught process of state formation. As noted in chapter 2, the legal system that was gradually being forged was not based on the principles of the separation of power or the rule of law. Rather, it was based on what has been termed "rule by law."[4] In order for the khedival household to transform itself into a bureaucratic state, the khedives had to ensure that the policies they passed were implemented and that there was a mechanism that ensured this implementation. Rule by law, then, meant that the state that the khedives were establishing in Egypt operated "on the basis of fixed and knowable law—which, implicitly or explicitly, must therefore bind state authorities themselves. There is no requirement for separation of powers or pluralism, and indeed no consideration of the process by which law is made."[5] Moreover, law in this case is deployed not only as an expression of sovereignty but as an essential element of it. In this respect, and as with Majlis al-Aḥkām's verdict to banish Khālid Efendi (see in chapter 2), Saʿīd Pasha's decision to banish ʿUmar Bey from Egypt was a powerful means of marking his own authority as separate from that of the Ottoman sultan and of distinguishing his realm, Egypt, from the larger Ottoman Empire.

But this independent realm that was being forged by law in Egypt was riven with contradictions. For one thing, Egypt was technically and legally an Ottoman province with the sultan as its legal sovereign, and the khedive was merely a provincial governor without the right to promulgate laws in his own name. Furthermore, within Egypt itself, the sovereignty of the khedive was being seriously challenged by other members of his extended family. As Ehud Toledano, F. Robert Hunter, and Adam Mestyan have shown, the middle decades of the nineteenth century witnessed deep divisions among Mehmed Ali's household.[6] During this period, many members of the ruling family established households of their own, and the political field was shaped considerably by competition and struggle among these rival households. Sulṭān's case illustrates this tension as it took place on an estate owned by Ilhāmī Pasha, who had been groomed by his father, ʿAbbās Pasha, to succeed him as governor of Egypt before ʿAbbās was mysteriously assassinated in his Banhā palace only four years before Sulṭān's case.[7]

The tension among Egypt's ruling households was vividly expressed in the remarkable confrontations between the senior police officers and Ilhāmī Pasha's employees at the gate of the estate. It was as if ʿUmar Bey, acting on behalf of Ilhāmī Pasha, was marking the estate as an independent realm and claiming exclusive jurisdiction for his master by denying the officers of the Cairo Police Department the right to set foot on the property. In ʿUmar Bey's mind, these officers were merely employees of another estate, that of Saʿīd Pasha, and as such lacked the right to enter Ilhāmī Pasha's estate without Ilhāmī's consent.

In response, the Cairo Police Commissioner, backed, as it turned out, by Majlis al-Aḥkām, was effectively arguing that Saʿīd Pasha's realm was not just any estate but rather *the state, al-ḥukūma*. This *ḥukūma,* moreover, had not only sovereign jurisdiction but also sanctity, *ḥurma,* which ʿUmar Bey had violated by beating a slave to death. And as Majlis al-Aḥkām argued in its strong recommendation to Saʿīd Pasha, in order to restore its momentarily injured sanctity, *al-ḥukūma* had to avenge itself by punishing ʿUmar Bey. In other words, a matter that had taken place inside the estate of a member of the ruling family was no longer a private affair; it was a matter of *national* importance, even though the victim was a black slave.

Lastly, the case illustrates how the different protagonists ascribed contrasting definitions to such interconnected concepts as *al-ḥukūma* (the state), *ʿadl* (justice), and *ḥaqq* (right). It is interesting, for example, that the term *al-ḥukūma* appears three times in the lengthy case record. While the estate slaves seemingly put their confidence in *al-ḥukūma,* took the risk of marching the long distance to the police headquarters in Cairo proper, and implored *al-ḥukūma*'s officials to "take necessary action" against what they considered to be mortal danger, 'Umar Bey countered their allegations by evoking the notions of *'adl* and *ḥaqq,* by which he believed *al-ḥukūma* should be bound. According to 'Umar Bey's notion of justice, *al-ḥukūma* should strive to restore order by backing him up in his attempt to impose deterrent punishment on recalcitrant slaves. 'Umar Bey appears to believe in an early definition of *'adl* as an act of balancing[8]—that is, putting things in their right place, to be juxtaposed with its opposite, *ẓulm,* which means to put a thing in a place not its own.[9] In contrast to these two notions of *al-ḥukūma*—as a refuge from *ẓulm* and as an enforcer of *'adl*—held by the slaves and the bey, respectively, both the Cairo Police Commissioner and Majlis al-Aḥkām viewed *al-ḥukūma* as possessing not only will and sovereignty but also sanctity.

Sulṭān's case and the seriousness with which it was handled acquires added significance when it is contrasted with an incident that occurred nearly thirty years earlier, where a public official flogged a man to death and got away with a mere verbal rebuke. In August 1829, Ṣāliḥ Efendi, the police commissioner of the Delta town of Mīt Ghamr, caught a man forging an official receipt. Ṣāliḥ decided to punish him by administering 1,800 lashes. As a result, the man died. When Mehmed Ali heard of the incident, he wrote to Ṣāliḥ, who happened to be his relative, mildly rebuking him: "O Ṣāliḥ! Administering such an excessive number of lashes without my permission, and in such a manner that leads to death, is a gross injustice and is against my wishes." He then warned Ṣāliḥ not to resort to such excessive beating in the future and to report similar incidents to him personally.[10]

The contrast between the gentle admonishment that Mehmed Ali gave Ṣāliḥ Efendi in 1829 and the drastic sentence—banishment—with which Sa'īd Pasha punished 'Umar Bey Waṣfī in 1858 is indicative of how far Egypt's rulers had come in their attempt to limit official violence. Over the course of thirty years, what had been considered an offense that could be straightened out by a mere written reprimand had somehow acquired such gravity that it was punished by nothing less than exile. By 1858, an attack on a black slave's body had become equated with a violation of the very sanctity of the state.

This chapter tells the story of this dramatic transformation. It shows how Sulṭān's body became the locus of competing sovereignties and the realm in which the law was being performed. The chapter argues that the case of

Sulṭān's death illustrates, first, the tensions that were inherent in a politico-legal system in which the *zevat* (Arabic: *dhawāt*)—the members of Egypt's ruling households—thought they could literally take the law in their own hands and, second, how, in contrast, the rising state, *al-ḥukūma* struggled to snatch the law from this elite and monopolize it for itself. As this chapter shows, this struggle expressed itself most vividly in the move to ban official violence, a move that was believed to be necessary in order for the unified, centralized state to impose its sovereign will on the ruling family's competing estates.

OFFICIAL VIOLENCE IN KHEDIVAL EGYPT

Three years after Sulṭān's dramatic case, Saʿīd Pasha issued an order banning flogging. On July 4, 1861, he wrote to the Cairo Police Department to ask it to draft a comprehensive decree replacing flogging, *ḍarb* (literally "beating"), with imprisonment. In response, the Cairo Police Department conducted a thorough search of its records and previous criminal legislation to find out how different crimes had been punished; in addition, they wrote to the Alexandria Police Department to compare notes. After much deliberation, the Cairo Police Department wrote to the Cairo Governorate, which then drafted a decree and forwarded it to Saʿīd Pasha for ratification.

This resulted in the Decree Replacing Beating with Imprisonment (Lāyḥat Istibdāl al-Ḍarb bi'l-Ḥabs), which had thirteen articles and proved to be a landmark in Egyptian penal legislation. It ended flogging as legal punishment and put serious limits on using beating and torture to extract confessions from criminal suspects. The preamble explained that an earlier nine-article draft had revealed that "cases reviewed by the police are [necessarily] varied and cannot be standardized. It was suspected that different verdicts might have been issued in cases where the crimes had been the same.... And in order to standardize the verdicts issued in cases that would hereafter be reviewed by the police, the following decree was drafted." Article 1 stated that first-time offenders who committed minor misdemeanors, such as tearing someone's clothes or spitting in someone's face, should be punished by being locked up in solitary confinement for a period ranging from twenty-four hours to three days, depending on the severity of the crime. Article 2 stipulated that repeat offenders and those caught drinking or gambling should be locked up, just like the offenders mentioned in Article 1, but that they should also be denied food, water, smoking, and coffee for a period ranging from three to seven days. Most significantly, Article 13 recognized that "it is impossible to list all the types of charges and offenses that the police are likely to encounter. Therefore, whosoever used to be punished with fifteen to twenty-five lashes will [henceforth] be imprisoned between twenty-four hours to three days; and whosoever used to be punished with thirty to seventy-five lashes will be imprisoned between three to fifteen days; and whosoever used to be punished with seventy-five to one hundred lashes will be imprisoned between nine to twenty-one days."[11]

As will be explained later in the chapter, beating had been widely used in police stations before this decree. What prompted the authorities to effect such a radical change in penal policy? To help explain the timing of the decree, it is worth noting that scholars working on other parts of the world have noted that there was a remarkably contemporaneous move to abolish corporal punishment, something they have attributed to the spread of Enlightenment ideas from Western Europe. Historians of Russia, for example, have argued that the ideas of justice, equality, and liberal humanism as expounded by such thinkers as Beccaria, Locke, and Montesquieu inspired an 1863 decree abolishing torture in the country.[12] Although the Russian political system seems not to have been directly affected, these scholars contend that the new, subversive ideas could not be prevented from crossing borders and increasingly affecting influential members of society. Gradually, these ideas spread to the rest of the body politic, and eventually a change in the law occurred. Bruce Adams emphatically stresses the role that principles of the Enlightenment played in Russia: "The men behind Russia's 1863 reform were well-educated, city-dwelling bureaucrats and reformers who found physical punishment barbarous and anachronistic."[13]

Was the 1861 Egyptian decree a result of a universal movement that saw torture as an affront to humanity? Can one argue that this decree belonged to a transcultural trend that signaled the appearance of a new social sensitivity to pain, a sensitivity that might have prompted similar movements to abolish torture at around the same time in Russia and in the British army in Colonial India?[14]

In *Formations of the Secular,* Talal Asad questions the ease by which the "progressivist story" has explained why the infliction of physical pain was banned in Western European legal systems two centuries ago. According to this story, torture suddenly appeared scandalous because its "intolerable cruelty emerged more clearly . . . [as] the pain inflicted in judicial torture was declared to be *gratuitous*."[15] But why was this shift so sudden? Why was torture not considered inhumane before Voltaire and Beccaria? Asad argues that Enlightenment thinkers were troubled not by physical punishment per se but by the problem of quantifying pain. It was the incommensurability of pain that forced them to regard torture as inhumane because it was difficult to compare it and to deduce that it affected people equally. Torture was thus seen as ill-suited for upholding the principles of justice. Taking his cue from Foucault, Asad adds that prison, by contrast, was seen as more egalitarian because it was based on a philosophical tradition that regarded freedom to be the natural condition: "Penal reformers reasoned that since the desire for liberty was implanted equally in every individual, depriving individuals of their liberty must be a way of striking at them equally. . . . No form of punishment accorded so precisely with our essential humanity, therefore, as imprisonment did. . . . By a reductive operation, the idea of a calculus has facilitated the comparative judgment of what would otherwise remain incommensurable qualities."[16]

In a similar vein, in a pathbreaking study that Asad partly relies on, John Langbein argues that the abolition of judicial torture in Europe in the seventeenth century had little connection to Enlightenment thought (he calls this the "fairy tale explanation").[17] Rather, he contends that torture was abolished after confession had lost its centrality as the prime means of establishing legal proof. That was prompted by the gradual emergence of a new system of proof in the seventeenth century that allowed for free judicial evaluation of criminal evidence. Courts increasingly relied on circumstantial evidence and theoretical arguments, and this new system eventually replaced the traditional means of establishing legal proof, which was based on Roman canon law and required a confession and two eyewitnesses. This was nothing less than a revolution in legal thought. What is noteworthy about Langbein's analysis is that he places this shift *before* the emergence of Enlightenment thinkers, such as Voltaire and Beccaria, who, according to the traditional narrative, had supposedly embarrassed European legislators into abolishing torture. In other words, Langbein claims that it was *after* the cumbersome and lengthy procedure of legal torture had become redundant that Enlightenment thinkers stepped onto the scene to theorize a process that had already taken place and condemn torture as inhuman and excessive.

If it seems implausible that the "fairy tale" explanation for the abolition of physical pain could account for such an important development in European legal development, can one at least use Asad's and Langbein's arguments to explain the 1861 decree in Egypt?[18] The only scholar of Egyptian legal history who has studied this significant decree is Rudolph Peters, and it is worthwhile to take a close look at his analysis. Over a period of fifteen years, Peters wrote a series of articles and book chapters that deal with various aspects of nineteenth-century Egyptian legal history, including criminal legislation, the condition of prisons, the role of the qadi in adjudicating homicide cases, and the use of fatwas as sources of legal history.[19] In one of his early studies, he wonders "why Egypt introduced penal reforms similar to those adopted in Western Europe at roughly the same period." He considers the possibility that "this was due to European influence mediated by European experts [working] in Egypt and Egyptian students who had been sent to the West," but quickly dismisses that explanation as inadequate and instead attributes the significant process of legal reform to local developments. "The main factor behind the reforms," he asserts, "was the spread of public security in most of Egypt as a result of Mehmed 'Alī's greater control over the country, better police surveillance, and greater efficiency in tracking and apprehending criminals."[20]

In a later study devoted to prison reforms, Peters specifically raises the question of what might have led to the promulgation of the 1861 decree.[21] Citing Pieter Spierenburg's *The Spectacle of Suffering,*[22] which argues that the spread of what Norbert Elias has called "the civilizing process"[23] played a significant role in developing new sensibilities against officially inflicted pain, Peters contemplates the possibility that Egyptian penal reformers might have been repulsed by the spectacle of public punishment; but, again, he is quick to dismiss this explanation as inadequate:

> In Egypt, there were reformers in the nineteenth century, but they have left no documents regarding their ideas on legal punishment. Nevertheless, it is my contention that they influenced penal policy, especially with regard to the abolition of torture and corporal punishment. They must have followed the example of the Ottoman Empire, where corporal punishment had been abolished with the introduction of the Penal Code of 1858. It is doubtful, however, whether the Egyptian reformers were motivated by growing sensibilities against public punishment.... The ethnic gap between the Turkish speaking elite and the native Egyptian peasants must have been an effective barrier to empathy.[24]

Instead of resorting to the spread of Enlightenment ideas to explain the 1861 decree, Peters offers two nuanced arguments as alternatives. The first is economic. By the middle of the nineteenth century, Egypt was moving away from the command economy that characterized Mehmed Ali's financial policies. Given his policy on monopolies, Peters argues, the Pasha was concerned about his peasants and their productive capacities and saw that imprisonment necessarily diminished the size of the labor force that he could rely on. When state monopolies were abolished, however, and when the state's extraction of the rural surplus became limited to tax collection, his concern about the imprisonment of peasants diminished. In addition, Peters contends, the rise of large estates and the dispossession of many small landholders caused peasants to become expendable, which meant that there was no longer any need to exempt them from imprisonment if they committed an offense.[25]

His second argument is that the need to monopolize the means of coercion was also behind the 1861 decree. Wielding the whip (*kurbāj*), like carrying out public executions, was a symbol of authority, and whipping peasants needed to be controlled by the central government: "Since the execution of capital punishment was the Khedive's prerogative, an official who killed a subject by an excess of beating or flogging, would intrude on the Khedive's rights. This rule was indeed enforced and officials who killed subjects were brought to justice."[26]

Building on Peters's insights, I will attempt to explain the promulgation of the 1861 decree as well as other measures taken to limit official violence by putting such measures in the historical context of the overall development of Egyptian law in the first two thirds of the nineteenth century. I argue that the 1861 decree cannot be explained except if viewed as belonging to a gradual trend of limiting official violence that started in the 1820s. I also contend that official violence had always been seen as problematic in that it was impossible to calibrate to deliver the required effect, namely the subjectification of peasants.

Finally, to understand this overall trend, it is important to bear in mind that flogging played two distinct functions in the legal system: it was a form of legal punishment and a means of establishing probative evidence. I trace the evolution of these two functions in the middle decades of the nineteenth century. In the remainder of this chapter, I argue that the move away from flogging, of which the 1861 decree was but one manifestation, occurred not only because there was growing anxiety about levels of public violence but also because alternatives to the functions of this violence became available.

During the first fifteen years of his reign, Mehmed Ali practiced what Foucault would call "sovereign power,"[27] and his penal policy relied on the public, spectacular performance of punishment. As we saw in chapter 4, the Pasha gave Cairo's *muḥtasib* free rein to punish many market offenses in a severe, physical manner. Currency counterfeiters were hanged from the city gates with coins clipped to their noses; butchers caught tampering with the weight of meat had their noses slit and pieces of meat hung from the cuts; and confectionary merchants caught manipulating weights and prices were forced to sit on their hot pans over the fire.[28] Thieves were paraded through the streets with their hands and heads set in stocks.[29] And up to the mid-1850s, murderers were hanged and their corpses left in the public thoroughfares for three days "as a deterrent to passersby."[30] After conscription had been introduced to Upper Egypt in the early 1820s, it became known that many women were helping their husbands and sons maim themselves to escape the draft. Mehmed Ali ordered these women to be hanged at village entrances "as example to others."[31] Furthermore, when a large rebellion against his authority broke out in Upper Egypt in 1824, the Pasha ordered the elderly and disabled villagers who had been involved to be hanged at their village entrances to remind others of the fate that awaited them if they joined the rebellion.[32]

The problem with these spectacles of punishment is that they proved nearly impossible to interpret accurately. Were they intended to deter onlookers by setting a horrible example in front of their very eyes of what might happen to them if they defied the will of the Pasha? Or were these spectacular punishments meant as expressions of the sovereign's unbridled fury, aimed to cow the populace into submitting to his whims? It is important to understand that these punishments were not given out by some rogue element of the newly formed bureaucracy; often, they were ordered by the Pasha himself or his closest kin. In one famous incident, Mehmed Ali wrote to his son, Ibrāhīm, complaining about one of his chief accountants, Muʿallim Ghālī, who had dared to express some hesitation in ordering the collection of a new tax on dates. Enraged, he commanded his son to kill the man. After Ibrāhīm had carried out the ugly deed and it became clear that the slain man's subordinates were horrified at what had happened to their boss, the Pasha wrote a new missive to his son telling him to do his best to pacify the shaken accountants.[33]

That this bloody violence was dangerously endemic in the ruling household, the very core of Egyptian political life during the early decades of the nineteenth century, is evident from following a few stories about its members. In 1963, one of the descendants of the royal family recounted what, a century later, was still remembered as a notorious legend within the family about Nazlı, Mehmed Ali's oldest daughter: "[Nazlı] is said to have been gay, witty, and charming, but cruel and passionately jealous of her husband [Mehmed Bey Defterdar, Mehmed Ali's treasurer], whom she worshipped. One day when he happened to remark on the long and wavy hair of one of her slaves, Nazlı listened in silence. At dinner that evening a large covered dish was served. The cover was removed, and the husband saw the head of the slave lying among her beautiful tresses. He rose and went away never to return."[34]

Nazlı's nephew, 'Abbās Pasha, who went on to become governor of Egypt, was said to have killed his baker with his own hands when he was still governor of Gharbiyya. On hearing about the incident, his grandfather, Mehmed Ali, wrote him a letter warning him of the grave repercussions of these impulsive acts and telling him that if he did not mend his ways, his subjects would "snub and be repulsed" by him.[35]

Despite these accounts of extreme violence within the very core of Mehmed Ali's household, there was a clear realization that it carried grave risks. By the mid-1830s, therefore, it is possible to detect a gradual move to limit official violence. For example, when Mehmed Ali heard that a provincial governor had cut off the nose and ears of a peasant caught uprooting his cotton field, he reprimanded him, saying that he preferred that such offenders be punished either by prison time or by execution.[36] Impalement ceased to be practiced as a form of execution, and the last recorded public impalement took place in 1839.[37] European travelers often remarked that convicted thieves were no longer punished by having their hands chopped off according to "the ancient law of Islamism."[38] This anecdotal remark is corroborated by Peters's meticulous research into judicial records, which "found no evidence that *qiṣāṣ* for injuries was applied in practice."[39] Even public executions became rare. Writing in 1837, John Bowring reported that "the numbers of execution have much diminished in Egypt," and he added that the public executioner lamented, "I have little now to do."[40] A British traveler writing in the early 1850s remarked that there were no public executions during the first three years of 'Abbās' rule.[41] Peters also remarks that due to tightened security and new laws that restricted the number of capital offenses, "executions had become relatively rare by the middle of the century."[42]

Legal codes were an important means of limiting official violence. Building on centuries of Ottoman legal practice, Mehmed Ali issued legal codes (*qānūns*) that not only defined what acts were to be punished corporeally but also restricted such physical punishment to flogging. For example, his first criminal code, passed in September 1829, stipulated lashing with the *kurbāj* in six out of its seventeen articles.[43] A few months later, he issued Qānūn al-Filāḥa, which dealt with offenses relating to damages to public property as well as to misconduct of government employees; this code stipulated the use of the *kurbāj* in thirty-one of its fifty-five articles.[44] In addition, the Humāyūnī Law of 1852 stipulated anywhere between three and ninety-nine lashes as punishment for a wide range of offenses.[45]

At first glance, there appears to be nothing new about how the penal laws passed from the late 1820s to the early 1850s showed an explicit preference for public flogging as the main method of punishment. Public, spectacular punishment was also an integral part of the legal system in Mamluk Egypt.[46] Under Ottoman law, the numerous types of physical punishment (amputation of body parts, impaling, branding, and capital punishment) were often performed publicly.[47] The criminal laws passed in Egypt in the first half of the nineteenth century could thus be seen as a continuation of an age-old politico-legal tradition that relied on the public performance of physical punishment to instill in the minds of onlookers the idea of the expendability of the body of the criminal and the huge gap that separated it from the body of the sovereign. Public torture was therefore seen as an essential step in reconstituting the momentarily injured sovereignty of the ruler. According to Foucault, it does so "by manifesting [that sovereignty] at its most spectacular. . . . Over and above the crime that has placed the sovereign in contempt [public punishment] deploys before all eyes an invincible force. Its aim is not to establish balance [as much] as to bring into play, as its extreme point, the dissymmetry between the subject who has dared to violate the law and the all-powerful sovereign who displays his strength."[48]

However, there are some novel features about the place occupied by public physical punishment in the numerous criminal laws passed between the late 1820s and the early 1850s that distinguish these laws from earlier legal traditions. Firstly, as Peters has shown, unlike Ottoman criminal codes, which merely defined some acts as illegal and hence deserving of punishment, these new Egyptian laws not only specified the kind of punishment that should be meted out but also attempted to quantify it.[49] It was no longer sufficient, for example, to say that those who violated market regulations were to be punished in the unqualified manner that Mehmed Ali's *muḥtasib* followed. Rather, a precise taxonomy of pain was introduced that attempted to take into consideration the seriousness of the offense, the physical constitution of the offender,[50] whether the culprit was a first-time or repeat offender, and the social standing of the offender.

Secondly, the number of lashes that were to be meted out for particular offenses depended on the social class of the offender. The fact that punishment was often tailored to fit an offender's social status was not, in and of itself, new or unique to these nineteenth-century Egyptian laws.[51] *Fiqh* requires judges to take social standing into account when using their discretionary power (*ta'zīr*) to pass sentences on convicted offenders. According to Ḥanafī *fiqh*, for example, there are four categories of offenders, and each category is to be punished differently. Thus, when dealing with land owners (*al-dahhāqūn*) and military chieftains (*al-quwwād*), the qadi should limit himself to sending his deputy to the offender to inform (*i'lām*) him, "Word has reached me [i.e., the deputy] that you have done such and such." When dealing with descendants of the Prophet and of 'Alī (*sādāt kirām*) and with the *'ulamā'*, the qadi is to summon them to court and verbally confront them (*bi'l-muwājahah*) with their offenses. Next come the middle classes (*awsāṭ*), who are to be informed of their offenses, summoned to court, and imprisoned (*ḥabs*). Finally come the riffraff (*al-safala*), who are to be punished with all of the above plus beating (*ḍarb*).[52] Taking the social standing of offenders into consideration was not unique to shari'a either. The Russian aristocracy, for example, was privileged for much of the eighteenth and nineteenth centuries by being exempt from punishment by the knout, which together with being exempt from conscription and paying poll tax, helped constitute the distinction between the upper and the lower classes in Russian society.[53] As a further example, the British army in India decided against punishing sepoys by lashing, preferring to dishonorably discharge them, the idea being that dismissal would be seen (in a caste-based society) as directly affecting the sepoy's self-esteem and sense of honor. Corporal punishment was seen as suitable only for soldiers, as it was believed that they had nothing but their bodies, meaning that imprisonment and fines could not be used as suitable punishment.[54]

While the idea of making allowances for the social position of the defendant when sentencing was not new, what was different about these nineteenth-century Egyptian laws was to whom they extended this legal privilege. For example, to the category including *'ulamā'* and *sādāt kirām*, the

Humāyūnī Law of 1852 added "notables" (*wujūh al-nās*) and high-ranking civil servants (*aṣḥāb al-rutab*).[55] The addition of these new social groups was not only a function of the "ruling class's *perception* of social distance vis-à-vis other groups in Egyptian society"[56] but also an indication of how these new laws now functioned as important tools of social engineering. In other words, the law not only reflected social distances that its drafters *perceived* as natural boundaries separating different classes but also served as a means of *establishing* these distances.[57] While the *'ulamā'* and *sādāt kirām* were traditionally thought to be entitled to exemption from the ignominy of public torture, the new criminal law added the state's civil servants and members of the ruling household to this list of privileged legal persons.[58]

There was another, more significant, change in the manner that punishment was decided on in these new laws. By comparing the Humāyūnī Law of 1852 to Mehmed Ali's first criminal legislation of 1829 or to Qānūn al-Muntakhabāt (Code of Selected Enactments of 1830–44[59]), one clearly sees that recidivism had become an important criterion in determining punishment, and it was arguably a defendant's criminal record more than the severity of the crime or his or her social standing that was the crucial factor. Article 5, Section 2 of the Humāyūnī Law of 1852, for example, stipulates that if drunkards and gamblers "commit their offense once and [then] twice, and if they are not deterred [by previous punishment] from following their whims and insist on [recommitting] their offense, then they should be exiled or sent to prison chained [in shackles] until they repent."[60] Article 11, Section 3 of the law, furthermore, stipulates that "he who has stolen three times, been punished, and has not been deterred ... is incorrigible [*ghayr qābil lil-istiqāma*] and is incapable of proper behavior. Accordingly, he should be exiled and banished to the Sudan."[61] As a further example, Article 19, Section 3 stipulates that those who have tampered with prices or weights should be given between three to seventy-nine lashes on the first offense. On the second offense, their punishment was increased to imprisonment, as this entailed "closing down their shops and losing their means of subsistence." If they persisted and repeated the offense a third time, "they should [first] pay any debts that they might have incurred and then be sent back to their villages in order not to be counted as merchants."[62]

These changes to the meaning and nature of punishment can also be detected in the way the laws were implemented and how punishments were carried out. As mentioned above, the problem of administering a "just measure of pain" was practically a question of quantification. It was the commensurability of pain that informed attempts to specify the exact number of lashes that different crimes deserved. It was not certain, for example, that the same offense would receive the same punishment when committed in different places and by different people. For even if the law specified a given number of lashes per offense, there was no way to standardize the severity of the blows throughout the realm so that the amount of the ensuing pain would be commensurate and comparable. In addition, it proved difficult to ensure that no excessive beating took place, and one can detect concern about "superfluous" beating as early as 1830. The preamble to Qānūn al-Filāḥa, which was passed in that year, for example, stated: "It has been known that convicted criminals are often beaten in an excessive manner [*yuḍrabūn ḍarban zā'idan 'an qānūnihim*]. Accordingly, they may be seriously injured [*yaḥṣul lahum talaf*]. Therefore, it became necessary to specify exactly the punishment they are to receive."[63] To drive this point home, Article 25 of the same law stipulated that "any village governor who causes the death of a convicted criminal by using excessive force in flogging him will be liable to pay the full [shari'a-stipulated] blood money [*diyya*] to the criminal's next of kin." It added that lashing should be limited to the buttocks and the soles of feet.[64] Despite these clear warnings, public officials continued to use excessive force against convicted offenders, and nearly thirty years later, the problem of how to define excessive force and how to quantify pain was still such an issue that Sa'īd Pasha had to warn his interior minister that "beating in excess of the limit stipulated by law is contrary to Our desire" and that under no circumstance should beating exceed 200 lashes, "and in this case, a physician should be present during the execution of the punishment."[65] This stipulation that a physician should be present during the administration of public flogging was mentioned in the records of some courts-martial.[66] The fear was that if the officials who carried out floggings, be they local governors (for civilian matters) or high-ranking officers (for military proceedings), were not effectively controlled, excessive beating would occur, which might lead to death or to incapacitation. In the case of soldiers, this would mean "the government [*al-mīrī*] would have lost the said soldier's services."[67] This abhorrence of waste (rather than concern for the humanity of the culprits) was another reason behind the occasional decisions of Majlis al-Aḥkām to repeal verdicts issued by lower courts involving corporal punishment and replace them with prison sentences.[68]

Besides the abovementioned problems with the process of carrying out physical punishment, namely the difficulty of quantifying and standardizing pain and the fear that excessive beating might lead to permanent physical injury or death, the authorities were also concerned about the impact that public beating had on the spectators.[69] Although there are no records of the minutes of any meeting that might have been convened to discuss such a problem, there are numerous criminal cases that refer to local disturbances breaking out as a result of beatings that must have been perceived as excessive and unjust.

Sulṭān's case, with which this chapter opened, is a good example of an incident in which a beating administered in an excessive manner could result in serious problems for the state. Admittedly, this case is not about disturbances breaking out following the execution of a court sentence. Nevertheless, given the fact that the legal system at that time made no distinction between the executive and the judiciary, and since the incident took place in a palace belonging to a very central figure of the ruling family, one can assume that the punishment, as severe as it was, was considered legal and not extralegal. This and other similar cases provided further impetus for the need to replace corporal punishment.

PRISON AS AN ALTERNATIVE TO FLOGGING

Given the clear awareness that flogging as punishment was problematic, there was an acute need to find an alternative to it. This is what Egyptian prisons provided starting in the late 1840s, namely a means of punishing offenders that was seen as a reliable and safe alternative to flogging. This must have been the main reason for the marked attention paid to health conditions in prisons and jails all over Egypt from the 1850s onward. Indeed, by the time the 1861 decree had been passed, the sanitation of Egyptian prisons had already improved significantly. To appreciate the steps undertaken to improve the condition of prisons, it may be useful to summarize what these prisons looked like in the first half of the nineteenth century.

Throughout much of the nineteenth century, Egyptian prisons did not fall under the jurisdiction of one single authority.[70] Rather, the various prisons and places of detention were under the control of separate bureaucratic agencies. At the top of the prison hierarchy was Līmān al-Iskandariyya, which was located in the Alexandria dockyards. This was certainly the most important prison in the land and was a truly convict prison (as opposed to a local prison that held people for short sentences). It was reserved for the most serious criminals; the various laws that were passed (Qānūn al-Filāḥa of 1829, Qānūn al-Muntakhabāt of 1830–44, and the Humāyūnī Law of 1852) all specified that prisoners receiving the longest sentences be sent to Līmān al-Iskandariyya.[71]

In Cairo, there seem to have been numerous prisons and other buildings that were used for interning convicted criminals, although they were not built for that purpose. The main one was the Citadel Prison (Ḥubūs al-Qal'a), which seems to have been reserved for holding suspects who had been arraigned for serious crimes while their cases were pending in front of Majlis Miṣr (the judicial body that dealt with criminal and civil cases in Cairo).[72] The main hard-labor prison in Cairo was initially the Iron Workshop (Dimirhane), in Būlāq.[73] Later, it seems to have been replaced by the Railway Workshop (al-Wābūrāt), also in Būlāq. The main jail for suspects being arraigned while their cases were viewed by the Cairo Police Department was located within the police headquarters in Azbakiyya, but suspects were also held at the police stations (*qarāqūls*) of the ten "quarters" (*atmān*) of the city. Furthermore, the Cairo Shari'a Court (Maḥkamat Miṣr al-Shar'iyya) had a small jail for detaining men and women for periods shorter than twenty-four hours.[74] Finally, women were interned, both before and after trial, in the Iplikhane, a textile workhouse in Būlāq.[75]

Given how many places of incarceration existed in Cairo, let alone in the country at large, it proved very difficult to put them all under the supervision of a single authority. Accordingly, there were no standardized regulations for the officials running these prisons to abide by. Nevertheless, some general points can be made regarding the health conditions of jails and prisons.

With the possible exception of Līmān al-Iskandariyya, none of Egypt's prisons occupied buildings that had been built to serve as jails. Rather, it was customary for orders to be issued to convert some old structures or reserve a section of a government building for prison use. For example, when it was discovered during Sa'īd's reign (1854–63) that women were being held in a jail very close to that of men at Cairo Police Department Headquarters, the Cairo Governorate wrote to Sa'īd Pasha requesting permission to rent a nearby house at the cost of 50–75 piastres a month and hire a literate male jailer (*sajjān*) at a monthly salary of 150 piastres.[76] During the same period, there were repeated concerns about the proximity of one of the jails in Cairo to the main safe of the Treasury Department (Khazīnat al-Māliyya); soon after Ismā'īl's accession, the jail was relocated to a disused stable to the south of al-Ghawrī Mosque.[77]

Since these buildings were not built to house prisons, they proved inadequate, and there were numerous reports issued by civilian health inspectors, who would occasionally visit these places, complaining of the alarming health conditions inside. As early as the 1820s, when the Iron Workshop was still being used as a prison, there were complaints about the dangerous health conditions there. In 1828, a peasant named ʿAbd al-Raḥmān ʿAbd al-Raḥīm, who had been imprisoned at the Iron Workshop for nine months on a theft charge, presented a petition requesting his release, stating that there was no one tending his fallow land in Sammalūṭ in Upper Egypt. When his case was investigated, it was discovered that six months after his internment he had contracted syphilis, a disease that made him incapable of working in the foundry. This, together with fear of contagion, justified his release.[78] When the Cairo Public Health Commissioner (Maʾmūr Dīwān Taftīsh Ṣiḥḥat al-Maḥrūsa) visited the jail at the Cairo Citadel in March 1851, he found the place "in such a bad state that [it] causes serious harm to health." Although he initially recommended that the whole place be completely rebuilt, he realized that this would cost a considerable amount and therefore suggested some minor alterations, such as building latrines, whitewashing the walls, and giving inmates wooden cots to sleep on instead of leaving them to sleep on the floor.[79] After his rounds of Ḥubūs al-Ḍābitkhāne, the jail at Cairo Police Department Headquarters, the same official wrote a damning report saying that he had found "a huge pile of stinking rubbish that is extremely nauseating and which could lead, God forbid, to an outbreak of infectious diseases. This in a place that should be an example of cleanliness."[80] Eight years later, the same jail was inspected by a doctor from the Azbakiyya Civilian Hospital who had been specifically dispatched for that purpose. His report was equally condemnatory. He noted how small the jail was and remarked that it lacked proper ventilation. He recommended building larger cells (*ḥawāṣil*) so that "prisoners would not be piled on top of each other as is currently the case, something that would necessarily cause them considerable harm."[81]

It is not clear if inmates were routinely shackled in iron chains in their cells. During Mehmed Ali's reign, there are some references to chains being used to tie prisoners together by their necks and feet.[82] It also seems that factory workers, who were mostly prisoners or individuals who had been pressed into service by force, were occasionally bound with fetters, apparently as an extra punishment.[83] When convicts were being taken to prison or prisoners were being moved from jail to jail, they had wooden stocks around their hands and iron chains around their necks.[84] In the army, although the training manuals and military legal codes did not stipulate the use of chains to restrain prisoners,[85] officers occasionally put their soldiers in shackles after beating them in the army jail.[86] It was common practice for prisoners who were sent to the hospital for treatment to be bound with iron chains; Clot Bey, however, succeeded in convincing Majlis al-Aḥkām to allow those afflicted with "heavy diseases" to be left unchained, although those with "light diseases" were kept shackled.[87]

Diet was another area that attracted the attention of prison officials.[88] As a rule, prisoners were responsible for feeding themselves, and police records abound with cases of prisoners who were fed regularly by their friends or families during occasional visits[89] or who bought food with money deducted from their belongings when they were detained.[90] Article 17, Chapter 3 of the Humāyūnī Law stipulated that destitute convicts who could not support themselves would be fed by the government "within reasonable limits." The daily ration seems to have been no more than three loaves of bread.[91] Supplying water to the Cairo jails was problematic.[92] After the city's water carriers were forbidden from drawing water directly from the Nile or the Khalīj, special fountains (*hanafiyyāt*) were built for the purpose. The water carriers' guild raised the fee of supplying water, and the authorities had no option but to agree to the higher rates.[93]

From what has been described so far, it does seem that the health conditions of Egyptian prisons in the first half of the nineteenth century left much to be desired. The image one gets from the reports drafted by the different health officials who occasionally visited these places of detention is one of dank, dark, airless places filled with unhealthy prisoners suffering from the effects of malnutrition and hard labor. Although health officials, penal legislators, and prison managers in Egypt never formulated a consistent and self-confident policy to justify and perpetuate such miserable conditions—as their British contemporaries had done with their principle of "less eligibility" and the implementation of unproductive, wasteful punitive devices such as the treadmill—Egyptian prisons were nevertheless dangerous places where it was more than likely that one would lose not only one's freedom but also one's life. Using the registers of the Līmān al-Iskandariyya, Rudolph Peters managed to calculate the mortality rate of the prison's inmates: in late 1840s, the average mortality rate per year was over 13 percent. To put this figure in perspective, at "the most insalubrious *bagne* (hard-labor prison) in France, that of Rochefort, the mortality rate between 1816 and 1827 was 9 percent per annum, which was higher than that of all other French *bagnes*."[94]

Considering the unhealthy conditions in Egyptian prisons, one can understand the concern of health authorities. In the mid-1830s, the khedives and their senior officials started to issue orders regarding the general conditions of prisons. For example, in 1834, as a result of various petitions presented by prisoners complaining that they were serving long detention periods without being sentenced, Mehmed Ali issued a general decree to his provincial governors telling them to deal with the cases in front of them promptly and without delay.[95] In 1849, when the same problem continued to come to the attention of various officials, the newly formed Majlis al-Khuṣūṣī (Privy Council) reiterated Mehmed Ali's previous order:

> Since detaining prisoners for long periods without being questioned causes them harm, and since dealing with every person according to his crime is only just, then delaying their detention periods unnecessarily while they might be the providers of their families and might accordingly lead their dependents to fall into destitution and misery, and some of [those detained] might die as a result of being so firmly tied to hardship—as a result of all this the Majlis has thereto ordered all provincial governors to check those detained in the cells [*ḥawāṣil*] of their provinces regularly and during heavy loads of work, at least once a week.[96]

One month later, Majlis al-Aḥkām endorsed this recommendation and issued a general order to the same effect to all provincial governors.[97] The following year, Majlis al-Aḥkām issued another order stipulating that provincial prisons should be checked at least once a fortnight.[98]

Nevertheless, the records show that many prisoners continued to present petitions complaining that they were being detained for long periods without their cases being looked into. Most of the preserved petitions are from the prison at Cairo Police Department Headquarters, which suggests that this was a nationwide problem, since it is difficult to imagine that provincial prisons were more relaxed about bringing their detainees to trial.[99] Confronted by repeated complaints from detainees, Saʿīd Pasha convened a special committee to investigate the conditions of Cairo prisons. Its findings were damning for the Cairo Police Department prefect, Hüseyin Fahmī, who was found to be particularly negligent of the conditions of his prisons. The khedive promptly sacked Fahmī and ordered him to "rest at home as punishment for yourself and an example for others."[100]

It was during Khedive Ismāʿīl's reign, though, that the health conditions of prisons and prisoners received the closest attention. Soon after his accession, Ismāʿīl issued an order "to remove all factors that might be harmful to the health of prisoners, to clean all prisons, and to renovate and rebuild all [prison buildings] that need repair so that such buildings will have clean, healthy air."[101] When he heard that as a result of this order, all prisoners were being subjected to a body search on being detained and that any money found on them was confiscated, he inquired about the reason for this. The response was that these measures were for the benefit of the prisoners, since many of them would have their money stolen once they were detained with thieves and other serious criminals. He was appalled to receive such an answer, and he immediately issued a decree demanding that prisons stop this practice at once and segregate prisoners according to the nature of crime they had committed: murderers, thieves, debtors, and those awaiting trial should be held in separate sections of prisons. He added that all prisons should take hygienic considerations and the well-being of the prisoners into account, and if that necessitated building or renovating prisons, then he would approve the expenses.[102] Soon afterward, many provincial governors wrote to the Pasha to say that they had checked the prisons in their provinces, and they requested considerable funds to renovate them and reconstruct them to meet the new demands.[103] When it was reported that the debtors' prison was overcrowded, that the families of many of the debtors were suffering, and that the debtors themselves were falling ill, Majlis al-Khuṣūṣī issued a ruling that creditors would have to pay the expenses of imprisoned debtors who could not genuinely support themselves while serving their sentences. The council justified this by saying that the health of a prisoner who could not feed himself might deteriorate while he was in prison, and "health matters are to take precedence over all other matters."[104]

These various measures to improve prison health conditions had a noticeable impact: according to Peters, the mortality rates dropped from 13 percent in the 1840s to 4.5 percent in the 1860s.[105] It thus appears that a significant shift took place in the nature and meaning of imprisonment during the mid-nineteenth century. While Egyptian prisons never developed into places of reform and rehabilitation in the way British Benthamite prisons did, they were nevertheless transformed from places of exile and banishment in which one was likely to lose one's life into places of incarceration where one's liberty, but not one's health, was taken away. By the early 1860s, Egyptian prisons presented themselves as viable alternatives to the whip as a means of punishment. This, and the fact that prison terms were more easily quantifiable than pain, helps explain why the authorities felt comfortable passing the 1861 decree banning flogging and replacing it with incarceration.

FLOGGING AS A MEANS OF ESTABLISHING PROBATIVE EVIDENCE

In addition to being an official punishment named in legal codes, beating was also used as a means of extracting confessions from suspects to establish probative evidence, and it is important to bear this in mind as we attempt to understand what prompted authorities to limit official violence. Shariʿa courts, however, dismissed confessions extracted under duress as invalid and baseless, and when the Grand Mufti dealt with homicide cases in which torture had been used to force defendants to confess, he would issue a fatwa saying, "The defendants cannot be convicted for manslaughter because their confessions have been obtained by what according to the *shariʿa* is regarded as coercion [*ikrah sharʿi*]."[106] However, the *siyāsa* councils readily admitted confessions extracted under duress, and the police often resorted to torture during interrogations, although these confessions were often contested and occasionally reversed.[107]

In the records of the al-Minūfiyya Governorate in the Delta, for example, we find a typical report in which the governor complained to one of his superiors that the suspects arraigned in a recent theft case had not confessed to their crime in spite of repeated beatings: "We lashed them with the whip numerous times until the flesh peeled off their legs [*ḥattā tanāthar laḥm arjulihim*]. One of the suspects was forced to stand up for forty-eight hours until his feet got swollen. But they did not confess, and alleged that they had been wrongly arraigned [*mazlūmīn*]."[108]

It is important to note that up until the 1850s, the authorities did not even try to hide the fact that torture was used as a means of extracting evidence from suspects. The notion of keeping this practice a secret because it was considered "'uncivilized' and therefore illegal"[109] belongs to a later period. It was commonly known and understood by both state officials and the populace that police inflicted pain on prisoners. It was not even a "public secret" that was effective precisely because it was both secretly performed and widely acknowledged.[110]

However, the public, official practice of torture was not without its problems. For one thing, and as the case mentioned above shows, torture did not guarantee a confession. Often, suspects did not break down or give the legally required confession. In other cases, torture resulted in false confessions. An 1855 theft case from Cairo illustrates this issue. An Abyssinian woman accused her female servant and five male neighbors of stealing jewelry from her house while she was away. The police quickly moved in to investigate the case, arrested the suspects, and "applied pressure on them" (*bi-l'taḍyīq 'alay-him*). The suspects confessed to the theft. Their houses were searched and some jewelry was indeed found. When the experts (in this case jewelers from the Cairo gold market) were summoned to examine the jewelry, they ascertained that it was in fact stolen jewelry but that it had been stolen from another house, whose owner had reported the theft earlier. During a second interrogation, the suspects all withdrew their confessions, insisting that they had given them under duress. The *siyāsa* council accepted this argument and had the suspects released, "since it transpired that their confessions were the result of the beating they had received [in custody]."[111]

The *siyāsa* councils did not always accept the claim that an earlier confession was "faulty" since it had been given under duress. This, for example, was the argument used by a certain Ḥanafī Muḥammad, who was accused of killing a Syrian Christian man named Khawāja Ibrāhīm in March 1853. After being caught red-handed by the neighbors robbing Khawāja Ibrāhīm's house, Ḥanafī was escorted to the village head and eventually to the provincial headquarters in Ashmūn, where he confessed to having killed Khawāja Ibrāhīm earlier in a nearby village using a double-barreled rifle and throwing his body in the Nile. Ḥanafī repeated his confession when he was interrogated by the qadi of Ashmūn. However, he later retracted his confession, claiming that he had given it "out of fear of beating and imprisonment" (*khawfan min al-ḍarb wa'l-ḥabs*) and that the provincial governor, Ma'jūn Bey, had threatened to beat him and forced him to confess to something he had not done. The investigating authorities, however, did not believe this denial and reasoned that even though "he had claimed that his confession was due to beating, this claim was not substantiated as it is obvious that he resorted to this [denial] in order to escape conviction. . . . He is heretofore sentenced to hard labor in al-Qal'a al-Sa'īdiyya for life."[112]

Significantly, even though Ḥanafī could not substantiate his claim of having been tortured while in police custody, the use of physical pain itself was not what was questioned in this case. Indeed, and as has been pointed out, the practice of inflicting pain on prisoners was, strictly speaking, legal, and it was not something that the authorities were attempting to hide. However, what was being increasingly questioned was its efficacy in securing a valid confession. As noted above, whereas the practice sometimes failed to force suspects to give a confession, in many cases it was discovered that it was, in fact, too successful, for it occasionally produced false confessions.

Of course, the concern about the efficacy of pain in producing truthful confessions was not new; nor was it unique to Egypt. In early modern Europe, confessions started to lose their centrality with the ascendency of circumstantial evidence and the concomitant marginalization of traditional means of establishing probative evidence according to Roman canon law, which relied on a confession and two eyewitnesses.[113] Similarly, throughout the first half of the nineteenth century, the *siyāsa* branch of the Egyptian legal system increasingly questioned the use of confession and eyewitness accounts as the prime methods of establishing probative evidence, and *siyāsa* authorities occasionally expressed concern that inflicting pain often resulted in false confessions and that a lack of reliable eyewitnesses often meant that suspects got off scot-free. What eventually made inflicting pain gratuitous in terms of providing probative evidence was the availability of forensic medicine as an alternative, something that had far-reaching implications not only on probative evidence but also on the entire legal system.

The following section offers a close analysis of the crucial role forensic medicine played in *siyāsa* adjudication of violent crimes. This analysis is informed by a comparison of how the *siyāsa* and *fiqh* systems used medical expertise.

MEDICAL EXPERTISE IN SHARIʿA COURTS

The presentation of medical information in Egyptian courts of law was not suddenly introduced in the mid-nineteenth century; rather, medicine and medical expertise have a long history in shariʿa. Nevertheless, the way medical expertise is accepted in shariʿa courts is fundamentally different from how it was accepted in the *siyāsa* councils. This accounts for why *siyāsa* councils viewed forensic medicine as a substitute for pain as a means of establishing probative evidence. A close look at the difference should clarify this point.

There are many instances in which classical *fiqh* permits medical expertise to be called on to resolve legal disputes. These include disputes between a seller and a buyer of a slave where the buyer claims to have discovered a defect or an illness in the slave and the question revolves around whether the defect or illness occurred before or after purchase; cases that involve determining "mortal illness" (*maraḍ al-mawt*), for according to *fiqh*, any transaction, such as making a last will and testament or founding a *waqf*, carried out by a person on their deathbed is considered void to preclude prejudices to that person's heirs that these transactions might involve; cases involving compensation for medical malpractice; and cases in which paternity must be proven through physiognomy (*qiyāfa*).[114]

While it is commonly agreed that the basis for accepting such expertise is the Quranic dictum "Ask those who know [*ahl al-dhikr*] if you do not know,"[115] there is considerable disagreement among jurists about the probative value of expert testimony and whether it should be classified as transmission (*riwāya*), the purest example of which is transmitting Prophetic traditions, or as testimony (*shahāda*), the purest example of which is court testimony. This disagreement has serious implications, for the conditions of validity of *shahāda* are considerably stricter than those of *riwāya*. Most importantly, because of the potential hostility associated with testimony, jurists have insisted that the number of witnesses be two, whereas no such condition was set for accepting transmission.[116]

More significant than the question of whether medical expertise should be considered an example of *shahāda* or *riwāya* in *fiqh* is the question of how this expertise should be established. In general, it appears that practical experience (*tajriba*) is prioritized following the Prophetic tradition "Only the experienced can be wise."[117] In explaining this tradition, Ron Shaham quotes the early twentieth-century Indian jurist Muḥammad ʿAbd al-Raḥmān al-Mubārkfūrī, who said, "The wise among the physicians is the one who is experienced in both the persistent and innate issues."[118] The *fiqh* literature requires that the medical expert, like all expert witnesses who appear in front of the qadi, be proficient in his trade, trustworthy, and reliable.[119] And as in many other professions, physicians are supposed to be closely monitored by the *muḥtasib*, who is supposed to keep a close eye on them, watching out for malpractice and weeding out quacks. In *Nihāyat al-Rutba fī Ṭalab al-Ḥisba*, for example, Shayzarī states that the *muḥtasib* should make physicians take the Hippocratic Oath, make sure that they do not prescribe poisons or harmful medicines to their patients or talismans to the commoners and that they do not suggest anything that could induce an abortion to pregnant women or anything that could cause impotence to men. He should also require them to maintain modesty when entering private homes and to respect the privacy of their patients.[120]

Most significantly, it is when we look at how and why medical expertise is presented to the shariʿa court in penal cases that the contrast with its deployment in the *siyāsa* council becomes most visible. The *fiqh* literature deals with three types of cases in which medical experts can be called on to provide their opinion in penal matters. The first type of case involves intentional killing (*qatl ʿamd*) where there is dispute about whether the death was caused by the defender's assault or by some other factor. In these cases, the qadi can summon physicians to the court to provide testimony about the signs they saw on the body of the victim. The Shāfiʿī jurist al-Nawawī mentions a case in which witnesses to a fatal bodily assault could not determine whether the victim had died due to the assault or had already been dead when he was hit. In this case, the physicians were supposed to check if the blood spilled from the victim was that of a living person (*damm ḥayy*) or that of a corpse (*damm mayyit*). If the medical experts assert that the blood was that of a living person, then the guardian of the victim would be entitled to blood money. However, al-Nawawī does not clarify the technique by which the experts could make the distinction between the two types of blood.[121]

That the jurists were aware that medical expertise could not determine if a wound could be fatal is indicated by the manner in which they addressed the thorny issue of determining who the offender is in the following hypothetical case: Zayd dies after ʿAmr stabs him with a knife in his belly and Bakr cuts his neck with a sword. This case is usually raised to tackle the question of complicity in murder, but it is also revealing of how *fiqh* relies on medical expertise. In this specific hypothetical case, Ḥanafī jurists ask if Zayd died instantaneously after the double attack, for if he did, ʿAmr is considered the killer; but if he lived for a day or more before expiring, then Bakr is considered the killer.[122]

The medical expertise that is deployed in this and many other hypothetical cases does not strive to establish the actual cause of death. Rather, the *fiqh* treatises are concerned with the verbal formulae that witnesses, including medical expert witnesses, have to utter in front of the qadi for their testimony to be taken as evidence of intentional homicide:

> The witness testimony [*al-shahāda*] in penal cases has to be explicit about explaining causality [*muṣarriḥa bi'l-gharad*]. It is necessary that the witness link death to the act being witnessed. So if he said, "He struck him with a sword," nothing is proven thus. Likewise, if he said, "He hit him and then [the victim] bled," or if he said, "He wounded him," or "He struck him with a sword and then [the victim] bled or died," nothing is proven, for death could have been the result of another cause. [But if the witness] said, "He wounded him, and so he killed him," or "[The victim] died of his wounds," or "He bled him and [the victim] died as a result," then homicide has been proven [*thabata al-qatl*].[123]

The second type of case involves intentional physical offenses that cause injuries (*qiṣāṣ fīmā dūn al-nafs*). If such cases can be retaliated physically, that is, "where injury can be inflicted in exactly the same area, without risking the life of the offender and without causing him graver harm than that he inflicted on the offended person,"[124] then this retaliation is to be carried out by physicians, not by the injured party. But such cases are the exception. The majority of cases to which jurists direct their attention are those that cannot be retaliated physically but must be dealt with by stipulating fixed monetary compensation. These offenses are divided into three types: wounding the body (*jirāḥ*) or the head (*shijāj*); cutting or severing organs (*ibāna*); and causing damage to the function of an organ (*ibṭāl manfaʿa*).[125] The *fiqh* treatises give a detailed taxonomy of body organs and, in case of injury, their corresponding financial compensation, known as *diyya* or *arsh*. In determining the value of *arsh*, careful attention is paid to the singularity of the organ (e.g., the *arsh* of the nose is one unit, whereas each eye is half a unit) and its functionality (e.g., the tongue is used for speech, taste, and swallowing, and each function is assigned a different *arsh*). Accordingly, the *arsh* of two eyes is fixed at one hundred camels, while the *arsh* of each eye set at fifty camels. The same goes for legs, ears, lips, and nipples. The compensation for organs that do not come in pairs, such as the nose, the male organ, the tongue, and the skin, is one hundred camels each. In addition, there is an equally elaborate list detailing financial compensation for the loss of intellect or any of the five senses.[126]

A good example of how *fiqh* treatises deploy medical expertise to come up with these retaliatory compensations is the manner by which head wounds (*shijāj*) are classified. The Ḥanbalī jurist Ibn Qudāma stated that only physicians can ascertain the different types of head wounds, which is a crucial step in determining the amount of blood money to be paid. In addition to the different kinds of bodily wounds, Ibn Qudāma mentions ten different types of head wounds: those that break the skin (*al-ḥāriṣa*); those that break the skin and spill the blood (*al-dāmiya*); those that break the skin, spill the blood, and cut the flesh (*al-bāḍiʿa*); those that break the skin, spill the blood, cut the flesh, and penetrate both skin and flesh (*al-mutalāḥima*); those that reach the periosteum (*al-sumḥāq*); those that penetrate the periosteum and reveal the bones of the skull (*al-mūḍiḥa*); those that break the bones of the skull (*al-hāshima*); those that break the bones and dislocate them (*al-munaqqila*); those that reach the pia mater but do not penetrate the brain (*al-āma* or *al-maʾmūma*); and those that penetrate the brain (*al-dāmigha*). After the physician identifies the kind of head wound, *fiqh* treatises say, the judge is to rule on the amount of blood money to be paid—for example, five camels for a *mūḍiḥa,* ten for a *hāshima,* fifteen for a *munaqqila,* thirty-three and a third of a *diyya* for a *ma'mūma,* and so on.[127]

The third type of case involves wounds to organs for which no exact financial compensation is specified. In these cases, the compensation is called *ḥukūmat 'adl,* the value of which is left to the discretion of the judge (hence the word *ḥukūma,* which is derived from *ḥukm,* the ruling of the judge) and is based

> not on the tariff but on an assessment of the disability caused by the injury in any particular case. Like the process of evaluating the worth of physical injuries in slaves, the evaluation of *ḥukūmat 'adl* involved both physicians and slave dealers. One finds legal formularies of disputes between the offender and the offended concerning the severity of the injury. First, the qadi summons physicians to define the sort of injury. Following that, the qadi summons experts for determining the value of bodily defects (*arbāb al-khibra bi-taqwīm al-abdan,* probably slave dealers) and instructs them to evaluate the price of the victim (as if he were a slave) before and after his injury. The difference between the two is the compensation sum.[128]

In determining the value of the *ḥukūmat 'adl* for an injury, the judge should use his own discretion while abiding by the general principle that the compensation he settles on should not exceed the prescribed *arsh.*[129] Crucially, he should also follow the general maxims that maintain and uphold social hierarchies. Accordingly, in the case of an intentional killing, the *diyya* of a woman is half that of a man, and in a case of grievous bodily harm, a woman's limbs are worth half a man's limbs. Similarly, the *diyya* of a Jew or a Christian is one-third that of a Muslim.[130] In his seminal article "The Valorization of the Human Body in Muslim Sunni Law," Baber Johansen explains the logic informing the law of retaliation by saying that what counts is "the generic classification of people according to gender, freedom and health. Families remain important as the group of agnatic male relatives who are . . . responsible for the compensatory payments of unintentional killing or grievous bodily harm, and as their heirs, who receive the payment of unintentional homicides. . . . The amount of compensation [therefore] depends on the generic classification of persons, i.e., their gender and their status as free persons or slaves."[131]

Indeed, it seems that while it obviously dealt with individual bodies, the medical expertise that was presented to shari'a courts aimed not so much at establishing cause of death or injury but at upholding and valorizing these social hierarchies.

MEDICAL EXPERTISE IN *SIYĀSA* COUNCILS

By contrast, starting in the early 1850s, the medical expertise that the *siyāsa* councils admitted in penal cases was constituted by and functioned in a radically different manner. Four features marked what came to be known as *siyāsa* medicine from the medical expertise that the qadi accepted in shari'a court. First, this new medical expertise went further than establishing the nature of a bone fracture or the depth of a wound; it was based on determining a causal link between visible bodily injury, on the one hand, and organ malfunction or death, on the other. A good example of this can be found in the report submitted by the forensic doctor in the case of the death of Muḥammad 'Abd al-Raḥmān, with which chapter 2 opened. After exhuming the body and conducting an autopsy, the doctor stated in his report that

> there is a circular wound facing the bladder between the sixth and seventh ribs. Bloody, foamy substance had excreted from it. Its diameter is about one centimeter. The rim is inverted inward, . . . and [the path of the wound] leads to the left lung. Also, by checking the abdomen, a small circular wound was detected in the epigastrium [*al-qism al-shurāsīfī*]. . . . [This wound] reaches the stomach. From the above it is clear that these wounds were caused by fine projectiles. . . . [These projectiles] hit the left lung and the stomach, causing death, which happened three days ago.[132]

Another example can be found in the case of Zahra bint Sayyid Aḥmad, a middle-aged woman who mysteriously died in November 1877. When it was rumored in the neighborhood that Zahra's son-in-law had been seen beating her hard in the stomach, he was arrested on suspicion of causing her death. After preliminary investigations, not enough evidence was found against him, and he was set free. Zahra's son, however, became suspicious of his brother-in-law, and he went to the police and insisted on an autopsy, even though Zahra's body had already been interred and would have to be exhumed. His petition for exhuming the body was accepted, and a doctor from Qaṣr al-'Ainī Hospital conducted the autopsy. It stated that one of Zahra's lungs was defective, that it was obvious that serious damage had been caused to the liver, and that the ninth rib had been broken. The report ended by clearly identifying the cause of death as "external pressure on the healthy right lung, which was the only lung that was capable of respiration and oxygenating the blood. This pressure caused a temporary halt in breathing, . . . [which], added to the damage caused to the liver, resulted in death."[133]

These two examples illustrate a medical expertise that was shaped by a deep knowledge of human anatomy, which, in turn, was informed by dissection. It stands in sharp contrast to an understanding of the human body based on physiognomy or the practical knowledge that a bonesetter accumulates through experience. Furthermore, it is a reflection of the high degree of professionalization that the medical establishment underwent in the first half of the nineteenth century. As shown in chapters 1 and 4, the manner in which physicians were trained, licensed, and monitored had been fundamentally altered, resulting in medical expertise itself being radically reconstituted.

As important as this first feature is, it is another feature that provides a better explanation of how forensic medicine eventually replaced confession as a reliable means of providing probative evidence. This second feature of *siyāsa* medicine was its textuality. Whether considered transmission (*riwāya*) or testimony (*shahāda*), the conclusions that medical experts presented to shari'a courts were verbal; they were not written reports. In his encyclopedic work *Al-Ḥāwī al-Kabīr,* al-Māwardī says that after conducting their inspections, physiognomists should deliver their conclusion to the court "verbally" (*bi-lafẓ al-ikhbār* or *bi-lafẓ al-shahāda*).[134] Research done on shari'a court records, furthermore, shows that this *fiqh* rule, namely that medical expertise be delivered orally, was indeed practiced. For example, in his study on shari'a courts in Ottoman Egypt, 'Abd al-Rāziq 'Īsā mentions two separate cases in which the plaintiffs went to the main court in Cairo, al-Bāb al-'Ālī, each claiming that they had bought a female slave whom they subsequently discovered to be "defective" (*bihā 'ayb shar'ī*). The medical experts that the court summoned to inspect the two slaves (two midwives in one case, and a senior physician, or *ḥakīm bāsh*, and the daughter of the chief physician of the Manṣūrī Hospital in the other) checked both slaves and confirmed that the defects (the pregnancy of one, and the intermittent insanity of the other) had occurred prior to the purchase. The qadis accepted the verbal testimony (*shahāda, qawl*) of the medical experts and nullified the sales contracts.[135]

By contrast, after conducting their investigations in *siyāsa* criminal cases, the forensic doctors presented their conclusions to the councils in written reports (*taqrīrs*), and the records of the *siyāsa* councils are replete with verbatim copies of these written reports. For example, in June 1878, the body of

Ilyās Efendi, the brother of Ismāʿīl Bey Yusrī, who would later become the head of the Railway Authority, was found dead in his own house. His sister, who had been living with him, testified that he had been "very depressed" (*ʿindahu kadar ʿaẓīm*) for four or five days prior. A forensic doctor was sent to conduct an inspection. He later presented a written report establishing that the wounds on the body were the result of shots that had been fired from the double-barreled rifle that was found lying next to the body. The report added that the wounds showed that the shots had been fired from a very close range and that they were self-inflicted, corroborating the sister's statement.[136]

The third contrast between this new medical expertise and that presented to the shariʿa court stems from the question of whether these medical experts were regular personnel of the *siyāsa* councils or were summoned in an ad hoc manner to submit their reports on a case-by-case basis. Once again, a comparison with shariʿa courts may be instructive.

In his study on expert witnesses in *fiqh,* Shaham raises this important question: did the qadi summon these witnesses to the court, "which would render the experts the qadi's advisers, or did the litigants summon the experts, with the latter serving as partisan witnesses?"[137] After surveying the relevant *fiqh* literature, Shaham concludes, "It seems that in cases of public law application, it was the qadi, the representative of state authority, who summoned the witnesses.... In private lawsuits however, it appears that the options of the experts as either the qadi's advisers or partisan witnesses were both practiced."[138] Given that in Islamic law, homicide is governed by the principle of private prosecution whereby the victim's next of kin are the ones who have the right to initiate prosecution, carry out the execution of the sentence, and pardon the defendant or accept financial settlement,[139] it is also up to them to fetch witnesses and/or solicit medical experts to prove their claim. Even when the qadi summoned medical experts, they did so on an ad hoc basis, and these experts were not part of the regular personnel of the court. Neither Emile Tyan nor ʿAbd al-Rāziq ʿĪsā mention expert witnesses in their respective lists of shariʿa court personnel.[140] Accordingly, there was no official by the title of *ṭabīb sharʿī* in shariʿa courts, and there is no such a thing as *ṭibb sharʿī* in *fiqh* literature.[141]

By contrast, medical experts were one of the central, permanent components of the *siyāsa* system. Referred to as *ḥukamāʾ al-siyāsa* (instead of *ḥukamāʾ al-ṣiḥḥa,* or "health doctors"),[142] these doctors were assigned to police stations and entrusted with investigating all reported accidents that occurred in their respective neighborhoods so as to rule out any criminal suspicions. As opposed to the medical experts that appeared in shari'a courts, these *siyāsa* doctors did not spring into action, so to speak, on an ad hoc basis; rather, they were regular employees of the recently formed public hygiene bureaucracy, and their duties included the routine investigation of reported cases in which foul play was suspected. When the police received a report of a street accident (most of which were caused by speeding carriages),[143] a local fight, or an accusation of sexual assault,[144] the local *siyāsa* doctor would go to the reported site and conduct a preliminary inspection. When a death occurred, if he ruled out foul play, the *siyāsa* doctor would issue a burial certificate (*tadhkarat dafn*), without which no corpse was to be buried.[145] If, on the other hand, the preliminary inspection proved inconclusive, the body would be sent to Qaṣr al-'Ainī for an autopsy and a clear statement on the cause of death.

The archives of both the Cairo Governorate and the Cairo Police Department contain numerous cases in which *siyāsa* doctors were dispatched to investigate suspicious cases not on a request by litigants or a qadi's summons but as part of their regular, routine duties. For example, when the body of Mubārak al-Sūdānī, a soldier in the Second Infantry Regiment, was found in the newly dug Ismā'īliyya Canal to the northeast of Cairo, the police opened an investigation to find out whether he had drowned or had already been dead when his body was dumped into the canal. His body was therefore sent to Qaṣr al-'Ainī for an autopsy; the *siyāsa* doctor there concluded that the cause of death was "asphyxiation due to drowning" (*asfiksiā al-gharaq*)—in other words, he had been alive when he fell in the water.[146] In a similar case, the unidentified body of an eighteen-year-old man was found in the Qulalī Canal in Būlāq in northern Cairo. The police sent the body to Qaṣr al-'Ainī in the hope of determining the cause of death and shedding light on the identity of the young man. The hospital's report established asphyxiation as the cause of death, but due to the "advanced state of putrefaction" (*ḥālat ta'affun shadīda)* in which the body was found, the *siyāsa* doctors could not give any further details that might have been helpful in identifying the victim. In response, the police said that the doctors should have been more diligent in providing such details as the height of the victim, whether he was bearded, and any other markers that could have helped in identifying him.[147]

In another case, the body of an eighty-year-old woman who had been living alone was found two months after she had died. The police were suspicious that the neighbors took such a long time to report her missing. Specifically, they found it odd that despite the fact that the incident had occurred in the busy quarter of Khān al-Khalīlī and that the woman had died at the height of summer, the neighbors did not detect the stench. These suspicions were somewhat put to rest when the neighbors explained that the dead woman's house was surrounded by high walls, that she had lived on the top floor, and that the windows of her room had been sealed with glass and paper. But what finally brought the case to rest was the *siyāsa* doctor's report, which stated that there were no fractures in any of her bones and concluded that the woman most probably had not met a violent death.[148]

In the countryside, the *siyāsa* doctors stationed at the provincial headquarters (*mudīriyyāt*) worked in the same way: when confronted with a suspicious murder case, the police would send a *siyāsa* doctor to conduct an external postmortem examination and then present a detailed written report. The 1865 case that was discussed in chapter 2 of two bodies that were exhumed in an agricultural field included a lengthy forensic report submitted by a *siyāsa* doctor that concluded that in spite of the fact that the men had died some fifteen days earlier (which made it difficult to detect any skin wounds), one body had a fractured knee, a broken nose, and a disjointed thigh, and the other had missing teeth and a fractured lower jaw, which were clear signs that the two men had met a violent death. The doctor suspected that an axe and a thick wooden stick (*nabbūt*) had been used to kill the victims.[149]

The fourth and final difference between *siyāsa* medical expertise and shari'a court medical expertise was that the former was not deployed to uphold social hierarchies. Indeed, in many cases, it was deployed for the exact opposite purpose: to disrupt and challenge these hierarchies. To illustrate this point, and the three preceding points as well, it may be useful to follow a murder case from 1857 that took place in al-Fashn, a town in the Banī Sweif Governorate, some 150 kilometers south of Cairo. In addition to shedding light on how non-elite Egyptians reacted to forensic medicine, the case provides valuable details about how the *siyāsa* councils came to rely on the expertise of forensic doctors in the absence of eyewitnesses and/or a confession; it also shows how the councils went about incorporating the medical reports of the *siyāsa* doctors in their rulings. Most importantly, it includes examples of all the features mentioned above that, among other things, allowed the *siyāsa* councils to rely on forensic medicine as a substitute for torture.

The case involved two elderly peasants, Isḥāq Ṭaniyūs and Basṭārūs Yūsuf, from Jirjā in Upper Egypt. On January 17, 1857, the deputy governor of their

FIGURE 10: *The Bastinado.* Image courtesy of the Art and Picture Collection, The New York Public Library.

province, ʿAlī Efendi Bahjat, had them conscripted to perform corvée labor. When they were late in knocking down an old wall, ʿAlī Efendi apparently got frustrated with them and decided to teach them both a lesson. So he had them both bastinadoed (see figure 10). He started with Basṭārūs, who was given six lashes on the soles of his feet. When Isḥāq saw his friend being beaten, he suddenly fainted and dropped dead then and there.

Or so ʿAlī Efendi claimed. Isḥāq's relatives, however, had another story. They said that after finishing with Basṭārūs, ʿAlī Efendi turned to Isḥāq and proceeded to beat him. Unaware that Isḥāq was mute, the deputy governor mistook his silence as a sign of defiance. So he went into a rage, lashing Isḥāq so severely that the old man later died of his wounds.

When news of the incident reached the provincial headquarters, a doctor was summoned to conduct a postmortem examination. In his report, the doctor claimed that he found no suspicious signs on the body and issued a burial certificate to that effect. He then had the body sent to the relatives' home for burial. Outraged by the forensic report, which they claimed was a result of intimidation by the deputy governor, Isḥāq's relatives refused to receive the body, blocked the street leading to the dead man's house, and ultimately had the entire town sealed off, barring the government officials from entering. In a dramatic gesture, they left the body lying outside the town on a small hill, guarded by two sentries. The following morning, in their quest for justice, they took the body to the *siyāsa* doctor of the nearby urban center of al-Fashn (in whose *majlis* the case was eventually reviewed).

However, the doctor refused to comply with their request for a second post-mortem examination, and so the relatives traveled all the way to the provincial capital, more than one hundred kilometers to the south, where the resident doctor agreed to examine the corpse. But he did not find any conclusive evidence that death had been caused by beating either. In their subsequent testimonies in front of the *siyāsa* council, the relatives said that by that time, Isḥāq had been dead for four days and his body "had gotten bloated and exploded" (*intafakh wa infajar*), making it impossible for the doctor to determine the exact cause of death.

In his defense, ʿAlī Efendi claimed that these were all false accusations concocted by the agent (*wakīl*) of the plaintiffs, a man named Tūmā Rufāʾīl, who had been a government employee at one point but had been expelled from public service. When Tūmā's request to be pardoned and reinstated in his job had been rejected, ʿAlī Efendi claimed, he concocted this fantastic story.

Tūmā responded that ʿAlī Efendi, the local qadi, and numerous scribes of the *mudīriyya* had been involved in countless illegal acts; that all these officials had been abusing the fellahin; and that most recently, they had conscripted some people who should have been exempted from corvée. (He was undoubtedly right in this last accusation. A decree issued in 1851 forbade provincial governors from enlisting the following people for corvée: pregnant women, mothers with children under three years old, children under eight years old, and men over seventy years old.)[150] The plaintiffs demanded that ʿAlī Efendi be suspended from his duties while the case was pending, arguing that he should not be supervising the very people who were accusing him. They also claimed that he was "biased in his investigations" (*ḥāṣil lahu al-mayl fiʾl-taḥqīq*) and added that he was a member of the Asyūṭ *siyāsa* council, insinuating at best that there was a conflict of interest and at worst that members of the different councils had formed a clique and were in the habit of covering up for each other. ʿAlī Efendi was temporarily suspended from his duties.

When they were asked to prove their claim that Isḥāq had died from the beating, the plaintiffs failed to produce an eyewitness who was willing to testify against the deputy governor. In their own testimony, they made clear that there had been many witnesses but claimed that these individuals had "concealed their testimony" (*takattamū al-shahāda*) "due to intimidation by the provincial officials" (*min al-takhwīf al-ḥāṣil lahum min khuddām al-mudīriyya*).[151] The only testimony they could procure was one that was written, signed, and sealed by the former qadi, who, however, retracted it when he was cross-examined. All other witnesses denied having seen Isḥāq being beaten by the deputy governor.

When the local *siyāsa* council, Majlis al-Fashn, finally reviewed the case, it refused to believe that Isḥāq had not been beaten. It argued that there had been a single offense, namely failure to knocking down an old wall; that the offense had been committed by both men; and that the punishment, the bastinadoing, was meted out for nonperformance. Accordingly, the council found it difficult to believe that only one of the culprits had been beaten. In its final verdict, the council concluded "that the deceased had indeed been beaten." However, the verdict continued,

> Since it is obvious that the beating was six blows only, which, in addition was administered to the soles of the feet, such a trivial amount [*mablagh juz'ī*] could not have constituted the cause of death. . . . And since the doctor stated in his report that . . . the cause of death was a stroke [*dā' al-sakta*] and that this disease is caused by advanced age, hot weather, extreme cold, fear, trepidation, drinking alcohol, or the like, . . . and since some of these signs were satisfied in the case at hand, namely that it was a hot day, that the deceased was an old man, and that he was disturbed, we see that there is a probability [*fa-yura annahu la mānī'*] that death was caused by this disease, which was, in turn, caused by these factors. . . . It was declared, therefore, that the case was dismissed.

'Alī Efendi Bahjat was reprimanded for not taking the old age of the deceased into consideration, and as a punishment, his salary was reduced while he was suspended. Majlis al-Aḥkām upheld the verdict of Majlis al-Fashn.[152]

What is remarkable about this case is the insistence of Isḥāq's relatives on securing a medical report that they hoped would prove foul play and show that 'Alī Efendi had administered excessive lashes that were the direct cause of the old man's death. How can we explain the fact that the victim's family insisted on seeking a medical report not once, not twice, but three times, all the while barring officials from entering the village to bury the dead body and risking the gruesome consequences of failing to bury their relative? What lay behind the dramatic gesture of refusing to bury the body of their loved one and leaving it at the village entrance until it got bloated and exploded? Was it revenge against 'Alī Efendi? The fellahin's deep-seated hatred of *khuddām al-mīrī* (government officials), something that was stated explicitly in a remarkably similar case in which a Copt died as a result of a beating by the local governor?[153] Or was it a profound belief in justice? Whatever the reason, what this case, like the case of Sulṭān, makes evident is the deep confidence that lower-class Egyptians had in forensic medicine. It also shows how much the *siyāsa* councils, unlike the shari'a courts, accepted the written reports of medical experts and how ready they were to use them to provide the missing probative evidence caused by the absence of eyewitnesses.

COMPARING MEDICAL EXPERTISE IN SHARI'A COURTS AND *SIYĀSA* COUNCILS

Having looked at some cases of violent crime, it is now possible to draw some preliminary conclusions about how *siyāsa* councils and shari'a courts accepted medical expertise differently and how this difference explains why it was easy for *siyāsa* authorities to see forensic medicine as an alternative to confession as probative evidence. Whereas *siyāsa* councils relied heavily on medical expertise, so much so that this expertise was known officially as *siyāsa* medicine, qadis admitted medical expertise in a markedly different manner. At first sight, this difference appears to be due to *fiqh*'s heavy reliance on confession and eyewitness testimony to establish legal proof, especially in *ḥudūd* cases.[154] But as indicated above, *fiqh* readily accepted expert opinions, most notably medical expertise. And as Shaham has shown, there was enough flexibility within *fiqh* to categorize medical expertise as *shahāda* (testimony) and thus allow it to carry the same weight as eyewitness testimony in establishing probative evidence. It is also incorrect to attribute the difference between these two branches of the legal system to the exactness of anatomoclinical medicine that the *siyāsa* doctors practiced as compared to the "imprecise" medical expertise of the physiognomist or the bonesetter that the qadi relied on. For as Foucault has shown, every medical system is bound by its discourse, which governs its own truth claims, and *fiqh* has developed elaborate rules to safeguard the reliability and validity of medical expertise.[155] Rather, it is the features of *siyāsa* medicine alluded to above that explain the relative ease with which this medicine came to play a central role in the deliberations of *siyāsa* councils.

To recapitulate, these features are that *siyāsa* medicine did not merely describe the shape of wounds but focused on establishing causal links between assault and organ failure or death; that *siyāsa* medical expertise was presented in a textual manner; that *siyāsa* doctors, as their title indicates, were part of the regular personnel of the *siyāsa* system; and that *siyāsa* medicine was not deployed to uphold social hierarchies. To elaborate further on the significance of these features, it is important to point out that, as shown in chapter 2, even though *fiqh* and *siyāsa* worked hand in glove, these two branches of the nineteenth-century Egyptian legal system were based on radically different epistemologies and functioned in fundamentally different ways. Whereas shari'a courts functioned in an adversarial manner whereby it was up to the litigants to initiate legal action, prove their cases, and provide their own legal defense and the judge acted as an unbiased arbiter, effectively making sure that *fiqh* rules were strictly followed (while the *'udūl* witnesses looked over his shoulder), the *siyāsa* councils functioned in an inquisitorial manner. In the *siyāsa* system, the police acted as both prosecutors and investigators. As such, the police initiated legal action and prosecuted cases, and the administrators manning the *siyāsa* councils did all the adjudicating. The police interrogated witnesses, gathered evidence, summoned technical experts (including medical experts), and established the facts. Then the administrators manning the *siyāsa* council deliberated on the cases based on the carefully prepared dossiers.

Crucially, this discussion took place in camera, behind closed doors, and on the basis solely of the written dossier. As shown in chapter 2, in contrast to the detailed procedures the qadi had to follow to make sure that the oral testimonies were delivered smoothly and immediately, equally detailed procedures were laid down by the *siyāsa* councils to make sure that the dossiers were written and read efficiently. Given that *siyāsa* councils discussed pending cases on the basis of dossiers, the fact that forensic doctors presented their expertise in written reports meant that this medical evidence could be more easily incorporated into the process of adjudication than it could in shari'a court trials, where the qadi was more concerned with the probity of the expert witness than with the content of the expertise.

Moreover, the fact that the medical report linked symptoms to organ malfunction or death in a causal manner, as shown in Isḥāq's case, meant that the structure of the medical report mirrored the argumentative style of the *siyāsa* council, which added to the ease with which the *siyāsa* system accepted forensic medicine as a means of establishing legal proof.[156]

It should be clear at this point how forensic medicine replaced eyewitnesses and confessions as the prime means of establishing probative evidence in mid-nineteenth-century Egypt. It was not that the dissection-based, anatomoclinical medicine that the Qaṣr al-'Ainī doctors had acquired enabled them to provide conclusive, incontrovertible evidence, something that shari'a courts were unable to provide given their reliance on the strict *fiqh* rules of evidence. For as we saw earlier in this chapter, these doctors occasionally admitted that they could not provide conclusive medical evidence. Moreover, *fiqh* had no compunction about admitting medical expertise as a means of establishing probative evidence. Rather, it seems that the new medical expertise of the Qaṣr al-'Ainī graduates proved to be a much more reliable method of establishing causal links between physical assault and death or organ failure than the medical expertise used in shari'a courts, which was aimed mainly at maintaining social hierarchies. On finishing their medical inspections, these doctors wrote lengthy reports about their findings and presented their reports to the police, who included them in the final dossiers that were presented to the *siyāsa* councils. Above all, the textual nature of the *siyāsa* doctors' reports and the fact that these doctors were not independent physicians but employees of the *siyāsa* system meant that their reports became an essential component in case dossiers, on which the *siyāsa* councils based their deliberations and issued their verdicts.

The ease with which the *siyāsa* councils came to depend on medical expertise contributed to defendants' confessions losing the centrality they once occupied in establishing probative evidence. With medical expertise firmly in place within the *siyāsa* system, there was no longer a need to resort to beating defendants to induce confessions.

CONCLUSION

Soon after British troops landed in Egypt in 1882, thus launching a military occupation that would last for seventy-two years, the Ministry of the Interior issued a decree expressing frustration that earlier decrees banning the use of the whip had been ignored. Dated January 16, 1883, this decree went on to say that "resorting to such bestial matter is opposed to the Khedival wishes, and also contrary to human affairs and violates the rights of humankind."[157] The argument that Britain had to interfere in Egypt to put an end to Ottoman despotism and restore law and order is one that the British government was keen on selling to a hostile domestic British public that was apprehensive about the financial burden of occupation and to European rivals that were skeptical about Britain's true motives. In his influential book *Modern Egypt,* Lord Cromer, the British consul-general and effective ruler of Egypt during the first quarter-century of the British occupation, reiterated what he had been arguing in his annual reports by boasting that it was the British who had "dealt a decisive blow to the system of government by flogging" and that it was thanks to them that "the three Cs: corvée, corruption, and courbash (that is, the whip),"[158] had been abolished.

However, as this chapter shows, there was deep anxiety within Egypt about the use of the whip long before the arrival of the British in 1882. The 1861 Decree Replacing Beating with Imprisonment seriously restricted the practice of whipping, but concern about the ease with which officials in the budding state resorted to inflicting pain as a means of extracting confessions or as a way of punishing wrongdoers can be traced back to the mid-1830s, if not earlier. And while it is true that "there was no public debate in nineteenth century Egypt about penal policies, [or] express statements laying down e.g. a philosophy of legal punishment or the principles of penal reform,"[159] this chapter has attempted to discern what might have prompted the authorities to ban the use of the whip.

The laws, decrees, and official correspondence that this chapter covered do not show that the elimination of the whip was prompted by concern about humanity or revulsion to bestiality.[160] Rather, the abolition of official violence in nineteenth-century Egypt is something that happened gradually over a period that spanned nearly half a century, from the mid-1830s to the early 1880s. It was a significant trend that was instigated not by intellectuals and thinkers inspired by Enlightenment ideas but by administrators, physicians, and bureaucrats who were intent on making Egypt more efficient and manageable. This trend was also supported by the khedives, who saw that the wanton use of the whip by members of their household undermined their ability to rule and threatened the independent realm they were struggling to establish in Egypt. But snatching the law, which members of the elite had proverbially taken into their hands, was no easy task. For as described in this chapter, to seize the whip from the hands of members of the ruling household and their retainers, the state needed to empower the newly founded bureaucracy and mandate that it function according to set rules and regulations. These rules and regulations, as chapter 2 showed, are what the *siyāsa* councils had come to symbolize by the mid-1850s.[161] The state also needed to transform prisons from places of banishment and death to places of temporary loss of liberty, with the concomitant change in the meaning of punishment that this entailed. Finally, the state needed to replace confession with forensic medicine as the prime means of establishing probative evidence. In short, official violence was as significant a sign of the deep tensions plaguing Egypt's politico-legal system throughout the first three quarters of the nineteenth century as abolishing it was indicative of how fundamentally the system had changed over the same period.

The clearest sign of the deep transformations that the fields of law and politics witnessed during the third quarter of the nineteenth century is the new name by which forensic medicine came to be known. In modern-day Arabic parlance, in Egypt and throughout the Arab world, legal medicine is known as *ṭibb sharʿī,* which erroneously gives the impression that it is based on shariʿa. However, as indicated in this chapter, *fiqh* never referred to the medicine that was presented to shariʿa courts as *ṭibb sharʿī.* Thus, the adjective *sharʿī* cannot be a reference to its traditional meaning of *fiqh* and shariʿa. Moreover, up until the early 1880s, legal medicine was known as *ṭibb siyāsī,* in reference to the *siyāsa* system, as this medicine played a decisive role in adjudicating criminal cases. A clue as to the timing and reasons behind the change in nomenclature can be gleaned by comparing two editions of the same book. The author is a certain Ibrāhīm Efendi Ḥasan, "a teacher at the Medical School" (*khūga bi-Madrasat al-Ṭibb*). The first edition was published in 1876–77 under the title *Rawḍat al-Āsī fī'l-Ṭibb al-Siyāsī* (The physician's garden of *siyāsa* medicine).[162] The second edition was published thirteen years later, by which time the author had been promoted to the position of public health inspector of Egypt (*mufattish al-ṣiḥḥa al-ʿumūmiyya bi'l-diyār al-Miṣriyya*) and had been granted the title pasha. The title of the second edition had been changed to *Al-Dustūr al-Marʿī fī'l-Ṭibb al-Sharʿī* (The strict guide to *sharʿī* medicine).[163] In the preface to the second edition, Ḥasan explains the reason behind the change from *al-ṭibb al-siyāsī* to *al-ṭibb al-sharʿī:*

> I named [the first edition] of my book *Al-Ṭibb al-Siyāsī,* for back then the courts of law in the country were exclusively those of the noble shariʿa [*maḥākim al-sharʿ al-sharīf*], which seldom had recourse to medicine when they adjudicated cases. By contrast, the bodies that did have the jurisdiction to adjudicate criminal disputes were nothing but civilian [*madaniyya*], *siyāsa* councils that functioned according to principles that were closer to being administrative [*idāriyya*] than legal [*shariʿyya qānūniyya*]. Hence, I called [the first edition] *Al-Ṭibb al-Siyāsī,* as this medicine was required in these councils. However, now courts rely on *qānūn* [*ṣārat al-maḥākim qānūniyya*], and so I called [the second edition] legal medicine [*ṭibb sharʿī*]. The meaning is the same, but the name has changed.[164]

If this quote appears confusing, it is because the author is trying to describe a situation in which the meaning of nearly every single noun and adjective he is referring to had recently witnessed radical change. In the thirteen years that separated the two editions of this book, as a result of profound changes in the fields of law, medicine, and politics that Egypt had witnessed over the previous three-quarters of a century, the meanings of such terms as *maḥkama, majlis, qānūn, sharʿiyya,* and *siyāsa* had been radically altered. Up until the 1870s, shariʿa courts had been referred to exclusively as *maḥkama,* but its referent was considerably expanded in 1875 to include the newly established Mixed Courts and in 1883 to include the National Courts. Similarly, *majlis* ceased to refer to a conflict-resolution body that adjudicated criminal disputes and instead came to mean an administrative council. *Qānūn* lost its Ottoman meaning of a piece of legislation that a sovereign enacts based on the *fiqh* principle of *taʿzīr* and instead acquired the new meaning of a positive legal code. *Sharʿiyya,* in addition to being an adjective of shariʿa, meaning shariʿa derived or shariʿa related, acquired the added meaning "legitimate" or "legal." And *siyāsa,* instead of referring to *taʿzīr*-based legislation and adjudication, now referred to the newly emerging field of politics.

This change in nomenclature explains the prescience of the Cairo Police Commissioner when, back in 1858, he wrote to Saʿīd Pasha in reference to the death by beating of the black slave, Sulṭān, at the hands of an employee working in one of the khedival estates, an act that he described as "violating the sanctity of the state." For in the twenty or so following years, not only did old words acquire new meanings but a state was founded and a political realm forged. While the khedive continued to play a central role in this newly forged political realm, *siyāsa* (the field of politics) was also being shaped by struggles over the bodies of people like Sulṭān and his fellow slaves. In addition to black slaves, this chapter has showed how prison wardens, physicians, health inspectors, coroners, government administrators, and magistrates, as well as non-elite Egyptians, like Isḥāq Ṭaniyūs and Basṭārūs Yūsuf, shaped this new political realm.

Conclusion

TWO YEARS AFTER CARRYING OUT the Massacre of the Mamluks (March 1811), which wiped out Egypt's ruling elite, Mehmed Ali appointed his twenty-four-year-old son, Ibrāhīm Pasha, as governor of Upper Egypt and ordered him to chase the remaining Mamluks all the way to Aswan in the south and extend his own authority in the "cleansed" lands. Jabartī, with his characteristic acuity, describes what this authority entailed:

> Ibrāhīm surveyed and registered all but a small amount of land in this region, recording in the *dīwān* all the government lands and fiefs assigned to tax farmers, amirs, irregular troops, and the lords of the old (Mamluk) Houses endowment incomes, ... debts, supervision for family and charitable *waqf*s, alms, offerings, etc. Also included were revenues that the original benefactors had allocated to administrators for charity and largess to the poor ... and hospices for the feeding of visitors and wayfarers, wonderers and travelers.... And when the [Pasha's] official was asked what these persons should do if guests descended on them in the usual numbers, he said, "They should buy their food from their own purses." Or, "[They] should lock their doors and live alone with their families, making economies in their way of life. They will grow accustomed to it. What they are doing now is wasteful and extravagant.... The *dīwān* is most deserving of this land, since it is responsible for expenses, salaries, and equipment required for military campaigns against armies."[1]

After describing the logic of the new system that Mehmed Ali and his son were putting in place and explaining how they envisaged the *dīwān* would replace the open houses of the old lords, Jabartī gives a vivid description of Ibrāhīm Pasha's tactics:

> [Ibrāhīm] did to them [i.e., the inhabitants of Upper Egypt] what the Tatars had done when they roamed the land: he degraded the grandees of Upper Egypt, afflicting them with the most vile of his evil deeds, stealing their livestock and money, sheep and cattle.... When they were unable to meet the demands ..., he put them to various kinds of torture: flogging, hanging, branding, and burning. An informant told me ... that Ibrāhīm Pasha had a man stretched out on a long plank; this was placed on a blazing fire, and turned by men on either end so that the man was roasted like meat on a spit.[2]

Throughout his chronicle, Jabartī makes little effort to hide his scorn of Mehmed Ali and the *dīwān* he was systematically erecting in Egypt. Above all, his chronicle is informed by a pathos for a vanishing world, a world in which the violence that was occasionally visited by the Mamluks on the peasants was always circumscribed by values of chivalry, honor, and charity. But this world had disappeared, and he was horrified to witness the unbridled violence being unleashed on the poor in the name of this new system with its insatiable military needs and none of the constraints of the old system.

Jabartī's narrative stops at events that took place a few years prior to his death in 1825. Had he lived long enough to witness the Pasha's *dīwān* come to fruition, he might have noticed that unbridled physical violence gradually disappeared from public life and that the Pasha's government eventually mushroomed into a full-blown bureaucracy with departments and offices, rules and regulations, new vocabularies and novel taxonomies.

In Quest of Justice tells the story of this new polity, whose beginnings Jabartī aptly sketched, showing how it evolved over the fifty-odd years between the early 1830s and the early 1880s. The advent of this polity, which we now call the modern Egyptian state, is always taken for granted, and there are only a few accounts of what it actually entailed.[3] In an earlier study, I sketched the military origins of that modern state and described the internal logic that informed its most pivotal institution, the army.[4] By contrast, *In Quest of Justice,* while acknowledging that the army did indeed occupy pride of place, goes beyond the military to provide an account of the other ways the modern Egyptian state touched the lives of Egyptians from different walks of life. Rather than follow the acts and deeds of powerful statesmen or the thoughts and words of great intellectuals, I chose to offer a thick description of novel practices that altered the daily lives of Egyptians in profound ways.

WHICH IMPERIAL CONTEXT?

The half-century during which this remarkable process of the formation of the modern Egyptian state took place—the early 1830s to the early 1880s—has traditionally been depicted as a period that witnessed a surge of capitalist imperialism and European expansion, and the 1882 British occupation of Egypt that marks the end of this period is seen as a prime example of nineteenth-century imperialism. Key moments in this story are the 1838 Anglo-Ottoman Commercial Convention, which outlawed monopolies and established a low external tariff of 8 percent; the 1841 settlement between Mehmed Ali and the Sublime Porte, which reduced the size of the Egyptian army to 18,000 troops, depriving the Pasha of a protected market for the products of his factories; the phenomenal export of European capital to Egypt and to other parts of the Middle East at very high interest rates; the series of foreign loans that Egypt's rulers took out at these high interest rates; the huge expansion of Egyptian cotton cultivation, especially during the American Civil War (1861–65), which deepened the economic ties between Egypt and Europe, particularly Britain; and the acute financial crisis of the mid-1870s, which resulted in a declaration of bankruptcy (1876), the deposition of Ismā'īl (1879), and the British occupation (1882).[5]

While cognizant of these profound transformations that saw Egypt being drawn ineluctably into the orbit of European imperialism, *In Quest of Justice* stresses another imperial context within which to view the unprecedented changes that Egyptian society witnessed during this half-century. It contends that viewing Egypt as struggling to carve an independent course within the Ottoman Empire is the best way to understand its history in the nineteenth century. As I have argued elsewhere, the significant reforms that Mehmed Ali instituted during his long reign were intricately tied to his army, which was the main instrument he utilized in attempting to carve out an independent rule for himself in Egypt.[6] The factories he founded, the publishing house he established in Būlāq, and the schools and polytechnics he opened (chief among which was the Qaṣr al-'Ainī Medical School) all had serving the army as their raison d'être. With that well-operated military machine, Cairo was transformed from a mere provincial capital into a powerful center within the Ottoman Empire, a center that challenged the empire's imperial capital and posed a serious threat to the very existence of the Ottoman Empire.

But the importance of the Ottoman context when it comes to making sense of the sociocultural developments that Egypt witnessed in the middle decades of the nineteenth century is not derived only from the military connection. After the 1841 settlement between Mehmed Ali and Sultan Abdülmecid, Egypt was effectively transformed into a hereditary province, and all the Pasha's successors were very keen to preserve and enhance Egypt's semiautonomous status within the Ottoman Empire. Crucially, they saw that waging further wars against Istanbul would not preserve their unique position as khedives. Instead, Mehmed Ali's successors—Ibrāhīm, 'Abbās, Sa'īd, and Ismā'īl—all made strategic use of the instruments of government to carve out an independent realm for themselves in Egypt. This khedival state did originate as an appendage to the military, but it soon developed a life of its own, so to speak, in the forty-odd years following the 1841 settlement. Thus, although the Qaṣr al-'Ainī Medical School and Hospital might have started as a military institution, it eventually became a center of a large civilian medical establishment. Similarly, Būlāq Press started out by printing military manuals and medical textbooks for army physicians, but it was rapidly transformed into an active press that published gems of Arabic literature and Islamic philosophy as well as numerous translations of European scientific works in medicine, physics, chemistry, mathematics, and history. Likewise, the census had its origins in the military's need to account for the available manpower, but it was quickly transformed into a demographic database that was of vital importance to the nationwide public hygiene establishment, which itself was run by former army physicians.

Having at their disposal this machinery of a modern state, the khedives were able to tighten their grip on Egypt's population in a way undreamt of by the Mamluk warlords and never achieved by the Sublime Porte. It was by having at its fingertips such devices as the census and the *tadhkara,* by implementing such policies as conscription and postmortem examinations, and by building such institutions as the police and the councils that *al-dīwān* mushroomed into *al-ḥukūma* and that the newly forged *ḥukūma* could think of the population of Egypt as being under its sovereignty. In bureaucratic parlance, a person would be considered *dākhil al-ḥukūma* (literally "inside the government") precisely because he or she had come under the jurisdiction of the khedival government by being counted in the census, vaccinated against smallpox, being issued a stamped *tadhkara,* or so on. By contrast, being *khārij al-ḥukūma* (outside the jurisdiction of the khedival government) meant that a person was not subject to the Egyptian government, and this is was what prompted the authorities to exile "foreigners," especially *awlād al-Turk* (Turks), to *barr al-Turk* (the Ottoman Empire).

Most importantly, though, this book privileges the Ottoman context because it is only within this context that legal reform, one of the most important developments that this book charts, can be understood. The profound changes that the Egyptian legal system underwent in the nineteenth century were not the result of Mehmed Ali "achieving his goal of following in Europe's footsteps in the legal field," as has been claimed by Egypt's preeminent legal historian.[7] Nor were these reforms informed by a desire to replace the Islamic legal tradition with French civil law, as has been more recently claimed.[8] Rather, the many legal codes that were drafted and passed in Egypt during this period were often translations from Ottoman Turkish, and the numerous legal bodies, the *majālis,* that dotted the Egyptian landscape were modeled not after European courts but after Ottoman ones. Even Majlis al-Aḥkām, which was founded in 1849 and occupied the highest position in the elaborate legal system, was named after the Ottoman Meclis-i Vala-yı Ahkam-ı Adliye, which had been founded in Istanbul in 1838. Most significantly, the principle of *siyāsa,* which lay at the core of the Egyptian legal system, was derived from the shariʿa principle of *taʿzīr,* and the entire Egyptian legal system was predicated on supplementing *fiqh* as practiced in the shariʿa court with *qānūn* as applied in the *siyāsa* council. This coupling of *fiqh* and *siyāsa* was no *bidʿa,* no innovation, but rather had been practiced by the Ottomans for centuries not only in the central lands of the empire but also in Egypt itself.[9] And there is no clearer testimony to the fact that it was the *siyāsa* legal tradition rather than French civil law that served as the basis of Egyptian law throughout much of the nineteenth century than the fact that forensic medicine, which played a key role in adjudicating penal cases, came to be known as *ṭibb siyāsī,* or *siyāsa* medicine.

SCIENCE AND RELIGION

It would not be correct to say that Egyptians experienced alienation or culture shock in regard to the many innovations that occurred within their society in the nineteenth century. The single most remarkable feature that emerges from the large volume of bureaucratic correspondence that forms the backbone of this book is the deep sense of self-confidence that these bureaucrats felt. These policemen, pharmacists, physicians, administrators, and *siyāsa* council members seemed not to have been bothered by the provenance of the many innovative practices they were implementing. The sciences of cartography, statistics, chemical forensics, postmortem examinations, and anatomoclinical medicine might have been borrowed from Europe, but this act of borrowing was never informed by a sense of anxiety that had its roots in identitarian crises. Indeed, adopting these innovations was never couched in a language of "catching up with the West" or "bridging the gap with Europe" or seen as signaling a sense of loss or abandonment. The question of identity was moot.

In an earlier study, I argued that peasant resistance to conscription into Mehmed Ali's army was uniform, persistent, and widespread.[10] By contrast, the reaction of non-elite Egyptians in urban centers as well as in the countryside to the profound changes that their society witnessed throughout the nineteenth century was nuanced and calculated. Like the administrators and bureaucrats who ran the machinery of *al-ḥukūma,* non-elite Egyptians do not seem to have viewed the practices associated with this new state through an identitarian lens. These practices were as profound as they were unprecedented, and they entailed an unmatched encroachment on personal lives. By the middle of the nineteenth century, all Egyptians were required to register their babies at birth, vaccinate their children against smallpox, carry stamped certificates when they moved from village to village, and approach police stations and *siyāsa* councils to redress their grievances; their cities and neighborhoods were redesigned along hygienic lines; their neighborhood food markets were inspected by a newly formed sanitary police force; and their dead were medically inspected before they could be buried. Yet nowhere in the historical record do we see non-elite Egyptians objecting that these unparalleled innovations violated their beliefs or contradicted their religious convictions.

Remarkably, the supposedly enlightened European administrators working in the khedival government were the ones who viewed these innovations as offensive to local religious sensibilities. It was Clot Bey, the founding director of the Qaṣr al-'Ainī Medical School, who assumed that Muslims would object to dissection because they believed corpses felt pain; and it was Francesco Grassi, the medical director of the Consular Board of Health in Alexandria, who believed that Muslims resisted quarantines due to their "want of faith in medicine and to their fanaticism."

Moreover, nowhere in the copious bureaucratic correspondence of the khedival government or in the numerous translated medical books published by Būlāq Press is it possible to detect a sense of a contradiction between science and religion or modernity and the Islamic textual tradition. Indeed, none of the bureaucrats running the newly founded state machinery, the administrators manning the *siyāsa* councils, or the physicians managing the nationwide public hygiene establishment seem to have thought that the modern practices they were implementing were culturally or religiously offensive. Opening *siyāsa* councils never meant closing down the shari'a courts, and promulgating *qānūn*s never entailed abandoning *fiqh*. The new science of urban planning, based as it was on cartography and vital statistics, did not require confiscating *awqāf* or declaring the entire system of Islamic charitable endowments obsolete. Shari'a courts might not have accepted forensic medicine as a means of establishing probative proof, but the *siyāsa* councils, the other branch of the shari'a-based legal system, did. Egyptian forensic doctors believed that opening up cadavers was the only way they could distinguish homicides from natural deaths, and they saw no contradiction between the two benefits of accomplishing this: enabling the state to collect accurate vital statistics and upholding the shari'a principle of *qiṣāṣ*. Furthermore, the Azhari students who went on to study medicine at Qaṣr al-'Ainī and then in Paris never viewed their scientific knowledge and their religious beliefs as belonging to two distinct modes of thought. The only exception to this seamless relationship between science and religion was the institution of the *muḥtasib,* a position that was abandoned after it was effectively taken over by the sanitary police and forensic chemists. But as explained in chapter 4, this was not so much the result of some deliberate attack on the role of religion in the marketplace as it was a reflection of deep anxieties about the physical violence the *muḥtasib* employed to carry out his job. And as stated in chapter five, the khedives preferred to practice violence—the violence of the modern state—in a much subtler way.

Throughout the voluminous records of the government bureaucracy on which this book is based, a deep sense not only of self-confidence but also of pride comes across most vividly. Without a doubt, the paths of the countless bureaucrats, policemen, and physicians who have animated this book were not problem free. But one always senses from reading the accounts of these state officials a conviction that the government machinery they had put in place was capable of coming up with practical, enforceable solutions to any problems they encountered. Thus, when the Cairo Public Health Commissioner wrote in 1874 that he was frustrated that despite all the efforts of his department, the mortality figures of the city had not shown the improvement that he had desired, he was confident that the twin sciences of cartography and statistics would correctly identify the root of the problem (overcrowding) and suggest a solution to it (building new neighborhoods). Similarly, when the administrators running Majlis al-Aḥkām were alarmed by the noticeable rise in the number of murder cases involving the *nabbūt,* they did not throw up their hands in despair because they were bound by the Humāyūnī Law, which required the adjudication of homicide cases according to *fiqh*. Rather, they went back to Ḥanafī doctrine, ruled that the *nabbūt* should be declared a murder weapon, and gave instructions to the *siyāsa* councils to handle deaths by the *nabbūt* as homicide cases rather than manslaughter cases. Likewise, when the Cairo Department of Health Inspection, keen on tightly controlling over food markets, was concerned that foreign merchants might be exempt from unannounced shop inspections, it insisted, against the recommendation of the police, on conducting these inspections, arguing that "no exceptions are ever to be made in matters of public hygiene."

SIYĀSA AND SHARIʿA

The central role that *al-ṭibb al-siyāsī* (forensic medicine) came to play in the evolving criminal legal system is also an indication of this same self-confidence. Postmortems and autopsies were performed as a matter of course in homicide cases, and such practices were not frowned on as examples of Western encroachment on shariʿa or of modern scientific methods replacing religiously informed techniques of establishing legal proof. Rather, as its name indicates, *al-ṭibb al-siyāsī* was understood to belong to *siyāsa,* an old, authentic component of shariʿa. And if there was a novel aspect of how forensic medicine came to play such a pivotal role in the criminal justice system, it was not the nature of Bichatian medicine or Lavoisian chemistry but the nature of the legal system. As this book illustrates, what stands out as most remarkable about the khedival legal system is the high degree of bureaucratization and standardization that it involved. For while *siyāsa* has always been a component of shariʿa, never before had its rules and procedures been so systematized and its records so well kept as in khedival Egypt.

Rather than relying on the often inaccurate descriptions of contemporary chroniclers or the hostile words of the *fuqahāʾ,* we can read the surviving archive of the khedival *siyāsa* system to study this central component of shariʿa. This archive gives us a more accurate understanding of the logic and the inner workings of the Islamic criminal legal system than ahistorical readings of shari'a that depict it as based on a happy marriage of law and morality. *Siyāsa,* this book argues, has always been an integral part of shari'a, and the central role it played in Islamic legal history shows that raison d'état and concern for law and order were as central to shari'a as morality and communal values. Therefore, if we take *siyāsa* seriously as we attempt to understand the historical evolution of shari'a, the possibility emerges that law and morality might have already been uncoupled prior to the onslaught of modernity. Only a *fiqhī* legality would insist on excising *siyāsa* from shari'a and on seeing law and morality as intricately bound together. By contrast, this book argues that a more accurate understanding of shari'a legality must grant *siyāsa* a central role in it, both as a legal concept and a historical practice.

GOVERNMENT BUREAUCRACY AND CONCEPTUAL CHANGES

This book also notes how remarkable it is that the newly founded state bureaucracy was able to coin a language of its own. The Arabic that this bureaucracy used has been described by subsequent observers as odd, ineloquent, and grammatically incorrect.[11] Be that as it may, what is noteworthy is the gradual refinement of the language of government correspondence, itself the result of the increased efficiency with which the bureaucracy conducted its business. In this process, a new language was born, not only by introducing neologisms (e.g., the term *mīzāniyyat al-mawtā* was used for mortality rates, and *ijtimā' al-nufūs* referred to overcrowding), but, more importantly, by giving modern meanings to old, traditional terms.

Thus, as discussed in chapter 5, *majlis* ceased to refer to a conflict-resolution body that adjudicated criminal disputes and came to be the term used for an administrative council. Similarly, *siyāsa* referred to the newly emerging field of politics rather than to *ta'zīr*-based legislation and adjudication. Other *fiqh*-related words that acquired new meanings are *ḍamān,* which used to mean compensation for damage done but came to mean a voucher for a missing person, and *ḥukūmat 'adl,* which in *fiqh* referred to compensation paid for bodily injury based on a ruling by a qadi but, by the end of the nineteenth century, came to mean government based on justice.

Most telling is the new meaning that the phrase *al-kashf 'alā al-amwāt* acquired. As we noted in chapter 1, in the seventeenth century this phrase referred to the process of registering the legacies of the deceased, which was carried out by officials of a government body called Bayt al-Māl. By the nineteenth century, the phrase came to mean a postmortem examination performed by forensic doctors. As this example shows, the conceptual changes that were part of the new bureaucratic idioms were not the result of a concerted effort of intellectuals to introduce European modernity to Egypt. Rather, they were the result of scribes, bureaucrats, physicians, and *siyāsa majlis* administrators reflecting on practices that had already been introduced in Egypt. Accordingly, *qānūn* lost its Ottoman meaning as a piece of legislation that the sultans enacted based on the *fiqh* principle of *ta'zīr* and acquired the new meaning of a positive legal code. However, this was not because Egyptian legal specialists were eagerly translating the French civil code into Arabic but because there was a phenomenal expansion in the legislating activity that the khedives engaged in as part of their efforts to tighten their sovereignty over Egypt. Similarly, the old meaning of *al-kashf 'alā al-amwāt* did not become obsolete because Qaṣr al-'Ainī physicians were translating French anatomical tomes into Arabic. They did translate these tomes, but more importantly, as this book explains, sovereignty came to be expressed by, among other things, the ability of the state to account for its population: the state kept track of who was born and where, and who died and how. This was different from an older notion of sovereignty whereby the state made sure that the precepts of the faith, as far as they related to death rituals, were implemented. In the seventeenth century, the Ottoman governor of Egypt was interested in divvying up the legacies of the deceased according to *fiqh* principles of inheritance. By the mid-nineteenth century, the modern Egyptian state became interested in the dead in order for it to be able to identify homicide cases and to rule out epidemics.

When Dead Bodies Dare to Speak. The fact that this modern Egyptian state was efficient and self-confident does not necessarily mean that it was popular or legitimate in the eyes of its subjects. As this book illustrates, Egyptians from all walks of life saw this modern state encroaching on their lives in an unprecedented manner, and they found their bodies being controlled in ever tighter and more effective ways. And it was not only through new discourses on health, public hygiene, law, and justice that their bodies were so thoroughly manipulated. State-ordained instructions were equally responsible for altering the daily lives and calibrating the bodies of Egyptians. Non-elite Egyptians were not always the docile, passive recipients of state fiat, but they did not always react to the new discourses and practices of the modern state with acts of armed resistance or outright rebellion. Rather, and as this book demonstrates, Egyptians, in their quest for justice, deployed numerous techniques and followed different strategies to accommodate the state and its multifarious agencies. In the process, state policy was refined and shaped, only to be altered again in response to further acts of accommodation, subterfuge, and resistance. It is in this nexus between power and resistance that the Egyptian state attained its modern form.

This book charts many instances of this exchange between power and resistance. More than in any other area, however, it is with respect to the dead that this relationship between the two poles of political subjectivity can best be detected, and it is in the field of necropolitics that the wide scope of non-elite engagement with the modern Egyptian state can best be charted. This engagement ranged from docile passivity to silent subversion to active appropriation of state discourse and practice. In chapter 3, we were introduced to Faḍl Wāsi', a helpless young woman from Upper Egypt who came to Cairo looking for the man who had gotten her pregnant. We followed her as she gave birth to a stillborn baby and then buried the body in a makeshift grave, claiming she knew nothing of the regulations to register newborn babies and report recent deaths. In chapter 1, we read about how two blind shaykhs who ran a *kuttāb* in Cairo's southern cemetery buried the body of one of their students without informing the authorities, their argument being that "any delay in a matter like this [i.e., burial] would be improper." But chapter 1 also told the story of how the residents of Alexandria approached the leading clergy of the city to present a petition complaining about the quarantine measures imposed to contain the plague epidemic that ravaged the city in 1834. Afraid of seeing their own houses quarantined or their own families divided because the dying were segregated in lazarettos, they avoided informing the authorities about plague-afflicted family members and instead dumped the bodies of their loved ones in the streets of the city. Finally, also in chapter 1, and in contrast to these examples of passivity and subversion, we saw the residents of Port Said actively engaging with the health authorities, appropriating their discourse, and presenting one of the most eloquent petitions written with beautiful Arabic orthography complaining about the resident European doctor, who, they argued, had not been conducting his medical rounds and had been neglecting his duty to perform postmortem examinations in person.

This tactic—whereby non-elite Egyptians actively appropriated the techniques of the modern state to defend their own interests—is most clearly expressed in the numerous cases in which ordinary citizens, not state agents, insisted on autopsies to determine cause of death. But whereas the state insisted on autopsies as a way of controlling both epidemics and serious crime, non-elite Egyptians did so in quest of justice. As we saw in chapter 5 in the case of Zahra bint Sayyid Aḥmad, Zahra's own son insisted on an autopsy to prove his suspicion that she had been beaten to death by his brother-in-law. In chapter 5, it was the same quest for justice that prompted the residents of the entire town of Jirjā to close off their town and prevent soldiers from burying Isḥāq Ṭaniyūs when they strongly believed the local governor, 'Alī Bahjat, had beaten him to death. When they suspected that the forensic doctors had faked the medical reports to exonerate the governor, they left Isḥāq's body unburied until it "got bloated and exploded."

But the case that best illustrates the Egyptians' readiness to use the practices of the khedival state, including forensic medicine, to protect their rights and achieve justice is that of Maḥbūba, a young woman from a small village in the Minyā province in Upper Egypt. Maḥbūba's story sums up better than any other case recounted in this book what the creation of a modern state meant for common Egyptians, how this state deployed techniques that enabled it to lay claim on their bodies, and how they fought back to reclaim their bodies, seek justice, and live—or die—in dignity.

In the summer of 1857, Maḥbūba's husband, 'Alī Jād Allah, was summoned for corvée labor on the Cairo-Suez railway line. On the way to perform his duty, 'Alī escaped, prompting his village shaykh, Muḥammad al-Sha'rāwī, to search for him. Al-Sha'rāwī went to 'Alī's home, thinking that he may have preferred to stay in the comfort of his small family, composed of his wife, Maḥbūba, their young son, and his mother-in-law. When al-Sha'rāwī did not find him there, he arrested Maḥbūba instead and had her imprisoned in the village jail. While she was in custody, al-Sha'rāwī beat her severely to get her to confess her husband's whereabouts. The longer she denied having any knowledge of where her husband was hiding, the harsher al-Sha'rāwī's lashes became. The jailer, seeing Maḥbūba's condition deteriorate in front of his eyes, advised al-Sha'rāwī to release her to relieve himself of any responsibility in case she died in custody. Al-Sha'rāwī accepted the advice and had Maḥbūba delivered to her home, and he arrested her young son instead. At home, Maḥbūba's condition continued to worsen, and when she realized she was dying, she sent her brother to al-Sha'rāwī to beg him to release her son so that she could lay her eyes on him one last time. Al-Sha'rāwī accepted a bribe of one hundred piasters, but he still refused to hand over the young boy to see his mother for the last time. Shortly thereafter, Maḥbūba died.

At this point, ʿAlī appeared from hiding and, together with his mother-in-law, went to the local shariʿa court to bring charges against al-Shaʿrāwī, accusing him of causing Maḥbūba's death. They laid Maḥbūba's body, wrapped in a shroud, in front of the qadi and demanded a postmortem examination. But the qadi refused the request, saying that only a physician could carry out such an examination. He then proceeded to handle the case according to *fiqh*. He questioned al-Shaʿrāwī about the charge, but al-Shaʿrāwī denied all accusations. The qadi then asked the claimants if they had any witnesses to the beating, but they answered that since the beating had taken place in jail, they could provide no witnesses. The qadi then asked them if they could provide any other witnesses to Maḥbūba's condition after she had been released from jail and sent home, but they said that as Maḥbūba had been a very poor woman, no one had come to check on her and she had received no visitors before she died. Finally, the qadi asked them to fetch the village female corpse-washer to inquire if she had detected any contusions on Maḥbūba's body while preparing it for burial. But as luck would have it, the woman who performed this ritual in the village happened to be Maḥbūba's mother, which meant that her testimony could not be accepted, and in any case, she was blind. Lacking a *bayyina* (a confession by the defendant or an eyewitness account), the qadi could not rule for the defendants, and according to *fiqh*, the case had to be dropped.

But neither ʿAlī nor his mother-in-law gave up. Confronted by what they believed "was a prejudice of the qadi, the agricultural overseer, and the local shaykhs," they took Maḥbūba's body, put it on top of a camel, and roamed the countryside seeking the help of a *siyāsa* doctor who would conduct a postmortem examination. In the provincial town of Quluṣna, the deputy doctor answered the claimants' request. In his report, he wrote that he "had found signs of severe beating by a palm leaf on [Maḥbūba's] chest up to her face and from her shoulders down to her wrists, and that blood had been oozing out of her mouth." He concluded by stating that Maḥbūba's death had been caused by beating.

The claimants felt vindicated and "clung to what had been revealed by the deputy doctor's report" (*tamasakkū bimā tawaḍḍaḥ bi-kashf wakīl al-ḥakīm*). With the medical report in hand, they marched to the local police headquarters and presented their case, per *siyāsa* rules. After the police had interrogated all parties, claimants, and defendants and taken into account the medical report, the *siyāsa* council, Majlis al-Fashn, found Muḥammad al-Shaʿrāwī guilty of causing Maḥbūba's death and sentenced him to five years in prison in the local jail. When Majlis al-Aḥkām viewed the case, it upheld the verdict but ruled that al-Shaʿrāwī should serve his prison sentence in the notorious Līmān al-Iskandariyya instead.[12]

There is no better case than Maḥbūba's to illustrate both the degree to which the Egyptian state, in a little less than half a century, managed to establish firm control over the natural resources of the country and the resourcefulness with which Egyptians accommodated this new machine that controlled all aspects of their lives, from birth to death. This tragic story shows that there was little about this modern state that Egyptians could be happy with. The Cairo-Suez railway line, completed just one year after Maḥbūba's death, is a good example not only of the diplomatic and technical proficiency that the Egyptian state had achieved by the middle of the nineteenth century but also of the efficient policing and precise census-taking that allowed tens of thousands of peasants like ʿAlī Jād Allah to be pressed into corvée labor to build the rail link between the two cities. While Egypt could pride itself for being the first country outside Europe and North America to build railways, for Maḥbūba, the Cairo-Suez railway line and the modern state that lay behind it were an unmitigated disaster: her husband was forced into corvée work, her only child was abducted by her village's strongman, and she herself paid with her life for a project that could hardly be less relevant to her happiness and wellbeing.

What Maḥbūba's case illustrates is how resourceful and quick non-elite Egyptians were in appropriating the novel techniques of the state for their own purposes. This state was not created to serve them, and it controlled their bodies in ever-tighter ways and even extended its gaze beyond the living, subjecting the dead to close scrutiny. But as Maḥbūba's husband and mother show, Egyptians, in their quest for justice, spared no effort in making this state serve them, and they stopped at nothing in their constant struggle to live in peace and die with dignity.

NOTES

INTRODUCTION

1. For a reproduction of the painting, see Maḥmūd Mināwī, *Tārīkh al-Nahḍa al-Ṭibbiyya al-Miṣriyya: Mathaf Qaṣr al-ʿAinī* (Cairo: Nahḍat Miṣr, 2000), 95.

2. Emily Savage-Smith, "Anatomical Illustration in Arabic Manuscripts," in *Arab Painting: Text and Image in Illustrated Arabic Manuscripts,* ed. Anna Contadini (Leiden: Brill, 2007), 158.

3. On the tension between classical learning and the evidence of practical dissection performed by Renaissance anatomists, see Andrea Carlino, *Books of the Body: Anatomical Ritual and Renaissance Learning,* trans. John Tedeschi and Anne C. Tedeschi (Chicago: Chicago University Press, 1999).

4. William S. Heckscher, *Rembrandt's Anatomy of Dr. Nicolaas Tulp: An Iconographic Study* (New York: New York University Press, 1958), 43.

5. For the significance of Vesalius's revolutionary approach to anatomical illustration as an effective visual tool replacing textual description, see Gül A. Russell, "Vesalius and the Emergence of Veridical Representation in Renaissance Anatomy," *Progress in Brain Research* 203, (2013): 3–32.

6. Anne Marie Moulin, "The Construction of Disease Transmission in Nineteenth-Century Egypt and the Dialectics of Modernity," in *The Development of Modern Medicine in Non-Western Countries: Historical Perspectives,* ed. Hormoz Ebrahimnejad (London: Routledge, 2009), 53. There were two Strekalovskys active in Egypt in the 1930s and 1940s, Roman and Nicholas. Both were Russian watercolor painters. Roman worked for a while at the American University in Cairo and, among other things, produced a number of watercolors that illustrated the 1941 Dar al-Maʿārif edition of *Kalīla wa Dimna.* In the 1930s, Nicholas painted posters for the newly founded Egyptian carrier, Misr Airlines, and also made watercolor etchings of St. Catherine's Monastery in Sinai. The two Strekalovskys collaborated to execute eighty-four exquisite paintings of Egyptian Bombyliids (bee flies). See Egyptian Bombyliids Collection, Watercolors, Record Unit 7468, Smithsonian Institution Archives, Washington, DC.

7. Clot was granted the honorific title of bey in recognition of his efforts to combat the devastating cholera epidemic of 1831–32.

8. Antoine Barthélémy Clot Bey, *Mémoires,* ed. Jacques Tagher (Cairo: IFAO, 1949), 71–72.

9. Clot Bey, *Mémoires,* 74.

10. Antoine Barthélémy Clot Bey, *Compte rendu des travaux de l'École de Médecine d'Abou-Zabel (Égypte), et de l'examen général des élèves* (Paris: D. Cavellin, 1833), 142, 146.

11. Naguib Mahfouz, *The History of Medical Education in Egypt* (Cairo: Government Press, 1935), 31.

12. Yoav Di-Capua, *Gatekeepers of the Arab Past: Historians and History Writing in Twentieth-Century Egypt* (Berkeley: University of California Press, 2009), 91–218.

13. Di-Capua, *Gatekeepers,* 110.

14. For a complete list of the publications of Ghurbāl's students, see Di-Capua, *Gatekeepers,* table 4, 192–93.

15. Aḥmad 'Izzat 'Abd al-Karīm, *Tārīkh al-Ta'līm fī 'Aṣr Muḥammad 'Alī* (Cairo: Maktabat al-Nahḍa al-Miṣriyya, 1938), 251–293; Jamāl al-Dīn al-Shayyāl, *Tārīkh al-Tarjama wa'l-Ḥayāh al-Thaqāfiyya fī 'Aṣr Muḥammad 'Alī* (Cairo: Dār al-Fikr al-'Arabī, 1951), 16–23, 53–68.

16. Di-Capua, *Gatekeepers,* 191.

17. 'Abd al-Karīm, *Tārīkh al-Ta'līm,* 266.

18. Al-Shayyāl, *Tārīkh al-Tarjama,* 18.

19. The use of the word "throne" is misleading, as Egypt was not an independent state, let alone a kingdom, at this point but rather a province of the Ottoman Empire, and its ruler was but a governor ruling on behalf of the Ottoman sultan in Istanbul.

20. Al-Shayyāl, *Tārīkh al-Tarjama,* xiv.

21. Al-Shayyāl, *Tārīkh al-Tarjama,* xiii–xiv. The theme of an impatient Europe waiting anxiously at Egypt's gates to bring in "great change" can also be found in the editor's introduction to the 1908 edition of William Lane's *Manners and Customs of the Modern Egyptians* (London: J. M. Dent, 1908), vii.

22. Di-Capua, *Gatekeepers,* 152–153. See also, Muḥammad Ismā'īl Zāhir, "Al-Ḥamla al-Firinsiyya: Al-Wa'i b'l-Tārkīh min Khilāl al-Ākhar," in *Mi'atā Ām 'Alā al- Ḥamla al-Firinsiyya: Ru'iya Miṣriyya,* ed. Nāṣir Aḥmad Ibrāhīm (Cairo: Al-Dār al-'Arabiyya lil-Kitāb, 2008), 570–615.

23. Luwīs 'Awaḍ, *Tārīkh al-Fikr al-Miṣrī al-Ḥadīth,* 2 vols. (Cairo: Al-Hilāl, 1969), 2:8.

24. 'Awaḍ, *Tārīkh al-Fikr,* 1:10.

25. 'Awaḍ, *Tārīkh al-Fikr,* 2:29–30. For a nuanced reading of the relationship between science and religion during the French Expedition, see Jane Murphy, "Locating the Sciences in Eighteenth-Century Egypt," *British Journal for the History of Science* 43, no. 4 (2010): 557–571.

26. 'Awaḍ, *Tārīkh al-Fikr,* 2:30–31.

27. On how Egyptian historians up until the 1970s treated the three centuries of Ottoman rule as Egypt's "dark ages," see Di-Capua, *Gatekeepers,* 151, 152, 191.

28. Ra'ūf 'Abbās, *Al-Niẓām al-Ijtimā'ī fī Miṣr fī Ẓill al-Milkīyāt al-Zirā'īya al-Kabīra, 1837–1914* (Cairo: Dār al-Fikr al-Ḥadīth lil-Ṭibā'a wa'l-Nashr, 1973). Also of relevance is Ra'ūf 'Abbās, *Al-Ḥaraka al-'Ummāliya fī Miṣr, 1899–1952* (Cairo: Dār al-Kitāb al-'Arabī li'l-Ṭibā'a wa'l-Nashr, 1967).

29. Ra'ūf 'Abbās, *Al-Tanwīr Bayna Miṣr wa-al-Yābān: Dirāsa Muqārana fī Fikr Rifā'a al-Ṭahṭāwī wa-Fukuzawa Yukitshi* (Cairo: Mīrīt, 2001). The comparison with Japan can also be found in Muḥammad Jalāl Kishk, *Wa Dakhalt al-Khayl al-Azhar* (Cairo: Al-Zahrā', 1990), 20–21; and Roger Owen, *Cotton and the Egyptian Economy, 1820–1914: A Study in Trade and Development* (Oxford: Clarendon Press, 1969), 357–364.

30. Ra'ūf 'Abbās, "Qudūm al-Gharb: Bidāya lil-Nahḍa am Ijhāḍ Lahā?" in *Kitābat Tārīkh Miṣr . . . Ilā Ayn? Azmat al-Manhaj wa Ru'ā Naqdiyya,* ed. Ra'ūf 'Abbās (Cairo: Dār al-Kutub wa'l-Wathā'iq al-Qawmiyya, 2009), 85–94.

31. 'Abbās, "Qudūm al-Gharb," 87.

32. 'Abbās, "Qudūm al-Gharb," 91–92.

33. 'Awaḍ, *Tārīkh al-Fikr,* 1:148–149.

34. 'Abbās, "Qudūm al-Gharb," 91–92.

35. 'Abbās, "Qudūm al-Gharb," 91–92.

36. 'Abbās, "Qudūm al-Gharb," 91–92.

37. A good example of the serious academic attention given to social history during the Ottoman period is Nāṣir Ibrāhīm's *Al-Azmāt al-Ijtimā'iyya fī Miṣr fī al-Qarn al-Sābi' 'Ashr* (Cairo: Dār al-Āfāq al-'Arabiyya, 1998), which deals with famines and epidemics. On the history of the Egyptian Historical Society, see Di-Capua, *Gatekeepers,* 210–213. On the increased attention given to studying the Ottoman period, see Di-Capua, *Gatekeepers,* 331–332.

38. Amira El Azhary Sonbol, *The Creation of a Medical Profession in Egypt, 1800–1922* (Syracuse: Syracuse University Press, 1990), 36.

39. Sonbol, *Creation of a Medical Profession,* 21.

40. Sonbol, *Creation of a Medical Profession,* 50–51.

41. Sonbol, *Creation of a Medical Profession,* 131.

42. Sonbol, *Creation of a Medical Profession,* 2.

43. Jane Hathaway, *The Politics of Households in Ottoman Egypt: The Rise of the Qazdağlis* (Cambridge: Cambridge University Press, 1997); Ehud Toledano, *State and Society in Mid-Nineteenth-Century Egypt* (Cambridge: Cambridge University Press, 1990); Alan Mikhail, *Nature and Empire in Ottoman Egypt* (Cambridge: Cambridge University Press, 2011); Adam Mestyan, *Arab Patriotism: The Ideology and Culture of Power in Late Ottoman Egypt* (Princeton: Princeton University Press, 2017); James Baldwin, *Islamic Law and Empire in Ottoman Cairo* (Edinburgh: Edinburgh University Press, 2017). While the title khedive was not officially granted by the Ottoman sultan to Egypt's rulers until after 1865, it was commonly used inside Egypt much earlier. I therefore refer to the years between 1805, when Mehmed Ali was instated as governor of Egypt, and 1879, when Ismā'īl was deposed, as the khedival period.

44. In addition to the works cited below, see Shula Marks, "What Is Colonial about Colonial Medicine? And What Has Happened to Imperialism and Health?" *Social History of Medicine* 10, no. 2 (1997): 205–219.

45. Daniel Headrick, *Tools of Empire: Technology and European Imperialism in the Nineteenth Century* (New York: Oxford University Press, 1981), 72. See also Raymond Dummett, "The Campaign against Malaria and the Expansion of Scientific Medical and Sanitary Services in British West Africa, 1898–1910," *African Historical Studies* 1, no. 2 (1968): 153–197.

46. David Arnold, *Colonizing the Body: State Medicine and Epidemic Disease in Nineteenth-Century India* (Berkeley: University of California Press, 1993), 9.

47. Frantz Fanon, *A Dying Colonialism,* trans. Haakon Chevalier (New York: Grove, 1967), 121.

48. Roger Jeffery, "Recognizing India's Doctors: The Institutionalization of Medical Dependency, 1918–39," *Modern Asian Studies* 13, no. 2 (1979): 301–326.

49. David Arnold, "Medicine and Colonialism," in *Companion Encyclopedia of the History of Medicine,* vol. 2, ed. W. F. Bynum and Roy Porter (London: Routledge, 1993), 1406.

50. Quoted in Nancy Gallagher, *Medicine and Power in Tunisia, 1780–1900* (Cambridge: Cambridge University Press, 1983), 95.

51. Radhika Ramasubban, *Public Health and Medical Research in India: Their Origins under the Impact of British Colonial Policy* (Stockholm: SAREC, 1982).

52. Arnold, "Medicine and Colonialism," 1399.

53. Radhika Ramasubban, "Imperial Health in British India, 1857–1900," in *Disease, Medicine, and Empire: Perspectives on Western Medicine and the Experience of European Expansion,* ed. Roy Macleod and Milton Lewis (London: Routledge, 1988), 40–41.

54. See, for example, Clot Bey, *Compte rendu des travaux de l'École de Médecine,* 147–148.

55. Georges Douin, *Mohamed Aly et l'expédition d'Alger* (Cairo: Royal Egyptian Geographic Society, 1930). See also Henry Dodwell, *The Founder of Modern Egypt: A Study of Muhammad 'Ali* (Cambridge: Cambridge University Press, 1931), 94–105.

56. For a history of Mehmed Ali's army, see Khaled Fahmy, *All the Pasha's Men: Mehmed Ali, His Army and the Making of Modern Egypt* (Cambridge: Cambridge University Press, 1997).

57. For standard versions of the history of science, see J. McClellan and Harold Dorn, *Science and Technology in World History: An Introduction* (Baltimore: Johns Hopkins University Press, 1999); and George Sarton, *The History of Science and the New Humanism* (New York: Braziller, 1956). For more recent critiques of these versions, see Peter Harrison, "'Science' and 'Religion': Constructing the Boundaries," *Journal of Religion* 86 (2006): 81–106; and Harrison, *The Territories of Science and Religion* (Chicago: University of Chicago Press, 2015).

58. For an analysis of the alleged antagonism in Islamic societies toward science, see H. Floris Cohen, *The Scientific Revolution: A Historiographical Inquiry* (Chicago: University of Chicago Press, 1994); and Toby Huff, *The Rise of Early Modern*

Science: Islam, China and the West (Cambridge: Cambridge University Press, 1993). For refutations of this viewpoint, see Dimitri Gutas, *Greek Thought, Arabic Culture: The Graeco-Arabic Translation Movement in Baghdad and Early 'Abbasid Society (2nd-4th/8th-10th Centuries)* (London: Routledge, 1998), 166–175; and Nahyan Fancy, *Science and Religion in Mamluk Egypt: Ibn al-Nafis, Pulmonary Transit and Bodily Resurrection* (London: Routledge, 2013), 4–5.

59. The literature on science and faith in the medieval Muslim world is vast, but see especially Fancy, *Science and Religion.*

60. On the "diffusion" of science, see George Basalla, "The Spread of Western Science," *Science* 156 (1967): 611–622.

61. On contact zones, see Simon Schaffer et al., eds., *The Brokered World: Go-Betweens and Global Intelligence, 1770–1820* (Sagamore Beach: Science History Publications, 2009); and Kapil Raj, *Relocating Modern Science* (Basingstoke: Macmillan, 2007).

62. My research into the way Egyptian doctors in the khedival period translated anatomoclinical medicine was informed by Marwa Elshakry's pioneering study of how Darwin's work was received in Egypt a generation later. See Elshakry, *Reading Darwin in Arabic, 1860–1950* (Chicago: University of Chicago Press, 2013).

63. Gyan Prakash, "Body Politic in Colonial India," in *Questions of Modernity,* ed. Timothy Mitchell (Minneapolis: University of Minnesota Press, 2000), 191.

64. Michel Foucault, "Governmentality," in *The Foucault Effect: Studies in Governmentality,* ed. Graham Burchell, Colin Gordon, and Peter Miller (Chicago: University of Chicago Press, 1991), 91.

65. Prakash, "Body Politic," 192.

66. Arnold, *Colonizing the Body,* 10.

67. Prakash, "Body Politic," 193.

68. Partha Chatterjee, *The Nation and Its Fragments: Colonial and Postcolonial Histories* (Princeton: Princeton University Press, 1993), 18.

69. For the "déjà vu effect," whereby British officials viewed Egypt as an instance of something they had experienced in India, see Aaron Jakes, "Peaceful Wars and Unlikely Unions: The Azhar Strike of 1909 and the Politics of Comparison in Egypt," *Comparative Studies in Society and History* (forthcoming); Roger Owen, "The Influence of Lord Cromer's Indian Experience on British Policy in Egypt, 1883–1907," in "St. Antony's Papers," special issue, *Middle Eastern Affairs* 4, no. 17 (1965): 103–139; and Robert L. Tignor, "The 'Indianization' of Egyptian Administration under British Rule," *American Historical Review* 68, no. 3 (1963): 631–661.

70. Timothy Mitchell, *Colonising Egypt* (Cambridge: Cambridge University Press, 1988).

71. For a history of shari'a courts in Ottoman Egypt, see Reem Meshal, *Sharia and the Making of the Modern Egyptian: Islamic Law and Custom in the Courts of Ottoman Cairo* (Cairo: American University in Cairo Press, 2014).

72. On the reasons why it is difficult to study the actual records of the shari'a courts before the Ottoman period in Egypt and elsewhere in the Muslim world, see

Wael Hallaq, "The *Qāḍī's Dīwān (Sijill)* before the Ottomans," *Bulletin of the School of Oriental and African Studies* 61, no. 3, (1998): 415–436.

73. On Egyptian secularists, see the commemorative two-volume book published on the occasion of the semicentennial of the National Courts: *Al-Kitāb al-Dhahabī lil-Maḥākim al-Ahliyya: 1883–1933* (Būlāq: Al-Maṭba'a al-Amīriyya, 1937–38). On Egyptian Islamists, see the final section of the introduction and chapter 2.

74. For a good example of this narrative, see Laṭīfa Sālim, *Tārīkh al-Qaḍā' al-Miṣrī Al-Ḥadīth,* 2 vols. (Cairo: Al-Hay'a al-Miṣriyya al-'Āmma lil-Kitāb, 2001). For a critical review of recent studies of the history of nineteenth-century Egyptian law, see chapter 2 of this book.

75. Talal Asad, *Formations of the Secular: Christianity, Islam, Modernity* (Stanford: Stanford University Press, 2003), 208 (emphasis added).

76. See especially Saba Mahmood, *Politics of Piety: The Islamic Revival and the Feminist Subject* (Princeton: Princeton University Press, 2005); and Charles Hirschkind, *The Ethical Soundscape: Cassette Sermons and Islamic Counter-Publics* (New York: Columbia University Press, 2006).

77. David Scott and Charles Hirschkind, eds., *Powers of the Secular Modern: Talal Asad and His Interlocutors* (Stanford: Stanford University Press, 2006).

78. Samuli Schielke, "Second Thoughts about the Anthropology of Islam, or How to Make Sense of Grand Schemes in Everyday Life," *Zentrum Moderner Orient Working Papers* 2 (2010): 6.

79. Asad, *Formations of the Secular,* 208–209 (emphasis added).

80. Asad, *Formations of the Secular,* 253.

81. Asad, *Formations of the Secular,* 209.

82. Asad, *Formations of the Secular,* 206 (emphasis added).

83. Asad, *Formations of the Secular,* 208.

84. Asad, *Formations of the Secular,* 250.

85. Wael Hallaq, *The Impossible State: Islam, Politics and Modernity's Moral Predicament* (New York: Columbia University Press, 2013).

86. Hallaq, *Impossible State,* 12, 49, 156, 75.

87. Hallaq, *Impossible State,* 166.

88. Wael Hallaq, *Sharī'a: Theory, Practice, Transformations* (Cambridge: Cambridge University Press, 2009), 15. For a critical study of the profound transformations of legal paradigms that colonialism brought about, see Samera Esmeir, *Juridical Humanity: A Colonial History* (Stanford: Stanford University Press, 2012).

89. Hallaq, *Impossible State,* 14.

90. Andrew Marsh, "What Can the Islamic Past Teach Us about Secular Modernity?" *Political Theory* 43 (2015): 843 (emphasis in original).

91. For an elaboration of this critique of Hallaq's *The Impossible State,* see Neguin Yavari, "Review Symposium: *The Impossible State,*" *Perspectives on Politics* 12, no. 2 (2014): 466–467.

92. Hallaq, *Sharī'a,* 549.

93. Hallaq, *Sharī'a,* 200.

94. Hallaq, *Sharīʿa,* 214.

95. Hallaq, *Sharīʿa,* 215.

96. See, most notably, Fariba Zarinbaf, *Crime and Punishment in Istanbul, 1700–1800* (Berkeley: University of California Press, 2010); Baldwin, *Islamic Law;* Başak Tuğ, *Politics of Honor in Ottoman Anatolia: Sexual Violence and Socio-Legal Surveillance in the Eighteenth Century* (Leiden: Brill, 2017); and Guy Burak, "Between the *Ḳānūn* of Qāytbāy and the Ottoman *Yasaq:* A Note on the Ottomans' Dynastic Law," *Journal of Islamic Studies* 26, no. 1 (2015): 1–23.

97. Leonard Wood, *Islamic Legal Revival: Reception of European Law and Transformations in Islamic Legal Thought in Egypt, 1875–1952* (Oxford: Oxford University Press, 2016).

98. For a background on this "March crisis," see Joel Gordon, *Nasser's Blessing Movement: Egypt's Free Officers and the July Revolution* (New York: Oxford University Press, 1992), 127–143; Hazem Kandil, *Soldiers, Spies, and Statesmen* (London: Verso, 2012), 15–42; and Sāmī Jawhar, *Al-Ṣāmiṭūn Yatakallimūn: 'Abd al-Nāṣir wa'l-Ikhwān* (Cairo: Al-Maktab al-Miṣrī al-Ḥadīth, 1975), 11–56.

99. For a good example of how highly 'Awda is regarded in Islamist circles, see 'Abd Allāh al-'Aqīl, *Min Aʿlām al-Ḥaraka al-Islāmiyya* (Cairo: Dār al-Tawzīʿ wa'l-Nashr al-Islāmiyya, 2010), 245–253.

100. 'Abd al-Qādir 'Awda, *Al-Tashrīʿ al-Jināʾī al-Islāmī Muqāranan bi'l-Qānūn al-Waḍʿī,* 2 vols. (Cairo: Dār al-Turāth, 1980).

101. 'Awda, *Al-Tashrīʿ al-Jināʾī,* 1:11.

102. 'Awda, *Al-Tashrīʿ al-Jināʾī,* 1:5.

103. 'Awda, *Al-Tashrīʿ al-Jināʾī,* 1:24–25.

104. 'Awda, *Al-Tashrīʿ al-Jināʾī,* 1:15.

105. Before he retired in 1989, Ṭāriq al-Bishrī was the First Deputy of the President of Majlis al-Dawla, Egypt's administrative court, modeled after the French Conseil d'Etat. His chief works include *Saʿd Zaghlūl Yufāwiḍ al-Istiʿmār* (Cairo: Al-Hay'a al-Miṣriyya al-'Āmma lil-Kitāb, 1977); *Al-Dīmūqrātiyya wa Niẓām 23 Yūliyū, 1952–1970* (Beirut: Mu'assasat al-Abḥāth al-'Arabiyya, 1987); and *Al-Muslimūn wa'l-Aqbaṭ fī Iṭār al-Jamāʿa al-Waṭaniyya* (Cairo: Al-Hay'a al-Miṣriyya al-'Āmma lil-Kitāb, 1980).

106. Ṭarīq al-Bishrī, *Al-Ḥaraka al-Siyāsiyya fī Miṣr, 1945–1953* (Cairo: Dār al-Shurūq, 2002), 50.

107. Ṭāriq al-Bishrī, *Al-Waḍʿ al-Qānūnī Bayna al-Sharīʿa al-Islāmiyya wa'l-Qānūn al-Waḍʿī* (Cairo: Dār al-Shurūq, 2005), 6–7.

108. Bishrī, *Al-Waḍʿ al-Qānūnī,* 12–18.

109. Ṭāriq al-Bishrī, *Māhiyyat al-Muʿāṣara* (Cairo: Dar al-Shurūq, 2007), 42.

110. Bishrī, *Māhiyyat al-Muʿāṣara,* 54.

111. Bishrī, *Māhiyyat al-Muʿāṣara,* 43. The story about Khedive Ismāʿīl and the shaykhs of al-Azhar is published in Rashīd Riḍā, *Tārīkh al-Ustādh al-Imām al-Shaykh Muḥammad 'Abdu,* vol. 1 (Cairo: Al-Manār, 1931), 620–621.

112. Note that al-Bishrī prefers *al-mawrūth* and not the more familiar word *al-turāth,* which is commonly translated as "heritage." The reason, he argues, is that

those who base their arguments on *turāth* do not actually use the term, preferring instead "the term that connotes identity, i.e., Islam, to resist the upheavals of uprooting in this civilizational encounter." However, those who adopt imported thought (*abnā' al-fikr al-wāfid*) use the word *turāth,* and they do so "after distancing themselves from it and after detaching it from identity. . . . We can then say that, paradoxically, the *turāthīs* prefer the term 'Islam,' while those of imported thought [*dhawī al-fikr al-wāfid*] prefer the term *turāth.*" Bishrī, *Māhiyyat al-Mu'āsara,* 9 (the article this citation is taken from was first published in 1983). For a sympathetic review of al-Bishrī's view of *al-mawrūth* and *al-wāfid,* see Roel Meijer, "Authenticity in History: The Concept of *al-Wafid* and *al-Mawruth* in Tariq al-Bishri's Reinterpretation of Modern Egyptian History," in *Amsterdam Middle East Studies,* ed. Manfred Woidich (Wiesbaden: Verlag, 1990), 68–83.

113. Bishrī, *Māhiyyat al-Mu'āṣara,* 8.

114. Bishrī, *Māhiyyat al-Mu'āṣara,* 11.

115. Al-Bishrī's volte-face was warmly embraced by the Islamist movement in Egypt and elsewhere, and he is considered one of the most respected ideologues of the Muslim Brotherhood, even though he never officially joined the group. For examples of how highly regarded al-Bishrī is within Islamic circles, see Muḥammad Salīm al-'Awwā, *Ṭāriq al-Bishrī Faqīhan* (Mansoura: Dār al-Wafā', 1999); and Muḥammad Mūrū, *Ṭāriq al-Bishrī: Shāhid 'alā Suqūt al-'Almāniyya* (Cairo: Dār al-Fatā al-Muslim, n.d.).

116. Bishrī, *Al-Ḥaraka al-Siyāsiyya,* 51.

117. Bishrī, *Māhiyyat al-Mu'āṣara,* 41.

CHAPTER ONE. MEDICINE, ENLIGHTENMENT, AND ISLAM

1. 'Alī Mubārak, however, mentions that there were three *tikiyyās*, or hospices for the poor, that were founded during the Ottoman period: al-Jalshāniyya, al-Ḥabbāniyya and al-A'jām. See 'Alī Mubārak, *Al-Khiṭāṭ al-Tawfīqiyya al-Jadīda,* 20 vols. (Cairo: Būlāq, AH 1304–06/1882–89 CE), 1:97. For the history of hospitals in Mamluk Egypt, see Ahmed Ragab, *The Medieval Islamic Hospital: Medicine, Religion, and Charity* (Cambridge: Cambridge University Press, 2015).

2. For a recent biography of Clot Bey, see Christian Jean Dubois, *Clot Bey: Médecin de Marseille, 1793–1868* (Marseilles: J. Laffitte, 2013).

3. Antoine Barthélemy Clot Bey, *Aperçu général sur l'Égypte,* 2 vols. (Paris: Fortin, 1840), 2:409–410.

4. "Lancet Gallery of Medical Portraits," *Lancet* 20, no. 502 (1833), 88.

5. J. A. St. John, *Egypt and Mohammed Ali,* 2 vols. (London, 1834), 2: 401–402.

6. For Clot Bey's arguments to have the school moved see Dār al-Wathā'iq al-Qawmiyya [Egyptian National Archives], Cairo (hereafter cited as DWQ), Ma'iyya Saniyya, Turkī, S/1/55/2 (original no. 47), doc. no. 421, AH 27 Ṣafar 1249 / 16 July

1833 CE; DWQ, Maʿiyya Saniyya, Turkī, S/1/52/2 (original no. 57), doc. no. 491, p. 106, AH 17 Dhū al-Qaʿda 1250 / 17 March 1835 CE; and DWQ, Maʿiyya Saniyya, Turkī, S/1/54/1 (original no. 61), doc. no. 265, AH 19 Rajab 1251 / 10 November 1835 CE. See also Clot Bey, *Aperçu général,* 2:418–419.

7. F. M. Sandwith, "The History of Kasr-el-Ainy," *Records of the Egyptian Government School of Medicine* 1 (1901): 11.

8. ʿAzza ʿAbd al-Hādī, "Muqāwamat al-Ahālī li-Taṭʿīm al-Judarī fī al-Qarn al-Tāsiʿ ʿAshr," in *Al-Rafḍ wa'l-Iḥtijāj fi'l-Mujtamaʿ al-Miṣrī fī al-ʿAṣr al-ʿUthmānī,* ed. Nāṣir Ibrāhīm (Cairo: Al-Jamʿiyya al-Miṣriyya lil-Dirāsāt al-Tārikhiyya, 2004), 303–312. See also Antoine Barthélémy Clot Bey, *Mabḥath Taʿlīmī fī Taṭʿīm al-Judarī,* trans. Aḥmad Ḥasan al-Rashīdī (Cairo: Būlāq, AH 1259/1843 CE).

9. For accounts of this census, see Kenneth Cuno and Michael J. Reimer, "The Census Registers of Nineteenth-Century Egypt: A New Source for Social Historians," *British Journal of Middle Eastern Studies* 24, no. 2 (1997), 193–216; Ghislaine Alleaume and Philippe Fargues, "La naissance d'une statistique d'État: Le recensement de 1848 en Egypte," *Histoire et Measure* 13, nos. 1–2 (1998): 147–193; Ghislaine Alleaume and Philippe Fargues, "Voisinage et frontière: Résider au Caire en 1846," in *Urbanite arabe: Homage à Bernard Lepetit,* ed. Jocelyne Dakhlia (Arles: Sindbad, 1998), 77–112; and Philippe Fargues, "Family and Household in Mid-Nineteenth-Century Egypt," in *Family History in the Middle East: Household, Property, and Gender,* ed. Beshara Doumani (Albany: State University of New York Press, 2003), 23–50. See also ʿAbbās Pasha's decree clarifying how to count the naval and military infirm and stating the ages of the dead when registering them in the annual tallies: DWQ, Maḥfaẓat al-Mīhī, malaf 1262, doc. dated AH 30 Dhū al-Ḥijja 1262 / 19 December 1846 CE.

10. See, for example, Sonbol, *Creation of a Medical Profession;* and Hibba Abugideiri, *Gender and the Making of Modern Medicine in Colonial Egypt* (Farnham, Surrey: Ashgate, 2010).

11. Mahfouz, *History of Medical Education,* 23–24.

12. Clot Bey, *Mémoires,* 74.

13. Antoine Barthélemy Clot Bey, "Clot Bey's Observations on Egypt," *Foreign Quarterly Review* 27 (1841): 377–378.

14. Antoine Barthélémy Clot Bey, *Kunūz al-Ṣiḥḥa wa Yawāqīt al-Minḥa,* trans. Muḥammad al-Shāfiʿī, ed. Muḥammad ʿUmar al-Tūnisī and Nicolas Perron (Cairo: Būlāq, 1844), 5.

15. Clot Bey, *Kunūz al-Ṣiḥḥa,* 15.

16. John Bowring, "Report on Egypt and Candia," *Parliamentary Papers, Reports from Commissioners* 21 (1840): 146 (emphasis added).

17. William Lawrence, *Ḍiyāʾ al-Nayyirīn fī Mudāwāt al-ʿAynayn* [*A Treatise on the Diseases of the Eye*], trans. Aḥmad al-Rashīdī (Cairo: Būlāq, 1840), 3–4. Al-Rashīdī would later teach gynecology at the School of Midwives, which was founded in 1837. He also became the first editor of the medical journal *Yaʿsūb al-Ṭibb,* which was launched in 1865. See DWQ, Muḥāfaẓat Miṣr, Ṣādir Riyāsat al-Isbītāliyya, L/1/4/3 (original no. 457), doc. no. 19, pp. 42, 58, AH 22 Ramaḍān 1281 / 18 February

1865 CE. On Lawrence's *Treatise,* see H. Stanley Thompson and Patricia G. Duffel, "William Lawrence and the English Ophthalmology Textbooks of the 1830s and 1840s," *Archives of Ophthalmology* 130, no. 5 (2012): 639–644.

18. Muḥammad al-Shāfi'ī, "Nubdha fī al-Ṭibb al-Tajribī," *Bulletin de l'institut Egyptien* 1 (1862): 505.

19. J. Worth Estes and LaVerne Kuhnke, "French Observations of Disease and Drug Use in Late Eighteenth-Century Cairo," *Journal of the History of Medicine and Allied Sciences* 39 (1984): 128. See also Clot Bey, *Aperçu général,* 2:383.

20. Shāfi'ī, "Nubdha," 507. On ophthalmia and eye diseases, see LaVerne Kuhnke, "Early Nineteenth Century Ophthalmological Clinics in Egypt," *Clio Medica* 7 (1972): 209–214.

21. Sandwith, "History of Kasr-el-Ainy," 3.

22. Peter Gay, *The Enlightenment* (London: Norton, 1966), 80.

23. Sandwith, "History of Kasr-el-Ainy," 4.

24. Earl of Cromer (Evelyn Baring), *Modern Egypt,* 2 vols. (London: Macmillan, 1908), 2:512.

25. Cromer, *Modern Egypt,* 2:510.

26. This analysis of Mehmed Ali's dynastic struggle with the Ottoman sultan is based on Khaled Fahmy, *Mehmed Ali: From Ottoman Governor to Ruler of Egypt* (Oxford: Oneworld, 2008).

27. Frédéric Cailliaud, *Voyage á Méroé, au Fleuve Blanc, au-delà de Fâzoql,* 2 vols. (Paris: L'Imprimerie Royale, 1826), 2:313, 2:316.

28. Dodwell, *Founder of Modern Egypt,* 64–65.

29. For a rare letter in Arabic from Mehmed Ali to his provincial governors reprimanding them for intentionally conscripting overage men to fulfill their quotas, see DWQ, Ma'iyya Saniyya, Turkī, S/1/13/4 (original no. 30), doc. no. 19, p. 7, AH 5 Ramaḍān 1250 / 5 January 1835 CE.

30. LaVerne Kuhnke, *Lives at Risk: Public Health in Nineteenth-Century Egypt* (Berkeley: University of California Press, 1990), 37.

31. For popular reaction to the new hospitals, see Khaled Fahmy, "Medicine and Power: Towards a Social History of Medicine in Nineteenth-Century Egypt," *Cairo Papers in the Social Sciences* 23, no. 2 (2000): 38–50.

32. For a thoughtful analysis of fatalism in modern-day Egypt regarding bioethics and specifically organ transplants, see Sherine Hamdy, *Our Bodies Belong to God: Organ Transplants, Islam, and the Struggle for Human Dignity in Egyp*t (Berkeley: University of California Press, 2012).

33. Alexander William Kinglake, *Eothen* (London: Ollivier, 1847), 211.

34. F. Grassi, "A Relation and Reflections on the Indian Cholera Which Raged in Egypt in the Year 1848," translation from the Italian, FO 78/759, Gilbert, 30 December 1848, National Archives, London.

35. 'Abd al-Raḥmān al-Jabartī, *'Abd al-Raḥmān al-Jabartī's History of Egypt,* 4 vols., ed. and trans. Thomas Philipp and Moshe Perlmann (Stuttgart: Verlag, 1994), 3:52. The page numbers given for this source are those of the first Būlāq edition of 1880, which Philipp and Perlmann display as a reference in their translated edition.

36. Michel Foucault, "Fourth Lecture, 1 February 1978," in *Security, Territory, Population: Lectures at the Collège de France, 1977–1978*, ed. Michel Senellart, trans. Graham Burchell (London: Palgrave Macmillan, 2009), 105.

37. Michael Dols, "The Second Plague Pandemic and Its Recurrences in the Middle East: 1347–1894," *Journal of the Economic and Social History of the Orient* 22 (1979): 167–168.

38. Nāṣīr Ibrāhīm, *Al-Azmāt al-Ijtimā'iyya fī Miṣr fī al-Qarn al-Sābi' 'Ashr* (Cairo: Dār al-Āfāq al-'Arabiyya, 1998), 184.

39. As Alan Mikhail has shown, there was a causal link between these three phenomena: low Niles usually led to famines, which weakened the natural immunity of the population, leaving people susceptible to an outbreak of plague and helping small outbreaks turn into epidemics. It was the close link between these three phenomena that led many people to believe that plague was endemic to Egypt. See Mikhail, *Nature and Empire.*

40. Aḥmad al-Damurdāshī Katkhudā 'Azabān, *Kitāb al-Durra al-Muṣāna fī Akhbār al-Kināna,* ed. 'Abd al-Raḥīm 'Abd al-Raḥmān 'Abd al-Raḥīm (Cairo: IFAO, 1989), 29.

41. Mikhail, *Nature and Empire,* 223.

42. Aḥmad al-Damurdāshī, *Kitāb al-Durra al-Muṣāna,* 31–33. See also Jabartī, *'Ajā'ib,* 1:99.

43. Mikhail, *Nature and Empire,* 224.

44. Jabartī, *'Ajā'ib,* 3:192.

45. Muḥammad Ibn Abī al-Surūr al-Bakrī, "Al-Kawākib al-Sā'ira fi Akhbār Misr al-Qāhira," fol. 80, quoted in N. Ibrāhīm, *Al-Azmāt,* 187.

46. Michel Foucault, *Essential Works of Foucault, 1954–1984*, vol. 3, *Power,* ed. James Faubion, trans. Robert Hurley et al. (New York: New Press, 2000), 90–105, 134–156, 298–326.

47. Kuhnke, *Lives at Risk,* 75.

48. Jabartī, *'Ajā'ib,* 3:149–150

49. Foucault, "Fourth Lecture," 105.

50. For a comparison with French public health measures in colonial Tunisia, see Richard Parks, "*Divide et Impera:* Public Health and Urban Reform in Protectorate-Era Tunis," *Journal of North African Studies* 17, no. 3 (2012): 533–546.

51. Kuhnke, *Lives at Risk,* 77.

52. Jabartī, *'Ajā'ib,* 4:176.

53. Foucault, "Fourth Lecture," 92.

54. Jabartī, *'Ajā'ib,* 4:257.

55. Foucault, *Essential Works,* 95–96.

56. St. John, *Egypt and Mohammed Ali,* 2:465–466.

57. Catherine J. Kudlick, *Cholera in Post-Revolutionary Paris: A Cultural History* (Berkeley: University of California Press, 1996).

58. Lane, *Manners and Customs,* 3n1. Kinglake, however, who was in Cairo during the peak of the epidemic, says that Cairo lost half its population. See Kinglake, *Eothen,* 207.

59. Kuhnke, *Lives at Risk,* chaps. 3 and 4; Shehab Ismail, "Engineering Metropolis: Contagion, Capital, and the Making of British Colonial Cairo, 1882–1922" (PhD diss., Columbia University, 2017), 32; Edward Bedloe and James F. Love, "Cholera in Egypt," *Public Health Reports* 11, no. 37 (September 11, 1896): 861–863.

60. DWQ, Dīwān Khidīwī, Turkī, S/2/40/22 (original no. 776), doc. no. 37, p. 16, AH 5 Ṣafar 1247 / 16 July 1831 CE.

61. DWQ, Ma'iyya Saniyya, Turkī, S/1/58/1 (original no. 41), doc. no. 354, AH 18 Rabī' I 1247 / 27 August 1831 CE; Kuhnke, *Lives at Risk,* 53–54.

62. DWQ, Ma'iyya Saniyya, Turkī, S/1/60/2 (original no. 59), doc. no. 159, p. 48, AH 10 Jumādā II 1250 / 14 October 1834 CE; DWQ, Ma'iyya Saniyya, Turkī, S/1/60/2 (original no. 59), doc. no. 189, p. 55, AH 29 Jumādā II 1250 / 2 November 1834 CE.

63. Kuhnke, *Lives at Risk,* 95; DWQ, Ma'iyya Saniyya, Turkī, S/1/60/2 (original no. 59), doc. no. 219, p. 65, AH 17 Rajab 1250 / 19 November 1834 CE.

64. See, for example, DWQ, Ma'iyya Saniyya, Turkī, S/1/60/2 (original no. 59), doc. no. 61, p. 20, AH 11 Rabī' II 1250 / 17 August 1834 CE, which contains a petition by tobacco merchants, who feared their cargo would perish during the quarantine period. See also DWQ, Ma'iyya Saniyya, Turkī, S/1/60/2 (original no. 59), doc. no. 489, AH 23 Dhū al-Ḥijja 1250 / 22 April 1835 CE.

65. DWQ, Ma'iyya Saniyya, Turkī, S/1/60/2 (original no. 59), doc. no. 316, p. 99, AH 13 Ramaḍān 1250 / 13 January 1835 CE.

66. DWQ, Ma'iyya Saniyya, Turkī, S/1/52/2 (original no. 57), doc. no. 534, p. 116, AH 17 Dhū al-Ḥijja 1250 / 10 February 1835 CE.

67. DWQ, 'Ābidīn, reg. no. 211, doc. no. 465, AH 11 Shawwāl 1250 / 10 February 1835 CE. See also what appears to be Ibrāhīm Pasha's response: DWQ, Shām, box no. 29, doc. no. 363, AH 14 Shawwāl 1250 / 13 February 1835 CE.

68. On the quarantines imposed on factories, see DWQ, Ma'iyya Saniyya, Turkī, S/1/53/7 (original no. 60), doc. no. 161, p. 29, AH 20 Dhū al-Ḥijja 1250 / 19 April 1835 CE; for the quarantines imposed on schools, see DWQ, Ma'iyya Saniyya, Turkī, S/1/53/7 (original no. 60), doc. no. 162, p. 30, AH 20 Dhū al-Ḥijja 1250 / 19 April 1835 CE.

69. DWQ, Ma'iyya Saniyya, Turkī, S/1/60/2 (original no. 59), doc. no. 319, p. 100, AH 14 Ramaḍān 1250 / 14 January 1835 CE; DWQ, Muḥāfaẓat Iskandariyya, box no. 1 Awāmir, doc. no. 148, AH 15 Ramaḍān 1250 / 15 January 1835 CE.

70. DWQ, Dīwān Khidīwī, S/2/18/1 (original no. 654), unnumbered doc., pp. 109–110, AH 27 Jumādā II 1261 / 3 July 1845 CE.

71. On the imposition of quarantines in the eastern Mediterranean, see Zlata Blažina Tomić and Vesna Blažina, *Expelling the Plague: The Health Office and the Implementation of Quarantine in Dubrovnick, 1377–1553* (London: McGill-Queen's University Press, 2015), 106–108. For Ottoman efforts to control the plague, see Nüket Varlik, *Plague and Empire in the Early Modern Mediterranean World: The Ottoman Experience, 1347–1600* (New York: Cambridge University Press, 2015). For premodern conceptions of contagion, the plague, and quarantines, see Justin Stearns, *Infectious Ideas: Contagion in Premodern Islamic and Christian Thought in the Western Mediterranean* (Baltimore: Johns Hopkins University Press, 2011).

72. DWQ, Muḥāfaẓat Iskandariyya, box no. 1, Awāmir, doc. no. 135, AH 14 Sha'bān 1250 / 16 December 1834 CE. On the antipathy to quarantines in European liberal capitalist countries, see Erwin Ackerknecht, "Anticontagionism between 1821 and 1861," *Bulletin of the History of Medicine* 22 (1948): 561–593.

73. Antoine Barthélémy Clot Bey, *De la peste observée en Egypte: Recherches et considerations sur cette maladie* (Paris: Fortin, Masson et Cie., 1840), 428.

74. Antoine Barthélémy Clot Bey, *Al-'Ujāla al-Ṭibiyya fīmā lā Budda minhu li-Ḥukāmā' al-Jihādiyya,* trans. August Sakākīnī (Cairo: Maṭba'at al-Madrasa al-Ṭibiyya bi-Abī Za'bal, AH 1284/1832 CE), 50–51.

75. Antoine Barthélémy Clot Bey, *Tanbīh Fīmā Yakhuṣṣ al-Ṭā'ūn* (Cairo: Maṭba'at Dīwān al-Jihādiyya, AH 1250/1835 CE), 5.

76. Antoine Barthélémy Clot Bey, *Leçon sur la peste d'Égypte et spécialement sur ce qui concerne la contagion ou la non contagion de cette maladie, donnée à l'hôpital de la Pitié* (Marseille: Vial, 1862). This was first published as "Résumé sur la contagion de la peste," *Gazette des Hopitaux,* April 28, 1840.

77. Antoine Barthélémy Clot Bey, "The Plague and Quarantine Laws," *Lancet* 31, no. 806 (February 1839): 743–744.

78. Clot Bey, *De la peste,* 212–223, 233–234.

79. F. Grassi, "A Relation."

80. Kuhnke, *Lives at Risk,* 80.

81. DWQ, Ma'iyya Saniyya, Turkī, S/1/60/2 (original no. 59), doc. no. 267, AH 12 Sha'bān 1250 / 14 December 1834 CE.

82. DWQ, Ma'iyya Saniyya, Turkī, S/1/60/2 (original no. 59), doc. no. 355, p. 112, AH 13 Shawwāl 1250 / 12 February 1835 CE; DWQ, Muḥāfaẓat Iskandariyya, box no. 1, doc. no. 160, AH 12 Shawwāl 1250 / 11 February 1835 CE. For an English translation of this letter, see LaVerne Kuhnke, "Resistance and Response to Modernization: Preventive Medicine and Social Control in Egypt, 1825–1850" (PhD diss., University of Chicago, 1971), 122–123. This is not the only example of Mehmed Ali's cavalier attitude to Prophetic Tradition. In 1846, when some Cairo *'ulamā'* raised questions about conducting a census, Mehmed Ali gathered them and, according to his Armenian advisor, Hekekyan, told them, "Surely in the mass of divine revelation [i.e., the Quran] which took twenty-three years to come down there must be not one but several passages authorizing the census, as some have been for the Nizam Gedeed [the conscript army], for the European costume, for quarantines, etc. Go and see—go and see." Quoted in Paul Sedra, "Observing Muhammad 'Ali Paşa and His Administration at Work, 1843–1846," in *The Modern Middle East: A Sourcebook for History,* ed. Camron M. Amin, Benjamin Fortna, and Elizabeth Frierson (Oxford: Oxford University Press, 2006), 42.

83. DWQ, Ma'iyya Saniyya, Turkī, reg. no. 66, doc. no. 9, p. 2, AH 19 Rabī' I 1251 / 15 July 1835 CE.

84. DWQ, Ma'iyya Saniyya, Turkī, reg. no. 66, doc. no. 587, p. 151, AH 22 Jumādā II 1251 / 15 October 1835 CE.

85. DWQ, Ma'iyya Saniyya, Turkī, S/1/60/2 (original no. 59), doc. no. 234, p. 72, AH 23 Rajab 1250 / 25 November 1835 CE.

86. For more on female doctors in khedival Egypt, see Khaled Fahmy, "Women, Medicine and Power in Nineteenth-Century Egypt," in *Remaking Women: Feminism and Modernity in the Middle East,* ed. Lila Abu-Lughod (Princeton: Princeton University Press, 1998), 35–72.

87. DWQ, Ma'iyya Saniyya, Turkī, S/1/60/2 (original no. 59), doc. no. 620, p. 185, AH 24 Ṣafar 1251 / 21 June 1835 CE.

88. DWQ, Ma'iyya Saniyya, S/1/79/1 (original no. 62), doc. no. 551, AH 26 Dhū al-Ḥijja 1250 / 25 April 1835 CE.

89. DWQ, Ma'iyya Saniyya, S/1/60/4 (original no. 64), doc. no. 64, AH 9 Ramaḍān 1251/ 29 December 1835 CE.

90. DWQ, Ma'iyya Saniyya, S/1/60/4 (original no. 64), doc. no. 138, AH 19 Ramaḍān 1251 / 8 January 1836 Ce.

91. DWQ, Shām, box no. 51, doc. no. 18, encl. no. 3, AH 7 Muḥarram 1256 / 11 March 1840 CE.

92. DWQ, Shām, box no. 51, doc. no. 18, encl. no. 1, AH 15 Muḥarram 1256 / 19 March 1840 CE.

93. DWQ, Shām, box no. 53, doc. no. 100/29, encl. no. 3, AH 4 Rabī' I 1256 / 6 May 1840 CE.

94. The mufti was referring to the famous plague of 'Imwās (ancient Emmaus) that struck in 638 or 639. This was the paradigmatic plague that shaped medieval Muslim ideas of the scourge. See Michael Dols, *The Black Death in the Middle East* (Princeton: Princeton University Press, 1977), 21–25.

95. DWQ, Shām, box no. 52, doc. no. 46, AH 2 Ṣafar 1256 / 5 April 1840 CE. On the notion that fear and panic could dispose one to the plagues, see Clot Bey, *Tanbīh,* 4: "Fear and panic [*al-khawf wa'l-wahm*] are two conditions that help one become stricken by the plague." On contagion in Islamic medical and religious traditions, see Stearns, *Infectious Ideas,* chap. 3; and Dols, *Black Death,* chap. 4.

96. DWQ, Shūrā al-Mu'āwana, Turkī, reg. no. 282, doc. no. 301, AH 20 Rabī' I 1256 / 22 May 1840 CE.

97. "General Regulations Concerning the Public Health at Alexandria and in the Interior to Be Put into Execution According to Order of His Highness the Vice Roy, dated 15 Rejeb 1257 (30 August 1841)," enclosure in FO 78/502, Barnett, 23 December 1842, National Archives, London. This is an English translation of the original Ottoman text, which I could not locate in the Egyptian National Archives. For more on these general regulations, see chapter 4. *Spolgio* involved taking off one's clothes, having the clothes fumigated, and then putting on the disinfected clothes.

98. The earliest order to this effect I could locate is from 1832. Citing a recommendation by Clot Bey's Shūrā al-Aṭibbā, it stipulated that burials in graveyards that were in close proximity to populated quarters of the city had to be stopped and that undertakers had to build high fences around graveyards to prevent the miasmas emanating from them from infecting the city. See DWQ, Dīwān Khidīwī, S/2/40/26 (original no. 785), doc. no. 18, p. 9, AH 6 Muḥarram 1258 / 5 June 1832 CE.

99. DWQ, Dīwān al-Jihādiyya, reg. no. 440, doc. no. 179, p. 215, AH 20 Sha'bān 1264 / 22 July 1848 CE. The authorities were so concerned about public peace that they

also forbade people from visiting the cemeteries during the 'Īd al-Fiṭr: DWQ, Dīwān al-Jihādiyya, reg. no. 440, doc. 246, p. 238, AH 28 Ramaḍān 1264 / 28 August 1848 CE.

100. DWQ, Majlis al-Aḥkām, S/7/33/1, p. 225, quoting an order from Majlis Mulkiyya dated AH 29 Muḥarram 1252 / 16 May 1836 CE. The latter stipulated that wailers caught practicing these "abominable acts" (*af'āl qabīḥa*) would be imprisoned for forty days.

101. DWQ, Dīwān al-Jihādiyya, reg. no. 440, doc. no. 212, p. 218, AH 2 Ramaḍān 1264 / 2 August 1848 CE; DWQ, Ma'iyya Saniyya, 'Arabī, S/1/8/5 (original no. 39, pt. 1), doc. no. 15, p. 114, AH 20 Muḥarram 1266 / 6 December 1849 CE. On the history of the School of Midwives, see Fahmy, "Women, Medicine and Power."

102. Kuhnke, *Lives at Risk,* 80, 81.

103. DWQ, Dīwān al-Jihādiyya, reg. no. 440, doc. no. 246, p. 238, AH 28 Ramaḍān 1264 / 28 August 1848 CE; DWQ, Dīwān al-Jihādiyya, reg. no. 440, doc. no. 247, p. 238, AH 4 Shawwāl 1264 / 3 September 1848 CE. These two documents explicitly say that because the Muslim 'Īd al-Fiṭr at the end of Ramaḍān would coincide with the beginning of the Coptic year, it would be necessary to prevent both Muslims and Copts from visiting cemeteries.

104. For a description of these funerary lamentations (*'adīd,* or *nadb*) see Lane, *Manners and Customs,* 517; Gaston Maspero, *Chansons populaires recuillies dans la Haute-Égypte de 1900–1914 pendant les inspections du services des antiguités* (Cairo: Imprémerie de l'Institut Français d'Archéologie Orientale, 1914), 134–136; and Samīḥ 'Abd al-Ghaffār Sha'lān, *Al-Mawt fī al-Ma'thūrat al-Sha'biyya* (Cairo: 'Ayn lil-Dirāsat wa'l-Buḥūth al-Insāniyya wa'l-Ijtimā'iyya, 2000), 271–340.

105. The religious opposition to dissection throughout human history, and not only in Islamic lands, is something that is stressed in the introduction to the first medical book that Būlāq Press published: A. L. J. Bayle, *Al-Qawl al-Ṣarīḥ fī 'Ilm al-Tashrīḥ,* trans. Yūḥannā 'Anḥūrī, ed. Aḥmad Ḥasan al-Rashīdī and Muḥammad al-Harrāwī (Cairo: Būlāq, 1832). This was a translation of A. L. J. Bayle, *Traité élémentaire d'anatomie, ou Description succincte des organs et des éléments organiques qui composent le corps humain* (Paris: Librarie de Deville Cavellin, 1833).

106. Marie-Christine Pouchelle, *The Body and Surgery in the Middle Ages,* trans. Rosemary Morris (New Brunswick, NJ: Rutgers University Press, 1990), 82.

107. Katharine Park, "The Criminal and the Saintly Body: Autopsy and Dissection in Renaissance Italy," *Renaissance Quarterly* 47, no. 1 (1994): 4.

108. Park, "The Criminal and the Saintly Body," 12.

109. Park, "The Criminal and the Saintly Body," 12.

110. Carlino, *Books of the Body,* 169.

111. Carlino, *Books of the Body,* 294–295, 202.

112. Carlino, *Books of the Body,* 84. See also Linebaugh's classical study: Peter Linebaugh, "The Tyburn Riot against the Surgeons," in *Albion's Fatal Tree: Crime and Society in Eighteenth-Century England,* ed. Douglas Hay et al. (New York: Pantheon Books, 1975), 65–117.

113. Michel Foucault, *The Birth of the Clinic: An Archaeology of Medical Perception,* trans. A. M. Sheridan Smith (New York: Vintage Books, 1994), 125–126.

114. On Bichat, see Foucault, *Birth of the Clinic,* chap. 8.

115. Emilie Savage-Smith, "Attitudes toward Dissection in Medieval Islam," *Journal of the History of Medicine and Allied Sciences* 50 (1995): 109.

116. Dr. Seisson, who was professor of physiology at Abū Zaʿbal, reiterates the same view. In an 1836 textbook on physiology, he wrote, "Physiology as an art did not exist when dissection was forbidden due to the prohibition [*taḥrīj*] against opening cadavers [that was believed] violated their sanctity [*intihāk ḥurmatihā*]." Seisson, *Isʿāf al-Marḍā min ʿIlm Manāfiʿ al-Aʿḍā,* trans. Yūḥannā ʿAnḥūrī, Ibrāhīm al-Disūqī, and ʿAlī Haybā, ed. Muḥammad al-Harrāwī (Cairo: Būlāq, AH 1252/1836 CE), 2.

117. On the different *isnād*s of this hadith and the *fiqhī* reasoning to allow for dissection regardless, see Ayman Muḥammad Ḥatmal, *Shahādat Ahl al-Khibra wa Aḥkāmuhā: Dirāsa Fiqhiyya Muqārana* (Amman: Dār al-Ḥāmid, 2007), 202–103. See also Muaḥmmad ʿAlī al-Bār, "Al-Tashrīḥ: ʿUlūmuhu wa Aḥkāmuhu," *Majallat al-Majmaʿ al-Fiqhī al-Islamī* 6, no. 8 (1994), 177–199.

118. Savage-Smith, "Attitudes toward Dissection."

119. Savage-Smith, "Attitudes toward Dissection," 71.

120. For *ḥisba* and the *muḥtasib,* see chapter 4.

121. Savage-Smith, "Attitudes toward Dissection," 82.

122. Savage-Smith, "Attitudes toward Dissection," 89.

123. Savage-Smith, "Attitudes toward Dissection," 92.

124. Emily Savage-Smith, "Medicine in Medieval Islam," in *The Cambridge History of Science,* vol. 2, *Medieval Science,* ed. David C. Lindberg and Michael H. Shank (Cambridge: Cambridge University Press, 2013), 156.

125. ʿAbd al-ʿAzīz ʿAbdallāh Ibn Bāz, *Ḥukm Tashrīḥ Juthath al-Muslimīn* (Cairo: al-Markaz al-Salafī lil-Kitāb, 1982).

126. Abū Muḥammad ʿAlī Ibn Aḥmad Ibn Saʿīd Ibn Ḥazm, *Al-Muḥallā,* 11 vols. (Cairo: Al-Munīriyya, 1929–34), 5:166 (question no. 606).

127. For a more recent study that summarizes theological debates for and against dissection, see ʿAbd al-ʿAzīz Khalīfa al-Qassār, *Ḥukm Tashrīh al-Insān Bayn al-Shariʿa wa'l-Qānūn* (Beirut: Dār Ibn Ḥazm, 1999), chap. 3.

128. Rashīd Riḍā, "Istftā' ʿan al-Kashf al-Ṭibbī ʿalā al-Mayyit," *Al-Manār* 10 (1907–8): 358–359; Riḍā, "Al-Kashf al-Ṭibbī ʿalā al-Mawtā wa-Ta'khīr al-Dafn," *Al-Manār* 13 (1910): 100–101.

129. Quoted in Vardit Respler-Chaim, "Postmortem Examinations in Egypt," in *Islamic Legal Interpretation: Muftis and Their Fatwas,* ed. Muḥammad Khalid Masud, Brinkley Messick, and David Powers (Cambridge, MA: Harvard University Press, 1996), 281.

130. Aḥmad al-Damanhūrī, "Muntahā al-Taṣrīḥ bi-Khulāṣat al-Qawl al-Ṣarīḥ fī ʿilm al-Tashrīḥ," unpublished manuscript, MS Maktabat al-Azhar, Ṭibb 5660 (Cairo, 1250), fol. 1. For the inherent ambiguity of the term *tashrīḥ,* see Savage-Smith, "Attitudes toward Dissection," 68–69.

131. Peter Gran, *Islamic Roots of Capitalism: Egypt 1760–1840* (Austin: University of Texas Press, 1979), 171. On Ibn al-Nafīs's practice of dissection, see Fancy,

Science and Religion, 111; and Sulaiman Qataya, "Ibnul-Nafees Had Dissected the Human Body," in *Proceeding of the Second International Conference on Islamic Medicine,* 6 vols., ed. Ahmed Ragai El-Gindy and Hakeem Mohammad Zahoorul Hasan, (Kuwait: Munaẓẓamat al-Ṭibb al-Islāmī, 1982), 2:306–312.

132. For more details on this point, see Fahmy, "Women, Medicine and Power."

133. DWQ, Ma'iyya Saniyya, S/1/8/10 (original no. 46), doc. no. 968, p. 1117, 7 Shawwāl 1266 / 16 August 1850.

134. DWQ, Ḍabṭiyyat Miṣr, L/1/5/2 (original no. 185), doc. no. 31, p. 95, AH 28 Sha'bān 1277 / 11 March 1861 CE.

135. DWQ, Dīwān Taftīsh Ṣiḥḥat al-Maḥrūsa, M/5/11 (original no. 226), doc. no. 27, p. 113, AH 11 Shawwāl 1290 / 2 December 1873 CE; DWQ, Dīwān al-Dākhiliyya, Daftar Qayd al-Awāmir al-Karīma, reg. no. 1310, order no. 141, p. 42, AH 27 Dhū al-Ḥijja 1274 / 10 July 1858 CE.

136. DWQ, Majlis al-Khuṣūṣī, S/11/3/1 (original no. 1), doc. no. 4, p. 1, AH 2 Jumādā II 1286 / 9 September 1869 CE. On the tension between the Islamic imperative of prompt burial and the authorities' insistence on a waiting period before internment, see On Barak, *On Time* (Berkeley: University of California Press, 2013), 108–110.

137. For a comparison with present-day Egypt examining the tension between religious scholars and doctors over the definition of death, see Hamdy, *Our Bodies,* chap. 2.

138. Pierre Augustin Béclard, *Al-Tashrīḥ al-'Āmm* [*Éléments d'anatomie générale, où Description de tous les genres d'organes qui composent le corps humain*], trans. 'Issawī al-Naḥrāwī (Cairo: Būlāq, 1845), 3.

139. Béclard, *Al-Tashrīḥ al-'Āmm,* 53.

140. The biographical information in this paragraph is from Muḥammad al-Shabāsī, *Al-Tanwīr fī Qawā'id al-Taḥḍīr* (Cairo: Būlāq, AH 1264/1848 CE), second preface, 4–5.

141. Jean Cruveilhier, *Al-Tanqīḥ al-Waḥīd fī al-Tashrīḥ al-Khāṣṣ al-Jadīd,* 3 vols., ed. Muḥammad Ibn 'Umar al-Tūnisī and Sālim 'Awaḍ al-Qanayātī, trans. Muḥammad al-Shabāsī (Cairo: Būlāq, AH 1266 /1850 CE). Būlāq Press could not reproduce the wonderful illustrations of the original French work, however, which remain unrivaled in the history of medical illustration.

142. DWQ, Dīwān al-Jihādiyya, reg. 437, doc. no. 54, p. 51, AH 6 Dhū al-Ḥijja 1262 / 1 December 1846 CE.

143. Shabāsī, *Al-Tanwīr,* second preface, 5.

144. Carlino, *Books of the Body,* 216.

145. Ruth Richardson, *Death, Dissection and the Destitute* (London: Penguin, 1988), 54.

146. Shabāsī, *Al-Tanwīr,* 2.

147. Shabāsī, *Al-Tanwīr,* 3.

148. Shabāsī, *Al-Tanwīr,* 4.

149. Shabāsī, *Al-Tanwīr,* 434.

150. Shabāsī, *Al-Tanwīr,* 443.

151. This is a reference to Quran 94:1 and also a play on the word *tashrīḥ,* or dissection.

152. Bayle, *Al-Qawl al-Ṣarīḥ,* 1.

153. Ḥusayn al-Rashīdī, *Kitāb al-Aqribādhīn* (Cairo: Būlāq, 1842), 1.

154. Nicolas Perron, *Al-Djawāhir al-Saniyya fī'l-A'māl al-Kīmāwiyya,* 3 vols., ed. and trans. Muḥammad al-Tūnisī, Muḥammad al-Harrāwī, Darwīsh Zaydān, and Ḥusayn Ghānim, (Cairo, Būlāq, AH 1260/1844 CE), 1:1.

155. DWQ, Muḥāfaẓat Miṣr, L/1/5/1 (original no. 183), doc. no. 150, from Taftīsh al-Ṣiḥḥa to al-Ḍabṭiyya, pp. 147–148, AH 18 Dhū al-Qa'da 1276 / 7 June 1860 CE; DWQ, Muḥāfaẓat Miṣr, L/1/20/5 (original no. 1043), case no. 36, pp. 162–165, AH 18 Shawwāl 1277 / 29 April 1861 CE. See also the significant follow-up that took place three years later: DWQ, Ma'iyya Saniyya, Awāmir, S/1/1/24 (original no. 1907), Khedival Order to Ḍabṭiyyat Miṣr no. 32, p. 80, AH 13 Sha'bān 1280 / 23 January 1864 CE.

156. DWQ, Muḥāfaẓat Miṣr, L/1/27/2 (original no. 1976), order no. 3716, p. 20, AH 14 Dhū al-Qa'da 1275 / 15 June 1859 CE. Despite the fact that exhumed body was in an advanced state of decomposition, the second postmortem revealed enough to lead authorities to suspect that the first exam had been faulty. As a result, the original doctor was accused of grave negligence and dismissed from service. See also the comparable case of 'Alī al-Qazzāz, a sixty-six-year-old village barber who claimed that a recently deceased woman from his village, Salīma, had died after her husband had burned her tongue. However, the autopsy established the cause of death to have been a stomach inflammation, and al-Qazzāz's claim was dismissed. The barber was sentenced to six months in prison for making a false accusation. See DWQ, Dīwān al-Tarsāna, M/14/4, p. 180, AH 3 Ṣafar 1285 / 26 May 1868 CE.

157. DWQ, Muḥāfaẓat Miṣr, L/1/27/2 (original no. 1976), doc. no. 446, p. 56, AH 29 Muḥarram 1276 / 29 August 1859 CE.

158. The police turned down her request for lack of sufficient evidence. See DWQ, Majlis al-Aḥkām, S/7/10/1 (original no. 663), case no. 178, pp. 92–93, AH 3 Muḥarram 1275 / 13 August 1858 CE.

159. DWQ, Niẓārat al-Dākhiliyya, Mukātabāt 'Arabī, box no. 15, petition, AH 24 Muḥarram 1292 / 2 March 1875 CE. There are two documents that gave information about the subsequent investigation of the matter: DWQ, Niẓārat al-Dākhiliyya, Mukātabāt 'Arabī, box no. 15, letter from Governor of Port Said to the Interior Minister, AH 4 Ṣafar 1292 / 12 March 1875 CE; and DWQ, Niẓārat al-Dākhiliyya, Mukātabāt 'Arabī, box no. 15, letter from Governor of Port Said to the Interior Minister, AH 10 Ṣafar 1292 / 18 March 1875 CE.

160. Sandwith, "History of Kasr-el-Aini," 10. A picture of the plaque can be found in Mināwī, *Tārīkh al-Nahḍa al-Ṭibbiyya,* 86.

CHAPTER TWO. *SIYĀSA,* THE FORGOTTEN CODE

1. On *ḥajb* (exclusion from inheritance), see Averroës, *Distinguished Jurist's Primer,* 2 vols., trans. Imran Ahsan Khan Nyazee (Reading: Garnet, 1996), 2:425–

246; and A. Hussain, *The Islamic Law of Succession* (Riyadh: Darussalam, 2005), 52–61.

2. DWQ, Majlis al-Aḥkām, S/7/10/109, case no. 362, AH 3 Rajab 1294 / 14 July 1877 CE.

3. Most notably Rudolph Peters, whose work is summarized in Khaled Fahmy, "Rudolph Peters and the History of Modern Egyptian Law," in *Legal Documents as Sources for the History of Muslim Societies: Studies in Honour of Professor Rudolph Peters,* ed. Maaike Van Berkel, Leon Buskens, and Petra Sijpesteijn (Leiden: Brill, 2017), 12–35. See also 'Imād Hilāl, *Al-Fallāḥ wa'l-Sulṭa wa'l-Qānūn* (Cairo: Dār al-Kutub wa'l-Wathāi'q al-Qawmiyya, 2007); and Khaled Fahmy, "Justice, Law and Pain in Khedival Egypt," in *Standing Trial: Law and the Person in the Modern Middle East,* ed. Baudouin Dupret (London: I.B. Tauris, 2004), 85–116; Fahmy, "The Police and the People in Nineteenth-Century Egypt," *Die Welt des Islams,* 39 (1999): 1–38; and Fahmy, "The Anatomy of Justice: Forensic Medicine and Criminal Law in Nineteenth-Century Egypt," *Islamic Law and Society,* 6 (1999): 224–271.

4. See, for example, Gabriel Baer, "Tanzimat in Egypt: The Panel Code," *Bulletin of the School of Oriental and African Studies,* 26 (1963): 29–49.

5. Sālim, *Tārīkh al-Qaḍā.*

6. Byron Cannon, "Social Tension and the Teaching of European Law in Egypt before 1900," *History of Education Quarterly* 15, no. 3 (1975): 299–315.

7. J. Anderson, *Islamic Law in the Modern World* (London: Stevens and Sons, 1959), 22–23.

8. This is very much the argument put forward by Bernard Lewis in his classic article "The Impact of the French Revolution on Turkey: Some Notes on the Transition of Ideas," *Journal of World History* 1 (1953): 105–125, esp. 118–119. See also Niyazi Berkes, *The Development of Secularism in Turkey* (Montreal: McGill University Press, 1964).

9. Aḥmad Fatḥī Zaghlūl, *Al-Muḥāmāh* (Cairo: Maṭba'at al-Ma'ārif, 1900), 158.

10. Farhat Ziadeh, *Lawyers, the Rule of Law and Liberalism in Modern Egypt* (Stanford: Hoover Institution, 1968), 10. For al-Jabartī's critique of this court, see Jabartī, *'Ajā'ib,* 3:19–20.

11. Ziadeh, *Lawyers,* vii.

12. Cromer, *Modern Egypt,* 2:516.

13. Jacques Tagher, *Ḥarakat al-Tarjamah bi-Miṣr Khilāl al-Qarn al-Tāsi' 'Ashr* (Cairo: Dār al-Ma'ārif, 1945), 99.

14. Sālim, *Tārīkh al-Qaḍā',* 1:28.

15. 'Azīz Khānkī, "Al-Tashrī' wa'l-Qaḍā' Qabl Inshā' al-Maḥākim al-Ahliyya," in *Al-Kitāb al-Dhahabī lil-Maḥākim al-Ahliyya,* vol. 1 (Cairo: Būlāq, 1937), 92, 93. See also Zaghlūl, *Al-Muḥāmāh,* 172, 183.

16. Muḥammad Nūr Faraḥāt, *Al-Mujtama' wa'l-Sharī'a wa'l-Qānūn* (Cairo: Dār al-Hilāl, 1986), 128–129, 137, 141.

17. The scholarship on the Mixed Courts is extensive, but see the following important works: Jasper Y. Brinton, *The Mixed Courts of Egypt* (New Haven: Yale University Press, 1968); and Byron Cannon, *Politics of Law and the Courts in*

Nineteenth-Century Egypt (Salt Lake City: University of Utah Press, 1988); and Will Hanley, *Identifying with Nationality: Europeans, Ottomans, and Egyptians in Alexandria* (New York: Columbia University Press, 2017). Significantly, Hanley's pathbreaking study uses court records from the Mixed Courts.

18. Jeremy Bentham, *Kitāb Uṣūl al-Sharā'i'*, trans. Aḥmad Fatḥī Zaghlūl (Cairo: Būlāq, 1892).

19. Edmond Demolins, *Sirr Taṭawwur al-Inkilīz al-Saksūniyyīn,* trans. Aḥmad Fatḥī Zaghlūl (Cairo: Al-Taraqqī, 1899).

20. For political and intellectual profiles of Zaghlūl, see Aḥmad Zakariyya al-Shilliq, *Aḥmad Fatḥī Zaghlūl wa'l-Āthār al-Fatḥiyya* (Cairo: al-Hay'a al-'Āmma li-Quṣūr al-Thaqāfa, 2006); and Shilliq, *Ru'ya fī Taḥdīth al-Fikr al-Miṣrī: Aḥmad Fatḥī Zaghlūl wa Qaḍiyyat al-Taghrīb* (Cairo: Al-Hay'a al-Miṣriyya al-'Āmma lil-Kitāb, 1987).

21. Zaghlūl, *Al-Muḥāmāh,* 222, 239–243.

22. See, for example, Zaghlūl, *Al-Muḥāmāh,* 169–170.

23. Khānkī, "Al-Tashrī' wa'l-Qaḍā'," 1:62–96.

24. Khānkī, "Al-Tashrī' wa'l-Qaḍā'," 1:95–96.

25. Di-Capua, *Gatekeepers.*

26. On the foundation of the Royal Archives, see Di-Capua, *Gatekeepers,* chap. 3.

27. On the changing meaning of the word *maḥkama,* see Ibrāhīm Pasha Ḥasan, *Al-Dustūr al-Mar'ī fī'l-Ṭibb al-Shar'ī* (Cairo: Al-Maṭba'a al-Ṭibbiyya al-Durriyya, AH 1306/1888–89 CE), 9. For more on this point, see chapter 5 of this book.

28. See, for example, Judith Tucker, *Women in Nineteenth Century Egypt* (Cambridge: Cambridge University Press, 1984); and Leslie Peirce, *Morality Tales: Law and Gender in the Ottoman Court of Aintab* (Berkeley: University of California Press, 2003). See also, Dror Ze'evi, "The Use of Ottoman Shari'a Court Records as a Source for Middle Eastern Social History: A Reappraisal," *Islamic Law and Society* 5, no. 1 (1998): 35–56.

29. See, for example, Kenneth Cuno, *The Pasha's Peasants: Land, Society and Economy in Lower Egypt, 1740–1848* (Cambridge: Cambridge University Press, 1992); and A. 'Abd al-Raḥmān Abd al-Raḥīm, *Al-Rīf al-Miṣrī fī al-Qarn al-Thāmin 'Ashr* (Cairo: 'Ain Shams University Press, 1974).

30. See, for example, Boğac Ergene, *Local Court, Provincial Society, and Justice in the Ottoman Empire: Legal Practice and Dispute Resolution in Cankiri and Kastamonu (1652–1744)* (Leiden: Brill, 2003).

31. For a background on this law and earlier penal legislation in Egypt, see Rudolph Peters, *Crime and Punishment in Islamic Law: Theory and Practice from the Sixteenth to the Twenty-First Century* (Cambridge: Cambridge University Press, 2005), 136–137.

32. Articles 1–3, chapter 1 of the Humāyūnī Law, reproduced in Zaghlūl, *Al-Muḥāmāh,* appendix, 157.

33. Peters, *Crime and Punishment in Islamic Law,* 39. On *ḥuqūq al-'ibād* and *ḥuqūq Allah,* see Peirce, *Morality Tales,* 89.

34. Bernard Weiss, *The Spirit of Islamic Law* (Athens, GA: University of Georgia Press, 1998), 152–153.

35. Article 12, chapter 1 of the Humāyūnī Law, reproduced in Zaghlūl, *Al-Muḥāmāh,* appendix, 159.

36. DWQ, Muḥāfaẓat Miṣr, L/1/20/8 (original no. 1108), case no. 10, pp. 171–172, AH 7 Ṣafar 1279 / 4 August 1862 CE. Due to the inconsistency of the eyewitnesses, Khālid Efendi could not be convicted in the shariʿa court. In the *siyāsa majlis,* however, he was found guilty of manslaughter and sentenced to five years in prison and banishment to Turkey after serving his prison sentence.

37. For the role of forensic medicine in adjudicating similar cases, see chapter 5.

38. DWQ, Majlis al-Aḥkām, S/7/10/29 (original no. 633), case no. 39, pp. 44–48, AH 19 Jumādā I 1282 / 10 October 1865 CE.

39. DWQ, Majlis al-Khuṣūṣī, S/11/8/8 (original no. 71), decree no. 28, pp. 113–116, AH 17 Jumādā I 1282 / 7 November 1865 CE.

40. DWQ, Majlis al-Khuṣūṣī, S/11/8/8 (original no. 71), decree no. 28, pp. 113–116, AH 17 Jumādā I 1282 / 7 November 1865 CE, esp. articles 10 and 11.

41. DWQ, Maʿiyya Saniyya, Turkī, S/1/55/23 (original no. 539), doc. no. 7, p. 98, AH 30 Rabī' I 1282 / 21 September 1865 CE.

42. See Jane Caplan and John Torpey, eds., *Documenting Individual Identity: The Development of State Practices in the Modern World* (Princeton: Princeton University Press, 2001); and Daniel Lord Smail, *Imaginary Cartographies: Possession and Identity in Late Medieval Marseille* (Ithaca: Cornell University Press, 2000), 188–221.

43. See, for example, Muwaffaq al-Dīn Abū Muḥammad ʿAbd Allāh b. Aḥmad b. Muḥammad Ibn Qudāma, *Al-Mughnī,* 10 vols. (Cairo: Maktabat al-Qāhira, 1970), 10:57.

44. Brinkley Messick, "Evidence: From Memory to Archive," *Islamic Law and Society* 9, no. 2 (2002): 256. See also Messick, "Written Identities: Legal Subjects in an Islamic State," *History of Religions* 38, no. 1 (1998), 25–51. Messick notes, "With respect to witnesses unknown to the court, which was the typical case, further identifiers were required," (40).

45. See, for example, 'Abd al-Rāziq Ibrāhīm 'Īsā, *Tārīkh al-Qaḍā' fī Misr al-ʿUthmāniyya, 1517–1798* (Cairo: Al-Hay'a al-Misriyya al-ʿĀmma lil-Kitāb, 1998), 304.

46. Claude Cahen, "A propos des shuhud," *Studia Islamica* 31 (1970): 75.

47. Ron Shaham, *The Expert Witness in Islamic Courts: Medicine and Crafts in the Service of Law* (Chicago: University of Chicago Press, 2010), 6.

48. Jeanette Wakin, *The Function of Documents in Islamic Law* (Albany: State University of New York Press, 1972), 7.

49. Ronald C. Jennings, "Kadi, Court, and Legal Procedure in 17th Century Kayseri: The Kadi and the Legal System," *Studia Islamica* 48 (1978): 146–147; 'Īsā, *Tārīkh al-Qaḍā',* 305.

50. Jennings, "Kadi," 143–145; Shaham, *Expert Witness,* 6.

51. DWQ, Mudīriyyat al-Daqahliyya, Maḥkāmat al-Manṣūra al-Sharʿiyya, reg. no. 2 (original no. 14), case no. 190, p. 20, AH 28 Rajab 1282/17 December 1865 CE.

For the role of the *shuhūd al-hāl* in identifying litigants, see Messick, "Evidence," 255–256; and Muḥammad Nūr Faraḥāt, *Al-Qaḍā' al-Shar'ī fī Misr ī al-'Aṣr al-'Uthmānī* (Cairo: Al-Hay'a al-Mirṣiyya al-'Āmma lil-Kitāb, 1988), 77.

52. DWQ, Majlis al-Aḥkām, 7/10/31 (original no. 635), case no. 26, pp. 15–17, AH 8 Jumādā I 1282 / 29 September 1865 CE.

53. DWQ, Ḍabṭiyyat Miṣr, L/2/67/4, case no. 33, pp. 11–13, AH 8 Rabī' II 1270 / 8 January 1854 CE. Dīwān Kethuda, also known as Dīwān Khidīwī, was concerned with domestic, nonmilitary affairs and was presided over by the pasha's deputy, his *kethuda,* hence its name. Most of its responsibilities were taken over by Dīwān al-Dākhiliyya (the Department of the Interior) when it was established during Ismā'īl's reign.

54. This is my best guess at the name, as the original document is nearly illegible at this point.

55. DWQ, Ḍabṭiyyat Miṣr, L/2/6/3 (original no. 2030), case no. 115, pp. 87–89, AH 3 Safar 1295 / 6 February 1878 CE. Sayyida was found guilty of theft, and it was explicitly stated that using an alias made her even more suspicious. See also this 1854 case involving a slave caught using three different names: DWQ, Muḥāfaẓat Miṣr, L/1/2/1, doc. no. 4, from the Muḥāfaẓa to the Ḍabṭiyya, p. 14, AH 8 Rabī' I 1271 / 29 November 1854 CE; and this 1877 case concerning a woman named Imbāraka, daughter of Muṣṭafā al-Sabbākh, who claimed that her name was Faṭma, daughter of 'Alī Muḥammad, when she was caught stealing some brass kitchen utensils: DWQ, Muḥāfaẓat Miṣr, L/2/6/1 (original no. 2027), case 48, pp. 89–91, AH 16 Sha'bān 1294 / 26 August 1877 CE.

56. DWQ, Ḍabṭiyyat Miṣr, L/2/6/2 (original no. 2028), case no. 113, pp. 23, 26, AH 8 Shawwāl 1294 / 5 October 1878 CE.

57. DWQ, Ḍabṭiyyat Miṣr, L/2/40/9 (original no. 529), Wārid 'Arḍḥālāt, letter from Muḥāfaẓat Misr no. 1117, p. 48, AH 8 Rabī' I 1279 / 3 September 1862 CE.

58. DWQ, Ḍabṭiyyat Miṣr, L/2/11/12 (original no. 565), Ṣādir 'Arḍḥālāt, letter to Muḥāfaẓat Miṣr no. 9, p. 7, AH 18 Rabī' I 1279 / 13 September 1862 CE.

59. DWQ, Ḍabṭiyyat Miṣr, L/2/11/12 (original no. 565), Ṣādir 'Arḍḥālāt, letter to Muḥāfaẓat Miṣr no. 214, p. 85, AH 18 Rabī' I 1279 / 13 September 1862 CE.

60. DWQ, Majlis al-Aḥkām, Daftar Majmū' Umūr Jinā'iyya, p. 47, law no. 4, AH 1261/1845 CE. This is a unique and highly important register compiled during Khedive Ismā'īl's reign in an attempt to assemble a list of previous criminal legislation. A heavily edited version of the register was published in 2011: 'Imād Hilāl, *Wathā'iq al-Tashrī' al-Jinā'ī al-Miṣrī: Sijill Majmū' Umūr Jinā'īyah* (Cairo: Maṭba'at Dār al-Kutub w'al-Wathā'iq al-Qawmīyya, 2011).

61. On modern techniques of establishing identity, see Caplan and Torpey, *Documenting Individual Identity.*

62. Smail, *Imaginary Cartographies,* 192.

63. Mine Ener, *Managing Egypt's Poor and the Politics of Benevolence, 1800–1952* (Princeton: Princeton University Press, 2003), 30–37.

64. DWQ, Ḍabṭiyyat Miṣr, L/2/6/3 (original no. 2030), case no. 95, p. 77, AH 22 Muḥarram 1295 / 26 January 1878 CE.

65. DWQ, Majlis al-Aḥkām, S/7/10/1 (original no. 663) case no. 123, pp. 55–56, AH 21 Dhū al-Ḥijja 1274 / 2 August 1858 CE.

66. DWQ, Dīwān al-Tarsāna, M/14/4, (original no. 955), p. 23, AH 8 Jumādā I 1283 / 18 September 1866 CE. This is the case file of of Muḥammad Ḥasanayn, who also called himself Muḥammad ʿAzzūz.

67. Quoted in Rudolph Peters, "'For His Correction and as a Deterrent Example for Others': Mehmed Ali's First Criminal Legislation (1829–1830)," *Islamic Law and Society* 6 (1999): 164–193.

68. DWQ, Maʿiyya Saniyya, ʿArabī, S/1/19/2 (original no. 1909), order no. 8, pp. 12–13, AH 12 Jumādā II 1280 / 24 November 1863 CE.

69. Filīb Jallād, *Qāmūs al-Idāra wa'l-Qaḍā'*, 7 vols. (Alexandria: Lāghūdākī, 1899), 3:153.

70. Yūsuf Āṣāf, *al-Taʿdīlāt al-Qānūniyya Allatī udkhilat ʿalā al-Qānūn al-Ahlī al-Miṣrī* (Cairo: Al-Maṭbaʿa al-ʿUmūmiyya, 1895), 23–29.

71. Fahmy, *All the Pasha's Men*, 106.

72. DWQ, Muḥāfaẓat Iskandariyya, Awāmir, box no. 1, doc. no. 4, AH 14 Rabīʿ II 1236 / 8 January 1821 CE.

73. DWQ, Dīwān Khidīwī, S/2/30/17 (original no. 793), doc. no. 156, p. 56, AH 12 Rabīʿ I 1249 / 30 July 1833 CE.

74. DWQ, Dīwān Khidīwī, S/2/18/1 (original no. 654), unnumbered doc., pp. 138–140, AH 24 Dhū al-Ḥijja 1266/1 October 1850 CE. When the Passport Department was late in compiling these registers, causing a backlog, the Alexandria Governorate wrote a reprimand letter: DWQ, Muḥāfaẓat Iskandariyya, L/3/1/33 (original no. 52), doc. no. 24, p. 35, AH 28 Dhū al-Qaʿda 1268 / 14 September 1852 CE.

75. DWQ, Majlis al-Khuṣūṣī, S/11/8/6 (original no. 68), doc. no. 63, pp. 99–100, AH 12 Dhū al- Qaʿda 1280 / 19 April 1864 CE.

76. Article 13, chapter 3 of the Humāyūnī Law, reproduced in Zaghlūl, *Al-Muḥāmāh,* appendix, 165.

77. DWQ, Ḍabṭiyya Miṣr, L/2/6/2 (original no. 2028), case no. 167, pp. 87–89, AH 8 Dhū al-Qaʿda 1294 / 14 November 1877 CE. This was a case of four peasants who arrived separately in Cairo and formed a gang to drug and rob people. After their case had been investigated, and while it was still pending a final sentence, only one of the peasants was released, as he could secure a *ḍamān.* The other three could not. Eventually, two of the others found people who could give them *ḍamān*s, and only one remained in jail. For more on this case, see chapter 5.

78. DWQ, Majlis al-Aḥkām, S/7/33/1, p. 236, decree dated AH 5 Rabīʿ II 1269 / 16 January 1853 CE.

79. DWQ, Majlis al-Aḥkām, S/7/33/1, order from Dīwān al-Māliyya, p. 179, AH 24 Shawwāl 1269 / 31 July 1853 CE.

80. DWQ, Majlis al-Aḥkām, S/7/33/1, order from Dīwān al-Māliyya, p. 179, AH 24 Rabī' I 1270 / 25 December 1853 CE.

81. Articles 1–3, chapter 1 of the Humāyūnī Law, reproduced in Zaghlūl, *Al-Muḥāmāh,* appendix, 157–158.

82. "Sūrat Ḥarakāt al-Afandiyya Ḥukkām al-Shar' fi Ijrā' al-Aaḥkām al-Shar'iyya," Article 4 of the Humāyūnī Law, reproduced in Jallād, *Qāmūs,* 2:104.

83. Rudolph Peters, "Murder on the Nile: Homicide Trials in 19th Century Egyptian Shari'a Courts," *Die Welt des Islams* 30 (1990): 111.

84. Baber Johansen, "Signs as Evidence: The Doctrine of Ibn Taymiyya (1263–1328) and Ibn Qayyim al-Jawziyya (d. 1351) on Proof," *Islamic Law and Society* 9, no. 2 (2002): 179.

85. Johansen, "Signs," 169.

86. Messick, "Written Identities," 40.

87. Johansen, "Signs," 169, 177, 178–179.

88. Peirce, *Morality Tales,* 380.

89. See Messick, "Evidence," 231–232.

90. In trials for crimes other than homicide, however, "testimonies conveying an admission made by the defendant out of court or what two other qualified witnesses have declared out of court (*shahāda 'alā al-shahāda*) are accepted" (Peters, *Crime and Punishment in Islamic Law,* 12). For more on this kind of *shahāda,* see Messick, *The Calligraphic State: Textual Domination and History in a Muslim Society* (Berkeley: University of California Press, 1993), 207.

91. By contrast, the defendant can present his or her evidence in the absence of the plaintiff. See Messick, "Evidence," 240.

92. Messick, "Evidence," 237.

93. Wael Hallaq, "*Qādī*s Communicating: Legal Change and the Law of Documentary Evidence," *Al-Qanṭara* 20 (1999): 439.

94. Wakin, *Function of Documents,* 4. For an example of the strong suspicion of *khuṭūṭ* (written documents), see Muḥammad Ibn Abī Bakr Ibn Qayyim al-Jawziyya, *Al-Ṭuruq al-Ḥukmiyya fi'l-Siyāsa al-Shar'iyya* (Cairo: Al-Ābāb, AH 1317/1899–1900 CE), 188. However, it is now evident that shari'a did accept written documents as valid means to establish legal proof, especially in cases concerning landed property, and Baber Johansen has demonstrated that jurists have accepted written documents to establish legal proof from as early as the eleventh century. See Baber Johansen, "Formes de langage et fonctions publiques: Stéréotypes, témoins et offices dans la preuve par l'Érit en droit Musulman," *Arabica* 44, no. 3 (1997): 333–376.

95. Wakin, *Function of Documents,* 7.

96. Messcik, "Evidence," 263. There is a similar attitude toward written evidence in English common law. See J. A. Jolowicz, "Orality and Immediacy in English Civil Procedure," *Boletín Mexicano de Derrecho Comparado* 8 (1975): 595–608.

97. Article 1736 states, "Writing and seals are not to be admitted alone. However, if they are free of forgery, then they can be relied on." Article 1737 states, "Sultanic edicts and the contents of imperial registers can be relied on as they are free of forgery." Reproduced in Jallād, *Qāmūs,* 2:68.

98. Rudolph Peters, "Administrators and Magistrates: The Development of a Secular Judiciary in Egypt, 1842–1871," *Die Welt des Islams* 39 (1999): 394.

99. DWQ, Ḍabṭiyyat Miṣr, L/2/67/4, case 33, pp. 11–13, AH 8 Rabī' II 1270 / 8 January 1854 CE.

100. Reproduced in Zaghlūl, *Al-Muḥāmāh,* appendix, 3. "Two o'clock" means two hours after sunrise. This is what was known as "Arabic time," which measured the start of the day by the sunrise and not by mechanical clocks.

101. Reproduced in Zaghlūl, *Al-Muḥāmāh,* appendix, 57.

102. Reproduced in Zaghlūl, *Al-Muḥāmāh,* appendix, 64. As significant as this line of questioning was, it is important to realize that only in the 1870s was the accused given the right to appear in the *siyāsa* council hearing his or her case. See Peters, *Crime and Punishment in Islamic Law,* 137.

103. Reproduced in Zaghlūl, *Al-Muḥāmāh,* appendix, 74.

104. Reproduced in Zaghlūl, *Al-Muḥāmāh,* appendix, 65.

105. Peters, *Crime and Punishment in Islamic Law,* 9. On torture, see chapter 5.

106. Peters, *Crime and Punishment in Islamic Law,* 12, 13. On the opinion of different *madhhabs* regarding *'ilm al-qāḍī,* see Ibn Qudāma, *Al-Mughnī,* 10:48–49; and Averroës, *Distinguished Jurist's Primer,* 2:565.

107. Thus, being in possession of an instrument of crime—e.g., a wine jug in a case of drinking alcohol, or a knife in a murder case—is not enough to be convicted of a crime; Peters, *Crime and Punishment in Islamic Law,* 15.

108. Averroës, *Distinguished Jurist's Primer,* 2:522.

109. Peters reproduces an 1860 case from Ṭanṭa in the Delta in which the qadi could not find for the plaintiff because there was a slight inconsistency in the witnesses' testimony: one of the witnesses said that the defendant had kicked the victim with his right foot, whereas another witness testified that he kicked him with the left foot. See Peters, *Crime and Punishment in Islamic Law,* 12–13. He also notes that "a testimony or confession to theft ... must mention the word 'theft', and not just 'taking away', and a testimony to unlawful sexual intercourse (*zinā*) must use this technical term and not just any word meaning sexual intercourse" (13).

110. On the strict rules of evidence in these cases, see 'Awda, *Al-Tahsrī' al-Jinā'ī,* 2:315.

111. The September 1858 Five-Article Circular is reproduced in Majlis al-Aḥkām, S/7/10/2 (original no. 664), unnumbered order, p. 32, AH 13 Ṣafar 1275 / 22 September 1858 CE; and Amīn Sāmī, *Taqwīm al-Nīl,* 3 vols. (Cairo: Dār al-Kutub, 1936), 3:294–298.

112. See, for example, DWQ, Dīwān Taftīsh Ṣiḥḥat al-Maḥrūsa, M/5/1 (original no. 163), letter from al-Taftīsh to Cairo Ḍabṭiyya, no. 197, p. 76, AH 14 Jumādā II 1267 / 16 April 1851 CE.

113. Somewhat counterintuitively, *baṣīr,* which literally means "sighted," was sometimes used to refer to the blind. See Fedwa Multi-Douglas, "*Mentalités* and Marginality: Blindness and Mamlûk Civilization," in *The Islamic World from Classical to Modern Times: Essays in Honor of Bernard Lewis,* ed. C.E. Bosworth et al. (Princeton: Darwin Press, 1989), 220.

114. The Iplikhane was a textile workshop located in Būlāq where convicted women were sent to serve their sentences. See Peters, "Egypt in the Age of Triumphant Prison," 27.

115. DWQ, Muḥāfaẓat Miṣr, L/1/20/5 (original no. 1043), case no. 30, pp. 150–151, AH 15 Shawwāl 1277 / 26 April 1861 CE.

116. DWQ, Majlis al-Aḥkām, S/7/10/31 (original no. 635), case no. 26, pp. 15–17, AH 8 Jumādā I 1282 / 29 September 1865 CE.

117. For example, the case of Muḥammad ʿAbd al-Raḥmān's murder, with which this chapter opened, ended with a verdict that stated, "While investigating cases of homicide should not be based on rumors [*ishāʿa*], yet, *there is doubt* that the defendant had been involved in this case; accordingly, he is to be sentenced to five years in prison" (emphasis added). DWQ, Majlis al-Aḥkām, S/7/10/109, case no. 362, AH 3 Rajab 1294 / 14 July 1877 CE.

118. The testimony of the son could not be accepted. See Ibn Qudāma, *Al-Mughnī,* 10:172–173.

119. DWQ, Majlis al-Aḥkām, S/7/10/31 (original no. 635), case no. 24, pp. 12–15, AH 28 Jumādā I 1282 / 19 October 1865 CE (emphasis added). On the different prisons and penal colonies in the Sudan, see Rudolph Peters, "Egypt and the Age of the Triumphant Prison: Legal Punishment in Nineteenth Century Egypt," *Annales Islamologiques* 36 (2002): 253–285, esp. 269–270.

120. DWQ, Majlis al-Aḥkām, S/7/10/31 (original no. 635), case no. 222, pp. 177–178, AH 28 Shawwāl 1282 / 16 March 1866 CE (emphasis added).

121. DWQ, Majlis al-Aḥkām, S/7/10/31 (original no. 635), case no. 222, pp. 177–178, AH 28 Shawwāl 1282 / 16 March 1866 CE.

122. This article stated that public employees who violated any of the regulations or orders of their superiors should be imprisoned for a period ranging from ten days to one month if their negligent act had not resulted in damage (*ḍarar*). If, however, damage did occur, then they should be sentenced for a period of one to six months. Reproduced in Zaghlūl, *Al-Muḥāmāh,* appendix, 176.

123. Rudolph Peters, "The Infatuated Greek: Social and Legal Boundaries in Nineteenth-Century Egypt," *Égypte/Monde Arabe* 34 (1998): 58. I was fortunate enough to find both Filippo's and ʿĪsā al-Ḥabbāk's entries in the prison records: DWQ, Dīwān al-Tarsāna, M/14/2, (original no. 954), p. 154, AH 11 Ṣafar 1281 / 16 July 1864 CE (for Filippo); and DWQ, Dīwān al-Tarsāna, M/14/2, (original no. 954), p. 161, AH 10 Rabīʿ I 1281/13 August 1864 CE (for al-Ḥabbāk).

124. DWQ, Ḍabṭiyyat Miṣr, L/2/6/2 (original no. 2082), case no. 199, pp. 176–178, AH 22 Dhū al-Qaʿda 1294 / 28 November 1877 CE; DWQ, Majlis al-Aḥkām, S/7/10/121 (original no. 751), case no. 441, AH 22 Dhū al-Qaʿda 1295 / 18 November 1878 CE.

125. Peirce, *Morality Tales,* 178–179.

126. D. R. Woolf, "Speech, Text, and Time: The Sense of Hearing and the Sense of the Past in Renaissance England," *Albion* 8, no. 2 (1986): 177.

127. Peters, *Crime and Punishment in Islamic Law,* 70–71.

128. Peirce, *Morality Tales,* 179.

129. On recidivism, see chapter 5.

130. Reproduced in Zaghlūl, *Al-Muḥāmāh,* appendix, 161–162.

131. Reproduced in Zaghlūl, *Al-Muḥāmāh,* appendix, 165.

132. Reproduced in Zaghlūl, *Al-Muḥāmāh,* appendix, 166–167.

133. Peters, "Egypt and the Age of the Triumphant Prison," 268.

134. DWQ, Majlis al-Aḥkām, S/7/10/20 (original no. 622), case no. 697, pp. 108–109, AH 28 Shawwāl 1280 / 6 April 1864 CE.

135. DWQ, Ḍabṭiyyat Iskanadriyya, L/4/18/4 (original no. 1675), case no. 226, pp. 21–22, AH 15 Rabīʿ I 1295 / 9 March 1878 CE.

136. DWQ, Majlis al-Aḥkām, S/7/10/18 (original no. 626), case no. 286, pp. 6–7, AH 28 Jumādā II 1280 / 10 December 1863 CE.

137. Peirce, *Morality Tales,* 315; and Hallaq, *Sharīʿa,* 212.

138. Peters, *Crime and Punishment in Islamic Law,* 135. Despite this, Peters oddly includes his analysis of this period of Egyptian legal history in a chapter titled "The Eclipse of Islamic Criminal Law."

139. Rudolph Peters, "The Origins of Pre-1883 Egyptian Criminal Legislation" (paper presented at the 1996 Annual MESA Meeting, Providence, RI, November 21–24, 1996), 9.

140. For the text of the 1850 Ottoman Penal Code, called Kanun-u Cedid, see Ahmet Akgündüz, *Mukayeseli Islam ve Osmanlı hukuku kılliyatı* (Diyarbakır: Dicle Üniversitesi Hukuk Fakültesi yayınları, 1986), 821–831.

141. According to Abū Ḥanīfa, "Homicide is regarded as intentional if the killer used fire or a sharp weapon or instrument that can cut though the body (such as a sword, a sharp piece of wood or a sharp stone), whereas killing by all other weapons and instruments (hitting with a blunt instrument such as a stick or a large stone, drowning or poisoning) is classified as semi-intentional" (Peters, *Crime and Punishment in Islamic Law,* 43).

142. DWQ, Majlis al-Aḥkām, S/7/10/2 (original no. 664), p. 32, ruling dated AH 13 ṣafar 1275 / 22 September 1858 CE. On this matter, see Peters, *Crime and Punishment in Islamic Law,* 162–163; and Colin Imber, *Ebu's-Su'ud: The Islamic Legal Tradition* (Stanford: Stanford University Press, 1997), 237.

143. The decree creating Majlis al-Aḥkām stipulated that the council should have two *ʿulamāʾ,* a *Ḥanafī* and a *Shāfiʿī,* among its permanent members. See Zaghlūl, *Al-Muḥāmāh,* appendix, 63.

144. The Maʿiyya did not normally adjudicate legal cases, and as such, it was not a *siyāsa* council. However, when Saʿīd Pasha decided to close down all *siyāsa* councils on April 15, 1860, after suspecting that some members were accepting bribes, his own cabinet, the Maʿiyya, took over the task of adjudicating pending cases. Eventually, Saʿīd Pasha was forced to reinstate the councils after a fourteen-month hiatus. For background on this incident, see Sālim, *Tārīkh al-Qaḍāʾ,* 1:34–35.

145. DWQ, Muḥāfaẓat Miṣr, L/1/27/2 (original no. 1976), doc. no. 44, pp. 183, 196, AH 5 Dhū al-Ḥijja 1276 / 24 June 1860 CE.

146. DWQ, Majlis al-Aḥkām, Daftar Qayd al-Iʿlāmāt al-Sharʿiyya, no. 420, case no. 35, p. 36, no date.

147. As an example of how the shariʿa judiciary was streamlined, Peters cites the order issued by Majlis al-Aḥkām in 1858 specifying the amount of the blood money (*diyya*) for a Muslim man: it was to be 15,093.75 piasters for payment in silver or

40,762 piasters for payment in gold. And according to classical doctrine, the choice was left to the defendant. See Peters, *Crime and Punishment in Islamic Law,* 135.

148. For an exhaustive survey of this law, see Peters, "For His Dorrection."

149. Hasanaine al-Besumee, *Egypt under Muḥammad Aly Basha* (London: Smith Elder, 1838), 10. Al-Besumee had obviously been commissioned to write this pamphlet, which was intended to curry favor with the British public and argue his patron's case in London. For a recent analysis of al-Besumee and his aims in writing this pamphlet, see ʻAbd al-Khāliq Lāshīn, *Misriyyāt fī al-Fikr wa-l-Siyāsa* (Cairo: Sīnā, 1993), 55–71.

150. *The Egyptian Railway, or The Interest of England in Egypt* (London: Hope, 1852), 36–37.

151. For information on this dispute, see Baer, "Tanzimat."

152. Peters, *Crime and Punishment in Islamic Law,* 138, 139.

153. As quoted in Zaghlūl, *Al-Muḥāmāh,* appendix, 159.

154. For the history of the foundation of these *siyāsa* councils, see Peters, "Administrators and Magistrates."

155. Burhān al-Dīn Abī al-Wafā' Ibrāhīm Ibn Shams al-Dīn Ibn Farḥūn, *Tabṣirat al-Ḥukkām fī Uṣūl al-Aqḍiyah wa-Manāhij al-Aḥkām,* 2 vols., ed. Jamāl Mar'ashlī (Beirut: Dār al-Kitub al-'Ilmiyya, 1995), 1:115.

156. Imber, *Ebu's-Su'ud.*

157. Johansen, "Signs as Evidence," 191–192.

158. Jørgen Nielsen, *Secular Justice in an Islamic State: Maẓālim under the Bahrī Mamlūks, 662/1264–789/1387* (Leiden: Nederlands Instituut voor het Nabije Ossten, 1985).

159. Yossef Rapoport, "Royal Justice and Religious Law: *Siyāsah* and Shariʿah under the Mamluks," *Mamluk Studies Review* 16 (2012): 89.

160. Rapoport, "Royal Justice," 88.

161. Al-Maqrīzī, among many others, objected to *siyāsa* by polemically arguing that it was based on the Mongol *yāsā.* See Taqī al-Dīn Aḥmad b. ʿAlī b. ʿAbd al-Qādir al-Maqrīzī, *Al-Mawāʿiẓ wa'l-Iʿtibār fī Dhikr al-Khiṭaṭ wa'l-Āthār,* 5 vols., ed. Ayman Fu'ād Sayyid (London: Al-Furqān Islamic Heritage Foundation, 2002), 3:714–715. For a clear explanation of the distinctions between the Mamluk *siyāsa,* the Ottoman *siyaset,* and the Mongol *yāsā/yasaq,* see Burak, "Between the *Ḳānūn* of Qāytbāy and Ottoman *Yasaq.*"

162. Rapoport, "Royal Justice," 92.

163. Mathieu Tillier, "*Qāḍīs* and the Political Use of the *Maẓālim* Jurisdiction under the Abbāsids," in *Public Violence in Islamic Societies: Power, Discipline, and the Construction of the Public Sphere, 7th-19th Centuries CE,* ed. Maribel Fierro and Christian Lange (Edinburgh: Edinburgh University Press, 2009), 42–66.

164. Abū al-Ḥasan ʻAlī Ibn Muḥammad al-Māwardī, *The Ordinances of Government: Al-Aḥkām al-Sultāniyya w'al-Wilāyāt al-Dīniyaa,* trans. Wafaa H. Wahba (London: Garnet, 1996), 88.

165. Baber Johansen, "Secular and Religious Elements in Hanfite Law: Function and Limits of the Absolute Character of Government Authority," in *Contingency in*

a Sacred law: Legal and Ethical Norms in the Muslim Fiqh (Leiden: Brill, 1999), 216–217.

166. Māwardī, *Ordinances of Government;* Abū Ya'lā al-Farrā', *Al-Aḥkām al-Sulṭ-āniyya* (Cairo: Muṣṭafā al-Bābī al-Ḥalabī, 1966).

167. For more on this point, see Kristen Stilt, *Islamic Law in Action: Authority, Discretion, and Everyday Experiences in Mamluk Egypt* (Oxford: Oxford University Press, 2011), chap. 1.

168. For a critical analysis of how the argument of the "closure of the gates of *ijtihād*" was formulated and how it has recently been challenged, see Baber Johansen, "The Muslim *Fiqh* as a Sacred Law: Religion, Law and Ethics in a Normative System," in *Contingency in a Sacred Law: Legal and Ethical Norms in the Muslim* Fiqh (Leiden: Brill, 1999), 1–71.

169. See, for example, Wael Hallaq, "Was the Gate of Ijtihad Closed?" *International Journal of Middle East Studies* 16, no. 1 (1984): 3–41; and Sherman Jackson, "Kramer versus Kramer in a Tenth/Sixteenth Century Egyptian Court: Post-Formative Jurisprudence between Exigency and Law," *Islamic Law and Society* 8, no. 1 (2001): 27–51.

170. Baber Johansen, "How the Norms Change: Legal Literature and the Problem of Change in the Case of the Land Rent," in *Contingency in a Sacred Law: Legal and Ethical Norms in the Muslim* Fiqh (Leiden: Brill, 1999), 446–464.

171. Dror, "Use of Ottoman *Shari'a* Court Records."

172. See, for example, Peirce, *Morality Tales;* and Iris Agmon, *Family and Court: Legal Culture and Modernity in Late Ottoman Palestine* (Syracuse, NY: Syracuse University Press, 2006).

173. Johansen, "Muslim *Fiqh* as a Sacred Law," 58. On the works of Sanhūrī and Chehata, see Wood, *Islamic Legal Revival.*

174. Asad, *Formations of the Secular,* 221.

175. Asad, *Formations of the Secular,* 227.

176. Asad, *Formations of the Secular,* 227–228.

177. Lawrence Rosen, *The Justice of Islam: Comparative Perspectives on Islamic Law and Society* (Oxford: Oxford University Press, 1999), 156.

178. L. Rosen, *Justice of Islam,* 165.

CHAPTER THREE. AN OLFACTORY TALE OF ONE CITY

1. DWQ, Ḍabṭiyyat Miṣr, L/2/6/4 (original no. 2032), case no. 597, pp. 45–47, AH 21 Jumādā I 1295 / 27 May 1878 CE.

2. On the festive inauguration of the bridge, see Sāmī, *Taqwīm al- Nīl,* 3:919–920.

3. John Marlowe, *Spoiling the Egyptians* (London: Andre Deutsch, 1974), 108.

4. Janet Abu-Lughod, *Cairo: 1001 Years of the City Victorious* (Princeton: Princeton University Press, 1971), 84–85. See also André Raymond, *Égyptiens et Français*

au Caire, 1798–1801 (Cairo: Institut Français d'Archéologie Orientale, 1998), 314–315.

5. Dodwell, *Founder of Modern Egypt.*

6. Abu-Lughod, *Cairo,* 87.

7. For a critical analysis of the origins of 'Abbās's negative image, see Toledano, *State and Society,* 108–134.

8. For a revisionist account of 'Abbās's reign, specifically of his palaces, and a history of the new neighborhood of 'Abbāsiyya, to the northeast of Cairo, see Nihal Tamraz, *Nineteenth-Century Cairene Houses and Palaces* (Cairo: American University in Cairo Press, 1998), 40–75.

9. Much of this section is based on Abu-Lughod, *Cairo,* 98–117.

10. On world's fairs, see Zeynep Celik, *Displaying the Orient: Architecture of Islam at Nineteenth-Century World's Fairs* (Berkeley: University of California Press, 1992).

11. For a background on Haussmann's efforts to redesign Paris, see David Jordan, *Transforming Paris: The Life and Labors of Baron Haussmann* (New York: Free Press, 1995).

12. Due to diplomatic problems with Istanbul, however, the opening ceremony was delayed for another year, giving the khedive much needed time to reform his capital city.

13. See Mubārak's autobiography, Mubārak, *Al-Khiṭaṭ,* 9:37–61. For a lucid English-language sketch of Mubārak's character and life, see F. Robert Hunter, *Egypt under the Khedives: From Household Government to Modern Bureaucracy* (Pittsburgh: University of Pittsburgh Press, 1984), 123–138.

14. Mubārak, *Al-Khiṭaṭ,* 9:49.

15. Celik, *Displaying the Orient.*

16. André Raymond, *Cairo,* trans. Willard Wood (Cambridge, MA: Harvard University Press, 2000), 276–279.

17. For the subsequent history of the statues of Süleyman Pasha and Mehmed Lazoughlu, see DWQ, Maḥfūẓāt Majlis al-Wuzarā', Niẓārat al-Ashghāl, box no. 4/4, folder no. 171 Ashghāl, memorandum dated 9 April 1893. For the statue of Muṣṭafā Kāmil, see DWQ, Majlis al-Wuzarā', Niẓārat al-Ashghāl, box no. 4/4, folder no. 471, memoranda dated 8 November 1908, 10 November 1908, and 17 January 1914. For the statue of Ibrāhīm Pasha, see DWQ, Majlis al-Wuzarā', Niẓārat al-Ashghāl, box no. 4/4, folder no. 171 al-Ashghāl, memoranda dated 8 April 1883 and 2 March 1890.

18. See, for example, 'Arafa 'Abdu 'Alī, *Al-Qāhira fī 'Aṣr Ismā'īl* (Cairo: Al-Dār al-Miṣriyya al-Lubnāniyya, 1998), 36–42.

19. Augustus Lamplough and R. Francis, *Cairo and Its Environs* (London: Sir Joseph Causton & Sons, 1909), xv, quoted in Abu-Lughod, *Cairo,* 98.

20. William Morton Fullerton, *In Cairo* (London: Macmillan, 1891), 6–7, quoted in Abu-Lughod, *Cairo,* 98.

21. Abu-Lughod, *Cairo,* 117.

22. For other examples of this narrative, see ʿAlī, *Al-Qāhira;* Ḥusām al-Dīn Ismāʿīl, *Madīnat al-Qāhira min Wilāyat Muḥammad ʿAlī ilā Ismāʿīl, 1805–1879* (Cairo: Dār al-Āfāq al-ʿArabiyya, 1997).

23. Jean-Luc Arnaud, *Le Caire, mise en place d'une ville moderne, 1867–1907: Des intérêts du prince aux sociétés privées* (Aix-en-Provence: Actes Sud, 1998). See also Mohamed Elshahed, "Paris Was Never on the Nile," *Cairobserver,* December 14, 2011, http://cairobserver.com/post/14185184147/paris-was-never-along-the-nile.

24. Arnaud, *Le Caire,* 365n6, 82.

25. Rifāʿa al-Ṭahṭāwī, *Takhlīṣ al-Ibrīz fī Talkhīṣ Bārīz* (Cairo: Būlāq, 1834). For an English translation, see Rifāʿa al-Ṭahṭāwī, *An Imam in Paris: An Account of a Stay in France by an Egyptian Cleric, 1826–1831,* trans. Daniel L. Newman (London: Saqi, 2004).

26. On the theme of mirrors in Ṭahṭāwī's description of Parisian cafés, see Sandra Naddaf, "Mirrored Images: Rifāʿah al-Tahtāwī and the West," *Alif* 6 (1986): 73–83.

27. Mubārak, *Al-Khiṭaṭ,* 9:49–50.

28. Donald Reid, *Paris Sewers and Sewermen: Realities and Representations* (Cambridge, MA: Harvard University Press, 1991), 39.

29. Lucy H. Hooper, "A Visit to the Sewers of Paris," *Appelton's Journal* 13 (April 1875): 430, quoted in Reid, *Paris Sewers,* 41.

30. Muhammad Badr, "Al-Ṣiḥḥa al-Tāmma wa-l'Minḥa al-ʿĀmma," *Rawḍat al-Madāris* 1, no. 1, (AH 15 Muḥarram 1287 / 17 April 1870 CE): 26.

31. DWQ, Majlis al-Wuzarāʾ, Niẓārat al-Ashghāl, box no. 1/5, titled "Lawāʾiḥ wa Qawānīn Khāṣṣa bi-l-Ashghāl," folder no. 17, titled "Qānūn Ṭāʾifat al-Miʿmār," n.d. The plan is reproduced in facsimile in Ghislaine Alleaume, "Politique urbaines et contrôle de l'entreprise: Une loi inédite de ʿAlī Mubārak sur les corporations du bâtiment," *Annales Islamologiques* 21 (1985): 147–188.

32. Marcel Clerget, *Le Caire: Étude de géographie urbaine et d'histoire économique,* 2 vols. (Cairo: Schindler, 1934), 1:256.

33. Alleaume, "Politique urbaines," 149.

34. Arnaud, *Le Caire,* 82.

35. Alleaume, "Politique urbaines," 148–149.

36. Abu-Lughod, *Cairo,* 104.

37. Raymond, *Cairo,* 227–228. For a discussion of the problems ensuing from the lack of a centralized authority in charge of Cairo, see Raymond, *Cairo,* 243–244.

38. Jabartī, *ʿAjāʾib,* 1:29–30.

39. On Alexandria's Urnāṭū Council, see Michael Reimer, "Reorganizing Alexandria: The Origins and Development of the Conseil de l'Ornato," *Journal of Urban History* 19, no. 3 (1993): 55–83; Gabriel Baer, "The Beginnings of Municipal Government in Egypt," *Middle Eastern Studies* 4, no. 2 (1968): 118–140; and Ḥilmī Ahmad Shalabī, *Al-Ḥukm al-Maḥallī wa al-Majālis al-Baladiyya fī Miṣr Mundhu Inshāʾihā Ḥattā ʿĀmm 1918* (Cairo: ʿĀlam al-Kutub, 1987), 15–33. On Cairo's Tanẓīm, see Abu-Lughod, *Cairo,* 96, 147–149; and Arnaud, *Le Caire,* 98.

40. It is probably the unlikely location of the documents of the Tanẓīm in its early years that confused and eluded previous researchers.

41. This section gives only a brief account of the early history of this important council. A proper study of the activities and accomplishments of the Tanẓīm council in the pre-Ismāʿīl period would require a careful consultation of the registers of the Department of Public Instruction (Dīwān al-Madāris) and the Department of Public Works (Dīwān al-Ashghāl).

42. DWQ, Dīwān Madāris, reg. no. 2091, p. 14, AH 8 Dhū al-Ḥijja 1259 / 30 December 1843 CE.

43. DWQ, Maʿiyya Saniyya, Turkī, reg. no. 376, February 1844, quoted in Shalabī, *Al-Ḥukm,* 35.

44. DWQ, Dīwān Madāris, M/1/6 (original no. 6), doc. no. 90, p. 3018, AH 28 Shaʿbān 1261 / 1 September 1845 CE.

45. DWQ, Dīwān Khidīwī, S/2/1/2 (original no. 506), doc. no. 410, p. 48, AH 9 Jumādā II 1261 / 15 June 1845 CE. See later in the chapter for how this matter was eventually settled in subsequent legislation.

46. DWQ, Dīwān Madāris, M/1/6 (original no. 6), unnumbered petition, p. 2963, AH 22 Shaʿbān 1261 / 26 August 1845 CE.

47. The fifty-article order of the Majlis Tanẓīm al-Maḥrūsa was originally published in *Al-Waqāʾiʿ al-Miṣriyya,* no. 83 (AH 29 Rajab 1263 / 13 July 1847 CE). It is reproduced in Sāmī, *Taqwīm al-Nīl,* 2:547–552; and Ḥasan ʿAbd al-Wahhāb, "Takhṭīṭ al-Qāhira wa Tanẓīmuhā Mundhu Nash'atihā," *Bulletin de l'Institut d'Égypte* 37 (1955–56): 23–31. Abu-Lughod is skeptical that this order was ever implemented, arguing that it does "not seem to have been followed very enthusiastically, if at all" (Abu Lughod, *Cairo,* 96n42). However, ʿAbd al-Wahhāb says that he personally saw some of the streets signs installed on buildings that predate Mehmed Ali's reign and written in the same ink color stipulated in the order, suggesting that they must have been hung there when the decree was implemented (ʿAbd al-Wahhāb, "Takhṭīṭ al-Qāhira," 32–33).

48. DWQ, Majlis al-Khuṣūṣī, S/11/8/2 (original no. 1960), decree no. 40, pp. 38–48, AH 2 Jumādā I 1276 / 27 November 1859 CE. On the Privy Council, see Hunter, *Egypt nuder the Khedives,* 49–50; and Sāmī, *Taqwīm al-Nīl,* 3:18.

49. DWQ, Majlis Khuṣūṣī, S/11/8/8 (original no. 71), decree no. 56, pp. 55–56, AH 4 Dhū al-Ḥijja 1282 / 20 April 1866 CE.

50. On exchanging *waqf* domains (*istibdāl*), see Jamāl Khūlī, *Al-Istibdāl wa-Ightisāb al-Awqāf: Dirāsah Wathāʾiqīyya* (Alexandria: Dār al-Thaqāfa al-ʿIlmiyya, 2000).

51. DWQ, Dīwān Khidīwī, Awāmir, box no. 2, document dated AH 5 Rabīʿ II 1282 / 28 August 1865 CE. For a description of these slums in Mamluk and Ottoman times, see Nelly Hanna, *Habiter au Caire: La maison moyenne et ses habitants aux XVIIe et XVIIIe siècles* (Cairo: IFAO, 1991), 70, 198–199.

52. DWQ, Majlis al-Khuṣūṣī, S/11/8/10 (original no. 73), order no. 6, pp. 9–16, AH 27 Jumādā I 1283 / 7 October 1866 CE.

53. See DWQ, Majlis al-Khusūsī, S/11/8/14 (original no. 76), order no. 90, p. 97, AH 15 Rabī' II 1287 / 15 July 1870 CE, where it is explicitly stated that "the Khedival wishes are against the demolition of old monuments, especially . . . shrines."

54. This is, of course, a variation on the larger theme of the "Islamic city." See Ira M. Lapidus, *Muslim Cities in the Later Middle Ages* (Cambridge, MA: Harvard University Press, 1967); Albert Hourani, "The Islamic City in the Light of Recent Research," in *The Islamic City*, ed. A. H. Hourani and S. Stern (Oxford: Bruno Cassirer, 1970), 9–24; and Janet Abu-Lughod, "The Islamic City: Historic Myth, Islamic Essence and Contemporary Relevance," *International Journal of Middle East Studies* 19 (1987): 155–176.

55. André Raymond, "Islamic City, Arab City: Orientalist Myths and Recent Views," *British Journal of Middle Eastern Studies* 21 (1994): 3–18.

56. Baer, "Beginnings of Municipal Government."

57. DWQ, Majlis al-Khuṣūṣī, S/11/8/8 (original no. 71), decree no. 56, pp. 55–56, AH 4 Dhū al-Ḥijja 1282 / 20 April 1866 CE.

58. DWQ, Majlis al-Khuṣūṣī, S/11/8/10 (original no. 73), order no. 6, pp. 9–16, AH 27 Jumādā I 1283 / 7 October 1866 CE.

59. DWQ, Dīwān al-Khuṣūṣī, S/11/8/14 (original no. 76), decree no. 61, pp. 66–69, AH 12 Muḥarram 1287 / 14 April 1870 CE. This decree comments on an earlier decree by the Legislative Council dated AH 24 Dhū al-Qa'da 1285 / 8 March 1869 CE.

60. Mitchell, *Colonising Egypt*.

61. See chapter 5 for a discussion of how the abhorrence of waste was one of the considerations behind canceling flogging as legal punishment.

62. It is noteworthy that Ibn Khaldūn's *Muqaddimah* was published by Būlāq Press in the nineteenth century and was one of the books that were sent to be exhibited in the International Exposition of 1867 in Paris. See Abul-Futūḥ Raḍwān, *Tārīkh Maṭba'at Būlāq* (Cairo: Al-Maṭb'a al-Amīriyya, 1953), 204. On the familiarity of Ottoman political and cultural elites with Ibn Khaldūn's work, see Cornell H. Fleischer, "Royal Authority, Dynastic Cyclism, and 'Ibn Khaldunism' in Sixteenth-Century Ottoman Letters," *Journal of Asian and African Studies* 18 (1983): 198–220. On the Khaldūnian concept of *'umrān*, see Laroussie Amri, "The Concept of *'Umran:* The Heuristic Knot in Ibn Khaldun," *Journal of North African Studies* 13 (2008): 351–361.

63. DWQ, Majlis al-Khuṣūṣī, S/11/8/2 (original no. 1960), decree no. 40, p. 48, AH 2 Jumādā I 1276 / 27 November 1859 CE.

64. DWQ, Majlis al-Khuṣūṣī, S/11/8/2 (original no. 1960), decree no. 40, p. 40, AH 2 Jumādā I 1276 / 27 November 1859 CE. See also Khālid Muḥammad 'Azab, *Takhṭīṭ wa 'Imārat al-Mudun al-Islāmiyya* (Doha: Wizārat al-Awqāf wal al-Shu'ūn al-Islāmiyya, 1997), 84–86.

65. W. F. Bynum and Roy Porter, eds., *Companion Encyclopedia of the History of Medicine,* vol. 1 (London: Routledge, 1993), esp. chapters by Vivian Nutton ("Humoralism," 281–291), Caroline Hannaway ("Environment and Miasmata,"

292–308), and Maragaret Pelling ("Contagion/Germ Theory/Specificity," 309–334). See also, David Burns, *The Great Stink of Paris and the Nineteenth-Century Struggle against Filth and Germs* (Baltimore: Johns Hopkins University Press, 2006), esp. 44–45.

66. An important influence on the zymotic theory, which believed that fermentation and putrefaction caused fevers by releasing poisons into the air, was the German chemist Justus von Liebig (1803–73). On his influence on English medicine in the mid-nineteenth century, see Margaret Pelling, *Cholera, Fever and English Medicine, 1825–1865* (Oxford: Oxford University Press, 1978), 113–145, esp. 140–141.

67. On the attempt to construct the eudiometer, an instrument to measure the quality of air, see Simon Schaffer, "Measuring Cirtue: Eudiometry, Enlightenment and Pneumatic Medicine," in *The Medical Enlightenment of the Eighteenth Century,* ed. Andrew Cunningham and Roger French (Cambridge: Cambridge University Press, 1990), 281–318.

68. Clot Bey, *Kunūz al-Ṣiḥḥa,* 158–162.

69. On the Paris school of medicine, see Kuhnke, *Lives at Risk,* 6; and John H. Warner, *Against the Spirit of System: The French Impulse in Nineteenth-Century American Medicine* (Baltimore: Johns Hopkins University Press, 1998), chap. 2.

70. Kuhnke, *Lives at Risk,* 165, quoting from Clot Bey, *De la Peste.*

71. Kuhnke, *Lives at Risk,* 6–7.

72. Alain Corbin, *The Foul and the Fragrant: Odor and the French Social Imagination* (Cambridge, MA: Harvard University Press, 1986), 43. On Bichat, see Foucault, *The Birth of the Clinic,* 127–146; and chapter 4 of this book.

73. Jabartī, *'Ajā'ib,* 1:79.

74. Raymond, *Cairo,* 243.

75. DWQ, Diwān Khidīwī, Turkī, S/2/40/16 (original no. 764), doc. no. 427, p. 164, AH 12 Ṣafar 1246 / 2 August 1830 CE. The division of the city into eight neighborhoods (*atmān,* literally "eighths") dates back to the time of the French Expedition. In time, Miṣr al-Qadīma (old Cairo) and Būlāq were added as independent neighborhoods, which meant that Cairo had ten "eighths."

76. DWQ, Majlis Mulkiyya, Ṣādir Khulāṣāt, reg. no. 45, p. 22, doc. no. 229, AH 3 Sha'bān 1251 / 24 November 1835 CE, as reproduced in DWQ, Maḥfaẓat al-Mīhī, doc. no. 16, folder no. 8. A key word is unclear, making it difficult to know what the punishment was. The document reads: "He who eases nature in the street . . . will have one of his [illegible] nailed on the spot till sunset as a deterrent to others."

77. See, for example, DWQ, Diwān Madāris, M/1/6 (original no. 6), doc. no. 83, p. 2964, AH 6 Sha'bān 1261 / 10 August 1845 CE.

78. DWQ, Ḍabṭiyyat Miṣr, L/2/6/2 (original no. 2028), doc. no. 160, pp. 78–79, AH 8 Dhū al-Qa'da 1294 / 14 November 1877 CE.

79. DWQ, Dīwān Taftīsh Ṣiḥḥat al-Maḥrūsa, M/5/1 (original no. 163), doc. no. 23, p. 39, AH 25 Jumādā I 1263 / 28 March 1851 CE.

80. DWQ, Majlis al-Aḥkām, S/7/33/1, p. 229, order dated AH 14 Rabi' I 1269 / 26 December 1852 CE. See also DWQ, Dīwān al-Dākhiliyya, Awāmir lil-Dākhiliyya, reg. no. 1322, order no. 113, pp. 25–28, AH 10 Rajab 1282 / 29 November

1865 CE, where it is stated that the Cairo Water Company was to water the streets twice a day during the summer (March 16 to October 15) and only once during the winter (October 16 to March 15). The "thickness" of each sprinkling of water should be 151 millimeters.

81. Corbin, *Foul and the Fragrant,* 32.

82. Rodolphe el-Khoury, "Polish and Deodorize: Paving the City in Late Eighteenth-Century Paris," in *The Smell Culture Reader,* ed. Jim Drobnick (New York: Berg, 2006), 23.

83. See, for example, DWQ, Dīwān al-Madāris, M/1/1/3 (original no. 3), unnumbered doc., p. 827, AH 6 Muḥarram 1261 / 15 January 1845 CE. This is about a report submitted by Linant Efendi, Cairo's chief architect, concerning the rubble resulting from the renovations done by a certain Mikhā'īl Kassāb on his house. The report stated that the rubble obstructed the main road, which was frequented by Mehmed Ali and other dignitaries (*zawāt*) "in addition to causing harm to people [living nearby]." Kassāb was issued a fine, which was doubled when he did not pay it. See DWQ, Dīwān al-Madāris, M/1/1/4 (original no. 4), doc. no. 278, p. 2184, AH 23 Rabī' I 1261 / 1 April 1845 CE.

84. DWQ, Muḥāfaẓat Miṣr, L/1/5/2 (original no. 185), doc. no. 108, p. 114, AH 19 Ramaḍan 1277 / 31 March 1861 CE.

85. DWQ, Dīwān Madāris, M/1/5 (original no. 5), doc. no. 72, p. 2641, AH 20 Jumādā II 1261 / 26 June 1845 CE.

86. DWQ, Muḥāfaẓat Miṣr, L/1/5/2 (original no. 185), doc. 51, p. 55, AH 21 Jumādā I 1277 / 5 December 1860 CE.

87. Khoury, "Polish and Deodorize," 26.

88. DWQ, Dīwān Madāris, M/1/1/4 (original no. 4), doc. no. 269, pp. 2136, 2160, AH 16 Muḥarram 1261 / 25 January 1845 CE.

89. DWQ, Dīwān al-Jihādiyya, Ṣādir Shūrā al-Aṭibbā, reg. no. 440, doc. no. 50, p. 49, AH 14 Dhū al-Ḥijja 1263 / 23 November 1847 CE.

90. It is not known exactly when the first of these decrees banning burials within cities was issued. The earliest explicit order to that effect that I found is dated 1851, but it referred to similar laws that were already in existence. See DWQ, Muḥāfaẓat Miṣr, M/5/2, doc. 19, p. 37, AH 7 Rabī' I 1268 / 31 December 1851 CE.

91. DWQ, Muḥāfaẓat Miṣr, M/5/11 (original no. 226), doc. 92, pp. 208, 211, AH 2 Dhū al-Ḥijja 1290 / 21 January 1874 CE. This was concerning Sayyida Nafīsa Cemetery.

92. DWQ, Muḥāfaẓat Miṣr, M/5/1, doc. no. 137, p. 64, AH 23 Jumādā I 1267 / 26 March 1851 CE. This was the case of a cesspool in Bāb al-Lūq, in the southwestern part of the city.

93. DWQ, Muḥāfaẓat Miṣr, L/1/5/1, doc. no. 86, p. 97, AH 4 Sha'bān 1276 / 26 February 1860 CE.

94. DWQ, Diwān Madāris, M/1/1/3 (original no. 3), doc. no. 197, pp. 862, 872, AH 17 Muḥarram 1261 / 26 January 1845 CE.

95. This is what happened to sixty-five-year-old Ibrāhīm 'Abd al-Shāfī, who came to Cairo to beg but slipped into a cesspool fifteen days later. He had two

serious fractures in his legs and later died in the hospital. The worker responsible for clearing the cesspool was found guilty of negligence and charged with manslaughter by the Cairo Police Commissioner. See DWQ, Ḍabṭiyyat Miṣr, reg. L/2/6/4, case no. 575, pp. 29–30, AH 17 Jumādā I 1295 / 19 May 1878 CE.

96. DWQ, Muḥāfaẓat Miṣr, L/1/5/2 (original no. 185), doc. no. 28, p. 41, AH 13 Rabīʿ II 1277 / 29 October 1860 CE.

97. DWQ, Muḥāfaẓat Miṣr, L/1/5/1 (original no. 183), doc. 199, p. 183, AH 18 Muḥarram 1277 / 6 August 1860 CE.

98. DWQ, Muḥāfaẓat Miṣr, M/5/1 (original no. 163), doc. 92, p. 35, AH 20 Ṣafar 1267 / 25 December 1850 CE. Also of interest is one of the first orders issued by ʿAbbās Pasha in his capacity as governor of Cairo, concerning the *fisīkh* market in Būlāq, which doctors suggested moving across the river to Imbāba. See DWQ, Majlis al-Aḥkām, box no. 1, doc. no. 8, AH 27 Jumādā I 1265 / 20 April 1849 CE.

99. Raymond, *Cairo,* 227, 219.

100. The correspondence on slaughterhouses and tanneries is immense, but see especially DWQ, Muḥāfaẓat Miṣr, L/1/5/2 (original no. 185), doc. no. 135, p. 135, AH 5 Dhū al-Qaʿda 1277 / 15 May 1861 CE; DWQ, Muḥāfaẓat Miṣr, M/5/1 (original no. 163), doc 1, p. 1, AH 5 Dhū al-Qaʿda 1266 / 12 September 1850 CE; and DWQ, Ḍabṭiyyat Miṣr, L/2/31/1, doc. 197, p. 141, AH 12 Dhū al-Qaʿda 1296/28 October 1879 CE.

101. DWQ, Dīwān al-Jihādiyya, Ṣādir Shūrā al-Aṭibbā, reg. no. 437, doc. no. 7, p. 12, AH 8 Shawwāl 1262 / 29 September 1846 CE.

102. DWQ, Dīwān Madāris, box no. 3, doc. no. 135, AH 22 Shaʿbān 1263 / 5 August 1847 CE.

103. Abu-Lughod, *Cairo,* 92–93.

104. ʿAbd al-Wahhāb, "Takhṭiṭ al-Qāhira," 17.

105. DWQ, Dīwān Taftāsh Ṣiḥḥat al-Maḥrūsa, M/5/11 (original no. 226), doc. no. 70, p. 140, AH 24 Shawwāl 1290 / 16 November 1873 CE.

106. Abu-Lughod, *Cairo,* 93. For a map of Ottoman Cairo that shows the position of these and other lakes, see Raymond, *Cairo,* 217.

107. DWQ, Muḥāfaẓat Miṣr, L/1/5/2 (original no. 185), doc. no. 23, p. 36, AH 6 Rabīʿ II 1277 / 22 October 1860 CE.

108. DWQ, Ḍabṭiyyat Miṣr, L/2/31/1, doc. no. 219, p. 15, AH 8 Rajab 1296 / 28 June 1879 CE.

109. Muḥammad ʿAlī al-Baqlī, "Fī al-Tamarruʿ," *Yaʿsūb al-Ṭibb,* no. 29 (AH Jumādā I 1285 / August 1868 CE): 6. *Yaʿsūb al-Ṭibb* was the first medical journal to be published in Egypt. Its first editor was Muhammad ʿAlī Bey al-Baqlī.

110. For a brief account of the history of the Khalīj, see Abu-Lughod, *Cairo,* 134.

111. Mubārak, *Al-Khiṭaṭ,* 1:82–83.

112. DWQ, Dīwān Madāris, M/8/1 (original no. 14), doc. no. 10, p. 19, AH 24 Shawwāl 1260 / 6 November 1844 CE.

113. DWQ, Dīwān Katkhuda, Ṣādir Taftīsh al-Ṣiḥḥa, M/5/1 (original no. 163), doc. no. 51, p. 31, AH 5 Ṣafar 1267 / 10 December 1850 CE.

114. DWQ, Dīwān Katkhuda, Ṣādir Taftīsh al- Ṣiḥḥa, M/5/2 (original no. 167), doc. 12, p. 28, AH 11 Ṣafar 1268 / 17 December 1851 CE.

115. DWQ, Muḥāfaẓat Miṣr, L/1/5/2 (original no. 185), doc. 47, p. 76, AH 8 Rajab 1277 / 19 February 1861 CE.

116. DWQ, Muḥāfaẓat Miṣr, L/1/5/11 (original no. 209), doc. 17, pp. 97, 127, AH 1 Dhū al-Qaʿda 1286 / 2 February 1870 CE.

117. DWQ, Majlis al-Wuzarāʾ, Niẓārat al-Ashghāl, box no. 1/3, series 563–23, folders titled "Khāṣṣ al-Khalīj al-Miṣrī." These folders contain a number of drafts dating from 1882 to 1887 of different proposals of how to drain the Khalīj.

118. DWQ, Dīwān al-Jihādiyya, reg. no. 440, doc. 41, pp. 51, 57, AH 22 Jumādā I 1263 / 8 May 1847 CE.

119. DWQ, Dīwān al-Jihādiyya, reg. no. 437, doc. no. 120, pp. 106–107, AH 4 Rabīʿ I 1263 / 20 February 1847 CE.

120. The date the Shūrā al-Aṭibbā was founded is from Aḥmad Muḥammad Kamāl, *Tārīkh al-Idāra al-Ṣiḥḥiyya fī Miṣr min ʿAhd Afandīnā Muḥammad ʿAlī Bāshā lil-ʾĀn* (Cairo: Al-Raghāʾib Press, 1943), 1. The date it was disbanded is from DWQ, Maʿiyya Saniyya, reg. no. 1618, pt. 5, doc. no. 393, p. 31, AH 1 Shaʿbān 1272 / 7 April 1856 CE. The council was also known as Mashūrat al-Ṭibb. The council that replaced it was called the Majlis al-Ṣiḥḥa, or the Health Council, and it also lacked independence as it was part of the Alexandria Governorate. See DWQ, Majlis al-Khuṣūṣī, S/11/8/8 (original no. 71), doc. no. 7, p. 21, AH 4 Jumādā I 1282 / 25 September 1865 CE.

121. DWQ, Dīwān Jihādiyya, reg. no. 440, doc. no. 45, p. 44, AH 7 Dhū al-Ḥijja 1263 / 16 November 1847 CE.

122. Tuesday seems to have been the day reserved for going through the backlog of work. See DWQ, Dīwān Madāris, M/1/6 (original no. 6), correspondence no. 90, p. 3018, AH 28 Shaʿbān 1261 / 1 September 1845 CE.

123. DWQ, Dīwān Taftīsh Ṣiḥḥat al-Maḥrūsa, M/5/2 (original no. 167), correspondence no. 11, p. 52, AH 12 Jumādā I 1268 / 4 March 1852 CE.

124. Edwin Chadwick, *Report to Her Majesty's Principal Secretary of State for the Home Department from the Poor Law Commissioners on an Inquiry into the Sanitary Condition of the Labouring Population of Great Britain* (London: W. Clowes and Sons, 1842), 341.

125. DWQ, Majlis al-Aḥkām, S/7/33/1, p. 24, order issued on AH 29 Muḥarram 1262 / 27 January 1846 CE. For more on hygienic policing, see chapter 4.

126. DWQ, Muḥāfaẓat Miṣr, L/1/5/15 (original no. 217), doc. no. 6, pp. 1, 61, AH 12 Shaʿbān 1288 / 27 October 1871 CE.

127. For a similar tension in nineteenth-century New York between individuals who used their nose to map the city locally and sanitarians who understood the olfactory geography of the city in regional terms, see Melanie Kiechle, "Navigating by Nose: Fresh Air, Stench Nuisance, and the Urban Environment, 1840–1880," *Journal of Urban History* 42, no. 4 (2015): 753–771. For a comparison with Paris, see David Barnes, "Scents and Sensibilities: Disgust and the Meanings of Odors in Late Nineteenth-Century Paris," *Historical Reflections/Réflexions Historiques* 28, no. 1 (2002): 21–49.

128. DWQ, Ḍabṭiyyat Miṣr, L/2/31/1, doc. no. 374, p. 157, AH 17 Dhū al-Qaʿda 1296 / 2 November 1879 CE.

129. DWQ, Ḍabṭiyyat Miṣr, L/2/31/1, doc. no. 242, p. 185, AH 28 Dhū al-Qaʿda 1296 / 13 November 1879 CE. On the social significance of the *efendiyya,* see Lucie Ryzova, *The Age of the Efendiyya: Passages to Modernity in National-Colonial Egypt* (Oxford: Oxford University Press, 2014).

130. DWQ, Muḥāfaẓat Miṣr, L/1/5/11 (original no. 209), doc. no. 17, p. 107, AH 15 Dhū al-Ḥijja 1286 / 18 March 1870 CE.

131. DWQ, Ḍabṭiyyat Miṣr, L/2/31/1, doc. no. 295, p. 85, AH 20 Ramaḍān 1296 / 7 September 1879 CE.

132. DWQ, Ḍabṭiyyat Miṣr, L/2/31/1, doc. no. 263, p. 57, AH 21 Shaʿbān 1296 / 10 August 1879 CE.

133. See, for example, DWQ, Ḍabṭiyyat Miṣr, L/2/31/1, doc. no. 347, p. 126, AH 29 Shawwāl 1296 / 16 October 1879 CE (concerning rubbish found on the street connecting the khedival palaces of Ismāʿīliyya and ʿAbidīn); doc. no. 373, p. 152, AH 17 Dhū al-Qaʿda 1296 / 2 November 1879 CE (concerning the tannery of Būlāq, which was on the wind path of the same two palaces and "many other notables' houses"); and doc. no. 359, p. 139, AH 11 Dhū al-Qaʿda 1296 / 27 October 1879 CE (concerning rubbish "thrown in Qasr al-Nīl Street, [which was] used for the carriage route of the Khedive and other notables in addition to being in front of the house of Sitt Zaynab Hānim").

134. DWQ, Muḥāfaẓat Miṣr, L/1/5/1, doc. no. 9, pp. 27, 33, AH 16 Rabīʿ I 1276 / 23 October 1859 CE. See also DWQ, Muḥāfaẓat Miṣr, reg. M/5/1, doc. 13, p. 7, AH 27 Dhū al-Qaʿda 1266 / 3 November 1850 CE; and DWQ, Muḥāfaẓat Miṣr, L/1/5/2 (original no. 185), doc. no. 51, p. 147, AH 28 Dhū al-Ḥijja 1277 / 7 July 1861 CE.

135. Gwendolyn Wright, *The Politics of Design in French Colonial Urbanism* (Chicago: University of Chicago Press, 1991), 85.

136. Wright, *Politics of Design,* 85.

137. Gyan Prakash, *Another Reason: Science and the Imagination of Modern India* (Princeton: Princeton University Press, 1999), 133.

138. Partha Chatterjee, "Two Poets and Death: On Civil Society and Political Society in the Non-Christian World," in *Questions of Modernity,* ed. Timothy Mitchell (Minneapolis: University of Minnesota Press, 2000), 35–48.

139. Vijay Prashad, "Native Dirt/Imperial Ordure: The Cholera of 1832 and the Morbid Resolutions of Modernity," *Journal of Historical Sociology* 7 (1994): 255.

140. Prashad, "Native Dirt," 254.

141. For a similar development in nineteenth-century Paris, see Corbin, *Foul and the Fragrant,* chap. 9.

142. ʿĀbidīn Khayrallah, *Irshād al-Insān ilā Ṣiḥḥat al-Abdān* (Cairo: Al-ʿĀṣima, AH 1312/1894–95 CE), 80.

143. ʿAbd al-Raḥmān Ismāʿīl, *Al-Taqwīmāt al-Ṣiḥḥiyya ʿalā al-ʿAwāʾid al-Miṣriyya* (Cairo: Būlāq, 1903), 44.

144. Aḥmad Fahmī Muḥarram, Maḥmūd Labīb Muḥarram, and ʿAlī Yāsīn Muḥarram, *Al-Qawāʿid al-Asāsiyya fī Muʿālajat al-Kūlīrā al-Āsiāwiyya* (Cairo: Al-Muqtaṭaf, 1893), 18.

145. Muḥammad Ṣāliḥ Ḥilmī and Muḥammad Shafī', *Al-Mabādi' al-Awwaliyya fī al-Tadābīr al-Ṣiḥḥiyya* (Cairo: Al-Ma'ārif, 1921), 31–33. On a comparable concern in nineteenth-century New York over the dangers of "vitiated air," see Kiechle, "Navigating by Nose," 4.

146. Aḥmad Fahmī Muḥarram, Maḥmūd Labīb Muḥarram, and 'Alī Yāsīn Muḥarram, *Al-Qawā'id al-Asāsiyya,* 20.

147. Ismā'īl, *Al-Taqwīmāt,* 48.

148. Aḥmad Muhammad al-Shāfi'ī, *Balāgh al-Umniyya bi'l-Ḥuṣūn al-Ṣiḥḥiyya* (Cairo: Al-Maṭba'a al- 'Āmira al-Sharafiyya, AH 1305/1887–88 CE), 9–10.

149. Muṣṭafā Efendi Naṣr, *Al-Minḥa fī Tadbīr al-Ṣiḥḥa* (Cairo: Maṭba'at al-Ādāb, AH 1306/1888–89 CE), 21.

150. Ismā'īl, *Al-Taqwīmāt,* 46.

151. Aḥmad Fahmī Muḥarram, Maḥmūd Labīb Muḥarram, and 'Alī Yāsīn Muḥarram, *Al-Qawā'id al-Asāsiyya,* 45–46.

152. The best example of this is Ismā'īl, *Al-Taqwīmāt.* On the hygienic background to the Islamic requirement of washing the body after copulation, see Khairallah, *Irshād al-Insān,* 104–109.

153. Prakash, *Another Reason,* 130.

154. See Prakash, *Another Reason,* 126.

155. DWQ, Majlis al-Khuṣūṣī, S/11/8/22, doc. no. 10, pp. 12–14, AH 17 Shawwāl 1291 / 27 November 1874 CE.

CHAPTER FOUR. LAW IN THE MARKET

1. R. P. Buckley, *The Book of the Islamic Market Inspector* (Oxford: Oxford University Press, 1999), 3–4. For a critical Arabic edition, see 'Abd al-Raḥmān Ibn Naṣr al-Shayzarī, *Kitāb Nihāyat al-Rutba fī Ṭalab al-Ḥisba,* ed. Al-Sayyid al-Bāz al-'Arinī, (Cairo: Lajnat al-Ta'līf wa'l-Tarjama wa'l-Nashr, 1946). On dating Shayzarī's death, see Shayzarī, *Kitāb Nihāyat al-Rutba,* ix.

2. DWQ, Muḥāfaẓat Miṣr, L/1/4/3 (original no. 457), doc. no. 25, p. 6, AH 19 Rabī' II 1281 / 21 September 1864 CE.

3. Muḥammad Kamāl al-Dīn Imām, *Uṣūl al-Ḥisba fī'l-Islām: Dirāsa Ta'ṣīliyya Muqārina* (Cairo: Dār al-Hidāya, 1986), 5.

4. In the terminology of the nineteenth century, "sophisticated" was used almost synonymously with "adulterated." See Mitchell Okun, *Fair Play in the Marketplace: The First Battle for Pure Food and Drugs* (Dekalb, IL: Northern Illinois Press, 1986), 3n2.

5. Hussein A. Agrama, *Questioning Secularism: Islam, Sovereignty, and the Rule of Law in Modern Egypt* (Chicago: University of Chicago Press, 2012).

6. These twentieth century texts are: 'Umar 'Abd al-Raḥmān, ed., *Mīthāq al-'Amal al-Islāmī* (Cairo: Maktabat Ibn Kathīr, 1989); Faḍl Ilāhī (not Fadl El-Hay, as mistransliterated by Agrama), *Al-Ḥisba: Ta'rīfuhā wa Mashrū'iyyatuhā wa Wujūbuhā* (Cairo: Dār al-I'tiṣām, 1996); and 'Abd al-Fattāḥ Muṣṭafā al-Ṣayfī,

Al-Talabbus bi'l-Jarīma: Dirāsa lil-Munkar al-Mūjib lil-Ḥisba fī'l-Fiqhayn al-Islāmī wa'l-Waḍ'ī (Cairo: Dār al-Nahḍa al-'Arabiyya, 1991). As can be seen from their publication dates, the secondary *fiqh* sources that Agrama uses do not support the argument he is making.

7. Agrama, *Questioning Secularism*, 20, 64.

8. Agrama, *Questioning Secularism*, 64.

9. Talal Asad, "Thinking about Tradition, Religion, and Politics in Egypt Today," *Critical Inquiry* 42 (Autumn 2015): 177.

10. Asad, "Tradition, Religion, and Politics," 173.

11. Asad, "Tradition, Religion, and Politics," 177.

12. Asad, "Tradition, Religion, and Politics," 178.

13. Abū Hamid al-Ghazālī, *Adab al-Suhba wa'l-Mu'ashara* (Beirut: Dar al-Kutub al-'Ilmiyya, 2007), quoted in Asad, "Tradition, Religion, and Politics," 178n24.

14. Quranī, *Al-Ḥisba*, 1:4.

15. Imām, *Uṣūl al-Ḥisba*, 9.

16. Ilāhī, *Al-Ḥisba: Tarīfuhā*, 80.

17. 'Abd al-Fattāḥ Muṣṭafā al-Ṣayfī, *Al-Ḥisba fī'l-Islam: Niẓāman wa-Fiqhan wa-Taṭbīqan* (Alexandria: Dār al-Maṭbū'āt al-Jāmi'iyya, 2010), 9.

18. Shawkat Muḥammad 'Alyān, *Dawr al-Ḥisba fī Ḥimāyat al-Maṣāliḥ* (Riyadh: n.p., 2000), 44–45.

19. For an exhaustive account of *ḥisba* in Islamic thought, see Michael Cook, *Commanding Right and Forbidding Wrong in Islamic Thought* (Cambridge: Cambridge University Press, 2000).

20. Muḥammad Ibn Mukarram Ibn Manẓūr, *Lisān al-'Arab*, 20 vols. (Cairo: Būlāq, AH 1300/1882 CE), 1:301–305.

21. Muḥammad Ibn Ya'qūb Fayrūzabādī, *Al-Qāmūs al-Muḥīṭ*, 4 vols. (Beirut: Al-Mu'assassa al-'Arabiyya lil-Ṭibā'a wa'l-Nashr, 1970), 1:56.

22. Muḥammad Murtaḍa al-Zabīdī, *Tāj al-'Arūs*, 40 vols. (Kuwait: Al-Majlis al-Waṭanī lil-Thaqāfa wa'l-Funūn wa'l-Ādāb, 2004), 2:267–268.

23. Ibn Manẓūr, *Lisān al-'Arab*, 1:301.

24. Cook, *Commanding Right*, 13. The eight verses are: Quran 3:104, 3:110, 3:114, 7:157, 9:71, 9:112, 22:41, and 31:17.

25. See, for example, Farīd 'Abd al-Khāliq, *Al-Ḥisba fī'l-Islām 'Alā Dhawī al-Jāh wa'l-Sulṭān* (Cairo: Dār al-Shurūq, 2011), 37; Ilāhī, *Al-Ḥisba*, 45; 'Alī Ibn Ḥasan Ibn 'Alī al-Quranī, *Al-Ḥisba fī'l-Māḍī wa'l-Ḥāḍir Bayna Thabāt al-Ahdāf wa-Taṭ awwur al-Uslūb* (Riyadh: Maktabat al-Rushd, 1994), 1:3; and 'Abdallāh Muḥammad 'Abdallāh, *Wilāyat al-Ḥisba fī'l-Islām* (Cairo: Al-Zahrā', 1996), 70.

26. Quoted in Cook, *Commanding Right*, 33. For a list of other hadiths on the subject, see Cook, *Commanding Right*, 32n2.

27. Cook, *Commanding Right*, 131 (on Ḥanbalīs), 206 (on Mu'tazilites), 270–272 (on Imāmīs), 336n206 (on Ḥanafīs), 349 (on Shāfi'ites).

28. Basim Musallam, "The Ordering of Muslim Societies," in *Cambridge Illustrated History of the Islamic World*, ed. Francis Robinson (Cambridge: Cambridge University Press, 1996), 176.

29. Jonathan Berkey, "The Promise and Pitfalls of Medieval Islamic Social History," *International Journal of Middle East Studies* 46, no. 2 (2014): 392.

30. Benjamin Foster, "Agoranomos and Muḥtasib," *Journal of the Economic and Social History of the Orient* 13 (1970): 128–144.

31. Sihām Muṣṭafā Abū Zayd, *Al-Ḥisba fī Miṣr al-Islāmiyya min al-Fath al-ʿArabī ilā Nihāyat al-ʿAṣr al-Mamlūkī* (Cairo: Al-Hay'a al-Miṣriyya al-ʿĀmma lil-Kitāb, 1986), 49–54. For a different view, one that still believes the *agoranomos* influenced pre-Islamic Arabia, see Aḥmad Ghabin, *Ḥisba, Arts and Crafts in Islam* (Wiesbaden: Verlag, 2009), chap. 1, esp. 26–27.

32. Yaḥyā Ibn 'Umar, "Kitāb Aḥkām al-Sūq," edited and annotated by M. 'A. Makkī, *Ṣaḥīfat al-Ma'had al-Miṣrī lil-Dirāsat al-Islāmiyya fi Madrid* 4 (1956): 59–151.

33. See, for example, Ibn 'Umar, *Aḥkām al-Sūq*, 108, 112. On of the nature, internal structure, and date of composition of Mālik's *Muwaṭṭa'*, see Wael Hallaq, "On Dating Malik's *Muwatta*," *UCLA Journal of Islamic and Middle East Law* 1 (2002): 47–75.

34. Ibn 'Umar, *Aḥkām al-Sūq*, sec. 36, p. 126. On this matter, see Cook, *Commanding Right*, 368.

35. Ibn 'Umar, *Aḥkām al-Sūq*, sec. 35, p. 125.

36. Ibn 'Umar, *Aḥkām al-Sūq*, sec. 33, p. 124. On this matter, see Ibn 'Abdūn's (fl. second half of the fifth century AH / eleventh century CE) treatise on *ḥisba:* "Risala fi'l-hisba," in *Documents arabes inédits sur la vie sociale et économique en Occident musulman au moyen âge*, ed. E. Lévi-Provençal (Cairo: IFAO, 1955), 48.

37. Ibn 'Umar, *Aḥkām al-Sūq*, sec. 39, p. 128.

38. Ibn 'Umar, *Aḥkām al-Sūq*, sec. 37, pp. 126–127.

39. Ibn 'Umar, *Aḥkām al-Sūq*, sec. 49, p. 137.

40. Ibn 'Umar, *Aḥkām al-Sūq*, sec. 42, pp. 130–132.

41. Ibn 'Umar, *Aḥkām al-Sūq*, sec. 45, p. 134.

42. Ibn 'Umar, *Aḥkām al-Sūq*, sec. 24, pp. 115–116.

43. Ibn 'Umar, *Aḥkām al-Sūq*, secs. 25 and 26, pp. 116–117.

44. Ibn 'Umar, *Aḥkām al-Sūq*, sec. 12, p. 109.

45. Ibn 'Umar, *Aḥkām al-Sūq*, sec. 13, p. 110.

46. Ibn 'Umar, *Aḥkām al-Sūq*, sec. 11, p. 109.

47. Ibn 'Umar, *Aḥkām al-Sūq*, secs. 20 and 21, pp. 113–114.

48. Ibn 'Umar, *Aḥkām al-Sūq*, sec. 7, p. 106.

49. Ibn 'Umar, *Aḥkām al-Sūq*, sec. 12, p. 109.

50. Ibn 'Umar, *Aḥkām al-Sūq*, sec. 17, p. 112.

51. On price setting, see Adam Sabra, "'Prices Are in God's Hands': The Theory and Practice of Price Control in the Medieval Islamic World," in *Poverty and Charity in Middle Eastern Contexts*, ed. Michael Bonner, Mine Ener, and Amy Singer (New York: State University of New York Press, 2003), 73–91; and Kristen Stilt, "Price Setting and Hoarding in Mamluk Egypt: The Lessons of Legal Realism for Islamic Legal Studies," in *The Law Applied: Contextualizing the Islamic Shari'a; A Volume in Honor of Frank E. Vogel*, ed. Peri Bearman, Wolfhart Heinrichs, and Bernard G. Weiss (London: I.B. Tauris, 2008), 57–78.

52. Ibn 'Umar, *Aḥkām al-Sūq,* sec. 9, pp. 107–108.
53. Ibn 'Umar, *Aḥkām al-Sūq,* sec. 43, p. 132.
54. Ibn 'Umar, *Aḥkām al-Sūq,* sec. 46, pp. 134–135.
55. Ibn 'Umar, *Aḥkām al-Sūq,* sec. 27, p. 117.
56. Māwardī, *Ordinances of Government.*
57. For a biographical sketch of Māwardī, see Aḥmad Akhtar, "Al-Māwardī: A Sketch of His Life and Works," *Islamic Culture* 18 (1944): 283–300. See also, H. A. R. Gibb, "Al-Māwardī's Theory of the Caliphate," *Islamic Culture* 11 (1937): 291–302; and Hanna Mikhail, *Politics and Revelation: Māwardī and After* (Edinburgh: Edinburgh University Press, 1995). For a more recent reading, see Frank Vogel, "Tracing Nuance in Māwardī's *Al-Aḥkām al-Sulṭāniyyah:* Implicit Framing of Constitutional Authority," in *Islamic Law in Theory: Studies on Jurisprudence in Honor of Bernard Weiss,* ed. A. Kevin Reinhart and Robert Gleave (Leiden: Brill, 2014), 331–359.
58. Patricia Crone, *God's Rule: Government and Islam* (New York: Columbia University Press, 2004), 303.
59. Māwardī, *Ordinances of Government,* 32–65.
60. Māwardī, *Ordinances of Government,* 268.
61. Māwardī, *Ordinances of Government,* 267.
62. Māwardī, *Ordinances of Government,* 272.
63. Māwardī, *Ordinances of Government,* 275.
64. Māwardī, *Ordinances of Government,* 275.
65. Māwardī, *Ordinances of Government,* 277.
66. Abū Ḥāmid al-Ghazālī, *Iḥyā' 'Ulūm al-Dīn,* 4 vols. (Cairo: Al-Maktaba al-Tijariyya al-Kubra, [1967?]), 2:306–335. For an extended summary and a textual analysis of Ghazālī's treatment of *ḥisba*, see Cook, *Commanding Right,* 427–468. For a critical reading, see Musallam, "Ordering of Muslim Societies," 173–186. I have greatly benefited from Cook's and Musallam's very thoughtful, if different, analyses of Ghazālī's *Iḥyā'*. For a biography of Ghazālī, see Eric Ormsby, *Ghazālī* (Oxford: Oneworld, 2008).
67. This was Ibn al-Ukhuwwa, whose treatise on *ḥisba* is mentioned briefly later in the chapter. See Cook, *Commanding Right,* 452n165.
68. On the legacy of Ghazālī's treatment of *ḥisba,* see Cook, *Commanding Right,* 450–459, 507–509.
69. Ghazālī, *Iḥyā',* 2:306.
70. Ghazālī, *Iḥyā',* 2:312.
71. Ghazālī, *Iḥyā',* 2:312–314.
72. Ghazālī, *Iḥyā',* 2:315.
73. Ghazālī, *Iḥyā',* 2:342.
74. Ghazālī, *Iḥyā',* 2:335–343. For an English summary of this section of the text, see Musallam, "Ordering of Muslim Societies," 174.
75. See, for example, Ibn al-Ukhuwwa [Muḥammad Ibn Muḥammad al-Qurashī] "Ma'ālim al-Qurbā fī Aḥkām al-Ḥisba," in *Fī al-Turāth al-Iqtiṣādī al-Islāmī* (Beirut: Dār al-Ḥadātha, 1990), 28–316. For a critical English edition of this treatise, see Ibn

al-Ukhuwwa [Muḥammad Ibn Muḥammad al-Qurashī], *Ma'ālim al-Qurba fi Aḥkām al-Ḥisba of Ḍiyā' al-Dīn Muḥammad Ibn Muḥammad al-Qurashī al-Shāfi'ī known as ibn as-Ukhuwwa*, ed. and trans. Reuben Levy (Cambridge: Cambridge University Press, 1938). But Abū Zayd argues that that it is not certain that Ibn al-Ukhuwwa was influenced by Shayzarī. See Abū Zayd, A*l-Ḥisba,* 20,

76. Muḥmmad Ibn Aḥmad Ibn Bassam, *Nihāyat al-Rutba fi Ṭalab al-Ḥisba,* ed. Ḥusām al-Dīn al-Sāmarrā'ī (Baghdad: Maṭba'at al-Ma'ārif, 1968). There is a controversy, however, about whether Shayzarī borrowed from Ibn Bassām or vice versa. See 'Abdallah Qārī, "Ḥawla Kitābayy al-Shayzarī wa Ibn Bassām: Man Minhumā Sabaq al-Ākhar?" *'Ālam al-Kutub,* 29, nos. 3–4 (2007–8): 361–366.

77. Buckley, *Book of the Islamic Market Inspector,* 47; Shayzarī, *Kitāb Nihāyat al-Rutba*, 23. Cf. Ibn al-Ukhuwwa, *Ma'ālim al-Qurba,* ed. and trans. Levy, 30.

78. Buckley, *Book of the Islamic Market Inspector,* 50; Shayzarī, *Kitāb Nihāyat al-Rutba*, 26. Cf. Ibn al-Ukhuwwa, *Ma'ālim al-Qurba,* ed. and trans. Levy, 36.

79. Buckley, *Book of the Islamic Market Inspector,* 52; Shayzarī, *Kitāb Nihāyat al-Rutba*, 27. Cf. Ibn al-Ukhuwwa, *Ma'ālim al-Qurba,* ed. and trans. Levy, 32.

80. Buckley, *Book of the Islamic Market Inspector,* 54; Shayzarī, *Kitāb Nihāyat al-Rutba*, 31.

81. Buckley, *Book of the Islamic Market Inspector,* 56; Shayzarī, *Kitāb Nihāyat al-Rutba*, 32. Cf. Ibn al-Ukhuwwa, *Ma'ālim al-Qurba,* ed. and trans. Levy, 34.

82. Buckley, *Book of the Islamic Market Inspector,* 57 ; Shayzarī, *Kitāb Nihāyat al-Rutba*, 33. Cf. Ibn al-Ukhuwwa, *Ma'ālim al-Qurba,* ed. and trans. Levy, 35–36.

83. Buckley, *Book of the Islamic Market Inspector,* 60–61; Shayzarī, *Kitāb Nihāyat al-Rutba*, 36. Cf. Ibn al-Ukhuwwa, *Ma'ālim al-Qurba,* ed. and trans. Levy, 35.

84. For an account of the *muḥtasib*'s use of stamps to calibrate and monitor currency, see Michael L. Bates, "The Function of Fatimid and Ayyubid Glass Weights," *Journal of the Economic and Social History of the Orient* 24, no. 1 (1981): 63–92.

85. Asad, "Tradition, Religion, and Politics," 179.

86. Ṣayfī, *Al-Ḥisba fi'l-Islam,* 10.

87. For more on the centrality of violence in the *fiqh* theory of *ḥisba,* see Ahmed Abdelsalam, "The Practice of Violence in the *Ḥisba*-Theories," *Iranian Studies* 38, no. 4 (2005): 547–554.

88. Māwardī, *Ordinances of Government,* 261.

89. Māwardī, *Ordinances of Government,* 262.

90. Buckley, *Book of the Islamic Market Inspector,* 124; Shayzarī, *Kitāb Nihāyat al-Rutba*, 108.

91. Christian Lange, "Where on Earth Is Hell?' in *Public Violence in Islamic Societies: Power, Discipline, and the Construction of the Public Sphere, 7th-19th Centuries CE,* ed. Christian Lange and Mirabel Fiero (Edinburgh: Edinburgh University Press, 2009), 175n59.

92. Jamāl al-Dīn Abū al-Maḥāsin Yūsuf Ibn Taghrī Birdī, *Al-Nujūm al-Zāhira fi Mulūk Miṣr wa'l-Qāhira,* 16 vols. (Cairo: Al-Mu'assasa al-Miṣriyya al-'Āmma lil-Ta'līf wa'l-Ṭibā'a wa'l-Nashr), 4:236.

93. Muḥammad Ibn Aḥmad Ibn Iyās, *Badāʾiʿ al-Zuhūr fī Waqāʾiʿ al-Duhūr,* 6 vols., ed. Muḥammad Muṣṭafā (Cairo: Dar al-Kutub wa'l-Watha'iq al-Qawmiyya, 2008), 3:67–68.

94. Aḥmad b. ʿAlī al-Maqrīzī, *Al-Sulūk li-Maʿrifat Duwal al-Mulūk,* 4 vols. (Cairo: Maṭbaʿat Lajnat al-Ta'līf wa'l-Tarjama wa'l-Nashr, 1956–73), 2:758. For an analysis of this case, see Stilt, "Price Setting," 65–67.

95. Maqrīzī, *Al-Sulūk,* 3:361–364. For an analysis of this case, see Carl Petry, "The Hoax of the Miraculous Speaking Wall: Criminal Investigation in Mamluk Cairo," in *Mamluks and Ottomans: Studies in Honour of Michael Winter,* ed. David Wasserstein and Ami Ayalon (London: Routledge, 2006), 86–95.

96. On Ibn Zawlāq and Subawayhi, see Y. Lev, "Aspects of the Egyptian Society in the Fatimid Period," in *Egypt and Syria in the Fatimid, Ayyubid and Mamluk Eras,* vol. 3, ed. U. Vermeulen and J. Van Steenbergen (Leuven: Uitgeverij Peeters, 2001), 1–32. On wise fools, see Michael Dols, *Majnun: The Madman in Medieval Muslim Society,* ed. D. E. Immisch (Oxford: Oxford University Press, 1992), chap. 12.

97. Sibawayhi is playing on the pun between *ajrās* (bells) and *aḥrās* (guards).

98. Al-Ḥasan Ibn Ibrāhīm Ibn Zawlāq, *Akhbār Sibawayhi al-Miṣrī,* ed. Muḥammad Ibrāhīm Saʿd and Ḥusayn al-Dīb (Cairo: Maṭbaʿat ʿal-Naṣr, 1933), 29.

99. Jonathan P. Berkey, "The *Muhtasib*s of Cairo under the Mamluks: Toward an Understanding of an Islamic Institution," in *Mamluks in Egyptian and Syrian Politics and Society,* ed. Michael Winter and Amalia Levanoni (Leiden: Brill, 2004), 245–276.

100. Berkey, "*Muhtasibs*," 252–253.

101. Berkey, "*Muhtasibs*," 259.

102. Berkey, "*Muhtasibs*," 262.

103. Berkey, "*Muhtasibs*," 268.

104. Berkey, "*Muhtasibs*," 270. The internal quote is from Carl Petry, *The Civilian Elite of Cairo in the Later Middle Ages* (Princeton: Princeton University Press, 1981), 224.

105. Berkey, "*Muhtasibs*," 274.

106. Stilt, *Islamic Law in Action.*

107. Stilt, *Islamic Law in Action,* 196.

108. Ghazālī, *Iḥyāʾ,* 2:318.

109. Imām al-Ḥaramayn Ḍiāʾ al-Dīn ʿAbd al-Malik Ibn Yūsuf al-Juwaynī, *Al-Irshād Ilā Qawāṭiʿ al-Adilla fī Uṣūl al-Iʿtiqād* (Cairo: Al-Khānjī, 1950), 368.

110. Juwaynī, *Al-Irshād,* 370.

111. Cook, *Commanding Right,* 457.

112. Ghazālī, *Iḥyāʾ,* 2:329. On the difference between *khabar* and *shahāda,* see chapter five of this book.

113. For further elaboration of how Ghazālī's text falls short of giving clear answers to these ambivalent points, see Cook, *Commanding Right,* 480–482.

114. Agrama, *Questioning Secularism,* 64.

115. Ghazālī, *Iḥyā'*, 2:323.

116. T. F. Glick, "'Muhtasib' and 'Mustasaf': A Case Study of Institutional Diffusion," *Viator* 2 (1971): 59–81.

117. Quranī, *Al-Ḥisba,* 1:4.

118. Asad, "Tradition, Religion, and Politics," 177.

119. Agrama, *Questioning Secularism,* 64.

120. DWQ, Dīwān Khidīwī, S/2/40/23 (original no. 777), doc. no. 48, p. 53, AH 14 Rajab 1245 / 10 January 1830 CE.

121. Zaghlūl, *Al-Muḥāmāh,* appendix, 5. Gabriel Baer provides another clue when he says that the duties of the *muḥtasib* were taken over by the chief of police "after the reign of Muḥammad 'Alī." See Gabriel Baer, *Egyptian Guilds in Modern Times* (Jerusalem: Israel Oriental Society, 1964), 101.

122. The ordinance was issued in Turkish, but I could not find a copy of it in the Egyptian National Archives. Luckily, an English translation is preserved in the British National Archives, and this is the version I consulted. See "General Regulations Concerning the Public Health at Alexandria and the Interior to Be Put into Execution According to Order of His Highness the Vice Roy, Dated 15 Rejeb 1257 (30 August 1841)," enclosure in FO 78/502, Barnett, 23 December 1842, National Archives, Kew.

123. "General Regulations Concerning the Public Health," National Archives.

124. Buckley, *Book of the Islamic Market Inspector,* 122; Shayzarī, *Kitāb Nihāyat al-Rutba*, 107.

125. Buckley, *Book of the Islamic Market Inspector,* 125; Shayzarī, *Kitāb Nihāyat al-Rutba*, 108.

126. Bernard, *Al-Minḥah fi Siyāsat Ḥifẓ al-Ṣiḥḥah,* trans. Jurjī Fīdāl and Muḥammad al-Harrāwī (Cairo: Būlāq, 1834), 27.

127. For a history of objectivity in the nineteenth century, see Loraine Daston and Peter Galison, *Objectivity* (New York: Zone Books, 2010).

128. For a list of medical titles published by Būlāq Press, see Shayyāl, *Tārīkh al-Tarjama,* appendix 1.

129. Bernard, *Al-Minḥah.* On Bernard, see Kuhnke, *Lives at Risk,* 188.

130. Bernard, *Al-Minḥah,* 3.

131. Clot Bey, *Kunūz al-Ṣiḥḥa.* A Turkish translation of Clot's book was done by Muṣṭafā Rasmī and published by Būlāq Press in 1845; see Shayyāl, *Tārīkh al-Tarjama,* appendix 1.

132. The other three sections are public hygiene ("aṣ-Ṣiḥḥa al-Ijtimā'iyya"), military hygiene ("aṣ-Ṣiḥḥa al-Ḥarbiyya"), and naval hygiene ("aṣ-Ṣiḥḥa al-Baḥariyya").

133. René Descartes, *The Treatise on Man,* trans. Thomas Steel Hall (Cambridge, MA: Harvard University Press, 1972), 2–4.

134. For an analysis of the role played by dietary regimens within a mechanistic conception of the human body, see Bryan Turner, "The Discourse of Diet," *Theory, Culture and Society* 1 (1982): 23–32.

135. Bernard, *Al-Minḥah,* 10–11.

136. Dimitri Gutas, "Medical Theory and Scientific Method in the Age of Avicenna," in Peter E. Pormann, ed., *Islamic Medical and Scientific Tradition: Critical Concepts in Islamic Studies,* vol. 1 (London: Routledge, 2011), 37.

137. Bernard, *Al-Minḥah,* 11.

138. Bernard, *Al-Minḥah,* 11.

139. On the *sex res non-naturales,* see Melitta Weiss-Adamson, "*Tacuinum Sanitatis,*" in *Medieval Science, Technology, and Medicine: An Encyclopedia,* ed. Thomas F. Glick, Steven J. Livesey, and Faith Wallis (New York: Routledge, 2005), 469–470; and Mirko Grmek, ed., *Western Medical Thought from Antiquity to the Middle Ages,* trans. Antony Shugaar (Cambridge, MA: Harvard University Press, 1998), 161–162. On Ibn Sīnā's treatment of these six categories, see Abū 'Alī al-Ḥusayn Ibn 'Abd Allāh Ibn Sīnā, *Al-Qānūn fī al-Ṭibb,* 4 vols., ed. Idwār al-Qashsh (Beirut: Mu'assasat 'Izz al-Dīn, 1987), 1:111–137.

140. Bernard, *Al-Minḥah,* 16.

141. Bernard, *Al-Minḥah,* 20. For Ibn Sīnā's comments on living in these places, see Ibn Sīnā, *Al-Qānūn,* 1:91–92.

142. Bernard, *Al-Minḥah,* 22.

143. Clot Bey, *Kunūz al-Ṣiḥḥa,* 92–97.

144. Clot Bey, *Kunūz al-Ṣiḥḥa,* 162–163.

145. Clot Bey, *Kunūz al-Ṣiḥḥa,* 61–62.

146. See, for example, Clot Bey, *Kunūz al-Ṣiḥḥa,* 55.

147. Clot Bey, *Nubdhah fi Uṣūl al-Falsafah al-Ṭabi'iyah; Uṣūl fi al-Tashrīḥ al-'Āmm; uabdhah fi Tashrīḥ al-Marḍa,* trans. Ibrahim al-Nabarawi (Cairo: Būlāq, AH 1253/1837 CE), 21.

148. Xavier Bichat, *Anatomie générale appliquée à la physiologie et à la medicine* (Paris: Brosson et Gabon, 1801), lxxxiii-lxiv.

149. Clot Bey, *Kunūz al-Ṣiḥḥa,* 16.

150. Clot Bey, *Kunūz al-Siḥḥa,* 44.

151. Clot Bey, *Kunūz al-Ṣiḥḥa,* 52.

152. Clot Bey, *Kunūz al-Ṣiḥḥa,* 326. Dāwūd al-Anṭākī, or David of Antioch, was a sixteenth-century Syrian physician and pharmacist, who was active in Cairo and died in Mecca in 1599. His *Tadhkara* was a popular treatise that alphabetically lists Arabic, Persian, and Greek pharmacological terms.

153. Muḥammad al-Shāfi'ī, *Aḥsan al-Aghrāḍ fi at-Tashkhīṣ wa Mu'ālajat al-Amrāḍ,* trans. Ḥusayn al-Rashīdī, Muḥammad al-Tūnisī, and Nicolas Perron (Cairo: Būlāq, AH 1259/1843 CE), 6. The other sciences were natural history, zoology, physiology, and pharmacology.

154. Grégoire, *Ghāyat al-Marām fi Adwiyat al-Asqām,* trans. Yūsuf Fir'awn and Ḥasan Kassāb (Cairo: Būlāq, AH 1255/1839 CE), 8.

155. Grégoire, *Ghāyat al-Marām,* 13.

156. Perron, *Al-Djawāhir al-Saniyya.*

157. Perron, *Al-Djawāhir al-Saniyya,* 1:2.

158. For a short biographical sketch of Orfila, see "Biographical Sketch of the late M. Orfila" *Lancet,* 61, no. 1544 (2 April 1853): 326–327. For a critical account of

Orfila's work, which connected toxicology with forensic medicine, see José Ramón Bertomeu-Sánchez, "Popularizing Controversial Science: A Popular Treatise on Poisons by Mateu Orfila (1818)," *Medical History* 53, no. 3 (2009): 351–378.

159. Perron, *Al-Djawāhir al-Saniyya,* 1: 2–11.

160. Antoine Barthélémy Clot Bey, *Compte rendu de l'état de l'enseignement médical et du service de santé civil et militaire de l'Égypte au commencement de mars 1849* (Paris: Victor Masson, 1849), 23.

161. William R. Wilde, *Narrative of a Voyage to Madeira, Teneriffe and along the Shores of the Mediterranean, Including a Visit to Algiers, Egypt, Palestine, Etc,.* 2 vols. (Dublin: William Curry, 1840), 1:341.

162. K. Baedeker, *Egypt: Handbook for Travellers* (London: Dulau, 1878), 242.

163. DWQ, Muḥāfaẓat Miṣr, L/1/4/3 (original no. 457), doc. no. 25, p. 6, AH 19 Rabīʿ II 1281 / 21 September 1864 CE. For reports written by other ad hoc chemical committees established to check food quality or suspicious poisonous material, see DWQ, Dīwān al-Jihādiyya, S/3/122/7 (original no. 446), doc. no. 216, p. 50, AH 1 Dhū al-Qaʿda 1274 / 13 June 1858 CE (about the impossibility of refining a certain kind of oil); and DWQ, Dīwān al-Jihādiyya, S/3/122/7 (original no. 446), doc. no. 218, AH 2 Dhū al-Qaʿda 1274 / 14 June 1858 CE (concerning a suspicious liquid that the committee found was not poisonous).

164. Kuhnke, however, says Figari was a professor of botany as early as 1827. See Kuhnke, *Lives at Risk,* 188.

165. Antonio Figari, *Projet pour l'établissement de colonies agricoles et d'une ferme modèle en Égypte* (Alexandria: P. Cumbo, n.d.).

166. Antonio Figari, *Al-Durr al-Lāmiʿ fī'l-Nabāt wa Mā Fīhi min al-Khawāṣ wa'l-Manāfiʿ,* trans. Muḥammad Ibn ʿUmar al-Tūnisī and Husayn al-Rashīdī (Cairo: Būlāq, 1841); and Figari, *Ḥusn al-Barāʿa fī ʿIlm al-Zirāʿa,* trans. Aḥmad Nadā (Cairo: Būlāq, 1866).

167. DWQ, Dīwān al-Jihādiyya, S/3/122/7 (original no. 446), doc. no. 33, p. 48, AH 18 Shawwāl 1274 / 1 June 1858 CE; DWQ, Majlis al-Khuṣūṣī, S/11/8/4 (original no. 66), doc. no. 25, p. 40, AH 9 Muḥarram 1280 / 26 June 1863 CE; Kuhnke, *Lives at Risk,* 188; and M. A. Cappelletti, "Antonio Figari," in *Dizionario Biografico degli Italiani,* vol. 47, ed. Fiorella Bartoccini and Mario Caravale (Rome: Istituto della Enciclopedia Italiana, 1997), 538–540.

168. This school seems to have been founded in 1829. It was originally located in the Citadel, but was later moved to Old Cairo. See J. Heyworth-Dunne, *An Introduction to the History of Education in Modern Egypt* (London: Frank Cass, 1968), 131, 357.

169. DWQ, Dīwān al-Jihādiyya, S/3/122/7 (original no. 446), doc. no. 35, p. 51, AH 27 Shawwāl 1274 / 10 June 1858 CE. This record also says that his annual salary was two thousand piasters; in 1863, it was raised to three thousand piasters. See DWQ, Majlis al-Khuṣūṣī, S/11/8/4 (original no. 66), doc. no. 25, p. 40, AH 9 Muḥarram 1280 / 26 June 1863 CE.

170. J. B. Gastinel, "Mémoire sur le haschich et ses applications dans la thérapeutique," *Répertoire de Pharmacie* 6 (1849): 129–142; Gastinel, *Monographie des opiums*

de la Haute-Égypte (Paris: Lainé et Havard, 1862); Gastinel, *Analyses de glutens retirés des farines examinées par la Commission des blés égyptiens* (Paris: Lainé et Havard, 1862); Gastinel, *Étude topographique, chimique et médicale sur les eaux minérales de Hélouan-les-Bains* (Cairo: Moniteur Égyptien, 1883).

171. J.B. Gastinel, *Nukhbat al-Adhkiya' fī 'Ilm al-Kimiya'*, 2 vols., trans. Aḥmad Nadā (Cairo: Būlāq, 1870).

172. For a short biographical sketch on Nadā, see 'Umar Ṭūsūn, *Al-Ba'thāt al-'Ilmiyya fī 'Ahd Muḥammad 'Alī Thumma fī 'Ahdayy 'Abbās al-Awwal wa Sa'īd* (Alexandria: Ṣalāḥ al-Dīn, 1934), 348–350. Official records state that in 1863, he had the position of professor of natural history at the Qaṣr al-'Ainī Medical School, with an annual salary of 1,500 piasters. See DWQ, Majlis al- Khuṣūṣī, S/11/8/4 (original no. 66), doc. no. 25, p. 40, AH 9 Muḥarram 1280 / 26 June 1863 CE.

173. Aḥmad Nadā, *Al-Āyāt al-Bayyināt fī 'Ilm al-Nabātāt* (Cairo: Būlāq, 1866); Nadā, *Al-Aqwāl al-Marḍiyya fī 'Ilm al-Tabaqāt al-Arḍiyya* (Cairo: Būlāq, 1871).

174. Ṭūsūn, *Al-Ba'thāt,* 562–564; Heyworth-Dunne, *An Introduction,* 329.

175. On Frank, see George Rosen, *A History of Public Health* (Baltimore: Johns Hopkins University Press, 1993), 137–143.

176. DWQ, Ma'iyya Saniyya, Turkī, S/1/58/1 (original no. 41), doc. no. 354, AH 18 Rabī' I 1247 / 27 August 1831 CE.

177. Kuhnke, *Lives at Risk,* 53–54, 92–99; E.C. Bernard, *Le Conseil sanitaire, maritime et quarantenaire d'Egypte* (Alexandria: Penasson, 1897); "The General Board of Health, Egypt," *Lancet* 116, no. 2979 (October 1880): 555.

178. Although she never uses these Arabic or Turkish names, it seems that this is what Kuhnke means when she refers to the Military Medical Council.

179. For more on the 1841 settlement, see Fahmy, *Mehmed Ali,* 91–98.

180. Kuhnke, *Lives at Risk,* 145–147; Tassos Demetrios Néroutsos, *Aperçu historique de l'organisation de l'intendance générale sanitaire d'Egypte: séant à Alexandrie, depuis sa fondation en 1831 . . . jusqu' . . . en 1879* (Alexandria: Mourès, 1880), 39–42.

181. Kuhnke, "Resistance and Response," 170.

182. Quoted in Kuhnke, "Resistance and Response," 171.

183. Muḥammad 'Alī al-Baqlī. "Fī al-tamarru'," *Ya'sūb al-Ṭibb,* no. 29 (AH Jumādā I 1283 / August 1866 CE), 8; Kuhnke, *Lives at Risk,* 167. Although the 1841 ordinance concerned Alexandria, similar regulations pertained to Cairo.

184. DWQ, Muḥāfaẓat Miṣr, L/5/2/ (original no. 185), doc. no. 35, p. 107, AH 21 Ramaḍān 1277 / 2 April 1866 CE.

185. DWQ, Dīwān Taftīsh Ṣiḥḥat al-Maḥrūsa, M/5/11 (original no. 226), doc. no. 115, p. 252, AH 26 Dhū al-Qa'da 1290 / 16 January 1874 CE.

186. DWQ, Ḍabṭiyyat Miṣr, L/2/31/1, doc. no. 390, pp. 165, 169, AH 20 Dhū al-Qa'da 1296 / 5 November 1879 CE.

187. DWQ, Ḍabṭiyyat Miṣr, L/2/31/1, doc. no. 414, p. 186, AH 1 Dhū al-Ḥijja 1296 / 15 November 1879 CE. It is also noteworthy that even cases of public drunk-

enness were handled by the police, not the *muḥtasib* or the qaḍi. In his exhaustive study of qadi sentences, Rudolph Peters found no convictions for drunkenness and thus concluded that such offenses "were dealt with summarily by the police." See Rudolph Peters, "Islamic and Criminal Law in Nineteenth Century Egypt: The Role and Function of the Qadi," *Islamic Law and Society* 4, no. 1(1997): 83.

188. DWQ, Ḍabṭiyyat Miṣr, L/2/31/1, doc. no. 380, p. 160, AH 19 Dhū al-Qaʿda 1296 / 4 November 1879 CE; and DWQ, Ḍabṭiyyat Miṣr, L/2/31/1, doc. no. 425, pp. 192–193, AH 3 Dhū al-Ḥijja 1296 / 17 November 1879 CE.

189. DWQ, Muḥāfaẓat Miṣr, L/1/5/2 (original no. 185), doc. no. 35, p. 107, AH 21 Ramaḍān 1277 / 2 April 1861 CE.

190. Clot Bey, *Kunūz al-Ṣiḥḥa,* 47.

191. DWQ, Muḥāfaẓat Miṣr, L/1/5/1, doc. no. 155, p. 151, AH 24 Dhū al-Qaʿda 1276 / 14 June 1860 CE. This case was about unripe, green dates, which were deemed "harmful to public hygiene."

192. DWQ, Muḥāfaẓat Miṣr, L/1/4/1, doc. no. 173, pp. 24, 26, AH 17 Jumāda II, 1280 / 29 November 1863 CE. For another examination of coffee, see DWQ, Muḥāfaẓat Miṣr, L/1/4/24 (original no. 464), doc. no. 62, p. 18, AH 20 Jumāda II 1284 / 18 October 1867 CE.

193. DWQ, Muḥāfaẓat Miṣr, L/1/4/9 (original no. 458), doc. no. 788, pp. 50, 53, AH 16 Rabīʿ II 1282 / 7 September 1865 CE.

194. DWQ, Dīwān al-Jihādiyya, reg. no. 446, doc. no. 437, pp. 61–62, AH 25 Dhū al-Qa'da 1274 / 8 July 1858 CE.

195. Ghazālī, *Iḥyā',* 2:338.

196. On how time of death was established by investigating the stiffness, color, and temperature of a corpse, see Shabāsī, *Al-Tanwīr,* 435–437. On how rigor mortis was detected in the Egyptian heat, see the memoirs of Sir Sydney Smith, the Australian chief forensic medical officer in Egypt in the 1920s: Smith, *Mostly Murder* (New York: David McKay, 1959), 58.

197. DWQ, Ḍabṭiyyat Iskandariyya, L/4/18/3 (original no. 1674), case no. 133, pp. 16–19, AH 5 Dhū al-Ḥijja 1294 / 11 December 1877 CE.

198. Cf. Timothy Mitchell, *Rule of Experts: Egypt, Techno-Politics, Modernity* (Berkeley: University of California Press), 91–92. Mitchell reflects on the implication of transferring cadastral knowledge from the village surveyors to the map.

199. For a modern-day commentary on the dangers inherent in performing the duty of *ḥisba,* see Usāma Ibrāhīm Ḥāfiẓ and ʿAlī Muḥammad ʿAlī al-Sharīf, *Al-Nuṣḥ wa'l-Tabyīn fī Taṣḥīḥ Mafāhīm al-Muḥtasibīn* (Cairo: Maktabat al-Turāth al-Islāmī, 2002). This book is significant partially because it was issued and endorsed by leading members of the Egyptian radical group al-Gamaʿa al-Islamiyya (which was responsible for assassinating President Anwar Sadat in 1981), including Karam Zuhdī, ʿĀṣim ʿAbd al-Māgid ʿIṣām Dirbāla, and Nāgiḥ Ibrāhīm. The book, the title of which translates as "Advice and correction of principles followed by *muḥtasibs,*" has an entire chapter cautioning private *muḥtasibs* against the overzealous use of violence (chapter 11).

CHAPTER FIVE. JUSTICE WITHOUT PAIN

1. In 1851, ʿAbbās Ḥilmī renamed the Cairo quarter of Qaysūn al-Ḥilmiyya after himself. See Sāmī, *Taqwīm al-Nīl,* 3:38.

2. DWQ, Majlis al-Aḥkām, S/7/10/3 (original no. 665), case no. 347, pp. 54–56, AH 22 Rabīʿ II 1275 / 29 November 1858 CE (emphasis added). The original letters from the Cairo Police Department to the Majlis al-Aḥkām can be found in DWQ, Ḍabṭiyyat Miṣr, L/2/186 (original no. 365), doc. no. 72, pp. 179, 185–188, AH 15 Rabīʿ II 1275 / 22 November 1858 CE; and DWQ, Ḍabṭiyyat Miṣr, L/2/186 (original no. 365), doc. no. 74, p. 188, AH 19 Rabīʿ II 1275 / 26 November 1858 CE. Saʿīd Pasha's decision is in DWQ, Maʿiyya Saniyya, Awāmir, reg. no. 1891, order no 12, p. 85, AH 28 Shaʿbān 1275 / 2 April 1859 CE. For a full transcription of the case, see Khaled Fahmy, *Al-Jasad wa'l-Ḥadātha: Al-Ṭibb wa'l-Qānūn fī Miṣr al-Ḥadītha* (Cairo: Dār al-Kutub wa'l-Wathā'iq al-Qawmiyya, 2005), 197–205.

3. Fahmy, "The Police and the People," 375.

4. Nathan Brown, *The Rule of Law in the Arab World* (Cambridge: Cambridge University Press, 1997).

5. Brown, *Rule of Law,* 242.

6. Toledano, *State and Society;* Hunter, *Egypt under the Khedives;* Mestyan, *Arab Patriotism.*

7. The 1841 *firman* that granted Egypt to Mehmed Ali in a hereditary manner stipulated that the governorship should be bestowed on the oldest male descendant in the family (as opposed to primogeniture). Accordingly, Ilhāmī was not entitled to succeed his father as governor of Egypt. Nevertheless, there is some evidence that ʿAbbās might have harbored such a desire, as is suggested by the attempt by some members of his entourage immediately after he was assassinated (on July 7, 1854) to stage a palace coup in the hope of blocking Saʿīd's accession until Ilhāmī had returned from a trip to Europe. See Sāmī, *Taqwīm al-Nīl,* 3:72.

8. On justice as an act of balancing and the use of terms such as *mizān* and *qisṭās,* which mean "scale," to express notions of justice in Islamic legal thought, see Rosen, *Justice of Islam,* 163–164.

9. For more on these early definitions of *ʿadl* and *ẓulm,* see Roy Mottahedeh, *Loyalty and Leadership in Early Islamic Society* (Princeton: Princeton University Press, 1980), 179. See also Boğaç Ergene, "On Ottoman Justice: Interpretations in Conflict (1600–1800)," *Islamic Law and Society* 8 (2001): 52–87. Ergene writes that among the many meanings of justice in Ottoman legal and political thought was the protection of the privileges of those who were thought to deserve them.

10. Ra'ūf ʿAbbās, ed., *Al-Awāmir wa'l-Mukātabāt al-Ṣādira min ʿAzīz Miṣr Muḥammad ʿAlī,* 2 vols. (Cairo: Dār al-Kutub wa'l-Wathā'iq al-Qawmiyya, 2005), 1:274.

11. DWQ, Muḥāfaẓat Miṣr, L/1/20/8 (original no. 1108), order no. 3, pp. 71–73, AH 11 Shaʿbān 1278 / 11 February 1862 CE.

12. Bruce F. Adams, "Progress of an Idea: The Mitigation of Corporal Punishment in Russia to 1863," *Maryland Historian,* 17 (1986): 57–74.

13. Adams, "Progress of an Idea," 71.

14. Douglass M. Peers, "Sepoys, Soldiers and the Lash: Race, Caste and Army Discipline in India, 1820–50," *Journal of Imperial and Commonwealth History* 23 (1995): 211–247.

15. Asad, *Formations of the Secular,* 107 (emphasis in original).

16. Asad, *Formations of the Secular,* 109.

17. John Langbein, *Torture and the Law of Proof: Europe and England in the Ancien Régime* (Chicago: University of Chicago Press, 1977).

18. For a thoughtful study about British colonial policy in Egypt during the half-century following the 1882 invasion and British claims that they abolished the whip, banned forced labor, and reformed the taxations system, see Esmeir, *Juridical Humanity.*

19. For a review of Peters's copious and pioneering work on the history of nineteenth-century Egyptian law, see Fahmy, "Rudolph Peters."

20. Peters, "For His Correction," 174. For a corroboration of this hypothesis, see Fahmy, "The Police and the People."

21. Rudolph Peters, "Egypt and the Age of the Triumphant Prison."

22. Pieter Spierenburg, *The Spectacle of Suffering: Executions and the Evolution of Repression from a Preindustrial Metropolis to the European Experience* (Cambridge: Cambridge University Press, 1984).

23. Norbert Elias, *The Civilizing Process,* trans. Edmund Jephcott (New York: Pantheon, 1982).

24. Peters, "Egypt and the Age of the Triumphant Prison," 277.

25. Peters, "Egypt and the Age of the Triumphant Prison," 278.

26. Peters, "Egypt and the Age of the Triumphant Prison," 277.

27. Michel Foucault, *Discipline and Punish: The Birth of the Prison,* trans. Alan Sheridan (New York: Vintage, 1979), 3–72.

28. Jabartī, *'Ajā'ib,* 4:277–279.

29. A. Paton, *History of the Egyptian Revolution,* 2 vols. (London: Trubner, 1863), 2:264.

30. DWQ, Ma'iyya Saniyya 'Arabī, Mustakhlaṣat min al-Ma'iyya al-Turkī, box no. 1, doc. no. 7/362, AH 14 Dhū al-Ḥijja 1271 / 28 August 1855 CE. This is one of the rare instances that I could find of a *qiṣāṣ* verdict being carried out.

31. DWQ, Ma'iyya Saniyya, Turkī, S/1/48/3, doc. no. 325, AH 7 Rajab 1243 / 24 January 1828 CE.

32. Fahmy, *All the Pasha's Men,* 130. See also Fahmy, "Mutiny in Mehmed Ali's New Nizamī Army, April-May 1824," *International Journal of Turkish Studies* 8 (2002): 135.

33. Zaghlūl, *Al-Muḥāmāh,* 169, quoting a letter dated AH 5 Sha'bān 1237 / 27 April 1822 CE.

34. Emine Foat Tugay, *Three Centuries: Family Chronicles of Turkey and Egypt* (London: Oxford University Press, 1963), 117.

35. Sāmī, *Taqwīm al-Nīl,* 3:5, document dated AH 21 Jumāda I 1250 / 9 September 1834 CE.

36. Sāmī, *Taqwīm al-Nīl,* 2:458, document dated AH 22 Ramaḍān 1251 / 10 January 1836 CE.

37. M. Gisquet, *L'Egypte, les turcs et les arabes,* 2 vols. (Paris: Amyot, 1848), 2:132.

38. Paton, *History of the Egyptian Revolution,* 2:264.

39. Peters, "Islamic and Secular Criminal Law," 84.

40. Bowring, *Report on Egypt and Candia,* 123.

41. *Egyptian Railway,* 33.

42. Peters, "Egypt and the Age of the Triumphant Prison," 258.

43. Peters, "For His Correction," 184–188.

44. The text of this law was first published as an appendix to *Lā'iḥat Zirā'at al-Fallāḥ* ([Cairo: Būlāq, AH 1245/1830 CE], 61–67). It was later published, with slightly different wording, in Jallād's *Qāmūs al-Idāra wa'l-Qaḍā'* (3:351–378), and in Zaghlūl's *Al-Muḥāmāh* (appendix, 100–111).

45. See, for example, Article 2, Section 2 (for infamy); Article 5, Section 2 (for gambling); Article 7, Section 2 (for public quarrels with no use of lethal weapons); and Article 19, Section 3 (for market irregularities). All reproduced in Zaghlūl, *Al-Muḥāmāh,* appendix, 156–177.

46. Tamer el-Leithy, "Public Punishment in Mamluk Society" (master's thesis, Cambridge University, 1997); M. Espéronnier, "La mort violent à l'époque mamlouke: Le crime et la châtiment," *Der Islam,* 74 (1997): 137–155.

47. Uriel Heyd, *Studies in Old Ottoman Criminal Law,* ed. V.L. Ménage (Oxford: Oxford University Press, 1973), 262–265.

48. Foucault, *Discipline and Punish,* 48–49.

49. Peters, "For His Correction," 167–172.

50. See specifically the Pricing Decree, passed on AH 25 Rajab 1245 / 20 January 1830 CE, which set fixed prices for different commodities and stipulated lashing for those merchants who violated the new regulations. Significantly, it stated that the physical condition and age of the merchant should be taken into consideration when determining the punishment; the younger and stronger the merchant, the more lashes he should receive. See Sāmī, *Taqwīm al-Nīl,* 2:360.

51. Christian Lange and Maribel Fierro, "Introduction: Spatial, Ritual and Representational Aspects of Public Violence in Islamic Societies (7th-19th Centuries CE)," in *Public Violence in Islamic Societies: Power, Discipline, and the Construction of the Public Sphere, 7th-19th Centuries CE,* ed. Christian Lange and Maribel Fierro (Edinburgh: Edinburgh University Press, 2009), 8.

52. Abū Bakr Al-Kāsānī, *Badā'i' al-Ṣanā'i' fī Tartīb al-Sharā'i',* 7 vols. (Cairo: Al-Maṭba'a al-Jammāliyya, 1910), 7:64.

53. Abby M. Schrader, "Containing the Spectacle of Punishment: The Russian Autocracy and the Abolition of the Knout, 1817–1845," *Slavic Review* 56 (1997): 613–644.

54. Peers, "Sepoys, Soldiers and the Lash."

55. Article 2, Chapter 2 of Al-Qānūn al-Sulṭānī, reproduced in Zaghlūl, *Al-Muḥāmāh,* appendix, 161.

56. Peters, "For His Correction," 178 (emphasis added).

57. For similar cases of law used as a tool of social engineering, see Schrader, "Containing the Spectacle of Punishment"; and Peers, "Sepoys, Soldiers and the Lash."

58. This use of the law to bring about the differences between rulers and ruled also had strong ethnic connotations, for members of the ruling elite were ipso facto Turkish speaking while the masses were Arabic speaking (*evlad-i Arab,* literally "sons of Arabs"). For an analysis of how this distinction was visible in Mehmed Ali's army and how Turkish-speaking soldiers were mostly spared the ignominy of public flogging, see Fahmy, *All the Pasha's Men,* 138.

59. Reproduced in Zaghlūl, *Al-Muḥāmāh,* appendix, 100–155.

60. Reproduced in Zaghlūl, *Al-Muḥāmāh,* appendix, 161–162.

61. Reproduced in Zaghlūl, *Al-Muḥāmāh,* appendix, 165.

62. Reproduced in Zaghlūl, *Al-Muḥāmāh,* appendix, 166–167.

63. *Lā'iḥat Zirā'at al-Fallāḥ,* 61.

64. *Lā'iḥat Zirā'at al-Fallāḥ,* 67. Another version can be found in Zaghlūl, *Al-Muḥāmāh,* appendix, 105.

65. DWQ, Dīwān al-Dākhiliyya, Daftar Qayd al-Awāmir al-Karīma, reg. 1310, order no. 80, p. 25, AH 9 Ramaḍān 1274 / 23 April 1858 CE.

66. See, for example, DWQ, Dīwān al-Jihādiyya, reg. no. 2538, case no. 27, pp. 46–49, AH 9 Ṣafar 1294 / 23 February 1877 CE.

67. DWQ, Dīwān al-Jihādiyya, reg. no. 2538, case no. 27, pp. 46–49, AH 9 Ṣafar 1294 / 23 February 1877 CE.

68. See, for example, DWQ, Majlis al-Aḥkām, S/7/10/1, case no. 107, p. 48, AH 20 Dhū al-Ḥijja 1274 / 1 August 1858 CE. In this case, which dealt with a servant who stole clothes valued at 1,600 piasters, a lower majlis verdict of seventy-nine lashes was replaced by a prison sentence of thirty days. For a critique of how humanity appears in colonial law, see Esmeir, *Juridical Humanity*; and Asad, *Formations of the Secular,* 109–113.

69. For various examples from early modern Europe of crowds' reactions to public executions and the spectacle of the gallows, see Spierenburg, *Spectacle of Suffering,* 92–109; and Foucault, *Discipline and Punish,* 58–65.

70. Rudolph Peters, "Prisons and Marginalization in Nineteenth-Century Egypt," in *Outside In: On the Margins of the Modern Middle East,* ed. Eugene Rogan (London: I.B. Tauris, 2002), 31–52; Peters, "Egypt and the Age of the Triumphant Prison," 253–185; Peters, "Controlled Suffering: Mortality and Living Conditions in 19th-Century Egyptian Prisons," *International Journal of Middle East Studies* 36 (2004): 387–407; Khaled Fahmy, "Medical Conditions in Egyptian Prisons in the Nineteenth Century," in *Marginal Voices in Literature and Society: Individual and Society in the Mediterranean Muslim World,* ed. Robin Ostle (Strasbourg: European Science Foundation, 2000), 135–153.

71. DWQ, Maḥfaẓat al-Mīhī, order no. 43, AH 25 Rabī' I 1260 / 15 April 1844 CE.

72. DWQ, Ma'iyya Turkī, S/1/62/10 (original no. 537), order no. 106, p. 53, AH 30 Dhū al-Ḥijja 1281 / 26 May 1865 CE.

73. There were numerous petitions presented to Mehmed Ali to release men from the Iron Workshop. See, for example, DWQ, Ma'iyya Saniyya, Turkī, S/1/49/4 (original no. 27), docs. no. 150, 178, 249, 360, 362, AH Rabīʿ I–Rabīʿ II 1242 / October–November 1826 CE. For examples of orders by Mehmed Ali to send public officials to the Iron Workshop, see DWQ, Diwān Khidīwī, S/2/40/1 (original no. 736), doc. no. 162, p. 35, AH 2 Dhū al-Qaʿda 1242 / 28 May 1827 CE; and DWQ, Diwān Khidīwī, S/2/40/1 (original no. 736), doc. no. 138, p. 15, AH 14 Dhū al-Ḥijja 1242 / 9 July 1827 CE.

74. Those to be detained for longer periods were to be sent to the Ḍabṭiyya, which was guarded by sentries sent from the nearby Gammāliyya Police Station. See DWQ, Diwān al-Khuṣūṣī, S/11/8/13 (original no. 75), doc. no. 8, p. 12, AH 17 Shaʿbān 1285 / 3 December 1868 CE.

75. There are various court sentences that confirm this. Of particular interest is an 1858 order issued by Majlis al-Aḥkām stipulating that women should be detained at the workhouse but not forced to labor while their cases were pending. See DWQ, Majlis al Aḥkām, S/7/33/1, p. 234, AH 19 Jumādā II 1274 / 5 February 1858 CE.

76. DWQ, Maʿiyya Saniyya ʿArabī, S/1/1/15 (original no. 1894), doc. no. 65, p. 125, AH 23 Shawwāl 1277 / 4 May 1861 CE. Saʿīd Pasha approved the request.

77. DWQ, Maʿiyya Saniyya ʿArabī, S/1/1/24 (original no. 1907), doc. no. 12, p. 47, AH 28 Jumādā I, 1280 / 11 November 1863 CE. The cost of preparing this stable for prison use was 11,904 piastres.

78. DWQ, Diwān Khidīwī, S/2/41/2 (original no. 741), doc. no. 300, AH 28 Rabīʿ I 1244 / 9 October 1828 CE.

79. DWQ, Diwān Katkhuda, Taftīsh Ṣiḥḥat Miṣr, Ṣādir Taftīsh, M/5/1 (original no. 163), doc. no. 47, p. 21, AH 19 Muḥarram 1267 / 24 November 1850 CE; DWQ, Diwān Katkhuda, Taftīsh Ṣiḥḥat Miṣr, Ṣādir Taftīsh, M/5/1 (original no. 163), doc. no. 128, p. 62, AH 4 Jumādā I 1267 / 7 March 1851 CE.

80. DWQ, Diwān Katkhuda, Taftīsh Ṣiḥḥat Miṣr, M/5/1 (original no. 163), doc. no. 142, p. 63, AH 4 Jumādā I 1267 / 7 March 1851 CE.

81. DWQ, Muḥāfaẓat Miṣr, Taftīsh Ṣiḥḥat Miṣr, L/1/5/1 (original no. 183), doc. no. 50, p. 58, AH 17 Jumādā I 1276 / 14 October 1859 CE.

82. DWQ, Dīwān Khidīwī, S/2/7/1 (original no. 729), doc. no. 703, p. 109, AH 6 Ṣafar 1244 / 18 August 1828 CE.

83. DWQ, Dīwān Khidīwī, S/2/40/1 (original no. 736), doc. no. 4, p. 1, AH 28 Shawwāl 1242 / 26 May 1827 CE. On the days workers were chained together, they would not receive their daily wages but only their food rations. However, some prisoners had their chains unlocked to perform hard labor. Peters discusses an 1849 case involving a prisoner who escaped from the bakery of the Līmān al-Iskandariyya after he had been uncoupled from a fellow prisoner so that he could work independently at a bellows. See Peters, "Prisons and Marginalization," 42.

84. DWQ, Ḍabṭiyyat Miṣr, L/2/5/6 (original no. 23), doc. no. 13, p. 21, AH 27 Shawwāl 1262 / 19 October 1846 CE; Maʿiyya Saniyya ʿArabī, S/1/1/30 (original no. 1915), order no. 4, p. 7, AH 4 Jumādā I 1282 / 25 September 1865 CE. See also Peters, "Controlled Suffering," 398.

85. See, for example, *Kanun-u Seferiye* (Cairo: Būlāq, AH 1258/1842 CE); and *Qānūn al-Dākhiliyya* (Cairo: Maṭbaʿat Dīwān al-Jihādiyya, AH 1250/1835 CE).

86. See, for example, the horrible case of the private Hilāl Bishara, who spent more than fifteen months in the hospital being treated for wounds he received after being beaten by his major, which were not helped by the shackles that were put around his ankles. See DWQ, Dīwān al-Jihādiyya, Daftar Qayd al-Maḍābit bi-Majlis al-ʿAskariyya, reg. no. 2538, case no. 27, pp. 46–49, AH 9 Ṣafar 1294 / 23 February 1877 CE.

87. DWQ, Dīwān al-Jihādiyya, Ṣādir Mashūrat al-Ṭibb, reg. no. 444, doc. no. 43, p. 8, AH 8 Rajab 1273 / 3 March 1857 CE. In another letter, Clot Bey recommended that the windows of the ward of Qaṣr al-ʿAinī Hospital where imprisoned patients were treated be built with a slope to prevent the prisoners from climbing on them to escape or receiving contraband things from outside the hospital. See DWQ, Dīwān al-Jihādiyya, Ṣādir Mashūrat al-Ṭibb, reg. no. 444, doc. no. 125, p. 24, AH 15 Dhū al-Qaʿda 1273 / 8 July 1857 CE.

88. See Peters, "Controlled Suffering," 395–396.

89. See, for example, the case of Faṭṭūma bint ʿAdawī, who used to live in Suez. She came to Cairo to pass on some money from her father and a neighbor of hers to her brother and her brother-in-law, who were imprisoned in one of the city's jails. While waiting in front of the jail to give the prisoners some bread, she discovered that her money had been stolen. DWQ, Ḍabṭiyyat Miṣr, L/2/6/2 (original no. 2028), case no. 99, pp. 1–2, AH 24 Ramaḍān 1294 / 3 October 1877 CE.

90. See, for example, the long and very interesting case of three Greek subjects arrested and detained in the Ḍabṭiyyat Miṣr for the murder of Andrāwus al-Zahhār. DWQ, Ḍabṭiyyat Miṣr, L/2/6/2 (original no. 2028), case no. 194, pp. 130–154, AH 19 Dhū al-Qaʿda 1294 / 25 November 1877 CE.

91. There are various orders to this effect. See, for example, DWQ, Majlis al-Aḥkām, S/7/33/1, order from Majlis Mulkiyya, p. 234, AH 10 Ramaḍān 1252 / 19 December 1836 CE; DWQ, Majlis al-Aḥkām, S/7/33/1, order from Majlis al-Aḥkām, p. 233, AH 19 Ramaḍān 1266 / 29 July 1850 CE; and DWQ, Maʿiyya Saniyya ʿArabī, S/1/1/23 (original no. 1902), order no. 2, p. 11, AH 11 Ramaḍān 1279 / 2 March 1863 CE.

92. It seems, moreover, that most jails lacked latrines, which officials recommend building long after the jails themselves had been constructed. See, for example, Ismāʿīl's order, based on the recommendation of Majlis al-Khuṣūṣī, to build latrines for twelve of Cairo's local prisons, the *qarāqūl*s: DWQ, Dīwān al-Dākhilyya, reg. no. 1317, order no. 109, p. 28, AH 20 Muḥarram 1287 / 22 April 1870 CE.

93. DWQ, Niẓārat al-Dākhiliyya, Mukātabāt ʿArabī, box, no. 12, doc. no. 12, AH 13 Shawwāl 1290 / 4 December 1873 CE. See also the letter from Ḍabṭiyyat Miṣr to the Cairo Governorate requesting a new mule to transport water to the Ḍabṭiyya, the reason being that it was "no longer possible to delay delivering water to the prisoners": Ḍabṭiyyat Miṣr, L/2/11/12 (original no. 565), doc., no. 52, p. 22, AH 22 Rabīʿ I 1279 / 18 September 1862 CE. Also of interest is the decree of Majlis al-Khuṣūṣī approving the appointment of a special water carrier to deliver water to the

Iplikhane in Būlāq: DWQ, Majlis al-Khuṣūṣī, reg. no. 33, decree 30, p. 140, AH 16 Sha'bān 1290 / 10 October 1873 CE.

94. Peters, "Controlled Suffering," 391.

95. DWQ, Majlis al-Aḥkām, S/7/33/1, p. 233, AH 2 Jumādā II 1250 / 8 August 1834 CE.

96. DWQ, Majlis al-Aḥkām, S/7/33/1, p. 334, AH 15 Rajab 1265 / 7 June 1849 CE.

97. DWQ, Majlis al-Aḥkām, box no. 1, doc. no. 89, AH 16 Sha'bān 1265 / 5 July 1849 CE.

98. DWQ, Majlis al-Aḥkām, S/7/33/1, p. 233, AH 19 Ramaḍān 1266 / 25 July 1850 CE.

99. See, for example, DWQ, Ma'iyya Saniyya 'Arabī, S/1/1/15 (original no. 1894), order no. 4, p. 20, AH 8 Jumādā I 1277 / 22 November 1860 CE.

100. DWQ, Ma'iyya Saniyya 'Arabī, S/1/1/15 (original no. 1894), order no. 24, p. 65, AH 19 Jumādā II 1277 / 3 January 1861 CE. For more on this incident, see Sāmī, *Taqwīm al-Nīl,* 3:366.

101. Order dated AH 6 Shawwāl 1279 / 27 March 1863 CE, quoted in DWQ, Ma'iyya 'Arabī, S/1/1/25 (original no. 1910), order no. 1, p. 1, AH 28 Rabī' I 1280 / 13 September 1863 CE.

102. DWQ, Ma'iyya 'Arabī, S/1/1/25 (original no. 1910), order no. 1, p. 1, AH 28 Rabī' I 1280 / 13 September 1863 CE.

103. DWQ, Ma'iyya Saniyya 'Arabī, S/1/1/25 (original no. 1910), order no. 15, p. 56, AH 23 Sha'bān 1280 / 3 February 1864 CE.

104. DWQ, Majlis al-Khuṣūṣī, S/11/8/13 (original no. 75), decree no. 32, p. 47, AH 5 Dhū al-Qa'da 1285 / 17 February 1869 CE.

105. Peters, "Controlled Suffering," 391.

106. Quoted in Peters, "Egypt and the Age of the Triumphant Prison," p. 261n50. On the absence of judicial torture in *fiqh,* see Christian Lange, *Justice, Punishment and the Medieval Muslim Imagination* (Cambridge: Cambridge University Press, 2008), 73–74.

107. In his seminal article on *siyāsa* in Mamluk Egypt, Yossef Rapoport quotes from Ibn al-A'raj, a minor religious scholar, who wrote the following in the last year of the Mamluk sultanate about what a *siyāsa* official could do in the court: "He [i.e., the *nāẓir fī al-maẓālim*] can examine crimes and grievances prior to any complaint; he can intimidate [*irhāb*] a suspect of injustice and crime before the crime has been proved by admission or by conclusive evidence. He can also stimulate [*al-ḥaml 'alā*] a confession of the truth, and imprison culprits for injustices. He can use physical force to gain a confession after circumstantial evidence of a crime has appeared." (Rapoport, "Royal Justice," 97).

108. DWQ, Mudīriyyat al-Minūfiyya, L/6/1/1, Ṣādir (outgoing letters), AH 24 Shawwāl 1260 / 6 November 1844 CE, p. 209. See also DWQ, Mudīriyyat al-Minūfiyya, L/6/1/1, Ṣādir (outgoing letters), AH 6 Dhū al-Qa'da 1260 / 17 November 1844 CE, in which deprivation of sleep and chaining in iron shackles are added as further examples of *'adhāb,* or torture. I thank Ruud Peters for bringing this case to my attention.

109. Talal Asad, "On Torture, or Cruel, Inhuman, and Degrading Treatment," in *Social Suffering,* ed. Arthur Kleinman, Veena Das, and Margaret Lock (Delhi: Oxford University Press, 1998), 289.

110. Anupama Rao, "Problems of Violence, States of Terror: Torture in Colonial India," *Economic and Political Weekly* 36 (2001): 4131.

111. DWQ, Muḥāfaẓat Miṣr, L/1/20/1 (original no. 794), case no. 8, pp. 7–9, AH 13 Ṣafar 1272 / 25 October 1855 CE.

112. DWQ, Muḥāfaẓat Miṣr, L/1/20/1 (original no. 794), case no. 26, pp. 28–30, AH 22 Rabīʿ II 1272 / 1 January 1856 CE. Although the accused confessed to having intentionally killed the victim, he was not sentenced to death because the plaintiff could not establish his relationship to the deceased using *fiqh* rules, an important procedural detail that frequently mitigated *ḥudūd* punishments.

113. Langbein, *Torture and the Law of Proof;* Foucault, *Discipline and Punish,* 36–39.

114. Anwar Maḥmūd Dabbūr, *Ithbāt al-Nasab bi-Ṭarīq al-Qiyāfa fi'l-Fiqh al-Islāmī* (Cairo: Dār al-Thaqāfa al-ʿArabiyya, 1985); Shaham, *Expert Witness,* 41–52, 66–75.

115. Quran 21:7. See Ḥasan Ibn Muḥammad al-Yandūzī, *Adillat al-Ithbāt al-Jināʾī wa-Qawāʿiduhu al-ʿĀmma fi'l-Sharīʿa al-Islmāiyya* ([Rabat ?]: Top Press, 2004), 286–287; and Shaham, *Expert Witness,* 28.

116. Shaham, *Expert Witness,* 31. On this point, compare the views of Shaham on the one hand and Baber Johansen and Mohammad Fadel on the other about whether expert testimony constitutes a *riwāya* or a *shahāda:* Shaham, *Expert Witness,* 38–39, 55; Johansen, "Signs as Evidence"; Mohammad Fadel, "Two Women, One Man: Knowledge, Power and Gender in Medieval Sunni Legal Thought," *International Journal of Middle East Studies* 29 (1997): 185–204.

117. The first part of this tradition is: "The modest person is the one who had stumbled" (*lā ḥalīm illā dhū ʿathra*). See Shaham, *Expert Witness,* 58, 211n9.

118. Shaham, *Expert Witness,* 58, 211n9.

119. Shaham, *Expert Witness,* 57.

120. Shayzarī, *Kitāb Nihāyat al-Rutba,* 98.

121. Shaham, *Expert Witness,* 71–72.

122. Muḥammad Amīn Ibn ʿUmar Ibn ʿĀbidīn, *Radd al-Muḥtar ʿalā al-Durr al-Mukhtār,* 12 vols. (Beirut: Dār al-Kutub al-ʿIlmiyya, 1992), 6:544–545. For a remarkably similar case that occurred in Egypt in 1879, see Peters, *Crime and Punishment,* 29. Zayd, ʿAmr, and Bakr are placeholder names.

123. Yaḥyā Ibn Sharaf al-Nawawī, *Rawḍat al-Ṭālibīn wa ʿUmdat al-Muftīn,* 12 vols. (Beirut: Al-Maktab al-Islāmī, 1991), 10:32.

124. Shaham, *Expert Witness,* 73.

125. For a concise summary of these offenses, see Ghazālī, *Al-Wajīz,* 2:143–149.

126. For a complete list of the retaliatory compensations, see Muḥammad Ibn Aḥmad al-Minhājī al-Asyūṭī, *Jawāhir al-ʿUqūd wa-Muʿīn al-Quḍāt wa'l-Muwaqqiʿīn wa'l-Shuhūd,* 2 vols. (Cairo: Maṭbaʿat al-Sunnah al-Muḥammadīyah, 1955), 2:262–263.

127. Ibn Qudāma, *Al-Mughnī*, 8:480–481, 8:469–474, 9:270. The number of camels should not be taken literally. Rather, this is a percentage of a full *diyya*, that for a Muslim male, which is typically calculated to be one hundred camels. Following this logic, the *arsh* of a *mūḍiḥa* is 5 percent of a full *diyya*, that of a *ma'mūma* is 33 percent, and so on. On using camels as the basic unit of *arsh*, see Ibn Qudāma, *Al-Mughnī*, 8:376–377. See also Ḥusayn bin 'Abd Allāh al-'Abīdī, *Al-Arsh wa Aḥkāmuhu* (Riyadh: Jāmi'at al-Imām Muḥammad ibn Sa'ūd al-Islāmīyya, 2004), 2:562–582.

128. Shaham, *Expert Witness*, 72–73.

129. Imām al-Ḥaramayn Ḍiā' al-Dīn 'Abd al-Malik Ibn Yūsuf al-Juwaynī, *Nihāyat al-Maṭlab fī Dirāyat al-Madhhab*, 21 vols. (Jiddah: Dār al-Minhāj, 2007), 17:361 (issue no. 11235).

130. Ghazālī, *Al-Wajīz*, 2:143.

131. Baber Johansen, "The Valorization of the Human Body in Muslim Sunni Law," *Princeton Papers in Near Eastern Studies* 4 (1996): 94–95.

132. DWQ, Majlis al-Aḥkām, S/7/10/109, case no. 362, AH 3 Rajab 1294 / 14 July 1877 CE.

133. DWQ, Ḍabtiyyat Miṣr, L/2/6/2 (original no. 2028), case no. 199, pp. 176–78, 22 Dhū al-Qa'da 1294 / 28 November 1877.

134. Abū al-Ḥasan Alī Ibn Muḥammad al-Māwardī, *Al-Ḥāwī al-Kabīr*, 19 vols., ed. 'Alī Muḥammad Mu'awwaḍ and 'Ādil Aḥmad 'Abd al-Mawjūd (Beirut: Dār al-Kutub al-'Ilmiyya, 1994), 17:391–392.

135. 'Īsā, *Tārīkh al-Qaḍā'*, 318.

136. DWQ, Ḍabṭiyyat Miṣr, L/2/6/4 (original no. 2032), case no. 779, pp. 160–161, AH 25 Jumādā II / 26 June 1878 CE.

137. Shaham, *Expert Witness*, 58.

138. Shaham, *Expert Witness*, 58–59.

139. Peters, *Crime and Punishment in Islamic Law*, 39.

140. Emile Tyan, "Judicial Organization," in *Law in the Middle East*, vol. 1, *Origin and Development of Islamic Law*, ed. M. Khadduri and H. J. Liebesny (Washington, DC: Middle East Institute, 1955), 245–248, 253–257; 'Īsā, *Tārīkh al-Qaḍā'*, 301–343.

141. This is despite the wide circulation of this term since the late nineteenth century. The reasons behind the modern adoption of this peculiar term to refer to what is known in English as legal medicine is dealt with in the conclusion of this chapter.

142. DWQ, Ḍabṭiyyat Miṣr, L/2/31/1, doc. no. 74, pp. 40, 63, AH 22 Sha'bān 1296 / 11 August 1879 CE.

143. There was an interesting petition presented by a woman called Khadra from Fumm al-Khalīj, in southern Cairo, who complained about the release from the Ḍabṭiyya's jail of the man who had been accused of killing her son with his speeding carriage. See DWQ, Dākhiliyya, Mukātabāt 'Arabī, box no. 14, AH 17 Dhū al-Qa'da 1291 / 26 December 1874 CE.

144. In rape cases, female doctors, *ḥakīmāt*, examined the victims. On the forensic duties of these female doctors, see Fahmy, "Women, Medicine and Power." For a case that illustrates how male relatives understood the importance of *ḥakīmāt* in adjudicating sexual assault cases, see DWQ, Ḍabṭiyya Miṣr, L/2/6/8 (original no. 2041), case no. 533, pp. 59–60, AH 16 Jumāda I 1296 / 8 May 1879 CE. See also Liat Kozma, *Policing Egyptian Women: Sex, Law, and Medicine in Khedival Egypt* (Syracuse: Syracuse University Press, 2011).

145. For a detailed account of how these certificates were issued and how they had to be double-checked against the daily reports handed in by the undertakers, see Article 1 of Lā'iḥat Bayt al-Māl, issued on AH 11 Dhū al-Ḥijja 1276 / 30 June 1860 CE, quoted in Jallād, *Qāmūs,* 2:5.

146. DWQ, Ḍabṭiyyat Miṣr, L/2/6/2 (original no. 2028), case 112, p. 24, AH 8 Shawwāl 1294 / 16 October 1877 CE.

147. DWQ, Muḥāfaẓat Miṣr, L/1/20/5 (original no. 1043), doc. no. 27, pp. 139–140, AH 8 Shawwāl 1277 / 19 April 1861 CE.

148. DWQ, Muḥāfaẓat Miṣr, L/2/20/8 (original no. 1108), doc. no. 9, pp. 163, 170, AH 7 Ṣafar 1278 / 14 August 1861 CE.

149. DWQ, Majlis al-Ahkām, S/7/10/29 (original no. 633), case no. 39, pp. 44–48, AH 19 Jumādā I 1282 / 10 October 1865 CE.

150. DWQ, Dīwān Khidīwī, S/2/18/1 (original no. 654), doc. no. 173, pp. 154–156, AH 11 Rabī' II 1267 / 14 January 1851 CE.

151. This phrasing echoes the Quranic injunction not to abstain from witnessing: "And do not conceal testimony, for whoever conceals it—his heart is indeed sinful, and Allah is Knowing of what you do" (Quran 2:283). Curiously, as is clear from the names of the victims, the plaintiffs and their agent were Copts, and it is unclear whether they or the *siyāsa* council scribe evoked this Quranic expression.

152. DWQ, Majlis al-Aḥkām, S/7/10/1 (original no. 663), case no. 144, pp. 64–66, AH 23 Dhū al-Qa'da 1274 / 7 August 1858 CE.

153. In this case, the doctor established that the deceased had in fact died as a result of excessive beating. However, the doctor's report notwithstanding, the defendant was not convicted. The Majlis stated that all the witnesses were biased and that their testimonies could not be relied on "since it is the custom of the fellahin to hate the governors." See DWQ, Majlis al-Aḥkām, S/7/10/1 (original no. 663), case no. 26, pp. 9–10, AH 13 Dhū al-Qa'da 1274 / 28 July 1858 CE.

154. Anwar Maḥmūd Dabbūr, *Al-Shubuhāt wa-Atharuhā fī Isqāt al-Ḥudūd* (Cairo: Al-Maktaba al-Tawfīqiyya, 1978), 59–106.

155. Foucault, *Birth of the Clinic.*

156. For a comparison with the respective roles played by forensic medicine in both the cannon law and common law traditions, see Catherine Crawford, "Legalizing Medicine: Early Modern Legal Systems and the Growth of Medico-Legal Knowledge," in *Legal Medicine in History,* ed. Michael Clark and Catherine Crawford (Cambridge: Cambridge University Press, 1994), 89–116. On the difference between

the adversarial nature of the English common law system and the inquisitorial nature of the Roman cannon law tradition, see John Langbein, *Prosecuting Crime in the Renaissance: England, Germany, France* (Cambridge, MA: Harvard University Press, 1974) 129–139.

157. Jallād, *Qāmūs,* 3:225.

158. Cromer, *Modern Egypt,* 2:397. On abolishing corvée, see Nathan Brown, "Who Abolished Corvée Labor and Why?" *Past and Present* 144 (1994): 116–137.

159. Peters, "Egypt and the Age of the Triumphant Prison," 256.

160. For a critique of colonial law's "deployment of the human" in Egypt, see Esmeir, *Juridical Humanity;* and Talal Asad, "Conscripts of Western Civilization," in *Dialectical Anthropology: Essays in Honor of Stanley Diamond,* vol. 1, *Civilization in Crisis: Anthropological Perspectives,* ed. Christine Ward Gailey (Tallahassee: University of Florida Press, 1992), 333–351.

161. For more on this, see Peters, "Administrators and Magistrates."

162. Ibrāhīm Efendi Ḥasan, *Rawḍat al-Āsī fī'l-Ṭibb al-Siyāsī* (Cairo: Maṭba'at al-Madāris al-Mulkiyya, AH 1293/1866–67 CE).

163. Ibrāhīm Pasha Ḥasan, *Al-Dustūr al-Mar'ī.* Ibrāhīm Pasha Ḥasan served as director of the Qaṣr al-'Ainī School of Medicine from 1893 to 1904. See 'Alī Ibrāhīm, "Kulliyyat al-Ṭibb: Māḍīhā wa Ḥāḍiruhā wa Mustaqbaluhā," *Al-Muqtaṭaf* 90 (1937): 272.

164. Ibrāhīm Pasha Ḥasan, *Al-Dustūr al-Mar'ī,* 9.

CONCLUSION

1. Jabartī, *'Ajā'ib,* 4:183–184.

2. Jabartī, *'Ajā'ib,* 4:184.

3. The most significant are Hunter, *Egypt under the Khedives;* and Mitchell, *Rule of Experts.*

4. Fahmy, *All the Pasha's Men.*

5. The literature on the economic and financial history of Egypt in the middle decades of the nineteenth century is huge, but of particular value are David Landes, *Bankers and Pashas: International Finance and Economic Imperialism in Egypt* (London: Hinemann Education, 1958); Owen, *Cotton and the Egyptian Economy;* Owen, "Egypt and Europe: From French Expedition to British Occupation," in *Studies in the Theory of Imperialism,* ed. Roger Owen and Bob Sutcliffe (London: Longman, 1972), 195–209; and Cuno, *The Pasha's Peasants.*

6. Fahmy, *All the Pasha's Men;* and Fahmy, *Mehmed Ali.*

7. Sālim, *Tārīkh al-Qaḍā',* 1:28.

8. Agrama, *Questioning Secularism.*

9. Baldwin, *Islamic Law and Empire.*

10. Fahmy, *All the Pasha's Men.*

11. ʿAbd al-Samīʿ Sālim al-Harrāwī, *Lughat al-Idāra al-ʿĀmma fī Miṣr fī al-Qarn al-Tāsiʿ ʿAshr* (Cairo: Al-Majlis al-Aʿlā li-Riʿāyat al-Funūn wa'l-Ādāb wa'l-ʿUlūm *al-Ijtimāʿiyya*, 1963); Zaghlūl, *Al-Muḥāmāh*.

12. DWQ, Majlis al-Aḥkām, S/7/10/1 (original no. 663), case, no. 75, p. 33, AH 29 Dhū al-Qaʿda 1274 / 12 July 1858 CE.

BIBLIOGRAPHY

ARCHIVAL SOURCES

Dār al-Wathā'iq al-Qawmiyya [Egyptian National Archives]. Cairo.

National Archives. Kew.

F. Grassi, "A Relation and Reflections on the Indian Cholera Which Raged in Egypt in the Year 1848," translation from the Italian, FO 78/759, Gilbert, 30 December 1848.

"General Regulations Concerning the Public Health at Alexandria and in the Interior to Be Put into Execution According to Order of His Highness the Vice Roy, Dated 15 Rejeb 1257 (30 August 1841)," enclosure in FO 78/502, Barnett, 23 December 1842.

UNPUBLISHED MANUSCRIPTS AND DISSERTATIONS

Damanhūrī, Aḥmad al-. "Muntahā al-Taṣrīḥ bi-Khulāṣat al-Qawl al-Ṣarīḥ fī 'Ilm al-Tashrīḥ." Unpublished manuscript, MS Maktabat al-Azhar, Ṭibb 5660. Cairo, 1250.

Ismail, Shehab. "Engineering Metropolis: Contagion, Capital, and the Making of British Colonial Cairo, 1882–1922." PhD diss., Columbia University, 2017.

Kuhnke, LaVerne. "Resistance and Response to Modernization: Preventive Medicine and Social Control in Egypt, 1825–1850." PhD diss., University of Chicago, 1971.

Leithy, Tamer el-. "Public Punishment in Mamluk Society." Master's thesis, Cambridge University, 1997.

PUBLISHED WORKS

'Abbās, Ra'ūf, ed. *Al-Awāmir wa'l-Mukātabāt al-Ṣādira min 'Azīz Miṣr Muḥammad 'Alī.* 2 vols. Cairo: Dār al-Kutub wa'l-Wathā'iq al-Qawmiyya, 2005.

———. *Al-Ḥaraka al-ʿUmmāliya fī Miṣr, 1899–1952.* Cairo: Dār al-Kitāb al-ʿArabī li'l-Ṭibāʿa wa'l-Nashr, 1967.
———. *Al-Niẓām al-Ijtimāʿī fī Miṣr fī Ẓill al-Milkīyāt al-Zirāʿīya al-Kabīra, 1837–1914.* Cairo: Dār al-Fikr al-Ḥadīth lil-Ṭibāʿa wa'l-Nashr, 1973.
———. "Qudūm al-Gharb: Bidāya lil-Nahḍa am Ijhāḍ Lahā?" In *Kitābat Tārīkh Miṣr . . . Ilā Ayn? Azmat al-Manhaj wa Ru'ā Naqdiyya,* 85–94. Cairo: Dār al-Kutub wa'l-Wathā'iq al-Qawmiyya, 2009.
———. *Al-Tanwīr Bayna Miṣr wa-al-Yābān: Dirāsa Muqārana fī Fikr Rifāʿa al-Ṭahṭāwī wa-Fukuzawa Yukitshi.* Cairo: Mīrīt, 2001.
ʿAbd al-Hādī, ʿAzza. "Muqāwamat al-Ahālī li-Taṭʿīm al-Judarī fī al-Qarn al-Tāsiʿ ʿashr." In *Al-Rafḍ wa'l-Iḥtijāj fi'l-Mujtamaʿ al-Misrī fī al-ʿAṣr al-ʿUthmānī,* edited by Nāṣir Ibrāhīm, 303–312. Cairo: Al-Jamʿiyya al-Miṣriyya lil-Dirāsāt al-Tārikhiyya, 2004.
ʿAbd al-Karīm, Aḥmad ʿIzzat. *Tārīkh al-Taʿlīm fī ʿAṣr Muḥammad ʿAlī.* Cairo: Maktabat al-Nahḍa al-Miṣriyya, 1938.
ʿAbd al-Khāliq, Farīd. *Al-Ḥisba fi'l-Islām ʿAlā Dhawī al-Jāh wa'l-Sulṭān.* Cairo: Dār al-Shurūq, 2011.
ʿAbd al-Raḥīm, A. ʿAbd al-Raḥmān. *Al-Rīf al-Miṣrī fī al-Qarn al-Thāmin ʿAshr.* Cairo: ʿAin Shams University Press, 1974.
ʿAbd al-Raḥmān, ʿUmar, ed. *Mīthāq al-ʿAmal al-Islāmī.* Cairo: Maktabat Ibn Kathīr, 1989.
ʿAbd al-Wahhāb, Ḥasan. "Takhṭīṭ al-Qāhira wa Tanẓīmuhā Mundhu Nash'atihā." *Bulletin de l'Institut d'Égypte* 37 (1955–56): 23–31.
ʿAbdallāh, ʿAbdallāh Muḥammad. *Wilāyat al-Ḥisba fi'l-Islām.* Cairo: Al-Zahrā', 1996.
Abdelsalam, Ahmed. "The Practice of Violence in the Hisba-Theories." *Iranian Studies* 38, no. 4 (2005): 547–554.
ʿAbīdī, Ḥusayn bin ʿAbd Allāh al-. *Al-Arsh wa Aḥkāmuhu.* 2 vols. Riyadh: Jāmiʿat al-Imām Muḥammad Ibn Saʿūd al-Islāmīyya, 2004.
Abugideiri, Hibba. *Gender and the Making of Modern Medicine in Colonial Egypt.* Farnham, Surrey: Ashgate, 2010.
Abu-Lughod, Janet. *Cairo: 1001 Years of the City Victorious.* Princeton: Princeton University Press, 1971.
———. "The Islamic City: Historic Myth, Islamic Essence and Contemporary Relevance." *International Journal of Middle East Studies* 19 (1987): 155–176.
Abū Zayd, Sihām Muṣṭafā. *Al-Ḥisba fī Miṣr al-Islāmiyya min al-Fath al-ʿArabī ilā Nihāyat al-ʿAṣr al-Mamlūkī.* Cairo: Al-Hay'a al-Miṣriyya al-ʿĀmma lil-Kitāb, 1986.
Ackerknecht, Erwin. "Anticontagionism between 1821 and 1861." *Bulletin of the History of Medicine* 22 (1948): 561–593.
Adams, Bruce F. "Progress of an Idea: The Mitigation of Corporal Punishment in Russia to 1863." *Maryland Historian* 17 (1986): 57–74.
Agmon, Iris. *Family and Court: Legal Culture and Modernity in Late Ottoman Palestine.* Syracuse, NY: Syracuse University Press, 2006.

Agrama, Hussein A. *Questioning Secularism: Islam, Sovereignty, and the Rule of Law in Modern Egypt.* Chicago: University of Chicago Press, 2012.

Akgündüz, Ahmet. *Mukayeseli İslam ve Osmanlı Hukuku Külliyatı.* Diyarbakır: Dicle Üniversitesi Hukuk Fakültesi yayınları, 1986.

Akhtar, Aḥmad. "Al-Māwardī: A Sketch of His Life and Works." *Islamic Culture* 18 (1944): 283–300.

'Alī, 'Arafa 'Abdu. *Al-Qāhira fī 'Aṣr Ismā'īl.* Cairo: Al-Dār al-Miṣriyya al-Lubnāniyya, 1998.

Alleaume, Ghislaine. "Politique urbaines et contrôle de l'entreprise: Une loi inédite de 'Alī Mubārak sur les corporations du bâtiment." *Annales Islamologiques* 21 (1985): 147–188.

Alleaume, Ghislaine, and Philippe Fargues. "La naissance d'une statistique d'État: Le recensement de 1848 en Egypte." *Histoire et Measure* 13, nos. 1–2 (1998): 147–193.

———. "Voisinage et frontière: Résider au Caire en 1846." In *Urbanite arabe: Hommage à Bernard Lepetit,* edited by Jocelyne Dakhlia, 77–112. Arles: Sindbad, 1998.

'Alyān, Shawkat Muḥammad. *Dawr al-Ḥisba fī Ḥimāyat al-Maṣāliḥ.* Riyadh: n.p., 2000.

Amri, Laroussie. "The Concept of *'umran:* The Heuristic Knot in Ibn Khaldun." *Journal of North African Studies* 13 (2008): 351–361.

Anderson, J. *Islamic Law in the Modern World.* London: Stevens and Sons, 1959.

'Aqīl, 'Abd Allāh al-. *Min A'lām al-Ḥaraka al-Islāmiyya.* Cairo: Dār al-Tawzī' wa'l-Nashr al-Islāmiyya, 2010.

Arnaud, Jean-Luc. *Le Caire, mise en place d'une ville moderne, 1867–1907: Des intérêts du prince aux sociétés privées.* Aix-en-Provence: Actes Sud, 1998.

Arnold, David. *Colonizing the Body: State Medicine and Epidemic Disease in Nineteenth-Century India.* Berkeley: University of California Press, 1993.

———. "Medicine and Colonialism." In *Companion Encyclopedia of the History of Medicine,* vol. 2, edited by W. F. Bynum and Roy Porter, 1393–1416. London: Routledge, 1993.

Asad, Talal. "Conscripts of Western Civilization." In *Dialectical Anthropology: Essays in Honor of Stanley Diamond,* vol. 1, *Civilization in Crisis: Anthropological Perspectives,* edited by Christine Ward Gailey, 333–351. Tallahassee: University of Florida Press, 1992.

———. *Formations of the Secular: Christianity, Islam, Modernity.* Stanford: Stanford University Press, 2003.

———. "On Torture, or Cruel, Inhuman, and Degrading Treatment." In *Social Suffering,* edited by Arthur Kleinman, Veena Das, and Margaret Lock, 285–308. Delhi: Oxford University Press, 1998.

———. "Thinking about Tradition, Religion, and Politics in Egypt Today." *Critical Inquiry* 42 (Autumn 2015): 166–214.

Āṣāf, Yūsuf. *Al-Ta'dīlāt al-Qānūniyya Allatī Udkhilat 'alā al-Qānūn al-Ahlī al-Miṣrī.* Cairo: Al-Maṭba'a al-'Umūmiyya, 1895.

Asyūṭī, Muḥammad Ibn Aḥmad al-Minhājī al-. *Jawāhir al-ʿUqūd wa-Muʿīn al-Quḍāt wa'l-Muwaqqiʿīn wa'l-Shuhūd.* 2 vols. Cairo: Maṭbaʿat al-Sunnah al-Muḥammadīyah, 1955.

Averroës. *Distinguished Jurist's Primer.* 2 vols. Translated by Imran Ahsan Khan Nyazee. Reading: Garnet, 1996.

ʿAwaḍ, Luwīs. *Tārīkh al-Fikr al-Miṣrī al-Ḥadīth.* 2 vols. Cairo: Al-Hilāl, 1969.

ʿAwda, ʿAbd al-Qādir. *Al-Tashrīʿ al-Jināʾī al-Islāmī Muqāranan bi'l-Qānūn al-Waḍʿī.* 2 vols. Cairo: Dār al-Turāth, 1980.

ʿAwwā, Muḥammad Salīm. *Ṭāriq al-Bishrī Faqīhan.* Mansoura: Dār al-Wafāʾ, 1999.

ʿAzab, Khālid Muḥammad. *Takhṭīṭ wa ʿImārat al-Mudun al-Islāmiyya.* Doha: Wiẓārat al-Awqāf wal al-Shuʾūn al-Islāmiyya, 1997.

Badr, Muhammad. "Al-Ṣiḥḥa al-Tāmma wa-l'Minḥa al-ʿĀmma." *Rawḍat al-Madāris* 1, no. 1 (AH Muḥarram 1287/April 1870 CE): 26–27.

Baedeker, K. *Egypt: Handbook for Travellers.* London: Dulau, 1878.

Baer, Gabriel. "The Beginnings of Municipal Government in Egypt." *Middle Eastern Studies* 4, no. 2 (1968): 118–140.

———. *Egyptian Guilds in Modern Times.* Jerusalem: Israel Oriental Society, 1964.

———. "Tanzimat in Egypt: The Panel Code." *Bulletin of the School of Oriental and African Studies* 26 (1963): 29–49.

Baldwin, James. *Islamic Law and Empire in Ottoman Cairo.* Edinburgh: Edinburgh University Press, 2017.

Baqlī, Muḥammad ʿAlī al-. "Fī al-tamarruʾ." *Yaʿsūb al-Ṭibb,* no. 29 (AH Jumādā I 1285/August 1868 CE): 1–11.

Bār, Muaḥmmad ʿAlī al-. "Al-Tashrīḥ: ʿUlūmuhu wa Aḥkāmuhu." *Majallat al-Majmaʿ al-Fiqhī al-Islamī* 6, no. 8 (1994): 177–199.

Barak, On. *On Time.* Berkeley: University of California Press, 2013.

Barnes, David. "Scents and Sensibilities: Disgust and the Meanings of Odors in Late Nineteenth-Century Paris." *Historical Reflections/Réflexions Historiques* 28, no. 1 (2002): 21–49.

Basalla, George. "The Spread of Western Science." *Science* 156 (1967): 611–622.

Bates, Michael L. "The Function of Fatimid and Ayyubid Glass Weights." *Journal of the Economic and Social History of the Orient* 24, no. 1 (1981): 63–92.

Bayle, A. L. J. *Al-Qawl al-Ṣarīḥ fī ʿIlm al-Tashrīḥ.* Translated by Yūḥannā ʿAnḥūrī. Edited by Aḥmad Ḥasan al-Rashīdī and Muḥammad al-Harrāwī. Cairo: Būlāq, 1832.

———. *Traité élémentaire d'anatomie, ou Description succincte des organs et des éléments organiques qui composent le corps humain.* Paris: Librarie de Deville Cavellin, 1833.

Béclard, Pierre Augustin. *Al-Tashrīḥ al-ʿĀmm* [*Éléments d'anatomie générale, où Description de tous les genres d'organes qui composent le corps humain*]. Translated by ʿIssawī al-Naḥrāwī. Cairo: Būlāq, 1845.

Bedloe, Edward, and James F. Love. "Cholera in Egypt." *Public Health Reports* 11, no. 37 (September 11, 1896): 861–863.

Bentham, Jeremy. *Kitāb Uṣūl al-Sharā'iʿ*. Translated by Aḥmad Fatḥī Zaghlūl. Cairo: Būlāq, 1892.
Berkes, Niyazi. *The Development of Secularism in Turkey*. Montreal: McGill University Press, 1964.
Berkey, Jonathan P. "The *Muhtasibs* of Cairo under the Mamluks: Toward an Understanding of an Islamic Institution." In *Mamluks in Egyptian and Syrian Politics and Society,* edited by Michael Winter and Amalia Levanoni, 245–276. Leiden: Brill, 2004.
———. "The Promise and Pitfalls of Medieval Islamic Social History." *International Journal of Middle East Studies* 46, no. 2 (2014): 385–394.
Bernard. *Al-Minḥah fi Siyāsat Ḥifẓ al-Ṣiḥḥah.* Translated by Jurjī Fīdāl and Muḥammad al-Harrāwī. Cairo: Būlāq, 1834.
Bernard, E. C. *Le Conseil sanitaire, maritime et quarantenaire d'Egypte.* Alexandria: Penasson, 1897.
Bertomeu-Sánchez, José Ramón. "Popularizing Controversial Science: A Popular Treatise on Poisons by Mateu Orfila (1818)." *Medical History* 53, no. 3 (2009): 351–378.
Besumee, Hasanaine al-. *Egypt under Muḥammad Aly Basha.* London: Smith Elder, 1838.
Bichat, Xavier. *Anatomie générale appliquée à la physiologie et à la medicine.* Paris: Brosson et Gabon, 1801.
"Biographical Sketch of the Late M. Orfila." *Lancet* 61, no. 1544 (April 1853): 326–327.
Bishrī, Ṭāriq al-. *Al-Ḥaraka al-Siyāsiyya fī Miṣr, 1945–1953.* Cairo: Dār al-Shurūq, 2002.
———. *Māhiyyat al-Muʿāṣara.* Cairo: Dar al-Shurūq, 2007.
———. *Saʿd Zaghlūl Yufāwiḍ al-Istiʿmār.* Cairo: Al-Hay'a al-Miṣriyya al-ʿĀmma lil-Kitāb, 1977.
———. *Al-Waḍʿ al-Qānūnī Bayna al-Sharīʿa al-Islāmiyya wa'l-Qānūn al-Waḍʿī.* Cairo: Dār al-Shurūq, 2005.
Blažina Tomić, Zlata, and Vesna Blažina. *Expelling the Plague: The Health Office and the Implementation of Quarantine in Dubrovnick, 1377–1553.* London: McGill-Queen's University Press, 2015.
Bowring, John. "Report on Egypt and Candia." *Parliamentary Papers, Reports from Commissioners* 21 (1840): 1–236.
Brinton, Jasper Y. *The Mixed Courts of Egypt.* New Haven: Yale University Press, 1968.
Brown, Nathan. *The Rule of Law in the Arab World.* Cambridge: Cambridge University Press, 1997.
———. "Who Abolished Corvée Labor and Why?" *Past and Present* 144 (1994): 116–137.
Buckley, R. P., trans. *The Book of the Islamic Market Inspector.* By ʿAbd al-Raḥmān Ibn Naṣr al-Shayzarī. Oxford: Oxford University Press, 1999.
Burak, Guy. "Between the *Ḳānūn* of Qāytbāy and Ottoman *Yasaq:* A Note on the Ottomans' Dynastic Law." *Journal of Islamic Studies* 26, no. 1 (2015): 1–23.

Burns, David. *The Great Stink of Paris and the Nineteenth-Century Struggle against Filth and Germs.* Baltimore: Johns Hopkins University Press, 2006.

Bynum, W. F., and Roy Porter, eds. *Companion Encyclopedia of the History of Medicine.* Vol. 1 London: Routledge, 1993.

Cahen, Claude. "A propos des shuhud." *Studia Islamica* 31 (1970): 71–79.

Cailliaud, Frédéric. *Voyage á Méroé, au Fleuve Blanc, au-delà de Fâzoql.* 2 vols. Paris: L'Imprimerie Royale, 1826.

Cannon, Byron. *Politics of Law and the Courts in Nineteenth-Century Egypt.* Salt Lake City: University of Utah Press, 1988.

———. "Social Tension and the Teaching of European Law in Egypt before 1900." *History of Education Quarterly* 15, no. 3 (1975): 299–315.

Caplan, Jane, and John Torpey, eds. *Documenting Individual Identity: The Development of State Practices in the Modern World.* Princeton: Princeton University Press, 2001.

Cappelletti, M. A. "Antonio Figari." In *Dizionario biografico degli italiani,* vol. 47., edited by Fiorella Bartoccini and Mario Caravale, 538–540. Rome: Istituto della Enciclopedia Italiana, 1997.

Carlino, Andrea. *Books of the Body: Anatomical Ritual and Renaissance Learning.* Translated by John Tedeschi and Anne C. Tedeschi. Chicago: Chicago University Press, 1999.

Celik, Zeynep. *Displaying the Orient: Architecture of Islam at Nineteenth-Century World's Fairs.* Berkeley: University of California Press, 1992.

Chadwick, Edwin. *Report to Her Majesty's Principal Secretary of State for the Home Department from the Poor Law Commissioners on an Inquiry into the Sanitary Condition of the Labouring Population of Great Britain.* London: W. Clowes and Sons, 1842.

Chatterjee, Partha. *The Nation and Its Fragments: Colonial and Postcolonial Histories.* Princeton: Princeton University Press, 1993.

———. "Two Poets and Death: On Civil Society and Political Society in the Non-Christian World." In *Questions of Modernity,* edited by Timothy Mitchell, 35–48. Minneapolis: University of Minnesota Press, 2000.

Clerget, Marcel. *Le Caire: Étude de géographie urbaine et d'histoire économique.* 2 vols. Cairo: Schindler, 1934.

Clot Bey, Antoine Barthélémy. *Aperçu général sur l'Égypte.* 2 vols. Paris: Fortin, 1840.

———. "Clot Bey's Observations on Egypt." *Foreign Quarterly Review* 27 (1841): 377–378.

———. *Compte rendu de l'état de l'enseignement médical et du service de santé civil et militaire de l'Égypte au commencement de mars 1849.* Paris: Victor Masson, 1849.

———. *Compte rendu des travaux de l'École de Médecine d'Abou-Zabel (Égypte), et de l'examen général des élèves.* Paris: D. Cavellin, 1833.

———. *De la peste observée en Egypte: Recherches et considerations sur cette maladie.* Paris: Fortin, Masson et Cie., 1840.

———. *Kunūz al-Ṣiḥḥa wa Yawāqīt al-Minḥa.* Translated by Muḥammad al-Shāfi'ī. Edited by, Muḥammad 'Umar al-Tūnisī and Nicolas Perron. Cairo: Būlāq, 1844.
———. *Leçon sur la peste d'Égypte et spécialement sur ce qui concerne la contagion ou la non contagion de cette maladie, donnée à l'hôpital de la Pitié.* Marseille: Vial, 1862.
———. *Mabḥath Ta'līmī fī Taṭ'īm al-Judarī.* Translated by Aḥmad Ḥasan al-Rashīdī. Cairo: Būlāq, AH 1259/1843 CE.
———. *Mémoires.* Edited by Jacques Tagher. Cairo: IFAO, 1949.
———. *Nubdha Fī Uṣūl al-Falsafah al-Ṭabi'īyya; Uṣūl Fī al-Tashrīḥ al-'Āmm; Nubdha Fī Tashrīḥ al-Marḍā.* Translated by Ibrāhīm al-Nabarāwī. Cairo: Būlāq, AH 1253/1837 CE.
———. "The Plague and Quarantine Laws." *Lancet* 31, no. 806 (February 1839): 743–744.
———. *Tanbīh Fīmā Yakhuṣṣ al-Ṭā'ūn.* Cairo: Maṭba'at Dīwān al-Jihādiyya, AH 1250/1835 CE.
———. *Al-'Ujāla al-Ṭibiyya fīmā lā Budda minhu li-Ḥukāmā' al-Jihādiyya.* Translated by August Sakākīnī. Cairo: Maṭba'at al-Madrasa al-Ṭibiyya bi-Abī Za'bal, AH 1284/1832 CE.
Cohen, H. Floris. *The Scientific Revolution: A Historiographical Inquiry.* Chicago: University of Chicago Press, 1994.
Cook, Michael. *Commanding Right and Forbidding Wrong in Islamic Thought.* Cambridge: Cambridge University Press, 2000.
Corbin, Alain. *The Foul and the Fragrant: Odor and the French Social Imagination.* Cambridge, MA: Harvard University Press, 1986.
Crawford, Catherine. "Legalizing Medicine: Early Modern Legal Systems and the Growth of Medico-Legal Knowledge." In *Legal Medicine in History,* edited by Michael Clark and Catherine Crawford, 89–116. Cambridge: Cambridge University Press, 1994.
Cromer, Earl of (Evelyn Baring). *Modern Egypt.* 2 vols. London: Macmillan, 1908.
Crone, Patricia. *God's Rule: Government and Islam.* New York: Columbia University Press, 2004.
Cruveilhier, Jean. *Al-Tanqīḥ al-Waḥīd fī al-Tashrīḥ al-Khāṣṣ al-Jadīd.* 3 vols. Edited by Muḥammad Ibn 'Umar al-Tūnisī and Sālim 'Awaḍ al-Qanayātī. Translated by Muḥammad al-Shabāsī. Cairo: Būlāq, AH 1266 /1850 CE.
Cuno, Kenneth. *The Pasha's Peasants: Land, Society and Economy in Lower Egypt, 1740–1848.* Cambridge: Cambridge University Press, 1992.
Cuno, Kenneth, and Michael Reimer. "The Census Registers of Nineteenth-Century Egypt: A New Source for Social Historians." *British Journal of Middle Eastern Studies* 24, no. 2 (1997): 193–216.
Dabbūr, Anwar Maḥmūd. *Ithbāt al-Nasab bi-Ṭarīq al-Qiyāfa fī'l-Fiqh al-Islāmī.* Cairo: Dār al-Thaqāfa al-'Arabiyya, 1985.
———. *Al-Shubuhāt wa-Atharuhā fī Isqāt al-Ḥudūd.* Cairo: Al-Maktaba al-Tawfīqiyya, 1978.

Damurdāshī Katkhudā ʿAzabān, Aḥmad al-. *Kitāb al-Durra al-Muṣāna fī Akhbār al-Kināna.* Edited by ʿAbd al-Raḥīm ʿAbd al-Raḥmān ʿAbd al-Raḥīm. Cairo: IFAO, 1989.

Daston, Loraine, and Peter Galison. *Objectivity.* New York: Zone Books, 2010.

Demolins, Edmond. *Sirr Taṭawwur al-Inkilīz al-Saksūniyyīn.* Translated by Aḥmad Fatḥī Zaghlūl. Cairo: Al-Taraqqī, 1899.

Descartes, René. *The Treatise on Man.* Translated by Thomas Steel Hall. Cambridge, MA: Harvard University Press, 1972.

Di-Capua, Yoav. *Gatekeepers of the Arab Past: Historians and History Writing in Twentieth-Century Egypt.* Berkeley: University of California Press, 2009.

Dodwell, Henry. *The Founder of Modern Egypt: A Study of Muhammad ʿAli.* Cambridge: Cambridge University Press, 1931.

Dols, Michael. *The Black Death in the Middle East.* Princeton: Princeton University Press, 1977.

———. *Majnun: The Madman in Medieval Muslim Society.* Edited by D.E. Immisch. Oxford: Oxford University Press, 1992.

———. "The Second Plague Pandemic and Its Recurrences in the Middle East: 1347–1894." *Journal of the Economic and Social History of the Orient* 22 (1979): 162–189.

Douin, Georges. *Mohamed Aly et l'expédition d'Alger.* Cairo: Royal Egyptian Geographic Society, 1930.

Dubois, Christian Jean. *Clot Bey: Médecin de Marseille, 1793–1868.* Marseilles: J. Laffitte, 2013.

Dummett, Raymond. "The Campaign against Malaria and the Expansion of Scientific Medical and Sanitary Services in British West Africa, 1898–1910." *African Historical Studies* 1, no. 2 (1968): 153–197.

The Egyptian Railway, or The Interest of England in Egypt. London: Hope, 1852.

Elias, Norbert. *The Civilizing Process.* Translated by Edmund Jephcott. New York: Pantheon, 1982.

Elshahed, Mohamed. "Paris Was Never on the Nile." *Cairobserver,* December 14, 2011. http://cairobserver.com/post/14185184147/paris-was-never-along-the-nile#.WkPhCq2cY_V.

Elshakry, Marwa. *Reading Darwin in Arabic, 1860–1950.* Chicago: University of Chicago Press, 2013.

Ener, Mine. *Managing Egypt's Poor and the Politics of Benevolence, 1800–1952.* Princeton: Princeton University Press, 2003.

Ergene, Boğaç. *Local Court, Provincial Society, and Justice in the Ottoman Empire: Legal Practice and Dispute Resolution in Cankiri and Kastamonu (1652–1744).* Leiden: Brill, 2003.

———. "On Ottoman Justice: Interpretations in Conflict (1600–1800)." *Islamic Law and Society* 8 (2001): 52–87.

Esmeir, Samera. *Juridical Humanity: A Colonial History.* Stanford: Stanford University Press, 2012.

Espéronnier, M. "La mort violent à l'époque mamlouke: Le crime et la châtiment." *Der Islam* 74 (1997): 137–155.

Estes, J. Worth, and LaVerne Kuhnke. "French Observations of Disease and Drug Use in Late Eighteenth-Century Cairo." *Journal of the History of Medicine and Allied Sciences* 39 (1984): 121–152.

Fadel, Mohammad. "Two Women, One Man: Knowledge, Power and Gender in Medieval Sunni Legal Thought." *International Journal of Middle East Studies* 29 (1997): 185–204.

Fahmy, Khaled. *All the Pasha's Men: Mehmed Ali, His Army and the Making of Modern Egypt.* Cambridge: Cambridge University Press, 1997.

———. "The Anatomy of Justice: Forensic Medicine and Criminal Law in Nineteenth-Century Egypt." *Islamic Law and Society* 6 (1999): 224–271.

———. *Al-Jasad wa'l-Ḥadātha: Al-Ṭibb wa'l-Qānūn fī Miṣr al-Ḥadītha.* Cairo: Dār al-Kutub wa'l-Wathā'iq al-Qawmiyya, 2005.

———. "Justice, Law and Pain in Khedival Egypt." In *Standing Trial: Law and the Person in the Modern Middle East,* edited by Baudouin Dupret, 85–116. London: I.B. Tauris, 2004.

———. "Medical Conditions in Egyptian Prisons in the Nineteenth Century." In *Marginal Voices in Literature and Society: Individual and Society in the Mediterranean Muslim World,* edited by Robin Ostle, 135–153. Strasbourg: European Science Foundation, 2000.

———. "Medicine and Power: Towards a Social History of Medicine in Nineteenth-Century Egypt." *Cairo Papers in the Social Sciences* 23, no. 2 (2000): 38–50.

———. *Mehmed Ali: From Ottoman Governor to Ruler of Egypt.* Oxford: Oneworld, 2008.

———. "Mutiny in Mehmed Ali's New Nizamī Army, April–May 1824." *International Journal of Turkish Studies* 8 (2002): 129–138.

———. "The Police and the People in Nineteenth-Century Egypt." *Die Welt des Islams* 39 (1999): 1–38.

———. "Rudolph Peters and the History of Modern Egyptian Law." In *Legal Documents as Sources for the History of Muslim Societies: Studies in Honour of Professor Rudolph Peters,* edited by Maaike Van Berkel, Leon Buskens, and Petra Sijpesteijn, 12–35. Leiden: Brill, 2017.

———. "Women, Medicine and Power in Nineteenth-Century Egypt." In *Remaking Women: Feminism and Modernity in the Middle East,* edited by Lila Abu-Lughod, 35–72. Princeton: Princeton University Press, 1998.

Fancy, Nahyan. *Science and Religion in Mamluk Egypt: Ibn al-Nafīs, Pulmonary Transit and Bodily Resurrection.* London: Routledge, 2013.

Fanon, Frantz. *A Dying Colonialism.* Translated by Haakon Chevalier. New York: Grove, 1967.

Faraḥāt, Muḥammad Nūr. *Al-Mujtama' wa'l-Sharī'a wa'l-Qānūn.* Cairo: Dār al-Hilāl, 1986.

———. *Al-Qaḍā' al-Shar'ī fī Misr ī al-'Aṣr al-'Uthmānī.* Cairo: Al-Hay'a al-Mirṣiyya al-'Āmma lil-Kitāb, 1988.

Fargues, Philippe. "Family and Household in Mid-Nineteenth-Century Egypt." In *Family History in the Middle East: Household, Property, and Gender,* edited by Beshara Doumani, 23–50. Albany: State University of New York Press, 2003.

Farrā, Abū Ya'lā al-. *Al-Aḥkām al-Sulṭāniyya.* Cairo: Muṣṭafā al-Bābī al-Ḥalabī, 1966.

Fayrūzabādī, Muḥammad Ibn Ya'qūb. *Al-Qāmūs al-Muḥīṭ.* 4 vols. Beirut: Al-Mu'assassa al-'Arabiyya lil-Ṭibā'a wa'l-Nashr, 1970.

Figari, Antonio. *Al-Durr al-Lāmi' fi'l-Nabāt wa Mā Fīhi min al-Khawāṣ wa'l-Manāfi'.* Translated by Muḥammad Ibn 'Umar al-Tūnisī and Husayn al-Rashīdī. Cairo: Būlāq, 1841.

———. *Ḥusn al-Barā'a fī 'Ilm al-Zirā'a.* Translated by Aḥmad Nadā. Cairo: Būlāq, 1866.

———. *Projet pour l'établissement de colonies agricoles et d'une ferme modèle en Égypte.* Alexandria: P. Cumbo, n.d.

Fleischer, Cornell H. "Royal Authority, Dynastic Cyclism, and 'Ibn Khaldunism' in Sixteenth-Century Ottoman Letters." *Journal of Asian and African Studies* 18 (1983): 198–220.

Foster, Benjamin. "Agoranomos and Muḥtasib." *Journal of the Economic and Social History of the Orient* 13 (1970): 128–144.

Foucault, Michel. *The Birth of the Clinic: An Archaeology of Medical Perception.* Translated by A. M. Sheridan Smith. New York: Vintage Books, 1994.

———. *Discipline and Punish: The Birth of the Prison.* Translated by Alan Sheridan. New York: Vintage, 1979.

———. *Essential Works of Foucault, 1954–1984.* Vol. 3, *Power.* Edited by James Faubion, translated by Robert Hurley et al. New York: New Press, 2000.

———. "Fourth Lecture, 1 February 1978." In *Security, Territory, Population: Lectures at the Collège de France, 1977–1978,* edited by Michel Senellart, translated by Graham Burchell, 126–145. London: Palgrave Macmillan, 2009.

———. "Governmentality." In *The Foucault Effect: Studies in Governmentality,* edited by Colin Gordon and Peter Miller Graham Burchell, 87–104. Chicago: University of Chicago Press, 1991.

Gallagher, Nancy. *Medicine and Power in Tunisia, 1780–1900.* Cambridge: Cambridge University Press, 1983.

Gastinel, J. B. *Analyses de glutens retirés des farines examinées par la Commission des blés égyptiens.* Paris: Lainé et Havard, 1862.

———. *Étude topographique, chimique et médicale sur les eaux minérales de Hélouan-les-Bains.* Cairo: Moniteur Égyptien, 1883.

———. "Mémoire sur le haschich et ses applications dans la thérapeutique." *Répertoire de Pharmacie* 6 (1849): 129–142.

———. *Monographie des opiums de la Haute-Égypte.* Paris: Lainé et Havard, 1862.

———. *Nukhbat al-Adhkiyā' fī 'Ilm al-Kīmiyā'.* 2 vols. Translated by Aḥmad Nadā. Cairo: Būlāq, 1870.

Gay, Peter. *The Enlightenment.* London: Norton, 1966.

"The General Board of Health, Egypt." *Lancet* 116, no. 2979 (October 1880): 555.

Ghabin, Aḥmad. *Ḥisba, Arts and Crafts in Islam*. Wiesbaden: Verlag, 2009.
Ghazālī, Abū Ḥāmid al-. *Iḥyā' 'Ulūm al-Dīn*. 4 vols. Cairo: Al-Maktaba al-Tijariyya al-Kubra, [1967?].
———. *Al-Wajīz fī Fiqh al-Imām al-Shāfi'ī*. 2 vols. Beirut: Dār al-Arqam, 1997.
Gibb, H. A. R. "Al-Māwardī's Theory of the Caliphate." *Islamic Culture* 11 (1937): 291–302.
Gisquet, M. *L'Egypte, les turcs et les arabes*. 2 vols. Paris: Amyot, 1848.
Glick, T. F. "'Muhtasib' and 'Mustasaf': A Case Study of Institutional Diffusion." *Viator* 2 (1971): 59–81.
Gordon, Joel. *Nasser's Blessing Movement: Egypt's Free Officers and the July Revolution*. New York: Oxford University Press, 1992.
Gran, Peter. *Islamic Roots of Capitalism: Egypt 1760–1840*. Austin: University of Texas Press, 1979.
Grégoire. *Ghāyat al-Marām fī Adwiyat al-Asqām*. Translated by Yūsuf Fir'awn and Ḥasan Kassāb. Cairo: Būlāq, AH 1255/1839 CE.
Grmek, Mirko, ed. *Western Medical Thought from Antiquity to the Middle Ages*. Translated by Antony Shugaar. Cambridge, MA: Harvard University Press, 1998.
Gutas, Dimitri. *Greek Thought, Arabic Culture: The Graeco-Arabic Translation Movement in Baghdad and Early 'Abbasid Society (2nd–4th/8th–10th Centuries)*. London: Routledge, 1998.
———. "Medical Theory and Scientific Method in the Age of Avicenna." In *Islamic Medical and Scientific Tradition: Critical Concepts in Islamic Studies*, vol. 1, edited by Peter E. Pormann. London: Routledge, 2011.
Ḥāfiẓ, 'Usāma Ibrāhīm, and 'Alī Muḥammad al-Sharīf. *Al-Nuṣḥ wa'l-Tabyīn fī Taṣḥīḥ Mafāhīm al-Muḥtasibīn*. Cairo: Maktabat al-Turāth al-Islāmī, 2002.
Hallaq, Wael. *The Impossible State: Islam, Politics and Modernity's Moral Predicament*. New York: Columbia University Press, 2013.
———. "On Dating Malik's Muwatta." *UCLA Journal of Islamic and Middle East Law* 1 (2002): 47–75.
———. "*Qāḍīs* Communicating: Legal Change and the Law of Documentary Evidence." *Al-Qanṭara* 20 (1999): 437–466.
———. "The *Qāḍī's Dīwān* (*Sijill*) before the Ottomans." *Bulletin of the School of Oriental and African Studies* 61, no. 3 (1998): 415–436.
———. *Sharī'a: Theory, Practice, Transformations*. Cambridge: Cambridge University Press, 2009.
———. "Was the Gate of Ijtihad Closed?" *International Journal of Middle East Studies* 16, no. 1 (1984): 3–41.
Hamdy, Sherine. *Our Bodies Belong to God: Organ Transplants, Islam, and the Struggle for Human Dignity in Egypt*. Berkeley: University of California Press, 2012.
Hanley, Will. *Identifying with Nationality: Europeans, Ottomans, and Egyptians in Alexandria*. New York: Columbia University Press, 2017.
Hardy, Anne. "Development of the Prison medical Service, 1774–1895." In *The Health of Prisoners: Historical Essays*, edited by Richard Creese, W. F. Bynum, and J. Bearn, 59–82. Atlanta: Rodopi, 1995.

Harrāwī, 'Abd al-Samī' Sālim al-. *Lughat al-Idāra al-'Āmma fī Miṣr fī al-Qarn al-Tāsi' 'Ashr.* Cairo: Al-Majlis al-A'lā li-Ri'āyat al-Funūn wa'l-Ādāb wa'l-'Ulūm al-Ijtimā'iyya, 1963.

Harrison, Peter. "'Science' and 'Religion': Constructing the Boundaries." *Journal of Religion* 86 (2006): 81–106.

———. *The Territories of Science and Religion.* Chicago: University of Chicago Press, 2015.

Ḥasan, Ibrāhīm Efendi. *Rawḍat al-Āsī fī'l-Ṭibb al-Siyāsī.* Cairo: Maṭba'at al-Madāris al-Mulkiyya, AH 1293/1866–67 CE.

Ḥasan, Ibrāhīm Pasha. *Al-Dustūr al-Mar'ī fī'l-Ṭibb al-Shar'ī.* Cairo: Al-Maṭba'a al-Ṭibbiyya al-Durriyya, AH 1306/ 1888–89 CE.

Hathaway, Jane. *The Politics of Households in Ottoman Egypt: The Rise of the Qazdağlis.* Cambridge: Cambridge University Press, 1997.

Ḥatmal, Ayman Muḥammad. *Shahādat Ahl al-Khibra wa Aḥkāmuhā: Dirāsa Fiqhiyya Muqārana.* Amman: Dār al-Ḥāmid, 2007.

Headrick, Daniel. *Tools of Empire: Technology and European Imperialism in the Nineteenth Century.* New York: Oxford University Press, 1981.

Heckscher, William S. *Rembrandt's Anatomy of Dr. Nicolaas Tulp: An Iconographic Study.* New York: New York University Press, 1958.

Heyd, Uriel. *Studies in Old Ottoman Criminal Law.* Edited by V.L. Ménage. Oxford: Oxford University Press, 1973.

Heyworth-Dunne, J. *An Introduction to the History of Education in Modern Egypt.* London: Frank Cass, 1968.

Hilāl, 'Imād. *Al-Fallāḥ wa'l-Sulṭa wa'l-Qānūn.* Cairo: Dār al-Kutub wa'l-Wathāi'q al-Qawmiyya, 2007.

———. *Wathā'iq al-Tashrī' al-Jinā'ī al-Miṣrī: Sijill Majmū' Umūr Jinā'īyah.* Cairo: Maṭba'at Dār al-Kutub w'al-Wathā'iq al-Qawmīyya, 2011.

Ḥilmī, Muḥammad Ṣāliḥ, and Muḥammad Shafi'ī. *Al-Mabādi' al-Awwaliyya fī al-Tadābīr al-Ṣiḥḥiyya.* Cairo: Al-Ma'ārif, 1921.

Hirschkind, Charles. *The Ethical Soundscape: Cassette Sermons and Islamic Counter-Publics.* New York: Columbia University Press, 2006.

Hourani, Albert. "The Islamic City in the Light of Recent Research." In *The Islamic City,* edited by A.H. Hourani and S. Stern, 9–24. Oxford: Bruno Cassirer, 1970.

Huff, Toby. *The Rise of Early Modern Science: Islam, China and the West.* Cambridge: Cambridge University Press, 1993.

Hunter, F. Robert. *Egypt under the Khedives: From Household Government to Modern Bureaucracy.* Pittsburgh: University of Pittsburgh Press, 1984.

Hussain, A. *The Islamic Law of Succession.* Riyadh: Darussalam, 2005.

Ibn 'Abdūn. "Risala fi'l-hisba." In *Documents arabes inédits sur la vie sociale et économique en Occident musulman au moyen âge,* edited by E. Lévi-Provençal, 3–65. Cairo: IFAO, 1955.

Ibn 'Ābidīn, Muḥammad Amīn Ibn 'Umar. *Radd al-Muḥtar 'alā al-Durr al-Mukhtār.* 12 vols. Beirut: Dār al-Kutub al-'Ilmiyya, 1992.

Ibn Bassam, Muḥmmad Ibn Aḥmad. *Nihāyat al-Rutba fi Talab al-Ḥisba*. Edited by Ḥusām al-Dīn al-Sāmarrā'ī. Baghdad: Maṭba'at al-Ma'ārif, 1968.

Ibn Bāz, 'Abd al-'Azīz 'Abdallāh. *Ḥukm Tashrīḥ Juthath al-Muslimīn*. Cairo: Al-Markaz al-Salafī lil-Kitāb, 1982.

Ibn Farḥūn, Burhān al-Dīn Abī al-Wafā' Ibrāhīm Ibn Shams al-Dīn. *Tabṣirat al-Ḥukkām fī Uṣūl al-Aqḍiyah wa-Manāhij al-Aḥkām*. 2 vols. Edited by Jamāl Mar'ashlī. Beirut: Dār al-Kutub al-'Ilmiyya, 1995.

Ibn Ḥazm, Abū Muḥammad 'Alī Ibn Aḥmad Ibn Sa'īd. *Al-Muḥallā*. 11 vols. Cairo: Al-Munīriyya, 1929–34.

Ibn Iyās, Muḥammad Ibn Aḥmad. *Badā'i' al-Zuhūr fī Waqā'i' al-Duhūr*. 6 vols. Edited by Muḥammad Muṣṭafā. Cairo: Dār al-Kutub wa'l-Wathā'iq al-Qawmiyya, 2008.

Ibn Manẓūr, Muḥammad Ibn Mukarram. *Lisān al-'Arab*. 20 vols. Cairo: Būlāq, AH 1300/1882 CE.

Ibn Qayyim al-Jawziyya, Muḥammad Ibn Abī Bakr. *Al-Ṭuruq al-Ḥukmiyya fi'l-Siyāsa al-Shar'iyya*. Cairo: Al-Ābāb, AH 1317/1899–1900 CE.

Ibn Qudāma, Muwaffaq al-Dīn Abū Muḥammad 'Abd Allāh Ibn Aḥmad Ibn Muḥammad. *Al-Mughnī*. 10 vols. Cairo: Maktabat al-Qāhira, 1970.

Ibn Sīnā, Abū 'Alī al-Ḥusayn Ibn 'Abd Allāh. *Al-Qānūn fī al-Ṭibb*. 4 vols. Edited by Idwār al-Qashsh. Beirut: Mu'assasat 'Izz al-Dīn, 1987.

Ibn Taghrī Birdī, Jamāl al-Dīn Abū al-Maḥāsin Yūsuf. *Al-Nujūm al-Zāhira fī Mulūk Miṣr wa'l-Qāhira*. 16 vols. Cairo: Al-Mu'assasa al-Miṣriyya al-'Āmma lil-Ta'līf wa'l-Ṭibā'a wa'l-Nashr, 1963–71.

Ibn al-Ukhuwwa [Muḥammad Ibn Muḥammad al-Qurashī]. "Ma'ālim al-Qurbā fī Aḥkām al-Ḥisba." In *Fī al-Turāth al-Iqtiṣādī al-Islāmī*, 28–316. Beirut: Dār al-Ḥadātha, 1990.

———. *Ma'ālim al-Qurba fi Aḥkām al-Ḥisba of Ḍiyā' al-Dīn Muḥammad Ibn Muḥammad al-Qurashī al-Shāfi'ī known as Ibn as-Ukhuwwa*. Edited and translated by Reuben Levy. Cambridge: Cambridge University Press, 1938.

Ibn 'Umar, Yaḥyā. "Kitāb Aḥkām al-Sūq." Edited and annotated by M. 'A. Makkī. *Ṣaḥīfat al-Ma'had al-Miṣrī lil-Dirāsat al-Islāmiyya fi Madrid* 4 (1956): 59–151.

Ibn Zawlāq, al-Ḥasan Ibn Ibrāhīm. *Akhbār Sibawayhi al-Miṣrī*. Edited by Muḥammad Ibrāhīm Sa'd and Ḥusayn al-Dīb. Cairo: Maṭba'at 'al-Naṣr, 1933.

Ibrāhīm, 'Alī. "Kulliyyat al-ṭibb: Māḍīhā wa Ḥāḍiruhā wa Mustaqbaluhā." *Al-Muqtaṭaf* 90 (1937): 269–279.

Ibrāhīm, Nāṣir. *Al-Azmāt al-Ijtimā'iyya fī Miṣr fī al-Qarn al-Sābi' 'Ashr*. Cairo: Dār al-Āfāq al-'Arabiyya, 1998.

Ignatieff, Michael. *A Just Measure of Pain: The Penitentiary in the Industrial Revolution, 1750–1850*. London: Macmillan, 1878.

Ilāhī, Faḍl. *Al-Ḥisba: Ta'rīfuhā wa Mashrū'iyyatuhā wa Wujūbuhā*. Cairo: Dār al-I'tiṣām, 1996.

Imām, Muḥammad Kamāl al-Dīn. *Uṣūl al-Ḥisba fi'l-Islām: Dirāsa Ta'ṣīliyya Muqārina*. Cairo: Dār al-Hidāya, 1986.

Imber, Colin. *Ebu's-Su'ud: The Islamic Legal Tradition*. Stanford: Stanford University Press, 1997.
ʿĪsā, ʿAbd al-Rāziq Ibrāhīm. *Tārīkh al-Qaḍā' fī Misr al-ʿUthmāniyya, 1517–1798*. Cairo: Al-Hay'a al-Misriyya al-ʿĀmma lil-Kitāb, 1998.
Ismāʿīl, ʿAbd al-Raḥmān. *Al-Taqwīmāt al-Ṣiḥḥiyya ʿalā al-ʿAwā'id al-Miṣriyya*. Cairo: Būlāq, 1903.
Ismāʿīl, Ḥusām al-Dīn. *Madīnat al-Qāhira min Wilāyat Muḥammad ʿAlī ilā Ismāʿīl, 1805–1879*. Cairo: Dār al-Āfāq al-'Arabiyya, 1997.
Jabartī, ʿAbd al-Raḥmān al-. *ʿAbd al-Raḥmān al-Jabartī's History of Egypt*. 4 vols. Edited and translated by Thomas Philipp and Moshe Perlmann. Stuttgart: Verlag, 1994.
Jackson, Sherman. "Kramer versus Kramer in a Tenth/Sixteenth Century Egyptian Court: Post-Formative Jurisprudence between Exigency and Law." *Islamic Law and Society* 8, no. 1 (2001): 27–51.
Jakes, Aaron. "Peaceful Wars and Unlikely Unions: The Azhar Strike of 1909 and the Politics of Comparison in Egypt." *Comparative Studies in Society and History* (forthcoming).
Jallād, Filīb. *Qāmūs al-Idāra wa'l-Qaḍā'*. 7 vols. Alexandria: Lāghūdākī, 1899.
Jawhar, Sāmī. *Al-Ṣāmiṭūn Yatakallimūn: ʿAbd al-Nāṣir wa'l-Ikhwān*. Cairo: Al-Maktab al-Miṣrī al-Ḥadīth, 1975.
Jeffery, Roger. "Recognizing India's Doctors: The Institutionalization of Medical Dependency, 1918–39." *Modern Asian Studies* 13, no. 2 (1979): 301–326.
Jennings, Ronald C. "Kadi, Court, and Legal procedure in 17th Century Kayseri: The Kadi and the Legal System." *Studia Islamica* 48 (1978): 133–172.
Johansen, Baber. "Formes de langage et fonctions publiques: Stéréotypes, témoins et offices dans la preuve par l'Érit en droit Musulman." *Arabica* 44, no. 3 (1997): 333–376.
———. "How the Norms Change: Legal Literature and the Problem of Change in the Case of the Land Rent." In *Contingency in a Sacred Law: Legal and Ethical Norms in the Muslim* Fiqh, 446–464. Leiden: Brill, 1999.
———. "The Muslim *Fiqh* as a Sacred Law: Religion, Law and Ethics in a Normative System." In *Contingency in a Sacred Law: Legal and Ethical Norms in the Muslim* Fiqh, 1–71. Leiden: Brill, 1999.
———. "Secular and Religious Elements in Hanfite Law: Function and Limits of the Absolute Character of Government Authority." In *Contingency in a Sacred Law: Legal and Ethical Norms in the Muslim* Fiqh, 189–218. Leiden: Brill, 1999.
———. "Signs as Evidence: The Doctrine of Ibn Taymiyya (1263–1328) and Ibn Qayyim al-Jawziyya (d. 1351) on Proof." *Islamic Law and Society* 9, no. 2 (2002): 168–193.
———. "The Valorization of the Human Body in Muslim Sunni Law." *Princeton Papers in Near Eastern Studies* 4 (1996): 71–112.
Jolowitz, J. A. "Orality and Immediacy in English Civil Procedure." *Boletín Mexicano de Derrecho Comparado* 8 (1975): 595–608.

Jordan, David. *Transforming Paris: The Life and Labors of Baron Haussmann*. New York: Free Press, 1995.
Juwaynī, Imām al-Ḥaramayn Ḍiā' al-Dīn 'Abd al-Malik Ibn Yūsuf al-. *Al-Irshād Ilā Qawāṭi' al-Adilla fī Uṣūl al-I'tiqād*. Cairo: Al-Khānjī, 1950.
———. *Nihāyat al-Maṭlab fī Dirāyat al-Madhhab*. 21 vols. Jiddah: Dār al-Minhāj, 2007.
Kamāl, Aḥmad Muḥammad. *Tārīkh al-Idāra al-Ṣiḥḥiyya fī Miṣr min 'Ahd Afandīnā Muḥammad 'Alī Bāshā lil-'Ān*. Cairo: Al-Raghā'ib, 1943.
Kandil, Hazem. *Soldiers, Spies, and Statesmen*. London: Verso, 2012.
Kanun-u Seferiye. Cairo: Būlāq, AH 1258/1842 CE.
Kāsānī, Abū Bakr al-. *Badā'i' al-Ṣanā'i' fī Tartīb al-Sharā'i'*. 7 vols. Cairo: Al-Maṭba'a al-Jammāliyya, 1910.
Khānkī, 'Azīz. "Al-Tashrī' wa'l-Qaḍā' Qabl Inshā' al-Maḥākim al-Ahliyya." In *Al-Kitāb al-Dhahabī lil-Maḥākim al-Ahliyy*, vol. 1, 62–96. Cairo: Būlāq, 1937.
Khayrallah, 'Ābidīn. *Irshād al-Insān ilā Ṣiḥḥat al-Abdān*. Cairo: Al-'Āṣima, AH 1312/1894–95 CE.
Khoury, Rodolphe el-. "Polish and Deodorize: Paving the City in Late Eighteenth-Century Paris." In *The Smell Culture Reader*, edited by Jim Drobnick, 18–28. New York: Berg, 2006.
Khūlī, Jamāl. *Al-Istibdāl wa-Ightisāb al-Awqāf: Dirāsah Wathā'iqiyya*. Alexandria: Dār al-Thaqāfa al-'Ilmiyya, 2000.
Kiechle, Melanie. "Navigating by Nose: Fresh Air, Stench Nuisance, and the Urban Environment, 1840–1880." *Journal of Urban History* 42, no. 4 (2015): 753–771.
Kinglake, Alexander William. *Eothen*. London: Ollivier, 1847.
Kishk, Muḥammad Jalāl. *Wa Dakhalt al-Khayl al-Azhar*. Cairo: Al-Zahrā', 1990.
Al-Kitāb al-Dhahabī lil-Maḥākim al-Ahliyya: 1883–1933. 2 vols. Cairo: Al-Maṭba'a al-Amīriyya, 1937–38.
Kozma, Liat. *Policing Egyptian Women: Sex, Law, and Medicine in Khedival Egypt*. Syracuse: Syracuse University Press, 2011.
Kudlick, Catherine J. *Cholera in Post-Revolutionary Paris: A Cultural History*. Berkeley: University of California Press, 1996.
Kuhnke, LaVerne. "Early Nineteenth Century Ophthalmological Clinics in Egypt." *Clio Medica* 7 (1972): 209–214.
———. *Lives at Risk: Public Health in Nineteenth-Century Egypt*. Berkeley: University of California Press, 1990.
Lā'iḥat Zirā'at al-Fallāḥ. Cairo: Būlāq, AH 1245/1830 CE.
"Lancet Gallery of Medical Portraits." *Lancet* 20, no. 502 (1833): 88.
Landes, David. *Bankers and Pashas: International Finance and Economic Imperialism in Egypt*. London: Hinemann Education, 1958.
Lane, William. *Manners and Customs of the Modern Egyptians*. London: J. M. Dent, 1908.
Langbein, John. *Prosecuting Crime in the Renaissance: England, Germany, France*. Cambridge, MA: Harvard University Press, 1974.

———. *Torture and the Law of Proof: Europe and England in the Ancien Régime.* Chicago: University of Chicago Press, 1977.

Lange, Christian. *Justice, Punishment and the Medieval Muslim Imagination.* Cambridge: Cambridge University Press, 2008.

———. "Where on Earth Is Hell?" In *Public Violence in Islamic Societies: Power, Discipline, and the Construction of the Public Sphere, 7th-19th Centuries CE,* edited by Christian Lange and Mirabel Fiero, 156–178. Edinburgh: Edinburgh University Press, 2009.

Lange, Christian, and Maribel Fierro. "Introduction: Spatial, Ritual and Representational Aspects of Public Violence in Islamic Societies (7th–19th Centuries CE)." In *Public Violence in Islamic Societies: Power, Discipline, and the Construction of the Public Sphere, 7th-19th Centuries CE,* edited by Christian Lange and Maribel Fierro, 1–23. Edinburgh: Edinburgh University Press, 2009.

Lapidus, Ira M. *Muslim Cities in the Later Middle Ages.* Cambridge, MA: Harvard University Press, 1967.

Lāshīn, ʿAbd al-Khāliq. *Misriyyāt fī al-Fikr wa-l-Siyāsa.* Cairo: Sīnā, 1993.

Lawrence, William. *Ḍiyāʾ al-Nayyirīn fī Mudāwāt al-ʿAynayn* [*A Treatise on the Diseases of the Eye*]. Translated by Aḥmad al-Rashīdī. Cairo: Būlāq, 1840.

Lesch, John E. *Science and Medicine in France: The Emergence of Experimental Physiology, 1790–1855.* Cambridge, MA: Harvard University Press, 1984.

Lev, Y. "Aspects of the Egyptian Society in the Fatimid Period." In *Egypt and Syria in the Fatimid, Ayyubid and Mamluk Eras,* vol. 3, edited by U. Vermeulen and J. Van Steenbergen, 1–32. Leuven: Uitgeverij Peeters, 2001.

Lewis, Bernard. "The Impact of the French Revolution on Turkey: Some Notes on the Transition of Ideas." *Journal of World History* 1 (1953): 105–125.

Linebaugh, Peter. "The Tyburn Riot against the Surgeons." In *Albion's Fatal Tree: Crime and Society in Eighteenth-Century England,* edited by Douglas Hay, Peter Linebaugh, John G. Rule, E. P. Thompson, and Cal Winslow, 65–117. New York: Pantheon Books, 1975.

Mahfouz, Naguib. *The History of Medical Education in Egypt.* Cairo: Government Press, 1935.

Mahmood, Saba. *Politics of Piety: The Islamic Revival and the Feminist Subject.* Princeton: Princeton University Press, 2005.

Maqrīzī, Taqī al-Dīn Aḥmad b. ʿAlī b. ʿAbd al-Qādir al-. *Al-Mawāʿiẓ wa'l-Iʿtibār fī Dhikr al-Khiṭaṭ wa'l-Āthār.* 5 vols. Edited by Ayman Fu'ād Sayyid. London: Al-Furqān Islamic Heritage Foundation, 2002–4.

———. *Al-Sulūk li-Maʿrifat Duwal al-Mulūk.* 4 vols. Cairo: Maṭbaʿat Lajnat al-Ta'līf wa'l-Tarjama wa'l-Nashr, 1956–73.

Marks, Shula. "What Is Colonial about Colonial Medicine? And What Has Happened to Imperialism and Health?" *Social History of Medicine* 10, no. 2 (1997): 205–219.

Marlowe, John. *Spoiling the Egyptians.* London: Andre Deutsch, 1974.

Marsh, Andrew. "What Can the Islamic Past Teach Us about Secular Modernity?" *Political Theory* 43 (2015): 838–849.

Maspero, Gaston. *Chansons populaire recuillies dans la Haute-Égypte de 1900–1914 pendant les inspections du services des antiguités.* Cairo: Imprémerie de l'Institut Français d'Archéologie Orientale, 1914.
Māwardī, Abū al-Ḥasan 'Alī Ibn Muḥammad al-. *Al-Ḥāwī al-Kabīr fī Fiqh Madhhab al-Imām al-Shāfi'ī.* 19 vols. Edited by 'Alī Muḥammad Mu'awwaḍ and 'Ādil Aḥmad 'Abd al-Mawjūd. Beirut: Dār al-Kutub al-'Ilmiyya, 1994.
———. *The Ordinances of Government: Al-Aḥkām al-Sultāniyya w'al-Wilāyāt al-Dīniyaa.* Translated by Wafaa H. Wahba. London: Garnet, 1996.
McClellan, J., and Harold Dorn. *Science and Technology in World History: An Introduction.* Baltimore: Johns Hopkins University Press, 1999.
Meijer, Roel. "Authenticity in History: The Concept of *al-Wafid* and *al-Mawruth* in Tariq al-Bishri's Reinterpretation of Modern Egyptian History." In *Amsterdam Middle East Studies,* edited by Manfred Woidich, 68–83. Wiesbaden: Verlag, 1990.
Meshal, Reem. *Sharia and the Making of the Modern Egyptian: Islamic Law and Custom in the Courts of Ottoman Cairo.* Cairo: American University in Cairo Press, 2014.
Messick, Brinkley. *The Calligraphic State: Textual Domination and History in a Muslim Society.* Berkeley: University of California Press, 1993.
———. "Evidence: From Memory to Archive." *Islamic Law and Society* 9, no. 2 (2002): 231–270.
———. "Written Identities: Legal Subjects in an Islamic State." *History of Religions* 38, no. 1 (1998): 25–51.
Mestyan, Adam. *Arab Patriotism: The Ideology and Culture of Power in Late Ottoman Egypt.* Princeton: Princeton University Press, 2017.
Mikhail, Alan. *Nature and Empire in Ottoman Egypt.* Cambridge: Cambridge University Press, 2011.
Mikhail, Hanna. *Politics and Revelation: Māwardī and After.* Edinburgh: Edinburgh University Press, 1995.
Mināwī, Mahmūd. *Tārīkh al-Nahḍa al-Ṭibbiyya al-Miṣriyya: Mathaf Qaṣr al-'Ainī.* Cairo: Nahḍat Miṣr, 2000.
Mitchell, Timothy. *Colonising Egypt.* Cambridge: Cambridge University Press, 1988.
———. *Rule of Experts: Egypt, Techno-Politics, Modernity.* Berkeley: University of California Press, 2002.
Mottahedeh, Roy. *Loyalty and Leadership in Early Islamic Society.* Princeton: Princeton University Press, 1980.
Moulin, Anne Marie. "The Construction of Disease Transmission in Nineteenth-Century Egypt and the Dialectics of Modernity." In *The Development of Modern Medicine in Non-Western Countries: Historical Perspectives,* edited by Hormoz Ebrahimnejad, 42–59. London: Routledge, 2009.
Mubārak, 'Alī. *Al-Khiṭāṭ al-Tawfīqīyya al-Jadīda.* 20 vols. Cairo: Būlāq, AH 1304–6/1882–89 CE.
Muḥarram, Aḥmad Fahmī, Maḥmūd Labīb Muḥarram, and 'Alī Yāsīn Muḥarram. *Al-Qawā'id al-Asāsiyya fī Mu'ālajat al-Kūlīrā al-Āsiāwiyya'.* Cairo: Al-Muqtaṭaf, 1893.

Multi-Douglas, Fedwa. "Mentalités and Marginality: Blindness and Mamlûk Civilization." In *The Islamic World from Classical to Modern Times: Essays in Honor of Bernard Lewis,* edited by C. E. Bosworth, Charles Issawi, Roger Savory, and A. L. Udovitch, 211–237. Princeton: Darwin Press, 1989.

Murphy, Jane. "Locating the Sciences in Eighteenth-Century Egypt." *British Journal for the History of Science* 43, no. 4 (2010): 557–571.

Mūrū, Muḥammad. *Ṭāriq al-Bishrī: Shāhid 'alā Suqūt al-'Almāniyya.* Cairo: Dār al-Fatā al-Muslim, n.d.

Musallam, Basim. "The Ordering of Muslim Societies." In *Cambridge Illustrated History of the Islamic World,* edited by Francis Robinson, 164–207. Cambridge: Cambridge University Press, 1996.

Nadā, Aḥmad. *Al-Aqwāl al-Marḍiyya fī 'Ilm al-Tabaqāt al-Arḍiyya.* Cairo: Būlāq, 1871.

———. *Al-Āyāt al-Bayyināt fī 'Ilm al-Nabātāt.* Cairo: Būlāq, 1866.

Naddaf, Sandra. "Mirrored Images: Rifā'ah al-Tahtāwī and the West." *Alif* 6 (1986): 73–83.

Naṣr, Muṣṭafā Efendi. *Al-Minḥa fī Tadbīr al-Ṣiḥḥa.* Cairo: Maṭba'at al-Ādāb, AH 1306/1888–89 CE.

Nawawī, Yaḥyā Ibn Sharaf al-. *Rawḍat al-Ṭālibīn wa 'Umdat al-Muftīn.* 12 vols. Beirut: Al-Maktab al-Islāmī, 1991.

Néroutsos, Tassos Demetrios. *Aperçu historique de l'organisation de l'intendance générale sanitaire d'Egypte: Séant à Alexandrie, depuis sa fondation en 1831 . . . jusqu' . . . en 1879.* Alexandria: Mourès, 1880.

Nielsen, Jørgen. *Secular Justice in an Islamic State: Maẓālim under the Bahrī Mamlūks, 662/1264–789/1387.* Leiden: Nederlands Instituut voor het Nabije Ossten, 1985.

Okun, Mitchell. *Fair Play in the Marketplace: The First Battle for Pure Food and Drugs.* Dekalb, IL: Northern Illinois Press, 1986.

Ormsby, Eric. *Ghazālī.* Oxford: Oneworld, 2008.

Owen, Roger. *Cotton and the Egyptian Economy, 1820–1914: A Study in Trade and Development.* Oxford: Clarendon Press, 1969.

———. "Egypt and Europe: From French Expedition to British Occupation." In *Studies in the Theory of Imperialism,* edited by Roger Owen and Bob Sutcliffe, 195–209. London: Longman, 1972.

———. "The Influence of Lord Cromer's Indian Experience on British Policy in Egypt, 1883–1907." In "St. Antony's Papers," special issue, *Middle Eastern Affairs* 4, no. 17 (1965): 103–139.

Park, Katharine. "The Criminal and the Saintly Body: Autopsy and Dissection in Renaissance Italy." *Renaissance Quarterly* 47, no. 1 (1994): 1–33.

Parks, Richard. "*Divide et Impera:* Public Health and Urban Reform in Potectorate-Era Tunis." *Journal of North African Studies* 17, no. 3 (2012): 533–546.

Paton, A. *History of the Egyptian Revolution.* 2 vols. London: Trubner, 1863.

Peers, Douglass M. "Sepoys, Soldiers and the Lash: Race, Caste and Army Discipline in India, 1820–50." *Journal of Imperial and Commonwealth History* 23 (1995): 211–247.

Peirce, Leslie. *Morality Tales: Law and Gender in the Ottoman Court of Aintab.* Berkeley: University of California Press, 2003.

Pelling, Margaret. *Cholera, Fever and English Medicine, 1825–1865.* Oxford: Oxford University Press, 1978.

Perron, Nicolas. *Al-Djawāhir al-Saniyya fi'l-A'māl al-Kīmāwiyya.* 3 vols. Edited and translated by Muḥammad al-Tūnisī, Muḥammad al-Harrāwī, Darwīsh Zaydān, and Ḥusayn Ghānim. Cairo: Būlāq, AH 1260/1844 CE.

Peters, Rudolph. "Administrators and Magistrates: The Development of a Secular Judiciary in Egypt, 1842–1871." *Die Welt des Islams* 39 (1999): 378–397.

———. "Controlled Suffering: Mortality and Living Conditions in 19th-Century Egyptian Prisons." *International Journal of Middle East Studies* 36 (2004): 387–407.

———. *Crime and Punishment in Islamic Law: Theory and Practice from the Sixteenth to the Twenty-First Century.* Cambridge: Cambridge University Press, 2005.

———. "Egypt and the Age of the Triumphant Prison: Legal Punishment in Nineteenth Century Egypt." *Annales Islamologiques* 36 (2002): 253–285.

———. "'For His Correction and as a Deterrent Example for Others': Mehmed Ali's First Criminal Legislation (1829–1830)." *Islamic Law and Society* 6 (1999): 164–193.

———. "Islamic and Criminal Law in Nineteenth Century Egypt: The Role and Function of the Qadi." *Islamic Law and Society* 4, no. 1 (1997): 70–90.

———. "The Infatuated Greek: Social and Legal Boundaries in Nineteenth-Century Egypt." *Égypte/Monde Arabe* 34 (1998): 53–65.

———. "Murder on the Nile: Homicide Trials in 19th Century Egyptian Shari'a Courts." *Die Welt des Islams* 30 (1990): 98–116.

———. "The Origins of Pre-1883 Egyptian Criminal Legislation." Paper presented at the 1996 Annual MESA Meeting, Providence, RI, November 21–24, 1996.

———. "Prisons and Marginalization in Nineteenth-Century Egypt." In *Outside In: On the Margins of the Modern Middle East,* edited by Eugene Rogan, 31–52. London: I.B. Tauris, 2002.

Petry, Carl. *The Civilian Elite of Cairo in the Later Middle Ages.* Princeton: Princeton University Press, 1981.

———. "The Hoax of the Miraculous Speaking Wall: Criminal Investigation in Mamluk Cairo." In *Mamluks and Ottomans: Studies in Honour of Michael Winter,* edited by David Wasserstein and Ami Ayalon, 86–95. London: Routledge, 2006.

Pouchelle, Marie-Christine. *The Body and Surgery in the Middle Ages.* Translated by Rosemary Morris. New Brunswick, NJ: Rutgers University Press, 1990.

Prakash, Gyan. *Another Reason: Science and the Imagination of Modern India.* Princeton: Princeton University Press, 1999.

———. "Body Politic in Colonial India." In *Questions of Modernity,* edited by Timothy Mitchell, 189–221. Minneapolis: University of Minnesota Press, 2000.

Prashad, Vijay. "Native Dirt/Imperial Ordure: The Cholera of 1832 and the Morbid Resolutions of Modernity." *Journal of Historical Sociology* 7 (1994): 243–260.

Qānūn al-Dākhiliyya. Cairo: Maṭba'at Dīwān al-Jihādiyya, AH 1250/1835 CE.

Qārī, 'Abdallah. "Ḥawla Kitābayy al-Shayzarī wa Ibn Bassām: Man Minhumā Sabaq al-Ākhar?" *'Ālam al-Kutub* 29, nos. 3–4 (2007–8): 361–366.

Qassār, 'Abd al-'Azīz Khalīfa al-. *Ḥukm Tashrīḥ al-Insān Bayn al-Sharī'a wa'l-Qānūn*. Beirut: Dār Ibn Ḥazm, 1999.

Qataya, Sulaiman. "Ibnul-Nafees Had Dissected the Human Body." In *Proceeding of the Second International Conference on Islamic Medicine,* 6 vols., edited by Ahmed Ragai El-Gindy and Hakeem Mohammad Zahoorul Hasan, 306–312. Kuwait: Munaẓẓamat al-Ṭibb al-Islāmī, 1982.

Quranī, 'Alī Ibn Ḥasan Ibn 'Alī al-. *Al-Ḥisba fī'l-Māḍī wa'l-Ḥāḍir Bayna Thabāt al-Ahdāf wa-Taṭawwur al-Uslūb*. Riyadh: Maktabat al-Rushd, 1994.

Raḍwān, Abul-Futūḥ. *Tārīkh Maṭba'at Būlāq*. Cairo: Al-Maṭb'a al-Amīriyya, 1953.

Ragab, Ahmed. *The Medieval Islamic Hospital: Medicine, Religion, and Charity*. Cambridge: Cambridge University Press, 2015.

Raj, Kapil. *Relocating Modern Science*. Basingstoke: Macmillan, 2007.

Ramasubban, Radhika. "Imperial Health in British India, 1857–1900." In *Disease, Medicine, and Empire: Perspectives on Western Medicine and the Experience of European Expansion,* edited by Roy Macleod and Milton Lewis, 38–60. London: Routledge, 1988.

———. *Public Health and Medical Research in India: Their Origins under the Impact of British Colonial Policy*. Stockholm: SAREC, 1982.

Rao, Anupama. "Problems of Violence, States of Terror: Torture in Colonial India." *Economic and Political Weekly* 36 (2001): 4125–4133.

Rapoport, Yossef. "Royal Justice and Religious Law: *Siyāsah* and Shari'ah under the Mamluks." *Mamluk Studies Review* 16 (2012): 71–102.

Rashīdī, Ḥusayn al-. *Kitāb al-Aqribādhīn*. Cairo: Būlāq, 1842.

Raymond, André. *Cairo*. Translated by Willard Wood. Cambridge, MA: Harvard University Press, 2000.

———. *Égyptiens et Français au Caire, 1798–1801*. Cairo: Institut Français d'Archéologie Orientale, 1998.

———. "Islamic City, Arab City: Orientalist Myths and Recent Views." *British Journal of Middle Eeastern Studies Studies* 21 (1994): 3–18.

Reid, Donald. *Paris Sewers and Sewermen: Realities and Representations*. Cambridge, MA: Harvard University Press, 1991.

Reimer, Michael. "Reorganizing Alexandria: The Origins and Development of the Conseil de l'Ornato." *Journal of Urban History* 19, no. 3 (1993): 55–83.

Respler-Chaim, Vardit. "Postmortem Examinations in Egypt." In *Islamic Legal Interpretation: Muftis and Their Fatwas,* edited by Muḥammad Khalid Masud, Brinkley Messick, David Powers, 278–285. Cambridge, MA: Harvard University Press, 1996.

Richardson, Ruth. *Death, Dissection and the Destitute*. London: Penguin, 1988.

Riḍā, Rashīd. "Istfitā' 'an al-Kashf al-Ṭibbī 'alā al-Mayyit." *Al-Manār* 10 (1907–8): 358–359.

———. "Al-Kashf al-Ṭibbī 'alā al-Mawtā wa-Ta'khīr al-Dafn." *Al-Manār* 13 (1910): 100–101.

———. *Tārīkh al-Ustādh al-Imām al-Shaykh Muḥammad 'Abdu.* Vol. 1. Cairo: Al-Manār, 1906.

Rosen, George. *A History of Public Health.* Baltimore: Johns Hopkins University Press, 1993.

Rosen, Lawrence. *The Justice of Islam: Comparative Perspectives on Islamic Law and Society.* Oxford: Oxford University Press, 1999.

Russell, Gül A. "Vesalius and the Emergence of Veridical Representation in Renaissance Anatomy." *Progress in Brain Research* 203 (2013): 3–32.

Ryzova, Lucie. *The Age of the Efendiyya: Passages to Modernity in National-Colonial Egypt.* Oxford: Oxford University Press, 2014.

Sabra, Adam. "'Prices Are in God's Hands': The Theory and Practice of Price Control in the Medieval Islamic World." In *Poverty and Charity in Middle Eastern Contexts,* edited by Michael Bonner, Mine Ener, and Amy Singer, 73–91. New York: State University of New York Press, 2003.

Sālim, Laṭīfa. *Tārīkh al-Qaḍā' al-Miṣrī Al-Ḥadīth.* 2 vols. Cairo: Al-Hay'a al-Miṣriyya al-'Āmma lil-Kitāb, 2001.

Sāmī, Amīn. *Taqwīm al-Nīl.* 3 vols. Cairo: Dār al-Kutub, 1936.

Sandwith, F. M. "The History of Kasr-el-Ainy." *Records of the Egyptian Government School of Medicine* 1 (1901): 3–20.

Sarton, George. *The History of Science and the New Humanism.* New York: Braziller, 1956.

Savage-Smith, Emilie. "Anatomical Illustration in Arabic Manuscripts." In *Arab Painting: Text and Image in Illustrated Arabic Manuscripts,* edited by Anna Contadini, 147–159. Leiden: Brill, 2007.

———. "Attitudes toward Dissection in Medieval Islam." *Journal of the History of Medicine and Allied Sciences* 50 (1995): 68–111.

———. "Medicine in Medieval Islam." In *The Cambridge History of Science,* vol. 2, *Medieval Science,* edited by David C. Lindberg and Michael H. Shank, 139–167. Cambridge: Cambridge University Press, 2013.

Ṣayfī, 'Abd al-Fattāḥ Muṣṭafā al-. *Al-Ḥisba fi'l-Islam: Niẓāman wa-Fiqhan wa-Taṭbīqan.* Alexandria: Dār al-Maṭbū'āt al-Jāmi'iyya, 2010.

———. *Al-Talabbus bi'l-Jarīma: Dirāsa lil-Munkar al-Mūjib lil-Ḥisba fi'l-Fiqhayn al-Islāmī wa'l-Waḍ'ī.* Cairo: Dār al-Nahḍa al-'Arabiyya, 1991.

Schaffer, Simon. "Measuring Virtue: Eudiometry, Enlightenment and Pneumatic Medicine." In *The Medical Enlightenment of the Eighteenth Century,* edited by Andrew Cunningham and Roger French, 281–318. Cambridge: Cambridge University Press, 1990.

Schaffer, Simon, Lissa Roberts, Kapil Raj, and 'James Delbourgo, eds. *The Brokered World: Go-Betweens and Global Intelligence, 1770–1820.* Sagamore Beach: Science History Publications, 2009.

Schielke, Samuli. "Second Thoughts about the Anthropology of Islam, or How to Make Sense of Grand Schemes in Everyday Life." *Zentrum Moderner Orient Working Papers* 2 (2010): 1–16.

Schrader, Abby M. "Containing the Spectacle of Punishment: The Russian Autocracy and the Abolition of the Knout, 1817–1845." *Slavic Review* 56 (1997): 613–644.

Scott, David, and Charles Hirschkind, eds. *Powers of the Secular Modern: Talal Asad and His Interlocutors.* Stanford: Stanford University Press, 206.

Sedra, Paul. "Observing Muhammad 'Ali Paşa and His Administration at Work, 1843–1846." In *The Modern Middle East: A Sourcebook for History,* edited by Camron M. Amin, Benjamin Fortna, and Elizabeth Frierson, 39–42. Oxford: Oxford University Press, 2006.

Seisson. *Is'āf al-Marḍā min 'Ilm Manāfi' al-A'ḍā.* Translated by Yūḥannā 'Anḥūrī, Ibrāhīm al-Disūqī, and 'Alī Haybā. Edited by Muḥammad al-Harrāwī. Cairo: Būlāq, AH 1252/1836 CE.

Shabāsī, Muḥammad al-. *Al-Tanwīr fī Qawā'id al-Taḥḍīr.* Cairo: Būlāq, AH 1264/1848 CE.

Shāfi'ī, Aḥmad Muhammad al-. *Balāgh al-Umniyya bi'l-Ḥuṣūn al-Ṣiḥḥiyya.* Cairo: Al-Maṭba'a al- 'Āmira al-Sharafiyya, AH 1305/1887–88 CE.

Shāfi'ī, Muḥammad al-. *Aḥsan al-Aghrāḍ fī al-Tashkhīṣ wa Mu'ālajat al-Amrāḍ.* Translated by Ḥusayn al-Rashīdī, Muḥammad al-Tūnisī, and Nicolas Perron. Cairo: Būlāq, AH 1259/1843 CE.

———. "Nubdha fī al-Ṭibb al-Tajribī." *Bulletin de l'institut Egyptien* 1 (1862): 505.

Shaham, Ron. The Expert Witness in Islamic Courts: Medicine and Crafts in the Service of Law. Chicago: University of Chicago Press, 2010.

Sha'lān, Samīḥ 'Abd al-Ghaffār. *Al-Mawt fī al-Ma'thūrat al-Sha'biyya.* Cairo: 'Ayn lil-Dirāsat wa'l-Buḥūth al-Insāniyya wa'l-Ijtimā'iyya, 2000.

Shalabī, Ḥilmī Ahmad. *Al-Ḥukm al-Maḥallī wa al-Majālis al-Baladiyya fī Miṣr Mundhu Inshā'ihā Ḥattā 'Āmm 1918.* Cairo: 'Ālam al-Kutub, 1987.

Shayyāl, Jamāl al-Dīn. *Tārīkh al-Tarjama wa'l-Ḥayāh al-Thaqāfiyya fī 'Aṣr Muḥammad 'Alī.* Cairo: Dār al-Fikr al-'Arabī, 1951.

Shayzarī, 'Abd al-Raḥmān Ibn Naṣr al-. *Kitāb Nihāyat al-Rutba fī Ṭalab al-Ḥisba.* Edited by Al-Sayyid al-Bāz al-'Arinī. Cairo: Lajnat al-Ta'līf wa'l-Tarjama wa'l-Nashr, 1946.

Shilliq, Aḥmad Zakariyya al-. *Aḥmad Fatḥī Zaghlūl wa'l-Āthār al-Fatḥiyya.* Cairo: Al-Hay'a al-'Āmma li-Quṣūr al-Thaqāfa, 2006.

———. *Ru'ya fī Taḥdīth al-Fikr al-Miṣrī: Aḥmad Fatḥī Zaghlūl wa Qaḍiyyat al-Taghrīb.* Cairo: Al-Hay'a al-Miṣriyya al-'Āmma lil-Kitāb, 1987.

Smail, Daniel Lord. *Imaginary Cartographies: Possession and Identity in Late Medieval Marseille.* Ithaca: Cornell University Press, 2000.

Smith, Sydney. *Mostly Murder.* New York: David McKay, 1959.

Sonbol, Amira El Azhary. *The Creation of a Medical Profession in Egypt, 1800–1922.* Syracuse: Syracuse University Press, 1990.

Spierenburg, Pieter. *The Spectacle of Suffering: Executions and the Evolution of Repression from a Preindustrial Metropolis to the European Experience.* Cambridge: Cambridge University Press, 1984.

St. John, J. A. *Egypt and Mohammed Ali.* 2 vols. London, 1834.

Stearns, Justin. *Infectious Ideas: Contagion in Premodern Islamic and Christian Thought in the Western Mediterranean.* Baltimore: Johns Hopkins University Press, 2011.

Stilt, Kristen. *Islamic Law in Action: Authority, Discretion, and Everyday Experiences in Mamluk Egypt.* Oxford: Oxford University Press, 2011.

———. "Price Setting and Hoarding in Mamluk Egypt: The Lessons of Legal Realism for Islamic Legal Studies." In *The Law Applied: Contextualizing the Islamic Shari'a; A Volume in Honor of Frank E. Vogel,* edited by Peri Bearman, Wolfhart Heinrichs, and Bernard G. Weiss, 57–78. London: I. B. Tauris, 2008.

Tagher, Jacques. *Ḥarakat al-Tarjamah bi-Miṣr Khilāl al-Qarn al-Tāsi' 'Ashr.* Cairo: Dār al-Ma'ārif, 1945.

Tahṭāwī, Rifā'a al-. *An Imam in Paris: An Account of a Stay in France by an Egyptian Cleric, 1826–1831.* Translated by Daniel L. Newman. London: Saqi, 2004.

———. *Takhlīṣ al-Ibrīz fī Talkhīṣ Bārīz.* Cairo: Būlāq, 1834.

Tamraz, Nihal. *Nineteenth-Century Cairene Houses and Palaces.* Cairo: American University in Cairo Press, 1998.

Thompson, H. Stanley, and Patricia G. Duffel "William Lawrence and the English Ophthalmology Textbooks of the 1830s and 1840s." *Archives of Ophthalmology* 130, no. 5 (2012): 639–644.

Tignor, Robert L. "The 'Indianization' of Egyptian Administration under British Rule." *American Historical Review* 68, no. 3 (1963): 631–661.

Tillier, Mathieu. "*Qāḍīs* and the Political Use of the *Maẓālim* Jurisdiction under the Abbāsids." In *Public Violence in Islamic Societies: Power, Discipline, and the Construction of the Public Sphere, 7th–19th Centuries CE,* edited by Maribel Fierro and Christian Lange, 42–66. Edinburgh: Edinburgh University Press, 2009.

Toledano, Ehud. *State and Society in Mid-Nineteenth-Century Egypt.* Cambridge: Cambridge University Press, 1990.

Tucker, Judith. *Women in Nineteenth Century Egypt.* Cambridge: Cambridge University Press, 1984.

Tuğ, Başak. *Politics of Honor in Ottoman Anatolia: Sexual Violence and Socio-Legal Surveillance in the Eighteenth Century.* Leiden: Brill, 2017.

Tugay, Emine Foat. *Three Centuries: Family Chronicles of Turkey and Egypt.* London: Oxford University Press, 1863.

Turner, Bryan. "The Discourse of Diet." *Theory, Culture and Society* 1 (1982): 23–32.

Ṭūsūn, 'Umar. *Al-Ba'thāt al-'Ilmiyya fī 'Ahd Muḥammad 'Alī Thumma fī 'Ahdayy 'Abbās al-Awwal wa Sa'īd.* Alexandria: Ṣalāḥ al-Dīn, 1934.

Tyan, Emile. "Judicial Organization." In *Law in the Middle East,* vol. 1, *Origin and Development of Islamic Law,* edited by M. Khadduri and H. J. Liebesny, 236–278. Washington, DC: Middle East Institute, 1955.

Varlik, Nüket. *Plague and Empire in the Early Modern Mediterranean World: The Ottoman Experience, 1347–1600.* New York: Cambridge University Press, 2015.

Vogel, Frank. "Tracing Nuance in Māwardī's *Al-Aḥkām al-Sulṭāniyyah:* Implicit Framing of Constitutional Authority." In *Islamic Law in Theory: Studies on Jurisprudence in Honor of Bernard Weiss,* edited by A. Kevin Reinhart and Robert Gleave, 331–359. Leiden: Brill, 2014.

Wakin, Jeanette. *The Function of Documents in Islamic Law.* Albany: State University of New York Press, 1972.

Warner, John H. *Against the Spirit of System: The French Impulse in Nineteenth-Century American Medicine.* Baltimore: Johns Hopkins University Press, 1998.

Weiss, Bernard. *The Spirit of Islamic Law.* Athens, GA: University of Georgia Press, 1998.

Weiss-Adamson, Melitta. "*Tacuinum Sanitatis.*" In *Medieval Science, Technology, and Medicine: An Encyclopedia,* edited by Steven J. Livesey, Faith Wallis, and Thomas F. Glick, 469–470. New York: Routledge, 2005.

Wilde, William R. *Narrative of a Voyage to Madeira, Teneriffe and along the Shores of the Mediterranean, Including a Visit to Algiers, Egypt, Palestine, Etc.* 2 vols. Dublin: William Curry, 1840.

Wood, Leonard. *Islamic Legal Revival: Reception of European Law and Transformations in Islamic Legal Thought in Egypt, 1875–1952.* Oxford: Oxford University Press, 2016.

Woolf, D. R. "Speech, Text, and Time: The Sense of Hearing and the Sense of the Past in Renaissance England." *Albion* 8, no. 2 (1986): 159–193.

Wright, Gwendolyn. *The Politics of Design in French Colonial Urbanism.* Chicago: University of Chicago Press, 1991.

Yandūzī, Ḥasan ibn Muḥammad al-. *Adillat al-Ithbāt al-Jinā'ī wa-Qawā'iduhu al-'Āmma fi'l-Sharī'a al-Islmāiyya.* [Rabat ?]: Top Press, 2004.

Yavari, Neguin. "Review Symposium: *The Impossible State.*" *Perspectives on Politics* 12, no. 2 (2014): 466–467.

Zabīdī, Muḥammad Murtaḍa al-. *Tāj al-'Arūs.* 40 vols. Kuwait: Al-Majlis al-Waṭanī lil-Thaqāfa wa'l-Funūn wa'l-Ādāb, 2004.

Zaghlūl, Aḥmad Fatḥī. *Al-Muḥāmāh.* Cairo: Maṭba'at al-Ma'ārif, 1900.

Zāhir, Muḥammad Ismā'īl. "Al-Ḥamla al-Firinsiyya: Al-Wa'i b'l-Tārkīh min Khilāl al-Ākhar." In *Mi'atā Ām 'Alā al-Ḥamla al-Firinsiyya: Ru'iya Miṣriyya,* edited by Nāṣir Aḥmad Ibrāhīm, 570–615. Cairo: Al-Dār al-'Arabiyya lil-Kitāb, 2008.

Zarinbaf, Fariba. *Crime and Punishment in Istanbul, 1700–1800.* Berkeley: University of California Press, 2010.

Ze'evi, Dror. "The Use of Ottoman Shari'a Court Records as a Source for Middle Eastern Social History: A Reappraisal." *Islamic Law and Society* 5, no. 1 (1998): 35–56.

Ziadeh, Farhat. *Lawyers, the Rule of Law and Liberalism in Modern Egypt.* Stanford: Hoover Institution, 1968.

INDEX

'Abbās, Ra'ūf, 11-13
'Abbās Pasha, 60, 69, 90, 121-122, 135, 145, 158, 231, 239, 274
'Abbāsiyya, 177
'Abd al-Karīm, Aḥmad 'Izzat, 7-8
'Ābidīn Palace, 7, 90
'Abdu, Muḥammad, 33
Abdülmecid, Sultan, 274
Abū Ḥanīfa, 118, 120, 149, 188, 311n141
Abu-Lughod, Janet, 140, 142, 145, 316n47
Abū Yūsuf, 149
Abū Za'bal, 1, 5, 13, 39-40, 300n116
'adāla, 97, 119, 130
'adl, 109, 194, 256, 279
'afw, 110, 123, 229, 259
agoranomos, 185
Agrama, Hussein, 181, 183, 201
alcoholic beverages, 197, 199-200, 205, 208-210, 220-221, 264
anatomoclinical medicine, 37, 79, 265-266, 276
anatomy, 3-4, 210-211, 258; Damanhūrī's treatise on, 68; Galen's writings on, 65; of the eye, 44; Muslim scholars' study of, 66; Naḥrāwī's writings on, 70-71; Shabāsī's writings on, 71-74
Anṭākī, Dāwūd al-, 211
appeal, 83, 89, 110, 123,
'Arīsh al-, 55
Aristotle, 4, 63, 68
Arnaud, Jean-Luc, 140-142
arsh, 255
Asad, Talal, 22-26, 128; on *ḥisba*, 182-183, 186, 198, 201
autopsy, 3, 6, 37; and non-elite Egyptians, 76; use for legal purposes, 21, 96, 110, 114, 221, 228, 257, 260, 282; use for medical purposes, 71
'Awaḍ, Luwīs, 9-12
'Awda, 'Abd al-Qādir, 29-31, 87, 124
Arnold, David, 15-16
'Aṭṭār, Ḥasan al-, 68-69
Azbakiyya, 96, 136-142, 169-170, 175, 178
Azbakiyya Civilian Hospital, 61, 70, 109, 217-219, 246
Azbakiyya Lake, 161
al-Azhar, 33, 43, 44, 62, 65, 68

Baer, Gabriel, 151
Bahjat, Muṣṭafā, 146
banishment. *See* exile
Baqlī, Muḥammad 'Alī al-, 161, 320n109
barbers, 64, 65, 81, 82, 302n156
Barillet-Deschamps, Jean-Pierre, 138
bastinado, 262, 264. *See also* flogging, torture
Bayt al-Māl, 50, 280, 343n145
bayyina, 82, 124, 283
Beccaria, Cesare, 234-235
Béclard, Pierre Augustin, 70
beggars, 100
Berkey, Jonathan, 196-197
Berthollet, Claude Louis, 10
Bichat, Xavier, 64, 74, 156, 210-212, 221, 224, 278

Diderot, Denis, 45
Dinshiwāī tribunal, 87
diet, 204, 207, 210-211, 215, 247
discretionary punishment, see *ta'zīr*
dissection, 1-6; and medical education, 1-6, 9, 266; church's position on, 63; Egyptian *'ulamā'*'s views on, 68-70; in postclassical *fiqh*, 65-68; Qaṣr al-'Ainī doctors' views on, 70-75; reaction of non-elite Egyptians to, 75-79, 257, 282-284
diyya, 118, 123, 243, 255-256
domicile, 98, 100-101, 130
"dual-city" model, 139-140, 168-170, 178

Edhem Bey, 145, 161
educational missions to Europe, 12, 43, 70-71, 75, 86, 137-138, 216
Egyptian Historical Society, 13
Egyptian National Archives, 35, 83, 90, 141
Enlightenment, 26, 39, 44, 48, 63, 65, 87, 131, 143, 234-236, 268
epidemics, 49, 52, 53, 56, 57, 153, 160, 162, 229, 280. *See also* cholera, disease, plague
equality, 32, 85, 89, 99, 130-131, 234
etiology, theories of, 16, 38, 46, 51, 56, 154-156, 168, 172, 209
exile, 38, 101, 115-116, 232, 242, 249, 268, 275
experts, 148, 221, 251, 253-254, 256. *See also* medical expertise

Fanon, Frantz, 16
Faraḥāt, Muḥammad Nūr, 86
fatwa, 58-60, 67, 149, 236, 250
female doctors. See *ḥakīma*
Figari, Antonio, 213-214
fishmongers, 154, 155, 160, 178
fisīkh, 160, 169, 320 n. 98
flogging, 38; as legal punishment, 226-228, 237-238, 243-244; as means to extract confession, 250-252; as practiced by *muḥtasib*, 197; banning of, 233-237; British claims of banning of, 267-268
food markets, 38, 160, 179-181, 204-208, 215, 218-220, 222, 224, 276, 278
forensic chemistry, 38, 220-222, 224. *See also* Chemical-Pharmaceutical Lab
forensic medicine: and non-elite Egyptians, 77, 226-229, 257-258, 261-264, 282-284; as alternative to confession, 252, 257-267; as circumstantial evidence, 83, 109-110, 123, 128, 220-221; as taught in Qaṣr al-'Ainī, 71-73, 206. See also *ṭibb shar'ī*, *ṭibb siyāsī*
Foucault, Michel, 19-20, 51, 53, 64, 129, 173, 235, 238, 240, 265
France, 31, 44, 65, 70-71, 75, 156, 167, 214, 216, 247
French Expedition to Egypt, 8, 10-12, 14, 84
funerals, 61, 63, 81, 186
funerary lamentations, 61-62, 186, 299n100
fuqahā', 25-26, 34, 68, 97, 124-127, 130, 224, 278

Galen, 1-2, 63, 65, 68, 71-72, 74, 207, 211
Gastinel, J. B., 213-214
General Health Council, 69, 71
Ghānim, Ḥusayn, 74
Ghazālī, Abū Ḥāmid al-, 183, 190-193, 198-201, 219, 220, 223, 224
Ghurbāl, Aḥmad, 7
Gran, Peter, 69
Grand Bey, 141, 151, 161
Grassi, Francesco, 48, 57, 276

ḥakīma, 77, 109, 114, 343n144
Hallaq, Wael, 26-27, 186
Harrāwī, Muḥammad al-, 74
Haussmann, Baron, 136, 138, 142-144, 153
Health offices of Cairo (*makātib al-ṣiḥḥa*), 81, 217, 219, 222
Hijaz, 50, 102, 116
Hippocrates, 1, 74, 154
Hippocratic Oath, 253
ḥisba, 38, 179, 205, 215, 217, 220, 222-224, 253. See also *muḥtasib*
homicide, 277, 278; in *fiqh*, 22, 93-94, 108-109, 117, 123, 250, 254, 254, 256, 259; in *siyāsa*, 94-97, 103; in both *fiqh* and *siyāsa*, 120-125, 229
Ḥudūd, 108-109, 120, 265
Ḥukūmat 'adl, 256, 279
Humāyūnī Law of 1852, 93-94; and *fiqh*, 102 117; and investigating homicides, 103, 109, 117, 123; and recidivism, 115